Business and Government Relations in Africa

T0362142

This book endeavors to take the conceptualization of the relationship between business, government, and development in African countries to a new level. In the twenty-first century, the interests and operations of government and business inevitably intersect all over the African continent. No government, federal or state, can afford to ignore the needs of business. But what are these needs, how does business express its needs to government, and which institutions organize government-business relations in African countries? How should government regulate business, or should it choose to let the markets rule? *Business and Government Relations in Africa* brings together many of sub-Saharan African leading scholars to address these critical questions.

Business and Government Relations in Africa examines the key players in the game—federal and state governments and business groups—and the processes that govern the relationships between them. It looks at the regulatory regimes that have an impact on business and provides a number of case studies of the relationships between government and economic development around the African continent, highlighting different processes and practices. It shows the latest state of knowledge on the topic and will be of interest both to students at an advanced level, academics and reflective practitioners. It addresses the topics with regard to business-government relations and will be of interest to researchers, academics, policy makers, and students in the fields of African politics, comparative politics, public policy, business and politics, sustainable development and sustainability, economic development, and managerial economics.

Robert A. Dibie is Professor of Public Policy, Public Management, and Environmental Studies at Indiana University Kokomo, United States.

Routledge Critical Studies in Public Management

Edited by Stephen Osborne

The study and practice of public management has undergone profound changes across the world. Over the last quarter century, we have seen

- increasing criticism of public administration as the over-arching framework for the provision of public services,
- the rise (and critical appraisal) of the "New Public Management" as an emergent paradigm for the provision of public services,
- the transformation of the "public sector" into the cross-sectoral provision of public services, and
- the growth of the governance of inter-organizational relationships as an essential element in the provision of public services.

In reality these trends have not so much replaced each other as elided or co-existed together—the public policy process has not gone away as a legitimate topic of study, intra-organizational management continues to be essential to the efficient provision of public services, whist the governance of inter-organizational and inter-sectoral relationships is now essential to the effective provision of these services.

Further, whilst the study of public management has been enriched by contribution of a range of insights from the "mainstream" management literature it has also contributed to this literature in such areas as networks and inter-organizational collaboration, innovation and stakeholder theory.

This series is dedicated to presenting and critiquing this important body of theory and empirical study. It will publish books that both explore and evaluate the emergent and developing nature of public administration, management and governance (in theory and practice) and examine the relationship with and contribution to the over-arching disciplines of management and organizational sociology.

Books in the series will be of interest to academics and researchers in this field, students undertaking advanced studies of it as part of their undergraduate or postgraduate degree and reflective policy makers and practitioners.

Public Governance and Strategic Management Capabilities
Public Governance in the Gulf States
Paul Joyce and Turki Al Rasheed

Ethics Management in the Public Service
A Sensory-based Strategy
Liza Ireni-Saban and Galit Berdugo

Public Management in Times of Austerity
*Edited by Eva Moll Ghin, Hanne Foss Hansen, and
Mads Bøge Kristiansen*

Public Policy, Governance and Polarization: Making Governance Work
Edited by David K Jesuit and Russell Alan Williams

Business and Government Relations in Africa
Edited by Robert A. Dibie

Business and Government Relations in Africa

Edited by Robert A. Dibie

Routledge
Taylor & Francis Group

LONDON AND NEW YORK

First published 2018 by Routledge

2 Park Square, Milton Park, Abingdon, Oxfordshire OX14 4RN
52 Vanderbilt Avenue, New York, NY 10017

Routledge is an imprint of the Taylor & Francis Group, an informa business

First issued in paperback 2019

Library of Congress Cataloging-in-Publication Data
Names: Dibie, Robert A., 1956– author.
Title: Business and government relations in Africa / edited by
    Robert A. Dibie.
Description: New York : Routledge, 2017. |
    Series: Routledge critical studies in public management |
    Includes index.
Identifiers: LCCN 2017011087| ISBN 9781138700093 (hardback) |
    ISBN 9781315204987 (ebook)
Subjects: LCSH: Trade regulation—Africa. |
    Administrative agencies—Africa. |
    Industrial policy—Africa. | Business and politics—Africa. |
    Economic development—Africa.
Classification: LCC HD3616.A35 D53 2017 | DDC 322/.
    3096—dc23
LC record available at https://lccn.loc.gov/2017011087

ISBN: 978-1-138-70009-3 (hbk)
ISBN: 978-0-367-24309-8 (pbk)

Typeset in Sabon
by Apex CoVantage, LLC

This book is dedicated to my son, Ajiri Dibie, and my late father, David Jones Dibie.

Contents

Figures

Tables

Preface

This book endeavors to take the conceptualization of the relationship between business, government, and development in African countries to a new level. In the twenty-first century, the interests and operations of government and business inevitably intersect all over the African continent. No government, federal or state, can afford to ignore the needs of business. But what are these needs, how does business express its needs to government, and which institutions organize government-business relations in African countries? How should government regulate business, or should it choose to let the markets rule? *Government and Business Relations in Africa* brings together many of sub-Saharan African leading scholars to address these critical questions.

The book examines the key players in the game—federal and state governments and business groups—and the processes that govern the relationships between them. It looks at the regulatory regimes which impact on business, such as the Ministry of Trade and Commerce, the Ministry of Economic Development, and in some countries the Prices Surveillance Authority. It provides a number of case studies of the relationships between government and economic development around the African continent, highlighting different processes and practices. The authors seek to understand the impact of weak economic policies, and the ability to adequately develop solid business and government relations in capacity building that could lead to wide-spread economic growth in Africa. Chapters take an open, explorative approach to the relationship between business and government relations on one hand and sustainable development on the other hand. To make business and government relations relevant in Africa's nations' development, the book has to reflect on the current economic and political environment. It includes chapters that consider the nature of the government-business relationship in the financial and manufacturing sectors and small business. It also includes an important chapter on ethics and corporate social responsibility in Africa. This is because the very visible hand of the government creates a constantly shifting business environment. The book also pays special attention to how changes in policies relating to financial and banking markets have affected the economic business cycles in several African countries.

This book intends to investigate business and government relations in several countries of Africa. It will show how the public sector influences private sector decision making, as well as provide an understanding of both sides of the relationship between business and government in Africa. It will cover the different ways in which government policy affects the activities of modern corporations and the key responses on the part of business. It will also examine the different tools that government use to influence business decision making in the African continent. Some chapters will explore traditional economic regulation and the trade toward deregulation in several African countries, and the ways public policy issues affect business in areas such as competitiveness, protectionism versus free trade, corporate bailouts, defensive or subsidies production, and consumer products.

The findings presented in this book will be very useful to policy makers, public administrators, public policy analysis, readers, researchers, graduate and undergraduate studies in business, economics, nonprofit, NGOs, development, and public policy disciplines. It examines fluctuating prices in commodities such as agricultural products, the nature and expansion of regulation, privatization of public corporations, government and the consumer, government and the workplace, traditional economic regulation, recent experiences in economic deregulation, reforming government regulation, and change in consumer behaviors. It will make use of examples and embedded content in order to help students and readers better appreciate the dynamics changes in the business-government relations world.

With the wide variety of cases, this book is able to provide conceptual insights to better understand how business-government relations in African countries have not been able to effectively integrate sustainable policies in order to stimulate poverty reduction, democratic governance, crisis prevention and recovery, and sustainable development. It reviews the extensive literature on business and government, capacity building strategies, and regulation policies, as well as examines the implication of sustainable development of countries in the African continent. The chapters present a wide range of new dimensions and variables that are not considered by other books.

Robert A. Dibie

Acknowledgments

I would like to express my appreciation to many individuals who directly or indirectly played a role in the development of this book. First, I wish to thank many people at Routledge, in particular my editor David Varley, who has strongly supported this project and provided exemplary leadership throughout the revision process. Collectively, they are an extraordinary team that demonstrated very high standards of excellence in their work.

I am also grateful to the reviewers who took time to review early draft of my work and provided helpful suggestions for improving the book. Their comments undoubtedly made the book better. My heartfelt thanks to all the scholars that contributed chapters or co-authored chapters with me: Professor Felix Edoho, Lincoln University, United States; Professor Ayandiji D. Aina, Caleb University, Nigeria; Professor Kealeboga J. Maphunye, University of South Africa; Dr. Chinyeaka Igbokwe-Ibeto, Nnamdi Azikiwe University, Nigeria; Dr. Yusuf Nur, Indiana University Kokomo, United States; Dr. Wilfred Gabsa, University of Yaoundé, Cameroon; Dr. Peter Nwafu, Albany State University, United States; Professor Saliwe Kawewe, Southern Illinois University, Carbondale, United States; Dr. Mariam Konete, Western Michigan University, United States; Professor Idrissa Quedraogo, University of Ouagadougou, Burkina Faso; Dr. Muawya Hussien, Dufar University, Oman; Dr. Josephine Dibie, Indiana University Kokomo, United States; Dr. Leonard Gadzekpo, Southern Illinois University, Carbondale, United States; and Dr. Omolara Quadri, University of Lagos, Nigeria.

I wish to thank my colleagues and graduate students at Indiana University Kokomo, United States; Babcock University, Nigeria; the University of the West Indies, Jamaica; Fort Hare University, South Africa; Central Michigan University, United States; and Caleb University Lagos, Nigeria, for their continued encouragement and interest in business and government relations in the economy, and sustainable development issues.

A special acknowledgement goes to Professor Toyin Falola, University of Texas, Austin; Professor Felix Edoho, Lincoln University, Jefferson City; Professor Sisay Aseda, Western Michigan University; and Professor Valentine James, Clarion University, Pennsylvania, for their exceptional support throughout this project. Their insights and contribution have added considerably to the quality of this book. I also want to acknowledge the business and government studies scholars whose research and analysis provide the foundation of this book. Their continuing efforts make me optimistic about continued progress in the study of how government need to enact regulatory reforms in order to help areas in any economy where the gains of structural reforms are potentially the greatest. Thus, in the African continent, regulation, which is often business sector specific, should be considered within a wider governance system whose policy objectives include a range of social and economic benefits to the citizens.

Finally, I am especially thankful for the efforts of my wife and best friend Dr. Josephine Dibie for her time, energy, commitment, and contribution to the quality and success of this book. Josephine and I have worked together in one capacity or another for 25 years, always around business and government relations, and appropriate fiscal and monetary policies issues. This volume represents the most recent culmination of that collaboration.

About the Contributors

Ayandiji Daniel Aina, PhD, is Professor of Political Science and Vice Chancellor and President at Caleb University in Lagos, Nigeria. He previously served as Provost, College of Management and Social Sciences, at Babcock University, Ilishan-Remo, Ogun State, Nigeria, and President of Adeleke University Ede, Osun State, Nigeria, respectively. He has consulted widely on matters of governance, public policy, and administration for universities, intergovernmental bodies and NGOs in Nigeria. Dr. Aina is an insightful scholar and writer. He has published several book chapters and peer-reviewed journal articles in the area of public policy, civil society, public administration, sustainable development, NGOs, international relations, political elections, and good governance. Dr. Aina has presented his research papers in more than fifty international conferences, in the United States, Canada, England, South Africa, Ghana, Kenya, Nigeria, and Cameroon. He is the current Managing Editor of the *Journal of International Politics and Development (JIPAD)*.

Josephine Dibie, DBA, is a Lecturer in Management and Accounting at Indiana University Kokomo. She has conducted several field researches in Africa. Dr. Dibie is the author and co-author of more than a dozen articles and book chapters. She has published extensively in the area of NGOs and women's empowerment in Africa. Her publications have appeared in the *Journal of Business and Social Sciences, International Journal of Politics and Development, Journal of Asian and African Studies,* and the *Journal of African Policy Studies.* Her research interests are in the areas of corporate executive compensation, political economy of leadership in Africa, NGOs, women's capacity building and empowerment, sustainable development, economic growth in Africa, and corporate social responsibility in Africa. She holds a Doctorate in Business Administration. She also earned a Master's of Public Administration from Indiana State University; an MBA from the University of Benin; a Master's of Arts in Economics from the University of Ibadan; and a Bachelor's of Science in Statistics from the University of Nigeria, Nnsuka.

Robert A. Dibie, PhD, is Professor of Public Policy, Public Management, and Environmental Studies at Indiana University Kokomo's School of Business. He has been Dean and Senior Higher Education Administrator for many years. Previously, Professor Dibie served as the Director of Graduate Programs in Public Administration at Western Kentucky University. Professor Dibie is the author of several books, book chapters, and more than ninety research articles in peer-refereed journals. His latest books are *Comparative Perspectives on Environmental Policy and Issues* by Routledge Press; *Women Empowerment for Sustainability in Africa* by Cambridge Scholars Press; and *Public Administration: Analysis, Theories and Application* by Babcock University Press. His research articles have appeared in the *International Journal of Public Administration*; *International Journal of Business and Social Sciences*; *Journal of African Policy Studies*; *Journal of Developing Societies*; *Journal of Sociology and Social Welfare*; *Journal of Social Justice*; *Journal of African and Asian Studies*; *Politics Administration and Change Journal*; *Journal of Business and Economic Policy*; and so on. He has presented more than 120 academic papers in national and international conferences, focusing on issues of sustainable development, public management, public policy, women's empowerment, environmental policies, development administration, and nongovernmental organizations (NGOs). As a nationally recognized leader in higher education, Professor Dibie has presented many seminars, workshops, and lectures in the areas of Higher Education Leadership, Public Policy, Environmental Policy, Gender Empowerment, and Sustainable Development in a number of universities around the world. He is a member of several professional academic organizations and currently serves on the Editorial Advisory Board of many scholarly journals. He has also consulted for several NGOs and universities in the United States, Europe, Africa, and the Caribbean Islands.

Felix M. Edoho, PhD, is a Professor in the School of Business Administration at Lincoln University Jefferson City, Missouri, United States. He was also the dean of the School of Business for several years. Dr. Edoho has written books in the areas of management challenges and economic development in Africa. His publications include *Management Challenges for Africa in the Twenty-first Century* by Praeger Press, and *Globalization and the New World Order: Promises, Problems and Prospects for Africa in the Twenty-first Century* by Praeger Press. Further, Dr. Edoho has also contributed more than 16 book chapters to various edited volumes. He has also published several journal articles and also serves as a track chair, discussant, panelist, and moderator at various domestic and international professional conferences. He has also received funds for various research projects. He was the director of a multimillion dollar international development project in Malawi that was funded by the US Agency for International Development. This project established an Agricultural Policy Research Unit to assist the Government of Malawi by providing inputs into agricultural policymaking process. He has also been actively involved in consulting work for a number of projects funded by the US Department of Housing and Urban Development. Dr. Edoho is a member of various professional associations. These include Academic of Management, Southern Management Association, International Management Development Association, and the Consortium for Faculty and Course development in international Studies.

Wilfred Gabsa, PhD, is an Associate Professor in the Faculty of Laws and Political Science at the University of Yaoundé II, Soa, Cameroon, West Africa. He received his doctoral degree from Georgia State University in Atlanta, United States. He has several years' experience working in both the public and nongovernmental sectors in Cameroon, West Africa. His research papers have been presented in several national and international conferences in Africa, Europe, Canada, and the United States. His research interests are in the area of governance, public law, government regulations and economic growth, political economy, and comparative political institution.

Leonard Gadzekpo, PhD, is an Associate Professor and Chair of the Department of Africana Studies at Southern Illinois University Carbondale. Dr. Gadzekpo was born in Côte d'Ivoire and grew up in Ghana. He got his first degree from the University of Science and Technology, Kumasi, Ghana, and taught in Ghana and Nigeria. He spent four years in Germany as an artist working on religious art pieces for the St. Stepanus Katholische Gemeinde in Oldenburg, and studied at Universitaet Oldenburg and Salzburg Universität, Austria. From 1990 to 1997 he did graduate studies at Bowling Green State University, Bowling Green, Ohio, and earned a MA in German, an MFA in Painting, and a PhD in American Cultural Studies. Dr. Gazekpo's writing and research interests are in the areas of business-government and the African society, empowerment for sustainable development in Africa, and comparative study of Africana history and culture. He has also presented his research papers in many national and international conferences. Dr. Gadzekpo is also presently working on a series of paintings dealing with the Africana experience in the world.

Muawya Hussien, PhD, is a Senior Lecturer and Acting Chairperson of the Department of Accounting and Finance in the College of Commerce and Business Administration at Dhofar University, Salalah, Sultanate of Oman, in the Middle East. He has presented his research paper at several national and international conferences in Ethiopia, Sudan, United Arab Emirates, and South Africa. His research is in accounting, business, and government relations in Africa, foreign investment in Africa, finance, international environmental policy, sustainable development, public sector partnership with NGOs, multinational corporations operations in Africa, and comparative trade policies.

Chinyeaka Justine Igbokwe-Ibeto, PhD, is a Senior Lecturer in the Department of Public Administration at Nnamdi Azikiwe University, Awka, Nigeria. He has published more than 60 peer reviewed journal articles, as well as 10 book chapters. His research work has appeared in the *Journal of Sustainable Development in Africa*; *Africa's Public Service Delivery and Performance Review*; *Review of Public Administration and Management (ROPAM)*; and *Journal of International Politics and Development*. Dr. Igbokwe-Ibeto is a member of the Advisory Board of Zainab Arabian Research Society for Multidisciplinary Issues (ZARSMI), United Arab Emirates. His research interest is in the areas of economic development and public administration. His research also focuses on sub-Saharan Africa's democratic governance, organizational management, sustainable development, and public policy.

Saliwe Kawewe, PhD, is a Professor and Acting Director of the School of Social Work at Southern Illinois University at Carbondale. She was the former Graduate Program Director in the same institution where she has been working since 1996. She obtained a PhD from Saint Louis University in 1985, an MSW from George Warren Brown School of Social Work, Washington University, in St. Louis in 1979, and a BSW from the University of Zambia in 1974. She has a diverse background experience entailing administration and social work practice in Zambia, and Zimbabwe in Africa, as well as child welfare in the United States. Dr. Kawewe has a commendable record of scholarship and has been recognized with more than fifteen academic awards and honors for teaching effectiveness, including community and professional service. In addition to publishing more than thirty-seven refereed articles, including book chapters and conference proceedings, she has attended more than 40 conferences, making more than 40 national and international professional presentations in the United States, the Caribbean Islands, Asia, Europe, and Africa. She is consulting editor for *Social Development Issues*; is on the editorial board of the *Journal of African Policy Studies*, *Journal of Women and Language*, and *Journal of Immigrant* and *Refugee Services*; has served on the editorial boards of the *National Women Studies Journal: NWSA*; and is a manuscript and abstract reviewer for various conferences.

Mariam Konaté, PhD, is an Associate Professor in the Department of Gender and Women's Studies at Western Michigan University. Her work examines the lives of women of African descent in the West as well as in Africa. Her newest research project explores the relevance of father absence to African American women's heterosexual dating experiences. The changing roles of African women who, through the interplay of gender, economics, and power, are redefining themselves in America and in postcolonial African societies are central to Dr. Konaté's research and teaching. Her book, *Heroism and the Supernatural in the African Epic* (Routledge, 2010), underscores the crucial role women play in the hero's life and rise to power, as well as in the initiation to supernatural powers. Women's empowerment and contribution to economic growth through self-determination is ubiquitous in the writings of many contemporary African and African American women writers, whose works Konaté teaches in her courses.

Kealeboga J. Maphunye, PhD, is the inaugural WIPHOLD-Brigalia Bam Research Professor and Chair in Electoral Democracy in Africa at the University of South Africa (UNISA). He conducts research on elections, governance and democracy in Africa, focusing on election management bodies and democratic systems. Professor Maphunye has observed elections and trained election officials in many African countries. He has written several journal articles, presented many papers at continental (Africa) and international forums, and regularly contributes to public and media debates on issues of elections, democracy, and governance in Africa. He has worked for the Botswana Women's Affairs Division as an NGO Project Officer; the School of Government, University of the Western Cape; and has conducted commissioned research for South African national government departments, including the presidency, as a researcher at the HSRC (Human Sciences Research Council). His work has appeared in the *Journal of African and Asian Local Government Studies; African Administrative Studies* (CAFRAD journal); *Journal of International Politics and Development; UK Public Management Review; Unisa Journal of Law, Society and Development; Politeia, Journal of Politics and Public Administration; Administratio Publica; Journal of African Elections;* and *Mediterranean Journal of Social Sciences.* Professor Maphunye's latest publications are *South Africa—Twenty Years into Democracy: The March to the 2014 Elections,* with Maphunye, K. J., Kibuka-Sebitosi, E., and Moagi, A. L. (2014); and "Post-Liberation Relapse and Aborted Social Contract? Isaias Afwerki and Eritrea, 1991–2015," in *The New African Civil-Military Relations,* edited by Rupiya, M., Moyo, G., and Laugesen, H. (2015).

Peter Ngwafu, PhD, is an Associate Professor and Director of the Department of Public Administration at Albany State University, Georgia. Dr. Ngwafu has consulted for several local government and nonprofit organizations in the United States and many countries in Africa. He has also conducted several field researches in Africa. His research interests are in the areas of public administration, human resources management, economic development, and public policy. Dr. Ngwafu's research papers have been presented in more than fifty national and international conferences. He is well published in the areas of business-government relations.

Yusuf Ahmed Nur, PhD, is an Associate Professor of Strategic Management in the School of Business at Indiana University Kokomo. He currently teaches strategic management, international business, and international marketing at the graduate and graduate levels. In his courses, Dr. Nur explores innovative ways to engage students so that they take full responsibility for their learning. Dr. Nur's research interests include strategic leadership, culture and leadership, entrepreneurship and economic development. His research has been published in *Business Horizons, Global Business Issues Journal,* and *The Business Renaissance Quarterly.* He holds a PhD in Strategic Management from Indiana University; an MBA from California State University, Fresno; and a Bachelor of Science in Electrical Engineering from Military Technical College in Cairo.

Omolara M. Quadri, PhD, is a Senior Lecturer at the Department of Political Science and Public Administration, University of Lagos, Nigeria, where she has taught since 2000. She has supervised several postgraduate students' research theses. Dr. Quadri received her PhD from the University of Lagos. She was a visiting scholar at Kennesaw State University, Atlanta, in the United States in 2011. She was also a recipient of the commonwealth professional fellowship at the University of Roehamton, London, United Kingdom, in 2012, as well as the American Political Science Association Africa Workshop Award, Maputo, Mozambique, in 2014. Dr. Quadri has published more than twenty-one peer reviewed journal articles, covering topics in urbanization, the role of the state in development in public policy, the feminization of poverty, poverty and stable economy, administration and management, Africa's health burden, and the nature of behavior in organizations. Her publications have appeared in *Africa's Journal of Institutions and Development;* the *Journal of Pan African Studies;* the *Journal of Society, Development and Public Health;* the *International Review of Politics and Development;* the *Nigerian Journal of Policy and Strategy;* and so on. She has also conducted consultancy services for a variety of government departments and NGOs in Africa. Dr. Quadri's research interests are in the area of public policy, development administration, sustainable development, and political economy.

Idrissa Quedraogo, PhD, is a Professor in the Faculty of Business Administration at the University of Ouagadougou, Burkina Faso, West Africa. He was also the Dean of the Business School for several years. He received his doctoral degree from the University of Tennessee, Knoxville, United States. He has consulted for several banks and nongovernmental organizations in Burkina Faso, including special African development bank projects. Dr. Quedraogo's research papers have been presented in several national and international conferences in United States, Africa, Europe, and Canada. Dr. Quedraogo is an accomplished scholar with a long list of outstanding publications. His research interests are in the areas of monetary policy, banking and finance, small business development, entrepreneurship, government regulations, privatization, and political economy in Africa.

About the Editor

Robert A. Dibie, PhD, is a Professor of Public Policy, Public Management, and Environmental Studies at Indiana University Kokomo's Department of Public Administration and Health Management. He has been Dean and Senior Higher Education Administrator for many years. Previously, Professor Dibie served as the Director of Graduate Programs in Public Administration at Western Kentucky University. He is a recipient of the prestigious Carnegie African Diaspora Fellowship award. A prolific and insightful researcher and writer, Professor Dibie has published 10 books and more than 85 peer-reviewed journal articles in the areas of environmental policy, civil society, public management, sustainable development, public policy, NGOs, women's empowerment, and ethics. His latest books includes *Comparative Perspectives on Environmental Policy and Issues* by Routledge Press; *Public Administration: Analysis, Theories and Application* by Babcook University Press; *Comparative Perspectives on Civil Society* by Lexington Press; *Public Management and Sustainable Development in Nigeria* by Ashgate; and *Nongovernmental Organizations and Sustainable Development in Sub-Saharan Africa* by Lexington Press. His recent research articles have appeared in the *International Journal of Public Administration*; *Journal of African Policy Studies*; *Journal of Developing Societies*; *Journal of Sociology and Social Welfare*; *Journal of Social Justice*; *Journal of African and Asian Studies*; *Politics Administration and Change Journal*; *Journal of International Politics and Development*; *Journal of African Business*; and so on. He has presented more than 120 academic papers in national and international conferences, focusing on issues of sustainable development, public management, public policy, women's empowerment, environmental policies, development administration, and nongovernmental organizations (NGOs). As a nationally recognized leader in higher education, Professor Dibie has presented many seminars, workshops, and lectures in the areas of higher education leadership, public policy, environmental policy, gender empowerment, and sustainable development in a number of universities around the world. Professor Dibie has also developed continuing education materials and taught professional development courses (in executive leadership, program evaluation, and ethics) for various professional organizations, including banks, city and county governments, nonprofit institutions, NGOs, and some national government departments in the United States and abroad. He has also consulted for several NGOs and universities in the United States, Europe, Africa, and the Caribbean Islands.

Dibie is committed to the pursuit of knowledge, wisdom, discovery, and creativity. He is a proven student-centered educator and has fostered personal and intellectual growth to prepare students for productive careers, meaningful lives, and responsible citizenship in a global society. Professor Dibie has also supervised more than 60 doctoral and masters' degree dissertations on public management, public policy, environmental policy, nongovernmental organizations, economic development policy, sustainable development, women's empowerment, business administration, environmental health and safety, and political science.

Acronyms

AA	Absolute Advantage
BBC	British Broadcasting Corporation
ERP	Enterprise Resource Planning
EU	European Union
FAO	Food and Agriculture Organization of the United Nations
FTA	Free Trade Area
G8	Group of Eight
GDP	Gross Domestic Product
GNI	Gross National Income
GNP	Gross National Product
ILO	International Labor Organization
IMF	International Monetary Fund
ITC	International Trade Centre
ODA	Official Development Assistance
OECD	Organization for Economic Cooperation and Development
OPEC	Organization of Petroleum Exporting Countries
PPP	Public-Private Partnerships
PPP	Purchasing Power Parity
R&D	Research and Development
SAP	Structural Adjustment Program
UN	United Nations
UNCTAD	United Nations Conference on Trade and Development
UNDP	United Nations Development Program
UNEP	United Nations Environment Program
UNESCO	United Nations Educational, Scientific and Cultural Organization
VAT	Value Added Tax
WTO	World Trade Organization

1 An Overview of Government and Business Relations

Robert A. Dibie

Introduction

It has been argued that Africa is a continent full of surprises. Looking at the bigger picture of Africa also reveals some surprises. For instance, if Africa were a single country according to World Bank data, it would have had more than $998 billion total gross national product (GNP) in 2006 and subsequent years (Mahajan, 2009; World Bank, 2014). The African continent is endowed with several natural resources. The continent's mineral reserves rank first or second for bauxite, cobalt, diamonds, phosphate rocks, platinum-group metals (PGM), vermiculite, and zirconium. Many other minerals are present in quantity. The 2005 share of world production from African soil was bauxite 9%; aluminum 5%; chromite 44%; cobalt 57%; copper 5%; gold 21%; iron ore 4%; steel 2%; lead (Pb) 3%; manganese 39%; zinc 2%; cement 4%; natural diamond 46%; graphite 2%; phosphate rock 31%; coal 5%; mineral fuels (including coal) & petroleum 13%; uranium 16%. (Yager et al., 2007; World Bank, 2014). However, there is much more to the business opportunities than natural resources. Although petroleum production has captured the attention of the media, a company called Bidco Refineries in Kenya has created a cooking oil business worth more than US$160 million (Mahajan, 2009). The previously listed mineral resources and agricultural products constitute the basis for local businesses, multinational corporations, and informal sectors' activities in the African continent.

Another important trend in business and government relations in Africa is that farmers, entrepreneurs, and miners have all collaborated to promote exports. In addition, groups of African countries have formed numerous trade blocs, which include the Common Market for Eastern and Southern Africa, the Economic and Monetary Community of Central Africa, the Economic Community of Central African States, the Economic Community of West African States, the Mano River Union, the Southern African Development Community, and the West African Economic and Monetary Union. Algeria, Libya, and Nigeria are members of the Organization of the Petroleum Exporting Countries (OPEC). The African Union was formally launched as a successor to the Organization of African Unity in 2002 to accelerate socioeconomic integration and promote peace, security, and stability on the continent (World Bank, 2014; OECD, 2010). Despite these initiatives, most African countries' governments have not done enough to promote small scale industry as either a complement or an alternative to large-scale modern manufacturing. Advocates of small industry promotion promise a wide range of benefits, including accelerated employment creation, income generation for the poor, dispersal of economic activity to small towns and rural areas, and mobilization of latent entrepreneurial talent (Johnson & Turner, 2016). It is also very important to argue at this junction that support for small enterprise and the informal sector could help African countries create a wider base of political support for capitalism and free-market policies.

As more businesses target their share of the African economy, there is ample need to critically examine the success factors in and obstacles to operating in the various African countries economies. By creating a positive business environment, providing the right tools for entrepreneurship and trade, and offering private sector partnership with government (Johnson & Turner, 2016), African nations could open the door to their people to pursue self-development. There is no development approach that is more edifying to person, and in turn, more durable in result, if there are no skilled entrepreneurs (Natsio, 2007; Johnson & Turner, 2016). In addition, several African countries businesses still do not have a clear pathway to profit. Private investors are not motivated enough by the government to meet the poor people needs in Africa (Nafziger, 1993; Sandbrook, 1993; Rangan et al., 2007). According to Rangan et al. (2007), many successful cases of business provision to poor consumers owe their profitability to enlightened government policies in some countries that enable adequate return of investors. In few countries in Africa, such policies seem to have common characteristics. For instance, government may provide just enough incentives to attract the private companies' entry to develop the infrastructure, but leave it to the businesses to collect the rest of the return from consumers of their services and products (Rangan et al., 2007; OECD, 2010). This very important relationship between government and business in Africa has forced innovative market mechanisms to emerge in terms of product and service design, on one hand, and delivery and compliance, on the other hand. In addition, in 2005 Europe received 35% of Africa's petroleum exports; the United States, 32%; China, 10%; Japan, 2%; and other countries in the Asia and the Pacific region, 12%. West African countries sent 45% of their exports to the United States and 32% to China, Japan, and other countries in the Asia and the Pacific region. North African countries sent 64% of their exports to Europe and 18% to the United States. Intraregional exports to African countries amounted to only 2% of total African petroleum exports (British Petroleum plc, 2006: 20).

Government, private sector, and nongovernmental organizations (NGOs) are essential components of economic development and poverty reduction in African countries. The relationship between these three sectors is also a very important source of innovation and employment generation (Griffin & Moorhead, 2014; Dibie, 2014a). Government has always been an influential actor in the economy of several African countries. This is because they own many public corporations and are able to enact public policies that assisted economic growth as well as promoted industrial development or the control of inflation and unemployment. The assessment of activities of government in several African countries in the past few decades could help readers better understand contemporary proposal for government action. In addition, an awareness of the changes that have occurred in business organizations will also help us appraise the corporate innovations that are taking place in the African continent.

The center objective of most African countries economic policy is to improve economic stability and welfare of its citizens. To successfully achieve these economic policies, five goals are important: (a) the creation of economic growth; (b) stability of prices; (c) positive balance of trade; (d) management of deficits of trade and debt; (e) and full employment. Economic growth is vital to nations in order to reduce poverty rates and unemployment, increase public resources, and avoid inflation (Dibie, 2014a; Pettinger, 2008). Price stability is the reduction of inflation or deflation of products and services, and reaching this goal is important to prevent the redistribution of wealth of citizens. Positive balance of trade promotes the act of exporting more than is imported, a goal that is very much interconnected with international economics. In addition, a well-regulated and vibrant competitive private sector can also empower poor citizens by providing them with better goods and services at more affordable prices. In the past two decades, government in several African countries have paid more attention to fostering private sector development as a major instrument of their national sustainable development strategic plan (OECD, 2010; World Bank, 2014).

Further, while ethics have long been of relevance to government and business relations in sub-Saharan African countries, what seems like an epidemic of ethical breaches in recent years has placed ethics in the lower mainstream of managerial responsibility both in the public and private sectors. According to Ferrell et al. (2015), two special aspects of government and business relations that have not taken increase importance are corporate governance and corporate social responsibility. Another significant area of government and business relations today involves employment relationships. Employment knowledge in the private sector is those values that are frequently transferred from the business sector to government agencies and vice versa (Geuras & Garofalo, 2010). For example, knowledge workers are those who add value to an organization because of what they know. How well governments in African countries are able to regulate businesses is seen as a major factor in determining how successful and ethical the economy may be in the future.

This chapter provides an overview of the nature of the economy of most African countries. It also investigates how the government of some African countries regulates business to preserve competition and protect consumers and employees. In some African countries, the national and regional governments also intervene in the economy with laws and regulations to promote competition and protect the environment, consumers, and employees. When necessary, the governments often would take steps through its central bank to minimize disruptive effect of economic fluctuation to spur growth so that consumers may spend more money and businesses may hire more employees. The chapter also describes how the governments of some African countries control the activities of businesses when the economy expands too much by raising the interest rate to discourage spending by businesses and consumers. It also examines how privatization, outsourcing, and contracting out are a practice of hiring other business organizations to do the work previously performed by the government. This practice is an increasingly popular strategy because it helps government to focus on their core activities or functions. A central issue in the past five decades revolves around the fact that rapid changes in government and business relationship, type of regulations policies, and the state of the economy pose unsurpassed difficulties in keeping accurate track of government's fiscal policies. It recommends that managers in government and business institutions in sub-Saharan Africa should be cognizant of both primary and secondary dimensions of diversity, as well as the many benefits to be derived from having diverse workforces that could propel sustainable development. Sustainable development cannot be achieved if there is a poor or weak government and business relations in any African country.

Globalization

Globalization is defined as the process of interconnecting the world's people with respect to culture, economic, political, technological, and environmental aspects of their live (Dibie, 2014a; Lodge, 1995). According to Griffin et al. (2017), a global perspective is distinguished by a willingness to be open and to learn from the alternative systems and meanings of other people and cultures, as well as a capacity to avoid assuming that people everywhere are the same. Globalization is playing a major role in the environment of the economy of many countries in sub-Saharan Africa. The globalization trend started soon after World War II. Managing in a global economy poses many different challenges and opportunities. An important consideration is how behavioral processes vary widely across cultural and national boundaries. For instance, a person with a global perspective tends to view the world from a broad perspective, always seeking unexpected trends and opportunities (Kedia & Muhkerji, 1999; Rhinesmith, 1992). In addition, people with global perspectives are more likely to see a broad context and accept life as a balance of conflicting forces.

Greenberg (2013) contends that the trend toward globalization has been widespread in past few decades as a result of three important forces. The forces include the following: (1) Technology has drastically lowered the cost of transportation and communication, thereby enhancing opportunities for international commerce and economic growth in many countries. (2) Globalization has also resulted to the enactment of new laws that have liberalized trades in many countries in Africa and around the world. It will be recalled that previously laws restricted trades, and most transactions were based on the principles of comparative advantage. (3) Globalization has also galvanized developing countries to seek to expand their economies by promoting exports and opening their doors to foreign companies seeking investment. Therefore, it could be argued that international trade is the major driver of globalization, while the primary vehicles are multinational corporations that have established more than 30% of their operations all over the world (Dibie et al., 2015; Greenberg, 2013; Daniels et al., 2011). Figure 1.1 shows the five changing environmental factors that have affected business and government relations in Africa.

Globalization just like what is proposed by the modernization theory requires the emergence of a rational and industrial individual or corporation that is receptive to new ideas, acknowledges different opinions and is punctual and optimistic, and believes that rewards should be distributed on the basis of universalistic rules. Therefore, globalization practice could

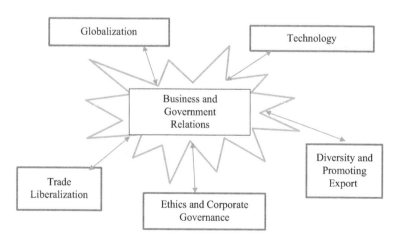

Figure 1.1 Changing environmental factors of business and government relations in Africa

Source: Designed by author

be argued to offer a better but still partial foundation for sustainable well-being for developing countries in Africa. For instance, the top nine largest multinational corporations in 2015 were forms from industrial countries. These multinational corporations include Royal Dutch Shell, Walmart Stores, ExxonMobil, British Petroleum, Sinopec (Chinese Petroleum and Chemical Corporation), General Motors, Toyota, and Ford Motors (Griffin et al., 2017; Fortune, 2011). It is important to note, however, that in the past three decades, despite the positive benefits of globalization, the number of experts throughout the world has risen, fallen, and changed direction, along with shifts in economic development throughout the world. At the same time, shrinking economies sometimes leave experts without jobs in their newly adopted countries (Greenberg, 2013). On the other hand, those working in another country as a result of globalization are exposed to different cultures. Difference in culture could lead to cultural shock; this means that people's recognition that others may be different from them in ways that they never imagined, and this takes some getting used to. According to Nelson and Quick (2013), the feelings of cultural shock are inevitable, although some degree of frustration may be expected when a person first enters a new country. However, the more time a person spends learning the new culture, the better they will come to understand and accept it (Janssens, 1995). Therefore, the fact that the world's economy is global in nature suggests that highly parochial and ethnocentric views have no place in business and government relations in respect of international trade. Despite the technical difficulties associated with globalization, government agencies must work on appropriate guidelines to ensure that their respective countries do not miss out on the benefits of globalization. At the same time, multinational and domestic companies in Africa need to develop internal guidelines, training, and leadership to ensure compliance of government regulations.

As a result of globalization, the volume of government and business relations has grown significantly and continues to grow at very rapid pace. There are five basic reasons for the growth of government and business relations in sub Saharan Africa:

1. Many local organizations have become international and have to seek approval to enter foreign and domestic markets;
2. Communication and transportation have advanced pragmatically over the past several decades;
3. Many local businesses have diversified into other markets to control costs, especially to reduce labor costs;
4. Government and business relations have grown due to new regulatory policies; and
5. In several countries government has increase the privatization of previously owned public corporation. In some cases the governments have

contracted out services to businesses and nonprofit institutions or non-governmental organizations.

(Greenberg & Baron, 2012; Griffin & Moorhead, 2014)

It is very important to observe that as a result of globalization trends and multicultural nature in Africa, business managers are increasingly required to have a global perspective and supportive set of skills and knowledge that are highly effective (Wankel, 2007; Levy et al., 2007). A related business challenge that is relevant to globalization is adopting broader stakeholder perspective and looking beyond shareholder value. This challenge calls for social responsibility. According to Nelson and Quick (2013), social responsibility requires businesses to live and work together for the common good and value of human dignity. Griffin et al. (2017) contend that when social responsibility issues involve the creation of a green strategy that is intended to protect the natural environment, it is often called corporate sustainability. In the past two decades, multinational corporations working in Africa are now increasingly interested in balancing their financial performance with their employees' quality of life, and improving the local community and brother society (Griffin et al., 2017; Daniels et al., 2011).

Some scholars have argued that globalization can be harmful to the poor if it opens markets for agricultural products from developed countries to African nations. Such importation of agricultural products to Africa could ruin subsistent farming, which is the traditional practice in the continent. Further, in this respect, globalization could also widen the gap between the rich and poor within a society, as wealthier citizens capitalize on information flow and quick transfer of goods and services leaving the poor further behind (Wright & Boorse, 2014; Ya Ni & Van Wart, 2016).

According to Wright and Boorse (2014), globalization is not always capable to promote some goods, such as financial stability and social justice. It also has the potential to dilute and even destroy cultural and religious ideals and norms when it is uncritically welcomed into Africa. However, regardless of whether globalization is helpful or harmful in Africa, it is already taking place in sub-Saharan Africa. African countries must therefore learn how to confront it head on and adapt its connections to their cultures and needs.

Corporate Social Responsibility

Corporate social responsibility (CSR) refers to businesses living and working together for the common good and valuing human dignity. In a nut shell, corporate social responsibility is a way of meeting the challenge of more ethical resource-efficient, sustainable consumption and production (Blewitt, 2015). Corporate social responsibility could also be viewed as a private sector development that incorporates the goals of environmental sustainability, inclusivity, global poverty reduction, and equity of all people (Ferrell et al.,

2015). It entails actions that enhance social good beyond the interest of the corporation, and that which is required by public policy (Griffin et al., 2017). In addition, corporation social responsibility practices are considered to be voluntary companies' actions designed to improve social or environmental conditions in a society or country (Calvera, 2015). Henderson (2007) and Hopkin (1999) contend that businesses have responsibilities other than those associated with the production of goods and services, and must give regard to the society which extends to a healthy physical environment.

The Global Compact initiative by the United Nations also postulates that responsible citizens must form a partnership with other bodies such as corporations and civil society organizations to realize the vision of more sustainable and inclusive global economy (UN Global Compact, 2005; UNEP, 2003). Therefore, corporate social responsibility could be seen as a vital part of the armory for achieving a stronger business and government relations, as well as sustainable development in all the countries that multinational corporations are manufacturing and selling goods and services. It is assumed that companies with good corporate social responsibility can enhance employee effective organizational commitment by improving their working environment, promoting employee participation in socially responsible actions, and fostering a good corporate image that makes employees feel proud of their companies' ethical, legal and discretionary actions (Wang, 2014; Calvera, 2015).

Several scholars contend that corporate social responsibility are set by Western corporations because they cover only cases from North America and Western Europe (Wang, 2014; Griffin et al., 2017; Daniel el. al 2011; Ferrell et al., 2015; Dibie et al., 2015; Henderson, 2007). In the care of Africa, some multinational corporations may adopt the policy of corporate social responsibility, however, their attitude and practices toward the environment and society are essentially not eco-friendly. Therefore, an argument could be presented that many multinational corporations in Africa are mostly directed by commercial dictates, self-interest, and political advantage in their philanthropy, and they are indulged in unethically exploitation of poor people.

Many multinational corporations operating in several African countries have not been able to effectively establish environmental policies and procedures that are consistent with both their domestic laws and those of other sub-Saharan countries where they have their operations (Dibie et al., 2015). According to Lehne (2013), the dual identity of multinational corporations makes both home country and host country governments suspicious because it renders conflict between governments and foreign companies almost inevitable. Lehne (2013) and Ya Ni and Van Wart (2016) also reported that most developing countries' governments often regard multinational corporations as vehicles to promote their political and economic interests. This is because foreign companies will gather up economic rewards in their countries and leave without helping to solve their social and political problems. Farrell et al. (2015) contend that many Western multinational corporations that tend to promote corporate social responsibility in the local home country turn around to play one country against another in the process of seeking research and developing funding, investment subsidies, job training, infrastructure projects, favorable pricing rules for their products, import and export incentives, as well as reduced tax relief. Jones (2013) argues that since corporate social responsibility has become more prominent publicly, many social and environmental indices of global progress have actually worsened. Further, Blewitt (2015) contends that there is evidence that large corporations do not always respect the environmental and other rights of indigenous people, or maintain their interest in the sustainable community development activities, even though these companies may feature prominently in corporate social responsibility communications. Such practice could be described as Machiavellian risk-management actions.

The mining multinational corporations are often culprit of the unethical practice in Africa. It could be argued that in extracting natural resources in Africa, these multinational corporations have a direct and unmistakable impact on the environment. This is because they constantly endanger the environment by contaminating the air, soil, or water during manufacturing processes, or by manufacturing products that release fossil-fuel contaminants into the environment (Wright & Boorse, 2014; Daniels et al., 2011; Wang, 2014). Although some multinational corporations in Africa provide access to capital, technology, management skills, and export markets, they are often criticized for deepening the economic dependence of local communities by importing inappropriate technologies interfering with domestic politics, and destroying traditional cultures (Lehne, 2013; Streeck & Schmitter, 1985). For example, while British Petroleum (BP) spent more than $30 billion to clean the oil spillage of the Gulf Coast of the United States between 2007 and 2010, it has not deemed it necessary to do the same for the Niger Delta of Nigeria, where it has been spilling crude petroleum for more than three decades (Dibie, 2014a; Okonta, 2008). It has also been argued that Shell and Chevron are engaged in the oil enclaves of the Niger Delta of Nigeria, pretending to be corporate responsible companies at the transnational outlook but local and selective in their eco-friendly policies in Nigeria (Okonta, 2008; Dibie & Offiong, 2012; Odogbor, 2005). Nigeria and several other African countries have enacted various environmental policies geared toward the regulation and control of the activities of both the public and private sectors. The policies include disposal of hazardous and toxic wastes that affect the health of the people directly and indirectly. It is also clear that the effectiveness of all these laws is in doubt, due to poor implementation strategies, corruption, and other numerous problems. The multinational oil companies that citizens of oil and mining communities complain about for oil spillage claims, loss of income from fishing and farming, pollution of drinking water and crops, or damage to health as a result of waterborne diseases always win cases against them on legal grounds, because they have a lot of financial capacity to fight their cases instead of obeying environmental laws that are expected to hold them accountable (Dibie, 2014a).

In order to establish a more robust business and government relations, multinational and local corporations must demonstrate environmental and community responsibility. The appropriate measures include ethics and equity in dealings with all stakeholders, as well as matters of efficiency, profitability, financial probity, and workforce quality (Maigan & Ferrell, 2001; Hopkin, 1999). In addition, socially responsible corporations in Africa must also provide employment and respect for both human and labor rights, as well as appropriate education. According to Maigan and Ferrell (2001) Blewitt (2015) and Wang (2014), good corporate social responsibility programs must work toward meeting their legal, ethical, economic, and discretionary obligations to society. Some scholars have identified important and appropriate activities that may be reasonably expected by corporations with good CRS policies. The activities include the following:

1. Full compliance of government regulations and a willingness to ethically exceed the provisions of these policies
2. Forging of partnerships with government and nongovernment organizations, including local community groups in such programs
3. Publication of meaningful and measurable social and environmental goals and regular reporting on progress towards achievements
4. Recruitment and training of local staff and purchase of goods and services from local suppliers
5. Investment and involvement in social welfare and environmental conservation and upgrading programs
6. Corporate public affairs program and the education and engagement of customers and staff about social and environmental issues of concern
7. Enactment of policies to avoid damaging social and environmental impacts of operations
   (Henderson, 2007; Lehne, 2013; Hopkin, 1999; Griffin et al., 2017; Maigan & Ferrell, 2001; Blewitt, 2015; Wang, 2014)

This means that domestic and international companies in Africa with high corporate social responsibility policy must engage in providing better quality product for customers inspiring high intrinsic motivation among employees by providing training and promotion opportunities and offering unique moral values to stakeholders (Blewitt, 2015; Wang, 2014; Calveras, 2015). Dibie and Dimitriou (2016) contend that good corporate social responsibility practices may help attract consumers, as well as galvanize a greater willingness to buy or use the companies' products or services when they feel that a company is ethical. According to Hart (2005), being eco-friendly and eco-effective could help a corporation meet the needs of the world's poor and make a good profit in the process. Therefore, the implementation of corporate social responsibility in Africa could benefit companies both financially and socially.

Dynamics of Business and Government Relations

Government and business relations have changed over several decades in the African continent as a result of outsourcing. Privatization, outsourcing, and contracting out involve the practice of hiring other business organizations to do the work previously performed by government (Hodge, 2000). The practice is an increasingly popular strategy because it helps governments focus on their core activities or functions. A central issue in the past five decades revolves around the fact that rapid changes in government and business relationship, type of regulations policies, and the state of the economy pose unsurpassed difficulties in keeping accurate track of government's fiscal policies. Diversity in both in the government and business sectors is also a crucial mechanism for enhancing partnerships. Unfortunately, many employees from both sectors tend to stereotype other agencies and institutions' staff within the two sectors in the economy (Greenberg, 2013; Geuras & Garofalo, 2010). Managers in government and business institutions in sub-Saharan Africa should be cognizant of both primary and secondary dimensions of diversity, as well as the many benefits to be derived from having a diverse workforce that could propel sustainable development. Sustainable development cannot be achieved if there is a poor or weak government and business relations in any African country (Dibie, 2014b).

Figure 1.2 shows that business efforts to influence public policy and government include not only individual company efforts but also business association efforts. In addition, for most business, some combination of the interaction and proactive approaches with government and other interest groups is most often the best policy-making approach (Anderson, 2015; Dye, 2013). On one hand, partnership or a combination of business, individual, and citizens' interest groups and NGOs all have influence on government policies. On the other hand, the media has a strong interest in giving visibility and setting the policy agenda. Businesses must view the media as an important influencing agent affecting their operating environment, and must be effective in its relations with the media (Anderson, 2015; Jon, 2000; Jon & Peters, 2000). Therefore, it could be argued that these entities often partner to influence public policy and a nation's governance system. The model provides an illustration that there are three general categories of business responses to public policy that are enacted by the government to regulate business. The categories include interactive, proactive, and reactive.

Unfortunately, African nations' debt is at an all-time high due to governmental spending and borrowing. Management of deficits and debt is important for nations' economic growth, because achieving this goal implies fiscal responsibility. Full employment is also beneficial to a nation's economy

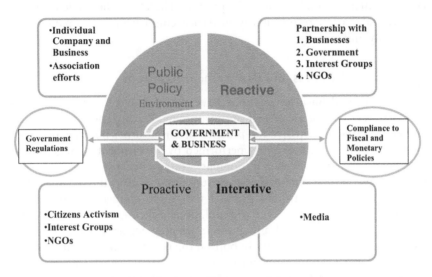

Figure 1.2 Governments and business relations model

Source: Anderson, J. (2015). *Public Policy-Making*. 8th Edition. Boston, MA: Wadsworth Press; Dye, T. (2013). *Understanding Public Policy*. 14th Edition. Boston, MA: Pearson Learning

because people will be paying taxes, there will be revenue to fund governmental programs, and lower numbers of people will be relying on welfare programs such as food stamps and other public foods (Kraft & Furlong, 2015).

Managing the African economy poses many challenges and opportunities. These challenges at a macro level include property ownership arrangements that vary widely. The availability of natural resources and components of the infrastructure, as well as the role of government in business, also enhance the managing of the economy of any country. While Pierre's (2009) definition of governance is society-centric, Ferrell et al. (2015) offer a definition of the term that is more State-centric. Even as they concede that governance relates to changing relationships between State and society and a growing reliance on less coercive policy instruments, they assert that the State is still the center of considerable political power. They perceive governance as processes in which the State plays a leading role, making priorities and defining objectives. This is in line with the notion of the role of the State as that of "steering" society and the economy.

Hirst (2000) offers a more general definition of the term *governance*. He asserts that governance can be generally defined as the means by which an activity or ensemble of activities is controlled or directed, such that it delivers an acceptable range of outcomes according to some established standard. In addition, the Canadian Institute of Governance (2002) offers another general definition, asserting that governance is the process whereby societies or organizations make important decisions, determine whom they involve and how they involve them, and how they render accounts.

According to the World Bank (2014), good governance entails sound public sector management such as efficiency, effectiveness and economy, accountability, exchange and free flow of information (transparency), and a legal framework for development in respect of justice, respect for human rights, and liberties. In addition, Surendra Munshi (2004) contends that good governance signifies a participative manner of governing that functions in a responsible, accountable, and transparent manner based on the principles of efficiency, legitimacy, and consensus for the purpose of promoting the rights of individual citizens and the public interest. Thus, governance entails indicating the exercise of political will for ensuring the material welfare of society and sustainable development with social justice.

Monetary and Fiscal Policies

There are many policy tools that can be used to achieve goals of economic development. Fiscal policy is used to allow policy makers to create budgets for government programs and revise the tax code. This is usually initiated by the president and legislative branch of government every year. Monetary policy is similar but is concerned more with controlling money supply in circulation. Government decrees are set in place with the policy tool of regulation to ensure quality and safety of the citizens, economy, and environment. Tax expenditures are subsidies and incentives given to companies or agencies when they do something that encourages regional economic development such as relocation to another area (Dibie, 2014a). Lastly, tax policy is used to generate revenue for expenditures by mandating income, property, and sales taxes (Kraft & Furlong, 2015; Dibie, 2014b).

Economic policies in several African countries are guided by the need to achieve economic growth and to address the high levels of poverty, inequality, and unemployment in the continent. One of the main failures of many African countries' economies in recent years has been their inability to create sufficient jobs. This has constrained growth, kept the tax base narrow, and forced the governments to use public finances in an increasingly redistributive manner. In light of this, the governments of several African countries have adopted a New Growth Path that seeks to restructure the economy in order to improve labor absorption and the composition and rate of economic growth.

Despite its focus on growth and job creation and the role of public spending on, for example, infrastructure, in supporting these aims, the New Growth Path reinforces some African governments' commitment to macroeconomic stability and low inflation. Further, industry has not been seen as a key to another goal in many African countries (UNECOSOC, 2012). If African countries governments really wanted the capability of doing without imports of essential commodities, they must develop both an integrated industrial structure and a productive agriculture. If they wish to exclude foreign political and cultural influence, they must also learn to operate their manufacturing plants without foreign help. Most of the discussion about government and business relations in Africa is about reducing dependence and increasing self-sufficiency (Mahajan, 2009; World Bank, 2014; OCED, 2010). This implies that African countries must learn how to establish manufacturing companies that could help them produce a majority of what they consume. In addition, an alternative strategy may be to develop the capacity of producing a wide variety of goods efficiently enough to trade them on world markets, and obtaining some goods overseas when it is advantageous to do so.

Appropriate fiscal and monetary policies are the mechanism that could galvanize a hidden development goal for African countries. However, many countries in the continent continue to establish the most capital intensive industries available. This cannot be attributed entirely to misguided policies in a particular country. The extent that modern manufacturing is a good development strategy in itself calls for a rethink on African nations' continuous dependency on industries that they do not have the manpower, electricity, or technology to maintain. Such endeavors are not sustainable. The sustainable development policies that African government should pursue must focus on how much could be accomplished with alternative polices and measuring the costs of industrialization in terms of other goals that remain to be achieved. Government liberalized policies with reduced control and market prices closer to scarcity values can help arrest the tendency toward capital intensity and inappropriate, modern technologies in manufacturing, and thus raise job creation in industries all over the African continent.

Role of Government in Business

The government has an important role to play in the business world. According to Ya Ni and Van Wart (2016), the government's role in business is as old as the history of any country's political economy. In most cases, a nation's constitution gives the government the power to regulate some commerce. Though the government's role in many African countries has increased over time, the business community still enjoys considerable freedom. The government, however, still exercises its authority in several ways. The following are some areas where government has played a major role in the past five decades.

Regulation

Regulation comprises agencies staffed by qualified public servants with expertise in carrying out an expanding array of responsibilities delegated to them by legislature (Hill & Lynn, 2016). It involves the regulation of a widening expanse of economic, political, and social activities and complex, often very large and politically, business organizations. One of the major roles of government is its ability to regulate society in order to preserve and enhance public welfare (Shafritz et al., 2011). Government regulation tends to affect each and every day of the African people's lives. For instance, people live in houses or apartments that have been built according to local building code; citizens drive cars that have many safety features required by the federal government; people drive to an intersection and stop at the red light; the Equal Employment Opportunity Commission requires a workplace free of sexual harassment; and in the hall of every business is a certificate indicating that the property is licensed to operate as a business. All over the African continents, many countries use two methods to carry out laws: (1) adjudication and (2) rule making.

On one hand, through adjudication, government agencies or ministries formulate enforcement orders backed by civil or criminal penalties and settle specific factual dispute. Adjudication can be informal or formal. In some countries, formal adjudication is known as hearing, which is similar to a trial. For example, if a company is charged with violating a law or regulation, it may defend itself before administrative law judges of the agency bringing the charges. Further, in most African countries, the informal procedures constitute the bulk of administrative adjudication. During informal adjudication, a government regulating agency determines the rights or liabilities of specific parties in a proceeding other than a formal hearing. Establishing rates, awarding licenses or permits, and both civil and criminal law enforcement are all examples of adjudication.

On the other hand, the ruling-making regulatory function of the government allows it agencies or ministries to issue general policy statements as well as detailed requirements. Rules or regulations are government agencies' statements that implement, interpret, or prescribe a law or policy (Lehne, 2013). The Administrative Procedure Act at the national level of most African countries requires a government agency to publish a notice of proposed rulemaking in the National Government Register, announcing the rule it intends to put into effect and soliciting public comments. For example, the Ministry of Environment in Nigeria has offered insurers and gives citizens and businesses the opportunity to comment on the feasibility of compliance with its proposals (Dibie, 2014b). Further, in Ghana and South Africa, various company and trade-association executives have consulted with government agency representatives to help them formulate specific environmental pollution rules. Traditional economic regulation by national and regional government agencies accounts for only two-thirds of the gross national product. The advent of social regulation has now extended to the remaining third in some countries' economy (Yandle & Young, 1986).

It is very important to note, however, that social regulation is characterized by the use of agencies or ministries organized along functional or issues rather than industry categories. Unlike the traditional economic regulation, the social regulation agencies have the power to regulate across all industries although their jurisdiction is limited to one aspect of business activity (Ya Ni, & Van Wart 2016; Stigler, 1976). Examples of agencies that are involved in social regulations are the Ministry of Environment or Environmental Protection Agency, the Occupational Safety and Health Administration, and the Equal Employment Opportunity Commission.

There are also other government ministries or agencies that are more specialized—for example, those charged with protecting consumers against unsafe products. Another example is the National Highway Traffic Safety Administration or the Road Safety Corps, as it is called in some African countries. This agency covers automobiles and traffic violations on highways (Inanga, 2005). The jurisdiction of the Food and Drug Administration extends to medical devices and cosmetics, in addition to food and drugs. The Consumer Product Safety Commission or Agency has a broad mandate, extending to most other consumer products, with little key exclusion such as alcoholic beverages, tobacco products, and firearms.

Permission and License

Before any company can open its doors for business, it is required to apply for license from the government. As a result, most businesses need to register with a national or regional government to operate. In most cases, businesses are required to register with both the national and regional governments. In addition, companies tend to need a charter, and other forms of operations, such as limited liability companies or partnerships, need other forms of registration. The function of this registration is usually to define the financial liability the owners of the company have (Lehne, 2013). These companies' registration requirement with the government helps protect businesses in respect to the limits on the risk associated with the amount they have invested in that particular organization. Registration also allows the government to monitor companies, to execute its other functions in the business and the national economy.

Taxation

Most governments in the African continent regularly exercise their power to provide incentives for designated private businesses or companies. Governments at all levels tax businesses, and the resulting revenue, is an important part of government budgets. A nation's public financial management covers its entire budget cycle from strategic planning to audit oversight (OECD, 211). Some revenue are taxed at the corporate level, and then taxed as personal income when distributed as dividends. This is in no way inappropriate, since it balances the tax burden between the company and individual, and allows the government to tax more equitably. Thus, public finance management through taxation ensures that resources are efficiently allocated based on identified needs and revenue collected from citizens and businesses, and expenditures are structured to benefit every person in the country. It is important to also note that using the tax incentives, the national government could foster what it considers to be the greater social responsibility of the part of business. Further, it is common for government to use taxes as a mechanism for control.

Consumer Protection

The government's role in business includes protecting the consumer or customer. The Consumer Product Safety Act of some African countries requires the government to create an independent regulatory agency to protect the public against unreasonable risks on injury associated with consumer products (OCED, 2010). It has been argued that one of the causes of market failure arise where individuals are not sufficiently informed to make sensible decision in the marketplace. Government regulation of consumer products takes many forms, ranging from out-right bans, to requirements for showing specific types of information on containers, to changes in the products themselves (Dye, 2013; Kraft & Furlong, 2015). When a vendor fails to honor the guarantee of its product, the purchaser has recourse in the law. Likewise, when a product causes harm to an individual, the courts may hold the vendor or manufacturer responsible. Labeling is another requirement the government imposes on marketers. Many foods, for example, must display nutritional content on the packaging (Lehne, 2013). The government of several African countries has been making advances in consumer rights for decades. However, the consumer movement still needs considerable development to protect the public, especially in the informal sector. The respective consumer product safety ministries or agencies have sought to mitigate any harm that might come to children exposed to hazard. The reason for government action in such a case is that consumers lack knowledge of either the chemicals with which the clothing is treated or the hazard that they give rise to. Therefore, correcting inadequacies in the information producers provide about the products they sell is a justification underlying much safety, health, and consumer protection regulations in many African countries. However, in order to protect the consumer government, regulation generates a wide variety of effects on the companies that produce and market to the consumer. As a result of the expanded role of government regulation of product safety, corporate marketing departments have had to develop the capability to handle reverse distribution or product recall (Lehne, 2013; Kraft & Furlong, 2015). Government also requires companies to provide greater information on labels and supporting literature, as well as restricting the types of claims that are made by companies in the advertisement of their products.

Employee Protection

In many African countries, national and regional government agencies work to protect the rights of employees. As a result government responsibility for ending job discrimination rests primarily with two national agencies: (a) the Equal Employment Opportunity Commission and (b) the Office of Contract Compliance in the Labor Department in some African countries. On one hand, some African government have established policies to ensure that all people have equal chance to compete for and hold positions of employment based on their job qualifications. The Equal Opportunity Commission protects employees from discrimination. On the other hand, some African governments also have affirmative action policies that ensure that women, handicapped, and other protected classes of people are equitably represented in the government ministries or agencies.

The Occupational Health and Safety Administration (OSHA), for example, is an agency under the Department of Labor. Its mission is to ensure a safe and healthful work environment. According to Dye (2013) and Kraft and Furlong (2015), the occupational Safety and Health Administration was created to ensure, as much as possible, that every working man and woman in the nation has safe and healthful working conditions, as well as to preserve a nation's human resources. The OSHA public implemented requires both voluntary and compulsory mandates.

Contract Enforcement

The Ministry of Trade and Industry of most African countries is required to enforce businesses' contracts with other companies (Greechie, 2003). These contracts may be complex, such as mergers, or they may be as simple as a warranty on supplies purchased. The government enforces these contracts. Most business litigates others whenever there is a breach of contract among them. As a result, companies often bring one another to court, just as individuals do, to get their conflicts resolved. An oral agreement can constitute a contract, but usually only a written agreement is provable (Hodge, 2000). If one party fails or refuses to meet its obligation under a contract, a company will turn to the legal system for enforcement. The Ministry of Trade and Industry could also disallow two companies from merging in order to prevent a monopoly.

Environmental Protection

A sustainable development strategy available to government is to draw down on natural resources assets, and to utilize environmental services that will produce greater long-term net benefits such as employment, income, gains, and reduction of poverty (Dibie, 2014b). As a result, when a marketing transaction impacts a third party—others besides the marketer and purchaser—the effect is called an "externality." The third party is often the environment. Thus, it is the government's role to regulate industry and thereby protect the public from environmental externalities (Lehne, 2013). Whether the government is effective in this role is a matter of much discussion. Greater attention by the government, however, to the environmental impact of development policies and development projects, may lead to more efficient resource use by government and business, as well as to more equitably distributed economic growth. As a result, social and environmental policies enacted by the government for managing current problems and addressing future hurdles are intricately intertwined (Dibie, 2014b). In addition, as a result of the relationship between air quality and respiratory illness such as emphysema, lung cancer, asthma, and bronchitis, the Environmental Protection Agency (EPA) or Ministry of Environment have been given mandates to regulate air pollution, water pollution, and hazardous and toxic substances (Dye, 2013; Kraft & Furlong, 2015). In some countries, the EPA and Federal Food and Drug Administration have also set standards for drinking water. The EPA has also set standards for noise emission for railroads. It is very important to note, however, that people as consumers and taxpayers pay the costs of cleaning up the environment and also receive the benefit that ensued from clean water, clean air, less noise, and minimal hazardous waste pollution.

Investment Protection

The value of multinational corporations' investment in Africa countries lays not so much in the capital it provides but in a number of other potential benefits, including employment creation, technology transfer, technical and managerial skills, and access to the world market. In some African countries, government policy provisions require companies to declare financial information public, thereby protecting the rights of investors and facilitating further investment (Mahajan, 2009; Nafziger, 1993). This is generally done through filings with the Securities and Exchange Commission. Whether federal regulation has been adequate in African countries is a matter of much debate.

Funding Research and Development

Many African countries, such as Nigeria, South Africa, Kenya, and Ghana, just to mention a few nations, spend billions of dollars to support federal research and development (R&D) activities. In addition, tax preferences are in place to encourage the private sector to increase its R&D spending (World Bank, 2014; OCED, 2010; Inanga, 2005). Some studies on federally supported research and development provide multifaceted but incomplete answers to questions about those governmental activities: whether the current level of spending is appropriate, what returns taxpayers receive for public investment in R&D, and whether funds are allocated to areas of inquiry and projects that will provide the highest return on that investment (Murphy & Topel, 2003; United States Government, 2007).

In addition, the incentive for businesses to deduct R&D expenses as they are incurred lowers a firm's costs for performing research and development. This tax incentive often stimulates many corporations to do more such work, because the lower cost may make R&D a more attractive alternative than other investment opportunities that do not have the same favorable tax treatment (Guenther, 2007; Kraft & Furlong, 2015). Thus, depending on the specification of the government, if your small business is engaged in scientific research and development (R&D), you may qualify for federal grants under the Small Business Innovation Research and the Small Business Technology Transfer program. In the United States, for example, the Small Business Innovation Research (SBIR) and Small Business Technology Transfer (STTR) programs are some of the largest sources of early stage capital for innovative small companies in the United States. These programs allow US-owned and operated small businesses to engage in federal research and development (R&D) that has a strong potential for commercialization.

Funding Small Business Development

In many African countries, business owners face both challenges and opportunities on a daily basis that often require them to have access to capital (Kuye et al., 2013; Inanga, 2005). The various Ministries of Commerce have now created Small Business Development Centers to assist entrepreneurs to write business proposals and apply for government loans. Such start-up loans could be used to purchase inventory and equipment, or invest in remodeling and advertising; small businesses need working capital for many reasons. Some African national and regional governments offer funding programs, often in the form of grants, and business support services to help new and established businesses grow and succeed (Kuye et al., 2013). Such government grants can help entrepreneurs develop their business through activities such as expansion, commercialization, research and development, innovation, and exports (Colebatch et al., 1997).

It is paramount for entrepreneurs in most African countries pursuing small business financial assistance in the form of loans, grants, or other aid programs to know where to look. Most government funding programs can help fund training employees, with product development, building a website, purchasing equipment, and lots more. It is very important to note, however, that a vast majority of government grants are given to nongovernmental organizations for programs and services that benefit the society or the public at large. There are other types of grants, such as those from foundations, public corporations, or private organizations (Bach & Unrah, 2004). These nongovernment organizations have specific requirements as to who is eligible to apply for and receive grant funding.

There are also well established financial institutions that finance government contracts. These financial institutions understand the challenges involved with government contract financing: start-up capital constraints, lack of traditional bank financing options, capacity to handle larger contracts, cash flow timing, and payroll issues.

Types of Business Responses

Nearly every company operating in African countries must have developed some capability to understand current and future development in government and public policy as they relate to their activities (Ya Ni & Van Wart, 2016; Lehne, 2013). Businesses' influence in determining the mixture of government functions a country selects in a particular period reflects the place of business in the brother political economy (Lehne, 2013). According to Blackford (2008), to be successful in a country, a company must have a better understanding of how government affects their operations and profitability, and the business can formulate strategies for how best to interact with government. Ya Ni and Van Wart (2015) and Blackford (2008) suggested three general types of business responses to the public policy environment: (a) reactive, (b) interactive, and (c) proactive.

Reaction to the government involves responding to government policy after it happens. The interactive approach of business involves collaborating with all other stakeholders in engaging with government policy makers and actors (including the media) to try to influence public policy outcomes, as well as to serve the interests of the business. The last of the three approaches is the proactive response approach, which entails acting to influence policies, anticipating changes, and trying to enhance competitive positioning by correctly anticipating changes in policy (Blackford, 2008). Ya Ni and Van Wart (2016) suggested that a combination of the interactive and proactive approaches is the best approach for most businesses. In meeting challenges from nongovernmental organizations (NGOs) and the media, businesses may respond in a variety of ways, including the following:

- **Anticipation.** Businesses may adopt issues management programs to forecast emerging issues and to adjust or change business practices in advance of the passage of stringent laws or regulations.
- **Confrontation.** Businesses may aggressively attack either the message or the messenger, and in extreme cases, businesses have felt justified to sue their critics for libel.
- **Participation.** Businesses may develop coalitions or partnerships with NGOs, as McDonald's did with the Environmental Defense Fund (EDF; see the following discussion) or as Home Depot did with the Rainforest Alliance.

(Kraft & Furlong, 2015; Ya Ni & Van Wort, 2016)

In some countries, when businesses are strongly affected by public policies, it is in their best interest to stay informed about policies and to try to influence governmental decision making and laws. Depending on the political economy of a country, there are different ways that businesses view and act on their relationship with government. First, it may be best for businesses to consider business and government on "two sides" and in opposition to each other. This perspective most often focus businesses' interactions with government on efforts to minimize government and reduce the costs and burdens on private business and the general economy associated with government taxes, regulations, and policies. An interactive or proactive approach is usually a better way to meet political and societal challenges while also protecting the reputation of the company (Ya Ni & Van Wort, 2015).

Second, government should favor businesses and incentivize business performance and investment because businesses are the main source of jobs, innovation, and societal economic well-being, and therefore government should support businesses with grants, tax credits, and subsidies (Blackford, 2008).

Third, businesses and government relations require partnership in addressing societal matters. This is in contrast to government being the regulator to ensure businesses act in a socially responsible manner. The author will like to suggest here that it is always important for sustainable businesses to understand how their efforts to achieve profits and to serve a social purpose are both strongly influenced by government policies. It is always important for sustainable businesses to manage their relationships with government (national, regional or state, national, and international) effectively. Nevertheless, business managers should be aware of the impact of business activities on the quality of life and the external pressures to promote these values. Despite these facts, production, marketing, and finance remain businesses' primary concern.

How Business Influence Government

Virtually all big businesses tend to form close relations with government regulatory agency staff and members of the National Assembly or their staff. The engagement is necessary in order to respond to the rising influence of government in business decision making. Businesses often use a variety of strategies to influence government policy. This includes supplying lobbying, political contributions, and interest group politics.

Supplying Information

Several big corporations have an office in the National Assembly or Congress to provide a listening post for the corporate headquarters. A constant flow of information is supplied to corporate officials on current government policies and future plans of action that might affect company operation. In addition, staff members interact with government and private planning groups, and with numerous public policy analysis organization that have been established at the national headquarters of the government (Lehne, 2013). Further, a substantial amount of business information and views are also provided to the government agencies that might be regulating their company. The two-way relationship between government and business helps provide a more cordial welcome to company personnel making inquiries at the national agency. This relationship might also enhance or give weight to the company's expressed concerns (Ya Ni &Van Wort, 2015). The good thing about sharing information with officials of government agencies and National Assembly members and their staff is that the corporate office in the national headquarters can help adapt corporate actions to changing national policies.

Business Lobbying

Lobbying is a communication with public officials to influence their decision in a manner harmonious with the interest of the individual or group communicating (Hill & Lynn, 2016). It is important to note, however, that a lobbyist's purpose may be selfish in the sense that he or she seeks to persuade others that his/her position is meritorious. The corporate office at the national headquarters serves as an essential mechanism for a company's relationship with the national government of a country. Officials of this office serve as the principal channel for communicating the company's views on the matters of major importance to legislators and executive branch officials.

The common practice is that businesses lobby in different ways. This can include the lobbying of National Assemblies or Congress and regional or state legislatures and executive branch agencies directly, through their own government relations specialists, through an industry trade association, through consultants, or through a combination of all those avenues. Big corporations may also engage in indirect or grassroots lobbying by appealing to their own employees, stakeholders, or the general public, to make their views known to policy makers (Anderson, 2015). Sometimes, in order to build a broad grassroots constituency, businesses may manage "issue advertising" campaigns on top-priority issues, or purchase issue ads in media outlets that target public policy makers or national headquarters insiders or stakeholders. Big companies could also choose to engage in social lobbying. Businesses showing a willingness to join such public interest coalitions can gain reputational rewards from NGOs, the media, and public policy makers. In some democratic countries in Africa, public policy does not directly restrict the activities of lobbyist. For example, in 2010 the energy companies in the United States spent more than $2.5 billion to lobby members of the US Congress, according to the Center for Responsive Politics. While oil, gas, and utility companies spent most of that money, renewable energy lobbying efforts were also sizable (Lacey, 2010).

Advising Government

Many businesses find it advantageous to provide personnel to serve on National Advisory Committees. In most cases, business representatives often serve on National Advisory Boards far more than any other interest groups (Ya Ni, & Van Wart 2016; Vehar, 1987). The opportunity to serve on these committees or board often permits company officials to obtain access to government decision makers and public policy officials. According to Anderson (2015), representing the big businesses to the executive branch of government may involve both attempts to influence future public policy and efforts to learn of current development and how the company might successfully adjust to them. It is very important to note that serving on government advisory committees is a desirable form of unpaid public service in that government becomes aware of a broad array of views before it enact any policy. Another very important function of advisory committees is to provide a sound board or at least a mechanism for the exchange of views by various private interest groups.

Interest Group Participation

An interest group is a group of individuals organized to seek public policy influence. There is tremendous diversity within interest groups (Dye, 2013). Interest groups and trade associations help in dealing with consumer complaints against member business companies, and reduce the pressure for greater government involvement in business. According to Lehne (2013), a vibrant system of interest group activity constitutes pluralist vision of how democracy should work. When a significant issue arises, groups appear to debate the concern. Group activities represent citizen opinion to government, and competition among various interests in which no single group is dominant, and then yield public policies broadly responsive to public preference (Anderson, 2015). Big companies' responses can include participation in interest group politics. Interest groups play a key role in all democratic systems of government. Business is just one of many interest group sectors trying to influence public policy. Businesses will encounter interest groups that may support or conflict with their position on an issue. It has been observed that business interests are still overrepresented: women, consumer, environmentalist, senior citizens, and advocates of human rights, conscience, and ideology must now be counted among the groups with an unmistakable national headquarters presence (Lehne, 2013; Kraft & Furlong, 2015).

Business Involvement in Politics

A successful functioning economy and an effectively operating business sector require a supportive policy environment (Ya Ni, 2015). As a result, a prohibition of business involvement in politics would in effect torpedo the policies needed to support a successful economy (Lehne, 2013). We would like to present an argument that in most cases business involvement in politics no longer safeguards societal diversity or checks abuse of government power by office holders in many African countries. Businesses also use campaign contributions to support their position and to try to influence public policies that can help them increase profits. Seven of the 10 largest corporations in the world are oil companies, based on revenues (Anderson, 2015). Business access to funds for lobbying and campaign contributions gives them a significant voice in the political system and on policies that can impact sustainable businesses. According to Lehne (2013), incumbents in the US Congress tend to capture the vast majority of campaign contributions from business sources, and they use these resources to prevent the emergence of meaningful challenges to their electoral position. In some African countries, there are a range of avenues a company might use in making political contributions. The most transparent and legitimate is that of forming a political action committee (PAC) to which voluntary contributions of employees are amassed and then given in legally limited amounts to selected candidates (Anderson, 2015; Dye, 2013). Apart from contributing directly to political candidates, firms can also advertise on ballot measure campaigns, and those contributions can come from corporate assets and are subject to no legal limitations. It could therefore be argued that corporate involvement in politics suppress rather promote social diversity and true democracy.

Business Interactions in Other Public Affairs

In several African countries, businesses are required to adopt positions that promote societal and industrial interest, and not just the interest of individual companies. Since businesses face a complex array of formal and informal public policy actors beyond government, their practices can be strongly influenced by citizen actions that bypass the formal institutions of government (Blackford, 2008). In a country that allows this type of practice, businesses could lobby and litigate, and they can get out large groups to demonstrate in public events and use exposure in the news media as a vehicle for getting their perspective heard. In Germany and Japan, citizen groups have both confronted and collaborated with corporations in order to foster change. NGOs often turn to collaboration with business to resolve issues. Indeed, as both sides have matured and grown less combative, business and NGOs have learned to work together to resolve problems. There are many examples of such productive collaboration, the most prominent of which have emerged on the environmental front.

In the United States, religious organizations, most prominently the Interfaith Center on Corporate Responsibility, have been the chief sponsors of such resolutions since the 1970s. More recently, they have been joined by mainstream shareholder groups, such as large institutional investors and pension funds, in calling for major changes in corporate governance and more recently for more attention to businesses' environmental footprint and contribution to greenhouse gas emissions and global warming (Dibie, 2014b). In addition, businesses have to also understand the importance of another actor in the business and public policy sphere—the news media. Business must constantly monitor the media and be ready to respond. In particular, since the media are usually a pivotal actor in any corporate crisis, company "crisis management" plans must include steps for dealing appropriately with the media and other critics. According to Useem (1984) and Green and Buchsbaum (1980) and Greechie (2003), business corporations have already dominated some nations political process. As a result, the only way to improve public policy is to restrict the political activities of individual corporations, rather than enhance the influence and effectiveness of business associations with public affairs.

What Is Special About Each Chapter?

Within this book, I have included all the important and traditional topics found in business and government relations courses. This book seeks to contribute to the larger federalization debate by considering the competence with which African governments regulate businesses within their domain. I have also added many case studies on business and government relations in Africa and sustainability issues. Each chapter includes unique materials that support economic and political decisions that positively or negatively affect the sustainable development processes in several African countries. The analysis of business and government relations in the different African countries will prepare students and practitioners to work effectively and understand the nature of such partnership in the sustainable development process of each nation.

Chapter 1 provides an overview of the nature of the economy of most African countries. It also investigates how the governments of some African countries regulate business to preserve competition and protect consumers and employees. In some African countries, the national and regional governments also intervene in the economy with laws and regulations to promote competition, and protect the environment, consumers, and employees. The governments, when necessary, often take steps through their central banks to minimize disruptive effect of economic fluctuation to spur growth so that consumers may spend more money and businesses may hire more employees. The chapter also describes how the governments of some African countries control the activities of businesses when the economy expands too much, by raising the interest rate to discourage spending by businesses and consumers. It also examines how privatization, outsourcing, and contracting out are practices of hiring other business organizations to do the work previously performed by government. This practice is an increasingly popular strategy, because it helps governments to focus on their core activities or functions. A central issue in the past five decades revolves around the fact that rapid changes in government and business relationship, type of regulations policies, and the state of the economy pose unsurpassed difficulties in keeping accurate track of governments' fiscal policies. The chapter recommends that managers in government and business institutions in sub-Saharan Africa should be cognizant of both primary and secondary dimensions of diversity, as well as the many benefits to be derived from having a diverse workforce that could propel sustainable development. Sustainable development cannot be achieved if there is a poor or weak government and business relations in any African country.

In Chapter 2, several approaches to business, government and society are examined. The chapter investigates three common approaches: (a) non-interference of the government (free market); (b) checking the exploitative power of business (socialism); (c) the mixed role of government in the economy. These three approaches help us understand what proper business-government relations should be in any economy. One purpose of economic models is to make economic ideas sufficiently explicit and concrete so that individuals, companies, or the government can use them to make positive decisions. The past two decades has been a time when globalization seems to press forward relentlessly on a host of fronts in the African continent; it is worth considering the central features of business and government, and the nature of their relationship, and to assess their limitations and strengths.

The main objective of Chapter 3 is to explore the formal or informal relations that exist between the private and public sectors in Burkina Faso. The chapter has a modest objective of identifying a number of elements of both continuity and change in business and government relations in Burkina Faso, as well as examining some of the effects they have on the pattern of policies that emerged in the country. It is organized into four sections. The first section is the review of the literature on the relationship between the government and the private sector. The second makes a critical analysis of these relations from both the traditional review of economic regulation and the deregulation, and the privatization of public enterprises and reforms in the private sector governance. The third section reviews the nature of private sector responses vis-à-vis the government and in terms of corporate governance. The fourth section provides some recommendations that could foster sustainable business and government relations to provide services for consumers, employees, and other stakeholders in Burkina Faso.

Chapter 4 examines the relationship between the Government of Botswana and Botswana's Confederation of Commerce, Industry, and Manpower (BOCCIM). It argues that the partnership between these two sectors in the implementation of the National Development Plan and the Economic Diversification Drive, if well-handled, could further enhance the nation's economic growth. It argues that a highly differentiated business community that includes a relatively large number of umbrella business organizations, a host of national association and trade organizations, and much representation by corporations individually and collectively in the process of shaping public policies has occurred in the past two decades. At the same time, there has been a remarkable stability with respect to the economic, legal, and institutional business and government frameworks in the country. However, in order for this partnership to yield positive results in the future, there is the need for stakeholders such as the reform agencies, developmental government departments, entrepreneurial trainers, venture capital and funding institutions, technology, business development consulting and research parastatals, quality control regulators, and the required regional and multinational corporations and marketing bodies to be up and functional in Botswana. The chapter recommends that the only precondition for businesses, government, trade, and economic growth to flourish in Botswana will require individual freedom reinforced by security for citizens, consumers' protection, entrepreneurship, and property.

The goal of Chapter 5 is to vividly explore the relationship between government, business, and society in Nigeria. Unfortunately, the controversy over business and government performance in Nigeria has been carried on, for the most part, with limited information or none at all. This chapter provides critical facts on the role of multinational corporations in Nigeria's industrial development. It brings together the available information on the operation of multinational firms in Nigeria. It argues that foreign direct investment and multinational corporations are neither inherently good nor bad. That is, foreign direct investment made in a context of high levels of aggregate demand and effective rules that limit the destructive aspects of competition may indeed have a positive impact on Nigerian citizens. However, foreign investment made in a context of high unemployment and destructive economic and political competition in the absence of effective rules can have a significantly negative impact on a nation such as Nigeria. This chapter seeks to make a modest contribution to the debate over the Nigerian competitiveness in the emerging global economy. The rationale underlying the chapter is that the instrumentality of public policy can be used to foster national competitiveness. Against this backdrop, the chapter proposes business-government partnership, and not the invisible hand of the market, as a viable framework for rejuvenating Nigeria's industrial base and competitiveness. This chapter is very important because of the new role government, business, and society has been playing since Nigeria started a representative democracy government in 1999.

Chapter 6 examines government, regulations, and practices in relation to business and business reaction and relation to and interaction with government. It investigates government-owned and partly government-owned business, multinational corporations, and private enterprises within the context of competitiveness and protectionism versus free trade. The chapter also explores corporate bailouts, defensive or subsidies production, consumer product regulation, and taxation in Ghana. External influences and impositions such as World Bank conditions, including deregulation, privatization, and removal of subsidies, are examined. It surveys how the Ghanaian government and businesses operate in a global economy, as well as a policy-making mechanism that affects business and government relations in drastic ways in the country. The chapter also presents problems that have dogged Ghana since independence in terms of the relationship between government and business and immerging strenuous conditions that put stress on healthy relations and collaboration between the two. It concludes by offering possible solutions to the problems, of corporate corruption, and lack of access to capital by the majority of Ghana's citizens. It projects those solutions onto the needs of a country poised to reach higher economic growth and heights, if not hindered by those problems.

Chapter 7 examines the role of the private sector in the economic development of Somalia. It argues that for-profit businesses have a unique role to play in the reconstruction of the Somalia economy. This chapter introduces a new perspective on the role of business in a stateless environment. Public goods have suffered in the anarchic environment that the civil war engendered in the Somali Republic. It proposes that economic development and infrastructure investment in the Somali Republic may take advantage of the innovative and successful business models that Somalia businesses have created. The chapter will first review the historical background of the economic and political change in the Somali Republic and focus on the role of business-government partnerships in economic development and infrastructure investment. Research studies, both conceptual and empirical, on business provision of public goods and services in Somalia will be discussed. Statelessness in the Somali Republic has created an environment in which new business models could flourish with minimal government interference, and minimal competition from international firms. Statelessness has effectively removed government institutions that had long hindered Somali entrepreneurship. The private sector in the Somali Republic swiftly adjusted to statelessness and created new operational models that can be tapped into in order to help the country rebuild its economy and infrastructure. Utilizing the experience and operating models of private enterprises in the provision of public goods and services is an alternative way forward for a successful Somalia economic development.

The objective of Chapter 8 is to investigate the nature of business and government relations in Sudan. It uses quantitative and qualitative methods of data collection in Sudan. Secondary data was obtained through an in-depth desk review and content analysis of relevant published and unpublished studies, policy and programs documents, regulations, and laws in Sudan. The chapter argues that one of the basic characteristic of government in Sudan is its right to make and enforce policies, rules, and regulations that are legally binding on businesses and citizens. It is such powers that confer legitimacy on a sitting government, not only to formulate polices but to ensure that they meet their targets and impact positively on the economy, welfare, and well-being of all citizens. This chapter provides a checklist of what the Government of Sudan is already doing well, and how it can improve the regulatory framework for investment, trade, and productivity. Analysis of data reveals that the central challenges for the Government of Sudan remains the increase of its capacity to adjust, so that it can better help its citizens take full advantage of the opportunities provided by technological innovation and a growing world economy. The chapter recommends that a more robust regulatory framework, supported by well-functioning institutions, should reduce the risks associated with unethical social responsibility of corporations in the country. The recommended robust framework could also help Sudan contribute to a more stable path for economic growth. In addition, appropriate domestic regulatory policies settings are more important than foreign pressure for business market access to realizing the benefits of sustainable development, consumer protection, and employees in the country.

Chapter 9 examines business and government relations in Zimbabwe. It argues that economic structural adjustment program (ESAP) is an inappropriate public policy for Zimbabwe, because it has negatively affected business and government relations in the country. It also uses primary and secondary data to present an argument that the Government of Zimbabwe is not doing enough to encourage businesses to conform to the nation's ethical standards, values, and attitudes. The chapter sought to explore the efficacy of laws and regulations as an effective tool for ethical dealing with consumers' protection, employees, safe products, investors, the communities, and societies in Kenya. This chapter demonstrates that ESAPs have further marginalized the Zimbabwean people, particularly women and children, more than they were ever before because the mandated budget austerity leads to the cutting of social spending and squeezing more from the taxpayer through increased education costs. This makes it harder for families to subsist in forcing them to withdraw their children from school, particularly girls in a patrilineal society devaluing females. Prioritizing export agriculture leads to reduced food production, which forces women to be exploited in the labor force, in which labor laws have been loosened through ESAPs' deregulation that undermines labor social rights. The result of the analysis of the study shows that successful business and government relations can contribute significantly to the quality of the nation's economic growth. Therefore, creating an environment that enhances peace and social justice could also promote economic growth in the country. In addition, some of the policies implemented after independence by the Zimbabwean government aimed at redistributing resources or alleviating poverty have been unsuccessful, or had perverse effects on the people and business corporations of the nation, complicated by the absence of democratic procedure in their adoption and implementation. It is therefore clear that no single alignment of government and business can offer a permanent solution to Zimbabwe's economic development problems. The chapter recommends strategies for the institutionalization of a successful business and government relations to improve the economy of Zimbabwe.

The objective of Chapter 10 is to investigate the nature of business and government relations in Uganda. It also explores how the public sector uses public policy and other means to influence the private sector's decision making and practices for the purpose of achieving economic development. The chapter provides a detail description of the important role of both sides of the relationship in respect to corporate social responsibility and government regulation in Uganda. It presents an argument that the Government of Uganda and its policies are crucial for the appropriate attainment of an effective business-government relation in the country. It uses data derived from primary and secondary sources to analyze the current relationship between business and government in Uganda. The conceptual framework is based on the new growth theory. The findings reveal that while there is a weak relationship between business and government in some industrial sectors due to inadequate enforcement of policies, the relationship in both institutions has improved over the years in other areas. In addition, government policies have not been able to effectively galvanize the private sector and NGOs to create a national system of innovation to technological progress and economic transformation. The national government and the leaders of Uganda are still very reluctant to leave economic outcomes in the country entirely up to market forces. The chapter recommends that national and appropriate collaboration between business and government could be major determinants of technological development and economic growth in Uganda in the future.

Chapter 11 examines business and government relations in Ethiopia. It argues that while the Government of Ethiopia should intervene in the economy with laws and regulations designed to promote competition and to protect consumers, employees, and the environment in the country business, entrepreneurs are also needed to risk their wealth, time, and efforts to develop for profit an innovative product or ways of doing something. The dynamics of development and participation at both national and grassroots levels in Ethiopia must involve business practices that foster new technology and innovative management techniques. At the same time government has to take steps to maximize the disruptive effects of economic fluctuation and reduce unemployment. The chapter uses data derived from primary and secondary sources to analyze the relationship between business and government in Ethiopia. The conceptual framework is based on the social constructionist, the building block model of development, and monetarist and Keynesian theories. The findings show that a stronger business and government relations in the country could galvanize the private and public sectors in addressing education, health care, welfare, and economic and social development issues in the country. In addition, the Ethiopian government policies have not been able to effectively galvanize the private sector and NGOs to create more jobs and entrepreneurs. There is a widespread recognition that the Government of Ethiopia does not have infinite resources and that they must satisfy important social needs without running unsustainable deficits. The chapter recommends government; private sector and NGOs should collaborate to establish a mechanism for a better and efficient approach to providing employment, goods, and services for all Ethiopians. It further suggests that appropriate monetary and fiscal policies are necessary for Ethiopia to effectively address its sustainable development and capacity building problems.

Chapter 12 examines the challenges faced by South Africa's economic sector in addressing corporate takeovers and how the country's transformation policies intersect with this process. It argues that the South African government has scored several achievements in the economic front, despite equally confronting some of the intractable problems ever faced by an African country. The chapter seeks to answer questions such as the following: What is the nature of economic takeovers in the South African economy? How are they affected by policy formulation and implementation, including other policy requirements that are related to the country's transformation process? To what extent can the South African case help us understand corporate takeovers in the sub-region and elsewhere in the African continent? The chapter relies on the extant literature, theoretical assumptions, media articles, and the country's laws and policies on transformation which promote or undermine corporate takeovers. It explores the nature of accountability and the challenges faced by the country's economic cluster in enhancing South Africa's economic system. The question of corporate takeover is an important subject that underlines a significant part of economic development, trade, and the role of private companies in the country's economic growth. Yet it is rarely linked with public policy in South Africa. Undoubtedly, this presents challenges for two sectors, i.e. business and government. These two sectors are usually keen to ensure that all the economic activities under their jurisdictions comply with policy obligations. The private sector, which often complains about government over-regulation and policy interference in the economic sphere, does not seem to appreciate the role of government to resolve the dilemma of the two formerly racially divided economic systems just after apartheid. The chapter recommends a nationwide transformation, which inevitably affects business and economic relations. Through such transformation, the government could seek to ensure the equitable participation of all the country's racial groups in the running of the economy and wealth creation.

The objective of Chapter 13 is to investigate the nature of business and government relations in Cameroon. It examines the strengths, weaknesses, opportunities, and threats to businesses, with a focus on the nature, role, and impact of public policy on the private sector in general. It argues that although the State remains the major regulator of the economy in Cameroon, its economic reform policy since the 1990s has been to strategically associate the private sector in the process of economic decision making. The sustainable development strategic plan of the country includes increasing production, enhancing trade and distribution of agricultural crops, and attracting appropriate technology and economic growth. The chapter uses secondary data to make an argument that the business sector has not been left out in economic policies of the nation, given the right to private ownership through privatization. It also evaluates the economic road maps of the country, such as Vision 2035, the Growth and Employment Strategy Paper (GESP), the Poverty Reduction and Employment Strategy Paper (DSCE), and recently, the Three Year Emergency Plan. The main thrust is a focus on government's role in the economy based on past and current experiences. It seeks to contribute to the course of economic policies with regard to the processes by which those policies are developed in Cameroon. The chapter concludes that the nature of business-government relations has improved significantly over the last two decades, to the extent that the roles played by the State as well as the private sector are complementary.

Chapter 14 adopts a qualitative approach of the disciplines of business management, political science, economics, and organizational management to explore business and government relations in Tanzania. Secondary data include review of statutory literature such as the Constitution of the United Republic of Tanzania, Acts of Parliament, Statutes, Ujamaa policy, codes, contracts, rules, and procedures and conventions for establishing institutions. The chapter examines how business and government relations have improved lives, strengthened communities, and foster civic engagement through consumer protection and employment. Both the private and public sectors in Tanzania have expanded the ability of informal organizations to fight poverty. Rather than providing services to low income individuals and communities, the government in Tanzania has collaborated with businesses in the country to strengthen and support entrepreneurs. This, in return, has helped NGOs, businesses, and governments by building infrastructure, enhancing technology, expanding community partnerships, securing long-term resources, coordinating training for citizens, and alleviating poverty in the country. The purpose here is to examine the characteristics of formal and informal rules and regulations governing the establishment and operation of businesses, how these have evolved over time, and how they may have impacted on economic growth in Tanzania.

Chapter 15 examines business and government relations in Kenya. It argues that the Government of Kenya is not doing enough to encourage businesses to conform to the nation's business ethics standards, values, and attitudes. The chapter also explores how the Government of Kenya has responded to basic ethical and corporate social responsibility concerns in the country in the form of codified laws and regulations. Data were derived through interviews, observation, and a review of print and electronic documentation on business and government relations in Kenya. The chapter explores the efficacy of laws and regulations as an effective tool for dealing with consumer protection, employees, safe products, investors, and communities and societies in Kenya. The chapter also suggests that although economic, social, and political environmental factors, emanating from globalization and related business competition, have stimulated increased demands, there is still a need to implement vigorous policy strategies on how to improve the performance of the national and regional governments in respect of how to better regulate businesses in the country. This intense policy strategy is necessary to effectively enhance business performance, quality, and ethical products, and corporate social responsible in Kenya. The chapter contributes to the body of literature on the techniques used by the government of any developing nation to promote competition and protect consumers, employees, and the environment. A result of the analysis of data shows that successful business and government relations can contribute significantly to the quality of the nation's economic growth. It recommends strategies for the institutionalization of successful business and government relations to improve the economy of Kenya.

Chapter 16 investigates how government and business in sub-Saharan Africa seek to enhance their human, institutional, and infrastructure capacity to secure a stable and sustainable economy. It argues that pragmatic sustainable and appropriate partnership between government and business could enhance capacity building and economic development. In all ramifications, capacity building of African countries requires good relationship between government and businesses. In addition, business should not be seen only a single contracting party in the economic and social developing process, but they should also be perceived as a major mechanism for coordinating different parties such as external and internal stakeholders in the sustainable development process in sub-Saharan Africa. Data derived from interviews, administration of surveys and content analysis of government reports, NGOs policies were used to analyze the nature of sustainable growth and trends in capacity building. The nexus of contract theory is used as a framework to discuss the nature of business and government relations. The findings reveal that there is a negative correlation between the nations' government policies, educational system, and the kind of skills needed to achieve sustainable development. In addition, government policies have not been able to effectively galvanize the business or private sector and NGOs to create more technical skills and jobs for citizens. The chapter recommends that the dynamics of development and participation at the grassroots level must involve a better nexus of internal and external stakeholders' partnership in all aspects of capacity building and economic development. This stakeholder partnership also requires a great amount of transparency and accountability between government and business that are participating. Sub-Saharan African nations need to establish capacity building projects that could help nurture changes in behavior, attitudes, methods, and the humanist paradigm, as well as offers not only based on self-reliance and participatory sustainable development but a means and end.

Conclusion

This chapter has examined the history of business and government relations in Africa. It argues that in most African countries, just like other nations of the world, the decision of government affects the environment in which business operates. Business practices can be strongly influenced not only by government but by direct citizen and NGO actions that bypass the formal institutions of government (Ya Ni & Van Wart, 2015). On one hand, government regulates businesses and of course serves as the largest single customer of business (Denhardt et al., 2014). On the other hand, businesses and their chief executive leaders recognize that governmental decisions affect the economic climate. For instance, government decisions affect the stock market. At the regional level, state governors have been campaigning to attract industries to their respective states, by providing incentives for plants and industries that might relocate.

Thus, it is clear that businesses all over the African continent recognize that the political climate of any nation or region directly affects the economic climate. In order to enhance government strategic goals (e.g., clean air, clean water, safe roads), regulation stands one of the most important tool and a cornerstone for public policy. According to Sharfitz et al. (2011) and Dibie (2014a), regulation allows public administrators the ability to take broad legislative directives and create specific rules that are designed to deliver desirable societal conditions. All over the African continent, governments are also very important as consumers of business products and services. The challenge of establishing a constructive partnership between government and businesses in Africa for the future requires public administrators, political leaders, and citizens to juxtapose democracy and market benefits. As a result of the essential role government plays in the economy, businesses are now developing public affairs offices to specialize in government operations, track policy development, and attempt to influence policy; however, they are also placing a greater premium on having executives at all levels who understand how government agencies operate in the respective African countries.

References

Akouwerabou, B. O. Bako, P. (2013). Marches's Public et Petites et Manyennes Entreprises au Burkina Faso: Quelle Gouvnance? Repport de Recherche du FR-CIEAN" 56/13.

Anderson, J. (2015). *Public Policy-Making*. 8th Edition. Boston, MA: Wadsworth Press.

Bach, D. and Unrah, G. (2004). *Business-Government Relationship in Global Economy: Broadening the Conceptual Map*. IE Working Paper DE8–109–1. www.latienda.ie.edu/working_ papers_economia/WP04–37.pdf. Accessed January 4, 2016.

Blackford, M. G. (2008). *The Rise of Modern Business in Great Britain, the United States, and Japan*. 3rd Edition. Chapel Hill, NC: University of North Carolina Press.

Blewitt, J. (2015). *Understanding Sustainable Development.* New York: Routledge Press.

British Petroleum plc. (2006). *Statistical Review of World Energy (2006).* London, UK: British Petroleum plc, 43 p.

Calveras, A. (2015). Corporate Social Responsibility Strategy in the Hotel Industry: Evidence From the Balearic Island. *International Journal of Tourism Research,* 17, 399–408.

Colebatch, H. K., Prasser, S. and Nethercote, J. R. (Eds.). (1997). *Business-Government Relations: Concepts and Issues.* Melbourne, Australia: Nelson Press. ISBN 0170092216.

Daniels, J. D., Radebaugh, L. H. and Sullivan, D. (2011). *International Business: Environments and Operations.* Upper Saddle River, NJ: Prentice Hall.

Denhardt, R., Denhardt, J. and. Blanc, T. (2014). *Public Administration: An Action Orientation.* Boston: Wadsworth Press.

Dibie, R. (2014a). *Public Administration, Analysis, Theory and Application.* Ilishan Remo: Babcook University Press.

Dibie, R. (2014b). Comparative Perspective on Environmental Policies and Issues. New York: Routledge.

Dibie, R. and Dimitriou, C. (2016). Evaluation of Sustainable Environmental Initiatives in Hotels in Southern Nigeria. *Journal of Applied and Theoretical Environmental Science,* 2(2), 29–50.

Dibie, R., Edoho, F. M. and Dibie, J. (2015). Analysis of Capacity-Building in Africa. *International Journal of Business and Social Sciences,* 4(12), 233–243.

Dibie, R. and Offiong, O. J. (2012). The Nature and Impact of Environmental Policy in Nigeria. *Journal of International Politics and Development,* 10, 113–142.

Djankov, S. and al. (2002). The Regulation of Entry. *The Quarterly Journal of Economics,* vol. CXVII, (February), 1–23.

Dye, T. (2013). *Understanding Public Policy.* 14th Edition. Boston, MA: Pearson Learning.

Ferrell, C., Fraedrich, J. and Farrell, L. (2015). *Business Ethics: Ethical Decision Making and Cases.* 10th Edition. Stanford, CT: Cengage Learning Press.

Fortune. (2011, May). *Global 500.* http://money.cnn.com/magazines/fortune/global500/2011/index.html. Accessed August 18, 2016.

Geuras, D. and Garofalo, C. (2010). *Practical Ethics in Public Administration.* 2nd Edition. Vienna, VA: Management Concepts.

Greechie, S. (2003). *Role of Government in Business.* http://smallbusiness.chron.com/role-government-business-803.html. Accessed September 11, 2015.

Green, M. and Buchsbaum, A. (1980). The Corporate Lobbies: Political Profile of the Business Roundtable and the Chamber of Commerce. Washington, DC: Public Citizen Press.

Greenberg, J. (2013). *Managing Behavior in Organizations.* 2nd Edition. Upper Saddle River, NJ: Prentice Hall Press.

Greenberg, J. and Baron, R. (2010). *Behavior in Organizations: Understanding and Managing the Human Side of Work.* 8th Edition. Upper Saddle River, NJ: Prentice Hall.

Griffin, R. and Moorhead, G. (2014). *Organizational Behavior Managing People and Organizations.* 11th Edition. Boston, M.A.: Cengage Learning.

Griffin, R., Phillips, J. M. and Gully, S. M. (2017). *Organizational Behavior: Managing People and Organizations.* Boston, MA: Cengage Learning.

Guenther, G. (2007, April 26). *Research Tax Credit: Current Status and Selected Issues for Congress.* CRS Report RL31181, Congressional Research Service, 2–9.

Hart, S. L. (2005). Capitalism at the Crossroads: The Unlimited Business Opportunities in Solving the World's Problems. Upper Saddle River, NJ: Wharton School Publishing.

Henderson, J. C. (2007). Corporate Social Responsibility and Tourism: Hotels Companies in Phuket, Thailand, After the Indiana Ocean Tsunami. *Hospitality Management, 26,* 228–239.

Hill, C. and. Lynn, L. Jr. (2016). *Public Management: Thinking and Acting in Three Dimensions.* Los Angeles, CA: Sage Press.

Hirst, P. (2000). Democracy and Governance. In Jon Pierre (Ed.), *Debating Governance: Authority, Steering, and Democracy.* Oxford: Oxford University Press, 20–39.

Hodge, G. (2000). Privatization: An International Review of Performance. Boulder, CO: Westview Press.

Hopkin, M. (1999). The Planetary Bargain: Corporate Social Responsibility Comes of Age. London: Macmillan Press.

Inanga, E. (2005). *Managing Nigeria's Economic System.* Ibadan, Nigeria: Heinemann Educational Books.

Janssens, M. (1995). Intercultural Interaction: A Burden on International Managers. *Journal of Organizational Behavior, 16,* 155–167.

Johnson, D. and Turner, C. (2016). *European Business.* 3rd Edition. New York: Routledge PressJones, B. (2013)." Sustainability and Corporate Social Responsibility." www.bennettjones.com/Publications%20Section/Speaking%20Engagements/Sustainability%20and%20Corporate%20Social%20Responsibility%20 (2013). Accessed April 29, 2016.

Jon, P. (2000). Debating Governance: Authority, Steering, and Democracy. Oxford: Oxford University Press.

Jon, P. and Peters, G. B. (2000). *Governance, Politics and the State.* New York: St. Martin's Press.

Kedia, B. L. and Mukherji, A. (1999). Global Managers: Developing a Mindset for Global Competitiveness. *Journal of World Business, 34,* 230–251.

Kraft, M. and Furlong, S. (2015). *Public Policy: Politics, Analysis, and Alternatives.* Washington, DC: CQ Press.

Kuye, O. I., Ogundele, O. J. and Alaneme, G. C. (2013). Strategic Roles of Business, Government and Society: The Nigerian Situation. International Journal of Business and Social Science, 4(12), 233–243.

Lacey, S. (2010). *Top 25 U.S. Energy Lobbyists of 2010.* Renewableenergyworld. com. www.renewableenergyworld.com/rea/news/article/2010/12/top-25-u-s-energy-lobbyists-of-2010. Accessed November 21, 2015.

Lehne, R. (2013). Government and Business: American Political Economy in Comparative Perspective. Washington, DC: Congressional Quarterly Press.

Levy, O., Beechler, S., Tyalor, S. and Boyacigiller, S. (2007). What We Talk About When We Talk About Global Mindset. Managerial Cognition in Multinational Corporations. *Journal of International Business Studies, 38,* 231–258.

Lodge, G. C. (1995). *Managing Globalization in the Age of Interdependence.* San Francisco, CA: Pfeifer Press.

Mahajan, V. (2009). *Africa Rising.* Upper Saddle River, NJ: Pearson Education Inc.

Maigan, I. and Ferrell, O. C. (2001). Antecedents and Benefits of Corporate Citizenship: An Investigation of French Businesses. *Journal of Business Research, 51,* 37–51.

Mankiw, N. G. (2018). Essentials of Economics. Eight Edition. Boston, M/ A.: Cengage Learning.

Murphy, K. M. and Topel, R. (2003). The Economic Value of Medical Research. In Murphy and Topel (Eds.), *Measuring the Gains From Medical Research,* 41–73. http://faculty.chicagobooth.edu/kevin.murphy/research/murphy&topel.pdf. Accessed April 29, 2016.

Nafziger, W. (1993). *The Debt Crisis in Africa.* Baltimore, MD: Johns Hopkins University Press.

Natsio, A. (2007). Building the Base of the Pyramid Value Chain. In V. Kasturi Rangan, John Quelch, Gustavo Herrero and Brooke Barton (Eds.), *Business Solutions for the Global Poor*. San Francisco, CA: Jossey-Bass Press, 133–159.

Nelson, D. and Quick, J. C. (2013). *Organizational Behavior: Science, the Real World, and You*. Mason, OH: South-Western/ Cengage Learning.

Odogbor, P. (2005). Effects of Environmental Degradation on Cultural Heritage of the Niger Delta and the Implication on Sustainable Rural Development. In Eke Orobator, Feturi Ifowodo and Emaruma Edosa (Eds.), *Federal State and Resources Control in Nigeria*. Benin City, Nigeria: F. Parker Publishing Company, 71–95.

Okonta, L. (2008). When Citizens Revolt: Nigerian Elites, Big Oil, and Ogoni Struggle for Self Determination. Trenton, NJ: African Press.

Organization of Economic Cooperation and Development (OCED). (2010). Accelerating Progress Towards the Millennium Development Goals (MDGs) Through Pro-Poor Growth: Messages From the DAC Network on Poverty Reduction. OECD, Paris.

Pettinger, T. (2008). *Economics Essays: The Importance of Economics*. www.economicshelp.org/2008/06/importance-of-economics.html. Accessed July 28, 2015.

Pierre, J. (2009). New Governance, New Democracy? University of Gothenburg, GÖTEBORG: The Quality of Government Institute. QoG Working Paper Series 2009: 4.

Rhinesmith, S. H. (1992). Global Mindset for Global Managers. *Training and Development*, 46, 63–69.

Sandbrook, R. (1993). *The Politics of Africa's Economic Recovery*. New York: Cambridge University Press.

Stigler, G. (1976). *The Citizen and the State: Essay on Regulation*. Chicago: University of Chicago Press.

Streeck, A. and Schmitter, J. (1985). The Prospect Contribution of Interest Governance to Social Order. In Streeck and Schmitter (Eds.), *Private Interest Government: Beyond Market and State*. London: Sage Publication, 57–91.

Surendra, M. (2004). Concern for Good Governance in Comparative Perspective. In Munshi Surendra and Biju Paul Abraham (Eds.), *Good Governance, Democratic Societies and Globalization*. New Delhi: Sage Publications, 1–24.

UN Global Compact. (2005). *What Is the Global Compact*. UN Global Compact Website: www.unglobalcompact.org. Accessed October 3, 2016.

UNEP. (2003). A Practical Guide to Good Practice: Managing Environmental and Social Issues in the Accommodation Sector. United Nations Environment Programme, Paris.

United Nations Economic and Social Council (UNECOSOC). (2012). *Mainstreaming a Gender Perspective Into All Policies and Programmes in the United Nations System*. www.un.org/en/ecosoc/docs/adv2012/gender_mainstreaming_report_for_distribution.pdf. Accessed April 19, 2015.

United States Government. (2007). *Federal Support for Research and Development (June)*. The Congress of the United States, Congressional Budget Office. United States Government Press.

Useem, M. (1984). The Inner Circle: Large Corporate and the Rise of Business Political Activity in the United States and United Kingdom. New York: Oxford University Press.

Vehar, N. (1987). The Business Role in Federal Advisory Committees. New York: Conference Board.

Wang, C. (2014). Do Ethical and Sustainable Practices Matter? Effects of Corporate Citizenship on Business Performance in Hospitality Industry. *International Journal of Contemporary Hospitality Management*, 26(6), 930–947.

Wankel, C. (2007). *21st Century Management: A Reference Hand Book*. Vol. 1. New York: Sage Press.

World Bank. (2014). *World Development Report (2013)*. New York: Oxford University Press.

World Statistics Pocketbook. (2010). "Burkina Faso Profile." http://data.un.org/CountryProfile.aspx?crName=Burkina%20Faso. Accessed April 29, 2016.

Wright, R. and Boorse, D. (2014). *Environmental Science: Towards A Sustainable Future*. Boston, MA: Pearson Press.

Yager, T. R., Bermúdez-Lugo, O. Mobbs, P. M., Newman, H. R. and Wilburn, D. R. (2007). *The Mineral Industries of Africa*. Minerals Yearbook (August), U.S. Geological Survey, PD License (U.S. Government Source, Public Domain).

Yandle, B. and Young, E. (1986). Regulating the Function, Not the Industry. *Public Choice*, 51(1), 59–70.

Ya Ni, A. and Van Wart, M. (2016). *Building Business–Government Relations: A Skills Approach*. New York: Routledge Press.

2 Theories of Business and Government Relations

Robert A. Dibie and Josephine Dibie

Introduction

There are approximately 1.5 billion people living on the African continent (World Bank, 2014). Africa is the second-largest and second most populous continent in the world. The continent is also home to 54 recognized sovereign states and countries, 9 territories, and 2 de facto independent states with very little recognition (World Bank, 2014).

Government agencies and business corporations in Africa are the two most important institutions in the continent. Rather than just attempting to explain the activities of government and business relations in this chapter, we shall present several approaches for understanding their relations. It should be made clear, however, that when looking at government and business in developing countries, their central focus is to organize society over ideological and religious means. However, in most developing or African countries, religion may be viewed as more central to society than business and ideological states (Ake 2005; Ya Ni & Van Wart, 2016). In this respect, more emphasis is place on social harmony and equity than wealth creation.

In today's world, understanding and managing the complex interactions between businesses and governments is crucial both for public and private managers. Economists and political scientists are deeply engaged by what they think about business and government relations. Some of them that are liberals promote the benefits of market and their capacity to solve virtually all problems in the most efficient way (Gilpin, 1987). On one hand, other scholars contend that policies should be framed around maximizing the power and interests of the country. Mercantilists call on governments to manipulate markets so as to capture special benefits for their nations. Radicals, other the other hand, believe the system of capitalism in the national and international system should benefit certain social classes within the most powerful capitalist nations (Gilpin, 2001; Sandbrook, 1993; Sachs, 2005; Lehne, 2013). These three perspectives sometimes have merit for understanding business and government relations. Governments restrict imports for cultural motives—such as the protection of national identity. Four common instruments to promote trade are subsidies, export financing, foreign trade zones, and special government agencies. Governments restrict unwanted trade through tariffs, quotas, embargoes, local content requirements, administrative delays, and currency controls.

This chapter examines several approaches to business-government relations. The chapter investigates three common approaches: (a) non-interference of the government (free market); (b) checking the exploitative power of business (socialism); (c) the mixed role of government in the economy. These three approaches help us understand what proper business-government relations should be in any economy. One purpose of economic models is to make economic ideas sufficiently explicit and concrete so that individuals, companies, or the government can use them to make positive decisions. The past two decades has been a time when globalization seems to press forward relentlessly on a host of fronts in the African continent; it is worth considering the central features of business and government, and the nature of their relationship, and to assess their limitations and strengths.

Theories and Framework

The Free Market—Capitalism Approach

Free market approach exists when the government places few restriction on how goods and services can be produced or sold, or how factors of production can be employed (Hubbard & O'Brien, 2015).

The theory of political economy revolves closely around the idea of free market or "laissez faire" capitalism. Translated effectively as "let it be," this system proposes that there be little or no formal relationship between business and government. Growing out of the theories of Adam Smith, the essentially free-market approach argues that the public good can be seen as synonymous with economic efficiency and gains in the standard of living for individuals (Mankiw, 2018). According to Smith, the "invisible hand" (the aggregate of undisturbed decisions by buyers and sellers in the open market) tends to produce better goods, at cheaper prices, for more people. These cheap, high-quality goods allow for a better standard of living through material abundance, utility, and comfort.

Checking the Exploitative Power of Business—Socialism Approach

Socialism is a way of organizing a society in which major industries are controlled by the government rather than by the individual people and companies. It is also a stage in Marxist theory transitional between capitalism and communism, and distinguished by unequal distribution of goods and pay according to work done (McAlister et al., 2010). Thus, socialism is a system or condition of society in which the means of production are owned and controlled by the government. This role is focused on distribution of wealth and income among everyone in society (Pettinger, 2008). Marx believed capitalism would end when the gap between wealth and poverty grew so large that workers would overthrow the capitalist system. In response to inequalities inherent in a system of open competition, socialism proposes actions to ensure economic equality for the entire population (Pettinger, 2008). Furthermore, Karl Marx argued that the essential structure of capitalism required that those who own the capital continually lower the wages of the working class (Mankiw, 2018. Additionally, Marx argued that free market capitalism was inherently dehumanizing and tended to force people into monotonous labor for the sake of producing massive quantities of goods in order to satisfy selfish profit motives (Lehne, 2013). According to socialism, the public good is seen in terms of economic equality and of checking the exploitative power of business (Pettinger, 2008). Therefore, the only remedy would be for the government, on behalf of the people, to take control of business and direct what goods would be produced at what prices.

The Mixed Roles of Government Approach

A mixed economy is an economy in which most economic decisions result from the interaction of buyers and sellers in market, but in which the government plays a significant role in the allocation of resources (Hubbard & O'Brien, 2015). A third option in terms of political economy was proposed by the economist John Maynard Keynes (Gordon, 1990; Pettinger, 2008). It was his contention that business fully controlled by government would inherently lead to inefficiency and a lowering of the standard of living (Blinder, 1991). On the other hand, he also argued that a purely free market system would tend to undermine itself in the long run, and lead to an unstable social situation due to inequalities and contradictions. It was the role of the government to push the private sector into socially desired outcomes, but to leave it alone in terms of how those outcomes should be accomplished (Keynes, 1936). For example, using monetary policy, the government can increase the supply of credit in the market, creating incentive for investment over savings and thus "stimulating" the economy (Mankiw, 2018; Keynes, 1936).

The Shareholder Model

The shareholder model sets the corporation at the center of a set of mutual relationships with persons and groups (Murray & Bell, 1985). It promotes the idea that firms have ethical duties and social responsibilities toward a wide range of shareholders due to their impacts on them. The shareholder model considers only business interests and asserts that business and government should be as separate as possible, with the implicit assumption that government should also be as small as possible (Ya Ni & Van Wart, 2016; Gilprin, 2001). This perspective expects corporate policy to emerge from the interplay of business associations, organized groups, and political agencies. It also expects government to play an active role in forging policy agreements that goes beyond the brokering of group preferences (Lehne, 2013). The shareholder model postulates that internal efficiency and external market analysis could lead to dynamic competition and innovation.

From this perspective, to produce good results, the model presents an argument that government and other institutions should not intervene in the activities of businesses so that corporations can focus more on their operations. The shareholders model advocates small government in terms of regulations, taxes, subsidies, and ownership, in order for the economy to have a relatively unrestricted market (Ya Ni & Van Wart, 2016). According the shareholders model, the major duty of the government should be to ensure that markets function properly and to correct market failures if there happen to be any. However, whenever governments intervene, they should do so with the least possible intrusiveness (Garrett & Rhine, 2006; Lehne, 2013). The shareholders model is closely related to the work of Adam Smith, as stated in his *Wealth of Nations* (1776). In his book, Adam Smith argued that the greatest good for society can be achieved by allowing businesses to compete freely. He contends that the market could produce an efficient economy that will optimally allocate resources and spontaneously coordinate activities among competitive producers (Ya Ni & Van Wart, 2016). Figure 2.1 shows the dynamics of the shareholders' model.

Figure 2.1 shows the relationship between shareholders and government, as well as the link between businesses and their shareholders. A positive outcome between internal efficiency and external market analysis could lead to dynamic competition and innovation. Thus shareholders have to

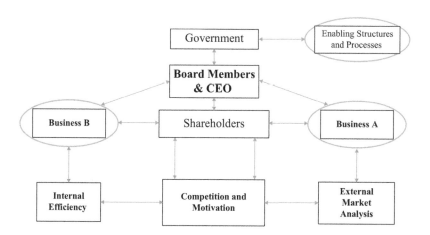

Figure 2.1 Dynamics of the shareholders' model

Source: Adopted from Ya Ni, A., and Van Wart, M. (2016). *Building Business–Government Relations*. New York: Routledge Press.

play a critical role with the government on one hand. On the other hand, shareholders have to work effectively with the corporate chief executive officers and board members to ensure positive outcomes. A proposed positive outcome, however, depends on the government enabling structures and processes.

McCann and Ward (2012) and Boddewyn (2015) argue from another perspective that the shareholder model fails to acknowledge the market failure problem. Market failure often leads to government intervention in a particular market. As a matter of fact, market failure demands government vigilance and intervention, such as regulation, wage and price control, bailout, and social and corporate insurance programs, as well as other welfare stabilization programs (Ya Ni & Van Wart, 2016). In most capitalist economies, businesses often call for small government; however, they are the ones that reap more benefit from the government. It is very important to note that monetary and material gain tends to erode humanity (Bach & Unruh, 2004; Rangan et al., 2007). This is true because businesses' excessive emphasis on profit could lead individuals and corporations to abuse and exploitation of disadvantaged, create legal loopholes, pollute the environment, and eliminate opportunities for future generation by fiscal mismanagement or ecological destruction, escalating poverty in the economy as a result (Dibie, 2014b). Thus, it is crucial that business interest should never be at the expense of society's long-term interest in order to achieve sustainable development and economic growth.

Regulatory State Model

The basic role of the government according to the regulatory state model is to lessen the negative results of market activity without losing the benefits of a completive market (Lehne, 2013). According to Derber (2002), the government regulates and rules products, productions, and processes of private firms and governs collective bargaining, equal opportunity, and human resource policies. Asch and Seneca (1989) contend that the government prohibits unfair market practices and regulates the operations of controversial industries. Government also enacts antitrust laws as well as outlaw monopolies, and institutes regulations to establish national standards in sensitive areas where markets function poorly, such as workplace safety and the employment of children. One of the major reasons for regulation is natural monopoly. A natural monopoly could occur where economies associated with large scale production makes it inefficient for more than one company to operate. Consequently, the largest company in the industry is also the most efficient. This because it has the lowest cost per unit of output. Such a company has the ability to underprice competitors and drive them out of business. The small company, as a practical matter, cannot compete and close down. The regulatory function of government is intended to provide benefits of marketplace competition when markets are not wholly competitive (Lehne, 2013). Non-regulatory monopolies could cause social losses because they restrict production and raise prices. As a matter of fact, such monopoly prices will enrich producers at the expense of consumers. Regulatory response typically involves setting rates or prices for the monopoly company and restricting or eliminating entry by competitors. For example, while the opportunities for competition in the railroad industry are still limited, railroad companies face intense competition from trucks and inland waterway barges on most freight they haul. As a result, competition from truckers ensures that for most commodities no monopoly of any significance can exist for the railroad today.

In addition, regulation or government control could be appropriate where a common resource must be allocated rationally or where there is no incentive to conserve natural resources. For example, if everyone were allowed full use and access of the electromagnetic spectrum, a resource owned by society as a whole, broadcasting using the same frequency would interfere with one another. This would cause poor reception of signal. Therefore, some amount of government intervention is necessary to allocate and manage the electromagnetic spectrum. Government intervention is also necessary in the form of regulation, so as to avoid wasting valuable non-reproductive resources. These measures are necessary to enable oil and gas to flow underground aa well as encouraging the ownership of these natural resources from been fragmented. In the absence of regulation, property owners would race to get the oil or gas out before the neighbors take it all (Johnson & Turner 2016). The economic justification for the regulation of nuclear power is similar but more complex (Forest 2009). Therefore, well designed government standards could reduce the hazard and, in the process, internalize in the company some of these external costs. In the process, the price of nuclear power would rise to reflect that cost. Such limitation of liability reduces the incentive to lower risk, and provides a justification for safety regulation by the Nuclear Regulatory Commission (Rolf 2006; Batch & Newman 2004).

In addition to the previously noted justification for government regulation, correcting inadequacies in the information producers provide about the products they sale is the reason underlying much health, safety, and consumer protection regulation in most countries. Similarly, because market incentives for voluntary health and safety programs by employers may be insufficient in some instances, regulation can be used to force employers to internalize the costs associated with job hazards to their employees.

As a result of the responsibilities and power of the regulator agencies and process, it is not surprising that many interests have cloaked their pleas for special treatment with a reference to some broader public purpose. At the same time, apart from the market failure justification for government regulation, it is often argued that distributive justice, or concern with political and social equity, is a reason for government intervention. Thus, the government's involvement is seen primarily as a way of bringing about the transfer of income or wealth tor everybody in the society (Ferrell et al., 2015; Dibie, 2014a). In most developed countries, regulation has been used as a way to redistribute income among the regions of the nation, to promote one industry at the expense of others, to provide services for small communities, and to give special protection to those deemed particularly worthy. Therefore it could be argued that regulation spawns and then protects certain groups, which subsequently have a vested interest in its continuation. One point that we should bear in mind is that although regulation is often used by government as a means of correcting market failures, regulatory actions are not the only means available to the people in any economy. Consumers can equally educate themselves and seek product information when they are making large purchases. In addition, taxes can be levied on polluters. Subsidies can be paid to those unfairly harmed by pollution, to compensate them for the cleanup burden imposed on them (Boddewyn, 2015). Thus, regulation is seen as a mixture of methods that involves more direct control and those that involve the use of indirect control mechanism such as taxes or subsidies.

At the other end of the spectrum, Lehne (2013) contends that although state regulation is intended to provide the benefits of marketplace competition when markets are not fully competitive, sometimes the regulator state could be captured by groups that use government authority to produce the policy result they prefer. Special interest groups have been known to effectively lobby the government to take action or not do anything that could undermine their interests. The National Raffle Association (NRA) is a good example in the United States. As a result, regulation is frequently argued to have asymmetric effects, on one hand, distributing benefit to some, and on the other hand, it imposes costs on others, thus pitting businesses against other stakeholders, including companies competing in the same industry (Johnson & Turner 2016; Lehne, 2013).

The Strategic Approach

The government department or agency and the business corporation are two of the most powerful institutions in modern society (Griffin & Moorhead, 2014; Lehne, 2013). The strategic approach accepts the role of government as a given and generally utilizes the many opportunities to prosper from the sale of products and services, via various types of cooperation with government. According to Greenberg (2012) and Greenberg and Baron (2010) many organizations use their influence to ensure that government policies are as favorable as possible, and ultimately appreciate government for doing things that are not very profitable (Ya Ni & Van Wart, 2016). The strategic approach to business and government relations tends to be more balanced and realistic than the shareholder perspective. It mobilizes business to be fully involved in the dynamic of society. It also enables business to play a central role in the economic growth of any nation. Companies that practice a highly strategic approach are various types of community and regional banks. For instance, community banks are careful to use their local connections strategically by having senior employees join local professional organizations, sponsoring local events, and participating in local nonpartisan policy making; in return, they benefit by getting the business of the largest local companies and agencies in the region (Ya Ni & Van Wart, 2016).

The shifting and complicated relationship between business and government exerts great influence on changing the performance of the economy and on the lives of citizens. This relationship ranges from cooperative to competitive, from friendly to hostile (Greechie, 2003; and Griffin & Moorhead, 2014). Competition impels a complicated rivalry for resources between two or more organizations, while cooperation has three sub-categories: bargaining refers to negotiation or an agreement for the exchange of goods and services between two or more organizations; cooperation is the process of absorbing the structure of an organization; and a coalition is a conscious combination of two or more organizations to achieve a common goal or purpose. The strategic approach is also a conscious combination of businesses and government to achieve a common goal for the growth of the economy. The adherence or result of these inter-organizational strategies has short- and long-term implications for business and government relations in any country.

The strategic approach is about competition and collaboration (Ferrell et al., 2015). It introduces a strategic social responsibility framework for courses that address the role of business in society. Social responsibility is presented as the extent to which a business adopts a strategic focus for fulfilling the economic, legal, ethical, and philanthropic responsibilities expected by all its stakeholders (Ferrell et al., 2015). It presents an argument that a good strategy of business-government relations must include networking and occasionally positioning oneself to be a part of a winning team rather than a sole winner. According to this perspective, networking provides market intelligence and goodwill. At the same time, being a corporate team player allows better supply chain management and cooperative and profitable ventures with other companies. An example of networking among government agencies is when the government purchases billions of dollars' worth of goods and services, so many businesses deem it necessary to liaison or keep themselves very informed about government procurement and contract sources or agents.

Government influences business decision making of all types, including planning, research and development, production, marketing, personnel, finance, facilities, and so on (Bach & Unruh, 2004). Therefore, the dynamic tension of competitive and collaborative roles that strategic companies want is demonstrated in business groups such as the Chamber of Commerce, where goals for low taxes may contrast with the price of substantial services useful for business (Ya Ni & Van Wart, 2016). While the static approach promotes collaboration between business and government, it could be so inclusive and relativistic that it is difficult to know what it stands for because circumstances change so frequently and dramatically. It could also be unclear, inconsistent, and ethically porous. In practice, the precise nature of the business and government relationship will vary by industry, size, location, type of production, and market serve.

Corporate Governance—Servant Leadership Theory

The corporate governance theory postulates that companies play a critical role in the governance of any economy. In order to estimate the needs of corporations and develop a practical regulatory environment, governments need both citizens and corporations to actively participate in the decision-making process. Government is not the only channel that citizens could use to control or influence the actions of private business (McAlister et al., 2010). According to Rod (2011) there is always the possibility that citizens would use government's authority to charter corporations to alter the basic function and organization of the modern company and, in the process, increase their access to the centers of economic power.

The governance of corporations in most developed and developing countries are regulated primarily by the requirements contained in government corporation status. Corporate boards of directors are characterized as self-perpetuating groups, accountable to themselves or to the chief executives who in practice may appoint them. In most cases, critics see corporations as private governments operating under legal constraints that are for the most part irrelevant; they advocate a variety of changes in the way that corporations are governed.

The stewardship theory assumes that managers are stewards whose behaviors are aligned with the objectives of their principals (Lussier & Achua, 2016). The theory argues and looks at a different form of motivation for managers drawn from organizational theory. Managers are viewed as loyal to the company and interested in achieving high performance (Hamid, 2011). The dominant motive that directs managers to accomplish their job is their desire to perform excellently. Specifically, managers are conceived as being motivated by a need to achieve, to gain intrinsic satisfaction through successfully performing inherently challenging work, to exercise responsibility and authority, and thereby to gain recognition from peers and bosses (Lussier, 2012). Figure 2.2 shows the attributes of the servant leadership model.

Servant leadership represents a shift in the leadership paradigm from a focus on leading to a focus on serving. Stewardship and servant leadership are related to charismatic and transformational leadership, in that they emphasize empowering followers to accomplish organizational goals (Lussier & Achua, 2016). Leadership is seen as an opportunity to serve at the ground level, not from the top. The main premise of servant leadership is self-sacrifice for others without regard to what one might receive in return

Figure 2.2 Servant leadership attributes model

Source: Greenleaf, R. F. (1977). *Servant Leadership: A Journey into the Nature of Legitimate Power and Greatness*. Mahwah, NJ: Paulist Press, p. 7.

(Greenleaf, 1977). Many corporate practices now include annual meetings at the sites convenient to large numbers of shareholders, issuing reports on actions taken at the annual meeting, and disclosing substernal amounts of financial data. In practice, however, the government remains the focal point for regulation for corporate control. The corporate charter and its bylaws define the fiduciary responsibilities of management toward shareholders and thereby determine the basic ground rules for takeover activity.

The theory also argues that an organization requires a structure that allows harmonization to be achieved most efficiently between managers and owners. In the context of a company's leadership, this situation is attained more readily if the CEO is also the chairman of the board. This leadership structure will assist them to attain superior performance to the extent that the CEO exercises complete authority over the corporation and that their role is unambiguous and unchallenged. In this situation, power and authority are concentrated in a single person. Hence the expectations about corporate leadership will be clearer and more consistent both for subordinate managers and for other members of the corporate board (Hamid, 2011). Thus, there is no room for uncertainty as to who has authority or responsibility over a particular matter. The organization will enjoy the benefits of unity of direction and of strong command and control. The spectrum of government intervention in corporate governance is no simple matter. Most of the citizen and interest group approaches are likely to generate serious and often unexpected side effects, such as the government failure that so frequently accompanies attempts to address the problem of market failure. The literature on government regulation of business shows that the costs of regulation often exceed the benefits. The real winners are the regulated corporations instead of the people that regulation is designed to protect.

The key argument is that government-business relations in Africa are transforming into a post-independent constellation that is in line with the pressures of globalization, technological, and structural adjustment in their political economy. In addition, the political goal of generating a class of domestic industrial entrepreneurs has not been adequately achieved. Instead, unproductive bureaucracies have contributed to the fact that companies in some African countries are characterized by inefficiency and technological backwardness (Sandbrook, 1993).

Economists have long been divided on the role of government in society. John Maynard Keynes and John Kenneth Galbraith have argued that an economy needs to be continually fine-tuned by an activist government to operate efficiently. Thus, as an economy grows, a growing government is also necessary to correct private-sector inefficiencies. This school of thought grew primarily out of the Great Depression, when markets seemed to fail and government intervention was viewed as a means to restore economic stability. Other twentieth-century economists, such as Frederick von Hayek and Milton Friedman, have argued that an activist government is the cause of economic instability and inefficiencies in the private sector. Government should exist to ensure that a private market operates efficiently; it should not act to replace the market mechanism (Garrett & Rhine, 2006).

Conclusion

This chapter has examined several business and government relations theories. It argues that although there are several benefits to business-government relations in any country, nations do not simply throw open their doors to free trade and force all their domestic businesses to sink or swim. The chapter also discusses how the relationships between business and government range from cooperative to competitive, from friendly to hostile. In addition, the chapter presents an argument that the basic power of the business firms in African countries lies in the widespread recognition that it is a fundamental mechanism for achieving citizens' social and economic progress.

In addition, it is paramount for national governments to continue to protect all or some of their industries in order for some companies to take advantage of their consumers. National government has an obligation to strike a balance between national desires for protection and international desires for free trade.

Finally, this chapter was based on the distinct logic of business and government relations in any economy. One point that is clearly stated is that businesses continuously feed government with critical information, assembling a transnational collaboration, cording simultaneous lobbying of different governments, supporting the strengthening of government regulations, and turning government into a partner. The outcome of business and government relations is that governments are not perceived to be super efficient in regulating businesses; at the same corporations in the private sector have not effectively played their role in mediating this resumed inefficiency. No doubt, a business or government manager who makes serious attempts to translate theory into reality is bound to increase productivity more than a counterpart who chooses to use the "fire brigade" or trial-and-error approach. Thus, the relative independence of business provides greater benefits than could have been achieved through tighter or more centralized government control.

References

Ake, C. (2005). The Feasibility of Democracy in Africa. Darker, Senegal: Codesria Press

Asch, P. and Seneca, R. (1989). *Government and the Marketplace*. Chicago: Dryden Press.

Bach, D. and Unruh, G. (2004, July 12). Business-Government Relations in a Global Economy Broadening the Economy Map. IE Working Paper, DE8–109–1.

Batch, D. and Newman, A. L. (2004). *Effective Market Power: The Domestic Institutional Roots of International Market Regulation.* Paper Presented at the Annual Meeting of the American Political Science Association, Chicago, Illinois, United States.

Blinder, A. S. (1991). Keynes, Lucas, and Scientific Progress. *American Economic Review*, 77(2) (1987), 130–136. Reprinted in Mark Blaug (Ed.), *John Maynard Keynes (1833–1946)*. Vol. 2. Brookfield, VT: Edward Elgar.

Boddewyn, J. (2015). International Business-Government Relations Research, 1945–2015: Concept, Typologies, Theories and Methodologies. *Journal of World Business*, 51(1), 10–22.

Derber, C. (2002). People Before Profit: The New Globalization in the Age of Terror, Big Money, and Economic Crisis. New York: Picador Press.

Dibie, R. (2014a). *Public Administration, Analysis, Theory and Application*. Ilishan Remo: Babcook University Press.

Dibie, R. (2014b). Comparative Perspective on Environmental Policies and Issues. New York: Routledge.

Ferrell, C., Fraedrich, J. and Farrell, L. (2015). *Business Ethics: Ethical Decision Making and Cases*. 10th Edition. Stanford, CT: Cengage Learning Press.

Forest, F. (2009). Introducing Government-Business Relations: History, Theories and Cases. Boston, MA: Pearson Custom Publishing.

Garrett, T. A. and Rhine, R. M. (2006, January–February). On the Size and Growth of Government. *Federal Reserve Bank of St. Louis Review*, 88(1), 13–30.

Gilpin, R. (1987). *The Political Economy of International Relations*. Princeton, NJ: Princeton University Press.

Gilpin, R. (2001). *Global Political Economy*. Princeton, NJ: Princeton University Press.

Gordon, R. (1990). What Is New-Keynesian Economics? *Journal of Economic Literature*, 28(3), 1115–1171.

Greechie, S. (2003). *Role of Government in Business*. http://smallbusiness.chron.com/role-government-business-803.html. Accessed September 11, 2015.

Greenberg, J. (2012). *Managing Behavior in Organizations*. 2nd Edition. Upper Saddle River, NJ: Prentice Hall Press.

Greenberg, J. and Baron, R. (2010). *Behavior in Organizations: Understanding and Managing the Human Side of Work*. 8th Edition. Upper Saddle River, NJ: Prentice Hall.

Greenleaf, R. F. (1977). Servant Leadership: A Journey Into the Nature of Legitimate Power and Greatness. Mahwah, NJ: Paulist Press, p. 7.

Griffin, R. and Moorhead, G. (2014). *Organizational Behavior Managing People and Organizations*. 11th Edition. Boston, MA Cengage Learning.

Hamid, A. A. (2011). *Corporate Governance and Stewardship*. http://ari-glcrc.blogspot.com/2011/12/corporate-governance-theories_07.html.

Hubbard, R. G. and O'Brien, A. P. (2015). *Macroeconomics*. 5th Edition. Boston, MA: Pearson Education Inc.

Johnson, D. and Turner, C. (2016). *European Business*. 3rd Edition. New York: Routledge Press.

Keynes, J. M. (1936). The General Theory of Employment, Interest, and Money. London: Macmillan.

Lehne, R. (2013). Government and Business: American Political Economy in Comparative Perspective. Washington, DC: Congressional Quarterly Press.

Lussier, R. (2012). *Management Fundamentals*. Mason, OH: South Western Press/Cengage Learning.

Lussier, R. and Achua, C. (2016). *Leadership: Theory, Application, & Skill Development*. Mason, OH: South Western Press/Cengage Learning.

McAlister, D. T., Ferrell, O. C. and Ferrell, L. (2010). *Business and Society: A Strategic Approach*. Boston, MA: Cengage Learning.

McCann, E. & Ward, K. (2012). Policy assemblages, mobilities and mutations: Toward a multidisciplinary conversation. *Political Studies Review*, 10(3), 325–332.

Mankiw, N. G. (1993). A Symposium on Keynesian Economics Today. *Journal of Economic Perspectives*, 7(Winter), 3–82.

Mankiw, N. G. (2018). *The Principles of Macroeconomics*. Boston, MA: Cengage Learning.

Murray, V. and Bell, M. (1985). *Theories of Business-Government Relations*. Toronto, Canada: Trans-Canada Press.

Pettinger, T. (2008). *Economics Essays: The Importance of Economics*. www.economicshelp.org/2008/06/importance-of-economics.html. Accessed July 28, 2015.

Rangan, V. K. Quelch, J. A., Herrero, G., and Barton. B. (2007). Business Solutions for Global Poor: Creating Social and Economic Value. San Francisco, CA: John Wiley & Son Inc.

Rod, M. (2011). Government—Business Relations: An Agency-Theory Perspective on the Procurement of Market Research. *International Journal of Procurement Management*, 4(1), 2–13.

Rolf, A. (2006). *Business-Government Trade Relations*. www2.dsu.nodak.edu/users. Accessed November 27, 2015.

Sachs, J. (2005). The End of Poverty: Economic Possibilities for Our Time. New York: Penguin Press.

Sandbrook, R. (1993). *The Politics of Africa's Economic Recovery*. New York: Cambridge University Press.

United Nations Development Programme. (1997). *Governance for Sustainable Human Development*. UNDP Policy Document, New York, 97–113.

World Bank. (2014). World Development Report. New York: Oxford University Press.

Ya Ni, A. and Van Wart, M. (2016). *Building Business—Government Relations: A Skills Approach*. New York: Routledge Press.

3 Business and Government Relations in Burkina Faso

Mariam Konaté, Idrissa Ouedraogo, and Pascal T. Kouaman

Introduction

Burkina Faso is a country in West Africa. The nation was formerly known as the Republic of Upper Volta. It achieved its independence from France in 1960. It had a population of about 18.1 million people in 2015 (World Factbook, 2016). Burkina Faso has boundaries with the Republic of Benin to the east, Ghana and Togo to the south, Mali to the north, Niger Republic to the east, and Ivory Coast to the southwest. According to a World Bank Group report in (2016), Burkina Faso's GPP was US$11.1 billion in 2015. The country's GDP per capita was estimated to be about US$1,777 in 2015 (GlobalEdge, 2016; World Factbook, 2016). Burkina Faso's government is regarded as semi-presidential. Under this semi-presidential system of democracy, the prime minister is the head of government, while the president is the head of state. This system also mandates both the prime minister and the president to execute executive powers. On the other hand, the legislative power of the country is vested in both the government and parliament.

The policies of privatization and economic liberalization were implemented in Burkina Faso in the beginning of the 1990s as a way to fight against poverty and to create wealth placed in the private sector at the heart of the development question. Several public policies were passed to cement the new role given to the private sector as a critical piece in the economic development puzzle. Among other actions, politics of state disengagement from some productive sectors, as well as the privatization of several companies previously under state control, were conducted. Although privatization has had some positive results, there have also been problems. Burkina Faso is a member of the UEMOA (West African Economic Monetary Union), an organization that is nowadays considered to be located in one of the most difficult regions to do business in (GlobalEdge, 2016). Indeed, the lack of administrative transparency, obsolete regulations, the lack of information accessible to entrepreneurs, as well as long and costly delays characterize countries in the UEMOA zone (World Factbook, 2016). The relations that exist between the government and the private sector are complex and diverse as it becomes more and more obvious that the public sector continues to impact the activities as well as the running of private companies (World Bank Group, 2016). Private companies, in return, also try to use the actions and decisions of the government to their advantage through forging personal relationships with public officials and political parties.

The nature of the relationships between the public and private sectors, and more specifically, the impact of those relationships on the private sector on one hand, and on the other hand, the strategies to envision in order to use those relationships to serve the economic development of Burkina Faso, have not been effectively researched by scholars. Therefore this chapter will contribute immensely to the literature on business and government relations in Burkina Faso.

The place and role of activities under private initiatives is very important in the economy of Burkina Faso. These activities represent the bulk of domestic production; their contribution was already around 76% in 2008. However, it should be noted that most of these activities are carried out either spontaneously or with a basic organization inconsistent with the standards provided by the regulations. The first case mainly includes family farms that are the means of livelihood of more than two-thirds of the population. The second case includes many very small, small, or medium-sized artisanal or semi-industrial or service provision units, run by individuals or groups of individuals. These units represent the share of private activities that, on the one hand, have no legal existence consistently with regulations, and on the other hand, have no organized management and operation in compliance with the modern business model; they are generally grouped under the term "informal sector." Such activities are difficult to identify; their contributions—though important—to production and employment cannot be accurately measured. Thus, they poorly participate in domestic income. The contribution of the informal sector to tax revenues increased from 0.61% in 2009 to 0.32% in 2011 (World Bank Group, 2016).

Private "formal" enterprises have been occupying an increasingly important place, enabling the liberalization of the economy since early 1990s. These enterprises are those under a legal status; they are normally registered in the Administrative and Trade Register (RCCM; in French, *Registre de Commerce et du Crédit Mobilier*), have a fiscal identification number called Unique Financial Identifier (IFU), and are reported to the National Social Security Fund (CNSS; in French, *Caisse Nationale de Sécurité Sociale*). Today there are 68,570 enterprises of different categories registered under the RCCM (World Factbook, 2016). More than half of these enterprises are made of trade businesses (53.6%). The industry sector represents only 13% of these enterprises, with more than three quarters operating in the construction and civil engineering; agro-food processing industries and the mining sector hardly account for respectively 6% and 2% of industrial businesses. The service sector enterprises account for over 26% of registered businesses; over 31% of these enterprises operate in the transport sector and over 28% provide education services (World Factbook, 2016).

Banks and financial institutions and insurance enterprises are relatively few in this category; they only represent respectively 1.19 and 0.54% of service companies. The last decade has seen an unprecedented dynamism over recent years (World Bank Group, 2016). Since 2001, over 3,000 enterprises have been registered per year, with an average 4034 starting businesses every year since 2000. This creation of businesses is worthy of consideration with regard to its potential contributions and disadvantages, but it is obvious that this particular dynamism can only take place in an enabling environment (GlobalEdge, 2016).

For half a century, Burkina Faso has made an economic system policy choice that now seems irreversible. Indeed, like many other African countries, the country chose in the early 1990s to restructure and liberalize its economy. This choice is obviously part of the implementation of structural adjustment programs (SAPs) with the support of international financial institutions. Like all countries that adopted such programs, that choice is clearly linked to the situation of public finances particularly undermined by the burden of debt. Two main reasons can justify this orientation. First of all, there was a continuous increase of expenditures to ensure public services; they were particularly affected by the burden of public enterprises marked by mismanagement. Second, the weakness of the economic fabric did not enable the state to generate substantial revenues to face such charges; the formal private sector was made virtually non-existent. The liberalization of the economy should therefore both reduce the government charges and increase revenues through a more active private sector. This is therefore a process of disengagement of the state from productive sectors and a promotion of the private sector that was thus triggered. Since then, several state companies were privatized; measures fostering the emergence of the private sector were implemented through the development baseline documents developed by the country (Poverty Reduction Strategy Papers; the Accelerated Growth and Sustainable Development Strategy). From the 2000s, the reforms of the business regulatory framework also helped improve the overall business environment.

The place granted to the private sector made it a major stakeholder in the development of the country and therefore a privileged interlocutor to the government. Several institutional frameworks exist to facilitate dialogue and effective relationships with the government and find appropriate responses to private sector concerns. Since 2001, the government has instituted an annual meeting with the private sector. It generally comes out from these meetings that the challenges encountered by enterprises are in more than 50% of cases linked to trade and taxation regulations. In particular, trade regulations related to the business environment, namely the rules governing the business operation, are the source of 29% of the concerns during 2001–2011, while the tax is the reason in a quarter of cases. The sectoral categorization of these concerns shows that 44% are cross-cutting, followed respectively by agriculture, animal and environmental resources (15%), and social sectors (6%). Trade, which occupies the majority of enterprises, is directly involved in only 1% of the concerns (World Bank Group, 2016).

The objectives of this chapter are to explore the formal or informal relations that exist between the private and public sectors in Burkina Faso. The rest of this chapter is organized into four sections. The first section is the review of the literature on the relationship between the government and the private sector; the second makes a critical analysis of these relations from both the traditional review of economic regulation and deregulation, and the privatization of public enterprises and reforms in the private sector governance; the third section reviews the nature of private sector responses vis-à-vis the government and in terms of corporate governance; and the fourth section makes recommendations that will allow for putting business and government relations at the service of economic development.

Framework of the Relationship

Literature on the link between business and government relations is relatively recent. Over the past two decades, development policies much addressed this issue and came to a conclusion that harmonious relations between the government and the private sector is key for development. The elements of the empirical and theoretical literature are numerous and complex. Achim Lang and Marc Tenbücken (2006) provided an overview of existing contributions by pointing at a thousand scientific articles dealing with the subject. These relations can be studied at two levels of analysis: the influences and interactions take place between the State and the company as a single entity or between the State and business groups through collective actions of these. Depending on the direction of the influence, a typology of these relations is established: the dependence of the private sector vis-à-vis the State and the interdependence between both actors and self-regulation of the private sector. We will review the concepts and theories according to this typology.

The literature that highlights the dependence of the private sector on the public sector underscores two major lines of analysis. One of them refers to the theory of organizational ecology and the other refers to the regulatory role of the State that designs the surrounding environment in which businesses operate. Organizational ecology draws ideas from ecology to explain the organizational processes and the dynamics of organizations. It likens the enterprise to an organization and justifies namely the start-up, survival, performance, or mortality of enterprises by the structure of their environment (Oertel & Walgenbach, 2009). In the particular case of the private sector, it seeks to determine to what extent changes in government policies affect businesses. For instance, it is indicated that the number of enterprises operating in a given industrial sector is a key element, the same as the structural conditions, in determining entry into and exit from the market (Hannan & Freeman, 1997). The government is also the key stakeholder in changing market forces and competition. The changes in the fiscal policy of a State particularly affect the entry rate in the relevant sector or region (Seade, 1980; Besley, 1989; Holmes, 1998). Regarding the performance drivers of firms, Porter (1990) sets forward the capacity of businesses to adapt based on their competitive advantages. The construction of these particular benefits is driven by the corporate responsibility and seriousness. Seriousness is expressed here by the continuing ability of the company to adapt to the environment. The responsibility is measured through the rationality of the behavior of the company in its action (Kieser & Woywode, 2006; Carroll & Hannan, 2000). Organizational ecology also provides insights into the influence of the government on the interest groups of the business community. On the basis of natural selection, associations evolve according to their degree of consistency with the economic and social environment (Baum & Amburguey, 2002). According to Schmitter and Streeck (1999), the political system represents an external constraint for these associations. In fact, governments influence the formation of associations by acting on either institutional tools such as the conditions to reach the decision making sphere, or on the process of recognition of these associations. In general, these actions are designed to reduce the formation of private sector interest groups. Other authors argue that it is rather linked to the characteristics of the economic and political situation such as growth, public sector activities, and regulations that determine the dynamics of business interest defense associations (Aldrich & Staber, 1988; Aldrich et al., 1994). By highlighting the importance of the environment as a driver of private sector corporate dynamics and interest groups, this theory of business ecology shows, at the same time, the role of regulations of business activities undertaken in the public sector.

As far as regulation is concerned, there are several studies showing that complex and cumbersome regulations hinder business development, while simple and transparent regulations enable to implement good performance business activities. This is also evidenced at both microeconomic and macroeconomic levels. At the aggregate level, the recent publications abundantly highlight the increased number of indicators measuring the burden and quality of regulations. Regarding starting businesses, countries with complex business start-up regulation and high input costs typically have a large informal economy and a stronger corruption (Djankov et al., 2002). A relaxation of the regulations generally leads to increased entrepreneurship (Kappler & Love, 2001) and ultimately to higher growth rates (Djankov et al., 2006) and increase in the investment rate (Eifert, 2009). At the micro level, Hallward-Driemeier et al. (2006) used data from the World Bank's World Business Environment Survey on 1,500 enterprises spread over five regions and came to the conclusion that business growth, productivity, and investment are influenced by the quality of infrastructure assets, complicated administrative procedures, the level of corruption practice, property rights, and the structure of employment. For the specific case of Morocco, Augier et al. (2010) showed that total factor productivity is highly correlated with access to credit; they emphasized the fact that tax heterogeneity and red tape are linked to poor productivity.

Interdependence is the second type of relationship between the private sector and the government. Interdependence covers interactions between the public and private spheres giving birth to mechanisms of institutional arrangements for regulation, coordination, and control in the society (Tenbücken & Lang, 2006). Interdependence is displayed through the governance concept that has become popular nowadays. This vague concept deriving from organizational sociology and management theories of the 1960s and 1970s has become not only a field of various scientific explorations, but also a pillar of development policies either at the national or international level. It is a concept dear to the World Bank since the early 1990s. It is defined by this institution as the way power is exercised in social and economic resource management in a country (World Bank Group, 2016). To the World Bank, the absence of good governance explains the failure of many projects and programs implemented in developing countries and may also explain the poor performance of sub-Saharan African countries in the 1980s (World Bank Group, 2016). Governance was initially a concept without theoretical foundation but is now equated with the expression of an extension of the theory of the State (Skocpol, 1985); it expresses—through the structures and institutions of the society—the various possible forms of coordination (Schneider, 2004). Traditionally, governance mechanisms rest with the State that performs control through the administration; this is administrative governance. The modern vision of governance highlights the engagement of all stakeholders in decision making; the private sector contributes in defining the means and the exercise of control tools and coordination relations with other stakeholders (Williamson, 1981). This is the market-driven situation. Interdependence between the private sector as a whole and the State is mainly treated by the neo-corporatism theory. Originally, traditional theories used to explain public policy making as the result of pressure and counter-pressure by various groups on the public sector (Oertel & Walgenbach, 2009). According to the neo-corporatism, understanding the economic and fiscal policy decisions and the relationships between and within industries assumes that we consider the business interest defense groups as full stakeholders in the policy-making process. Ultimately, public policy decisions result from engagements between the public sphere, trade associations, and workers.

There are various theories analyzing the influence of the private sector on the government. The direct theory of lobbying explains the influence exerted by a sole proprietorship on decision-making bodies; it was particularly developed in the light of the experience of the European Union. Direct lobbying is mainly performed by large enterprises; regarding the European Union, the action of these enterprises has significantly changed the mode of operation of the European Union Commission and its position in relation to these big enterprises (Coen, 1997). However, big enterprises can only perform direct lobbying through associations defending the interests of enterprises. An important aspect of direct lobbying theory is the ability of large enterprises to influence the strategies of their umbrella interest groups. Based on the experience they have with small and medium enterprises, they then search within those groups for a dominant position that gives them a central role in framing the actions of these groups (Greenwood, 1997).

Several theories focus on the influence of corporate interest defense groups on governments, including the class theory, the elite theory, and the annuity theory. The class theory originated from Marxism and categorizes individuals in groups based on their particular economic status in the production scale. It argues that the private sector advocacy groups representing the interests of the capitalists in this context do not need pressure tactics over governments. The social structure is naturally conducive to the interests of capitalists; according to Offe (1975), for example, this is justified by the dependency of government on capital. There is also the proximity between rulers and capitalists that support this fact. Other authors think that there is a tacit understanding between the rulers and capitalists in such a way to always preserve or set forward the interests of the latter (Lindblom, 1977). These interests can be maintained even in the absence of pressure for two reasons: first, the loss of trust in businesses under a capitalist system may cause a drop in the system as a whole, and second, enterprises are the main economic performance drivers of a nation, and any offense to their interests may affect the whole economy.

The elite theory considers that the society is made up of an elite class and the masses. The elite class is the holder of the wealth and knowledge and power in the society. Its influence on political decisions mainly results from its being close to the class of rulers and the fact that it shares the same habits and interests with it. Its influence also comes from the individualism of this class using its position in order to sway direct decision-making toward its interests (Mills, 1956). Finally, this situation is encouraged by the role that the managers of major enterprises fulfill in the public opinion and in decision-making processes in extensor.

The annuity theory results from two developments. The first development is based on Stigler's idea (1971) that the producer class is the most able to defend its interests. Becker (1983) describes the process as follows: if the state decides, for example, to increase taxes and the owners of capital withdraw from the production process, the consequences may be detrimental to economic performance; since the goal of the State is rather to promote this performance, the State is then obliged to comply with capital owners' requirements. The second development highlights the action of businesses on politicians and bureaucrats to create annuities by paying bribes arrangements in return (Tullock, 1980). Some business groups particularly influence decisions by funding electoral campaigns or political activities.

Nature of Business-Government Relations

The regulation governing the conduct of private business activities is difficult to assess comprehensively. With regard to the stakeholders in this sector, it is differently assessed, depending on the business sector. Its characterization is yet less complex to establish with respect to the actors it directly influences. This is less easy to establish because it has indirect effects on workers and consumers. This section is intended to explore the following: the nature and expansion of the regulation, the privatization of State enterprises, the relations between the government and workers, the relations between the government and consumers, and new experiences in economic deregulation.

Nature and Expansion of the Regulation and New Deregulation Experiences

The regulation governing the private sector has gone through a clear evolution in Burkina Faso, starting from the early 2000s. According to *Doing Business* indicators by the World Bank, the overall business environment has improved. However, not all the various aspects of business regulation went through the same change. Some aspects experienced a significant shift toward the private sector while others experienced no reform. Only some aspects are discussed here in order to provide an overview of the business environment and its evolution.

In the regulatory and institutional business framework, starting a business is one of the aspects considered because it can act as a barrier to the start of potential businesses. In particular, it requires the implementation of administrative procedures entailing for a cost and a minimum capital to be paid on starting the business. Indicators from the World Bank show that each of these aspects has been improved during the 2004–2014 decade. The number of procedures to be fulfilled for starting a business moved from 12 to 3, and their lead time moved from 40 to 3 days; the cost for starting the business moved from 147% to 49.8% of the income per capita, and the minimum capital as a percentage of income per capita moved from 531.1 to 416.2. The reduction in the business start-up lead time was enabled by the establishment of the Business Formalities Centres (CEFORE, *Centres de Formalité des Entreprises*).

In clear terms, the complexity and costs associated with starting a business have been substantially reduced. However, the minimum capital required remains very important, considering the low income of the large proportion of the population; no capital is required in some countries such as Sierra Leone, for example. Moreover, two important elements can be pointed out: first, procedures are actually a burden on the promoters but their lead time matters more than their number; secondly, the costs associated with business start-up (cost of procedures and minimum capital) seem to be more critical when deciding on whether to start a business or not; a decrease in these costs should significantly relieve the burden of starting up a business.

While investors are influenced by business start-up conditions on the one hand, they care less for the closure-related conditions. The conditions wherein insolvent firms can be saved and closed are critical for both the company and the workers and business partners. As a whole, the regulatory framework of the closure is not conducive. The closing lead time takes four years (since 2004) and the recovery rate is very low. This rate has increased from 6.3% to 26.8% but remains quite low. Although these conditions are supposed to protect social stakeholders in the business, they remain dissuasive especially in high risk areas (World Bank Group, 2016).

An important issue for the development of private investment is the ease of dealing with land properties and construction permits. Significant improvements were made in this respect, particularly regarding the lead time and costs of getting such documents, which makes Burkina Faso the top West African country for dealing with construction permits (Doing Business in Burkina Faso, 2011). This progress was enabled by the establishment of Construction Authorisation Formalities Centres (CFAC; in French, *Centres de Formalités des Actes de Construire*) and the one-stop land tenure centre.

Since 2004, the business environment has gone through significant reforms to ease the performance of private activities. Some aspects—not yet reformed—including constraints act as obstacles to the private sector, to be addressed. Others have already been reformed, and it would be advisable to deepen these reforms. In fact, for reforms to produce the expected effect on the private sector, they must reach a critical level (Kappler & Love, 2012).

Privatization of State-Owned Enterprises

From 1960 to 1990, political economy was strongly influenced by the interventionism of the State. The weakness of the economic fabric after the independence underpins this attitude of the State but also the economic policy vision of that period. Through a service responsible for planning the development of the various sectors, many industrial units and State-owned financial institutions were created to expand the economy. The organization that did not provide any room for the private sector enabled the country to achieve fairly good performance. So, while most African countries had already developed the Structural Adjustment Programs (SAPs) in the 1980s, Burkina Faso did not adhere to these programs until 1991, particularly because of the unbalanced state of its public finance. Public enterprises were blamed for causing the accrual of budget deficit, leading to their being liquidated or opened to private engagement. The SAPs acted as a turning point in the development of the private sector. Forty-five public companies were identified to be entirely or partly transferred to the private sector. In 2007, 26 of them were actually transferred; 13 were liquidated or under liquidation process, while 3 were withdrawn from the privatization program. It is interesting to note the role played by the private sector during these privatizations. The choice of the State to transfer its place to the private sector led to a shortfall over a certain period. The contribution of enterprises did not enable to offset the cost of support measures such as tax rebates, equity contributions or subsidies. It should be noted that the level of investments achieved was significant. Thus, in 1995–1998, the buyers of public enterprises invested 19.8 for the equipment renewal and FCFA 15.5 billion between 1999 and 2000 (Government of Burkina Faso, 20030. The outcome of these business activities is mixed. While some were able to expand their operations and create jobs, others simply closed, putting many workers in a challenging social situation (Somé, 2007). Privatizations were supposed to also lead to competition-driven reduction in prices. This expectation was rather improbable, because most public enterprises were operating in a monopoly or quasi-monopoly environment. As a whole, privatization programs have had the merit of providing room for the private sector in economic activity. However, the performance was not up to the expected results. Like the SAPS, privatization contributed in exacerbating social problems, even if its failures cannot be attributed to the private sector alone.

The Government and the Labor Market

The regulation of the labor market has long remained without significant change in Burkina Faso. Two reasons can justify this fact. The first reason is the willingness of the State to protect workers mainly because of poor living conditions. The second reason is related to the dynamism of labor unions and their strict opposition to any amendment of the regulations for employers. Despite this situation, the labor market has undergone reforms following the decision of the authorities to improve the business climate. In 2008, a new law was passed and introduced a relaxation of labor regulations at two levels. It removed or reduced certain rigidities. This particularly covers the conditions for employment contracts establishment and the settlement of conflicts related to the complete termination of contracts. This law also improved the efficiency of the labor administration (Government of Burkina Faso, 2008). This labor regulation reform, though audacious, is considered by many stakeholders as incomplete.

Furthermore, the quality and adequacy of the workforce remain a critical issue to enterprises. In the first 11 government-private sector meetings, the specific concern regarding capacity building was frequently raised. The government therefore undertook to support vocational training. Several vocational training centers were built, and a vocational training and learning support fund (FAFPA) was set up. All these measures, however, did not lead to the expected results, particularly in terms of job creation. The public sector remained the main source of employment. It is therefore possible that the scale of the reforms is not yet sufficient to encourage enterprises to create more jobs.

The Government and the Consumer

Part of the rationale for regulating business activities is linked to consumer protection. While the economic theory supports that laissez-faire leads to optimize the objectives of both the producer and the consumer in the presence of market failures, enterprises are tempted to market lower quality products. There is an institutional and legal system that protects consumers by regulating the production or import of products. These products are subject to quality standards set by international institutions or by the National Public Health Laboratory. This laboratory is responsible for tracking compliance with these standards. There are also consumer interests safeguarding organizations such as the League of Burkina Consumers or the Association of Electronic Communication Services Consumers (ABCE) that receive operating grants from the State. These organizations are supposed to work for the defense and protection of consumer rights. Furthermore, a section under the Ministry of Commerce is responsible for price control. In fact, the prices of a number of—mostly commodity—products are set through negotiations between the private sector, trade unions, consumer associations and the government. Other products also benefit from government grants entailing for price control (Government of Burkina Faso, 2015). The possibility emerges that while the State successfully enforces these prices on large size enterprises, this enforcement is more hardly achievable on small business and particularly retailers. The consumer support measures have therefore always had mixed results. That is why in 2011, riots against the high cost of living led the government to partially replace the private sector. The government set up commodity marketing shops to improve access for vulnerable people. As a whole, product and service quality and price control remains incomplete and ineffective in practice (Government of Burkina Faso, 2015).

The Power of Government

Government and Foreign Trade

Like many countries in sub-Saharan Africa, foreign trade in Burkina is based on the export of primary products against import of manufactured goods. The country has no oil and cotton, which has long been the main export product as inherited from colonization. Until 2013, cotton was unquestionably the leading export product followed by gold (African Economic Outlook, 2013). Trade with the countries of the sub-region remains undeveloped, despite the existence of a common market. There are several institutional structures to oversee and promote foreign trade. This role is played by the National Foreign Trade Board (ONAC; in French, *Office National du Commerce*) at the country level. The Burkina Shippers Council (CBC; in French *Conseil Burkinabé des Chargeurs*) and the Chamber of Commerce and Industry of Burkina (CCI-BF) play an important role in developing and facilitating trade. For this purpose, the CCI-BF has representations in various West African countries to provide support to importers and exporters.

Most products can be imported by any operator. Prior import permits are required for some products. Importing licenses are exclusively provided to specific bodies for some specific products, including hydrocarbon, cigarettes, and beverages. Over the last decade, foreign trade operating conditions changed without causing the expected improvements. In 2011, one document was taken out from the documents required for export and import operations. The time required was also reduced. However, this relaxation was accompanied by an increase in costs associated with the importation and exportation (World Bank Group, 2016). The overall outcome of these changes is mixed. In 2011, Burkina Faso was considered as the most difficult foreign business transactions country in the sub-region.

Tax Policy

In general, taxation is a point of disagreement between the public and the private sectors, as the private sector considers that the taxes are a big burden against its development. In 2008, over 65% of sample enterprises surveyed felt that taxation was the main obstacle to their development (Government of Burkina Faso). The tax burden is felt at two levels. The first level consists of the time needed to make the tax and duty payments, which in turn depend on their number. In this respect, the reforms have not been consistent. According to the Doing Business report, 2011, a typical firm takes on average 270 hours in the year to make payments on 46 different taxes. These procedures are still expensive for enterprises on one hand and difficult to implement on the other hand. The second level covers the tax rates applied to enterprises. The latest changes on tax and investment codes provided a substantial relaxation in the corporate tax burden. In addition to the willingness to promote the development of the local private sector, the government wanted to establish an attractive taxation for foreign investors. The income tax; the non-commercial profit tax; and the industrial, the commercial, and crafts profit tax experienced a decline by seven and a half points, moving from 35% to 27.5%. It is still worth noting that tax payment procedures remain complex and long.

Government and the Financial Sector

Access to credit is a concern for enterprises in Burkina Faso. This issue has repeatedly been raised during annual meetings between the private sector and the government. The banking sector has significantly expanded over the recent years. Between 2005 and 2011, the number of banks increased from 8 to 12. Domestic credit as a percentage of GDP was 20.1 in 2011. According to the World Bank surveys, in 2009, three quarters of firms felt that access to credit was a major constraint to their development. West Africa recorded the biggest difficulties for enterprises to access credit. In fact, only 28% out of 85% of enterprises in need of financing actually access it (World Bank, 2009; World Statistics Pocketbook 2010). The credit granting conditions, the banking regulations, the characteristics of applicants, and the information asymmetries are the main factors underpinning this situation. The harsh bank management conditions imposed by EU standards reduce the credit supply capacity of banks. The poor equity contributions of credit applicants combined with low managerial capacity of business owners make banks highly reluctant to grant them credits. Moreover, as in most sub-Saharan African countries, the lack of reliable information on credit applicants lead to often binding guarantees requested by banks. In Burkina Faso, the guarantee reliability index that reflects the harshness of the legislation is 3 out of 10; the extent of information is only 1 out of a scale of 6.

To address these issues that seriously hinder the development of small and medium enterprises, the government set up public financing fund to ease access to credit by lighter conditions. In 2011, these funds accounted for 4.44% of financial institutions. So far, their actions have not very significantly addressed the corporate financing issues. In fact, enterprises requested the establishment of a guarantee fund enabling them access credit. To this effect, the operationalization of the Interbank Guarantee Finance Corporation (SOFIGIB, *Société Financière de Garantie Interbancaire*) is a major step forward. The challenges for the government to improve access to business financing are linked to the judicial system, better regulation of the status of enterprises and the establishment of a truly operational guarantee fund.

The Responsibility in the Operating the National Economic System

The government has always been committed in the management of the national economic system. However, its role has evolved. Having long been the main stakeholder in all sectors of the economy, the government, from 1991, began to withdraw from the service production sectors. The economic liberalization enabled the government to confine itself to its role as regulator and support the economy. In fact, the government embarked on its economy management mode upgrading process. In the public sector, several reforms were undertaken to improve the efficiency of the administration. Public financial management strategies enabled the country to get a debt relief under the Heavily Indebted Poor Countries (HIPC) initiative. Since the first Structural Adjustment Program (SAP), managing the macroeconomic framework has become quite effective despite both internal and external shocks. The macroeconomic environment was generally stable. In terms of support to the private sector, the government developed a private sector development policy letter; the numerous reforms implemented were beneficial for businesses. The government is now in the sector promotion logics. This was evidenced by the structures put in place to support this sector and improve the legal and regulatory framework governing businesses. All these actions are part of the wider good governance promotion policy framework. Two national good governance programs were developed (1998–2003 and 2005 to 2015). To achieve a harmonious development, the government is nowadays building on the prospective to develop strategies likely to channel the forces in the various sectors of the economy toward a more harmonious development.

Nature of Private Sector Response

Since liberalization, the business and policy communities have always been very close to being often confused. The reasons for this acquaintance are shared by both types of stakeholders. The objective of policy stakeholders is to especially receive financial support in conducting their campaigns against promises to business operators. In turn, the rationale for business operators would be to be granted easy business arrangements and various benefits from the administration. To this purpose, the business community greatly contributes in funding electoral campaigns. Until October 2014, many major economic operators had pledged allegiance to the ruling party. This situation has very often gone beyond the provision of funds to parties; some stakeholders even integrated the political agenda and won electoral seats in the parliament or in municipalities. Though the compensation of that interest is not directly observable, the benefits in awarding public contracts and other benefits granted in the application of regulations can be mentioned. Regarding taxation, for example, large enterprises have accrued several years of large debts vis-à-vis the tax administration without being worried at any time. This behavior of private stakeholders is much from individual operators and to a lesser extent from sectoral groups or businesses with similar interests. The policy and business communities were strongly close, to the point of sometimes creating a complete collusion between both environments.

Response of Private Associations to the Autocratic Government Regulation

According to the supply theorists, for corporate taxes to be effective and bring the most revenue to the government, taxes and duties should not be too high. Otherwise, these enterprises feeling a low profit can stop their business or dodge tax regulations. Today, it is clearly recognized that costly and complex regulations discourage private investment or lead enterprises to circumvent regulations (Djankov et al., 2002). In fact, an effective regulation is one that is simple, less costly, flexible, and affordable to many. The most obvious observation in the case of Burkina Faso can be observed with business start-up. In the light of the effects of reforms, poorly enabling regulations maintain several private actors outside the formal sector. Operating in the poorly regulated informal sector indeed bears drawbacks, such as the extreme difficulty to get credit and expand one's activities. Yet, some stakeholders rather operate in such an environment, instead of undergoing the current regulations. This is the way not yet formalized businesses behave.

Enterprises operating in a formal environment may also be observed in a sense of bypassing these rules when, in overall terms, there are rules crippling their activities. This is the context in which they happen to pay bribes to administration actors to be exempted from some obligations or to enjoy special benefits. In the previous section, we have already pointed out the laxity some enterprises enjoyed from the tax authorities. These practices are more generally aligned to a culture of government being corrupted by private operators. Corruption is sometimes initiated by public officials as well (Akouwerabou & Bako, 2013). More recently, and in the framework of private sector business associations, the private sector response to restrictive regulations has been better organized. The National Council of Employers of Burkina Faso (CNPB, *Conseil National du Patronat Burkinabé*) prompted enterprises to cluster as sectoral groups or shared interests to safeguard their own interests. The private sector reacted specifically to regulations through advocacy. Thus, it successfully led to the establishment of annual meetings with the government, enabling it to raise concerns. This approach has the advantage of allowing the sharing of concerns and developing common solutions that benefit all.

Corporate Activism and Corporate Governance

A very small proportion of the enterprises are listed on stock exchanges. The shareholding system remains poorly developed in Burkina Faso. The government only recently made it compulsory in the privatization operations for a share of the corporate capital to be reserved for the public sector. The *Office National des Telecommunications* (ONATEL, National Telecommunications Utility) has a number of minority shareholders. The involvement of individuals in business capital is very recent. Hence the culture of activist engagement of a minority of shareholders in major corporate decisions remains underdeveloped. Several reasons may underpin this situation: firstly, these shareholders are unaware of their rights; secondly, there is a complexity in the legal and judicial procedures relating thereto; finally, enterprises are in such a constant progress in the stock market that there is truly no risk related to profit shares of those shareholders. The lack of follow-up by investors reduces the need for transparency and dissemination of information. Except for few large enterprises, some of which are branches of multinationals, corporate governance is not yet a shared business culture. This derives from the weakness of the legislation in force but also the status of most enterprises. In fact, more than half of the enterprises are sole proprietorships or family companies and therefore not subject to accountability. The lack of good corporate governance affects the government revenue and the efficiency of the private sector itself. In fact, the major reasons given by financial institutions to grant limited credits include the lack of transparency and poor corporate governance. Poor dissemination of information to the various departments and employees within enterprises is also an obstacle to the development of businesses activities. The CNPB initiated training sessions for business leaders to build their capacity on corporate governance means and its benefits. Eventually, for a true business development, leaders must integrate transparent governance rules into their management style. This is the only way they will successfully manage to address some constraints to their expansion.

Recommendations

The role of governments was largely broadened in recent years to now encompass the redistribution and security, and the definition and implementation of national development strategies, in addition to the activity regulation. This positioning of the government has been instated since the late 1990s, but this role should be refocused on core issues. Above all, it remains clear that no government can truly develop without a healthy economic environment. The point is about setting an institutional and macroeconomic stability environment. Institutional stability is a primarily political issue; on this point, it is accepted that the key to guarantee this stability is the establishment of a democratic system and culture. It is thus important to also create national conditions for a permanent dialogue between the various components of society to support the country building process. This question is the more relevant to the country, as it is disadvantaged in many ways, including geography, climate conditions, or even the structure of the economy.

Macroeconomic stability covers the establishment of a sustainable balance of external and internal accounts. Internally, effective management of public finances should be ensured through a better allocation of government resources, the fight against corruption and misappropriation of public funds, and addressing public administration issues. A healthy internal management would make the maintenance of external balance easy, which is a key indicator for external actors. In addition, in a stable environment safeguarding the security of investments and more generally the exercise of business, it is easier to create the conditions for a successful economy. The country is already engaged in reforms to facilitate the emergence of a dynamic private sector. It would be important to continue and reinforce these reforms. The reforms already carried out are certainly displaying the willingness to simplify business performance. But some important aspects are worth consideration. It is clearly key to continue the reforms of the regulatory framework and procedures governing the private sector by focusing on the most critical elements to this sector. In addition, good sector governance is not sufficient but must be accompanied by a strengthening of support for production sectors. The development of activities depends on several factors including factors of production and the availability and quality of infrastructure. In Burkina Faso, the production factor on which private actors are requesting actions is energy, because its cost is one of the highest in West Africa. Reducing the cost of energy is also a recurring concern of the private sector. In this sense, the establishment of development growth poles provides a great opportunity. In fact, within these areas, it would be interesting to apply more conducive rates to enterprises. To support production, it is also essential to continue the expansion and improvement of infrastructure to open up many parts of the country that have potential for some activities. Finally, in a more holistic vision, the strategic planning approach should be continued and extended to the whole economy. So far relatively neglected, aspects such as education, health, and foreign trade should have a better place in the planning.

Corporate Social Responsibility

The debate on private sector governance is largely focused on the easy arrangements it should receive in order to play its leading role in the economy. However, it is not appropriate to limit the role of the private sector to economic development, because its responsibilities also extend to social and environmental aspects. At first glance, it is acknowledged that complex and costly regulations are a burden to businesses; they must always comply with the rules and fulfill their obligations. These include the duty of transparency to the tax authorities, social obligations to workers, and so on. In particular, in labor market environment deregulation depriving workers of a number of protections, enterprises are to strictly comply with their social obligations toward workers. In addition to complying with the obligations binding them, the role of enterprises extends to the whole society. For a country with a mostly poor population, private sector actors could help supply services or goods to the poor. Social sectors including education and health that constantly suffer from the lack of resources could be strengthened through donations and aids from businesses. They also have an important role in the professional integration of young people by providing young graduates with internship opportunities. The country's mining boom led to a proliferation of mining sites causing a significant destruction of the environmental cover. It is therefore important for these mining enterprises to particularly take action in maintaining the environment in addition to the obligations imposed by their terms of references. The corporate social responsibility is an essential aspect on which enterprises can act not only to support the development as a whole but to also deserve the corporate citizenship brand.

Corporate Governance and Ethical Responsibility

Corporate governance has become a central issue in business management, particularly in line with strategy and competitiveness development. However, very few enterprises have already integrated this concept into their operations. The main reason for this delay is clearly the predominance of sole proprietorships and family businesses. In the context of market opening, increased competition control requires more transparent management that integrates all stakeholders in running a business. Good corporate governance helps reassure the owners of capital and ease the external financial flows to increase the level of business, especially industrial capital. It is also a means for harmonizing the efforts of all stakeholders in the company and pushing in the same direction. The establishment of internal institutions and global transparent tools to meet objectives clearly defined and known by all stakeholders reinforces the confidence of managers, workers, owners, and financial institutions. Corporate governance should no longer apply to only enterprises listed on stock exchanges but also cover individual enterprises in achieving their goals. In this respect, many private enterprises still managed traditionally could raise their level of performance by using real and modern management skills. More generally, the performance of the private sector depends on managers' and workers' capacities, which adds on the relevance of moving from a traditional opaque and family business management to a transparent, modern, and actual skill-based management. Furthermore, this transparency should not be limited to corporate stakeholders but to the whole company. Beyond being transparent, this suggests that enterprises should operate in compliance with the corporate values of the companies. It is clear that when requested to deregulate markets and prices and reduce controls on the private sector, the company needs to then ensure the actions of this sector. If enterprises operate under an ethical approach, they can reassure consumers and the government on their expectations for less control. This ethics applies to all aspects of a business activity: price, nature and quality of products marketed, and so on. It appears that businesses are primarily responsible for their corporate credibility and their performance. It is therefore urgent for many enterprises to reform their management systems to comply with these requirements.

Conclusion

This chapter has examined business and government relations in Burkina Faso. It presents the argument that the choice to liberalize the economy since the early 1990s has clearly altered the relations between the government and the private sector in the country. Since that time, the private sector has rapidly expanded especially through privatization of formerly state-owned enterprises. Over the last decade, the relations between these two groups went through a conducive evolution and even ended up being institutionalized. Many reforms have been implemented in many business life areas. In terms of regulations, procedures and costs have been significantly alleviated, thereby making it easy to start new businesses. Taxation and investment regulatory measures are attractive enough for businesses.

The reforms already carried out show the willingness of the government to make the private sector the basis of development.

The overall effect of these actions on the economy is encouraging. The contribution of the private sector to employment is significant even though it falls short of the government unemployment reduction targets. The share of state revenues from the private sector is also increasingly significant. These effects may continue and go to a larger scale in time, should the reforms continue, especially in the areas of promoting competitiveness and foreign trade, development, and modernization of infrastructure. Companies will then gain more dynamism and competitiveness by improving their governance and internal organization. In addition, political stability over the past three decades has been a key incentive for both national and foreign investors. The country's political future therefore remains the critical element that will not only drive the continuation of reforms but also the place and role that will be devoted to the private sector.

References

African Development Bank. (2014). *African Economic Outlook 2013*. AfDB 2013. www.africaneconomicoutlook.org/en.

Akouwerabou, B. D. and Bako, P. (2013). Marchés Publics et Petites et Moyennes Entreprises au Burkina Faso: Quelle Gouvernance? Rapport de Recherche du FR-CIEA N° 56/13.

Aldrich, H. and Staber, U. (1988). Organizing Business Interests: Patterns of Trade Association Foundings, Transformations, and Deaths. In G. R. Carroll (Ed.), *Ecological Models of Organizations*. Cambridge, MA: Ballinger, 123–155.

Aldrich, H., Zimmer, C., Staber, U. and Beggs, J. J. (1994b). Minimalism, Mutualism, and Maturity: The Evolution of the American Trade Association Population in the 20th Century. In J. A. C. Baum and J. V. Singh (Eds.), *Evolutionary Dynamics of Organizations*. New York: Oxford University Press, 55–78.

Augier, P., Dovis, M. and Gasiorek, M. (2010). The Business Environment and Moroccan Firm Productivity. Economics of Transition, Volume 20, Issue 2 (April), 369–399.

Baker, G. S. (1983). "Antitrust and the Economics of Federalism." 26 *Journal of Law and Economics*, 23–37.

Baum, J. A. C. and Amburgey, T. L. (2000). Organizational Ecology. Rotman School of Management, University of Toronto: University of Toronto Press.

Besley, T. (1989).Commodity Taxation and Imperfect Competition: A Note on the Effects of Entry. *Journal of Public Economics*, 40(3), 359–367.

Central Intelligence Agency. (2016). World Factbook. www.cia.gov/library/publications/the-world-factbook/geos/uv.html. Accessed October 10, 2016.

Coen, D. (1997). The Evolution of the Large Firm as a Political Actor in the European Union. Journal of European Public Policy, 4(1), 91–108.

Djankov, S., Freund, C., and Cong P., S., (2006). "Trading on time," Policy Research Working Paper Series 3909, Washington DC: The World Bank.

Djankov S., La Porta, S. R., and Lopez-de-Silanes, F. and Shleifer, A. (2002, February). The Regulation of Entry. *The Quarterly Journal of Economics*, CXVII. 37–64.

Doing Business (2011). Burkina Faso - Making a Difference for Entrepreneurs: Comparing Business Regulation in 183 Economies." http://documents.worldbank.org/

curated/en/866881468016254084/Doing-business-2011-Burkina-Faso-making-a-difference-for-entrepreneurs-comparing-business-regulation-in-183-economies. Accessed May 3, 2016.

Feng, W. (2014). Is There an Implicit Contract Between Government and Business? The Disclosure Regulation of Corporate Political Spending Through the Nexus of Contract Lenses. http://docplayer.net/42659400-Is-there-an-implicit-contract-between-government-and-business.html. Accessed April 28, 2017.

Foch, A. (2012). Un soutien appuyé malgré des effets limités: comment expliquer le paradoxe de la privatisation des infrastructures de la BM en Afrique sub-saharienne? Document de travail du Centre d'Economie de la Sorbonne, Maison de Sciences Economiques. http://centredeconomiesorbonne.univ-paris1.fr/bandeau-haut/documents-de-travail/.

GlobalEdge. (2016). *Burkina Faso Country Insight.* http://globaledge.msu.edu/search?q=Burkina+Faso. Accessed October 11, 2016.

Government of Burkina Faso. (2015). https://www.bing.com/news/search?q= Government+Of+Burkina+Faso%2c+2015.&qpvt=Government+of+Burkina+Faso%2c+2015.++&FORM=EWRE. Accessed May 27, 2016.

Government of Burkina Faso. (2008). http://listings.findthecompany.com/l/9811653/Government-Of-Burkina-Faso-in-Washington-DC. Accessed April 30, 2016.

Government of Burkina Faso. (2003). http://globaledge.msu.edu/countries/burkina-faso/government/. Accessed October 10, 2016.

Greenwood, J. (1997). *Representing Interests in the European Union.* Houndmills: Macmillan.

Hallward-Driemeier, M., Wallsten, S. and Xu, L. C. (2006). Ownership, Investment Climate and Firm Performance, Evidence From Chinese Firms. *Economics of Transition, 14*(4). 27–51.

Hannan, M. T. and Freeman, J. (1977). The Population Ecology of Organizations. *American Journal of Sociology, 82*(5), 929–964.

Kappler, L. and Love, I. (2001). *The Impact of Business Environment Reforms on New Firms Registrations.* Washington, DC: The World Bank, June 2011.

Kieser, Alfred; Michael Woywode (2006): Evolutionstheoretische Ansätze. In: Kieser, Alfred; Mark Ebers (Hg.): *Organisationstheorien.* Stuttgart: Kohlhammer, S. 309–352.

Lang, A. and Tenbücken, M. (2006). *State-Business-Relations: Mapping the Theoretical Landscape.* IPSA World Congress, Section 38–Business and Politics.

Lindblom, C. E. (1977). Politics and Markets: The World's Political Economic Systems. New York: Basic Books.

Marks, G., Scharpf, F. W., Schmitter, P. C. and Streeck, W. (1996). *Governance in the European Union.* London: Sage.

MEF. (2010). *SCADD 2011–2015.* Version définitive.

Mills, C. W. (1956). *The Power Elite.* New York: Oxford University Press.

Ministère de l'Economie et des Finances. *Code des impôts.* Direction générale des impôts, Burkina Faso.

Ministère de la Fonction Publique et de la Réforme de l'Etat. (2010). *Politique Nationale de Bonne Gouvernance 2005–2015.* www.fonction-publique.gov.bf/. Accessed May 4, 2016.

Ministère de l'Industrie du Commerce et de l'Artisanat. Politique sectorielle 2011–2020 du commerce de l'industrie et de l'artisanat. Burkina Faso.

Oertel, S. and Walgenbach, P. (2009, July). *How the Organizational Ecology Approach Can Enrich Business Research on Small and Medium-Sized Enterprises—Three Areas for Future Research.* SBR 61, 250–269.

Offe, C. (1975). The Capitalist State and the Problem of Policy Formulation. In Leon Lindberg (Ed.), *Stress and Contradiction in Contemporary Capitalism*. Lexington: Lexington Books.

Ouédraogo, I. M. (2011). Amélioration de l'environnement des affaires au Burkina Faso: problématique de l'accroissement de l'investissement privé. Conseil Economique et Social, Observatoire Economique et Social, Rapport.

Porter, M. (1990). *The Competitive Advantage of Nations*. New York: Free Press.

Seade, J. (1980). The stability of Cournot revisited. Journal of Economic Theory, 23(1), 15–27

Skocpol, T. (1985). Strategies of Analyses in Current Research. In Peter B. Evans, Dietrich Rueschemeyer and Theda Skocpol (Eds.), *Bringing the State Back*. Cambridge: Cambridge University Press, 3–37.

Soubeiga, S. and Strauss, J. (2013). Financial Sector Policy Note: Financing Small and Medium-Sized Businesses in Burkina Faso.

Schmitter, P., C., and Wolfgang Streeck, W. (1999). "The Organization of Business Interests: Studying the Associative Action of Business in Advanced Industrial Societies." http://www.mpifg.de/pu/dp_abstracts/dp99-1.asp. Accessed May 4, 2016.

Stampini, M., Leug, R., Diarra, S. M. and Pla, L. (2011). How Large Is the Private Sector in Africa? Evidence From National Accounts and Labor Markets. IZA Discussion Paper No. 6267.

Stigler, G. C. (1971). The Theory of Economic Regulation. *Bell Journal of Economics and Management Science*, 2(1), 3–21.

Tullock, G. (1980) Efficient Rent Seeking. In: Buchanan, J., Tollison, R. and Tullock, G., Eds., Toward a Theory of Rent Seeking Society, Texas A & M University Press, College Station, 97–112.

Williamson, O. E. (1981). "The Economics of Organization: The Transaction Cost Approach." *The American Journal of Sociology*. 87 (3): 548–577.

World Bank. (1994). *Governance: The World Bank's Experience*. Washington, DC: The World Bank.

World Bank Group. (2016). *Burkina Faso*. www.worldbank.org/en/country/burkinafaso. Accessed October 11, 2016.

The World Bank and International Finance Corporation. (2008). *Burkina Faso Country Profile, Enterprise Surveys*. 1818 H, Street NW, Washington, DC 20433.

The World Economic Forum. (2013). *The Africa Competitiveness Report (2013)*. The World Economic Forum, Geneva.

World Statistics Pocketbook. (2010)."Burkina Faso Country Profile." http://data.un.org/CountryProfile.aspx?crName=Burkina%20Faso. Accessed May 5, 2016.

United States Government. (2015). *U.S. Relations With Burkina Faso*. www.state.gov/r/pa/ei/bgn/2834.htm. Accessed October 11, 2016.

4 Business and Government Relations in Botswana

Robert A. Dibie and Ayandiji Daniel Aina

Introduction

Botswana is a democratic country in the southern part of Africa. It shares borders with South Africa, Zimbabwe, Zambia, and Namibia. Botswana is almost engulfed by the Kalahari Desert, thereby making the country a sparsely populated nation with little agricultural activity. The nation's population is approximately 2.1 million. Its gross domestic product (GDP) in 2014 was $34.1 billion (World Bank, 2015). The nation is one of Africa's most stable democratic countries. It has consistently maintained a democratic government, responsibly managed its natural resources, and invested in its people and infrastructure since 1966 (Kamrany & Gray, 2014). The country is regarded as the African continent's longest continuous multi-party democracy (Lange, 2009). According to Acemoglu et al. (2003), the nation is a landlocked sub-Saharan African country that was administered indirectly by the British. The British assumed the protectorate would eventually be absorbed into South Africa as an unskilled labor reserve. Botswana was formerly the British protectorate of Bechuanaland; the nation adopted its new name after becoming independent within the Commonwealth of the United Kingdom on September 30, 1966. Since then, it has maintained a strong tradition of stable representative democracy, with a consistent record of uninterrupted democratic elections (Woodberry, 2011).

The country has a mixed economic system, which includes a variety of private freedom, combined with centralized economic planning and government regulation. The business environment in the country is reported to be relatively good (GlobalEdge, 2014). However, there are times when it might be difficult for the government to respond to corporations and investor needs on time. Corporate financial information is often available, but debt collection and institutional framework may have some shortcomings. Business and government relations and inter-corporation transactions often may run into occasional difficulties, especially when there is slow growth in the economy (United States and Foreign Commercial Service and U.S. Department of State, 2012).

Botswana is also the world's largest producer of diamonds, and the trade has transformed it into a middle-income nation (Yager et al., 2007). In the past few decades, production has increased at the Jwemeng, Lethalake, and Orapa mines. Another new mine was also opened in Damtshaa (Bram, 2006). Botswana has for a long time relied on its diamond industry wealth, and the need to step up efforts to diversify the economy is not very clear. Botswana is reported to currently account for 35% of African diamonds (Yager et al., 2007). During the past 10 years the negative economic impact of low diamond prices has galvanized some frustration in the Government of Botswana's inability to promote development of its non-mining sectors. According to a Botswana Country Forecast report (2014), lower mineral prices feed directly into potential export earning and have spillover into reducing unemployment in the country. The challenge has been growing as the investment climate continues to fail to improve over the past decade. According to the World Bank (2014) Doing Business Survey, the conditions in the country are virtually getting worse, as indicated by Botswana's 8 position fall in the global ranking to 79th out of 189 countries surveyed. The Government of Botswana has not been very willing to adopt a tough confrontation with the nation's union militants, even when at risk of provoking disruptive strike. This position of the government tends to contribute to an economically damaging industrial action. Unfortunately, the combination of low diamond prices, shortage of energy supply, and low employment has made the country less attractive to new industries (World Bank, 2014). The country is trying to reduce its economic dependence on diamonds, moving to boost local business and employment by encouraging more value to be added to diamonds locally; however, the process has been very slow.

In addition, growing reliance on imports has nevertheless negatively affected the nation's export and balance of trade. This economy predicament has in turn reduced the current account surplus to less than $1 billion USD in 2014, creating the possibility for the return of a current deficit in 2016 (Botswana Country Forecast, 2014). Further, although Botswana is relatively free of corruption and has a good human rights record, there is the growing frustration among members of the urban middle class over the government's inability to enact good monetary and fiscal policies to alleviate the hardships that have persisted since the global economic downturn in 2009. The citizens' frustrations are especially associated with the high unemployment rate of 20% between 2013 and 2015 (World Bank, 2015).

The level of corruption in Botswana is the lowest in Africa (World Bank, 2015). An independent judiciary enforces contract effectively and protects property rights, buttressing competitiveness. However, there are some concerns that many corporations do not pattern their corporate social responsibility agenda, and lobbying is not interconnected with unethical management activities (Botswana Country Report, 2013). This is because it has not been uncommon for companies operating in the country to have corporate social responsibility policies, but they turn around at the same time to pursue actions that are far different and socially or environmental irresponsible in the political context (Botswana Country Report, 2013). Constructive engagement has often given way to an approach based on an adversarial view of business and government relations (Schepers, 2010).

Like most countries in Africa, Botswana is faced with the challenge of world competitiveness and industrialization. On one hand, Botswana's economy is based only on natural resources. This is what is called the factor-driven economy. On the other hand, the country is also suffering from efficiency-driven economics because it tends to seek technologies vacated by developed countries while trying to develop its own good market efficiency, labor market, efficiency, financial market efficiency, and so on (Republic of Botswana, 20143). As a result of these two economic challenges, the country has not been able to break into the global value and supply network in order to become a global player. Further, Botswana has not been able to develop pragmatic and appropriate strategies that could allow the nation to catch-up with emerging market economies such as the newly industrialized countries (Republic of Botswana, 2014).

The process of managing business and government relations in any country includes the nature of the interaction between companies, entrepreneurs, government, and its political stakeholders. In the case of Botswana, the size of citizen enterprises and the lack of drive to grow tend to restrict the major stakeholders and entrepreneurs from qualifying for high value and better contracts (GlobalEdge, 2014). To add to the business and government relations predicament, past and existing programs have not adequately addressed the issue of growth and graduation out of the micro and medium enterprise sector to larger scale enterprises. An official Government of Botswana report (2013) confirmed the small domestic market for goods and services, coupled with the lack of an entrepreneurial tradition and culture, were factors that severely limited the country's economic growth. It is also argued that the limited pool of potential entrepreneurs were potential threats to the small micro and medium enterprise sector growth in the country (Bureau of Economic and Business Affairs, 2012).

This chapter examines the relationship between the Government of Botswana and Botswana's Confederation of Commerce, Industry and Manpower (BOCCIM). It argues that the partnership between the two sectors in the implementation of the National Development Plan and the Economic Diversification Drive, if well-handled, could further enhance the nation's economic growth. It proposes that a highly differentiated business community that includes a relatively large number of umbrella business organizations, a host of national association and trade organizations, and much representation by corporations individually and collectively in the process of shaping public policies has occurred in the past two decades. At the same time, there has been a remarkable stability with respect to the economic, legal, and institutional business and government framework in the country. However, in order for this partnership to yield positive results in the future, there is the need for stakeholders such as the reform agencies, developmental government departments, entrepreneurial trainers, venture capital and funding institutions, technology, business development consulting and research parastatals, quality control regulators, and the required regional and multinational corporations and marketing bodies to be up and functional in Botswana. The chapter recommends that the only precondition for businesses, government, trade, and economic growth to flourish in Botswana will require individual freedom reinforced by security for citizens, consumers' protection, entrepreneurship, and property.

Government and the Economy Framework

The role of government in managing the economy of any country has been extensively studied (Sanyal & Guvenli, 2000; Schepers, 2010; Celik, 2013). On the other hand, corporate governance is not carried out in a vacuum, either. This is because the success of corporate governance depends on its owners, board members, managers, stakeholders, company owners, as well as the environment in which the corporation operates. The business cycle patter in any country may also affect the performance of corporate governance due to changes in trade practices, equity market change, variation in investment strategies, participation, and government policies. At the same time, government policy makers tend to evaluate the costs and benefits of their regulations before they are formulated and implemented (Celik, 2013). It is very important to note at this point that adopting to appropriate public policy plays a crucial role in corporate governance. While the government often enacts public policies, it is also required to understand the reality in which rules and regulations are to be implemented effectively (Danhrendorf, 2006; Porter, 2002). Celik (2013) contend that without knowledge about the relative significance and the nature of the businesses involved, regulation will be ineffective and most probably tainted by costly unintended consequences. Therefore, one could argue that to foster a positive relationship between business and government requires a certain degree of enabling regulations and contractual freedom.

The growth of lobbying and its various conceptual approaches is closely related to the number of fundamental changes in many countries. These approaches also tend to galvanize an uneasy relationship between democracy, capitalism, and the neoliberal market (Schepers, 2010). It has been argued that government policy makers need to use impact assessment at appropriate stages, ex-post evaluation, and other public governance tools to ensure technical efficiency and socially just regulation in both their fiscal and monetary policies implementation (Dahrendorf, 2006; Podolny, 2009). In Botswana and most liberal democracies in Africa, lobbying belongs to the fundamental civic rights to be able not only to choose but also to influence government and the national and regional assemblies on how to define the public interest, what to regulate, and how to regulate businesses. As a result, it could be argued that the modern corporation is a social institution for production and distribution of goods and services resulting from political intervention in the economy by government.

The interpenetrating system model by Griffin and Moorhead (2014) stipulates that business and government relations as well as the broader corporate and society relations are not simply an exchange relationship, but rather interactive processes in which each party has scope for independent initiative and yet is subject to stimulation and influence by the other. In order to enhance this point of view, Ferrell et al. (2014), Wood (1985), and Danhrendorf (2006) contend that business and government relations extend beyond the cooperation, and this is best described by using not simply an exchange relationship, but rather the principle of the greatest good for the greatest number. In other words, business and government act in a manner most consistent with their perceived interests.

Another approach for understanding business and government relations is the inter-organizational relations theory (Thompson & McEwen, 1958). According to the inter-organizational theory, certain interactions are based on primary competition or primary cooperation. On one hand, competition implies a complicated rivalry for resources, costumers, and markets between two or more organizations (Ferrell et al., 2014). Other the other hand, cooperation has three categories (i.e., bargaining, coalition, and cooperation). While coalition is a conscious combination of two or more organizations to achieve a common purpose, cooperation is the process of absorbing new elements into the leadership or policy determining structure of an organization (Thompson & McEwen, 1958). It also involves strategies whereby resources are shared, and competitive strategies imply a zero-sum posture with regard to resources. Sometimes cooperation and coalitions are the outcome of positive bargaining among business and government institutions (Dibie, 2014; Ferrell et al., 2014). It often involves negotiation of agreement for the exchange of goods and services between private and public organizations during the contracting out of services delivery or privatization (Dibie, 2014). It is observed that some organizations enter into inter-organizational relations because they are dependent upon other organizations and desire to develop coping strategies for obtaining resources (Porter, 2002). It is very important to note that an inter-organizational strategy to deal with government may then have cooperative, conflictual, or adversarial components based upon the perception of how business resources will be best allocated Ferrell et al., 2014). From a monetary and fiscal policies perspective, government as controllers of the economy of a country may directly affect the costs of production, thereby reducing profit, return on investment, assets, and return to stakeholders (Dibie, 2014). What is obvious, however, is that businesses produce tangible economic benefits for the society on one hand. On the other, government directly controls the corporations, through values added to products or services wages or taxes on corporation earning and regulation.

Several scholars have argued that since the government plays an overarching role in the economy of any country, and business frequently deals with government officials, agencies, and regulations, directives are unavoidable (Danhrendorf, 2006) In addition, the Government of Botswana is positively inclined toward inward foreign direct investment, and multinational corporations are more likely to be able to develop positive relations with the government.

One of the important premises of the contingency theory is that corporations must appropriately fit together their strategy and structure if they are to improve performance (Blumentritt, 2003) The theory stipulates that corporate performance depends on a variety of factors. As a result corporations must consider their internal capabilities as well as external conditions in plotting their strategy for success. According to Harris and Rueli (2000) a company's strategy and structure must fit each other if performance is to be enhanced. However, following Miles's (1987) reasoning, a bridging strategy is where a company attempts to quickly identify changing social expectations in order to align organizational conformation to those expectations (Miles, 1987; Blumentritt, 2003). Business and government relations performance is contingent on the extent to which a company successfully achieves its political objectives within the context of its competitive environment (Griffin & Moorhead, 2014). Therefore it could be argued that positive business and government relations are dependent on the interaction between a company and its political stakeholders. The stakeholders may include regulatory agencies, legislators, public relations, media, shareholders, political leaders, trading partners, and so on. Figure 4.1 shows the premises of how the contingency can be applied to business-government relations.

Figure 4.1 shows that the process of business-government relations involves the nature of interaction between the corporations, its internal capability (i.e., political stakeholders, political action committee, lobbying,

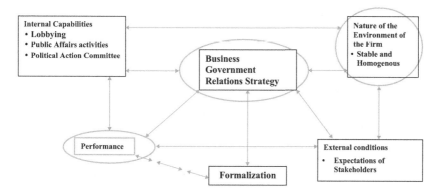

Figure 4.1 Business-government relations and contingency theory
Source: Designed by Authors of this Chapter 2016.

and public affairs activities) on the one hand. On the other hand, positive business and government relations also depend on a stable and homogenous environment. When the environment in which the corporation operates is stable and homogenous, boundary spanning can be developed into routine activity. However, when the environment is complex and turbulent public affairs activities will tend to be more non-routine and difficult to formalize (Griffin & Moorhead, 2014), there is also the need for some level of formalization in order to carry out the corporations' functional duties. According to Jennings and Seaman (1994), the relationship between formalization and performance may not be linear. However, too little formalization or too much formalization may hinder the ability of the public affairs function.

The review of literature and theories shows that there are many reasons why business and government relations activities may vary from one country to another in respect of the environmental context in which they are carried out. As a result, appropriate strategies are those that achieve a fit between organizational characteristics such as size and market power and environmental conditions such as turbulence and complexity (Hofer & Schendel, 1978; Ferrell et al., 2014). In the case of Botswana, positive business and government relations are necessary to encourage foreign investment; however, too many societal demands may saturate joint private and public managerial decision making. In addition, negative reaction such as workers striking against business practices has often increased when the tempo of government and society increases. The Government of Botswana is, however, open to developing joint programs with businesses to incrementally deal with routine industrial problems as well as achieve its industrial development policy goals.

Analysis of Business and Government Relations

The Botswana Democratic Party has governed the nation's multi-party democracy political system since independence from Britain in 1966. Ian Khama assumed the presidency in 2008 upon his predecessor's resignation, and won a five-year term in 2009. President Khama also won a second term in October 2014 (Lange, 2009). With abundant natural resources and a market-oriented economy, Botswana has Africa's highest sovereign credit rating. Diamonds account for one-third of its GDP (about US$3.3 billion), and the diamond industry has transformed Botswana into a middle-income country (World Bank, 2014). In an attempt to diversify the economy through tourism, the country has focused on conservation and developing extensive nature preserves. Botswana has one of the world's highest HIV/AIDS infection rates but is also working collaboratively with the World Health Organization to address the problem (Government of Botswana, 2013).

During the colonial regime, Britain invested as little as possible in the country and actively undermined efforts by Batswana's citizens to set up businesses (Parsons, 1988; Morton & Ramsay, 1987). In was only between

1957 and 1966 that the colonial regime of Britain invested significantly in infrastructure and education (Kamrany & Gray, 2014; Lange, 2009: 154). This practice of the British colonial government made Botswana, at independence, to be one of the poorest countries in the world before the 1960s (Lange, 2009). At independence in 1966, the new country had a per capita GNP of $97 and almost no middle class or working class. The closest thing to a working class was migrant peasants who worked intermittently in South African mines (Frank, 1981: 189; Ramsay et al., 1996: 237; Lange, 2009: 152). Cattle and goat herding were the traditional means of wealth and thus were tied to control of land and water, which are not transportable, and thus in many theories of democracy should inhibit democratization.

According to the World Bank (2014), the nation enjoyed one of the fastest growth rates in per capita income in the world between independence in 1966 and 2006. In spite of this positive growth Botswana's economy, particularly the mining sector is susceptible to global economic shocks. The US Foreign Commercial Service and US Department of State (2012) reported that Botswana's growth slowed to 3% in 2008, expanding to 3.7% in 2009, 10.8% in 2010, and an estimated 8% in 2011. The 2012 GDP also reached an estimated level of 5.9%. (World Bank, 2014). Further, by maintaining a sound fiscal policy and low levels of foreign debt, Botswana will continue to approach global economic downturns from a position of strength. Foreign exchange reserves were estimated to be $8.3 billion in September 2011, representing a healthy 18 months' cover of imports of goods and services. Botswana's per capita income of roughly US$14,800 (IMF estimate) makes it a middle-income country (US Foreign Commercial Service and US Department of State, 2012).

After almost five decades Botswana's economic freedom score is 69.8, making its economy the 36th freest in the 2015 Index. Its overall score is 2.2 points worse than last year, reflecting considerable declines in half of the 10 economic freedoms, including trade freedom, the management of government spending, and investment freedom. Although Botswana has registered the fourth-largest score drop in the 2015 *Index*, it remains the second-freest economy in the sub-Saharan Africa region, and its overall score is well above the regional and world averages (World Bank, 2015). A significant increase in the trade-weighted tariff rate has resulted in a decline in Botswana's trade freedom score. This increase, along with deterioration in the management of public spending, has moved Botswana out of the mostly free category. Table 4.1 shows elements of the Botswana industrial policy.

Despite these shortcomings, Botswana's scores on many of the 10 economic freedoms are consistently among the regions highest. The level of corruption is the lowest in Africa. An independent judiciary enforces contracts effectively and protects property rights, buttressing competitiveness (World Bank, 2015).

In order to rejuvenate the industrial sector of the country, the Government of Botswana enacted a new industrial development policy in 1998. The goal

Table 4.1 Botswana industrial development pathway

Industrial development path 1: 1984 to 1998	Industrial development path 2: 1998 to 2014	Industrial development path 3: 2014 to 2028
Import substitution	Export-led growth	Export-led growth
Domestic market	Both export and domestic markets	Both export and domestic markets
Private sector development	Private sector development	Creation of opportunities for private sector development
	Creation of institutional structure for privatization	Strategic use of privatization
	Competitive manufacturing and service industries	Development of high-priority high impact sector/initiative
	Creation of industry Development institutes	Strengthening implementation of industrial development initiatives
	Human resource development and training (institution)	Strengthening development relevant industry skills
	Policy for technology and industrial development	Effective use of technology for industrial development and global competitiveness
	Institutional support for Small Micro and Macro Enterprise (SMMEs participation in industrial development	Strengthening SMMEs participation in industrial development initiatives

Source: Government of Botswana. (2014). *Industrial Development Policy for Botswana.* Government Gaborone: Government Press.

of this policy was to enhance Botswana's ability to compete globally in the labor intensive manufacturing sector and high value market. In addition, the industrial policy was expected to expand the country's industrial based through the development of diversified, sustainable, and globally competitive industries (Government of Botswana, 2014). The country also proposed to diversify investment into any profitable and sustainable sector of the economy to ease current dependence on mining. Its intention was to encourage investment in manufacturing, tourism, infrastructure, knowledge economy, and financial services through the new International Financial Service Center (Bureau of Economic and Business Affairs, 2012).

The policy also stipulated the creation of (a) citizen economic empowerment; (b) industrial creation development; (c) industrial promotion and facilitation; (d) industrialization; (e) development of infrastructure and industry relevant skills; and (f) private sector capacity development. Despite the enactment of the policy, the nation continues to seek investment in labor intensive manufacturing sectors. Due to failure to achieve the goals of its 1998 industrial policy, the country has now realigned its economic diversification efforts toward natural resource beneficiations and service areas (Government of Botswana, 2013). The industrial development policy was based on the assumption that required markets and market institutions exist and are efficient; however, this was not the environmental situation in Botswana.

The strategic policy of Botswana defines the core elements of the industrial development policy. Its main goal is to invest in new manufacturing activities, sectoral diversification, and enhancing citizens' economic empowerment. The citizens' economic empowerment involves promoting active participation in the country's industrial development (Government of Botswana, 2014). To this end, the national government is now committed to ensure that vulnerable citizens such as women, disabled people, and youths have access to appropriate industrial skills, education, employment opportunities, as well as entrepreneurship skills.

The Botswana Export Development and Investment Authority (BEDIA) serve as the main point of contact for foreign investors and have expressed eagerness for working with established businesses seeking to expand their operations to Botswana (Bureau of Economic and Business Affairs, 2012). The BEDIA agency also ensures that investors—in particular, those seeking to establish export-oriented manufacturing enterprises—obtain the clearances, residence permits, work permits, factory space, and land they need with minimal delays (Government of Botswana, 2014). The export development and investment agency also nurtures and provides services to help new corporations address any problems they might encountered while doing business in the country (US Foreign Commercial Service and US Department of State, 2012).

As a result of the current slowdown in the country's economy, the national government seeks to diversify the economy away from diamonds into goods such as pharmaceuticals, textiles, clothing, and leather products; commodities such as coal; and services such as tourism, financial products, business process outsourcing, and research (Government of Botswana, 2014). Requests by investors for government support from BEDIA and other agencies are evaluated based on the extent to which the proposed project assists in the government's diversification efforts, contributes to the growth of priority sectors, and provides employment and training to Botswana citizens (Bureau of Economic and Business Affairs, 2012). In addition, foreign investors are also encouraged to transfer technology and skills to the nation's citizens, with a view to preparing them for promotion into management positions in the future.

The economy of Botswana has been reported to start experiencing some modest levels of diversification over the years (World Bank, 2015; Bureau of Economic and Business Affairs, 2012). The areas of notable improvement in average shares of GDP for 1998, 2008, and 2012, respectively, are agriculture (3.1%; 1.8%, and 2%); mining (40.1%; 38.3%, and 20.3%); manufacturing (4.6%; 4.0%, and 5.8%); construction, water, and electricity (8.1%; 7.4%, and 8.6%; services (28%; 32%, and 41.5%); and government services (15.5%; 17.0%, and 15.6%) (Government of Botswana, 2014; US Commercial Service, 2015). It should be noted that these changes are fairly significant for the services sector. Manufacturing, which has higher potentials for reducing Botswana's dependence on minerals, has remained fairly constant over the past few decades. In order to effectively address constraints identified as impeding the growth of business as well as improving delivery of services by the private sector, much needs to be done by the government. In addition, local private business has not been able to adequately take advantage of the available market opportunities within the country, regionally and globally (US Commercial Service, 2015). Table 4.2 shows patterns of trade in the past two years in Botswana.

As part of the 1998 industrial policy of Botswana mandate, there is a trade Act. The Trade Act stipulates that a license is required to operate a variety of businesses in Botswana. These include banking, non-bank financial services, transportation, medical services, mining, energy provision, and the sale of alcohol (Government of Botswana, 2014). The Government of Botswana's justifies its license requirements on public interest grounds and notes that its requirements are consistent with international best practice (US Commercial Service (2015). Concerns about trade policy from the business sector have led to the amendment of the Trade Act. In as much as the amendments to the Trade Act have eliminated the catch-all miscellaneous business license category, several owners report that some local authorities

Table 4.2 Pattern of trade 2013 to 2014

Item of trade	Millions USD—% years	Year
Imports of goods and services	$6,846, 681,744	2014
Export of goods and services	$7,875,859,226	2014
Total merchant trade (% of GDP)	98.335%	2014
FDI, net inflow (BoP)	$188,606, 246	2013
Commercial service exports	$471, 399, 053	2013
Total export	$7, 915, 468.177	2014
Total imports	$7, 830, 451, 251	2014
Exports of goods and services (% of GDP)	49.81%	2014
Imports of goods and services (% of GDP)	43.3%	2014

Source: US Commercial Service (2015). Botswana http://globaledge.msu.edu/countries/botswana/memo

will insist that a business apply for a license, even though the business clearly does not fall into one of the established categories of businesses requiring a license (US Commercial Service, 2015). The concerns reveal that business owners are not given the flexibility to choose a category in which to be licensed. In addition, some business people have observed that enforcement of licenses varies widely across local government authorities.

It has also been reported that the Government of Botswana reserves some business sectors solely for citizens' participation. The business sectors include butcheries, general trading establishments, gas stations, liquor stores, super-markets (excluding chain stores), bars other than those related to hotels, certain types of restaurants, boutiques, auctioneers, car washes, domestic cleaning services, curio shops, fresh produce vendors, funeral homes, hair-dressers, various types of rental/hire services, laundromats, specific types of government construction projects under a certain dollar amount, certain activities related to road and railway construction and maintenance, and certain types of manufacturing activities, including the production of furni-ture for schools, welding, and bricklaying (US Commercial Service, 2015). The Government of Botswana (2014) stipulates that its citizen participation initiative has taken an expansive interpretation of chain stores to mean any store with more than one outlet, and has allowed the exemption to apply to supermarkets. This is why large general merchandise markets, restaurants, and the dominant grocery network, all of which are owned by foreigners, operate without restriction. Therefore, foreign investors are permitted to participate in all other sectors.

One of the good initiatives of the industrial policy of Botswana (2014) is that foreign investors are given equal access to investment incentive schemes (grants and loans) for medium and large projects, provided they partner with a citizen of Botswana. However, foreign investors do not have access to government loans and grants designed specifically for citizen-owned con-tracting firms or for small enterprises, defined as those involving invest-ments of less than Pula 75,000, roughly US$10,710 (US Commercial Service (2015).

According to the US Commercial Service (2015), several public policies in Botswana have affected business results due to formal government action with respect to issues that appear on the public agenda. The Government of Botswana is perceived as a social control mechanism that provides incen-tives (positive and negative) for businesses to respond to social values that may not be adequately addressed through the fiscal and monetary policies and the market system. Despite adversarial in nature, inspectors, tax col-lectors, regulators, and punishers of business transgressions are part of the mechanism of these policies to achieve the goals of the country's govern-ment. On one hand, government officials often view business as selfish, materialistic, insensitive to the public interest, manipulative, and dishonest. On the other hand, business views government as obstacles, delayers, and impediments to economic progress (GlobalEdge, 2014).

In most cases, observers have noted that government policies are often contradictory to the imperatives of business efficiency. At the same time, businesses are often ignorant and not understanding of the constraints and problems faced by government officials (Porter, 2002; Cammett, 2007). Based on the evidence from other countries, large managerial business hierarchies were created before the extensive class of public administrators. As a result, the political economy of Botswana could be more organized in the future to help its business communities be better equipped to pursue the kinds of business and government relations linkages associated with later phases of upgrading the nation's industrial sector. Like many developing countries, the Government of Botswana still faces major obstacles in expanding its local research and development capabilities, and lacks a highly skilled workforce. This predicament tends to hinder its capacities to pursue more advanced processes of its local industries.

Privatization Efforts

Botswana's promotion of industrial efficiency is further galvanized by strategic privatization policies. The government believes that privatizing state-owned enterprises could foster investment returns. In addition, privatization could also attract private sector investment and efficiency gains, and increase productivity cost saving, improved customer service, new enterprises, and industrialization in the country (Bureau of Economic and Business Affairs, 2012). As a result of the previously listed reasons, the Government of Botswana has embarked on privatizing a number of state-owned businesses. As part of this effort, it has established the Public Enterprise Evaluation and Privatization Agency (PEEPA). This agency has developed policies that have impacted the extent of foreign participation in the nation's privatization agenda. The government would like to use privatization to increase foreign direct investment in the country, but there are significant concerns in the government circles that the political costs of privatization are high (e.g., extensive job losses). These concerns have created some controversy and led to delays surrounding the privatization effort (Government of Botswana, 2014; Botswana Country Forecast, 2014).

The nation's privatization efforts initially focused on the national airline, Air Botswana. However, after more than 15 years of effort and multiple attempts to reach agreement with strategic partners, however, the airline has still not been privatized (GlobalEdge, 2014). The implementation of the privatization of six other state organizations, including the Botswana Telecommunications Corporation (BTC) and the National Development Bank (NDB), is behind schedule. It has been reported that the ability of PEEPA to manage the privatization of state-owned enterprises is hampered by the fact that there is no privatization-implementing legislation (Botswana Country Forecast, 2014; GlobalEdge, 2014). As a result, the decision for privatizing particular parastatals remains with the relevant ministry or agency that has the discretion to advance privatization at the pace and when necessary for the benefit of improving the nation's economic growth.

Regulation

Several factors have characterized regulatory policy over the past four decades in Botswana. Social regulation was accompanied by the creation of several social regulatory agencies and a multitude of new legislations designed to improve safety, health, and the environment. Initial success of the social regulation was measured by the enforcement and adversarial relationship between business and government. It is important to note that sometimes judicial confrontations created much tension between the regulatory agency and the affected business corporation. The economic regulations of the country were geared toward fundamental reforms that could improve the nation's productivity and enhance performance as well as rejuvenate competition. Despite these good intensions of the government, some regulatory agencies started imposing policies designed to stop price reduction as well as create cartel-like price increases (Bureau of Economic and Business Affairs, 2012; Botswana Country Forecast, 2014).

According to the Botswana Country Forecast (2014), the nation's average tariff rate is 6.4%. Importing goods can be costly. There are some limits on land sales to foreign investors. In addition, the country's competitive banking sector is one of Africa's most advanced (Bureau of Economic and Business Affairs, 2012). Credit is allocated on market terms, although the government provides some subsidized loans. The government has abolished exchange controls, and the Botswana Stock Exchange is growing (GlobalEdge, 2014; Botswana Country Forecast, 2014). A more streamlined licensing process has eased business start-up procedures, but the overall pace of reform has slowed. Employment regulations are moderately flexible, and the non-salary cost of hiring a worker is relatively low. The inefficient agricultural sector is highly subsidized by the government, which also influences prices through state-owned enterprises and service providers (Government of Botswana, 2014). It is anticipated that the industrial development policy of Botswana may lead to some form of deregulation by the government in the near future. The adoption of cost-benefit analysis to guide policy makers in the decision of whether to issue new regulation or alter an old one might help the country achieve its sustainable economic growth goals (Porter, 2002).

The Way Forward

Market economy and government policies act to counterweight each other to meet goals of efficiency and economic growth, as well as egalitarian and humanitarian values of justice, equity, and fairness (Sanyal & Guvenli, 2000; Scheper, 2010). The unifying principles that help us reach a consensus on specific issues despite differences in values and ideology include

(a) government actions must be subjected to tests of efficiency; (b) the market and government need each other; (c) government should mitigate inhumane penalties of the market (i.e., poverty, discrimination); (d) the competitive system is the best system for organizing production; and (e) government must look after the interest of third parties that are negatively affected by externalities (Lehne, 2013; Ferrell et al., 2014).

The previously listed principles lead to a middle ground that blends democracy and capitalism. However, dangers exist from extreme positions that threaten to polarize society. On one hand, the extreme left has been the primary threat in the past, as they clamor for more government solutions and regulations, regardless of the cost. On the other hand, the extreme right makes a blanket indictment against all government intervention and regulation, and redefines poverty and discrimination as the freedom to fail in a laissez-faire economy. What we should learn from all this in respect to business and government relations in Botswana is that corporations leaders in the future must know the facts and should be trusted by government officials to know what they are talking about in respect to industrial development and investment. In addition, business leaders are developing alternative solutions to problems rather than just negative opposition. What is also interesting is that business leaders are also willing to work with the Government of Botswana on matters far removed from immediate corporate interests. It should be noted that privatization and business input will lend expertise to solving society's problems with greater efficiency and less negative impact on incentives needed to promote the productive use of scarce resources (Meznar & Johnson, 2015).

Finally, it is important to stress that stimulating private investment is the key to private sector development in Botswana. As a result, government policies and behavior tend to affect the business environment, just as public investment complements private investment. This means in essence that government policies and behavior can either increase or decrease the costs, risks, and barriers associated with doing business in Botswana. Therefore, it could be argued that the Government of Botswana has a key role to play in the development of the private sector in the country. Its 2014 industrial policy is the first and right initiative; however, there is much left to be done. The rejuvenation of access to credit, micro level reform, macroeconomic environment, increased entry growth and survival, and an improved informal sector are the right steps to take. All reform initiatives should be regularly revised and inclusive of the concerns of all stakeholders, including workers' organizations, business networks, professional organization groups, and chambers of commerce.

Conclusion

This chapter has examined business and government relations in Botswana. It argues that while the Government of Botswana has consistently welcomed foreign investment and multinational business corporations, there is a need for stakeholders to be up and functional in Botswana. Consequently, maintaining good relations with the Government of Botswana is crucial and very important to multinational corporations that operate in the country. It is also observed that many foreign corporations in the country tend to seek the help of the government in order to avoid any deleterious effect of a change in government policy. The practice of seeking the assistance of the government to address any difficulties it experience is a positive sign of mutual respect and good business and government relations in the country.

One of the outcomes of this study on business and government relations in Botswana is that, despite the major role of the regulatory agencies in the country and the size of the public sector, multinational corporations (especially those involved in mining) have not encountered major difficulties in their dealing with the Government of Botswana (Bram, 2006). There is the need for the Government of Botswana to inculcate entrepreneurship culture among citizens and encourage partnership among businesses in order to enhance private sector activities and growth. It is believed that such collaboration could develop capacity and eventually promote the growth of small and micro and medium enterprises. Transparency in the functions reform agencies, developmental government departments, entrepreneurial trainers, venture capital and funding institutions, technology, business development consulting and research parastatals, quality control regulators, and the required regional and multinational corporations and marketing bodies is strongly recommended.

Finally, the Government of Botswana should adopt performance standards in order to enable future discussion to shift from a highly adversarial approach to a partnership between government regulatory agencies and businesses in the country. Such strategic partnership or collaboration with the business sector of the country could galvanize infrastructure for industrial and sustainable development. It should be realized that a simple, transparent, predictable, and cost-effective business environment forms the basis upon which dynamic and prosperous enterprises can be developed in Botswana. No business and government relations problems stand alone; many of the current predicaments are directly related. Therefore, a solution proposed for one area may have beneficial effects in other areas.

References

Acemoglu, D., Johnson, S. and Robinson, J. A. (2003). An African Success Story— Botswana. In Dani Rodrick (Ed.), *In Search of Prosperity: Analytic Narratives on Economic Growth*. Princeton: Princeton University Press, 80–119.

Blumentritt, T. (2003). Foreign Subsidies' Government Affairs Activities: The Influence of Managers and Resources. *Business & Society*, 42(2), 202–233.

Botswana Country Forecast. (2014). New York: The Political Risk Services Group Inc. Publication.

Botswana Country Report. (2013). New York: The Political Risk Services Group Inc. Publication.

Bram, J. (2006, August 18). Diamond Exploration: The Worldwide Search Continues Unabated. *Mining Journal*, vol. 2, 8–26.

Bureau of Economic and Business Affairs. (2012). *Investment Climate Statement—Botswana*. www.state.gov/e/eb/rls/othr/ics/2012/191114.htm.

Cammett, M. (2007). Business-Government Relations and Industrial Change: The Politics of Upgrading in Morocco and Tunisia. *World Development*, 35(11), 1889–1903.

Celik, S. (2013). "Micro Credit Risk Metrics: A Comprehensive Review." In Intelligent Systems in Accounting, Finance and Management, Volume 20, Issue 4, 233–272.

Dahrendorf, L. (2006). *Democracy and Capitalism*. London: Hansard Society.

Dibie, R. (2014). *Public Administration, Analysis, Theory and Application*. Ilishan Remo: Babcook University Press.

Ferrell, O. C., Hirt, G. A. and Ferrell, L. (2014). *Business: A Changing World*. New York: McGraw-Hill Press.

Frank, L. (1981). Khama and Jonathan: Leadership Strategies in Contemporary Southern Africa. *Journal of Developing Areas*, 15(2), 173–198.

GlobalEdge. (2014). *Botswana*. globalEdge.msu.edu and Export.Gov. Accessed February 10, 2016.

Government of Botswana (2013). Tender Notice. http://photos.state.gov/libraries/botswana/19452/pdfs/Tenders%20Weekly%20Update_04152013.pdf. Accessed May 27, 2016.

Government of Botswana. (2014). *Industrial Development Policy for Botswana*. Government Gaborone: Government Press.

Griffin, R. and Moorhead, G. (2014). *Organizational Behavior Managing People and Organizations*. 11th Edition. Boston, M. A. Cengage Learning.

Harris, L. and Rueli, T. (2000). The Strategy/Structure Debate: An Examination of the Performance Implications. *Journal of Management Studies*, 37(4), 587–603.

Hofer, C. W. and Schendel, D. (1978). Strategy Formulation: Analytical Concepts. St. Paul, M.N.: West Publishing Company.

Jennings, D. and Seaman, S. (1994). High and Low Levels of Organizational Adaptation: An Empirical Examination of Strategy, Structure and Performance. *Strategic Management Journal*, 15, 459–475.

Kamrany, N. and Gray, J. (2014). *Botswana: An African Model for Progress and Prosperity*. www.huffingtonpost.com/make-m-Kamrany/botswana-economic-growth_b_ 2069226.html. Accessed February 11, 2016.

Lange, M. (2009). Lineages of Despotism and Development: British Colonialism and State Power. Chicago: University of Chicago Press.

Lehne, R. (2013). Government and Business: American Political Economy in Comparative Perspective. Washington, DC: Congressional Quarterly Press.

Miles, R. H. (1987). Managing the Corporate Social Environment: A Grounded Theory. Englewood Cliff, NJ: Prentice Hall.

Morton, F. and Ramsay, J. (Eds.). (1987). The Birth of Botswana: A History of the Bechuanaland Protectorate From 1910 to 1966. Gaborone: Longman Botswana.

Parsons, N. (1988). Prologue and Epilogue. In Neil Parson and Michael Crowder (Eds.), *Monarch of All I Survey: Bechuanaland Diaries, 1929–37 by Sir Charles Rey*. London: James Currey, xi–xxiv, 269–276.

Podolny, J. M. (2009). The Buck Stop and Start at the Business School. *Harvard Business Review*, 87(6), 62–67.

Porter, R. B. (2002). *Government-Business Relations in the United States*. Paper presented at Conference hosted by the John F. Kennedy School of Government in Celebration of the Schumpeter Program at Harvard University, April 11–12.

Ramsay, J., Morton, B. and Morton, F. (1996). *Historical Dictionary of Botswana*. 3rd Edition. Lanham, MD: Scarecrow Press.

Republic of Botswana. (2014). *Industrial Development Policy for Botswana*. Gaborone, Botswana: Government Printer.

Sanyal, R. and Guvenli, T. (2000). Relations Between Multinational Firms and Host Government: The Experience of American Owned Firm in China. *International Business Review*, 9, 119–134.

Schepers, S. (2010). Business-Government Relations Beyond Lobbying. *Corporate Governance*, 10(4), 475–483.

Thompson, J. D. and McEwen, J. W. (1958). Organizational Goals and Environments: Goals Setting as an Interaction Process. *American Sociological Review*, 23, 23–31.

United States and Foreign Commercial Service and U.S. Department of State. (2012). *Doing Business in Botswana: A Country Commercial Guide for U.S. Companies International*. http://photos.state.gov/libraries/botswana/19452/pdfs/2012%20 Country%20Commercial%20Guide.pdf. Accessed February 9, 2016.

US Commercial Service. (2015). *Botswana Trade Statistics*. http://globaledge.msu. edu/countries/botswana/memo. Accessed February 11, 2016.

Wood, D. J. (1985). Strategic Uses of Public Policy: Business and Government in the Progressive Era. Boston, MA: Pitman Publishing.

Woodberry, R. D. (2011). Ignoring the Obvious: What Explains Botswana's Exceptional Democratic and Economic Performance in Sub-Saharan Africa. Project on Religion and Economic Change Working Paper #05.

World Bank. (2014). *World Bank Development Report*. New York: Oxford University Press.

World Bank. (2015). *World Bank Development Report*. New York: Oxford University Press.

Yager, T. R., Bermudez-Lugo, O., Mobbs, P. M. Newman, H. P. and Wilburn, D. R. (2007). *The Mineral Industries of Africa*. Minerals Year Book, US Geological Survey Publication.

Case Study

Ethical Dilemma in Alibaba Hospital Kokomo

A new health center called Alibaba Hospital in Kokomo has 530 beds and provides services to the Howard County community, with a large elderly patient population that is predominately on Medicare. The Alibaba Hospital was registered as a nonprofit organization with the Internal Revenue Service (IRS). The mission statement of the Alibaba Hospital describes the hospital's "passion" for serving the community. However, the geriatric clinic consistently loses money, and making up the shortfall is stressing the hospital and preventing it from offering other services. A large state-funded hospital three hours away in Chicago offers geriatric services, and it has incrementally made $37 million profit in four years. The CEO of Alibaba Hospital, Dr. Ajiri, is thinking of closing the clinic because of lack of profit.

The Alibaba Hospital management staff was experiencing compliance issues that were directly impacting physician and patient satisfaction. Space constraints in the department interrupted the flow of work and affected employee morale. Symptomatic issues included loose reports, misfiled reports, missing charts, and incomplete charts. Loose reports were measured in inches of paper, because it would be too time consuming to count the actual number of loose sheets. Audits revealed that 75% of all charts in the facility contained at least one misfiled sheet, creating a potential risk to patient safety. In order to improve the process and workplace organization issues affecting the department's performance, Dr. Ajiri introduced a variety of methodologies from the Lean Healthcare toolkit. An initial health policy initiative focused on removing waste from the physical layout and creating visual management systems. Immediate gains were realized in employee morale and the amount of workspace available to the departments. Areas that had previously been cluttered or obstructed with unnecessary materials were now available for use in a productive manner.

The Emergency Department, with 50 beds, struggled to provide timely, effective care for even its most critical patients. With wait time high and communication problems rampant, many patients were leaving the hospital without even seeing a physician. The Emergency Department had to make dramatic changes if it hoped to fulfill its lifesaving mission. Under the guidance of Dr. Ajiri a team of hospital staff used a variety of Lean Healthcare tools to uncover inefficiencies in the Emergency Department. With problems identified, the staff were then able to craft solutions that could resolve even their biggest challenges. First, the team relied heavily on value stream mapping. This process revealed that patients were spending, on average, almost 5 hours in the Emergency Department from triage to discharge. Of that time, only 36 minutes was value-added for the patient; the rest was spent simply waiting for paperwork, a bed, or attention from staff. The value stream map revealed that poor communication and a lack of standardized staff roles were the primary causes behind such inefficiency. Senior staff and doctors were found to be engaged in issues of bribery, theft, mismanagement, and waste of hospital resources, reaching into such areas as deliberate acts of distortion of patients' information in order to deceive them. Patients were falsely billed for treatments that they did not receive. Some of the ethical problems also involved using hospital position for self-aggrandizement.

Dr. Kome, one of the team members, suggested how they could address the hospital's problems by creating standardized roles and establishing a code of ethics for Emergency staff, and setting up a communications board, as well as installing a new phone system. These tools revealed barriers to patient care in the form of poor department layout and disorganized supply and equipment rooms. The most frequently used rooms, such as those designated for trauma patients, were located farthest from nurses' stations. In addition, patients with minor illnesses and injuries were spread throughout the department, sometimes occupying space needed for life-or-death treatment. Triage nurses were separated from the department entry area, and staff struggled to locate necessary equipment and supplies. As a result, Dr. Kome suggested the following changes, which led to a dramatic but positive impact on Emergency operations of the Alibaba Hospital.

- The hospital realized an annualized savings of $4.3million profit in triage and primary nursing time combined.
- Patient waits time decreased by 59%, with total patient time in the department dropping to 2 hours.
- Better communication and physical layout markedly improved the department's ability to provide a physician's care to all patients who needed it.

In another situation, at the children's section of the hospital, the manager of the section competes for physicians and leadership with some of the foremost children's institutions in the Midwest region of the country. The Alibaba Hospital was a proven leader in the development and application of innovative technology in treating children's illnesses and injuries. The hospital endorsed the values of stewardship, honesty, and integrity in all its relationships, among other values. To date, Alibaba Hospital has been responsible for the compensation packages of its top performing doctors. It also used pay and performance metrics to determine the compensation for nurses and other administrators in the hospital. The hospital has tried to be fair and impartial in its compensation procedure, and also tried to benchmark its salary package with outside information. Dr. Ajiri recently announced in one the board meetings that doctors' compensation would be tied to their performance, while the nurses and other administrators would not receive any salary increase for five years, because they were already paid more than their counterparts in nearby hospitals. Many of the nurses and administrative staff had strong feelings about the salary plan just announced by Dr. Ajiri, while some opposed the idea because they were afraid of arbitrary goals being set. They contended that the new salary goals were unrealistic and therefore unattainable.

As a result of opposition to the new salary goals by the nurses, Dr. Ajiri decided to eliminate layers of nurse and administrative positions. Implementing changes in a hospital that had more than 520 patients constituted another set of problems. Furthermore, from a moral perspective, some doctors and managers found it difficult to accept that there was an immediate need for a change in culture and the way business used to be. This is because of the major tasks that Dr. Ajiri had to deal with in the transformation of the hospital. There was little doubt that the Alibaba Hospital needed to change radically in order to survive. Indeed, the changes in the hospital were dramatic, but this experience is far from unique in the world of hospital business. Clearly, change has become the rule rather than the exception. While Dr. Ajiri announces the changes in the compensation package of doctors, nurses, and administrators, he secretly increased his salary and that of the vice-president of finance by 40%.

In another development, most female nurses 35 years and older in the hospital complained about the glass ceiling in the company. However, since Dr. Ajiri took over as the chief executive officer of Alibaba Hospital three years ago, no woman had been promoted into senior management positions. As a matter of fact, women workers in the hospital had refused to serve as protégés under their male superiors. Because of this weak mentor orientation, the hospital has been known to have a strong "old boy network." Dr. Ajiri was expected to address the issue of female staff refusing to serve as protégés or mentors. But he felt that was a problem associated with the past.

A few weeks later, some Department of Health officers visited the Alibaba Hospital. The head of the visiting team was Dr. Onoja. When Dr. Onoja and her team toured the hospital, they found that some of the most productive workers were using substandard procedures and poorly made products. One nurse said, "Yes, the surgical gloves are somewhat of a problem, but we were told that the quality met the minimum requirement and so we have to use them." Dr. Onoja brought this medical violation incident to Dr. Ajiri's attention. He called Dr. Onoja to his office and offered to pay her $200,000 if she agreed not to report the ethical incidence in Alibaba Hospital to the State Medical Board. Dr. Onoja reminded Dr. Ajiri that, under current laws, chief executive officers can be held liable for the unethical and illegal actions of subordinates in their hospital. Thus ethical issue intensity involves individuals' cognitive state of concern about an issue or whether or not they have knowledge that an issue is unethical, which in turn affects their decision making. The identification of ethical issues often requires the understanding of complex business relationships. Further, ethical issue intensity reflects the ethical sensitivity of the individual and work group that faces the ethical decision-making process. Dr. Ajiri thanked Dr. Onoja for her long ethics statement and changed his offer from $200,000 to $500,000, and Dr. Onoja accepted. Dr. Ajiri then issued a personal check for that amount to her. Thus, Dr. Ajiri and Dr. Onoja had engaged in deceptive practices to advance their respective interests over those of their organizations or some other groups.

Further, a nurse called Ms. Moji in Alibaba Hospital with an excellent reputation maintained her clinical competence by reading not only nursing journals but also any publications related to her primary area of nursing. After being hired by Alibaba Hospital six years ago, she received frequent promotions and is presently head nurse for the Obstetrics (OB) ward. One of the floor nurses with the name Ms. Uzezi came to her recently and asked to talk privately. This nurse told the head nurse that one of the prominent OB doctors (Dr. Bolarin) was noted to "smell of alcohol" at three recent deliveries and asked what she should do. Ms. Uzezi stated that she did not want any trouble but was concerned about the issue, even though there had been no discernible difficulties related to patient care. The head nurse (Ms. Moji) thanked the floor nurse for the information and told her she would take care of the matter. That evening the physician (Dr. Bolarin) in question was making rounds and the head nurse asked to speak with him. The nurse told him of the rumor of his drinking, which caused him to become angry and demand to know who had started the rumor. The head nurse (Ms. Moji) refused to name the source of her information and told Dr. Bolarin (the physician) that she had to report this incident to the hospital administration. Dr. Bolarin informed her that he was a member of the hospital's board of directors, and he would see to it that the head nurse was fired if this rumor resulted in any further fallout. He also noted that the person who reported him would be punished in some manner. He then left.

In another development, Ms. Kekelomo, the daughter of Dr. Tataw, the vice-president of Alibaba Hospital, graduated from Indiana University's Master of Public Health program about two years ago. She is known for putting in 60 hours a week and for her meticulous management style, which has generated some criticism in the past. The last area that she managed showed record increases, despite the loss of some older accounts. For some reasons, few administrative staff and nurses did not like dealing with Ms. Kekelomo. Ms. Bola was the daughter of Dr. Balogun, a senior physician, and a close friend of Dr. Ajiri. Ms. Bola was known for coming to work late and leaving before 4.30 p.m., while the official closing hour was 5 p.m.

As Mr. Ibioro, the director of human resources at the Alibaba Hospital, was going over some of his notes, another senior management staff in the human resources division at the hospital, Ms. Olga, came to his office and said, "Do you know that Ms. Bola is engaged to Dr. Ajiri's son, Dr. Sam-Okere? Dr. Ajiri has asked me to make Ms. Bola's file look very productive. I have just reviewed her file again and she looks like a rising star, which would indicate that she should be promoted as quickly as possible before her wedding in two months. I realize that you are not in my division, but the way people get promoted, you never know. I would really like Ms. Kekelomo to get this promotion, but the boss (Dr. Ajiri) told me to recommend Ms. Bola."

As he was considering Ms. Bola as the choice for promotion, Mr. Ibioro indicated that Ms. Kekelomo was one of the very few African American women with an MPM degree that is qualified for promotion in the hospital. Ms. Kekelomo's excellent performance evaluation came up in their previous human resources staff meeting due to her diligent duty and accomplishments. Mr. Ibioro also noted that he had been going over the hospital's hiring and promotion figures, and it would be very advantageous for Alibaba Hospital to promote Ms. Kekelomo. Mr.

Ibioro had also spoken to the public relations officers, and they indicated that Ms. Kekelomo's promotion would be a tremendous boost for the hospital.

The next week seemed very long and was punctuated by the announcement that Dr. Ajiri's son (Dr. Sam-Okere) was getting married to Ms. Bola, the daughter of Dr. Balogun. The wedding would be in three months' time and sounded as though it would be a company affair. By 4 p.m. that day, Mr. Ibioro had gone through four aspirins and two antacids. His decision was due in two days. If he did not fulfill Dr. Ajiri's wishes, he might be fired. Due to his corruption, Dr. Ajiri views self-aggrandizement as the ultimate goal of an enterprise, and therefore may not be concerned about the impact of the hospitals' decision on patients and employees. On the due date, Mr. Ibioro recommended Ms. Kekelomo instead of Ms. Bola. He personally took the letter to Dr. Ajiri's office. After delivering the letter, he told Dr. Ajiri that he was not feeling well and needed a week off. By the time Dr. Ajiri had a chance to open the promotion letter, Mr. Ibioro had left for his one week sick leave. Mr. Ibioro had also distributed the promotion letter to all the senior administrators and board members of the hospital. This action made it difficult for Dr. Ajiri to change the promotion of Ms. Kekelomo, which was based purely on merit.

In a final instance, Dr. Balogun's decision-making capability had fallen short of his superior expectations. First, there was the problem of an Indianapolis-based medical company wanting to sell nicotine and caffeine patches to Alibaba Hospital. With new research showing both drugs to be more problematic than previously thought, the manufacturing medical company had decided to attempt a rapid penetration marketing strategy, requiring them to price the product very low or at cost in order to gain market share and then over time slightly increase the margin. With two billion potential customers, a one cent markup could result in millions of dollars in profit. Dr. Ajiri had invested in this Indianapolis medical company, called Medico and Maro Inc. Dr. Ajiri had rejected the deal, and Medico and Maro had gone to market their product to another hospital. Dr. Balogun told Dr. Ajiri, "Do you realize that you had the perfect product? One that was low cost and both physically and psychologically addictive? You could have services and extra money for years, as well as enough for early retirement. You are nuts for turning it down." Dr. Balogun was wrestling with the problem of the amount of money that he would have made if Alibaba Hospital had purchased the product from Medico and Maro Inc. However, he turned around and told Dr. Ajiri, a longtime friend from graduate school, "I applaud your moral courage, but it's negatively impacting the bottom line. We cannot have that all the time."

Assignment

1. You have been hired by Alibaba Hospital in Kokomo as a consultant by the new board of directors of the hospital to help them solve the ethical dilemmas in the institution.
2. Provide a critical analysis of the ethical problems and challenges facing the Alibaba Hospital.
3. Discuss the implication of each unethical decision that was made in Alibaba Hospital.
4. Discussed the moral philosophies that may be relevant to this situation in Alibaba Hospital.
5. Provide some recommendations that could help the hospital resolve its unethical dilemmas in the future.

5 Business and Government Partnership in Nigeria

Robert A. Dibie, Felix M. Edoho, and Josephine Dibie

Introduction

It has long been recognized that direct investment conveys both benefits and costs to the government and business sector of the receiving nation (Ake, 1995; Lussier & Achua, 2016; McGuigan et al., 2014). The benefits consist, in the first instance, of fostering the receipt of capital, of techniques of various kinds, and of market contacts. The costs involve the payment of interest, dividends, and fees for business services; they also involve the need, faced by nation living in an open economy, to maintain equilibrium in its international payments over time (Ferrell et al., 2011; Kuye & Ogundele, 2013).

Everywhere you go in Nigeria, there are elements of development gap between rural and urban income. The city promises desirable jobs and lucrative opportunities in government ministries and agencies, business corporations, and manufacturing industry. According to Oluwagbuyi and Ogungbenle (2013), the explosive rural to urban migration is a product of this urban bias, along with stagnant or diminishing real incomes in small-scale agriculture. Technology gap studies have shown that the Nigerian domestic capacity to absorb knowledge spillover and R&D processes from abroad is a key factor in explaining growth rate differentials over space between rich and poor countries, and rural and urban economies (Idemudia, 2010; Lussier & Achua, 2016). In addition, a supportive infrastructure, a well-developed home market, and a secured investment climate are all essential for the successful pursuit of business enterprise. Again, Nigeria has not been able to establish an appropriate and secured investment climate. Both during the colonial period and since independence, the Nigerian federal and state governments have tended to act in ways that obstruct rather than encourage national capitalism (Onimode, 1991). This is because of their inability to provide direct assistance and to create a favorable national economic climate within the limitations set by the international situation.

Debate over the ability of the Nigeria's business corporations to compete in the emerging global economy has been raging on since the nation adopted its structural adjustment programs in 1986. Certain analyses believe that the inability of the Nigeria's corporations to compete translates into the country's apparent decline (World Bank, 2014). The nature of the concern about Nigeria's competitiveness and doubts about its economic future are well reflected in the literature as evidenced by questions such as "Can Nigeria compete?" (Olukoshi, 1994) and "Is Nigeria in decline?" (Edoho, 1997) The resurgent concern about Nigeria's competitiveness is rooted in its debt crisis, low productivity and industrial performance, which resulted in the World Bank and International Monetary Fund's suggestion for a structural adjustment program (Idemudia, 2010). There has been a gradual shift in the role of business and government in Nigeria since 1999, when the country became a representative democracy after several years of military rule. According to Idemudia (2010) and Kuye and Ogundele (2013), the new conceptual shift of Nigeria reinforced the idea that business is not just part of the economic problem; it is also the solution to sustainable development.

With this connection, what do Nigerians mean by performance? The intended meaning goes far beyond the usual concept of profitability and includes a number of other aspects of the subsidiaries operations that significantly affect the citizens and stakeholders. Among these aspects are, for example, the levels and growth of production, the sources of financing and of inputs of goods and services, the destination of finished products, the subsidiary composition of senior personnel, and the distribution between the subsidiary and its foreign parent of the powers to make decisions and of the facilities that conduct research and development (R&D). Nigeria's concern over multinational corporations' performance extends beyond the question of what all these operations may imply for the subsidiaries themselves; it focuses on the question of what contribution MNCs operations may make, or fail to make, to Nigeria's society and economy. In certain aspects, the performance of subsidiaries can be measured objectively against that of other firms in Nigeria or abroad but in other aspects. As we shall see, the performance can be judged only in terms of more subjective criteria.

It is often suggested that the performance of multinational corporations in Nigeria is adversely affected by conflicts of interest and outlook—whether actual or potential—between the multinational firm and its parent company. Two reasons are usually offered for these conflicts: First, it is often claimed that decisions which may appear reasonable and profitable from the standpoint of the multinational firm may conflict with the interest of the Nigerian economy. The argument runs that to the extent that the international firm may try to maximize its global profit over time. This may not necessarily foster or permit the maximum feasible development of the subsidiary company. Second, it is sometimes also claimed that the centralization of some key decisions in the multinational firm may work against the interests of the subsidiary and of the Nigerian economy if for no other reason than that head office personnel may be insufficiently informed about, or insufficiently interested in, achieving the subsidiary's potential, while retaining some power over decisions affecting it.

The goal of this chapter is to vividly explore the relationship between government, business, and society in Nigeria. Unfortunately, the controversy over business and government performance in Nigeria has been carried on, for the most part, with limited information or none at all. This chapter provides critical information on the role of multinational corporations in Nigeria's industrial development. It brings together the available information on the operation of multinational firms in Nigeria. It argues that foreign direct investment and multinational corporations are neither inherently good nor bad. That is, foreign direct investment made in a context of high levels of aggregate demand and effective rules that limit the destructive aspects of competition may indeed have a positive impact on Nigerian citizens. However, foreign investment made in a context of high unemployment and destructive economic and political competition in the absence of effective rules can have a significantly negative impact on a nation such as Nigeria. This chapter seeks to make a modest contribution to the debate over the Nigerian competitiveness in the emerging global economy. The rationale underlying the chapter is that the instrumentality of public policy can be used to foster national competitiveness. Against this backdrop, the chapter proposed business-government partnership, and not the invisible hand of the market, as a viable framework for rejuvenating Nigeria's industrial base and competitiveness. This chapter is very important because of the new role government, business, and society has been playing since Nigeria started a representative democracy government in 1999.

Business and Government Framework

Business and government relations in Nigeria are conducted in many ways and through numerous government ministries and agencies. According to Alfredo (2011) and Boddenwyn (2015), the relationship between government and business is very complex. These scholars also contend that government and business relations may also lead to both positive and negative public good. In order to better understand the government-business relationship in the context of Nigeria, we shall explore socialism and mixed economy theory, the free market economy, and the political economy theories.

According to Ya Ni and Van Wart (2016), mixed economy is an economic system where the state and private sector direct the economy. The mixed economic system involves some degree of business economic freedom, with a minimum government regulation of the market. The mixed economy theory is such that the government would wield considerable influence over the economy by using fiscal and monetary policies (Daniels et al, 2011; Waddell, 2002).

Unlike the mixed economy that is a combination of private ownership and government regulation, the socialism approach is characterized by collective ownership of the means of production and distribution (Lehne, 2013). In addition, socialism opposes the idea that what is good for the individual and for the privately owned business is good for the society. Thus, socialism is critically opposed to the capitalism. Proponents have proposed that government should take control of business and direct what good should be produced at what price to remedy capitalism (Lehne, 2013). Socialism indicates that capitalism promotes selfish tendencies; as a result, it is a formula for dehumanizing citizens.

According to Altvater (1993) and Gregory and Stuart (2004), the free market economy is a system whereby decisions regarding production, investment, and distribution of goods and services are based on the forces of supply and demand. McGuigan et al. (20014) contend that the free-market approach grew out of the classical economy theory proposed by Adam Smith, which is a hands-off or laissez-faire approach to managing the economy. At the other end of the spectrum, the stakeholder model asserts that business interest should never be at the expense of society's long-term interest, that cooperation for social benefit is for everybody's benefit, and that when business self-regulates, there can be less government or common good (Lehne, 2013; Subair 2011).

The most important conduits in the past decade or postmilitary regimes are the Ministry of Finance and the Ministry of Economy, Trade and Industry. The Ministry of Finance has operational responsibilities for all fiscal affairs, including the preparation of the national budget. It initiates fiscal policies through its indirect control over the Central Bank of Nigeria. In addition, the Central Bank of Nigeria is responsible for monetary policy, On the other hand, the Ministry of Finance allocates public investment, formulates tax policies, collects taxes, and regulates foreign exchange (Central Bank of Nigeria, 2014).

According to Idemudia (2010) and Iwu-Egwuonwu (2011), Nigeria's economic development has not primarily been the product of private entrepreneurship; the government has directly contributed to the nation's prosperity. Its actions have helped initiate new industries, cushion the effects of economic depression, create a sound economic infrastructure, and protect the living standards of the citizenry (Central Bank of Nigeria, 2014). Further, the link between the corporate world and government in Nigeria is maintained through the Nigerian Labor Union and the Ministry of Trade and Commerce (CIA World Fact book, 2004). There is evidence, however, that the federation's power is not what it had been, partly because major corporations, especially the multinational oil companies that had amassed huge amounts of money in the past three decades, are increasingly capable of operating without the assistance of both the federal and state governments in Nigeria (Dibie, 2014).

A multinational company or transitional enterprise (hereafter referred to as MNC) can be defined as a firm that owns or controls income-generating assets in more than one country (Paquet, 1972). The substance has existed for more than a century, but it was only about three decades ago that it was given a special name within the framework of foreign direct investment

(FDI), and it has become a defined concept (Safarian, 1969; Fieldhouse, 1986) associated with multinational corporations.

The most important question concerning the MNC in Nigeria is why its character and activities should be registered as special problems. At one level, of course, the MNC is liable to the same criticism as any capitalist enterprise—that is, it exists to extract surplus value and thus exploit the people of Nigeria. Its two special features are in common with all forms of FDI, it operates across national frontiers, and control is retained by one global center. It might, therefore, have been expected that the first and main attack on MNCs would have come from Marxists.

Claude Ake's (1995) central message on multinational oil corporations in Nigeria was that, although MNC might increase the world's wealth through their efficient use of resources, the benefit would go mainly to the nations in which the MNC's parent company is based, while the rest of Nigeria, especially the people living in the oil producing areas, paid the price of their monopoly profits. The result would be a hierarchical world order, as corporations developed a complex division of labor within individual firms and throughout the international economy. These ideas form the starting point of most recent assessments of the impact of MNC on host nations. The essence of Claude Ake's (1985) and Lall Sanjaya's (1998) concept of an international hierarchy was that the interests of its lower echelons must be subordinated to those of the higher level—that subsidiaries exist only to serve the shareholder in the parent company at the top of the pyramid, so that, when a conflict of interest arises, the interests of the base will necessarily be sacrificed to those of the apex. Without this assumption, the debate over the role of the MNC would be merely technical, concerned with its motivation, organization, and profitability. By contrast, most of the literature since 1970 has turned on two different issues (Aaronson & Reeves 2002, 1993; Essia & Yearoo 2009): first, whether there is a necessary conflict of interest between MNCs and the host nations; and second, whether the specific methods adopted by MNCs in particular nations are to the disadvantage of their hosts, even if the MNC performed a generally useful role.

What measure should the host adopt to minimize or reduce their disadvantages (Kuye & Ogundele, 2013)? This indeed is the basic assertion made by a number of critic of MNCs who do not seriously question their utility in the developed world but argue from very diverse standpoints, that they are of dubious benefit to the less developed nations. To adopt Sanjaya Lall's (1977, 1999) typology, there are three common ways of looking at the deficiencies of the MNC in poor nations: that of nationalists, who accept the potential benefits of FDI but have reservations about certain aspects of it; the dependency approach, which (according to Lall) cannot be incorporated into any formal economic analysis; and that of some Marxists, who deny all possibility that since most criticism of MNC falls under the exploitation mode, let us consider the reservations made by Boddenwyn 2015 from a nationalist's standpoint.

Their starting point is that dual proposition that the proper criterion for assessing the role of MNCs in less developed nations must be social welfare in the broader sense, but also that there is no possibility of making a final objective judgment on their welfare implications. This is because there is limited information on many aspects of MNC's activities that are immeasurable "externalities"—different economic theories of development, differing value judgments on "welfare," and wide contrasts in defining "alternative situations." If we accept the neoclassical partisan welfare paradigm, then the adverse effects can simply be blamed on the policies of the host's government: transfer prices within MNC alone lie to some extent beyond state control. Thus, to obtain any grip on the subject, we must look for limitations in this basic welfare critique.

To explain the common dynamics of the economic benefits and industrial activity normally associated with MNC, one will have to weigh the economic costs included in the "package" in which they are imported or, alternatively, by the fact that they are "inappropriate" by other, non-economic criteria. In either case, the standard answer is that it is up to the government to decide and to control. This notion also stimulates most radical critics of MNCs to question whether governments in less developed nations can match up to their assigned role—whether they are too weak or class-dominated, if their officials are too ignorant or corrupt to promote "suitable" policies, and whether their sovereignty has any defense against MNC exploitation their resources. So, ultimately, our assessment of the probable and potential impact of MNC on host nations must lean on how effectively the host government performs its role as a maker of policy and defender of the national interests.

Multinational corporations view government as both friend and enemy (Wood, 1990). In Nigeria, business-government relationships "range from cooperative to competitive, from friendly to hostile" (Datomasi, 2007). Corporate executives and certain scholars are prone to complain about government intrusion in business affairs. This sentiment is grounded in the argument that "the rise of big business preceded the rise of big government" in the United States (McCraw, 1984: 42). This historical fact is often interpreted as a confirmation that government is best which governs least. Wood (1990) identifies three models for understanding the nature of business-government relations: adversarial, partnership, and pragmatic models. In the discussion that follows, modified versions of these models will be utilized to examine the changing nature of government-business relations, and how Nigeria can perhaps respond to the new brand of competition orchestrated by globalization.

Adversarial-Antagonistic Model:

This model considers government and business as natural enemies and major competitors. Competition stems largely from the fact that government and business struggle for the same scarce economic resources and power (Wood, 1990). The dysfunctional nature of the competition forms the basis of mutual suspicion and antagonism. Proponents of this model argue that the confrontations are inevitable because the missions and interests of business are diametrically opposed to those of government (Lehne, 2013). The goals of government and business are considered to be not only perennially incompatible, but also inherently conflictual. This model posits that the overriding goal of business is profit maximization. Corporate profitability will inevitably result in public welfare. To achieve this goal, business needs maximum operational freedom and conducive environment to grow and prosper. These contrast with the primary goal of government, which centers largely on maximizing welfare for all citizens (Albareda et al 2008; Chris et al 2007).

Partnership-Cooperative Model: This model is rooted in the complementary role of government and business in society. Advocates of this model suggest that government and business work toward the same goal (strong, virile, and dynamic economy). Moreover, the complementary role of government and business stimulates positive synergistic relationships between them. Each derives enormous benefits from the activities of the other. The aggregate benefits that accrue to the society as a result of this symbiotic relationship exceed what either the government or business could generate alone. Systems thinking provides the intellectual foundation for this model.

Pragmatic-Dynamic Model: The underlying idea in this model is that government-business relations continuously change according to circumstances. The model postulates that government and business seek to protect their individual interests. Therefore, both government and business necessarily seek to maximize their individual benefits and minimize their losses. As Wood (1990: 313) succinctly put it: "At different times and under different circumstances, this means that business and government units will act as partners, act independently of each other, behave as enemies, or engage in dissonant roles.

To come to grips with the question of how much of a contribution multinational corporations and domestic firms have contributed to the development in Nigeria, it is necessary to shift from the micro perspective to the macro level, and examine how Nigeria has been affected by foreign direct investment since 1999.

Expertise of Multinational and Domestic Corporations

Multinational firms perform many essential functions for government (Daniels et al. 2011), not the least of which is to provide information. Their structurally privileged position contributes to what Daniel et al (2011) refers to as "impairment" in the marketplace of ideas. Private actors need the government, but the government relies upon information provided by the private actors. As Claude Ake (1995) and Sanjaya Lall (1999) suggest, big multinational firms in Nigeria can provide information about foreign countries that could be useful to government officials; not all rivals can compete politically, and their industry associations consistently have provided information about foreign governments' failures to provide adequate intellectual property protection. Availing themselves of private policy networks, such as private law firms based abroad, these corporations have been the source of detailed substantive information about intellectual property laws, practices, and infractions.

An additional resource provided by the multinationals or private business sector is expertise in issue areas not well understood by government. In this regard, intellectual property agreement is especially unusual. Intellectual property right is an issue area requiring considerable technical expertise; it is extremely complex and relatively inaccessible to the general public. This provides opportunities for MNCs to frame issues in ways that will benefit them. Facts do not stand on their own; they must be imbued with social meanings and translated into political discourse (Collins et al., 2009).

The question of intention is very important in the discourse about MNC. There are a number of alternative theoretical explanations of why large business firms should wish to establish overseas subsidiaries, and everybody assumes that they do so to obtain a high overall profit by internationalizing their business enterprise. Their reasons, however, vary according to the nature of their activities and the environment in which they operate, and the main contrast is between the extractive and utility companies, on the one hand, and those which manufacture in host nations, on the other.

Standard foreign direct investment (FDI) theories rely on firm-specific advantages to explain why it occurs. Foreign investors must have some advantages over local firms to compensate for the fact that the multinational corporation (MNC) incurs additional costs because of (1) cultural, legal, institutional, and linguistic difference; (2) a lack of knowledge about local market conditions; and (3) lengthier lines of communication and therefore an increase in communication failures.

Foreign investors' advantages can take many forms. Technology is the primary advantage; access to large amounts of capital superior management and products differentiated by successful advertising are also important. Multinational firms bring much needed capital, but at a greater cost than the Government of Nigeria would be charged. They bring technology, but the technology may not be appropriate for the nation, and in most cases, is almost as efficient as is available in a contraction company of their home nation. Multinational firms also bring managerial techniques, but these might not be appropriate for the Nigerian society.

What are the criteria that one could use to evaluate the various MNC mechanisms of technology transfer in Nigeria? Let us examine this question from the point of view of Nigeria importing the technology. The following is a list of some criteria, which are not necessary listed in order of their relative importance (Aderemi, 2010).

The first criterion is the cost of the technology obtained through the various channels. It is hardly necessary to stress the importance of this criterion, but let us delineate how the question can be put. The transfer of technology that often accompanies direct investment has brought considerable benefits to Nigeria. As a result of the privilege conditions that Nigerians enjoy and the advantages derived from the nation's ties with the parent company, the subsidiaries of multinational corporations can often produce at a lower cost than national producers. It has often been emphasized that the most important function or direct investment is the better economic performance that results from capital and technology transfer from one nation to another. One question, however, remains unanswered. Can the advantages of direct investment be obtained in more economical ways? Nigeria should most certainly consider this question when it is realized that the parent company has a marked preference for local ownership of the subsidiary, because of the greater flexibility in production, choice of technology, management of the corporation, market sharing, and so on. It is not impossible that Nigeria could obtain the technology in other ways at lower cost (monetary or otherwise) or more efficiently.

The second criterion would be the degree of availability. In certain cases, there is no choice; the technology is available with the multinational firm (as in the oil multinational companies in Nigeria), or it is not available at all. The degree of adaptation of the technology to Nigeria is another concern. This argument is often cited to illustrate and support the doubt expressed about the usefulness of imported inappropriate technology in Nigeria. Often the economic conditions in Nigeria (supply of the various factors of production, relative prices of these factors, etc.) are very different from the economic conditions in the exporting nations. This argument can also be applied to technological transactions between nations, which have a similar degree of development.

What are the various channels of MNC transmission of technology? Without claiming to give a complete list, one could easily mention 10. For most of them, we shall simply mention the mechanism; for some, we shall add a few words of explanation. The order of presentation should not be interpreted as reflecting their relative importance.

1. Trade in producer goods constitutes a well-known means of transition. Some scholars go as far as saying that in some cases there seems to be a more important national comparative advantage in producer goods than in consumer goods. But this is probably not the principal source of gains from international trade.

2. The purchase of specialized services is another channel. Some firms specialize in the marketing of management and engineering services to foreign firms with which they are connected. These transfers will be done principally in the form of sales, especially where the firm has only a minority holding in the foreign enterprise.

3. Personal contacts (in particular, scientific missions, etc.) often give good results when well organized and when the delegates are chosen with care.
4. Technical assistance and joint production agreements play quite an important part for the developing nations and in North (developed nations) and South (less developed nations) relations.
5. The presence of foreign military troops in a nation.
6. Involuntary leakage of technological information (mobility of personnel, etc.) and industrial espionage are yet another channel. Of course, Nigeria cannot count on this method to obtain foreign technological information, but it is practiced just the same.
7. The observation and imitation of existing technological information is another channel that the Japanese have used with notable success. Nigeria can do the same with full commitment and the enactment of the appropriate industrial policy.
8. Licensing agreement or intellectual property agreement. From this point of view, for those that grant licenses, and the nation importing technology, there are two types of costs: the payments made in return for services received and the restriction contained within most agreements. These restrictions can be profitable to the firm that imports the technology in Nigeria, but they may not necessarily be so for the importing nation.
9. Joint ventures. Innovative firms that have agreements with foreign firms for the exchange of technical information show great foresight. Under joint-ventures, several enterprise prefer to negotiate with the foreign firm or foreign government) from a position of strength rather than to wait until the foreign competitor has found a similar method of production or a substitute product.
10. The multinational firm. Multinational firms, with their great productive and engineering capacity and access to foreign markets, are in a particularly favorable position to conduct research and development (R&D) and help develop production roles that are suitable to Nigeria.

(Idemodia 2007; Iwu-Egwuonwu, 2011)

The role that government and business plays in society is contextual. Social environment provides legitimacy for the role of government and business in any society. Although government and business are the two most powerful human institutions in modern society, government is the custodian of public trust. Corporations are not isolated from the society of which they are a part. They are creatures of it, and are nurtured and supported by it to accomplish specific purposes. They will survive only so long as they accomplish those purposes. The relationships between government and business exert tremendous influence on the performance of the economy and the lives of mass citizenry. As Weidenbaum (1990: 3) stated, each side of the government-business equation possesses powers, and yet each has an

Table 5.1 Mutual benefits in the business-government relationship

What does business do for government?	What does government do for business?
Performs society's necessary functions—production and distribution of goods and services	Provides legitimacy and legal protection, private property, contract enforcement, liability, charters
Pays taxes	Provides infrastructure support: money system, weather services, zoning, traffic control, public
Utilities, roads, airports, sea harbors, weights, measures	Build sustainable roads and seaports that could better serve the nation's economy
Generate income for others who pay taxes	Provides subsidies: low postal rates, land grants, strategic mineral stockpiles
Collect taxes as an agent of government	Safeguards markets: export promotions, import restrictions, tariffs, monitoring of export-import balance, domestic content regulations
Provides technical expertise to government and the public	Absorbs business risks: price floors, fair trade laws, loan guarantees, subsidies, bankruptcy laws
Produces and disseminates knowledge	Offers tax benefits: depreciation, tax deduction, or suspension as incentive for desired behavior
Provides products and service to government	Purchases much of business's output
Invents and develops new products and technologies through funding, and direct research	Supports invention and development through patents, copyrights, research

Source: Wood (1990: 311).

important need for the other. Wood (1990) lists the benefits business derives from government and vice versa in Table 5.1.

Let us now consider the capacity of the Nigerian government for coordinating the potentials of MNC in the nation, and whether the multinational corporations in the nation have constituted a form of economic imperialism since Nigeria obtained its independence from Britain in 1960.

Nigeria's Sovereignty and Multinationals

How effectively has the Nigerian government performed its role as maker of public policy and defender of the nation's interests? We also argue that in the current neoliberal economic regime, FDI and MNC have more negative than positive effects on Nigeria. The neo-classical policy or structural adjustment program is composed of strong forces that lead to insufficient levels of aggregate demand and therefore chromic unemployment, coercive competition, and destructive domestic and international rules of the game— that is, precisely those factors that undermine the potentially positive effects of foreign domestic investment. Some of the most important components of the neo-classical policy include budgetary austerity, financial liberalization, privatization, increased labor market flexibility, and trade and investment liberalization. Unfortunately, the listed factors were prescribed for Nigeria by the World Bank and International Monetary Fund (IMF), and it adopted them as its structural adjustment program in 1986. Looking at the MNC and FDI within the structural adjustment perspective will help us solve several puzzling issues. First, there is very little information on the operations of MNCs in the nation. Their operations can be studied at two levels: the general and the specific. Most published information by the Central Bank of Nigeria is general, based on surveys of a very large number of firms and their activities in the country. Such survey makes possible broad statements indicating the importance of the economic role of the MNC in the modern motivation and internal operations of individual corporations or attitudes and policies of the Nigerian government. Consequently, it cannot provide the evidence by which we might assess the welfare implications of FDI as we have defined it. The first need can only be met by detail research on particular corporations, with deliberate emphasis on the issues raised by theorists.

National ownership of certain activities is especially likely in defense related activities, utilities, and resources-extractive industries upon which Nigeria depends heavily for its foreign exchange. Indigenous managerial control over certain economic activities is an objective that is closest to our concerns in this study, and it is pursued apparently because the state either assumes that indigenous managerial control is more manipulate or because it is more consonant with Nigerian government interests (Kuye & Ogundele, 2013).

The fact about petroleum, mineral, and agricultural multinational corporations in Nigeria is that, by and large, they grew in a more or less free-trade environment—that is, the things they dealt in were seldom subject to protective duties, quantity controls, or tariffs (Moran, 1985; Subair 2011). These firms engaged in production and trade commodities for many reasons, but most did so either to achieve vertical integration within a single firm, or to sell to third parties on the international market. In both cases, however, one of the primary aims of public utility firms was to erect some form of monopoly as a defense against the risks of a competitive free-trade market. Petroleum companies, primarily concerned with drilling, refining, and marketing, nevertheless bought leases of oil deposits so that they could control the price of their global operations. Mineral firms and agricultural producers were both notorious for using monopoly, cartels, and rings to force down the price paid to the Nigerian government, peasant producers, and so on, and conversely to force up the price they could charge to consumers (Idemudia, 2010).

The manufacturing multinationals in Nigeria are interested in freedom of trade outside their protected home base. They do not need physical control over their markets. Above all, they normally engage in manufacture in other nations as a direct response to some form of obstruction in the market, which either threatens an established export trade in West Africa or offers opportunities for higher profit through some form and degree of monopoly in a previously competitive market.

Thus if the power held by the MNC in Nigeria is in any sense "a new imperial system" (or perhaps "a third colonial occupation"), then it must be said that the gates were opened from the inside. But we must not beg this question. Empire means the imposition of external authority, and the transfer of the power to make final decisions to a central metropolis. Sanjaya Lall's (1999) concept of a world hierarchy assumed that senior corporate executives in New York, London, and Paris could determine what happens in Lagos, Abuja, Aba, and Port Harcourt, and that the power of the great corporations was greater than that of small or even middling military government in Nigeria. This is true, from the way the multinational petroleum corporations have been handling environmental degradation matters in the Niger Delta areas of the nation (Ogundele, 2012; Muraina et al., 2010).

To understand the processes and problems of capital accumulation in the Nigerian economy, one must consider the strategic importance of foreign investment. Nigeria economic policy has had the preoccupation of providing investment incentives to foreign capital right from colonial times. Beginning from 1957, five key legislative provisions were put in place to provide incentives to foreign investors: (1) the Industrial Development (Import Duties Relief) Act of 1957; (2) the Industrial Development (Income Tax Relief) Act of 1958; (3) the Customs Duties (Dumped and Subsidized Goods) Act of 1958; (4) the Custom (Drawback) Regulation Act of 1959; and the Income Tax (Amendment) Act of 1959 (Dike, 1994; Biersteker, 1987). This legislations provided for tax holdings accelerated depreciation allowances, market protection, freedom to import capital, repatriate profits, and so on.

In the postcolonial decades, these legislations were reinforced. The First National Development Plan of 1962–1968, while recognizing the ultimate goal of economic independence, was quick to reassure foreign investors that Nigeria will continue to need and indeed welcome foreign capitals and skills (Dike, 1994). Apart from that, the Tafawa Balewa regime (1960–1966) made explicit statements against nationalization as a policy strategy. In the postcolonial decades of the 1970s, when control of foreign capital became a strategy of economic policy, indigenization was preferred to outright nationalization; joint or mixed ventures became preferred to outright ownership by foreign investors and MNC.

The Nigerian Enterprise Promotion Decree (NEPD) of February 1972 implemented the transfer of foreign capital ownership to Nigerians, a process otherwise known as indigenization. Originally there were two schedules of economic activity, the degree of technological and financial sophistication of the activity, involved constituting the major criteria for classification. Second, a Capital Issue Commission (CIC) was established to take charge of proper evaluation of shares to be sold by the MNCs. Thirdly, the Nigerian government established the Nigerian Bank for Commerce and Industry (NBCI) to provide development finance to Nigerians to enable them buy divested foreign equities and or set up new investments altogether.

All business enterprises assigned to schedule 1 of the degree were required to sell 100% of their equity to Nigerian subscribers. No new foreign enterprise could be established in those areas after 1972.

Schedule II of the decree listed economic activities in which expatriates would be barred under certain conditions. Small firms, defined as those with equity under 200,000 Nigerian pounds ($608,000) or sales turnover under 500,000 Nigerian pounds or ($1,520,000), were required to sell all of their equity to Nigerian subscribers. Large MNCs, which accounted for nearly all of the enterprises operating in these sectors, were required to make 40% of their equity available to Nigerians. The rest of the economy was not affected by the decree at all.

Most of the multinationals in Nigeria at the time were engaged in high-technology and large-scale operations that were not affected by the first decree. The largest employer in Nigeria, the textile industry, was excluded from either schedule I or II. Other large industries, such as chemicals, plastic, sugar refining, and telecommunications, were similarly excluded. Notably, petroleum, petroleum service, petrochemicals, iron and steel, and fertilizer production (the areas reserved for state in the second plan) were omitted from any mention in the first decree. Banking, insurance, and vehicle assembly, areas of future state investment, were also left out. The mining sector (including tin, coal, and columbite) was already mostly state-owned, and it was also omitted. The decree contained a provision to extend the list of affected enterprises, and at least one prominent state official described it as a way of checking the activities of MNCs in the nation (Muraina et al., 2010).

In anticipation of future implementation problems, the decree specifically prohibited "fronting" (that is, Nigerian operating enterprises on behalf of an expatriate who really manages all essential operations from a back room), and it forbade employment of the previous owner of an indigenized enterprise on a full-or part-time basis. In the spirit of Pan-Africanism, the decree defined all non-Nigerians and Africans owning enterprises in the nation as indigenous, as long as they were from an Organization of African Unity member state and their home country treated Nigerian businesspeople with reciprocity. A relatively long period, slightly more than two years, was given for the firms to comply with the decree, and the appointed day for the full implementation was set for March 31, 1974.

As indicated in Table 5.2, nearly 79% of the firms affected by the decree complied with its terms. Approximately 90% of the firms located in

Table 5.2 The nationality of affected enterprise

	Multinational capital	Indian capital	Levantine capital	Others	Total
Schedule I					
Compliance	52	17	98	42	209
Defaults	14	22	77	27	140
Compliance rate	79%	44%	56%	61%	60%
Total affected	66	39	175	69	349
% of total	19%	11%	50%	20%	–
Schedule II					
Compliances	342	66	89	36	533
Defaults	27	9	15	11	62
Compliance rate	93%	88%	86%	77%	90%
Total affected	369	75	104	47	595
% of total	62%	13%	17%	8%	–
Schedule I and II Combined					
Compliances	394	83	187	78	742
Defaults	41	31	92	38	202
Total affected	435	114	279	116	944
% of total	46%	12%	30%	12%	–

Sources: Compiled from Federal Ministry of Trade and Industry data, Lagos, Nigeria 1997. Biersteker, T. (1987). *Multinational, the State and Control of the Nigerian Economy.* Princeton University Press.

Schedule II complied, while 60% of those in schedule I complied. In both cases, the compliance rate of multinational capital is generally higher (considerable higher in the case of schedule I firms) than the compliance rate of Levantine and Indian capital. The latter are consistently below the average compliance rate in both schedules for reasons that led to 1977 revision of the decree. The impact of the 1972 Indigenous Degree fell most heavily on Indian and Levantine investors (Lebanese, Syrians, Greeks, etc.) and other firms owned mainly by developing nation's investors. The Levantine and Indian firms particularly had occupied the intermediate rungs of the modern sector—separating the large-scale Europeans and North American firms from the indigenous investors. The large European and North American firms operating financial services, oil, whole import and export trade, import substitution manufacturing, and so on went virtually unaffected by the 1972 measures. It was in recognition of this defect that the 1972 decree was amended in 1977.

The 1977 Indigenization Decree revision did provide for worker participation, and stipulated that 10% of stock divested should be allocated to employees of the firms concerned, such that at least 50% should come to junior employees. It also stipulated the socialization of the indigenization processes, so as to broaden the social base of private capital. The policy required that no individual Nigeria should own more than 5% of the stock of any single enterprise. This later aspect was more difficult to implement. The 1977 decree also led to the establishment of the Nigerian National Petroleum Company (NNPC). The aim of establishing the NNPC was to encourage an indigenous public corporation to oversee and participation in all phases of the petroleum industry—drilling, refining, and marketing. The Nigerian Government also acquired majority shareholding in all the foreign firms (in lieu of full nationalization) of 60%.

To tie up this section with the business-government partnership in Nigeria, we argue that in the process of indigenization, the Government of Nigeria was able to stimulate private indigenous participation in Nigeria's industry and commerce, and hence was able to maximize local retention of profits and, probably, raise the level of domestic investment in capital goods production. The indigenization policy was aimed at redirecting MNC capital from low-technology commercial activities into the major high-technology sectors whose development is considered important to the long-run growth of the Nigerian economy.

Indeed, the indigenization policy marked the finest hour for the Nigerian business classes. Nevertheless, indigenization created several other problems which should be noted:

1. It exacerbated an already skewed pattern of income distribution in favor of the business classes; it marked a major step in the accumulation and concentration of financial and real capital in the hands of the entrepreneurial and bureaucratic classes (Ite 2007). This includes the military juntas, senior bureaucrats, and their business class associates who have access to the institutional structures erected by the Nigerian military government.

2. It stemmed the inflow of new capital as a source of financing foreign direct investment, now that foreign firms have access to the domestic capital market and financial savings of the population through sale of equities.

3. Indigenization seems to encourage further flow of indigenous private investment into commerce and services now largely reserved for local entrepreneurs; on the other hand, it seems to have encouraged the business of linking foreign investors with the state bureaucracy for a fee (corruption in the public sector). This has become a legalized activity in Nigeria (Okomoh 2004).

4. Some indigenous business people were opposed to the revision of the indigenization policy in 1977, yet it was those same individuals who

were relied upon to assume managerial control of enterprises, and help implement the objectives of the policy. Although they were not in the position to influence significantly the formulation of the policy, they certainly were in a position to affect its implementation.

5. The combination of the countervailing measures employed by the multinationals and the opposition of some indigenous businessmen made it extremely difficult to affect the control of operations, even when a majority of the equity was acquired by Nigerians.

6. Making political appointments to the board of indigenized companies also did little to advance the cause of securing control. Due to personal interests, most political appointees were more willing to help their joint-venture partners obtain additional expatriates, negotiate away their managerial responsibilities in technical-service agreements, accept the rewritten articles of association, and ignore some the unilateral violations of the of the 1977 decree that was committed by their foreign partners (Biersteker, 1987; Dike, 1994). It was not that local businessmen were venal, ignorant, or unpatriotic. It is just that they had an acute sense of how to maximize their own interests and did not share all the objectives of the government technocrats who constructed the second decree.

7. The increased pace of personnel indigenization at the senior level has simultaneously increased learning about operations and created a vocal constituency for further personnel indigenization from the ranks of middle managers. The increase in wages and employee benefits has had an important effect on urban wages in general and on the growing disparity between urban and rural income in Nigeria.

In Nigeria, as soon as the government does R to counter the D1 strategy of the multinational corporations, the MNC would respond with D2. Lebanese firms and a few multinationals developed fronting as a means of neutralizing the first indigenization policy. The second indigenization policy specifically forbade fronting and developed enforcement mechanism to deal with it. Hence the MNC responded with regroupings, the two-company formula, and the careful selection of joint-venture partners. Even the measures introduced by the structural adjustment programs of the nation have not been able to address these countervailing measures. Table 5.3 shows multinational corporations in selected sectors in Nigeria.

Table 5.4 shows Nigerian foreign trade between 1977 when the second indigenization policy was enacted, and 1994, a few years after the structural adjustment programs was introduced in the nation.

The data in Table 5.4 would help us clarify our discussion on business-government partnership in Nigeria, and how their relationship has helped to improve or lower economic development and balance of trade in the nation. Table 5.3 shows a significant expansion of trade surplus between 1977 and 1994. It was in 1978, 1981, and 1982 that Nigeria had trade deficit. As

Table 5.3 Multinational corporations in selected sectors in Nigeria

MNC Name	Country of Parent Company
Petroleum Sector	
Shell	Holland
BP	England
Chevron	United States
Mobile	United States
Agip	Italian
Total	France
Elf	France
Texaco	United States
Pan Ocean	United States
Gulf	United States
Automotive Sector	
General Motors	United States
Ford Motor Co.	United States
Nissan	Japan
Mazda	Japan
Toyota	Japan
Deawood	South Korea
Volkswagen	Germany
Puogeot	France
Leyland	England
Electric Equipment	
General Electric	United States
N.V. Phillips Lamp	Netherlands
Siemens Group	Germany
Cie Generale d'Electric	France
Westinghouse	United States
R.C.A.	United States
Thompson-Brandt Group	France
Singer	United States
Sanyo	Japan
Chemical Sector	
Bayer Group	Germany
Basf Group	Germany
Imperial Chemical Industrial Ltd.	United States
Dow Chemical	United States
Union Carbide	United States
Montedison	Italy

MNC Name	Country of Parent Company
Beverage and Pharmaceutical Products	
Cadbury	England
Liver Brothers	England
Coco-Cola	United States
SmithKline and Becham	United States
Guinness	Ireland
Glasco	England
Johnson and Johnson	England
Construction	
Julius Beger	Germany
Niger Cat	Italy
Strabarg	Germany

Source: Data collected from the federal Ministry of Trade and Industry, Lagos, Nigeria 1998.

Table 5.4 Nigerian foreign trade 1977–1994 (US$ million)

Year	Imports	Exports	Balance of trade
1977	7,159.7	7,881.7	+722.0
1978	8,132.0	6,380.5	−1,751.5
1979	6,161.9	10,397.5	+4,235.6
1980	9,095.6	14,198.7	+5103.3
1981	12,599.1	11,033.8	−1,565.1
1982	10,100.2	9,196.6	−903.8
1983	6,555.7	7,751.8	+1,196.1
1984	4,484.5	9,138.8	+4,654.3
1985	5,536.9	11,720.8	+4,6183.9
1986	5,974.7	9,047.5	+3072.8
1987	15,695.4	29,578.1	+13,882.7
1988	18,088.4	31,191.8	+13,882.7
1989	30,8660.2	57,971.2	+27,111.0
1990	45,717.9	109,8886.1	+64,168.2
1991	989,488.2	121,533.7	+32,045.5
1992	143,151.2	205,613.1	+62,461.9
1993	185,629.4	218,765.2	+53,,135.8
1994	66,938.9	105,492.3	+38,553.4

Source: Central Bank of Nigeria 1998. Statistical Bulletin.

from 1983, its balance of trade expanded progressively from N1, 196.1, to a plus of N38, 553.4, in 1994. Between 1983 and 1994 the highest balance of trade surplus was N64, 168.2. This was achieved in 1990.

Further, in so far as there is a latent tension between the power of the MNC and that of the Nigerian government, it is the government that now holds most of the cards and determines the rules of the game. At the macro-economics level, the government can adjust its policies in such a way that it is no longer possible for MNCs to make excessive profits or make it attractive for MNC to import factors of production. At the administrative level, it is always possible to use anti-trust laws against excessive concentration, to improve quotas, limit prices, and above all to insist on a minimal level of local participation in equity holding and employment. Nationalization should be a rare last resort, simply because experience shows that very large foreign corporations will normally accept bids from other small nations if they are attractive.

Evaluating Industrial Policy in Nigeria

Business-government relations in Nigeria are characterized by a love-hate syndrome. Those in business recognize that government decisions affect the economic climate. Most obvious are the effects of governmental decisions at the federal level; note, for example, the impact of government economic pronouncements on the structural adjustment programs and the indigenization policies. Policies at the state and local governments also affect the business climate. The governors of many states have begun a major campaign to attract industry to their states, providing not only information and advice, but specific incentives for plants and industries that might relocate. Similar activities are being undertaken in more and more local communities, as cities recognize that the political climate of any locality directly affects the area's economic climate (Dibie, 2014).

The influence of government on business is, however, more specific in Nigeria. At the federal level, major regulatory agencies provide guidelines within which certain businesses must operate. Similarly, at the state level, some government agencies directly regulate specific businesses, while others act more generally to prevent unfair or unsafe practices. Even at the local level, through licensing and zoning practices, public organizations directly regulate business practices. Government is also important as a consumer of business products and services. For all these reasons, people in business are becoming increasingly aware of the need to understand in detail the work of government, how policies are made, how they are implemented, and how they may be influenced.

At present, Nigeria remains an underdeveloped, dependent, and technologically backward economy (Ake, 1995; Ihonvbere, 1994). In the context of sub-Saharan Africa, however, the structures of the Nigerian state and economy appear relatively developed, but viewed on a worldwide basis, they are less so. The fact remains that the economy is dominated by foreign interests and MNC, and the society is characterized by indiscipline, political instability, ethnic, religious and regional cleavages, and a general absence of basic human needs for the vast majority. Under these type of circumstances, foreign direct investment would have a negative impact on the nation.

A decline in technology development activities has been reported by the Central Bank of Nigeria for the years following the introduction of the structural adjustment programs. This was reflected in the drop in the aggregate index of industrial production estimated at 22.8% in the fourth quarter of 1997 (1985 being 100%). Similarly, decline of 5.0% and 5.1% were recorded in 1992 and 1993, respectively. The contraction in industrial production is traceable to the manufacturing and mining sub-sectors, where output fell by 8.3 and 9.8% in 1996 and first quarter of 1997. This decline was also observed in the third quarter of 1997 when the index fell by 15.7%, owing largely to the lingering political crisis in Nigeria and the problem of access to foreign exchange for import of raw materials and machinery spare parts (Central Bank of Nigeria, 2014).

The poor performance of the manufacturing sub-sector was confirmed by the outcome of a nationwide survey conducted by the Central Bank of Nigeria in 1995. This survey covered 509 manufacturing establishments in 29 industrial groups, with a response rate of 61.3%. The survey showed that the average rate of capacity utilization in the manufacturing industry fell from 37.2% in 1993 to 30.4 in 1995. Five manufacturing sub-groups operated above 50% capacity utilization—namely, beer (54.3%), wood and cork products (51.1%), soft drinks (50%), and soap and perfumes (50%). Eight others operated above 30%—namely, textile (46.6%), cement and cement products (45%), plastic products (42%), drugs and medicine (41%), tires and tubes (32%), vegetable and grain milling (30.5%), fabricated metal products (30%), and bakery products (30%). All the other groups operated less than 30% of their installed capacity—namely, structural metal products (24%); paints (23.8%); basic metal products (23%); paper products (23%); printing and publishing (23%); miscellaneous food preparation (26.5%); roofing sheets (21%); radio, television, and electrical equipment (18%); sugar and confectionery (17.5%); auto vehicle assembly (15%); and glass products (8%) (Central Bank Report, 1995).

Expenditure on research and development (R&D) fell 0.9% in 1995 and 26.6% in 1997 from 100% in 1985. As in previous years, the expenditure on R&D continued to account for a dismal fraction (1.7%) of total investment expenditure in Nigeria. The performance of public and private sectors deteriorated further at the ending of 1997, reflecting decline in levels of output and low overall capacity utilization rates. This unsatisfactory performance was attributable largely to the poor implementation of the structural adjustment programs; inadequate funding, especially working capital; foreign exchange constraints to procure essential raw materials and spare parts; high costs of operation; frequent breakdown of equipment; and political instability.

In addition, technology in Nigeria continues to be pervasive, as all sectors of the economy use it and are influenced and affected by it. Technology also acts as an interface between production and employment, between economic system and ecosystem. It follows, therefore, that effective public-private control over technology has been necessary for realizing the development strategy. To steer the development process, Nigeria must be able to choose appropriate products and technologies and ensure their supply. Sachs (1979) contends that suppliers may be obtained by means of an indigenous design and development effort or by purchase from abroad, followed by adaptation and modification to suit local conditions.

The harmonization of social, economic, and ecological objectives can be achieved only by a careful redefinition of the goals (the demand side) and means (the supply side) of Nigeria. Technology weighs on both sides through the appropriate production processes. This, in turn, requires that Nigeria not only limits its consideration of technology to its capital and labor aspects, but also treats it as a multidimensional entity between the public and private sectors.

As stated earlier, neither government nor business operates in a social vacuum. What business or government does is informed by the dominant values and ideology in the society. The constellation of societal values and politico-economic system necessarily provides not only the philosophical rationale, but also the institutional legitimacy for government-business interactions. In Nigeria, certain core values are central to political philosophy and economy ideology. Frederick et al. (1992: 159–160) and Lussier & Shermen (2009) list some of these core values which underpin the free market ideology. Prominent among these values are individualism, materialism, rationality, and freedom.

Wood (1990: 172; Steiner & Steiner 2006) suggests that "rationality is the basis or justifying materialism and individualism as the best way for the society to attain its ends." These values are the pillars of laissez-faire economic theory, which views government as a cog in the wheel of corporate progress. Liberal democracy assumes individualism, but there is little individualism in Nigeria. It assumes the abstract universals of legal subjects, but in Nigeria that would apply only in the urban environment. The political parties of liberal democracy do not make sense in societies where associational life is rudimentary and interest groups remain essentially primary groups. Claude Ake (1993) noted that some developed nations and many developing ones do not share the World Bank and IMF beliefs in the market allocate efficiency. As an example, the study argued that the Government of Japan has never trusted the markets, and it "has never been as sold on the tenets of neoclassical economics as the Government of the United States."

The adversarial-antagonistic approach to government-business relations is based on the notion that intensifying conflicts is a better way of resolving them and achieving several related goals. This approach is known as "escalate intervention" (Van de Vliert, 1984), a phenomenon whereby incompatible goals are emphasized. The reasoning behind this strategy is that increasing the intensity of a conflict brings matters to a head, the underlying causes of conflicts are clarified, and the motivation to search for acceptable and integrative corporations to present a united front and face the threats posed by globalization.

Positive Synergies Between Business and Government

Since business and government play complementary roles in the society, their relations are not necessarily that of perpetual conflicts as enunciated in the adversarial-antagonistic model. Pragmatic-dynamic model accurately portrays the changing nature of government-business relations. In the context of the aggressive global competition, however, the partnership-cooperative model provides a useful paradigmatic framework for government-business relations. This framework has the potential of nurturing positive synergies between the Nigerian Government and business as a means of reinvigorating the ability of the nation's corporations to compete effectively in the global markets. Partnership-cooperative framework is necessary to transform the vicious cycle of mutual suspicion and legacy of distrust into a virtuous cycle of mutual cooperation and legacy of trust. To achieve these objectives, government-business relationships need to be reconstructed on the basis of "superordinate" goals.

Superordinate goals are those ones that cannot be attained by any one party to a conflict (Robbins, 1974; Waddel 2002). Superordinate goals tie the interests of government and business together. Strategic partnership rooted in superordinate goals has the potential of widening the domains of cooperation, while constricting the zones of conflicts. In this framework, government and business are induced to focus on and work toward common national goals. Indeed, the OTA (1991: 87) study on US competitiveness concluded that such a "fit between corporate interests and government's objectives is growing more important to the United States." Superordinate goals that should govern government-business strategic partnership can be defined in terms of the overreaching goals of society—maintaining a virile economy and improving a standard of living for the citizens.

Ademola Oyejide (1998) argues that "the changing terms of global competition . . . represent a particular crisis for the institutions of Nigeria's society—companies, government, educational institutions, and the like." Confronting this crisis requires rethinking the government-business strategic partnership. A major approach to this is formulating a national industrial policy for critical areas, such as education, human resource development and training, R&D investment, and science and technology, as well as strategic alliance and consortia among corporations.

Partnership in Education

The weaknesses of Nigeria school systems often are cited as a major reason for declining national competitiveness. Functional literacy exists among a large proportion of the workforce (Marcus, 1993: 303). Lall's (1999) study reported that "the typical Sub-Saharan Africa education leaves many young people ill-prepared for work." Reports of various commissions recommend educational excellence designed to prepare students for a future economy based on high-technology. If such a recommendation is adopted, the Nigerian government could recapture its economic vigor and regain its competitive advantage in the world economy (Lall & Wangwe, 1998).

The task of improving Nigeria's education so that the future workforce is adequately prepared for the global challenges should be a joint undertaking among governments at all levels (national, state, and local governments) and between public and private sectors. Partnership is crucial in providing good education for Nigeria's future workforce. In the twenty-first century, production workers must sharpen reading and mathematics skills. To the extent that private industry has supported education, attention has been focused largely on the college and university levels. More resources need to be channeled to support elementary and secondary education.

Partnership for Human Resource Development

There is no substitute for the educated, skilled, and disciplined workforce. The Conference Board indicated that corporate executives ranked education and human resource the as key issues of public policy that would improve Nigeria's competitiveness (Tuodolo 2009; Urbach 2006). A report by the World Bank (1998) indicated that the Nigerian competitors "offer more and better training, both to young people preparing for work life and to activate workers," whereas for Nigeria's firms "training of people already in the work force is . . . deficient." The quality of the workforce is the key to national competitiveness (see Porter, 1990: 69–131). Germany is widely acknowledged for its high-quality scientific and technical education and specialized training. Japan is reputed for having a disciplined workforce.

The World Bank (1998) concluded that unless government and business undertake a vast increase in their investment in human capital, sub-Saharan African companies will not be able to hire the types of workers they need to compete in international markets." In the twenty-first century, one of the most challenging aspects of global competition will be training the workforce to keep place with rapidly advancing technology. Labor-management conflicts must be curtailed as a means of promoting labor productivity.

Partnership for Research and Development (R&D)

Oyejide (1998) and Lall and Wangwe (1998) addressed the managerial issues in Nigeria's declining productivity by focusing on how corporate managers allocate capital resources among technological alternatives. They emphasize the role of R&D in improving worker productivity. During the last decade, many Nigerian corporations have reduced total R&D budgets (Oyejide, 1998). The adverse consequence of this is the inability of Nigerian firms to compete in high technology industries. Research shows that a company's R&D intensity is a major means of gaining market share in global competition (Franko, 1989). To regain competitive strength, Nigerian corporations need considerable investments in R&D.

Government support of R&D through tax policy is a desideratum in this regard. Lall (1999) describes the least intrusive and lease expensive of various possible risk-sharing options between government and business as "strategic technology policy, an R&D partnership for developing new technologies of commercial interest."

The policy challenge arising from recent development is to consolidate macroeconomics policy improvements and address more effectively the structural impediments at the microeconomics level. Industrial restructuring, privatization, and private sector development pose critical policy concern. Policy improvement will be needed to sustain trade expansion and to stimulate domestic and foreign investments. Industrial policy will need to address the following areas:

1. Promoting competitiveness, especially improving technological capabilities in a market economy;
2. Shifting the incentive structure strongly toward export orientation;
3. Helping import-substituting industries restructure and upgrade their technologies and skills;
4. Investing in infrastructure, education, training, and technological support services;
5. Promoting regional cooperation to enlarge markets.

Conclusion

The analysis in this chapter suggests that business and government should continue to play an important role in promoting industrial development in Nigeria. However, this role should be very different from before, set in a different policy context and driven by a different set of objectives, aimed at promoting efficient markets and technical efficiency. Merely "getting prices right" or "indigenization" will not be sufficient to improve Nigerian industrial growth and competitiveness. Thus, government, business, and civil society organizations' partnership needs clear roles and terms for engagement to be defined.

The first step in any industrial reform process should therefore be to raise the skills of government officials and insulate the officials from political pressures. Officials should be provided with more, and more objective, information on ways in which industrial policy can be used. All this may be easier said than done, but without this base of administrative capabilities, it is difficult to see how Nigeria will emulate even a little of the industrial success of other developed nations.

Globalization, multinational operations, and foreign direct investment in Nigeria embody both opportunities and threats. Countries that adapt their systems of beliefs to the global reality are inclined to devise national strategies in response to its imperatives. Nigeria will derive maximum benefit from the ever expanding business opportunities if the educational system in the nation is improved considerably. However, foreign investment and MNC operations made in a context of high unemployment and destructive economic and political competition in the absence of effective rules (as is currently in Nigeria) can have a significantly negative impact on the nation. Another observation is that Nigeria has been unable to exploit the already imported advanced technology and develop an appropriate technological system for itself. It must be recognized that the guiding hand of governments has become the norm in the global business where politics and economics converge. For Nigerian firms to regain their competitive edge in the global business environment, there must be cooperation among all segments of the society, but especially between the government and business sectors.

The importance of technology as the prime factor of economic and structural transformation in Nigeria can never be stressed enough. If government capabilities can be improved, policy reform should involve a more gradual liberalization than what happened with the indigenization decree. Future policy should be backed by a comprehensive supply-side support system, especially in the development of the indigenous private sector. Rapid, wholesale liberalization such as the structural adjustment programs could make matters worse. There are different ways to expose industrial firms to a stimulating environment, and an ideal strategy may involve a great deal of active business-government partnership in policy making and guidance.

Multinational corporations (especially in the Nigerian petroleum industry) and foreign investors have been accused of being neither humanitarian nor generous in their economic dealings in Nigeria (Detomasi 2007; Ayanwale 2007). They have been regarded as egoistic and egocentric, and prefer to give their interest more priority over any appeal to sentimentally or morally help develop a sustainable economy for Nigeria. On the contrary, the effect of FDI and MNC depends crucially on the domestic and international context within which it occurs. Different domestic and international contexts governing MNC and FDI produce different outcomes. As we have shown, the environment of Nigeria is what has contributed to their present impact.

As a result of continued devaluation of the Naira (Nigerian currency), the cost of imported raw materials rose by 229% between 1987 and 1994, while that of locally produced raw materials rose by 96% (Central Bank of Nigeria, 2014). In a climate in which borrowing has become exorbitant, many private manufacturers have found themselves unable to compete for loans to develop a local technology or pay for the foreign exchange needed to bring in foreign inputs or even reorganize their production techniques or cover their basic overhead costs. The Nigerian government should introduce more industrial policies to correct the present situation. Such policies should be directed at regulating the wild fluctuation in the economy, as well as to further encourage the private sector to continue in business. Nigeria cannot build a self-reliant economy without a self-reliant indigenous and appropriate technology. Nigeria seems to have the private sector requisite, but lacks political will from the government (public sector) to implement policies that would fasten the technology development process.

References

Aaronson, S. and Reeves, J. (2002). *Corporate Responsibility in the Global Village: The Role of Public Policy*. Washington, DC: National Policy Association.

Aderemi, P. J. (2010, November 2). Governance and Corporate Social Responsibility in Nigeria. *The Nigerian Observer*. www.nigerianobservernews.com/. Accessed October 2011.

Ake, C. (1985). *Political Economy of Nigeria*. London: Longmans.

Ake, C. (1993). The Unique Case of African Democracy. *International Affairs*, 69(2), 241–252.

Ake, C. (1995). Nigerian Development and the Ogoni Crisis. *Policy Magazine*. Lagos, Nigeria: Daily Times Press.

Albareda, L., Lozano, J. M., Tencati, A., Midttun, A. and Perrini, F. (2008). The Changing Role of Governments in Corporate Social Responsibility: Drivers and Responses. *Business Ethics: A European Review*, 17(4), 347–363.

Albareda, L., Lozano, J. M. and Ysa, T. (2007). Public Policies on Corporate Social Responsibility: The Role of Governments in Europe. *Journal of Business Ethics*, 74(4), 391–407.

Alfredo, D. (2011). *The Relationship Between Government and Business*. www.ehow. com/about_5427693_relationship-between-government-business.html#ixzz1oVn A37Xf. Accessed October 13, 2016.

Altvater, E. (1993). The Future of the Market: An Essay on the Regulation of Money and Nature After the Collapse of Actually Existing Socialism. London: Verso.

Boddewyn, J. (2015). International Business-Government Relations Research, 1945–2015: Concept, Typologies, Theories and Methodologies. *Journal of World Business*, 51(1), 10–22.

Central Bank of Nigeria. (2014). *Annual Report*. Abuja, Nigeria: CNB Publication.

Chris, G., Philips, C. and Bhatia-Panthaki, S. (2007). The Private Sector, Poverty Reduction and International Development. *Journal of International Development*, 19, 723–734.

CIA World Factbook. (2004). United States Department of State. Area Handbook of the US Library of Congress.

Collins, K., Gittell, R., Holcomb, J. and Magnusson, M. (2009). *Exploring Business. Chapter 3 Frameworks for Understanding the Relationship Between Business, Government, and Society*. www.flatworldknowledge.com/pub/1.0/exploring-business/47923#. Accessed March 30, 2011.

Daniels, J., Radebaugh, L. and Sullivan, D. (2011). International Business: Environments and Operations. Upper Saddle River, NJ: Prentice Hall Press.

Detomasi, D. A. (2007). The Multinational Corporation and Global Governance: Modelling Global Public Policy Networks. *Journal of Business Ethics*, 71(3), 321–334.

Dibie, R. (2014). Comparative Perspective of Environmental Policies and Issues. New York, NY: Routledge Press.

Edoho, F. M. (1997). Globalization and the New World Order: Promises, Problems and Prospects for Africa in the 21st Century. Westport, CT: Praeger.

Essia, U. and Yearoo, A. (2009). Strengthening Civil Society Organizations/Government Partnership in Nigeria. *International NGO Journal*, 4(9), 368–374.

Ferrell, O. C., Hirt, G. and Ferrell, L. (2011). Business: A Changing World. New York: McGraw-Hill Press.

Idemudia, U. (2007). Corporate Partnerships and Community Development in the Nigerian Oil Industry: Strengths and Limitations. United Nations Research Institute for Social Development Markets, Business and Regulation Programme, Paper No. 2.

Idemudia, U. (2010). Corporate Social Responsibility and the Rentier Nigerian State: Rethinking the Role of Government and the Possibility of Corporate Social Development in the Niger Delta. *Canadian Journal of Development Studies*, 30(1–2), 131–153.

Ihonvbere, J. O. (1994). *Nigeria: The Politics of Adjustment and Democracy*. New Brunswick: Transaction Publishers.

Ite, U. E. (2007). Partnering With the State for Sustainable Development: Shell's Experience in the Niger Delta, Nigeria. *Sustainable Development*, 15, 216–228. Published online 10 October 2006 in Wiley InterScience. www.interscience.wiley. com. doi:10.1002/sd.312. Accessed December 29, 2011.

Iwu-Egwuonwu, R. C. (2011). Behavioral Governance, Accounting and Corporate Governance Quality. *Journal of Economics and International Finance*, 3(1), 1–12.

Kuye, O. L., and Ogundele, O. J. K. (2013). Strategic Rules of Business, Government and Society: The Nigerian Situation. *International Journal of Business and Social Sciences*, 4(12), September Special Issue, 233–243.

Lall, S. (1999). The Technological Response to Import Liberalization in Sub-Saharan Africa. New York: St. Martin's Press.

Lall, S. and Wangwe, S. (1998, June). Industrial Policy and Industrialization in Sub-Saharan Africa. *Journal of African Economics*, 7(Suplement 1), 70–107.

Lehne, R. (2013). Government and Business. Washington DC: Congressional Quarterly/ Sage Press

Lussier, R. and Achua, C. (2016). Leadership, Theory, Application and Skill Development. Boston, MA: Cengage Learning.

Lussier, R. N. and Sherman, H. (2009). *Business, Society and Government Essentials: An Applied Ethics Approach*. Long Grove III: Waveland Press.

McCraw, T. K. (1984). Business and Government: The Origin of Adversarial Relationship. *California Management Review*, 26 (Winter), 45–61

McGuigan, J., Moyer, C. and Harris, F. (2014). *Managerial Economics: Application, Strategy and Tactics*. Boston, MA: Cengage Learning.

Maravcsik, M. (1983). The Role of Science in Technology Transfer. *Research Policy*, 12(5), October Issue, 287–296.

Marcus, A. A. (1993). Business and Society: Ethics, Government, and the World Economy. Homewood, IL: Richard D. Irwin, Inc.

Moran, T. (1985). Multinational Corporations: The Political Economy of Foreign Direct Investment. Lexington: Lexington Books.

Muraina, A., Okpara, E. and Ahunanya, S. (2010). Transparency in Corporate Governance: A Comparative Study of Enron, USA and Cadbury PLC, Nigeria. *The Social Sciences*, 5(6), 471–476.

Ogundele, O. J. K. (2012). Introduction to Entrepreneurship, Corporate Governance and Small Business Management. Lagos: Molofin Nominees.

Okomoh, P. F. (2004). *The Role of Business in Society: Foreign Direct Investments (FDI) and their Impact on Sustainable Development in Nigeria*. Paper for 2004 World Bank Institute (WBI)/Wharton Business School International Research/ Essay Contest on CSR for Future Leaders. Accessed October 29, 2011.

Olukoshi, A. (1992). *The Politics of Structural Adjustment in Nigeria*. London: James Carrey Publishers.

Oluwagbuyi, O. & Ogungbenle, S. (2013). "Cost Implications of Unemployment on the Nigeria Economy." *Journal of Accountancy and Economics,3* (14), 27–42

Onimode, B. (1991). *Alternative Development Strategies for Africa*. London: Institute for African Alternatives.

OTA [Office of Technology Assessment]. (1991). *United State Congress. Competing Economies: America, Europe, and the Pacific Rim, OTA-ITE-498*. Washington, DC: U.S. Government Printing Office.

Oyejide, A. (1998, June). Trade Policy and Regional Integration in the Development Context: Emerging Patterns Issues and Lessons for Sub-Saharan Africa. *Journal of African Economics*, 7(Suplement 1), 108–145.

Porter, M. E. (1990). The Competitive Advantage of Nations. New York: The Free Press.

Robbins, S. P. (1974). *Managing Organizational Conflict: A Nontraditional Approach*. Englewood Cliffs, NJ: Prentice-Hall.

Sachs, I. (1979, April). Controlling Technology for Development. *Development Dialogue, (1.)*, 1–9.

Safarian, A. E. (1969). *The Performance of Foreign-Owned Firms in Canada*. Canadian-American Committee, National Planning Association.

Steiner, G. and Steiner, R. (2006). *Business, Government and Society*. Boston: Irwin/ McGraw-Hill Press.

Subair, G. (2011). Nigeria Records $6.099m Foreign Direct Investment. *Nigerian Tribune*, 28 July, 2011 www.tribune.com.ng/index.php/news/25784-nigeria-records-6099m-foreign-direct-investment. Accessed May 23, 2015.

Tuodolo, F. (2009). Corporate Social Responsibility: Between Civil Society and the Oil Industry in the Developing World. *ACME: An International E-Journal for Critical Geographies*, 8(3), 530–541.

Urbach, H. (2008). *Young International Ltd (UHY): Doing Business in Nigeria*. UHY Maaji and Co. Lagos. www.mittlererniederrhein.ihk_business_080701.pdf. Accessed October 13, 2016.

Waddell, S. (2002). Core Competences: A Key Force to Business-Government and Civil Society Collaborations. JCC 7, Autumn, Greenleaf Publishing.

Weidenbaum, M. L. (1990). *Business, Government, and Public Policy*. 4th Edition. Englewood Cliffs, NJ: Prentice-Hall.

Wood, D. J. (1990). *Business and Society*. Glenview, IL: Scott, Foresman and Company.

World Bank. (2014). *World Bank Development Report*. New York: Oxford University Press.

World Bank. (1995–1998). *Annual World Development Report*. New York: Oxford University Press.

Ya Ni, A. and Van Wart, M. (2016). *Building Business–Government Relations: A Skills Approach*. New York: Routledge Press.

Case Study

Management Dilemma at the City of Ozoro

Mr. Karo sat in his office at the city of Ozoro, and pondered his ethical dilemma. During his 35 years of service to the city, Mr. Karo had worked in different capacities. He had served as Assistant Manager, Manager, and Acting Director, respectively, in the budgeting, transportation, tax, auditing, major's office, payroll, accounting, and planning departments. Mr. Karo has a brother called Mr. Maro who he trained in college. Mr. Maro graduated from Delta State University and became a successful businessman in the city of Ozoro.

Three months after Mr. Karo had made a presentation to the city council, the new mayor hit it off and became friends with him. Over lunch two weeks after they became close friends, the mayor mentioned to Mr. Karo that his brother Mr. Maro had a good chance of getting a $5 million a year contract from the city. The contract was a five-year deal to build a new school and as well as install pumps for the city of Ozoro's City Hall. The mayor also informed Mr. Karo that Mr. Maro's bid was somewhat higher than the rest, and that he should lower it. Mr. Karo thanked the mayor for the information and asked his brother Mr. Maro to resubmit a bid slightly lower than the previous edition.

A week later, the major called Mr. Karo and told him that there is the probability that Mr. Maro would get the contract for the new school and the replacement pumps. The mayor, however, requested a small gift of $50,000 for the contract—in essence, a bribe. At first Mr. Karo told the mayor that he would think about it. Mr. Karo called his brother Mr. Maro and delivered the mayor's message. Mr. Karo told Mr. Maro that it was against US law to offer bribe to anyone in order to secure privileged information or a contract. Mr. Maro was, however, more concerned about how he could get the contract than obeying the law. Mr. Maro told his elder brother Mr. Karo to do whatever it takes to secure the contract for him. This seems to be a black and white decision, but Mr. Karo knew differently. After 35 years with the local government civil service, Mr. Karo recognized that if he was caught giving the mayor a bribe, he could be fired. With retirement only a few years away, he needed his pension. Mr. Karo, however, had to succumb to the pressure from his brother, and they went ahead and fulfilled the demands of the mayor.

In another development, Mr. Karo's boss, Dr. Oyigbo, the chief accountant of the local government, denied Mr. Karo's promotion to become senior accountant. Six weeks after the incident, Ms. Bola, an accountant with the local government, noticed Mr. Karo behaving in an odd manner. He left early and came into work late. One Sunday morning, Ms. Bola went into the office to complete the job she had started on Friday afternoon. She found Mr. Karo in the office that morning copying some of the software that the local government uses in auditing and consulting. A few weeks later at a dinner party, Ms. Bola overhead a conversation about Mr. Karo doing consulting work for some small firms. At work next Monday morning, she asked Mr. Karo if what she heard was true. It was the policy of the city for their senior employees not to do business with any of their clients' organizations. This is because such an act could constitute a breach of ethics or the code of conduct. The city is strongly committed to implementing its policies and regulatory programs.

Mr. Karo responded, "Yes, it is true. I have a few clients that I do work for on occasions, but they are located outside the city." Ms. Bola asked, "Don't you think there is a conflict of interest between you and the local government?" Mr. Karo replied, "I was counting on that promotion to help pay some extra bills. My oldest son decided to go to a private university, which is an extra $20,000. In addition, our medical plan at the local government does not cover some problems my wife has. In addition, you do not want to know the cost. The only way I can afford to pay for all these things is to do some extra work on the side."

Apart from this incident, Ms. Bola knew that Mr. Karo, one of her valued employees, was stealing from the local government office—not much, and in a way that no one but Ms. Bola would ever know. Ms. Bola also knew that without Mr. Karo, her unit could never complete a newly assigned task on time. She decided to do nothing about bringing the stealing incident to a stop and secretly hoped that success in the new assignment would bring about a long-desired promotion and get her out of the awkward situation.

After the new project ended, Ms. Bola was promoted the city senior accountant. Ms. Biola arrived at work one morning and found an envelope delivered by the mayor filled with receipts from a recent trip he took to an economic development conference. Included were receipts from a four-day vacation the mayor and his wife took to a Caribbean Island resort. It was clear that the mayor wanted the city to reimburse him for everything included in the envelope.

Six months into her new position as the city senior accountant, Ms. Bola conducted a random check on long distance telephone calls at the city mayor's office. She found that 30% of the long distance calls were personal calls (though charged to the city government). The cost of the calls were estimated at $43,000 for three months and, by extrapolation, almost $200,000 a year for the whole city. Many calls were placed to homes of employees or their relatives, while others were calls to prerecorded messages, such as time and temperature, horoscope, financial information, and so on. Penalties for unauthorized use of city telephone lines include fines, suspension, and dismissal. Ms. Bola was very reluctant to fire several of the guilty staff at the local government, so she decided to cover up her findings about the wrongful use of the telephone lines.

In another development, Dr. Obaro assumed duty as the new state governor of Delta State. The constitution of the country requires the local government mayors to report directly to the state governors. As the governor and the chief executive of the state, Dr. Obaro decided to change the structure of the civil service and all the departments by retiring all the women that were in the director positions and above. He redesigned the department without consulting with the State House of Assembly. Members of the State Assembly (Legislature) threatened to impeach him for violating the standard operating procedure according to the mandates of the state constitution. Dr. Obaro later decided that he would make peace with the members of the State Legislature. He invited the 100 members of the State Legislators in groups of 10 to pay him a visit on a weekend. During their visit, he gave each of them $5 million. On the next Monday, the State Legislator proposed a bill in the House to recognize the governor for his statesmanship. At the end of that same month, teachers in the state were not paid their salary, due to lack of funds in the state treasury. The teacher's union decided to go on strike and more than 700,000 children in primary and secondary schools all over the state could not go to school for five weeks before the federal government gave a loan to the State to pay the teachers.

As part of Dr. Obaro's reorganization of the State Department, he retired all the employees that were 55 years and older. He also removed women from all sectional head positions, because he felt they were always taking time off from work. The redesigning of the Department was contrary to the affirmation action and equal employment opportunity laws. It further led to a high rate of turnover in the Department. Another consequence of this reorganization was that some local government mayors could no longer award contracts to rebuild schools or reconstruct bad roads that were not federal government or state designated roads within their respect local government. It was also ironic that some local government mayors who were Dr. Obaro's friends were allowed to perform these centralized functions in their respective local governments.

Assignment

As the new director of the code of ethics or conducts for the local government, evaluate the ethical issues in this case study. Who is affected? What should be done to Mr. Karo, the mayor, Mr. Maro, and others? Analyze and discuss what Ms. Bola can do or the options available to her. Discuss any extra information you feel you need before making your decision.

6 Government and Business Relations in Ghana

Leonard Gadzekpo

Introduction

The Republic of Ghana is located in West Africa. It has boundaries with the Republic of Togo to the east, the Ivory Coast to the west, and Burkina Faso to the north. The Atlantic Ocean is to the south of the country. According to a World Bank Group (2016) report, Ghana's population was 27.4 million in 2015. The nation's GDP was estimated to be about US$37.86 billion in 2015 (World Bank Group, 2016; GlobalEdge, 2016). Ghana gained its independence from the United Kingdom on May 6, 1957. It currently has a unitary constitutional democracy government.

Healthy relationships between business and government remain the root of robust growth and sustained development, and a lack of both generates weak economic activity and resultant socio-political stagnation and instability. In the past two decades Ghana has been experiencing constant economic growth, and as of 2012 had a GDP growth of at least 8% (World Bank Group, 2016). How do government and business work together to achieve such a growth for the country to be identified as one of the top-10 fastest growing economies in the world, and the fastest growing economy in Africa? Given a very optimistic vision, Ghana should become a developed country between 2020 and 2030. Can government and business unleash public and private resources, energy, and potential to achieve such a goal and lead Africa to attain real economic development, just as it did over half a century earlier in leading sub-Saharan Africa in overcoming colonization and gaining political independence?

Colonial economic legacy may be trumpeted as a continuing economic reality in Ghana, especially in government business relations that were inherited at independence, relations that were not only entrenched in laws and regulations, but also deeply embedded in business practices. The land tenure system, business laws and regulations, tax laws and taxes, public corporations, government investment in infrastructure, and utilities are some examples of the colonial legacy that dogs the country, while attempts at changes and restructuring are often met with resistance from the business community that may perceive them as detrimental to their stability, time-tested practices, and their bottom-line, profits. It is, however, significant that privatization and trade liberalization policies instituted by government for most part of the last two decades induced by external pressures, for example from the International Monetary Fund (IMF) and the World Bank, have created two conflicting reactions (World Bank Group, 2016). On one hand, older Ghanaian-owned businesses, in some cases, see aspects of the policies negatively, while on the other hand, some foreign-owned businesses, especially those that seize opportunities offered by the policies and new Ghanaian-owned businesses that expanded and were spurned by them, react positively. The junction where government interests, business interests, and international economic and financial institutional interests and pressures converge is the site that presents conditions, developments, and evolving local business climates that best attest to the nature of government-business relations in Ghana.

The chapter examines government policies, regulations, and practices in relation to business and business reaction and relation to and interaction with government. It investigates government-owned and partly government-owned business, multinational corporations, and private enterprises within the context of competitiveness, protectionism versus free trade, corporate bailouts, defensive or subsidies production, consumer product regulation, and taxation. External influences and impositions such as World Bank conditions, including deregulation, privatization, and removal of subsidies, are brought into to focus not only as parameters within which the Ghanaian government and business operate in a global economy but also as policy-making areas that affect government and business relations in drastic ways.

The chapter also presents problems that have dogged Ghana since independence in the relationship between government and business and immerging strenuous conditions that put stress on healthy relations and collaboration between the two. It concludes by offering possible solutions to various problems—for example, corruption, general lack of capital, and particularly lack of access to capital by a majority of Ghanaian women. It projects those solutions onto the needs of a country poised to reach higher economic growth and heights if not hindered by those problems.

Regulation: Land, Sea, Business, and Government

Land and sea could not be overemphasized as critical elements in the economic and business life of a nation. These factors could be considered to be next to human resources (Lehne, 2013). Since national borders and claims to national sovereignty are hinged on specific demarcated geographical location and area, government authority within those borders over access to land and land use encoded in the land tenure system is the first point of contact between business entities and Ghanaian government. The nature and expansion of regulations within the Ghanaian land-tenure system exemplify the overlapping of indigenous and local centuries-old and modern national regulations. Land traditionally is owned by communities and not by individuals, so that local leaders, chiefs, and kings are custodians of the land that is accessible to members of the communities as individuals and for community projects. In the modern era, with colonization, the British took ownership of the then Gold Coast, which at independence became Ghana. But even during colonization, communal land ownership persisted, except when the British expropriated land for projects, in most cases through negotiations with local leaders, who when faced with awesome military and political pressure yielded their custodial authority. At independence, government inherited authority as owner of all land in Ghana, in that through the constitution and statutes vested power in the president to hold in trust the whole land mass for the landholding communities, but the government had to negotiate with local communities through their leaders to access tracks of land for public projects: Administration of Lands Act, 1962 (Act 123); Office of the Administrator of Stool Lands Act, 1994 (Act 481); Lands Commission Act, 1994 (Act 483); Local Government Act, 1993 (Act 462). As a result, 20% of land is public and directly controlled by government, while 80% is privately controlled by customary authorities and private owners, often under leases issued by the customary authorities to Ghanaian non-indigenes of communities and foreigners. Indigenes who needed land to build structures and establish enterprises readily have access to land with permission from customary custodians, while outsiders and government had to negotiate with the custodians.

News reports in 2012 indicate that Ghana produced about 5.9 million barrels of crude oil, generating an accumulated revenue of US$903 million (Myjoyonline, 2012). Oil finds off the coast of Ghana brought indigenous and modern national land-use regulations to a head (Modern Ghana, 2007). Fishing rights of coastal communities that for centuries have never been questioned nor undermined, however, with oil finds, have to be negotiated and regulated at the governmental level. Regulation has always been in place, even at the local indigenous level in the form of some days of the week being set aside as non-fishing days to control overfishing. Introduction of outboard motors and powered fishing boats heightened competition on the waters, only for all local fishing activities to be threatened, first, by foreign industrial fishing-boats that did not involve any onshore contacts and, second, by oil drilling and extraction activities. Local regulatory measures cannot address industrial fishing nor oil extractive activities, and where government and international conglomerates are in agreement, local regulation becomes moot. The Land Administration Project, started in 2003, lists laws and regulations to enhance stewardship and management of communal or stool lands through traditional authorities that had been relatively beneficial in gold, diamond, bauxite, manganese, and other mineral mining areas, does not hold much sway in the regulation of offshore activities (Toulmin et al., 2004). The minerals and mining law, PNDC Law 153, passed in 1986, is an attempt to create a favorable climate for investment and gives the government 10% equity in all mining companies, with an option to purchase an additional 20%. The nature of investments in mining, oil exploration, and extraction involving foreign companies and interests, leave farmers and fishermen and other small businesses dependent on utilization of land and water mass vulnerable and unprotected, since government has stake in such companies, in that the law pegs corporate tax at 45% and there is an applicable additional profit tax, if the rate of return exceeds agreed levels.

Other laws and regulations since the 1980s, including the Local Content and Local Participation Policy Framework, 2011; the Petroleum Revenue Management Act, 2011 (Act 815); the Petroleum Commission Act, 2011; and the Petroleum Exploration and Production Bill, 2013, point to ensuring that the developmental benefits of mining are maximized without active state participation. Thus, governance of the sector is largely limited to regulations that have little bearing on smaller businesses and individuals whose activities are not within the sector but have been negatively affected, especially in land and ocean offshore use. If minerals, oil, and gas are exported in their raw form with hardly any value added as result of the absence of processing, so that the mining sector contributes barely 2% of Ghana's gross domestic product (GDP), regulation that enhances their expansion without taking into account how their extractive activities affect other sectors that generate more revenue represents unsustainable economic direction presently and dire ecological consequence in the future. If short-term profits are a bottom line in mining and oil and gas business relationship with government, a precedent is set that is being replicated in other sectors.

Privatization of Public Corporations

Water resources, air space, and bandwidth are constitutionally included in public property held in trust by the President of the Republic of Ghana for all citizens. Public corporations had been established since the 1960s to manage these resources and make them available to Ghanaian citizenry. By the 1980s, with the realization that government had accumulated a large portfolio of state-owned corporations that were underperforming and were a threat to economic and financial stability of the country, arguments and positions abounded for their privatization, with the goal of making them more efficient, competitive, and profitable. The introduction of the 1983 Economic Recovery Programme (ERP) that was formalized in 1987 with establishment of the Commission by the State Enterprises Commission Law, 1987 (PNDCL 170), institutionalized privatization. The law seeks to improve the efficiency of the economy by encouraging private sector participation and investment and to develop a domestic capital market, as well as to motivate the private sector, reduce fiscal deficit, and raise foreign exchange. Government actions are not taken in a vacuum and are not only induced by internal national development but also by external international economic and financial demands and pressures.

Pressure from the International Monetary Fund and the World Bank for fiscal discipline and to keep the government from investing in state-owned enterprises, thus denying them support during economic hard times, stoked the push toward privatization (Grusky, 2001). Divesture of the mining sector, especially Ashanti Goldfields Corporation, that started in 1994 when the Government of Ghana, the major shareholder, floated 20–25% of its interest in the corporation and its merger in 2004 with AngloGold to create the world's second-largest gold producer, AngloGold Ashanti Company, after approval by the High Court of Ghana, is readily offered as an excellent example to be followed by state-owned enterprises (AngloGold Ashanti Company, 2004). Although there was little interest in the Ghanaian private sector and from foreign private entities in investing in utilities, pressure mounted and forced government to yield to divesture of public corporations.

The case of Ghana Water and Sewage Corporation presents a trend that in Ghana is still being offered as a solution to the underperformance of public utility corporations, even after divesture failed to make the privatized corporation efficient in delivery of water to Ghanaians, while it made significant profits. Pressure from donors mounted on indebted government to privatize public utility corporations, especially open urban water sector to private capital, although private capital was very limited in the country. But to access funds offered by donors, especially the IMF and World Bank, Ghana yielded to privatization. Foreign private corporations were unwilling to invest in Ghanaian utility, given failed results in Latin America and elsewhere in Africa. The government, therefore, contracted Aqua Vitens Rand Limited (AVRL), a company formed by Vitens Evides International of the Netherlands and Rand Water of South Africa to take over water distribution in urban areas (Shang-Quartey, 2014). AVRL managed US$120 million from donors and was paid US$5 million as management fees for 5 years, meaning it did not invest in any infrastructure but had access to huge funds.

With no change in the underlying infrastructure needed for water distribution, performance followed the pattern of inefficiency and worker dissatisfaction, leading government to revoke the contract with AVRL. The argument that privatization leads to efficiency and private capital forces corporations to deal with the market creating competition and robust development of infrastructure and excellent water delivery across the board did not materialize. Only the private corporation, AVRL, maximized huge profits, investing virtually nothing in Ghana but collecting substantial management fees, and left the country in debt and without improved water delivery. Ghana Water Company Limited, again, took over potable water production and distribution. With further investment in infrastructure, by 2014 GWC was producing and delivering daily in Accra, the capital of Ghana, up to 158.3 million gallons, and an increase from 93 million gallons from previous years (Chronicle, 2014). With the failure of privatization of Ghana

Water Company, however, there is still an argument emerging on the privatization of another state-owned corporation, Electricity Company of Ghana (ECG).

Incorporated in 1963 with shares of the limited company being sold since 1997, ECG has been charged with the distribution of electricity. When in 1967 a military government decree, the Electricity Corporation Decree (NLCD 125), and the repeal of the Electricity Act put production of electric power in the hands of another government-owned entity, Volta River Authority (VRA), with limited power production support from a private company, the Takoradi International Company (TICo), a joint venture ship between VRA and CMS Energy Inc. of the United States, ECG, and its subsidiary, the Northern Electricity Department (NED), were obligated to purchase in bulk power from VRA for redistribution across the nation (Edjekumhene, 2003). ECG faces similar developments and problems as Ghana Water Company.

Since 1997, Ghanaians and commercial electric power consumers have seen a continuing decline in delivery of service, and as with Ghana Water Company before the failed privatization, production has not grown to match demand as the population grew and commercial use increased steadily. Attempts to augment gigawatts, including the Kpong Hydroelectric Project on the Kpong Rapids and the Power Station at Penu, construction of the Bui Hydroelectric Plant on the Black Volta, and expansion of the Akosombo Plant with the installation of additional plants and development of the Pra, Tano, and lower White Volta rivers, have not improved power production and delivery. Hydroelectric power production is dependent on water volume and its flow through turbines built into dams, and because rainfall is unpredictable and droughts are regular, often blamed on global warming, various hydroelectric plants could not generate enough megawatts to sustain growing demand.

The West African Gas Pipeline (WAGP) Project that involved the construction of a natural gas pipeline of 678 kilometers to supply natural gas from Nigeria to meet the energy requirements of Ghana and other West African countries to be deployed in generating electricity in gas-fired turbine has hardly made a dent in demand, intermittently hamstrung by technical issues (Daily Independent, 2013). Oil and gas finds in Ghana and the promise of raw energy resource use in generating electricity follow an example in Nigeria, where instead millions of cubic liters of gas are flared. Despite technical glitches, when gas via WAGP and oil in tankers are delivered to be used in firing turbines to support and augment megawatts mainly generated by Akosombo Hydroelectric Plant and other plants, accrued financial burden on ECG regularly leads to default in payment of the energy commodities.

Compounding the problem of inadequate electric power production is ageing infrastructure and reported corruption of both ECG and Volta River Authority (VRA) officials. Out of 24 projects undertaken in 2015 by ECG, half are to repair and upgrade substations, switches, and the grid in general

(ECG, 2015). Ghanaian customers go without electric power for days, named locally "dumsor." They are so regular that they spurn the development of mobile phone applications to track such power outages. ECG could only offer load shedding schedules: The Electricity Company of Ghana wishes to inform its cherished customers that due to generation shortfall, it has become necessary to publish this load shedding guide (ECG, 2015). The clarion call in the media and in the private sector is that privatization would solve the problems, using another example of the privatization of Ghana Telecom, a state-owned telecommunication corporation that was sold to Vodafone, to become Vodafone Ghana instead of the failed privatization of GWC.

Privatization of Ghana Telecom started in 1997, allowing Telekom of Malaysia to acquire a 30% share in the corporation, along with control over operations and management for five years, while the government retained 70% share. At the end of the five-year exclusivity arrangement, a newly elected government ended the contract in 2002 and bought back the entire 30% share as WESTEL, Celtel, France Telecom, Portugal Telecom, and Vodacom all showed interest in owning majority share in Ghana Telecom (New Africa 2010). In 2008, Vodafone paid US$900 million for 70% equity in Ghana Telecom, which became Vodafone Ghana thereafter. Vodafone assumed control of One Touch, Ghana Telecom's mobile arm, which took ownership of Ghana's fixed telecom network, and gained monopoly over the provision of international, long distance telephone, and fixed broadband services in addition to the national fiber optic backbone hitherto owned and controlled by the state-owned Volta River Authority (AfricanLiberty.org, 2008). Critics are quick to draw attention to transfer of a public monopoly to a private one so that government's future e-government, ICT initiatives for schools, and other public institutions, as well as national security ever-expanding dependence on telecommunication, are not controlled by government but by a private corporation that is not answerable to Ghanaians constitutionally as citizens in a democratic republic and also as customers, but to mostly foreign shareholders of a multinational conglomerate.

Citizens and Consumers

The argument that market forces would determine if a business entity thrives or fails and that competition is health in the free market has limitations because the market is not a force of nature independent to itself, but a human creation that is regularly managed and often manipulated by both political and economic interests and exigence. As in the case of Vodafone and its assumption of control over the national fiber optic backbone, what protections do Ghanaians have against a private corporation's monopolistic hold on core telecommunication infrastructure?

Consumers themselves and consumer protection agencies work in concert to make protection possible. The National Communications Authority

(NCA) has the core responsibility to promote and ensure fair competition in the telecommunications industry and also to protect communications service providers from misuse of market power or anti-competitive and unfair practices by other service providers (NCA, 2015). The authority has provided space for consumers to make complaints and demand redress from service providers. While a consumer may sue a service provider over a breach of contract, an aggrieved consumer must first seek redress with the service provider, and if the matter is not resolved, report to the NCA as stipulated in the Electronic Communications Act 2008, Act 775 84 (1), thus making a court action a last option. Given that the average Ghanaian consumer's use of services and cost of those services are relatively small, unless complains are bundled up into a class action lawsuit, a consumer does not have the financial resource to go against a multinational conglomerate. There are hardly any class action lawsuits in Ghana.

As of 2015, there are nine telecommunication service providers in Ghana: MTN (Scancom), Gateway Communications, Mobile Choice, Teligent Wireless, Airtel Ghana, Tigo (Milicom), Vodafone Ghana, Globacom Ghana, and Expresso Telecom Group. Competition among them, while robust in branding and in call units size and bundling of services, are not reflected in price differences, which are infinitesimal. To maximize profit, they make minimal infrastructure upgrades, and Ghanaian users of cell phones are stuck with GSM 3G networks. With no new technologies to offer, thus giving a particular service provider a competitive advantage over others, in consonance with previous studies, the companies no longer compete on cost but on their ability to satisfy customers (Kotler & Keller, 2006). An area in which competition is constant, therefore, is in customer support and complaint resolution. Comparison of two service providers, Airtel and Vodafone, indicate customers are more satisfied with Airtel than Vodafone, even though Vodafone has an expanded nationwide infrastructure inherited from Ghana Telecom and more financial clout (Nimako, 2012; Ubink 2008).

Public monopolies do not fare any better in their relations with consumers as exemplified by Ghana Water Company and the Electric Company of Ghana. The Public Utilities Regulatory Commission (PURC) is an independent agency that calculates and sets electricity tariffs, educates customers about electricity services, as well as energy efficiency and conservation, and ensures the effectiveness of investments. It is constitutionally charged with duties to protect consumer interest and investor interest, control the cost of production of the service, and ensure the financial integrity of the public utility. Being a public independent agency, the seeming conflict in protecting both consumer and investor interests cannot be overemphasized. Erratic electric power supply, load shedding, and days of blackouts underscore the frustration consumers face, and no amount of complaints would yield better results if infrastructure fails. Since ECG is a public monopoly, consumers do not have any competing service providers to which to migrate. Good products and services attract customers and resultant profit for business, but Ghanaian captive customers have no options, and Public Utilities Regulatory Commission (PURC price controls and price hikes seem to be meaningless to customers if there are no services to use.

Business in Politics: Politicians, Investors, and Citizenry

Capitalism is not equal to democracy, although both coexist. While democracy is rooted in mechanisms within a system giving voice to people and that generates actions for the common good, capitalism is driven by profits, built on, and for profit only. When democratic processes do not put checks on capitalists' exploitative tendencies and mechanisms, untrammeled greed and oppression overwhelm democracy, leaving in their wake business and financial oligarchies and oppression. Within capitalist nations, citizens are also consumers of goods and services, and their purchasing power may act as a tool of control over businesses and corporations, small and large. Another tool is public opinion. Both businesses and politicians want to develop positive opinion in their favor and garner it for financial and political capital. Unpredictability of public opinion makes it a double-edged sword that can be deployed by a mass of people and translated into denial of support for politicians or loss of customers for businesses. Politicians and businesses thrive on masses of people and, therefore, often become allies.

Political campaigns and organizational activities require substantial funds that Ghanaian politicians do not have, so they are forced to raise them from a variety of sources. They may access mass small donations from supporters that trickle into their coffers and/or call upon larger donor funds from affluent businesspersons. Their affluence is built on profits made from their investments and businesses and, even if it is apparent, they want no returns for their donations; politicians so funded tend to lean toward and treat donors favorably. Profit from political party-owned businesses, while legal, when the party is in government may create a conflict of interest, if government contracts are awarded to the ruling party-owned businesses (van Biezen, 2003; Ninsin, 2006).

As Ghana gears up for general elections in 2016, questions are being raised about political party relations with businesses. An opposition party had a loan from a bank guaranteed by an investment banker, and is on the verge of defaulting (Ghanaweb, 2015). The ruling party also has to contend with a won civil lawsuit against a major donor and businessman who was paid millions of dollars in settlement with the help of the state attorney for financial engineering a stadium rehabilitation project (Myjoyonline, 2015). He, however, won a criminal case against him. The two cases highlight how financial support from businesspeople became a negative source of opinion, should an adverse issue arise from the funding process and funds, or the political party financier face accusations.

Conclusion

This chapter has examined business and government relations in Ghana. It argues that the healthy business and government relations have benefited both public and private sectors because they guarantee economic growth. If government sees to the welfare of Ghana's citizenry, business's goal is to grow profits for investors. There are instances in which government and business interests are divergent, as was exemplified in the relation Ghana government had with AVRL. To strike a good balance, both have to reach consensus and develop a working relationship. The ability to levy taxes and institute regulations and control mechanisms gives the government awesome power. Businesses, however, hold the economic growth of the country within their activities and are essential providers of employment.

Public and private monopolies may project stability, but inefficiencies that riddle their operations, as is the case with ECG, may be overcome through divesture and deregulation. Four independent electric power producers are now in Ghana. If one were privatizing ECG, would the government sell Akosombo Hydroelectric Dam and the grid managed by VRA, as it did with Ghana Telecom and VRA's national fiber optic backbone? Given limited capital in Ghana, public corporation and core infrastructure during divesture would be controlled by foreign entities and investors. In the face of a desire to maximize profits, even with expressed corporate social responsibility, the bottom line would override all decisions. The relation between government and business directly affects the populace as citizens and consumers, therefore, both have an obligation to sustain and expand economic growth.

References

AfricanLiberty.org Forum. (2008). *Selling Ghana Telecom: Crony Capitalism or Real Privatisation?* www.africanliberty.org/selling-ghana-telecom-crony-capitalism-or-real-privatisation/. Accessed October 9, 2016.

AngloGold Ashanti. (2004). *Completion of Merger of Anglogold Limited/Ashanti Goldfields.* News Release. Johannesburg. www.marketwired.com/press-release/ anglogold ashanti publishes annual report for 2004 nyse au 658484.htm Accessed October 7, 2016.

Biezen, I. V. (2003). Financing Political Parties and Election Campaign—Guidelines: Making Democratic Institutions Work. Brussel: Council of Europe Publishing.

The Chronicle. (2014). *State of the Nation Address by H.E. John Dramani Mahama.* http://thechronicle.com.gh/2014-state-of-the-nation-address-by-h-e-john-dramani-mahama-3/. Accessed October 1, 2016.

Daily Independent. (2013). *Perez Takes Over at WAGPCo.* http://dailyindependent-nig.com/2013/11/12/perez-takes-over-at-wagpco/. Accessed October 8, 2016.

Edjekumhene, A. and Hammond, B. (2003). Power Sector Reform in Ghana in the 1990's: The Untold Story of a Divided Country Versus a Divided Bank. Kumasi, Ghana: KITE Publication.

Electric Company of Ghana Limited (ECG). (2015). *Current Load Shedding Guide.* www.ecgonline.info/index.php/news/latest-news/238-current-load-shedding-guide. Accessed October 1, 2016.

Ghanaweb. (2015). *NPP Not Liable for Prudential Bank Loan – Ken Ofori Atta*. www.ghana-news.adomonline.com/politics/2015/may-28th/npp-not-liable-for-prudential-bank-loan-ken-ofori-atta.php. Accessed October 1, 2016.

GlobalEdge. (2016). *Ghana*. globalEdge.msu.edu and Export.Gov. Accessed February 10, 2016.

Grusky, S. (2001). Privatization Tidal Wave: IMF/World Bank Water Policies and the Price Paid by the Poor. *Multinational Monitor, 22*(9), 14–19.

Kotler, P. and Keller, K. (2006). *Marketing Management*. 12th Edition. Upper Saddle River, NJ.: Prentice Hall Press

Lehne, R. (2013). Government and Business: American Political Economy in Comparative Perspective. Washington, DC: Congressional Quarterly Press.

Modern Ghana. (2007). *Oil—Huge Field Discovered at Cape Three Points*. www.modernghana.com/news/137981/1/oil-huge-field-discovered-at-cape-three-points.html. Accessed October 1, 2016.

Myjoyonline. (2012). *Ghana Earns $903m From Oil*. http://business.myjoyonline.com/pages/news/201207/89789.php. Accessed October 1, 2016.

Myjoyonline. (2015). *Woyome Freed in 51m Judgement Debt Scandal*. www.myjoyonline.com/news/2015/March-12th/live-update-woyome-verdict.php. Accessed October 7, 2016.

National Communications Authority (NCA). (2015). *What We Do*. www.nca.org.gh/19/142/What-We-Do.html. Accessed October 9, 2016.

Nimako, S. G. (2012). Customer Dissatisfaction and Complaining Responses Towards Mobile Telephony Services. *The African Journal of Information Systems, 4*(3), 84–99.

Ninsin, K. A. (2006). *Political Parties and Political Participation in Ghana*. KonradAdenuer Stiftung. www.kas.de/ghana. Accessed October 9, 2016.

Shang-Quartey, L. (2014). *Post Privatisation Challenges of Public Water in Ghana*. The Transnational Institute (TNI). www.tni.org/en/article/post-privatisation-challenges-public-water-ghana#1.

Toulmin, C., Brown, D. and Crook, R. (2004). Project Memorandum: Institutional Reform and Development: Strengthening Customary Land Administration. Ghana Land Administration Project. Accra.

Ubink, J. M. (2008). Negotiated or Negated? The Rhetoric and Reality of Customary Tenure in an Ashanti Village in Ghana. *Africa: Journal of the International African Institute, 78*(2), 264–287.

Word Bank Group. (2016). *Burkina Faso*. www.worldbank.org/en/country/burkinafaso. Accessed October 11, 2016.

Case Study

The Dynamics of Executive Leadership

For 10 years the production division at Johnson and Jombo National Company was under the leadership of Dr. Afolabi. As the vice-president of the division, Dr. Afolabi was autocratic (by almost anybody's definition), but he had the personal qualities necessary to command respect and loyalty. He made and enforced all rules, regulations, and policies (which were not the domain of the chief executive officer or Board of Trustees) in almost infinite detail. For example, he assigned secretaries and office space and decided who had to manage all the lines of production in the company. Dr. Afolabi was always willing to accept complete responsibility not only for his actions but for those of his subordinates, as long as their actions were within the well-defined limits of the company's policies. Consequently, the employees as a group were always careful to adhere strictly to his wishes. He can best be described as a paternalistic autocrat.

Dr. Afolabi's methods left little to the individual staff members' imagination about experimentation, and freedom in doing their job according to the standard operating procedures. He also micromanaged employees' handling of customers as well as vendors relations. Despite Dr. Afolabi's production oriented leadership style, he often provided an atmosphere in which all staff and vendors knew exactly what to expect. As a result of Dr. Afolabi's leadership philosophy, employees' motivational acumen seemed generally high, and staff turnover was modest during his tenure. The following statement by one of the senior staff in his division adequately summarizes the frequently expressed sentiments of the employees and may reveal some indication of their performance:

"I've been working in the production division for 14 years under three different vice-presidents. There were times when I wanted to strangle the old vice-president, but we always knew what he was talking about."

Attitudes could generally be termed passive, subservient, respectful, dependent, and ambivalent, as some employees comments suggested. A senior production officer called Mr. Oguntoye asked 10 of his line staff if they thought Dr. Afolabi's manner impaired their production abilities. Only four believed that the quality of their production would have been better if a less restrictive work environment was available in the company. Practically all professional contacts between administration and staff originated at the top. Individually, employees rarely sought help from Dr. Afolabi, except when a special problem arose that needed his intervention. Vice-president Afolabi always remained somewhat aloof on the job, but frequently visited socially at the homes of staff members. Dr. Afolabi was also extraordinarily adept at handling his employees who did not do their jobs properly. The senior vice-president (Dr. Susan Drake) and the president (Dr. Joseph Deshon) appreciated his organizational skills, high production achievement of production division, and the fact that all the employees and their respective union never caused any problems that could stop production. Dr. Afolabi frequently had lunched with senior administrators in his division, and occasionally invited a junior staff member to come along. The president and the trustees were on the division's mailing list to receive a quarterly newsletter and advance notice of important speakers. It was not easy to get a good picture of how well the company's production division was performing to achieve the corporate goals. On one hand, while some products produced were of high quality, there were other products that the quality control inspectors have destroyed due to defective reasons. On the other hand, production achievement, measured in terms of the percentage of products manufactured on a timely bases for shipment to dealers, was always on target. The production division budget was ample and had increased more rapidly than any other division in the company.

Vice-president Afolabi's sudden death two weeks before Christmas created a turmoil for the busy production season. He was replaced at the beginning of the New Year by Dr. Daniel Aluko. The new production division Vice-president Dr. Aluko had several years' experience as a senior staff and interim assistant vice-president of production at a sister company called Jones and Sarah Breweries in a neighboring city. The search committee had selected him from a set of 50 applicants. Most senior staff and junior employees saw Dr. Aluko for the first time at the first division meeting of the New Year.

At that meeting, Dr. Aluko clearly voiced a strong belief in the principles of shared governance and a democratic administration. He contended that the division could best achieve the goal of higher productivity through a cooperative effort of senior and junior employees. He then pointed out several administrative, scheduling, and other matters normally decided by the former vice-president Afolabi. It was strange to the staff that Dr. Aluko was encouraging more inclusive and greater participation in the decision-making role for all employees of the division.

Specifically, Dr. Aluko suggested that the employees in the division should not be engulfed with the complexities and paradoxes of environmentalism advocacies. He contended that employees in the division and company as a whole are responsible to the communities in which they live and work, as well as to the world community. Staff in the division must be good citizens, support good works and charities, as well as bear their fair share of taxes. Everyone in the division must encourage civic improvements and better health and education. All staff must maintain in good order, the property they are privileged to use, as well as protect the environment and natural resources. He suggested that research must be carried on, innovative programs developed, and mistakes paid for. New equipment must be purchased, new facilities provided, and new products launched. On the other hand, reserves must be created to provide for adverse times. As a result if all employees in the production division operating according to these principles, the stockholders of the company should be able to realize a fair return of profit. He offered to help with administrative arrangements for these activities if the staff needed help.

Dr. Aluko also said that not only did he feel that staff administrative cooperation was desirable but he wanted to make genuine shared participation in his administration a reality. Dr. Aluko requested that all employees should cooperate to achieve that end. In concluding the meeting, he asked the employees to give these matters some thought before the next meeting, when the whole group could discuss them.

Two weeks later, at that next staff meeting, Dr. Aluko asked for discussion of the issues previously mentioned, but no discussion was forthcoming. He attempted to evoke discussion by mentioning several alternatives, but still no discussion followed. Dr. Aluko then asked for a vote on each proposal. The senior staff in the division voted almost unanimously to reject each proposal, and several colleagues openly expressed the belief that Dr. Aluko should handle these problems himself, the way late Dr. Afolabi did. After the meeting adjourned, many employees regrouped informally, minus Dr. Aluko, in the café lounge. Their comments varied and were pessimistic on the issues proposed. Yet, one recurrent theme was a feeling that the topics on which Dr. Aluko wanted junior staff cooperation were not matters for them. They amounted to a burden, and as a result the vice-president should bear the responsibilities the way his predecessor had done. He should not try to impose his duties on the staff. Morale was low due to Dr. Aluko's invitation for shared governance. One senior administrator said: "When they pay me a vice-president's salary and give me the corner office and a staff car, I'll do a vice-president's work and not before."

The senior vice-president (Dr. Drake) became concerned about these shared governance problems and invited Dr. Aluko over for a "chat." A few of the staff had gone so far as to complain to some Board of Trustee members. This was not helping the division's budget request that was pending in the company's board. More importantly, Dr. Drake lamented that she and the president (Dr. Deshon) "no longer know what's going on in the production division" and were concerned that perhaps Dr. Aluko was not up to the job of vice-president. Dr. Aluko pondered why the request for shared governance, competent management, and ethical behavior is wrong.

Assignment

Critically analyze the leadership problems in the production division and make recommendations to the president of Johnson and Jombo National Company. Do you think Dr. Aluko was given the support that he needed to do his job effectively by Dr. Deshon and Dr. Drake? Can the principles of authoritarian leadership style be better than those of shared governance? What was wrong with the hiring process of Dr. Aluko?

7 Business and Government Relations in Somalia

Yusuf Ahmed Nur

Introduction

The Somali political and economic systems have been in flux for a long time. Since the collapse of Siad Barre's regime in 1991, one feeble and ineffectual transitional government after another has succeeded in the Somali Republic. On September 10, 2012, the Somali people finally put together a new parliament, which chose a new president. The new dispensation will also remove the "transitional" designation from the government, parliament, and other federal institutions, thus giving them more permanency, a crucial prerequisite for finding a lasting solution to the political chaos that had enveloped the country for more than two decades. The new Somali administration has been in power for more than three years now. Unfortunately, successes have been few and far apart. Whoever takes over the helm of the country in the 2016 presidential election will still be facing daunting challenges, the most important of which will be the task of economic development.

Despite the anarchy and destruction that ensued soon after Siad Barre—the Somali military dictator who had ruled the country since 1969—was ousted in a popular revolt in 1991, and despite the lawlessness and insecurity that became part of the landscape in the Somali Republic, businesses have boomed and many services that were hard to obtain during Barre's 21-year dictatorial near-monopoly of the public and private sectors have become readily available to those who can afford them (Mayoux, 2001). The highly risky business environment has not deterred enterprising domestic and foreign firms from investing in the Somali Republic. The civil war transformed Somalis from a people dependent on an all-encompassing and pervasive government to entrepreneurs imbued with ingenuity, initiative, and acute business savoir-faire. If resourcefulness, opportunity recognition exploitation, innovation, and creativity are counted among the essential characteristics of entrepreneurship (Rangan et al., 2007), Somali businesses of the civil war era have fully embodied them. In some respects, the absence of a central government has turned out to be a blessing in disguise (Leeson, 2007). It has removed all state imposed obstacles and hindrances, allowing the entrepreneurial spirit of the Somali people to flourish.

Kirchoff (1991) presents a lot of evidence on private sector entrepreneurship's significant contributions to growth and development. Somali entrepreneurial successes are not limited to the wholesale, retail, and import-export sectors traditional for the nation. Private clinics, hospitals, health care centers, and pharmacies have sprung up. Private schools at all levels have been established and staffed—some with outside help and others with local initiative and resources. There are several new universities/institutes in the capital city alone that started to offer degrees in Arabic, Islamic law, business administration, computer science, as well as medicine and engineering (Little, 2003). Granted, these educational institutions suffer from a dearth of qualified instructors and severe scarcity of other resources, but they provide strong evidence of the successful provision of some public goods with little involvement of the Somali government.

In contrast, the public sector has suffered tremendously since 1991. Leeson (2007), as well as Powell et al. (2008), demonstrate that growth in the private sector has not translated into some major categories of public goods. No public building, utility, or infrastructure has escaped the destruction of the civil war and the underinvestment that was the result of a long period of statelessness. In order to succeed, the government will have to replace the old mentalities in public sector management with new thinking that may take a page from the successes of the private sector in order to bridge the gap between statelessness and having a working government that provides public goods and services to its citizenship. In this study, we argue that a business-government partnership between the government and the burgeoning entrepreneurial sector has the potential for improving the infrastructure investment and economic development in the Somali Republic.

The remainder of the chapter consists of four sections. It starts with reviewing the features of the entrepreneurial experiment in the stateless environment in the Somali Republic. This will be followed by a section reviewing evidence supporting business provision of public goods. Then literature review of the literature on business-government partnerships (BGPs). The chapter will conclude with the exposition of the benefits BGPs could have for sustainable economic development in the Somali Republic.

This chapter examines the role of the private sector in the economic development of Somalia. It argues that for-profit businesses have a unique role to play in the reconstruction of the Somalia economy. This chapter introduces a new perspective on the role of business in a stateless environment. Public goods have suffered in the anarchic environment that the civil war engendered in the Somali Republic. It proposes that economic development and infrastructure investment in the Somali Republic may take advantage of the innovative and successful business models that Somali businesses have created. The chapter will first review the historical background of the economic and political change in the Somali Republic, and focus on the role of business-government partnerships in economic development and infrastructure investment. Research studies, both conceptual and empirical, on business provision of public goods and services in Somalia will be discussed. Statelessness in the Somali Republic has created an environment in which new business models could flourish with minimal government interference, and minimal competition from international firms. Statelessness has effectively removed government institutions that had long hindered Somalia entrepreneurship. The private sector in the Somali Republic swiftly adjusted to statelessness and created new operational models that can be tapped into in order to help the country rebuild its economy and infrastructure. Utilizing the experience and operating models of private enterprises in the provision of public goods and services is an alternative way forward for a successful Somalia economic development.

Entrepreneurship in a Stateless Environment

There is an abundance of literature on the crucial roles governments play in fostering entrepreneurship (see AAARI, 2005). In the entrepreneurship literature, however, the existence of governments is typically taken for granted. In the existent literature there is little discussion of entrepreneurship in an environment where is no government or state institutions. That is why the Somali situation characterized by the absence of government institutions presents such an intriguing case (Little, 2003). Hisrich et al. (2008) defines entrepreneurship as a process of creating something new of value, both for profit and non-profit, which requires the expenditure of the necessary time and effort while assuming the risks. This definition of entrepreneurship perfectly describes the entrepreneurial experiment that has been going on in the Somali Republic for the past two decades. The necessities created by the absence of government have liberated the entrepreneurial talents of the Somali people.

The current entrepreneurial climate in the Somali Republic has come about after the collapse of the Siad Barre's dictatorial regime that stifled new business formation with cumbersome regulations and government fiat. The regime's collapse followed the popular armed uprising of 1991, which in turn led to the destruction of state institutions during "the four-month war" when the two faction leaders whose forces deposed Siad Barre's regime, General Aidid and Ali Mahdi, could not agree to share power. This crisis culminated in a civil war fought on the streets of Mogadishu. It is not by accident that the most devastated parts of the city were state buildings, such as government offices, schools, universities, and factories. Somalis had no state or state institutions of their own before the British, French, and Italian forces gradually colonized all Somali territories in the nineteenth century. Perhaps because of the nomadic nature of most Somalis, neither colonial state institutions nor those created after the 1960 independence of Somalia were deeply rooted in the psyche of the Somali people. In fact, in the Somali mind there is no distinction between state and government. To the average Somalia, Siad Barre and his government *were* the state. Therefore, during the anarchy of the "four-month war" in Mogadishu, state buildings and properties were not only thoroughly looted but destroyed as well. The jagged remains of these buildings today testify to the destructive anger against state institutions unleashed by the fall of the Siad Barre regime.

Since then, there have been multiple attempts at reestablishing state institutions, but with minimal success. The lack of strong state institutions, however, has not destroyed the Somalia economy. On the contrary, the Somalia economy has become more robust since 1991 (Leeson, 2007). The existent literature provides much empirical and anecdotal evidence that the private sector in the Somali Republic has helped the country improve its position since the collapse of the state in 1991, with respect to a number of economic and social indicators (Powell et al., 2008; Webersik, 2006; Menkhaus, 2003). Mubarak (1997) shows that the Somali central government, similar to the Soviet system it had been emulating since the military coup of 1969, presided over a bloated centrally planned economic system that failed to provide many of the goods and services which the government monopolized. Throughout Siad Barre's 21-year dictatorship, there had been extensive capital controls that led to the flourishing of black market, as the informal economy sprung up to provide the goods and services not otherwise available. As Leeson (2007) amply demonstrates, despite statelessness (or perhaps because of it), 13 out of 18 economic development indicators for the Somali Republic improved for 2000–2005, as compared with the same indicators for 1985–1990.

Somali entrepreneurship was born out of necessity. One of the early entrepreneurial business enterprises could be traced to the second half of the 1980s before removal of the Siad Barre regime. Those enterprises were formed to facilitate remittances from the Somali diaspora to the families and relatives they had left behind, the labor seeking emigrations from the Somali Republic to Saudi Arabia and Gulf countries in response to the petro-dollar-fueled economic boom. These enterprises called *hawala* (Arabic for exchange or transfer) became veritable financial institutions based not on government oversight and guarantees but on trust. Since then Somali *hawala* have undergone tremendous growth. At present they hold offices in many of the major cities around the world. Any person who wishes to send money to the Somali Republic may walk into a *hawala* office, and after paying the 4–5% fee, can complete the remittance within minutes (Africa Research Bulletin, 2008).

It was not long before the entrepreneurial enterprises expanded into other areas of business. One example is in the telecommunications sector. There was need for Somalia families to communicate with their members widely dispersed throughout the world. Thus three private wireless telecom firms appeared, and at present Mogadishu boasts one of the cheapest wireless telecom services in the world (Davis, 2007; Feldman, 2007). Powell et al. (2008) discuss the dramatic improvement in the access to main phone lines since Somalia became stateless, moving from 29th to 8th among the African countries included in their survey. Their study points out that while in many African countries state monopolies and licensing restrictions may raise prices and hinder the growth in telecommunication services, in Somalia it takes just three days for a land-line to be installed and prices for telecom services are generally low. Statelessness has played a major role in the telecom sector growth as the absence of regulation has led to intense competition in the Somali telecom market that resulted in good access to services (Powell et al., 2008).

Entrepreneurial success in the Somali Republic is evident in the economic and political environment in other industries as well. The most successful enterprises are in fact benefiting from the highly volatile and insecure political situation. Since there are no government regulations, there are no licensing requirements and few restrictions on imports or exports. Import and export businesses managed to develop despite the multi-year conflict-induced closure of the main sea port and airport of Mogadishu. Entrepreneurs prospected for and found a number of alternative shipping points along the Indian Ocean, the Somali Sea, and the Gulf of Aden.

While economic statistics are difficult to obtain for many aspects of the Somalia economy (World Bank, 2012), multiple measures collected by the World Bank and the UNDP (2012) demonstrate improvement in the availability of goods and services provided by the private. Table 7.1 compares the figures for such goods and services provided by the private sector with the indicators of the public sector performance in Somalia, as well as the other IGAD nations. Note that the indicators for privately furnished goods for the Somali Republic are comparable to or better than those for some of the IGAD nations, despite the fact that many of these countries have enjoyed more political stability than the Somali Republic for the last two decades. In contrast, the Somali Republic fares worst in all indicators for publicly provided goods. The Human Development Index (HDI) for the Somali Republic remains the lowest among its neighbors.

The differences in the performance of the private and the public sector are highlighted by a look at the change in the development indicators in the periods before the collapse of the Somali government in 1985–1990 and after statelessness in 2000–2005. In particular, Leeson (2007) notes large increases in the access to telephone lines and the internet, as well as the numbers of radios, TVs, and mobile phones. Table 7.2 presents a comparison of the available data for the neighboring countries of Kenya and Somalia. The contrast is particularly stark between the extraordinary growth of telecommunications provided by the private sector in Somalia, with an increase in telephone lines of 1,150%, and the public goods measured by adult literacy and access to improved water supply that are stagnant or in decline. In the same time period, the measures of literacy and water accessibility in Kenya improved, while growth in telecommunications was far behind the one observed in Somalia.

Table 7.1 Development indicators for the IGAD countries

	Private goods			Public goods			
	Internet users/ 100[1]	Telephone main/ 1000[2]	Mobile phones/ 1000[3]	Infant mortality (per 1000)[4]	Life expectancy[5]	HDI[6]	HDI[7]
Kenya	28.0	17.2	501.6	048	57	0.470	0.509
Uganda	13.0	05.4	138.6	058	54	0.422	0.446
Djibouti	07.0	13.6	090.7	072	58	0.402	0.430
Ethiopia	01.1	11.5	015.8	052	59	0.328	0.363
Somalia	01.3	11.0	065.8	108	51	0.285	–
Eritrea	06.2	08.3	014.3	046	61	–	0.349
Sudan	10.2(*)	08.8	189.5	057	61	–	0.408

[1]2011 figures (http://data.worldbank.org/indicator/IT.NET.USER.P2)
[2]2007 figures (www.nationmaster.com/graph/med_tel_mai_lin_in_use_percap-main-lines-use-per-capita)
[3]2007 figures (www.nationmaster.com/graph/med_tel_mob_cel_percap-telephones-mobile-cellular-per-capita)
[4]2011 figures (http://data.worldbank.org/indicator/SP.DYN.IMRT.IN)
[5]2011 figures (http://data.worldbank.org/indicator/SP.DYN.LE00.IN)
[6]www.undp.org/content/undp/en/home/librarypage/hdr/Somalia-human-development-report-2012.html

Table 7.2 Percentage change in development indicators in Somalia and Kenya from 1990 to 2005

	Kenya	Somali
Life expectancy (years)	–15.6	+5.4
Adult literacy (%)	+3.7	–20
Population with access to improved water (%)	+35.6	0
Telephone mainlines (per 1000)	+28.6	+1150

Source: Leeson (2007)

Private Market Failure and the Rule of Government

In spite of the significant successes of entrepreneurship and private markets in the stateless environment of the Somali Republic, economic theory predicts that private markets will fail to achieve efficiency or robust growth in regards to several areas of the provision of goods and services in an economy. One of the main requirements for a fully functioning market-based economic system is the need for property rights to be protected. This ensures that the rewards earned by profit-seeking individuals who create successful businesses in a market system will be protected, affirming the incentive for businesses to innovate and provide goods and services for their potential clients. The new entrepreneurs have been able to reap the rewards of lax business regulations due to the existence of property rights that are protected through trust and social contracts inherent in the Somali social order. As these businesses continue to move farther and farther outside of their trusted circle of individuals, it will become very difficult to rely on social contracts to protect their business interests, creating a role for the new Somali government to support the burgeoning business sector.

In economic theory, public goods have the property of being non-excludable. When the users of a good or service cannot be excluded from their consumption, the private organizations providing such goods or services will face a free-rider problem leading to a market failure. One solution to the free-rider problem is government provision of public goods. This option, however, has not been available in the Somali Republic, due to its statelessness.

Public goods in the Somali Republic have been underfunded in the stateless environment. Such public goods as roads, soil, and water for irrigation, drinking water, and sanitation have declined and will have to be the primary areas of concern for the new Somali government. Not only have these goods been grossly under-provided in the current economic environment, but their under-provision may considerably affect the growth of the private sector, as households must spend a considerable amount of their time and resources on providing transportation, nutrition, and health. When a government ensures that these concerns are addressed, households can shift their resources into other productive activities that can create value in the economy.

Other sectors that are traditionally assisted by governments such as education and medical care have not had government support in Somalia for the past two decades. Not only are these valuable services that can be provided to the public, but economic issues such as economies of scale and information asymmetries lead to their under-provision, especially in less-populated rural areas of the country. Basic health care concerns such as control of malaria, TB, childhood diseases, childbirth, and nutrition have not been addressed, as evidenced by the statistics presented in the latest UNDP (2012) Human Development Report for the Somali Republic and discussed in Table 7.1. This report supports the need for a more pervasive government presence in the provision of the public goods mentioned previously. Although the private sector Somali economy has improved since 1991, while many other African countries have been stagnant or declining, the Somali Republic is still considered a low human development country (World Bank, 2012; UNDP 2012).

One experience that the Somalis learned from their long and costly civil war is that they can accomplish a lot without a government. The entrepreneurial spirit of the Somalis has flourished not only in Somalia proper but also in the neighboring countries where there are large populations of Somali inhabitants. The Somali economic performance has been impressive considering the stateless environment that it has blossomed from, but the Somali performance in human development has lagged behind. Statelessness has protected the private sector from stifling regulation but has also precluded the public sector from access to funding and development policy. Studies suggest that an acceleration of economic and human development may be achieved through small incremental policy changes, which in turn may lead to long-term institutional reforms (Glaeser et al., 2004; Hausmann et al., 2004). A major challenge for the new Somali government is to strike a balance between the two extremes: to avoid stifling the private sector, and to provide guidance in the development of the public sector. A policy that helps achieve both goals is establishing business-government partnerships.

Business and Government Partnership

As the Somali government faces a variety of political and economic challenges, business-government partnerships provide an innovative way to bridge the gap between the present and future states of public good provision. In the early 1990s, entrepreneurial activities in the Somali Republic were still rudimentary. Sources of financing were mostly based on diaspora remittances and venture capital from overseas Somalis. There were no ties between the new entrepreneurial enterprises and the public sector. Eventually, private enterprises started delivering the essential services, which were previously exclusively provided by the state. Until the collapse of Siad Barre's regime in 1991, both education and health care were exclusively in the public sector. Within a few years after the collapse of the Barre regime, neighborhoods started organizing private primary schools, soon to be followed by secondary schools, and then higher education institutions. Exact statistics are difficult to obtain, but in the Mogadishu environs, private institutions have provided over a third of the educational needs (for a detailed treatment of the education situation in the Somali Republic, see Cassanelli & Abdikadir, 2007).

There is extensive literature that explores business-government partnerships (BGPs). This literature shows that BGPs have been employed in the provision of such public goods as transportation, energy, water and sewage, telecommunications, health, and education. The literature offers a number of BGP definitions. For instance, De Bettignies and Ross (2004) follow the definition of the British Columbia (Canada) Ministry of Finance (2002): "BGPs are contractual arrangements between government and a private party for the provision of assets and the delivery of services that have been traditionally provided by the public sector." Akintoye (2009) considers a

BGP to be "a contractual agreement of shared ownership between a public agency and a private company, whereby, as partners, they pool resources together and share risks and rewards, to create efficiency in the production and provision of public or private goods."

Besley and Ghatak (2001) note that BGPs run the gamut from the state contracting out the completion of projects while maintaining ownership, to complex arrangements and outright privatization. The form any individual BGP takes depends on the compatibility of goals between the private and public participants, the coordination of decisions and the commitment of resources (Schaeffer & Loveridge, 2002). De Bettignies and Ross (2004) discuss the economics of BGPs, citing instances of BGPs used in Canada such as airports, schools, incineration facilities, water and wastewater treatment, medical facilities, recreation facilities, property management, and utilities. The authors point out, however, that independent evaluation of these BGPs successes and failures are rare. In all the examples cited, the government limits itself to regulating the BGPs, leaving the financing and actual provision of services to the private partner.

The very terminology of "business-government partnership" suggests a collaboration between the public and private entities aimed at delivering increased efficiency (e.g., Pollock et al., 2001; Shaw, 2004), utilizing the private sector to absorb and manage project risks (Gaffney et al., 1999; Shaoul, 2003), and offer new forms of accountability (Mayo & Moore, 2001). Several conditions have been proposed for achieving success in BGPs, one of which is the establishment of horizontal relationships between the parties and utilizing consensual decision making (see Lowndes & Skelcher, 1998; Kooiman, 2003; Wettenhall, 2004, 2005).

In discussing the role of BGPs in the optimal procurement of public services, Crocker and Masten (1996) as well as De Bettignies and Ross (2004) present a model of the three potential choices for providing public goods. One key determinant of the form of public good delivery is the presence of relationship-specific assets or specialized investments. Such investments typically have little use outside of the relationship between the parties, and may not be easily converted to alternative uses. Examples of relationship-specific investments include infrastructure such as roads or bridges that cannot be relocated. Presence of relationship-specific assets leads to increased transaction costs, as the compensation for such investments becomes difficult to determine in the absence of a true market price. In the case of a good or service that does not require any relationship-specific assets, private enterprises may reap the gains of specialization and reach higher levels of efficiency in providing the good or service in question. This is the reason why private enterprises may efficiently participate in delivering food for public programs such as food stamps using the spot market environment of grocery stores, but do not build specific infrastructure such as roads, bridges, or water mains without complex contract. If a contract cannot be written, the government may have no other option but to deliver the good or service

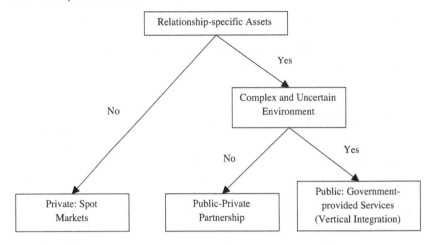

Figure 7.1 Optimal provision of public services
Source: Designed by the author, 2015

through vertical integration. Figure 7.1 summarizes the model of optimal public good procurement.

BGPs provide an efficient alternative to government provision of public goods as they allow the private organizations to reach gains of specialization while at the same time avoid skimping on specialized investments when the parameters of the relationship are specified in a long-term contract. In the 1990s, BGPs became popular in the developed world, where the public sector was undergoing budget cuts in the face of government budget deficits. BGPs became a viable alternative to government issued bonds as a funding source for development projects. The existent literature points out those BGPs are not as prevalent in the developing world as they are in the developed world. This is an interesting finding since governments in the developing world do not have the monetary resources to fund the provision of public goods. According to Akintoye (2009), this lag in BGP adoption is due to the high transaction cost for BGPs arising from the lack of efficient and transparent policies, mechanisms, and institutions. However, the potential for BGPs in developing economies is great, as their governments lack the resources to undertake the infrastructure projects necessary for development. BGPs provide a viable alternative in financing economic development.

Non-state providers of public goods in Somalia are as old the state itself if not older. Historically the most important and popular non-state providers of services were the Qur'anic schools. These have been around since the advent of Islam in Somalia in the 7th century CE. As Great Britain, France, and Italy started colonizing the Horn of Africa in mid-19th century, missionaries followed them establishing church run schools and clinics. However, the non-state providers of services that have proliferated in Somalia after the advent of the civil war are quite different from those historical ones. Their numbers, the scope, the scale, and types of services they provide have tremendously expanded. This phenomenon is worldwide. One of the major causes is attributed to market failure (Kushner & MacLean, 2015). But in Somalia this mainly came about because of the utter collapse of virtually all state institutions close to the beginning of the civil war.

In the case of the Somali Republic, the state has not been in a position to provide infrastructure or other public goods for more than two decades. Furthermore, the state has not been in a position to issue bonds or raise domestic funding for infrastructure development. This is in stark contrast to the private sector. Some private enterprises have even developed reputations in issuing highly profitable shares. Reputation and access to financing make such enterprises important potential partners for the state in any BGP undertaking.

The private sector also gained valuable popular goodwill during the 2012 severe draught that decimated Somalia. For the first time in the history of Somalia, the private sector rose to the occasion. Without waiting for government initiative or international aid to arrive, Somali businesses swiftly organized and coordinated relief effort for the stricken regions of Somalia. This was the main reason that the Somali Republic recovered from the devastating effects much faster than any other time in the draught strewn history of the country.

The World Bank maintains a database of all public projects with private participation—The World Bank Private Participation in Infrastructure Database. The database tracks four areas of investment: (1) energy generation; (2) telecommunications; (3) transportation; and (4) water, including sewage. Akintoye (2009) demonstrates that sub-Saharan Africa is among the regions of the world where BGPs in the listed four areas are least employed. Latin America and the Caribbean, and East Asia and Pacific lead the way, as BGPs are more prevalent there than they are in Europe and Central Asia. Akintoye (2009) concludes that with the proper business regulatory environment, developing countries could take advantage of BGPs in reducing the risks and costs of infrastructure development and attracting infrastructure project investments that could provide efficient and high quality services.

There are a number of problems that are noteworthy with respect to BGPs. The first major problem that the literature cites is accountability. This is doubly so in Somalia, since that state institutions are corrupt through and through. But since private enterprises have a better reputation in this regard, it may be best if the state just got out of the way. The best that the Somalia state can do is to ensure transparency and public participation in how public-private partnership (PPP) contracts are awarded. The second problem arises when circumstances change, necessitating demand for renegotiation of the contract on the part of the private partner; this could prove costly for the public. Third, the state may not be in a position to provide the necessary supervision of the private partner, which could lead to declines in the quality of the services provided (De Bettignies & Ross, 2004). One possible remedy lies in the ex ante establishment of a rigorous and comprehensive bidding process and contractual safeguards. Four, non-state provision of public goods may not bode well for state building. It exacerbates the already weak legitimacy of the state and weakens any loyalty that the citizen may have for it. There is evidence of this happening in other African countries (Bleck, 2013). There are also anecdotal indications that citizens are more likely to be critical of the state and thus may seek fundamental reforms. That kind of sentiment cannot be bad for the long term viability of state institutions. Five, it will not be easy for the Somalia state to develop its own capacities in funding and building infrastructure in the future. However, it is clear from the current situation of the Somali state that it will take decades before it is strong and stable enough to develop such capacities.

The advantages of BGPs to the Somali Republic should be weighed against the potential problems that may arise from their implementation. As pointed out by De Bettignies and Ross (2004), there are many advantages that could accrue to countries that implement BGPs as an integral part of their infrastructure development. Some of these advantages are quite relevant in the Somalia situation. In particular, the private sector is more skilled in management than the public sector. Furthermore, a competitive bidding process could be used to help lower costs and improve potential outcomes. Private partners may be better suited to manage economic risks associated with infrastructure projects than the new Somali government. Finally, private partners can take advantage of economies of scale and complementarities if they provide similar services in multiple jurisdictions.

Conclusion

This chapter has examined business and government relations in Somalia. It argues that the Somali Republic faces a shortfall in infrastructure investment and the provision of public goods and services. This dilemma continues to affect business and government relations in many areas. A way to overcome this issue is to implement BGPs in the areas of the economy where the public sector or the private sector acting independently will come up short. In the case of many traditional public goods, such as infrastructure, education, and health, the new Somali government does not yet have the full trust of the Somalia people or the financial wherewithal to invest the appropriate amount of money into development. Private enterprise comes up short in providing these goods, due to the risks inherent in markets with non-excludable goods and services. This creates a middle ground for the public and the private sectors to work together.

The private sector in the Somali Republic has developed quickly and has become efficient in providing such services as money transfers and banking, telecommunications, as well as certain public services such as education, electricity, and health care. One of the most important developments of the private sector is the crafting of locally effective business models, financing, transfer of knowledge, skills, and technology, as well as the recruitment and training of human resources. Such models and skills may contribute to development projects in a BGP setting.

Whereas the private sector has made major strides for the last 20 years, the public sector has lagged behind. If BGPs are structured to be managed similarly to Somali private enterprises, they will achieve efficiencies not available in the Somalia public sector before the civil war. An important factor in support of the BGPs is the problem with corruption endemic in the public sector management in the Somali Republic. BGPs may provide a disincentive for the graft, nepotism, and embezzlement that have traditionally plagued the public sector in the Somali Republic.

The economic and political situation in the Somali Republic faced by the new government is quite daunting, but at the same time it furnishes opportunities to try out new models of economic development. As prior state institutions have been laid to waste, the new government has an opportunity to start from scratch. BGPs allow for bottom-up economic development. Somalis have attained many entrepreneurial successes in the past two decades. The Somali experiment has been one of entrepreneurship without government oversight or regulation. However, facing the challenge of stagnant human development requires growth in public goods and infrastructure investment. BGPs have the potential to provide a viable way forward in the economic development of the Somali Republic.

References

AAARI. (2005). Global Entrepreneurship: Economic Development for Asia and the U.S. *CUNY Bulletin of Asia American/Asian Affairs*, 4(1), 23–52.

Africa Research Bulletin. (2008, March 16). Somalia: Hawala Remittances. *African Research Bulletin*, 17780–17781.

Akintoye, A. (2009). BGPs for Physical Infrastructure in Developing Countries. In A. Akintoye and M. Beck (Eds.), *Policy, Finance & Management for Business-government Partnerships*. London: Blackwell Publishing, 79–105.

Besley, T. and Ghatak, M. (2001). Government Versus Private Ownership of Public Goods. *The Quarterly Journal of Economics*, 116(4), 1343–1372.

Bleck, J. (2013). Do Francophone and Islamic Schooling Communities Participate Differently? Disaggregating Parent's Political Behavior in Mali. *Journal of Modern African Studies*, 51(3), 377–408.

British Columbia. (2002). *An Introduction to Business-government Partnerships*. Victoria, BC: Ministry of Finance and Corporate Relations.

Cassanelli, L. and Abdikadir, F. (2007). Somalia: Education in Transition. *Bildhaan: An International Journal of Somali Studies*, 7, 91–125.

Crocker, K. and Masten, S. (1996). Regulation and Administered Contracts Revisited: Lessons From Transaction-Cost Economics for Public Utility Regulation. *Journal of Regulatory Economics*, 9, 5–40.

Davis, P. (2007). *Entrepreneurs: Making Good in Somalia*. Available at: www.allafrica.com/stories/200704090038.html. Accessed August 1, 2012.

De Bettignies, J. E. and Ross, T. (2004). The Economics of Business-Government Partnerships. *Canadian Public Policy/Analyse de Politiques, 30*(2), 135–154.

Feldman, B. (2007). Somalia: Amidst the Rubble, a Vibrant Telecommunications Infrastructure. *Review of African Political Economy, 34*(113), 565–572.

Gaffney, D., Pollock, A., Price, D. and Shaoul, J. (1999). PFI in the NHS: Is There an Economic Case? *British Medical Journal, 319*, 116–119.

Glaeser, E., La Porta, R. and Lopez-de-Silanes, F., Shleifer, A. (2004). *Do Institutions Cause Growth?* NBER Working Paper No. 10568, National Bureau of Economic Research.

Hausmann, R., Pritchett, L. and Rodrik, D. (2004). *Growth Accelerations.* NBER Working Paper No. 10566, National Bureau of Economic Research.

Hisrich, R. D., Peters, M. and Shepherd, D. (2008). *Entrepreneurship.* New York: Irwin/ McGraw-Hill Press.

Kirchoff, B. B. (1991). Entrepreneurship's Contribution to Economies. *Entrepreneurship: Theory and Practice, 16*(2), 93–112.

Kooiman, J. (2003). *Governing as Governance.* London: Sage.

Kushner, D. C. and MacLean, L. M. (2015). Introduction to the Special Issue: The Politics of the Nonstate Provision of Public Goods in Africa. *Africa Today, 62*(1), vii–xvii.

Leeson, P. (2007). Better off Stateless: Somalia Before and After Government Collapse. *Journal of Comparative Economics, 35*, 689–710.

Little, P. (2003). *Somalia: Economy Without State.* Bloomington: Indiana University Press.

Lowndes, V. and Skelcher, C. (1998). The Dynamics of Multi-Organizational Partnership: An Analysis of Changing Modes of Governance. *Public Administration, 76*(2), 313–333.

Mayo, E. and Moore, H. (2001). *The Mutual State: How Local Communities Can Run Public Services.* London: New Economics Foundation.

Mayoux, S. (2001, November 15). Somalia: The Land of Opportunity. *BBC.* http://news.bbc.co.uk/1/hi/world/africa/1615258.stm. Accessed August 1, 2012.

Menkhaus, K. (2003). State Collapse in Somalia: Second Thoughts. *Review of African Political Economy, 30*(97), 405–422.

Mubarak, J. (1997). The 'Hidden Hand' Behind the Resilience of the Stateless Economy of Somalia. *World Development, 25*(12), 2027–2041.

Pollock, A., Shaoul, J., Rowland, D. and Player, S. (2001). *Public Services and the Private Sector.* London: Catalyst.

Powell, B., Ford, R. and Nowrasteh, A. (2008). Somalia After State Collapse: Chaos or Improvement? *Journal of Economic Behavior & Organization, 67*, 657–670.

Rangan, V., Quelch, J., Herrero, G. and Barton, B. (2007). *Business Solutions for the Global Poor: Creating Social and Economic Value.* San Francisco: John Wiley & Sons.

Schaeffer, P. and Loveridge, V. (2002). Toward an Understanding of Types of Business-government Cooperation. *Public Performance & Management Review, 26*(2), 169–189.

Shaoul, J. (2003). A Financial Analysis of the National Air Traffic Services BGP. *Public Money and Management, 23*(3), 185–194.

Shaw, E. (2004). What Matters Is What Works: The Third Way and the Private Finance Initiative. In S. Hale, W. Leggertt and L. Martell (Eds.), *The Third Way and Beyond.* Manchester: Manchester University Press.

UNDP. (2012). *Somalia Human Development Report 2012.* UNON, Publishing Services Section, Nairobi, Kenya.

Webersik, C. (2006). Mogadishu: Economy Without a State. *Third World Quarterly, 27*(8), 1463–1480.

Wettenhall, R. (2004). *Much Business-Government Partnership Mixing, But How Many Real Partnership?* Paper presented at the 10th International Conference on Business-government Partnerships: Axis of Progress, University of Algarve, Faro, 4–7 April.

Wettenhall, R. (2005). The Business-Government Interface: Surveying the History. In G. Hodge and C. Greve (Eds.), *The Challenge of Business-government Partnerships: Learning From International Experience*. Cheltenham: Edward Elgar, 22–43.

World Bank. (2012). *World Bank Data*. http://data.worldbank.org. Accessed October 10, 2012.

8 Business and Government Relations in Sudan

Muawya Hussien and Robert A. Dibie

Introduction

Sudan is an extremely poor country in North Africa that has experienced pro-tracted social conflict, civil war, and as of July 2011, the nation has lost three-quarters of its oil production due to the secession of South Sudan. The oil sector had driven much of Sudan's GDP growth since 1999 (United Nations, 2012; IMF, 2013). For nearly a decade, the economy boomed on the back of rising oil production, high oil prices, and significant inflows of foreign direct investment. Since the economic shock of South Sudan's secession, Sudan has struggled to stabilize its economy and make up for the loss of foreign exchange earnings. The interruption of oil production in South Sudan in 2012 for over a year and the consequent loss of oil transit fees further exacerbated the fragile state of Sudan's economy. Sudan is also subject to comprehensive US sanctions. Sudan is attempting to develop non-oil sources of revenues, such as gold mining, while carrying out an austerity program to reduce expenditures (Deng, 2007). The world's largest exporter of gum Arabic, Sudan produces 75–80% of the world's total output. Agriculture continues to employ 80% of the workforce (Sudan Central Bureau of Statistics, 2010). Sudan introduced a new currency, still called the Sudanese pound, following South Sudan's secession, but the value of the currency has fallen since its introduction. Khartoum formally devalued the cur-rency in June 2012, when it passed austerity measures that included gradually repealing fuel subsidies. Sudan also faces rising inflation, which reached 47% on an annual basis in November 2012, but subsided to 25% in 2013 (Sudaress, 2013; Elbeely, 2013). Ongoing conflicts in Southern Kordofan, Darfur, and the Blue Nile states; lack of basic infrastructure in large areas; and reliance by much of the population on subsistence agriculture keep close to half of the population at or below the poverty line (World Bank, 2015; Elbeely, 2013).

Despite the economic and political predicaments stated previously, Sudan is a country of extraordinary economic potential. It enjoys a strategic loca-tion at the confluence of the two Niles and has direct access to the Red Sea. The third-largest country in Africa, its land is rich with mineral resources, notably gold, silver, iron, zinc, copper, chrome, uranium, gypsum, mica, and other building materials, and benefits from favorable conditions for agriculture, including a varied climate, fertile soil, and water resources in the form of rains, rivers, and underground water. The country's historical attractions, natural parks, and seacoast are also assets for tourism development. Sudan attracted important amounts of foreign direct investment (FDI) after the mid-2000s. FDI inflows totaled less than $100 million per annum until 1998and then reached $2.6 billion in 2006 (UNCTAD, 2014a). Subsequently, they fluctuated but remained at a level generally surpassing $2.5 billion per year. Over the period 2006–2011, Sudan's inflows were surpassed only by Egypt in North Africa (and by Nigeria and South Africa on the whole African continent). As of 2011, Sudan's inward FDI stock stood at $24 billion, the fourth-highest in North Africa behind Egypt, Morocco, and Tunisia (and the sixth in Africa; UNCTAD, 2014a).

This chapter investigates the nature of business and government relations in Sudan. It presents an argument that the process of achieving sustainable development in Sudan is no longer a matter of choosing between the state and the market; instead, it is a matter of creating the appropriate mix of government and private sector actions to maximize welfare for the citizens of Sudan. Underpinning this position is the proposition that corporate social responsibility (CSR) is not just about the business-society relationship; rather, it is a way of rethinking the roles of companies in society that takes governance and sustainability as core values and that favors social co-responsibility among government, business, and civil society. It uses qualitative methods of data collection in Sudan. Secondary data was obtained through an in-depth desk review and content analysis of relevant published and unpublished studies, policy and programs documents, regulations and laws on Sudan. This chapter provides a checklist of what the Government of Sudan is already doing well, and how it can improve the regulatory framework for investment, trade, and productivity. Analysis of data reveals that the central challenges for the Government of Sudan remains the increase of its capacity to adjust so that it can better help its citizens take full advantage of the opportunities provided by technological innovation and a growing world economy. The chapter recommends that a more robust regulatory framework, supported by well-functioning institutions, should reduce the risks associated with unethical social responsibility of corporations in the country. The recommended robust framework could also help Sudan contribute to a more stable path for economic growth. In addition, appropriate domestic regulatory policies settings are more important than foreign pressure for business market access to realizing the benefits of sustainable development, consumer protection, and employees in the country.

Mixed Economy Framework

The relationship between government and business is neither laissez faire nor socialist, but rather a combination of both. This integration of both is called a mixed economy (Lehne, 2013; Ferrell et al., 2015). In other words, it is about creating an enabling environment with a strong regulatory framework to mobilize resources for development in any country (Ebert & Griffin, 2015). As a result, the changing roles of all stakeholders a country could create new opportunities for civil society-business-government on one hand and civil society on the other hand, to engage in a matter that could reshape each sector's role and redefine their mutual obligations (Ferrell et al., 2015).

Several scholars have focused on developed economies (Hubbard & Obrien, 2015; Lehne, 2013; Ferrell et al 2015). Such studies focused specifically on the relationship among business, civil society, and governmental sectors, and on the interdependence and interconnectedness of the three entities (Lussier & Sherman, 2009; Steiner & Steiner, 2006). While in Sudan, some studies have looked at corporate partnership and community development, as well as CSR and re-thinking the role of government and the possibility of corporate social development in the country (Dagdeviren, 2006; Sudaress, 2013; Elbeely, 2013), no known study has been able to integrate this tripartite relationship in the Sudanese context. As a result, one of the objectives of this chapter is to discuss the tripartite relationship between government, business, and society within the Sudanese context, with a view to ascertaining the state of affairs regarding their strategic roles. This analysis is relevant at this point in time because of the changing role of government and business on one hand, and that of society and citizens on the other hand.

The mixed economy concept argues that business and society have many nonmarket interactions, as there are social influences on business stemming from cultural and political forces in society (Lehne, 2013; Ferrell et al., 2015), while business also has an influence on the political life and culture of any society (Ebert & Griffin, 2015; Post et al., 1999). Many countries in the world use a variation of mixed economy policies. These policies allow a large degree of private business, while maintaining strict regulation of certain aspects of the economy through the government. As a result of these approaches the relationship between government and business can be argued to be either laissez faire or socialist, but rather a combination of both, essentially what is called a "mixed economy" (Hubbard & Obrien, 2015).

According to Ferrell et al. (2015) there a feeling that the increased business-government-civil society integrations are so valuable that they are evolving a new form of governance. The government, business, and society relationship cannot be discussed in isolation of the concept of CSR, which has evolved over the years. According to Nelson and Quick (2013), corporate social responsibility is the obligation for an organization to behave in ethical ways in the social environment in which it operates. Socially responsible actions such as protecting the environment, promoting worker safety, supporting social issues, and investing in the community are actions expected of organizations. Kraft and Furlong (2014) contend that companies can have a win-win situation when they go green, by displaying a sense of community while improving economic performance or economic growth. In the modern global economy, a corporation's success depends on its managers' ability to address the three challenges of globalization, workforce diversity, and corporate social responsibility (Lehne, 2013; Ebert & Griffin, 2015).

The corporate social responsibility concept, which was hitherto the major focus of multinationals, is now being used by government, businesses, and other types of organization as a framework for sustainable development (Nelson & Quick, 2013; Kraft & Furlong, 2014). Some authors aver that the real definition of sustainable development is a subject of much debate, and a consensus seems not realistic in the near future (Miller et al., 2014; Kraft, 2011; Dye, 2014). Given this new outlook, two key concepts that reflect the "new" role(s) of business in the society have emerged (Nelson & Quick, 2013). These are the stakeholder and sustainable concept. Dibie (2014) contends that sustainable development is a new approach to social and economic activities for all societies, rich and poor, which is compatible with the preservation of the environment. In addition, the World Commission on Environment and development conceives of sustainable development as development that meets the needs of the present without compromising the ability of future generations to meet their own needs (Dibie, 2014). What should be underscored here is the need to ensure that there is regeneration of finite resources, so that their exploitation today will not prevent others from using same over a long period of time. This is particularly important today, given the rush for both finite and non-finite resources by both national and international businesses, desirous of quick profits to line up their bank accounts.

Dye (2013) and Kraft and Furlong (2014) contend that the concept of sustainable development spawned the emergence of the "triple bottom line" concept, which lies at the heart of corporate responsibility and corporate citizenship. The concept of sustainable development seems to be made up of three fundamental and inseparable pillars: (a) generation of economic wealth; (b) environmental improvement; and (c) social responsibility (Dibie, 2014). The analysis of these three dimensions of sustainable development provides a better understanding of corporate social responsibility. Corporate social responsibility, as used in this chapter, refers to the continuing commitment of business to behave ethically by contributing to economic development while improving the quality of life of the workforce and their families as well as of the local community and society at large where a company operates its business.

Talisman launched a CSR campaign to improve its public image in Sudan. In 2000, two years after the investment in Sudan, the company issued its first independently verified CSR report. In it, Peter Widdrington, chairman of the board, acknowledged that "shareholders, employees, governments, interest groups and the general public demand more from corporations than just profitability. They expect businesses to be responsible in all areas of social and environmental performance." The report enhanced the company's transparency by monitoring its compliance with the International Code of Ethics for Canadian Business (the Code). This gave Talisman an ostensibly legitimate moral benchmark on which to measure its social and environmental impacts in Sudan. After consulting with experts in business ethics, social auditing and international law, and comparing the Code to similar agreements such as the Amnesty International Guidelines for Companies and the United Nations Global Compact, Talisman derived its own "Sudan Operating Principles." The Principles set standards in six key areas: human rights, community participation, employee rights, environmental protection, and business conduct and stakeholder engagement. Furthermore, each of the Principles was linked with three categories of measurable, or at least identifiable, objectives, depending on Talisman's ability to influence their achievement. The first category of the Talisman's objectives included those objectives that were under Talisman's direct control and responsibility. The second, GNPOC objectives, included objectives that depended on the support of Talisman's GNPOC business partners. The third, advocacy objectives, included objectives over which Talisman had little control but for which they had the responsibility to advocate.

In Sudan as well as many developing areas of the world, government at all levels has fallen short of expectations of the governed in the area of successful implementation of policies that center on improving the living condition of the people. It is, however, very important to note that what is suitable for development in Europe may be unsuitable in Sudan from a different context, unless necessary adaptation is made for it to be useful and sustainable in the country.

The modernization approach to development in the 1970s did not succeed much in Africa, just as privatization is not working today in Sudan because of a high dose of foreign ideas, values, and methods in them. Thus, the domestic policy settings are more important than foreign pressures for multinational corporations' access to realizing the benefit of sustainable development. The central challenges for the Government of Sudan remains the increase of its capacity to adjust so that it can better help its citizens to take full advantage of the opportunities provided by technological innovation and a growing world economy. Any method of development that would succeed in Sudan and most African countries must first empower the citizens and bring them into the mix of the development process as partners in the drive toward social change. A right step in this direction might involve decentralizing State powers and adjusting the policy process to give the citizens a sense of belonging in matters that affect their lives. Figure 8.1 shows the hierarchy of corporate social responsibility.

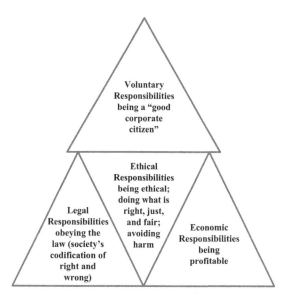

Figure 8.1 Hierarchy of corporate social responsibility
Source: Ebert and Griffin (2015)

Analysis of Business and Government Relations

One of the mechanisms of business and government relations in Sudan is direct foreign investment in the country, especially due to the large exploration of petroleum by foreign multinational corporations. Like most developing countries that are blessed by mineral resources, Sudan is not different in the way it uses foreign direct investment (FDI) as a strategy for achieving economic growth and development (Dibie et al., 2015). The discovery of oil in the late 1950s and improvement in the fortunes from the oil exploration in the mid-1970s attracted major investors to the country in order to tap the huge oil deposits. By the late 1980s the country had been reduced to a mono-income economy. Budgets were based on estimated revenue from the international sales of crude oil.

The relationship between business and government in Sudan over the past five decades has not been very smooth due to problems in its institutional, social, and structure. The most areas crucial aspect of the nation's economic problems lies in the division of country into two nations—for structural factors, clear lines of relationship between North Sudan on one hand and South Sudan on the other (FAO, 2013; World Bank 2016; UNDP 2011). The resulting civil war in both countries has made it very difficult for civil society and the state to be able to establish a cordial relationship. This is an indication that the governments of both North and South Sudan have yet to come to terms with the role civil society organizations (CSOs) should play in the economy. Consequently, civil society groups on the other hand are not in tune with better ways of applying themselves to shared governance issues. That is, both sides need further education on participatory governance art and practice.

Until recently, Sudan was an oil-exporting low-income country (LIC) with a history of mixed macroeconomic performance. In the mid-1990s, the predominantly agricultural economy with a large and inefficient public sector was in economic distress. The narrow revenue and export base was insufficient to finance large fiscal expenditure and balance of payments (BOP) needs. Large fiscal deficits were monetized by the Central Bank of Sudan (CBOS), while external arrears were building up. Inflation reached triple digits and the premium on the dollar on the curb market was in the double digits. Supported by Fund re-engagement in 1997, the authorities' decisive reform efforts and the coming on stream of oil production in 1999 helped restore macroeconomic stability (UNDP 2011; World Bank 2014). For more than a decade, real growth was strong and non-oil growth robust, almost quintupling per capita GDP by 2010. Oil production remained modest in the real sector (accounting for about 16% of total GDP in 2010), but crucial in the financing of the budget and the BOP (covering about 50% of current spending and imports of goods and services in 2010, respectively). Thanks to curtailed fiscal deficits and tightened monetary policy, average annual inflation remained contained at around 10% until the food and fuel price shocks in 2008. The exchange rate was gradually depreciated and the current account deficit returned to single digits.

The secession of South Sudan in July 2011 resulted in a major permanent external shock to Sudan, leading to deterioration in economic condition similar to that of the early 1990s (UNDP 2008; World Bank 2007a). The loss of about three quarters of the country's oil production hit the real sector, as well as the fiscal and external sectors: it left Sudan with roughly half of its previous fiscal revenues and a third of export proceeds. Macroeconomic fundamentals deteriorated, putting severe pressures on the fiscal position and the exchange rate. As in the mid-1990s, the authorities resorted to monetizing the fiscal deficit, driving up inflation and widening the spread between the official and the curb exchange rates. Continued uncertainties as to future relations with South Sudan have further aggravated the situation.

At the end of June 2012, the Sudanese authorities embarked on a reform path, aiming at addressing the macroeconomic imbalances resulting from the secession of South Sudan. The key measures adopted are (1) a devaluation of the Sudanese pound and the reform of the exchange rate regime; (2) an increase in taxes; (3) a reduction of fuel subsidies and non-priority spending; and (4) an expansion of social safety nets. While these measures will help reduce near-term pressures and improve the economic outlook, over the medium term there is a need to continue these reforms in order to restore domestic and external stability.

Table 8.1 Overview of the economy of Sudan

Region	Sub-Saharan Africa
Income category	Lower middle income
Population	38,764,090
GNI per capita	(US$): 1,740
Currency	Sudanese pound
Fiscal year	Calendar year
Trade organizations	Arab League, COMESA, WTO
GDP	$ 159.5 billion (PPP) (2014 est.) $70 billion (Nominal) (2014 est.)
GDP growth	3.9% (2013 est.)
GDP by sector	Agriculture: 44.5%; industry: 45.3%; services: 10.2% (2010 est.)
Inflation rate (consumer prices)	25% (2013 est.) 37.4% (2012 est.)
Labor force	11.92 million (2007 est.)
Labor force by occupation	Agriculture: 45%; Industry: 40%; Services: 15% (2011 est.)
Unemployment rate	20% (2012 est.) 18.7% (2002 est.)
Main industries	oil, cotton ginning, textiles, cement, edible oils, sugar, soap distilling, shoes, petroleum refining, pharmaceuticals, armaments, automobile/light truck assembly
Ease-of-doing-business rank	159th (2015)
Exports	$8.464 billion (2009 est.)
Export goods	oil and petroleum products; cotton, sesame, livestock, groundnuts, gum Arabic, sugar
Imports	$6.823 billion (2009 est.)
Import goods	Foodstuffs, manufactured goods, refinery and transport equipment, medicines and chemicals, textiles, wheat
Gross external debt	$36.27 billion (31 December 2009 est.)
Debt—external	$40.92 billion (31 December 2013 est.) $39.54 billion (31 December 2012 est.)
Public debt	111% of GDP (2013 est.) 101.7% of GDP (2012 est.)
Revenues	$9.046 billion (2009 est.)
Expenses	$10.83 billion (2009 est.)
Foreign reserves	US$14.300 billion (31 December 2011 est.)

Source: Doing Business database and CIA World Factbook

According to UNCTAD (2014), the largest investment projects were concentrated in the oil industry, with some FDI in other industries. Although official data on FDI, including its distribution by industry and key impact indicators, are incomplete, estimates show that oil attracted the largest share of foreign investment. For instance, all but one Greenfield projects of $1 billion or more over the period of 2003–2010 were carried out by international oil firms (China National Petroleum, Petronas). However, several smaller projects of $100 million to $1 billion took place in electricity (Bharat Heavy Electricals), mining (ASCOM Geology and Mining), telecommunications (Investcom), food (Bin Omeir Holding), hotels (Rotana Hotels), and building materials (RAK Ceramics) (UNCTAD, 2014).

It is often and truly said that Sudan is a country of great potential. For example, 57% of total land in Sudan is suitable for agricultural development, but only 8.5% is currently being cultivated—this is a stark statistic at a time when global demand for food is rising, yet land is scarce. The loss of oil may be a blessing in disguise, for it will force the country to focus on developing its own economic strengths: agriculture, minerals, and the provision of services to its rapidly urbanizing population.

It's hard to do business in Sudan in the current environment. Sanctions make a difference. But even without sanctions, investing or trading with a country with such a conflicted relationship with its neighbor and with serious internal conflicts unresolved is a risky business. And it is businesses, not governments, that take these decisions. Even setting aside conflict, the business environment is tough. The World Bank ranks Sudan as one of the most difficult countries in the world to do business (World Bank, 2015; Table 8.2). The new investment law is good, but not effectively implemented. And the financial and legal environments are opaque. So many companies stay away, but not all: a number of British companies are active here, or are attracted by the potential. Some of them have long-standing historical links. Others are approaching Sudan for the first time. It is sometimes said that British companies have walked away from Sudan, as though that it is the fault of the UK. Of course trading relationships are not what they were 50 years ago. The world (and Sudan and the UK) have changed. But the EU collectively is Sudan's third largest trading partner, and the UK accounts for around 20% of that business. The UK does more trade with Sudan than with many African countries. The UK will offer support and advice to any British company interested in Sudan. But if in the event they go elsewhere, that's not because the UK has "walked away." It's because in a competitive global market, the Sudan offer is not sufficiently attractive.

All companies recognize the importance of the private sector to Sudan. It is the private sector in Sudan, as elsewhere that is the most effective driver of prosperity. Historically countries only thrive, politically as well as economically, where there is a strong private sector that can create more economic opportunities for people. Until the second half of 2008, Sudan's economy boomed on the back of increases in oil production, high oil prices, and

Table 8.2 Summary of time, cost, and procedures for starting a business in Sudan

No.	Procedure	Time to complete	Cost to complete
1	Apply for registration and reserve a company name To apply for registration, the entrepreneur must submit an informal draft copy of the company memorandum and articles of association, including the company objectives, nominal capital, capital distribution, and the names of founding shareholders, whether natural or legal personalities, to the Companies Registrar for preliminary approval. This is accompanied by a request containing the required legal stamps and name reservation form proposing potential company names subject to availability. The preliminary approval to proceed with the company registration is usually issued by the Companies Registrar within 2–3 days, along with additional rules and guidelines to be incorporated within the provided Articles and Memorandum of Association before submission in its final form. The Companies Registrar may reject granting the preliminary approval if a similar or identical company name already exists. Agency: Commercial Registrar of Companies	3 days	SDG 200
2	Notarize the memorandum and articles of association Three copies of the Memorandum and Articles of Association, along with Forms C2 and C2a, must be completed according to the rules contained under the preliminary approval. These forms must be signed by all founding shareholders, and authenticated by a designated lawyer with authentication authority. Agency: Notary	2 days	SDG 350
3	Notify the taxation chambers Before applying for final approval and registration, the company must submit a preliminary approval request to the Taxation Chamber, along with the memorandum and articles of association duly stamped by the Chamber in acknowledgement of the notification, and Forms C2 and C2a. These documents shall then be submitted before the Zakat Chamber for its approval. Agency: Taxation chambers	1 day	0.2% of start-up capital
4	Register with the commercial registry Stamps must be affixed to the Articles and Memorandum of Association. The company documents, including Forms C2 and C2a and a copy of the lease agreement or property certificate of the company premises, must be submitted to the Commercial Registrar to finalize the company registration. Agency: Commercial Registry	4 days	Stamp duty and other application/ administrative fees (see comment)

(Continued)

Table 8.2 (Continued)

No.	Procedure	Time to complete	Cost to complete
5	Receive site inspection A representative from the Companies' Registry inspects the company premises to confirm its existence before delivering the certificate of incorporation. It is also mandatory for the company to obtain and post a sign board on the exterior of its office/business location. Agency: Companies' Registry	2 days	no charge
6	Apply for a tax identification number (TIN) The following documents are required to apply for a tax identification number: Shareholder information; Memorandum and articles of association (notarized); Certificate of incorporation (two copies); Completed registration forms; Company resolution delegating a person to act on the company's behalf Agency: Taxation chambers	1 day on average	SDG 5
7	Register for VAT The company registers for VAT at a separate department within the same building. It is not mandatory to register for VAT at the same time. Agency: Taxation chambers	2 days	no charge
8	Register with the labor authorities The company must deposit the basic work and penalties regulations with the competent labor office. Agency: Labor authorities	14 days	SDG 192
9	Enroll employees in social security The company must subscribe to the Social Insurance Fund. The required documents for this procedure are: Copy of Company Certificate of Incorporation and Memorandum and Articles of Association; Completed registration form. Simultaneously, the company registers its employees for social insurance. The social insurance registration procedure is free of charge, and requires the submission of the following documents: List of the employees' names and salaries; Completed registration form. Agency: Social Insurance Fund	5 days on average	SDG 25
10	Make a company seal The cost to make a company seal depends on the kind of material used. Costs vary starting at SDG 50 per seal. Agency: Seal maker	2 days	SDG 50—SDG 80

* Takes place simultaneously with another procedure.

Source: Doing Business database.

large inflows of foreign direct investment. GDP growth registered more than 10% per year in 2006 and 2007. From 1997 to date, Sudan has been working with the IMF to implement macroeconomic reforms, including a managed float of the exchange rate. Sudan began exporting crude oil in the last quarter of 1999. Agricultural production remains important, because it employs 80% of the workforce and contributes a third of GDP. The Darfur conflict, the aftermath of two decades of civil war in the south, the lack of basic infrastructure in large areas, and a reliance by much of the population on subsistence agriculture ensure much of the population will remain at or below the poverty line for years, despite rapid rises in average per capita income. In January 2007, the government introduced a new currency, the Sudanese pound, at an initial exchange rate of $1.00 equals 2 Sudanese pounds.

Privatization of Public Corporations

In 1990, the present Government of Sudan initiated a privatization program by establishing the Technical Committee for the Disposal of Public Enterprises (TCDPE). Based on financial viability, the TCDPE listed 117 state-owned enterprises SOEs for privatization in 1992. There were two phases for application of the program. In the first phase (1992–1997), 57 SOEs were privatized. During the second phase (1998–2003), however, the proposed sales and liquidations of 31 SOEs were not completed. Out of the 57 enterprises divested in the first phase, 25 were freely transferred to state government, farmers, and government and voluntary organizations (Table 8.3). Privatization activity peaked in 1994, but gradually tapered off as an increasingly wary public began to suspect the government's motives.

Consider the legal and institutional constraints on self-dealing; there was an absence of democratic institutions which bolster economic and social participation and minimize corruption. The presence of these institutions is a vital prerequisite for privatization to be successful. It is abundantly clear that Sudan wholly lacks the institutional infrastructure to control self-dealing. Prosecutors, judges, and lawyers are mostly political appointees. Business laws and accounting regulations are violated with impunity. There is a lack of democratic accountability, poor application of the rule of law, and rampant corruption. Dagdeviren (2006) argued that several weak institutional factors have negatively affected the outcomes of privatization in Sudan: (1) the absence of appropriate accounting practices led to inaccurate valuation of assets; (2) there were no appropriate workers' compensation mechanisms included when privatization policies were first launched; (3) capital markets were very rudimentary and the Khartoum Stock Exchange was not operational before a substantial part of privatization had been completed; (4) the absence of anti-monopoly and other legislative frameworks and regulatory organizations led to problems; and (5) corrupt methods of privatization and intentional lack of transparency (such as sales without tender and lack of documentation) eroded the credibility of the privatization endeavors. Examples abound. The privatization of telecommunication services occurred with no tender and, as reported by Dagdeviren (2006), some "specific personalities" were invited to become joint stock partners in Sudatel. Sudatel was essentially a government protected monopoly until 1997, when another communications company (Mobitel) was established, albeit under the auspices of the ruling elites. Moreover, as Dagdeviren (2006) asserts, the asset valuation of Sudatel and initial sale price was substantially downgraded by an unknown company (East-West Co.) selected by the controlled government groups. Awad (1999) reported that by raising the connection charges, after only three months of privatization, Sudatel was able to reap a profit of US$5 million.

Self-dealing is almost inevitable in the Sudanese case where the system is controlled by the ruling party managers. It is not surprising that most of the privatization stock shares are held by the government and ruling party managers. Non-ruling party citizens are directly excluded from participation, because most of the potentially profitable ventures' stocks were sold by invitation. Indirect methods of overtaxation and confiscation threats also exist. Selective tax audits have become a potent political weapon against businesses that are not supportive of the ruling party members. Further, the lack of appropriate institutions discourages workers' ownership and public participation. Falsified books preclude strong public capital markets. Companies that are deliberately allowed to get away with tax avoidance cannot report honestly to investors. Hidden transactions also preclude using the courts to enforce contracts. It is no coincidence, therefore, that the seven most profitable companies are dominated by ruling party managers, and mostly located in the central area of Sudan around Khartoum (Deng (2007). The rest of the companies that are either barely surviving or working at a loss have been privatized mainly through free transfer of ownership to regional states, farmers, other public sectors, or voluntary organizations. The latter are mostly ill-equipped agricultural schemes located in the peripheries of the country. It is noteworthy that all the regional conflicts in Southern Sudan (before separation), Darfur, and Eastern Sudan erupted partly because of concentration of wealth and power around Khartoum, leading to disproportionate regional development. The result is a massive migration to Khartoum and a drastic increase in open unemployment. Deng (2007), succinctly, points out that since independence in 1956, the fundamental root cause of regional conflicts in Sudan lies in the concentration of governance and development around Khartoum, and the ensuing marginalization of rural Sudanese in the governance of their country.

Ali (2006) reported that the Sudanese Gini coefficient of inequality shows a high degree of inequality approaching 0.5, and the existence of relatively low Kuznets' elasticities (a measure of the sensitivity of inequality to changes in income) indicates that changes in the distribution of consumption expenditures are expected to stay at relatively low values, averaging to 0.1132 during the decade of the 1990s. Besides the existence of self-dealing, which widens the inequality gap between the rich and the poor, other privatization and market liberalization effects that may worsen income distribution include an increase in the cost of living indexes and higher unemployment. As a matter of fact, most of the retrenchments of operations were applied with no compensatory plans for the displaced labor. The TCDPE contends that no retraining or compensatory early retirement programs were offered to workers. Furthermore, many privatized enterprises did not adjust their pension regulations to advance their contributions to the Pension and Social Insurance Fund for the existing or newly entering workers. That is why workers' unions in many of these firms (e.g., Nyala Tannery, Kadogli Textiles, etc.) were disgruntled and fought for a just solution to the problem. Following these massive layoffs, real wages deteriorated while the cost of living continued to rise.

The self-imposed market liberalization policies of Sudan (equivalent to structural adjustment policies elsewhere) of the early nineties, coupled with the self-serving privatization policies of the Ruling Party–controlled government, resulted in pernicious income distribution effects on society. With the urge of acquiring more economic and political power, existing public finance imperatives, inflationary debt monetization policies, high foreign debt (over one and a half billion dollars owed to the IMF in 1992), the government launched an aggressive privatization program, removed most of the subsidies, floated the Sudanese pound, and increased user fees.

Table 8.3 Profitability of selected privatized corporations*

Name/Sector/Method of sale/Year	Profitability
Commercial Bank (Service)—Sold to the Farmers Union in 1992	Since privatization, annual profits are estimated to be 71 million SD.
Gezira Tannery (Manufacturing)—Joint stock in 1993	Profits were estimated to be 242 million SD from 1995–1999.
Grand Hotel (Service)—Leased for 25 years in 1996	Profits were 47.8 million SD in 2001 and 24.6 million SD in 2000.
International Nile Textile Factory (Manufacturing)—Sold for debt settlement to Dawoo (Korea) in 1995	Production increased to 4760 tons per year after privatization.
Kirikab Corp. (Manufacturing)—Sold in 1991	Made 33.2 million SD profit in 2001.
Sudanese Cotton Co. (Service)—Sold in 1993	Made 460 million SD average yearly profit from 1994 to 2001.
White Nile Tannery (Manufacturing)—Sold to Dawoo (Korea) in 1992	Profit from 1994–2000 was estimated at 12 million SD.

Source: Technical Committee for the Disposal of Public Enterprises (TCDPE) (2004)

*Other companies struggling to survive or working at a loss include Wafra Chemicals, National Project for Poultry, Rabak Cotton Ginnery, Delta Toker, Blue Nile Agricultural Project, and White Nile Agricultural Project.

Table 8.4 Employment in selected privatized sectors*

Name/Sector/Method of sale/Year	Employment
Commercial Bank (Service)—Direct sale to the Farmers Union in 1992	Increased by 12% after privatization, from 729 to 817
Gezira Tannery (Manufacturing)— Joint stock in 1993	Declined by 50% after privatization, from 440 to 181
Grand Hotel (Service)—Leased for 25 years in 1996	Declined by 55% after privatization, from 339 to 152
Nile Textile Factory (Manufacturing)— Sale for debt settlement to Dawoo (Korea) in 1995	Increased by 1674% after privatization, from 72 to 1258
Kirikab Corp. (Manufacturing)— Direct sale in 1991	Declined by 22% after privatization, from 90 to 70
Sudanese Cotton Co. (Service)— Direct sale in 1993	Declined by 59% after privatization, from 972 to 399
White Nile Tannery (Manufacturing)— Direct sale to Dawoo (Korea) in 1992	Declined by 20% after privatization, from 368 to 296
Sudatel	Declined by 50% after privatization, from 6041 to 3021

Source: TCDPE (2004)
* For all of the companies working at a loss (see note under Tables 8.3 and 8.5), employment decreased significantly. In some cases (e.g., Delta Toker and White Nile Agricultural Project), all employees were dismissed after privatization.

The abysmal living conditions of the poor have, furthermore, been worsened by the continuous depreciation of the Sudanese pound against the US dollar, due to the ill-founded adoption of a floating exchange rate system. Such privatization policies are not only punitive to the poor, but are also incompatible with the development of a small, capital-poor economy. With poverty rates well above 50%, export-led growth and minimalist state views cannot succeed without democratic social and economic institutions, which buttress a sound development process by regulating self-dealing and encouraging an equitable income distribution. Such inequity has not been alleviated by the recent higher growth in the Sudanese economy bolstered by higher oil revenues.

Government and the Consumer

Results from the government lead crop and food security assessment indicate that most of the basic consumer good prices are increasing and expected to increase more like sorghum and millet, the basic food for more than half of the population in Sudan. Also, wheat prices increase where it showed a more than 30% increase, which is attributed to the decrease in supply and escalating prices in the international market. December 2010 prices are still above the 2005–2009 average levels. Prices of livestock are significantly higher than normal for all classes of livestock in almost all observed markets. This is ascribed to increased demand from local slaughterhouses and increase in demand from international markets. Improved physical condition of livestock resulting from good forage availability and improved body condition of the animals and their products are also the main reasons for good prices. The inflation rates have significantly increased with serious implications on the poor. The food inflation reached 19.7% in 2011 from its 11% in 2010. This is the highest since the food crises in 2008, while the non-food inflation reaches to 8.9% from its 6.9% level in the same period. The increases are mainly attributed to government policies, devaluation of Sudanese pounds, and the speculation of possible removal of subsidies on petro products and sugar with serious implications on other sectors. The food inflation rise is also related to increases in international food prices, in which Sudan is a net food importer. As the food inflation rate increases much higher than non-food, relative price increases continue to jump. Similar inflation rate changes have been observed for both urban (from 9.5% in 2010 to 15.1% in 2011) and rural (from 10% to 15.5% for the same period) settings. Given the unsettled situation in the ground, and possible removal of fuel and sugar subsidies and more demands in foreign currency, inflation rates are expected to increase further in the coming years, and this will reduce the purchasing power of poor households as prices of other commodities and public services are also anticipated to rise. Figure 8.2 shows Sudan baseline household and food ratio survey data.

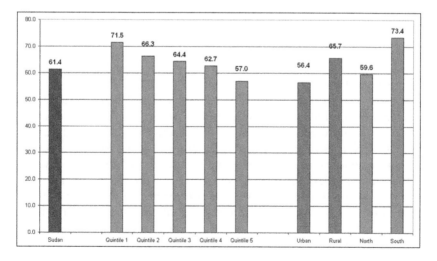

Figure 8.2 Food ratio in Sudan (%)

Source: The Sudan Baseline Household Survey (SBHS-2009), CBS—FAO-SIFSIA-MoAF, July 2009.

There is a growing concern in Sudan over the impact of current swings in inflation rates. This will have a serious impact on the poor, who are more than 60% of the population and dominantly relying on the market for accessing their food. According to World Food program (WFP), there are already about 3.2 million people who are still unable to secure adequate food access in the 15 Northern states of Sudan during 2011 (Figure 8.1). These are mainly conflict-affected populations, including IDPs, refugees, returnees, and vulnerable residents. Protection of consumers from the adverse effects of escalated food prices remains both a marketing policy and social policy challenge. With very limited purchasing power (ability to pay), Sudan needs to explore measures to protect the vulnerable, including the use of Zakat resources innovatively for safety nets and to reinforce the best use of the strategic reserve resources to mitigate price hike consequences by providing poor people direct access to food. In the medium to long run, increasing agricultural productivity and diversification of income sources and consumptions that proves both competitive and sustainable are viable ways of moving forward.

Regulation and Deregulation

Sudan has a significant but largely unexploited potential to attract foreign investors, notably due to ongoing internal conflicts. The country is also facing the consequences of the secession of South Sudan, in particular the loss of the bulk of its oil reserve. In this context, reassuring and rebuilding the trust of investors is essential to attract them to Sudan. By adopting national development plans and new legislation, Sudan has made efforts to diversify the economy and attract FDI into new industries. However, more is needed to build a transparent and predictable business environment. The analysis of the Investment Policy Review (IPR) completed by UNCTAD shows that Sudan has put in place a relatively open investment legislative framework with several of the existing laws being modern and in line with good practices. However, their implementation is often impeded by the absence of secondary legislation, insufficient institutional capacity and lack of coordination among different levels of the government. This is notably the case for the FDI-specific, environment, and competition regimes. Key remaining policy gaps include the need to clarify and streamline the process of investors' establishment, including access to land, and to review the tax regime to generate much-needed public revenue. The effectiveness of the recent legislative effort also relies on operationalizing the institutions foreseen in the law. In this regard, the anti-monopoly council and the anti-corruption commission are priorities. Further attention should also go to areas where improvement would be highly beneficial to the country. Examples include the development of free zones and local skills, in particular given the objective of reorienting and upgrading Sudan's participation in global value chains.

Reforming Government Regulation

The Government of Sudan has undertaken several positive measures over the past six or seven years to improve the business climate in Sudan. These include the Investment Encouragement Act of 1999, which incorporates a one stop facilitation process. However, many administrative barriers remain in the areas of business registration and licensing, land allocation, building permits, and customs and tax administration. Sudan is currently living through a period of substantial political upheaval and realignment, which are likely to affect the investment landscape for years to come. Purely technical solutions to constraints embedded in Sudan's investment climate are unlikely to prove effective without some fundamental agreement on economic policies and reforms that are susceptible to joint action among parties that may still be divided politically. In the wake of protracted inter-regional conflicts, it may be a huge challenge to find tremendous goodwill in the near term. It may, however, be possible to find a space for discussion and negotiation based on the interest all parties have in expanding the size of the economic pie, as well as in how it is ultimately divided. Also, Sudan has to prioritize reforms in such a way that they do not overwhelm existing budgets and institutional capacities (UNDP, 2011; World Bank 2016). Some of these reforms may require legislative changes, and some measure of political consensus and intensive implementation assistance. Others, however, can be addressed at an administrative level, and may provide some evidence to potential investors and to Sudanese stakeholders that the peace process may bring some near-term economic gains. Many of the critical reforms will require a long-term effort and can succeed only in the context of a national dialogue, involving both the public and private sectors and all regions of the country. This report contains several proposals as to how this dialogue can be established and sustained, but even these proposals depend on high-level and continued political leadership for their success.

Restoring political and macroeconomic stability will be key to achieving the country's diversification objectives. There is substantial theoretical and empirical evidence that factors such as political and macroeconomic stability are key determinants of the performance of developing countries in non-extractive industries in attracting FDI (Sadaress 2013; Ridell, 1999; Shafaeddin 2007). More generally, uncertainty related to the political and economic situation negatively impacts a country's economic and social development. In this respect, peace and stability remain pre-conditions for achieving the country's economic diversification and sustainable development objectives. Significant improvements to the legal and regulatory framework for investment are also needed to attract FDI in support of diversification. While several initiatives to improve the legal and regulatory framework for investment have been undertaken, they have not yet yielded the expected results, as reflected in the country's international investment climate rankings.

The goal of the Investment Policy Review is to assist the government in its efforts to enhance the climate for FDI in order to achieve its national development objectives. The IPR is in line with the UNCTAD Investment Policy Framework for Sustainable Development (IPSFD), which consists of a set of core principles for investment policymaking, guidelines for national investment policies and guidance for policy makers on how to engage in the international investment policy regime (UNCTAD, 2014).

The analysis of the Invest Policy Review (IPR) shows that although Sudan has put in place a relatively open investment legislative framework with several laws and regulations being modern and in line with good practices, issues regarding implementation remain. In this regard, the business climate is hampered by institutional weakness or the absence of regulations in a number of areas, in particular in the labor, environment, and competition regimes. These issues are compounded by coordination challenges between the federal and the state levels of the government, and the difficulties to enforce the laws in certain areas, notably land and anticorruption.

The regulatory framework often lacks the clarity and operational details required. Secondary legislation is often absent, notably the environmental protection and competition regulations. At the institutional level, several entities provided for by the legislations are not established or are only functioning partially, notably in labor, competition, and anti-corruption, due to a large extent to a lack of resources. The secession of South Sudan in 2011 strongly impacted the Sudanese economy. The associated loss of a large number of oilfields, in particular, resulted in a decline in GDP, a loss of more than half in budget revenues and a dramatic decrease in exports, which fell by two-thirds (IMF, 2013). Although official data collected in 2012 and 2013 suggest that FDI inflows remained at pre-secession levels, it seems unlikely that there was no decline, given that the bulk of oil investment projects are located in the territory that now constitutes part of South Sudan. This might be due to a weakness in data collection. The shock was expected to be counterbalanced partly by the transitional financial agreement between Sudan and South Sudan for the period 2013–2016. However, the civil war in South Sudan has interrupted part of oil production in that country, thus affecting expected transfers (Deutsche, 2014a; Market Research Reports, 2014). This added to chronically high inflation, which peaked at 48% in March 2013 and is expected to remain above 20% up to the end of 2016 (IMF, 2013), and a shortage of foreign currency caused by various factors, including the economic sanctions imposed on the country since 1997.

Sudan enacted a development plans that seek economic diversification. Oil and related activities remain important. The 25-year development (2007–2031) plan set out the long-term vision for sustainable development recognizes the need to diversify the economy by supporting agriculture, manufacturing and the processing of agricultural goods as well as developing services, notably the tourism industry. Sudan also adopted a four-year

2012–2016 economic salvation program, which comprises a set of concrete measures to cope with the consequences of the secession of South Sudan, including the development of productive capacities in non-oil industries. The strategy calls for improvements in the regulatory regime for investment and support to private sector development.

Agricultural development is needed to achieve food security and generate export earnings. Agriculture represents 40% of the country's GDP and 65% of employment (Ministry of Agriculture, 2014, during the UNCTAD fact-finding mission). The sector has the potential to become a driver in attaining two concurrent development goals: (1) achieving food security through the production of basic staples (sorghum, millet and wheat), as well as the production of livestock, fish and poultry; and (2) increasing export revenue through the sales of cash crops (e.g., cotton, groundnuts, gum Arabic sugar cane and alfalfa). The plan is to create up to 400 jobs in the implementation phase, and 200 more in the longer term.

Broader Government Power

Promoting Competitiveness

Promoting competitiveness and inclusive growth will require reforms on a number of fronts while simultaneously continuing to safeguard macroeconomic stability. The business environment needs to be more conducive to private sector development. According to the World Bank's Doing Business (2015) report, regulations governing investment and banking in Sudan are opaque and subject to frequent change, discouraging entrepreneurial activity. In order to boost the economy and ensure sustained and inclusive growth, government policies need to remove impediments to private sector investments and promote a wage policy, linking wages to the economy's productivity. Also, encouraging exports would contribute to rebalance the country's external accounts. While active internal demand management policies would help increase the country's export potential, they would need to be accompanied by supporting policies, including provision of advice and services to exporters that could be provided by specialized agencies and banks. SMEs could be a key driver in promoting economic diversification. Opening up the economy to foreign investors would (1) attract external resources to finance badly needed investments that would increase employment and the country's economic potential; and (2) enhance the local know-how, the best recipe for private sector development. To support these actions, the government should focus on developing the physical infrastructure and human capital, and improving basic public services. Relative to its peers, Sudan's share of world total exports had steadily increased, while its share of world nonoil exports had decreased. After the secession of South Sudan, total exports dropped with the loss of oil, masking a pickup in non-oil exports thanks to stronger gold proceeds.

Price Competitiveness

The exchange rate and developments in Sudan have been peg to the US dollars for most of the recent past two decades. However, the measures introduced at the end-June 2012 has effectively reinstate Sudan's official floating exchange rate system (World Bank 2016; UNCTAD 2014). Notwithstanding the authorities' stated objective, the monetary policy framework was until recently a de facto exchange rate anchor of the Sudanese guinea (SDG) vis-à-vis the USD. The official exchange rate was last depreciated by 0.06 USD to 2.67 to the USD in April 2011. Yet, the secession of South Sudan weakened the CBOS ability to manage the de facto peg. Furthermore, the introduction of administrative measures and exchange restrictions during 2011 fostered the expansion of the parallel foreign exchange market. This later led the authorities to devalue the Sudanese pound and reform the exchange rate regime. After a decade of widespread tamed exchange rate fluctuations, the SDG's bilateral exchange rates vis-à-vis major trading partners depreciated again.

External Non-Price Competitiveness

Sudan's competitiveness also suffers from structural impediments. These inhibit its ability to produce goods and services of international quality more cost effectively than other countries. Progress in creating a stable, competitive, and diversified economy hinges on expediting reforms. Both relative to historic performance and peers, structural competitiveness in Sudan is either stagnating or deteriorating. Available survey-based business and governance indicators identify cost-increasing production factors that adversely affect productivity and, thus, overall economic activity. More specifically:

1. *World Bank's Doing Business Indicators (2015).* Sudan is ranked among the upper lowest countries assessed in the midfield of its regional competitors. Since last year, Sudan did not change its overall ease of doing business rank, but it lost ranks on most sub-indicators. Priority structural areas for improvement are access to credit, trading across borders, investor protection, and the enforcement of contracts.
2. *World Bank's Worldwide Governance Indicators (WGIs).* For nearly a decade, Sudan's already weak governance indicators have been fluctuating mostly below their 2002 levels, widening the gap with its peers. Most notably, Sudan's political instability and violence have worsened in absolute and relative terms.
3. *World Bank's Country Policy and Institutional Assessment Ratings (CPIA).* For nearly a decade, Sudan's CPIA has been weak and on a slow downswing to 2.36. This is well below the threshold for medium performers (3.25) and well below its peers. The low quality of Sudan's

policy and institutional framework continues to impede poverty reduction, sustainable growth, and the effective use of development assistance.

4. *Transparency International's Corruption Perception Index.* Over the last decade, also, Sudan's index of perceived public sector corruption has deteriorated significantly and more than its regional peers, making it seventh to worst in the ranking of 183 countries in 2011. This particularly highlights the need for strengthening institutions, bureaucratic effectiveness, governance, and security.

Government and Foreign Trade

The structure of the Sudanese economy comprises many sectors; however, the agriculture sector predominates at both national and international levels before the export of oil in the last quarter of 1999; it contributed about 95% of the country's export. The Sudan economy is an open one in the sense that the foreign sector is an important sector in the economy. This openness has an important consideration for the policy makers and planners. Like many developing countries, Sudan's exports are mainly raw materials or primary products. These products are: cotton and cotton seed, gum Arabic, sesame, hides and skins, cattle and sheep, durra, groundnuts, oil and its derivatives, minerals (specially gold), and others. Import of consumer goods has the largest share, followed by machinery and equipment, raw materials, and finally others. Most imports were from Europe during the period 1960–1999, which changed after the year 2000; export followed a similar path. Currently the major economic problem is severe shortage of foreign exchange caused mainly by deterioration in the conventional export. Trade is largely affected by political and economic situations both internally and externally. Internally the change of governments brings new attitudes toward foreign trade, while the international factors such as trade embargo and economic sanctions affect foreign trade. Since 1960 up to now, seven governments have held power in Sudan.

Revitalizing non-oil exports can play an important role in achieving Sudan's tremendous potential for international integration, sustaining and broad-based economic development, and promoting widely shared improvements in living standards. The trade agenda can thus contribute to achieving the vision of national integration and gains for marginalized areas. Oil has driven the recent surge in real economic growth, but to sustain growth and provide broader income opportunities, Sudan will need to pursue a strategy of diversifying its sources of growth, including enhancing its non-oil exports. Thus the trade agenda should be further integrated into national strategies of development and poverty reduction, including near term focus on revitalizing traditional agricultural exports that have provided export earnings over the past half century and finding new markets for old products.

Concerning internal and external constraints to Sudan's integration into the world economy, it seems that the major constraints are primarily, although not exclusively, internal. Sudan's exports face relatively few barriers in foreign markets, with the notable exception of the embargo imposed by the United States. Few countries in the world impose high customs duties on Sudan's principal export, oil. Most-favored nation (MFN) tariffs on Sudan's agricultural exports are generally low, although there are notable exceptions: Korea restricts sesame imports using a tariff rate quota that has a 630% tariff on out-of-quota shipments, for example. Importing countries' animal health regulations have at times been a binding constraint on exports of live animals. Sudan enjoys preferential access to major industrial markets and is a member of several important regional free trade agreements, such as the Greater Arab Free Trade Area (GAFTA) and the Common Market for Eastern and Southern Africa (COMESA) free trade agreement (FTA). These preferential arrangements have been an important means of avoiding high tariffs on sugar, especially in the European Union and Kenya. Otherwise they do not deliver much value to Sudan at present because, in most cases, MFN duties are low on most products that Sudan currently ships to markets where it enjoys preferences.

As Sudan succeeds in diversifying into new products, particularly more processed products, however, these preferential arrangements will become more important, since many countries increase tariffs with the level of processing: collecting higher duties on leather shoes than on leather, for example, and higher duties on leather than on raw hides and skins. Sudan's import tariff regime is among the world's most restrictive. The average tariff rate is 20%, which although much less protectionist than what existed before the reforms of the 1990s, is well above levels imposed by most other developing countries. This tariff regime creates disincentives to exporting. High tariffs raise domestic prices above world prices. This encourages producers to sell locally instead of exporting, discourages them from importing inputs that could raise productivity, and limits their ability to integrate into global supply chains. This further undermines the competitiveness of Sudan's exports in world markets.

Sudan's export competitiveness is further undermined by high transport costs and recent exchange rate appreciation. Charges at Port Sudan are the highest in the region. Shipments are frequently delayed at the port for five to six weeks before being released, which further increases costs. The relative absence of international trade logistics firms limits the country's access to efficient global logistics services, thereby making it hard for Sudanese firms to take full advantage of the containerized shipping revolution and to integrate into global supply chains. Long marketing chains increase the cost of getting goods to Port Sudan. Sudan's internal transportation infrastructure is in the process of being rehabilitated (in the North) and constructed (in the South). These improvements are essential for connecting rural producers to world markets. Exchange rate appreciation has also hurt Sudanese exporters in recent years.

Trends in International Trade Flows

Sudan's real growth of trade of 25% in 2007 represents the second highest growth in the world for that year among all countries. This is a substantial increase from the already high historical trade growth rates since the oil export boom. While total exports grew dramatically from 7% of GDP in 1996 to 14% in 2006, imports remained higher at 16 periods of GDP and led to a trade deficit averaging 2% of GDP since 1999. The oil export boom raised the value of total exports from $620 million in 1996 to $4,522 million (1996 prices) in 2006, representing more than a 700% increase over the decade. The large import demand of the country, the huge transportation and other expenses related to oil operation, and the moderate performance of the non-oil exports contributed to the current account deficit. The magnitude of current account and balance of payments during 1999–2006, however, were smaller compared with pre-oil exportation levels. It is important to note that due to the prolonged history of conflict in the South, statistical data on trade with and within the South is very limited.

Tariff and Incentive Regime: Does It Facilitate Integration?

Sudan took great strides during the 1990s to open the economy to world trade. The government eliminated foreign currency restrictions, reduced import tariffs, eliminated commodity boards, privatized state-owned enterprises, and opened the economy to more foreign investment. Sudan's import duties, taxes, exemptions, and other policies that shape the incentive regime continue to discourage international integration, however. Import duties are high and variables, taxes, and fees imposed by different levels of government raise the costs of trading, and policies to compensate for high trade taxes are weak.

Sudan's Tariffs and Variable

With a simple average tariff rate of 20.2%, Sudan's MFN tariffs are among the highest in the world and considerably higher than most countries in Africa and the Middle East (GlobalEdge, 2016). High tariffs on final goods raise the prices of competing goods above world levels, thus encouraging local producer to supply the local market rather than selling internationally. In short, a tax on imports is effectively a tax on exports. High variation of tariffs across industries and stages of production distorts incentives to invest—investors allocate resources according to tariff policies rather than productivity—and impose greater economic costs on society than a more uniform tariff with the same average rate.

A number of government agencies at both local and national levels impose taxes, charges, and fees that raise the cost of international trade. Livestock face local fees and taxes as they move from locality to locality on their way to export (e.g., locality fees, jihad tax, pastoralists union tax, martyr tax, and wounded tax). Data compiled by the DTIS team finds that these can reach 33% of the FOB export price. Local taxes and fees charged on major export crops can also make up large shares of export prices: 17% for sesame and 15–20% for groundnuts. Manufacturers report paying a range of taxes and fees to national government agencies on imported inputs, which in turn reduce their ability to compete in export markets. The presence of these many taxes suggests the need for the rationalization of taxes imposed at different levels of government and by different government agencies.

Business and Tax Policy

Although taxation levels are generally low, the tax regime is complex and characterized by a wide array of industry-specific corporate income rates and incentives. Corporate income tax rates (called business profit tax) are 0% for agriculture, 10% for industry, and 15% for most services. The corporate income tax on banks recently increased from 15–30% (discussed later). Mining and oil are taxed at 30% and 35%, respectively. Dividends are not subject to tax (FAO, 2013). Other direct taxes include capital gains taxes on the earnings in the country, withholding taxes, rental tax, and a social development tax when exemptions are in place, notably under the 2013 Investment Law. Other taxes are stamp duties, transfer taxes, real property taxes, and in the case of a company owned by Muslim shareholders, Zakat at a rate of 2.5% applied to the working capital, although no indication on the required percentage of shares is given. There is no labor tax, but the employer is required to contribute 17% of the monthly salary of a Sudanese employee for social security. Value-added tax (VAT) is generally rated at 17%, and several industries are exempted from it. It is levied by and mostly for the federal government, and 40% of the total revenue is then transferred to the states transfers (IMF, 2013). VAT applies to the supply of goods and services by taxable persons in the country, as well as on the imports of goods and services into Sudan. The rate increases to 30% for telecommunication services, and an unusually wide range of activities are exempted: agriculture, banking and insurance services, rental, health, education, exports of fertilizer, chemicals, drugs, electricity, water, mining (including gold mining) and minerals, and investment related exports. There is no refund scheme for non-resident companies.

Foreign investors benefit from a specific regime, which add to the low corporate income tax rates applying to certain industries. An initial depreciation allowance of 20% is granted for the purchase of machinery

Table 8.5 Overview of the main corporate direct taxes

Type of taxes	Explanation
Corporate income tax	0% for agricultural companies, public and private educational institutions licensed as universities or general educational organizations, and registered charitable non-profit organizations 10% for industrial companies 15% for commercial, trading, service, real estate rental, fund management and insurance companies; 30% for mining companies, banks, cigarette and tobacco companies 35% for companies engaged in the exploration, extraction and distribution of oil and gas, and their subcontractors 2.5% minimum tax on annual turnover for telecommunication companies
Capital gains taxes	5% on gains from the sale of lands and buildings owned for at least consecutive three years 2.5% on gains from the sale of vehicles 2% on gains from the sale of securities, shares and bonds, subject to certain exceptions
Withholding taxes	No taxes on dividends Resident companies: 2% creditable withholding tax on import of goods 7% final withholding tax on payments to non-resident subcontractors for interest and other services 5% creditable withholding tax on payments to entities registered in Sudan as branches of a foreign company Non-resident companies: No branch remittance tax 7% on interest payments 15% on royalty payments 15% on technical services fees 15% on management consulting fees
Rental tax	10% final tax on rental payments exceeding SDG 3,000 (equivalent to $528 on April 3, 2014).
Social development tax	5% only on companies exempt from tax under the 2013 Investment Law or any other law
Social security	17% of the monthly salary of a Sudanese employee
Stamp duty	Rates vary on the type of instrument (more than 260)
Transfer tax	2% on transfer taxes
Royalties	7% on gold mining
Zakat	2.5% on the working capital of companies owned by Muslim shareholders

Source: UNCTAD (2014), based on information from the Taxation Chamber of the Ministry of National Economy and Finance during the fact-finding mission; Deloitte; FAO, (2013).

or equipment to be used in production (FAO, 2013). Investors are also exempted from VAT on the imports for the capital equipment of national investment projects, subject to the approval of the National Investment Authority. As mentioned previously, investment projects that are considered strategic might benefit from additional fiscal incentives granted on a case-by-case basis by the authority in coordination with the line ministry. This raises serious concerns with regard not only to their transparency, but also their effectiveness, which is difficult to monitor. To obtain at least partial compensation of the revenue loss associated with these incentives, the government introduced a 5% tax on companies that are exempt from taxes under the 2013 Investment Law or any other law. Such differential tax treatment, both in terms of general rates and project-specific incentives, adds to an already complex tax administration (IMF, 2013).

Tax rates remain generally low. Corporate income tax ranges from 0–15% in Sudan, except in certain industries. In comparison, the standard rate in neighboring African and Arab countries is of 25% in Egypt, 30% in Ethiopia, Kenya (and 37.5% for non-resident companies), and Nigeria (FAO, 2013). Sudan also faces challenges in collecting tax revenues. The country's tax-to-GDP ratio is indeed very low (table 5.2). The IMF reports that in 2012, Sudan collected 6.2% of its GDP in tax revenue, while the simple average in the region was 17% (World Bank, 2016).

Sudan is reported to have lost almost 55% of its fiscal revenues after 2011. Measures have been taken to compensate the fiscal shock. As mentioned, the corporate income tax on banks was doubled from 15–30%, the VAT rate and the social development tax increased by 2% (UNCTA, 2014). Gradual removal of the subsidies in the framework of the 2012–2014 Emergency Program is also under way. Consequently, the prices of diesel and petrol increased by 75%, while cooking gas rose by 66% (EIU, 2014).

Accountability in Managing the Nation's Economic System

Accountability has long been recognized as the cornerstone of successful public management. Kettl (2002) reminds us that government's performance is only as good as its ability to manage its tools and to hold its tool users accountable (491). In an environment of proliferating partnerships, the tools of government needed to maintain accountability are not the same as those needed for insular agency activities (Posner, 2002). While governments work to serve the public in capital investment projects, private partners are understandably "focused on recouping [their] investment and on generating a profit" (Buxbaum & Ortiz, 2007: 8). Accountability in PPPs requires the creation of proper safeguards to ensure that public services are not compromised for the sake of private profits. Achieving this oversight is complicated by the structural conditions that are inherent in organizational partnerships. Public–private alliances often feature an imbalance of responsibility among the partners, wherein some organizations have greater responsibility to the partnership (Wettenhall 2007, Shafaeddin 2007) Public managers need to be aware of the levels of accountability among partnership members. Brinkerhoff points out that unlike the principal–agent relationships that are inherent in hierarchical organizations or in contracts for services, the idea of a partnership "encompasses mutual influence, with a careful balance between synergy and respective autonomy, which incorporates mutual respect, equal participation in decision-making, mutual accountability, and transparency" (Lederman et al 2006; Mitchell 2007). Sound public finances have been identified as a central "pre-requisite for the efficient utilization of resources for post conflict recovery and the fight against poverty." A recent World Bank Study (2007) assessed that pro-poor spending of the government in 2006 "increased significantly," but with 5.5% of GDP, pro-poor spending was still below budget plans at 6.6%, and below the average spending in Highly Indebted Poor Countries (HIPC) by 7% and in Ethiopia with a high of 19% (World Bank, 2006).

Similarly, inclusive and transparent budgeting processes aimed at achieving enhanced responsiveness of, and accountability for, government policy priorities and actions also remain a challenge. Social accountability mechanisms in the budgeting process broadly depend on available space for informed participation and the transparency and responsiveness of government institutions to citizen input. The budget process is a central tool for the implementation of pro-poor policy and is divided in four different phases: formulation, adaptation, execution, and control. An examination of some aspects of this component highlights the less than optimal inclusiveness and participation of citizens' input in Sudan.

Nature of Business Response

Business Participation in Policies by Supporting Candidates for Election

The current Sudanese government (1989–present), dominated by the National Congress Party (NCP) who are supporting candidates for election, has expanded privatization programs. Motives behind privatization are complex and controversial. While ostensibly claiming the efficiency gains, and public finance imperatives of privatization, the ruling party in Sudan expediently used privatizing state-owned enterprises (SOEs) to acquire more economic and political power for the NCP (supporting candidates for election) and to support candidates for election. The consequences of such relation-based (crony) capitalism, of which political patronage is an integral part, were grave on the Sudanese economy. There are three main social losses (hypotheses): (1) increased prices as firms capitalize on market power, and hence, (2) increased inequality through accelerated self-dealing, and (3) profit incentives to restructure privatized businesses swamped by official corruption, bureaucracy, and a punitive tax system. The discussions on self-dealing and inequality, respectively, encapsulate these three issues.

Callaghy (1990) and World Bank (2015) argued that as independence came to Africa in the late 1950s, political rather than economic logic prevailed. He contends that a new class of elites emerged and used the state as its instrument of action and source of power, status, rents, and other forms of wealth. With the advent of the Sudanese privatization programs in the nineties, the government has been widely accused of practicing favoritism in selling SOEs to NCP members. At the same time, overtaxation and confiscation have forced established businesses to leave. The World Bank Report (2000) reveals that in 1997 alone, 374,110 Sudanese sought asylum in other countries, and in 1994, 282.6 per 100,000 people were jailed. As Campbell-White and Bhatia (1998) contend, self-dealing prevails when noncompetitive methods of privatization exist, where preemptive rights are absent, and in systems with unclear bidder selection processes. Although published data indicate that legal ways of privatization, such as asset sales on a competitive basis, have seemingly been followed, it is naïve to believe that the government will execute income distribution reforms that challenge their political interests (Ridell, 1999). The government controls the banking system and individuals with political patronage are able to carry more debt, giving them an unfair advantage in bidding for state assets. This hypothesis is based upon the institutional setup of policy objectives, the nature of the banking sector, and the lack of a viable bond market.

In Sudan, privatization is perceived as unfair, hurting the poor (especially those living in the peripheries of the country), and empowering the powerful and privileged NCP affiliates. Consistent with Birdsall and Nelllis (2003) and Buchs (2003), privatization is seen as causing layoffs and demotions, increases in the price of goods and services, enrichment of a corrupt leadership, and ultimately a widening of the gap between rich and poor. The main complaint is that even if privatization contributed to improved efficiency in some sectors (such as telecommunications), it had a negative effect on the distribution of wealth, income, and political power. Birdsall and Nelllis (2003) argue that the distributional effect of privatization matters in three ways: (1) most societies have a limit on their tolerance of inequality, regardless of the effects on growth and efficiency; (2) inequality hinders growth, particularly in developing countries where institutions and markets are weak; and (3) inequality can perpetuate itself by affecting the nature and pace of economic policy and establishing unproductive political arrangements. In a very similar way to the Russian case documented by Hellmann et al. (2000) and Nellis (1999), in Sudan a lack of institutional checks against corruption has helped a set of connected people illegally acquire resources and property rights. As their resources and economic power increased, this leadership became capable of blocking subsequent competition-enhancing and redistributive reforms.

Trade Unions Respond to Government Autocratic Regulations

The direct participation of the workers in the government, together with other "non-traditional" forces, marked a dramatic turn in state-union relations. The Sudan Workers Trade Union Federation (SWTUF) perceived its position as a "partner" in a government whose primary responsibility was to restore democracy and implement workable economic and social programs that would alleviate the country's economic crisis and set it on the right track. Rising up to their responsibility, the SWTUF declared that it will postpone all workers' demands that involved a burden on public expenditure, donate one day's pay of each of its members to the government's treasury, and to resolve peacefully all disputes between the government and the employers, on the one hand, and between the employees and their employers, on the other (Taha, 1970).

Demonstrations and marches were organized, and numerous petitions were presented to the government, but to no avail. In a move to step-up protest, the SWTUF announced a one-day general strike on June, 15, 1966. Again, the SWTUF realized that this was not a well calculated action when the SRWU, still a stronghold of the NUP, refused to participate, falling in step with the government, which denounced the strike as a political action engineered by the communists.

Sudan Divestment Initiatives

The Sudan Divestment Taskforce UK outlines why targeted divestment represents an efficacious method, whereby companies may make a difference in the behavior of the Sudanese government.

Targeted divestment seeks to withdraw foreign involvement in those sectors that provide revenues directly to the Sudanese government and elite but do not benefit the wider population. Cutting these foreign ties will cut the flow of revenue from foreign firms to the Sudanese government and Janjaweed militia. Although much of the initial divestment took place pursuant to the US Sudan Divestment Bill (around 2007–2008), efforts by the taskforce still continue. Divestment from Sudan is ongoing because of inaction by the Sudanese government on the issue. To pressure the Sudanese government, TIAA-CREF, a New York-based fund house, recently pulled out its investments in the ONGC (Oil and Natural Gas Corporation Ltd., the public sector petroleum company in India). In addition, TIAA-CREF pulled out of three other Asian oil groups due to concerns over human rights in Sudan. In response, the Sudanese government dismissed the fund's move, citing economic reasons why divestment was a foolhardy measure.

The Government of Sudan responded that the company which withdrew its deposits was mostly suffering from financial problems rather than attempting to establish a political position," according to a state news agency (Government of Sudan, 2016). It added that such a step will likely not have any effect on the Asian investments in Sudan. It pointed out that several other American companies have rejected the call on them to take their investments and deposits out of Sudan. Given that the crisis in Darfur is still ongoing, the cumulative effect of divestment on the region and the conflict remains to be seen, though skepticism of this method clearly exists among many quarters.

Conclusion

This chapter has examined the nature of business and government relations in Sudan. The quest for sustainable national development in Sudan remains a daunting challenge that requires a partnership between businesses, government, and nongovernmental organization in the country. The analysis of data reveals that business and government relations affect a substantial proportion of the people of Sudan. Unfortunately, the current laws and regulations have had mixed results. Since Sudan is a petroleum producing nation, regulating the oil corporations has become intensely controversial. As a result of political reasons, business in Sudan tends to use estimates at the high end of the range to argue against additional regulations, whereas NGOs, environmental groups, and government agencies invariably use lower estimates (Dibie, 2014; Deutsche, 2014a).

The common practice is that national regulatory agencies use federal standards and guidelines; however, implementing laws, regulations, and statute requires more than setting economic and environmental standards. What is lacking in Sudan is that most agency officials are not able to interpret statutory language and develop the means to achieve them. Although such statutes might reflect judgment about public health, emission control technologies, environmental science, consumer protection, and where permitted economic representation of regulator decision, the Government of Sudan tends to fall behind such expectations.

The way forward for the Government of Sudan to address this pressing concern is that a pragmatic national regulatory goal should be designed to guarantee the needs of the citizens for better condition of living. According to Kraft and Furlong (2014) and Kraft (2011), thoughtful assessment of what might be done to improve regulatory policies are not hard to come by. The Government of Sudan needs the political will to pursue these goals with diverse strategies. Such strategies may include market incentives, public education, regulation, information disclosure, and business and government partnerships (Dibie, 2014; Ebert & Griffin, 2015).

Therefore, the Government of Sudan must try to integrate economic, environmental, and social values at all levels of its administration and institutions. The most important requirement is for the Government of Sudan to take a far more comprehensive approach to ethical economic growth, environmental policy, and concentration on the long-term goal of sustainable development. In addition, effective public participation in these critical decisions requires that citizens become far better informed about the nature of business and government relations in the country, as well as the dimension of environmental problems and risk. It is very important that the citizens should be able to compare with one another the cost of dealing with their economic and environmental problems and risks, the trade-offs involved, and the policy choice that Sudan may face as a country. It is therefore paramount that certain categorical steps need to be taken in order to redress the situation and jump-start the transformation process that will bring about sustainable national development.

References

Ali, A. A. G. (2006). The Challenges of Poverty Reduction in Post-Conflict Sudan. Dubai: Arab Planning Institute.

Awad, M. H. (1999). *Poverty in Sudan: Anatomy and Prognosis*. Khartoum: University of Khartoum, Mimeo.

Birdsall, N. and Nelllis, J. (2003). Winners and Losers: Assessing the Distributional Impact of Privatization. *World Development, 31*(10), 1617–1634.

Buchs, T. (2003). Privatizations in Sub-Saharan Africa: Some Lessons From Experiences to Date. Working Paper, International Financial Corporation.

Buxbaum, J. N. and Ortiz, I. N. (2007). *Protecting the Public Interest: The Role of Long-Term Concession Agreements for Providing Transportation Infrastructure*. Los Angeles: University of Southern California, Keston Institute for Public Finance and Infrastructure Policy.

Callaghy, T. (1990). Lost Between State and Market: The Politics of Economic Adjustment in Ghana, Zambia, and Nigeria. In J. M. Nelson (Ed.), *Economic Crisis and Policy Choice: The Politics of Adjustment in the Third World*. Princeton, NJ: Princeton University Press, 257–320.

Campbell-White, O. and Bhatia, A. (1998). *Privatization in Africa*. Washington, DC: The World Bank.

Dagdeviren, H. (2006). Revisiting Privatization in the Context of Poverty Alleviation: The Case of Sudan. *Journal of International Development, 18,* 469–488.

Deng, L. (2007). *The Sudan Comprehensive Peace Agreement: A Framework for Sustainable Peace and Democratic Transformation of Sudan*. A Statement Before the United States Congress Sub-Committee on Africa and Global Health, Washington, DC.

Deutsche, W. (2014a, January 1). *South Sudan Government, Rebels Set to Enter Peace Talks*. www.dw.de/southsudan-government-rebels-set-to-enter-peace-talks/a-17336359.

Dibie, R. (2014). Comparative Perspective of Environmental Policies and Issues. New York, NY: Routledge Press.

Dibie, R., Edoho, F. M., and Dibie, J. (2015). "Analysis of Capacity Building and Economic Growth in Sub-Saharan Africa." International Journal of Business and Social Science. Vol. 2, no. 12, 1–25.

Dye, T. (2014). *Understanding Public Policy*. 13th Edition. New York: Longman, 210–231.

Ebert, R. and Griffin, R. (2015). *Business Essentials*. Boston, MA: Pearson.

Economist Intelligence Unit. (2014). *Country Report Sudan, Economic Growth*. Economist Intelligence Unit. www.sudestada.com.uy/Content/Articles/421a313a-d58f-462e-9b24-2504a37f6b56/Democracy-index-2014.pdf. Accessed 24 March.

Elbeely, K. H. (2013). The Economic Impact of Southern Sudan Secession. *International Journal of Business and Social Research (IJBSR)*, 3(7), 78–83.

FAO. (2013). Trends and Impacts of Foreign Investment in Developing Country Agriculture—Evidence From Case Studies. Rome: United Nations. www.fao.org/docrep/018/i3107e/i3107e00.ht. Accessed May 7, 2016.

Ferrell, O. C., Hiirt, G. and Ferrell, L. (2015). *Business: A Changing World*. New York, NY: McGraw-Hill Press.

GlobalEdge. (2016). *Sudan*. GlobalEdge.msu.edu and Export.Gov. Accessed February 10, 2016.

Government of Sudan (2016). " Government Bodies and Federal Ministries of Republic of Sudan." www.nationsonline.org/oneworld/sudan-government.htm. Accessed May 7, 2016.

Hellmann, J., Jones, G. and Kaufmann, D. (2000). *Seize the State, Seize the Day: State Capture, Corruption, and Influence in Transition*. Washington, World Bank, Report Prepared for World Development Report 2001 Workshop.

Hubbard, R. G. and Obrien, A. P. (2015). *Macroeconomics*. 5th Edition. Boston, MA: Pearson Publication.

IMF. (2013). Article IV Consultation Sudan, IMF Country Report No. 13/317. "IMF Revises Sudan's 2013 GDP Forecast Upwards." Sudan Tribune. Accessed January 22, 2014.

Kettl, D. F. (2002). Managing Indirect Government. In Lester M. Salamon (Ed.), *The e Tools of Government: A Guide to the New Governance*. New York: Oxford University Press, 490–510.

Kraft, M. (2011). *Public Policy: Politics, Analysis, and Alternatives*. New York: Longman Press, 250–267.

Kraft, M, and Furlong, S. (2014). *Public Policy: Politics, Analysis, and Alternatives*. Washington, DC: Congressional Press, 322–337.

Lehne, R. (2013). Government and Business: American Political Economy in Comparative Perspective. Washington, DC: Congressional Quarterly Press.

Lussier, R. N. and Sherman, H. (2009). *Business, Society and Government Essentials: An Applied Ethics Approach*. Long Grove III: Waveland Press.

Market Research Reports. (2014). *Sudan and South Sudan Oil and Gas Report Q2 2014*. www.marketresearchreports.com/business-monitor-international/sudan-and-south sudan-oil-and-gas-report-q2-2014.

Miller, R., Benjamin, D. and North, D. (2014). *The Economics of Public Issues*. Boston, MA: Pearson.

Mitchell, D. (2007, March). Trade Prospects and Competitiveness Issues for the Sudan Sugar Sector. Mimeo.

Nellis, J. (1999). *Time to Rethink Privatization in Transition Economies?* International Financial Corporation Discussion Paper No. 38, Washington, DC.

Nelson, D. and Quick, J. C. (2013). *Organizational Behavior*. Boston, MA: Cengage Learning.

Posner, P. L. (2002). Accountability Challenges of Third-Party Government. In Lester M. Salamon (Ed.), *The e Tools of Government: A Guide to the New Governance*. New York: Oxford University Press, 523–551.

Ridell, R. (1999). The End of Foreign Aid to Africa? Concerns About Donor Policies. *African Affairs*, 98(392), 309–335.

Shafaeddin, M. (2007, April). Trade Policy and Accession to the WTO: A Background Report for the Sudan DTIS. Mimeo.

Steiner, G. and Steiner, R. (2006). *Business, Government and Society*. Boston: Irwin/McGraw-Hill Press.

Sudan Central Bureau of Statistics. (2010). *The Fifth Sudan Population and Housing Census*.

Sudaress, A. (2013, November 7). Al-Bashir Chairs the High Council for Investment's Meeting Beginning of December. www.sudaress.com/alwatan/37593 (in Arabic).

Taha, A. (1970). *The Sudanese Labor Movement: A Study of Labor Unionism in a Developing Society*. PhD Thesis, University of California, Los Angeles.

UNCTAD. (2014). *World Investment Report (2014). Investing in the SDGs: An Action Plan*. United Nations: New York and Geneva.

United Nations Country. (2012, January). *Team in the Republic of Sudan: Sudan Country Analysis*. Draft Report. New York: Oxford University Press.

United Nations Development Programme. (2006, June). *Sudan. Macroeconomic Policies for Poverty Reduction: The Case of Sudan*. New York: Oxford University Press.

United Nations Development Programme. (2008, June). *Sudan Institutional Mapping of Government Economic Policy Institutions*. Prof. Ali Abdalla Ali/Dr. Khalid Hassan Elbeely (UNICONS/UNDP). New York: Oxford University Press, p. 14.

United Nations Development Programme. (2011). *Human Development Report*. New York: Oxford University Press.

Wettenhall, R. (2007). ActewAGL: A Genuine Public—Private Partnership? *International Journal of Public Sector Management, 20*(5), 392–414.

World Bank. (2007a, December). *Sudan—Public Expenditure Review*. Washington DC: The World Bank, Publication, p. 5, viii.

World Bank. (2007b, March). *Policy Note: Export of Gum Arabic From Sudan*. Prepared for the Oversight Committee of the MDTF, Washington, DC: World Bank.

World Bank. (2014). *Doing Business Data for Sudan*. Washington, DC: World Bank Publication.

World Bank. (2015). *World Development Report 2015: Mind, Society, and Behavior*. Washington, DC: World Bank. doi:10.1596/978-1-46480342-0. License: Creative Commons Attribution CC BY 3.0 IGO.

World Bank. (2016). *Doing Business 2016: Measuring Regulatory Quality and Efficiency*. Washington, DC: World Bank Group. doi:10.1596/978-1-4648-0667-4. License: Creative Commons.

9 Business and Government Relations in Zimbabwe

Saliwe Kawewe and Robert A. Dibie

Introduction

Zimbabwe is a landlocked country located in Southern Africa that borders the countries of Botswana, Mozambique, South Africa, and Zambia. The geography of Zimbabwe is mostly high plateau and mountains in the east. The government system is a parliamentary democracy (Government of Zimbabwe, 2014). The chief of state is the executive president and the head of government is the prime minister. Zimbabwe has a mixed economy in which there is limited private freedom, but the economy remains highly controlled by the government (OECD, 2014). Zimbabwe is a member of the African Union (AU), African Economic Community (AEC), and the Common Market for Eastern and Southern Africa (COMESA) (United Nations Human Development Report, 2014).

Approximately 80% of malnourished children in developing countries are found in countries where farmers have been forced by structural adjustment policies (SAPs) to shift their agricultural production from subsistence to export production for industrialized nations (Global Exchange, 2000; United Nation Human Development Report, 2014). Whereas Africa accounts for one-tenth of the world population, it generates almost half of the world's displaced people and refugees, most of whom are women and children. The International Monetary Fund (IMF) and World Bank (WB) capitalist model of development operationalized through economic structural adjustment programs' (ESAPs) prescriptions to debtor countries, enforced by the World Trade Organization (WTO), prioritizes export production over cultivating a diversified domestic economy. Such an approach is in contrast with the route taken by industrialized nations that created these organizations prescribing ESAPs for the South. This economic reform policy, which was designed to strengthen multinational corporations, also ensures its operation efficacy by integrating elites from all developing countries through its reward-and-punishment system, while alienating the masses of these countries (Mankiw, 2018).

Despite the fact that Zimbabwe and Tanzania were economic success stories of the 1980s and early 1990s (Word Bank, 2016), they have both plunged into economic crises, with Zimbabwe's GDP recording far much lower than before the adoption of the SAPs (French, 1998). Thus, problems of Africa are directly linked to ventures of Western exploitation of Africa. The African elites have become closer, while alienating the majorities who have sunk into further impoverishment due to the strings attached to ESAPs' policy prescriptions to the debtor governments, allowing international corporations to gain easy entry and access into the countries' labor force and resources unabated and at bottom line bargain prices compounded by privatization (selling of publicly owned assets to the private-sector/ corporations).

When it became independent in 1980, Zimbabwe had a diversified economy, well-developed infrastructure, and an advanced financial sector. It is now one of Africa's poorest countries. In July 2013, President Robert Mugabe of the Zimbabwe African National Union, Patriotic Front, was re-elected to his seventh five-year term, and his party won three-quarters of the seats in parliament in a peaceful but flawed election. In March 2013, voters approved a new constitution that would roll back presidential power. After decades of corruption and mismanagement, Zimbabwe now faces a cash crisis and declining support from China. In 2014, poor harvests left 2.2 million people in need of food assistance (Index of Economic Freedom, 2015).

The elitist governments that have historically and steadfastly manipulated the sentiments of the masses in order to gain the initial tacit approval that legitimizes their regimes were pressured to adopt ESAPs, an ill-fated decision leading to what looks like the recolonization of Africa as the debtor governments loose the following of their own people, control over land, services, and industries. Once independent, broad participation in the formulation and implementation of public policy such as structural adjustment programs (SAPs) dwindles, a major weakness across sub-Saharan Africa. Additionally, African elites have lost their role in competitive imperialism of the Cold War era, in which their role entailed playing off one imperial power against the other, but are now victims of monopolistic imperialism. Instead of propagating self-reliance, the African elites are now adopters and implementers of Western imposed SAPs (OECD 2014; Word Bank 2012; (Mazrui, 1996).

With Africa's external debt rising from US$212.2 billion to US$271 billion between 1986 and 1990 (World Bank 2012; Jamal, 1994), business and government relations became negatively affected. It is not surprising, even after independence, that the post-colonial era mirrors the colonial one. The rising debt trend continues well into the twenty-first century, accompanied by sharp declines in living standards witnessed by increases in absolute poverty from 270 million in the mid-eighties to 335 million people in 1990 (Jamal, 1994; Global Exchange, 2000). The interests of primary beneficiaries, mostly northern educated Africans and the skillful lobbyist-descendants of colonialists, have flourished at the expense of the subordinate large classes of workers and peasants, women, and children under the IMF and WB economic development model. Zimbabwe's proclamations of national-ism; indigenization; promotion of popular peace, social, and human rights; and welfare environmental conservation have rarely been translated into practice. Worse still, building sustainable democracy is difficult during peri-ods of national economic difficulties. Also given the mechanisms by which the WB and IMF used in the imposition of structural adjustment policies (ESAPs) on many African governments prior to the seal of approval to get loans for economic liberalization and globalization, and given the underpin-nings of democracy, some policy analysts argue that the two processes are antithetical (Jeon, 1998; Jamal, 1994; Boafo-Arthur, 1991).

Zimbabwe's economy had been characterized by weak growth in the pro-ductive sector, with crises of varying degrees during the 1970s, and with much more severity in the late 1980s when export performance declined as reflected in the falling shares of Zimbabwe exports in world trade and an unchanged export structure. Since pre-independence, Zimbabwe's industrial base owed much to import-substitution (local production of goods as an alternative to imported ones) and to the incentives provided during its long period of isolation under international sanctions; there had clearly been economic benefits in past industrial strategies. At independence in 1980, Zimbabwe had the advantage of a sophisticated industrial economy, higher levels of entrepreneurial talent, and general human capital, which allowed it to use import substitution to better effect than its neighbors did, and it was considered a vibrant economy.

By the end of the 1980s, foreign debt rose sharply and the socioeco-nomic infrastructure deteriorated concurrently with environmental degra-dation (Dibie, 2014). Debates on the causes of the crises centered on two sets of factors. The first comprised exogenous factors such as bad weather, deteriorating terms of trade, fluctuation of international interest rates, reduced inflows of foreign aid, and non-performing state-owned enter-prises as constituting a huge drain on government finances. The second emphasized endogenous factors such as inappropriate domestic policies and incentive structures, and the mismanagement of public resources. The crises had important implications for transforming Zimbabwe's economy as envisaged by the WB and IMF, who recommended SAPs under the sec-ond premises that endogenous policy measures would improve the nation's economic growth. Zimbabwe's adoption of ESAPs in 1991 was a reversal of a previous government's position, rejecting the same structural reforms with the same conditionalities in the 1980s, when many sub-Saharan African early birds to SAPs adopted them. Whereas government ministries that deal with education, health, social services, and other social spending programs were not included, the process of ESAPs' adoption was domi-nated by officials of commercial banks and finance ministry (the most con-servative Western educated and wealthy members of the government), and the experienced white lobbying groups (the economic backbone). All these participants would be the potential primary beneficiaries of ESAPs. Even these collaborators felt pressured by the IMF and WB, because countries that do not comply with these Washington-based institutions, controlled by the Group of Seven (G7; the United States, United Kingdom, Japan, Germany, France, Canada, and Italy), would be isolated with their chances of getting loans and international aid thwarted. Thus, Zimbabwe's adoption of economic policy reforms was considered compatible with contemporary style for achieving sustainable national economic development. As will be demonstrated in proceeding sections, the initial Zimbabwean spurt of import-substituting industrial growth faltered not long after adopting ESAPs, a trend in many African countries.

This chapter examines business and government relations in Zimbabwe. It argues that economic structural adjustment programs (ESAP) are an inappropriate public policy for Zimbabwe because they have negatively affected business and government relations in the country. It also uses primary and secondary data to present an argument that the Government of Zimbabwe is not doing enough to encourage businesses to conform to the nation's ethical standards, values, and attitudes. This chapter seeks to explore the efficacy of laws and regulations as an effective tool for ethical dealing with consumers' protection, employees, products safety, investors, communities, and societies in Kenya. This chapter demonstrates that ESAPs have further marginalized the Zimbabwean people, particularly women and children, more than they were ever before, because the mandated budget austerity leads to the cutting of social spending and squeezing more from the taxpayer through increased education costs. This makes it harder for families to subsist forcing them to withdraw their children from school, particularly girls in a patrilineal society devaluing females. Prioritizing export agriculture leads to reduced food production, which forces women to be exploited in the labor force, in which labor laws have been loosened through ESAPs' deregulation that undermines labor social rights (Dibie et al. 2015). Results of the analysis of the study show that successful business and government relations can contribute significantly to the quality of the nation's economic growth. Therefore, creating an environment that enhances peace and social justice could also promote economic growth in the country. In addition, some of the policies implemented after independence by the Zimbabwean government aimed at redistributing resources or alleviating poverty have been unsuccessful, or had perverse effects on the people and business corporations of the nation, complicated by the absence of democratic procedure in their adoption and implementation. It is therefore clear that no single alignment of government and business can offer a permanent solution to Zimbabwe's economic development problems. The chapter recommends strategies for the institutionalization of a successful business and government relations to improve the economy of Zimbabwe.

Premises of Business and Government Relations

This section addresses the premise of business and government relations and explained why such relationship might have both positive and negative impact of the economy of Zimbabwe. According to Ebert and Griffin 2015 and Lahne (2013), several of the problems nations face today are too big to be resolved by government alone, and global businesses will inevitably be affected. As a result, most business should form partnership with government to tackle the fiscal and monetary problems that are associated with unemployment, inflation, and regulations with their respective nation. In addition to the argument presented previously, the stakeholders approach contends that businesses are stakeholders too. They have a voice and should make it heard. Responsible businesses can serve their shareholders well by putting their case to government. Keeping your head down and hoping that politics might go away is unwise. Engage constructively, openly, and straightforwardly in order to collectively address the economic problems in the country (Ya Ni & Van Wart, 2016). Further, the relationship between corporations and other stakeholders such like employees, shareholders, community-based organizations, consumers, and ethical consideration can best describe as paramount to foster economic growth in any country (Carroll & Buchholtz, 2015; Mankiw 2018). This why a stakeholder approach becomes very useful in business and government relations.

Sengupta (2011) contends that government agency and the business corporation are two of the most powerful institutions in modern society. The shifting and complicated relationship between them exerts great influence on the changing performance of the economy, as well as on the lives of citizens. These relationships range from cooperative to competition, from friendly to hostile. It is also very important to note that although each side possesses basic powers, each has an important need for the other. For instance, the basic power of the business corporation lies in the widespread recognition that it is a fundamental mechanism for achieving human progress. According to Lahne (2013), the public's strong belief in the role of private markets, completion, and the independent business corporation ultimately limits the ability of government to dominate the economy in which the public and private sectors interacts in many ways.

Other scholars describe one of the hindrances to effective partnership between business, government, and civil society as secrecy. One of the hindrances is dealing with administrative practices, and laws that enthrone secrecy and "ad hoc-ism" in government affairs (Dibie et al. 2015; Lehne et al., 2011). As a result, government may not be a willing partner with the business corporation or civil society organization (CSOs), because oftentimes CSOs blow up perceived failure, but are unable to supply crucial recommendations for the public policy (Dibie, 2014). A brief reconnaissance of national experiences in modern times reveals that capitalistic economies generally perform much better than those with a much larger government presence. Most notable are those in societies ruled by communist and socialist regimes (Lahne, 2013). Moreover, the capitalist nations, on balance, provide their citizens with more personal freedom.

The neoclassical approach to economic growth has used two basic premises (Sengupta, 2011). The first is the competitive model of Walrasian equilibrium, where markets play a critical role in allocating resources efficiently. The second premise of the neoclassical model assumes that technology is given. This means that the model did not recognize investment, research and development, and human capital through learning. It could therefore be argued that the neoclassical growth model developed by Slow fails to explain the most basic fact of actual growth behavior (Mankiw, 2018). The implication of the omission is that the long-term rate of national growth is determined outside the model, and is independent of preferences and most aspects of the production function and policy measures.

The public sector influences private sector decision making in a great variety of ways. Most analyses of the interaction between business and government focus on the pros and cons of public policy action. This chapter turns the table on that conventional approach. Rather than just attempting to play public policy maker, we will also examine the interaction between business and government from the vantage point of the private business corporation and its management. Clearly, the reconciliation between the pressure of the private marketplace and reinvigoration of the public sector is a matter requiring careful balance.

The Untapped Unique National Economic Capacity

Competition can create values for the consumers of any country far greater than the wealth it bestows on successful entrepreneurs and their financial backers. Further, those consumer benefits must be widely distributed in order to achieve economic growth (Mankiw, 2018; OECD 2014). The failure of the Government of Zimbabwe to distribute consumer benefit is one of the reasons for its inability to achieve progressive economic growth over the past three decades. The nation's regulatory framework remains costly and time-consuming. Incorporating a business costs more than the level of average annual income, and completing licensing requirements takes more than 400 days. The formal labor market remains rudimentary. Dollarization, instituted in 2009 to end hyperinflation, now raises the specter of deflation as the U.S. dollar strengthens and the government continues to delay meaningful structural reforms (Index of Economic Freedom, 2015).

The United Nations Human Development Report (2014) reveals that Zimbabwe's economic freedom score is 37.6, making its economy the 175th freest in the 2015 Index. Its score has increased by 2.1 points from last year, driven by a particularly large gain in the control of government spending and improvements in six other economic freedoms, including trade freedom and fiscal freedom. Nonetheless, Zimbabwe is ranked last out of 46 countries in sub-Saharan Africa, and its overall score remains far below the world and regional averages (Index of Economic Freedom, 2015). It is interesting to note that after near economic collapse in the late 2000s, Zimbabwe has experienced five consecutive years of improvements in economic freedom. Over the past five years, economic freedom in Zimbabwe has improved by 15.5 points, the largest improvement of any nation. The biggest score gains have been in monetary freedom and the control of government spending. A move to dollarize the economy has brought the hyperinflation of 2008 and 2009 under control (Index of Economic Freedom, 2015).

Despite this minor growth, the nation remains one of the world's least free economies. President Robert Mugabe's government is corrupt and inefficient. The labor market is one of the most restricted in the world, and business licensing forces most workers to seek employment in the informal sector. The violent seizure of land has underscored poor government land reform policies and upset investor confidence in a once-vibrant agricultural sector (Index of Economic Freedom, 2015).

The fundamental macroeconomic problem in Zimbabwe in the early1990s and two decades after was that the sum of what the government of President Mugabe wanted and planned to do was greater than the resources available. Such a situation was probably inevitable, but the government's difficulty in discerning the macroeconomic limitations on new initiatives was greatly increased by the unusual circumstances of the first two ESAP years: a commodity boom; promises of more international aid than what was eventually delivered; expectations of a peace dividend that did not come; initial high rates of economic growth; and initial reduction in foreign debt. All of these circumstances created unrealistic expectations, concealing the probability that the government's plans would be impossible to finance. The government has been very slow to meet adjustment time lines, being disappointed by unmet promises of international aid (Index of Economic Freedom, 2015). This created a debt problem. Drought and terms-of-trade shocks made things worse. Drought was bound to occur periodically; only the timing was unpredictable. No allowance was made for the likelihood of these shocks in ESAP agreements. The severe drought of 1991–1992 in Zimbabwe provided justification for the government's reluctance to engage in cutting expenditure. When, however, the government made no progress with reducing the size of the budget deficit after the agricultural sector recovery in 1993–1994, the IMF began to apply pressure for compliance. This marked a turning point in the ability of the government to maintain autonomy in deciding on economic policy.

Globalization of world markets became one of the greatest challenges facing Zimbabwe, even in past two decades. Globalization enlightened us on the limitations of statehood autonomy, particularly after the end of the Cold War when abuse and exploitation of Africa was accompanied by its loss of the geopolitical strategic value. More African countries have become classified as least developed nations, and not one African country became classified as a developed nation as a result of efforts by the United States and Russia or the United Nations. The adverse effects of trade restrictions and protectionism increased in the 1990s. Marginalization of the masses from political and decision-making processes, declining competitiveness in Southern Africa Development Commission and the global market, excessive state intervention in the economy, militating against investment and productivity, deteriorating social services, and standard of living became the norm.

Social development and progress of the 1980s was clearly being eroded in the early 1990s with falling per capita incomes, unemployment, and underemployment, accelerating ecological degradation and hunger. In the mid-1990s, Zimbabwe was confronted with serious internal and external contradictions, which intensified marginalization. The crisis became more pronounced, with mounting foreign debts, declining exports, refugee problems, servicing foreign debt, urban strife due to increased food prices, and retrenchment. The failure of wage employment to keep up with formal sector wage-employment created unemployment and underemployment. Zimbabwe's crisis reached alarming proportions in the late 1990s (Kadenge et al., 1992).

When Zimbabwe adopted the structural adjustment policies in 1990, the major features of the policies pursued included labor retrenchment, trade liberalization and currency devaluation, subsidy withdrawal, and an increase in user fees (which rendered basic services like health and education unaffordable to the average worker). As elsewhere, macroeconomic reforms have had very serious political implications in Zimbabwe. These measures were seen by many as politically risky because of independent Zimbabwe's colonial experience with unfair adjustment policies. Industrial restructuring and the upgrading of industrial competitiveness have been components of these reforms prescribed by the IMF and World Bank. An implicit assumption of SAPs has been that enterprise-level inefficiencies are primarily a reflection of inappropriate macro-economic policies and distortions in resource allocation precipitated by selective industrial policies. Reforms, therefore, are based on the premise that appropriate adjustment at the macro-level, accompanied by the "freeing up" of market forces, liberalization of trade, and privatization of parastatals, would provide the necessary and sufficient conditions for industrial recovery and growth. Inefficient activities, which exist only because of government induced distortions rather than the presence of learning sequences and market failures will die out, while resources will move to efficient activities that emerge in response to market incentives (Mkandawire, 1992; Remmer, 1993). As a result, Zimbabwe and other debtor African nations' industry would exhibit the dynamism and competitiveness that characterized East Asian economies between 1980 and 1996.

The theory underlying adjustment and market-friendly policies does not offer a satisfactory explanation for rapid industrialization in the type of economic culture that prevails in Zimbabwe, especially under the leadership of

President Mugabe. This is because the theory ignores the capability of development and the need to overcome market failures in its process. This has an important bearing on the general issue of business and government relations in the country. The existence of pervasive market failures raises the costs of adjustment to import competition, and holds back the creation of new manufacturing activities and exports (United Nations Human Development Report, 2014). The EU's verdict on the fairness of the 2013 elections is crucial to a decision on how to continue to place sanctions against Zimbabwe. The United States also believed that the 2013 presidential elections were flawed and decided to continue to place economic sanctions on the government of almost 91-year-old President Robert Mugabe that had been ruling for 35 years. It is noted that the sanctions from the United States and the European Union has made business and government relationships in the country very weak.

It is clear that SAPs policies have also failed in Zimbabwe, because once the usual simplifying assumptions on learning are dropped, merely removing government interventions may not catalyze industrial growth and competitiveness. This is another factor that has seriously affected cordial business and government relations in the country. Even in economies with relatively advanced levels of technology capability like the United States, rapid liberalization imposes severe costs if not accompanied by a strategy of upgrading and gearing liberalization to the learning needs of different activities. By contrast, where the pace of opening up and support policies adopted to help firms upgrade is both guided by a clear strategy, the results are far better (Jamal, 1994; Jeon, 1997). The liberalization policy itself lacks full credibility and was not properly communicated to firms in Zimbabwe, inducing them to remain passive and wait for policies to revert to old, less threatening patterns. What is surprising is that the disappointing reaction to liberalization was not anticipated, even a basic understanding of technological processes would have led to a different design of the liberalization program (Jeong, 1997; Gibbon, 1992; Nelson, 1990). On the contrary, enterprise-level reactions are still not fully appreciated by those who designed and propagate adjustment programs, at least in their pronouncement on policy reform.

An alternative argument has been that most of sub-Saharan Africa, including Zimbabwe, is not really suited to industrialization, beyond the elementary level of resources-based and low technology activities that do not compete with imports. Indeed, some classical economists prescribe this while forgetting that the endowments that lead to successful industrialization are not given but made as a result of deliberation policy. For example, would they have said that the Asian Tigers had a natural comparative advantage in industrial activity 30 years ago? The logic of the structural adjustment programs argument leads to the efficiency outcome that very little industry may survive in Zimbabwe, with growth proceeding mainly from primary and service sector activities.

Policy measures have deliberately ignored industrialization and rather have given greater incentives to the production of primary commodities. Recent figures show that Zimbabwe's foreign debt rose from 45% of GDP in 1990 to 75% in 1994, falling to 67% of GDP at the end of 1995 (Jenkins, 1996). Around 95% of this is government debt, including the parastatals or government-owned business organizations. This increased aid sought and received during the 1992 drought meant that the debt service ratio rose to 30%, although it subsequently fell to 22% in 1995. The nation is, however, vulnerable to external shocks, which may again force it to raise its external borrowing.

A combination of structural adjustment and the rising economic crisis has not lead to public expenditure cuts in Zimbabwe and similarly situated countries worldwide. Many economic problems of Zimbabwe are directly related to deregulation. Since 1996, Zimbabwe has been facing potential collapse (Mupedziswa 1999; Mhone 1993; United Nations 2014). For the government to get the 176 million dollars from the IMF for crisis management, the government had to give up land reforms and restrict government spending. The civil service, with a personnel of 180,000, including social workers, eats up one-third of the government's annual budget expenditure, leading to a general inequitable decrease of incomes. For example, government officials have had their incomes increased by 130%, while other workers have received 3%–20% increases, and many have lost employment due to retrenchment and worse still the number of the unemployed rose to a record high of over 50% by 1995 (Carnoy, 1995). The introduction of ESAP also had deleterious impacts on some small industries, leading to their closure due to high operation costs and interest rates on loans (Kawewe, 1998a). The development of grassroots and small companies has been constrained by high interest rates on bank loans and inflation. Because urban populations of sub-Saharan Africa comprise a majority of the urban poor, the decline in their living standards has become massive and devastating over the SAP years. Even the rural dwellers who had previously utilized the urban kin as a safety net in times of hardship have become more vulnerable, especially within the context of an inherited a distorted colonial land distribution and ownership pattern (Kawewe, 1998a; Palmer & Burich, 1992).

Higher unemployment leads to declining nutrition, health, and education standards, and increasing school absences, while at the same time increasing the national demand for tertiary and secondary schooling. These factors combined lead to a corresponding decline in income (Carnoy, 1995). As food prices rise, some families have cut down on nutrition and food intake. For example, some families have stopped buying chicken, beef, bread, and fish. They have also cut back on the staple food (corn meal), vegetables, and the number of meals per day, from the standard three to two or one, in order to make ends meet. Obviously such conditions adversely affect the health of children and women, especially female children (Kawewe, 1998a). Urban families scramble for any available patch of land to grow crops and vegetables for consumption and for hawking. Even professionals' efforts at imparting nutrition knowledge are not translated into better nutrition when clients cannot afford the bare minimum food requirements. Such urban conditions of women have serious implications for children, childcare, and women's health and welfare, compounded by the burden women experience through overwork. As elsewhere in the world, the burden of extra work is usually unevenly distributed, with most of it shouldered by women (Kawewe, 1998a).

Zimbabwe's socioeconomic disparity, particularly the colonial legacy of unequal land distribution by race, is directly related to employment and sustainable economic development. Of the 11.5 million population of Zimbabwe, 7 million (75%) are blacks who live in the overcrowded and underdeveloped rural reservations, with some as squatters who are landless. There are 100,000 whites that comprise 1% of the Zimbabwean population, and 4% (4,000) of whites control 80% of the private enterprise and 50% of the country's arable land. Numerically, 4,000 whites own the country's best farmland, consisting of 11 million hectares, and generate 40% of the country's commercial agricultural-goods export revenue (Wanmali et al., 1997).

It is interesting to note that despite these unequal land privileges in Zimbabwe, the World Bank and IMF recommendation for structural adjustment did not address the land issue. The pre-existing post-independence national corrective measures such as racial reconciliation, nationalization, and indigenization, in which the government would redistribute land equitably for peasant resettlement, were not effectively accomplished, as these national policies would undermine corporate rights and the fundamental economic bases of ESAPs (Bello, 1993; Global Exchange, 2000). For example, the IMF and WB finance big rural projects like dams, roads, and power plants to facilitate economic development projects under SAPS, but these devastate biodiversity and the environment, and lead to social and population dislocation. Additionally, SAPS reduce labor and environmental protection, leaving small farmers and businesses to compete with large multinational corporations, which leads to workers being paid starvation wages and unable to fend for their families, to the point of being forced to live in inhumane conditions or left homeless. Without enough land, the urban-retrenched workers have no hope of subsisting in overcrowded rural areas whose inhabitants have historically viewed urban-employed relations as privileged and as their safety net in periods of hardship (Dibie et al 2015; Sengura 2011). Thus, ESAPs have been predictably devastating to the poor, further suffocating them without adequate public welfare, without control of their economy and access to basic services, even more so than in the United States, because Zimbabwe is a poor country to begin with. The cycle of impoverishment is perpetuated and not eliminated.

Urban unemployment created a surge in the rural areas, while the land equation had not been addressed successfully, because it faced opposition from a historically powerful white lobbying group, the Commercial Farmers Union (CFU), one of the strong advocates for ESAPs. The CFU has steadfastly opposed land reforms since colonial times, by claiming that changing from large-scale farming to small-scale peasant farming with communal tenure would devastate the economy. Such a stance is inherited from racist colonial assumptions that indigenous African peasants are inefficient, and that they would degrade the new land in the same way as the communal lands, which were called Tribal Trust Lands during the colonial period. These assumptions have been challenged and refuted by progressive Africanists (Moyo, 1994, 1995; Velempini & Traver 1997; Palmer & Burich, 1992). The fact is that colonialism cultivated the soil erosion of the semi-arid communal lands by packing the peasants and their domestic animals like sardines in these areas, and by introducing agricultural methods that were not environmentally friendly. Land reforms also faced opposition from the peasants, which included mass protest and public disturbance when they found out that the land was changing hands from the white elite to the black elite for the purpose of satisfying commercial agricultural production for export to meet ESAPs' donor obligations (Kawewe, 1998a; Goga 1996). The promotion of macroeconomic agricultural policies supported by ESAPs has perpetuated peasant impoverishment.

Even the Social Dimensions Program, a WB and IMF social services program and stop-gap measure to alleviate the so-called temporary hardships arising out of the ESAPs, benefits a selected minority of former middle-class victims of retrenchment in cities, and for only a limited period of time, leaving the rural and urban poor in devastating impoverishment. Additionally, for the past 50 years, there has existed an apparent discrepancy between stated objectives of the WB and other multinational institutions of capitalism and the free market economy and implementation goals. Araghi (1997) revealed information from a secret World Bank document that spells out the institution's hidden philosophy and global economic development plans that are intended to purposefully force four million people from their lands in order to create room for Western projects in the South. It would appear then that Zimbabwe's indigenization and land repossession programs to resettle peasants would be contrary to this financial donor's thesis or secret plan. Thus, ESAPs erosion of the social welfare of indigenous peoples of Zimbabwe, with much severity on women and children already marginalized, seems in line with SAP's goals being primarily driven by the economic interests of the industrialized nations.

When these most powerful political and sociocultural and ideological institutions of the world, fashioned after trickle-down economics, now make proclamations to improve women's education and productivity in the emerging economies (World Bank, 1999), they reflect a double standard in that they steadfastly impose SAP policies that require drastic cuts in social spending, of which education is a part, and then when poverty becomes an eye sore, debtor governments are blamed. These donors then intervene and assume a rescuer/savior role for the poor, while at the same time undermining the authority of the state on its people. For example, when many rural women and children died during the drought of the early 1990s, the World Bank intervened by forcing the government to drop education and health fees, which had been introduced to meet budget austerity measures under ESAPs.

However, SAP had mixed impacts on economic development and growth. While macroeconomic indicators show positive effects of structural adjustment on development and growth, many Zimbabwe citizens find it difficult to cope with the overall effects of adjustment. The problems affected too many citizens by the high cost of utilities; the withdrawal of subsidies on health, education, transportation, and agricultural inputs; the retrenchment of labor and the consequent high unemployment rate; and chronic low salaries for workers, especially in the public sector, which continue to engage the attention of many. There has been, therefore, a genuine fear that democratization and its embedded freedom would lead to a revolt by the masses against further imposition of draconian adjustment policies.

Another negative aspect of adjustment is the heavy reliance on external financial support. Zimbabwe faces a bleak future because of the over-dependence on external financial inflows. The high levels of dependence on foreign aid equally cast a shadow on the impact of structural adjustment. Because of abnormally high levels of assistance from donors, there is much difficulty in disentangling the effects of external aid from the effects of adjustment programs on Zimbabwe's development (Jenkins, 1996). Jenkins (1996) and Kawewe (1998b) therefore call into question the resilience of the much-touted economic turnaround. Contrary to the IMF-WB recent rush at bailing out the Asian economies with quick loan packages worth tens of billions of dollars, in Africa the economic relief efforts have been a never-ending stingy effort, in which negotiations can drag on for months; when approved, the allotments reflect more of a lifelong dependency program for sub-Saharan Africa (French, 1998). Furthermore, Asian nations can recover from the meltdown through IMF-WB bailouts to pay creditors and to absorb the immediate severe economic shock arising from credit and banking systems (Rotberg, 1998).

The impact of public policy on the citizens of the United States is parallel somewhat to the situation in Zimbabwe. In the 1960s and 1970s, the number of homeless Americans began to increase gradually in the wake of a series of public policy shifts. Most significant were those affecting the availability of low-income housing and the treatment of the mentally ill. It was the contraction in national social spending during this period, however, which broadened and deepened the problem of homelessness. Beginning with President Reagan's own Omnibus Reconciliation Act of 1981, federal funding for a vast array of social programs was slashed or capped, in a process that soon resonated throughout all levels of government and community. While military spending increased by more than 40% in the 1980s, funding for both health and job-training programs was slashed by the same amount, and federal support of housing programs was reduced by almost 80%. Included in the cuts were programs that helped low-income families avoid the worst ravages of poverty, such as Aid to Families with Dependent Children (AFDC), where eligibility levels stiffened and benefit levels that already left families well below the poverty line were sharply lowered. As more Americans were sinking into poverty, billions of dollars were also taken away from the Food Stamp Program, eliminating one million recipients (Reich, 1989; da Costa Nunez, 1995).

The policies of the 1980s were devastating to the American poor and, to a large extent, account for the unprecedented rise in poverty and homeless rates, as well as the increased complexity of the problems now facing poor families. Economic trade agreements and liberalization have had a devastating impact on the poor in both developed and developing countries. The North American Free Trade Agreement (NAFTA), for example, had adverse effects on the middle class and poor Americans through retrenchment without corresponding increases in social spending on human capital development, job creation, and training in marketable skills, welfare, and social service benefits (Kawewe, 1999). IMF mismanagement in the South creates financial crises that translate into poverty for both developing and developed countries. For example, when the IMF mismanagement led to the financial crises in Indonesia, South Korea, Thailand, and others, resulting in a deep depression, 200 million newly poor were created in these countries. Worse still, the IMF, using conditions for noncompliance, directed these countries to export their way out of the crises by dumping their steel in the US markets, resulting in over 12,000 American steel worker layoffs (World Bank, 2012; Danaher, 2000). Free trade agreements have translated into lost jobs as companies folded up, relocated, or operated their industries in the South in order to exploit a cheap labor force—hence the 1999 Seattle rallies by people from all over the world opposing the WTO's effort to have total control of the world's economy and resources for the benefit of the wealthy and corporations (Global Exchange, 2000; Danaher, 2000). Not only has the total number of homeless Americans increased substantially in the past 10 years, but also there has been a marked change in the composition of this group in the 1990s. Even the best designed education and training programs produced only small gains for the poor, especially welfare recipients. Economic feasibility has historically translated into reduction in welfare rolls, while compromising the social cost, as in the case of workfare and managed care. Welfare reforms of the 1990s have been successful in shrinking the welfare rolls and reducing cost, but not poverty reduction (Caputo, 1993, 1994; US Government, 1996; Freedman, 1990; Dibie et al 2015).

Conclusion

This chapter has examined the relationship between business and government in Zimbabwe. It argues that the partnership that exists between government and business in Zimbabwe is symbolic in the sense that some corporations exited like monopoly. As a result, maintaining competitive economy does not come easily in the country. The truth is that the typical cases of monopoly of power arise from the actions of the Government of Zimbabwe under President Mugabe's watch. In other instances, the Government of President Mugabe awarded monopoly power to private companies, notably in the area of communication, transportation, and utilities (United Nations Human Development Report, 2014).

The way to move forward is for the business sector in the country to aim toward satisfying the stakeholder, at the same time contributing to the sustainable development process in Zimbabwe. On one hand, business definitely needs the society to consume its goods and services, serve as a labor force, and help fight its cause when needed. On the other hand, society benefits from business in the supply of its needs in terms of goods and services (Lahne, 2013). Furthermore, while society is organized, protected, and enriched by government and business partnership, government institutions, on the other hand, foster and provide the enabling macro-environment, and regulate the economy to ensure that business organizations conform to the rules of the game (Moorhead & Griffin, 2015). Trust in government is an important ingredient of economic success. This is especially true in the case of representative democracies (Ferrell et al., 2015). Any revolving elections and unethical political candidate practices could only decrease trust in government, and in turn result in losses for the entire business corporations and citizens in the long run.

Additionally, some parallels have been drawn between the impact of economic policies on social welfare of the poor in Zimbabwe and the United States. In both cases, there is a need to integrate social and economic development by addressing issues of human capital development and budget austerity versus consumption. Once one of Africa's vibrant economies, Zimbabwe has stagnated, to the detriment of women and children. There is a possibility of serious instability and unrest in Zimbabwe as a wave of political turmoil sweeps the country (Schillinger, 1998). Social workers can work collaboratively with various groups, including the trade unions, to find peaceful and productive life-saving solutions to the country's problems. The general impression held about Africa is filled with mythology, as there are smart Africans, leaders, women, men, and children, as anywhere in the world, but the existence of very real problems in sub-Saharan Africa with people still surviving is not deniable (Toler, 1998). Progressive human service professionals can contribute to effective public policy formulation and implementation, which requires direction toward economic and social rights, commitment, and resources. It is paramount that the new era of

Zimbabwe must strive to reform and revitalize both government and business so that each sector can be a source of strength for the other.

References

Araghi, F. (1997). 50 Years Is Enough: The Case Against the World Bank and the International Monetary Fund/Faith and Credit: The World Bank's Secular Empire Mortgaging the Earth: The World Bank, Environmental Impoverishment, and the Crisis of Development. *Contemporary Sociology, 26*(2), 184–187.

Bello, W. (1993). *Dark History: The U.S. Structural Adjustment and Global Poverty*. Oakland, CA: Institute for Food and Development Policy.

Boafo-Arthur, K. (1991). Ghana: Structural Adjustment, Democratization, and the Politics of Continuity. *African Studies Review, 42*(2), 41–72.

Caputo, R. K. (1993). *Welfare and Freedom American Style II*. Lanham, MD: University Press of America.

Caputo, R. K. (1994). Family Poverty, Unemployment Rates and AFDC Payments: Trends Among Blacks and Whites. *Families and Society, 74*, 515–526.

Carnoy, M. (1995). Structural Adjustment and the Changing Face of Education. *International Labour Review, 134*(6), 653–671.

Carroll, A. and Buchholtz, A. (2015). *Business and Society: Ethics, Sustainability and Stakeholder Management*. Stamford, CT: Cengage Learning.

Da Costa, N. (1995). The New Poverty in Urban America: Family Homelessness. *Journal of Children*, Vol. 1, (3) 23–37.

Danaher, K. (2000). *A New Approach to the Third World Debt Crisis*. Global Exchange Web Page, 1–3. www.globalexchange.org/economy/alternatives/debt Crisis.html. Accessed October 14, 2016.

Dibie, R. (2014). *Comparative Perspective of Environmental Policies and Issues*. New York, NY: Routledge Press.

Dibie, R., Edoho, F. M., and Dibie, J. (2015). "Analysis of Capacity Building and Economic Growth in Sub-Saharan Africa." *International Journal of Business and Social Science*. Vol. 2, no. 12, 1–25.

Ebert, R. and Griffin, R. (2015). *Business Essentials*. Boston, MA: Pearson.

Ferrell, O. C., Hiirt, G. and Ferrell, L. (2015). *Business: A Changing World*. New York, NY: McGraw-Hill Press.

Freedman, H. D. (1990). Special Employment Programs in Developed and Developing Countries. *International Labor Review, 129*(2), 165–184.

French, W. H. (1998). Africans Resentful as Asia Rakes in Aid. *New York Times*, 8–12.

Global Exchange. (2000). *Global Economy: World Bank/IMF Factsheet*. Author, 1–4. www.globalexchange.org/wbimf/facts.html. Accessed October 14, 2016.

Goga, S. (1996). The Politics of Economic Reform in Zimbabwe: Continuity, Change and Development. *Journal of American Planning Association, 62*(4), 542–543.

Index of Economic Freedom. (2015). *Zimbabwe*. www.heritage.org/index/pdf/2015/countries/zimbabwe.pdf. Accessed October 14, 2016.

Jamal, T. (1994). Have Structural Adjustment Programs Worked. *Africa Quarterly*, 4(4), 17–30.

Jenkins, C. (1996). *The Politics of Economic Policy-Making in Zimbabwe After Independence*. Institute of Economics and Statistics, Oxford: University of Oxford.

Jeon, H. W. (1997). The Role of African States in Economic Development. *Africa Insight, 27*(2), 85–90.

Jeon, H. W. (1996). Ghana: Lurching Toward Economic Rationality. *World Affairs, 159*(2), 71–81.

Kadenge, P. G., Ndoro, H. and Zizwi, B. M. (1992). *Zimbabwe's Structural Adjustment Program: The First Year Experience*. Harare: Government Press.

Kawewe, S. M. (1998a). Social-Networking Zimbabwean Families: An African Traditional Approach to Waging a War Against HIV/AIDS. *Social Development Issues, 18*(2), 34–51.

Kawewe, S. M. (1998b). The Impact of Gendered Unequal Land Distribution, Population Movement and HIV/AIDS on the Welfare of Zimbabwean Women and Children: Implications for Peace and Social Justice in Southern Africa. Paper Presented to the Joint World Congress of IFSW & IASSW, Peace and Social Justice: The Challenges Facing Social Work: Symposium on Women, Jerusalem, Israel.

Kawewe, S. M. (1999). The Impact of Trade Agreements and Monetary Policies on Global Communities: A Case Study of the Zimbabwe's Economic Structural Adjustment Programs' Impact on Social Welfare. Paper Presented at the 45th Annual Program Meeting, Council on Social Work Education: Opening the Golden Gate of Opportunity. San Francisco, CA.

Lahne, R. (2013). *Government and Business*. Washington, DC: Congressional Quarterly Press.

Mankiw, G. (2015). *Macroeconomic*. 7th Edition. Boston, MA: Cengage Learning.

Moyo, S. (1995). *The Land Question in Zimbabwe*. Harare: SAPES.

Mazrui, A. A. (1996). The New Dynamics of Security: The United Nations and Africa. *World Policy Journal, 13*(2), 37–43.

Moorhead, G. and Griffin, R. (2014). *Organizational Behavior: Managing People and Organization*. Stamford, CT: Cengage Learning.

Moyo, S. (1994). Economic Nationalism and Land Reform in Zimbabwe. Harare: SAPES.

Mupedziswa, R. (1996). The Challenge of Economic Development in an African Developing Country: Social Work in Zimbabwe. *International Social Work, 39*(1), 41–54.

Mupedziswa, R. (1999). "Bruised and battered: the struggles of older female informal traders in urban areas of Zimbabwe since the economic reforms." *Southern African Journal of Gerontology, 8* (1), 9–13.

Mhone, G. (1993). The impact of structural adjustment on the urban informal sector in Zimbabwe. Discussion Paper 2. Geneva: International Labour Organisation.

Mundy, V. 1995. The urban poverty datum line in Zimbabwe. Harare: Catholic Commission for Justice and Peace in Zimbabwe.

Nelson, J. (1990). The Politics of Economic Adjustment in Developing Countries. In Joan Nelson (Ed.), *Fragile Coalitions: The Politics of Economic Adjustment*. Princeton, NJ: Princeton University Press, 123–151.

OECD Factbook (2014). Economic, Environmental and Social Statistics. www. oecdilibrary.org/economics/oecd-factbook-2014_factbook-2014-en. Accessed May 7, 2016.

Palmer, R. and Burich, I. (1992). *Zimbabwe: A Land Divided*. Oxford: Oxfarm.

Potts, D. (1995). Shall We Go Home? Increasing Urban Poverty in African Cities and Migration Processes. *The Geographical Journal, 161*(3), 245–271.

Reich, R. (1989). As the World Turns. *New Republic*, no 3876:28.

Remmer, K. (1993). The Political Economy of Elections in Latin America. *American Political Science Review, 87*(2), 71–93.

Rotberg, R. (1998, January 21). Asian Nations Aren't Alone; Zimbabwe Needs Help Too. *Christian Science Monitor*, 19–20.

Schillinger, K. (1998). Wave of Political Turmoil Sweeps Zimbabwe: Longtime Leader Loses Grip as Economy Deteriorates. *Boston Globe*, A10–A12.

Sengupta, J. (2011). Understanding Economic Growth: Modern Theory and Experience. New York: Springer Press.

Toler, D. L. (1998). Secrets and Lies: Debunking the Myths About Africa. *Essence*, 28(12), 74–80.

United Nations. (2014). *Human Development Index*. New York, NY: Oxford University Press.

United States Government. (1996). *The Personal Responsibility and Reconciliation Act*. Pub.L.No. 104–193.

Velempini, E. and Traver, K. D. (1997). Accessibility of Nutritious African Foods for Adequate Diet in Bulawayo, Zimbabwe. *Journal of Nutritional Education*, 29(3), 120–127.

Wanmali, S. and Islam, Y. (1997). Rural Infrastructure and Agricultural Development in Southern Africa: A Centre-Periphery Perspective. *The Geographical Journal*, 163(3), 259–269.

World Bank. (2012). *World Development Report*. New York: Oxford University Press.

World Bank. (2014). The World Bank Group in Africa: An Overview of the World Banks's Work in Sub-Sahara Africa. 1–11. www.worldbank.org/html/extdr/offrep/afr/overview.html.

World Bank. (20016). *World Bank Development Report*. New York: Oxford University Press.

Ya Ni, A. and Van Wart, M. (2016). *Building Business–Government Relations: A Skills Approach*. New York: Routledge Press.

Case Study

Kome and Ojanigo Limited Liability Company (KOLLC)

Kome and Ojanigo Limited Liability Company (KOLLC) was founded in January 1986 in Indianapolis by a group of physicians and pharmacists as a social welfare organization. In its earliest stages of development, some of the founders had a clear picture of the obstacles to delivering excellent medical services in Indiana and across the United States. The founding chief executive officer Dr. John Deshon and other associate directors pinpointed the predominant reasons for flagging competitiveness. They indicated that the duplication of efforts among manufacturing innovators, difficulties in transferring technological breakthroughs from university to industry, and the inability of individual industry members to commit the time and funds to research projects needed for continued technological advances were among the crucial problems.

As a social organization, KOLLC was tax-exempt because it worked in the IRS's view to further the common good and general welfare of the people of a community such as bring about civic betterment and social and health improvement. The founders of KOLLC, however, wanted to know how their newly formed company was different from a charitable nonprofit company. Dr. Deshon explained to the founders that the major difference between 501(c)(3) and 501(c) organizations is that the later do not face the same limitation on political activity that are imposed on the former. He states that because of these differences, 501(c)(4) organizations are tax-exempt, but gifts made to them are not tax deductible. Thus, organizations that are qualified under section 501(c) of the IRS code are tax-exempt—that is, they are not required to pay federal taxes on their income. However, only those classified under section 501(c) (3), the charitable nonprofits, are both tax-exempt themselves and also eligible to receive gifts that are tax deductible for the donors.

The goal of KOLLC is to empower people to have better lives by proving them with low cost medical products and other means to get a better life, whether it is health education, employment, or even simple entertainment. KOLLC is also committed to a mission not based on profit, but on social change. The company also tries to be innovative in order to be successful, self-sustaining in its business ventures. One of the reputations that KOLLC has achieved is that of an organization that has a social goal and has been involved in an economic venture.

In the next few years, the steering committees and Dr. Deshon met regularly to define common research needs and locate funding sources.

They also sought industry sponsors from high-technology companies with an understanding of the problems in manufacturing of medical products, and a desire to do more than merely supplying money.

For the first 30 years KOLLC managed to stay in the black. In the early 1990s things started to get much better for KOLLC. The organization made more profit and opened branches across the state. The company's profit was, however, reinvested in the organization, due to its status as a tax-exempt charitable organization. It established accounting and finance, material management, and human resources systems to effectively coordinate its different facilities. Of particular concern to the organization, however, was a market share that had been declining since May 1996 for six months. Senior management recognized that other medical supply companies in the state of Indiana were newer, had better facilities, were more "user friendly," and had captured the interest of referring physicians. Management, therefore, requested the help of some consultants to make recommendations on how KOLLC could be more innovative in implementing a new total quality management process in the organization. One of the consultants noted that implementing a quality process was a major organizational change, requiring a thorough diagnosis of the company, a considerable commitment of resources, and a high level of involvement by senior management. For most companies, the loss of even a small percentage of profit is considered to be a notable setback. KOLLC is a non-profit health care organization that provides a wide range of health care services and products.

During the 1990s when KOLLC had more business than it could handle, there was little incentive for its CEO to manage smartly. The company services and sales tripled from $10 million to $30 million within six years. Today, however, innovation or smart management is the key to KOLLC's success and survival. The KOLLC has been, however, plagued with problems since 1997. The company was faced with the problem of cutting $3.6 million from its budget due to reduced business and steep competition. The company's survival called for innovation in restructuring and trimming costs. KOLLC restructured its workforce by cutting 25 positions. It also reduced its plant space and made maximum use of what space was left. KOLLC was able to save $8.6 million annually for three years. The priority during the time of crisis was to ensure that employee output increased incrementally. In an attempt to change the company's predicament, a new chief executive officer (CEO), Dr. Oputa, was hired to take charge of the organization. The previous CEO, Dr. John Deshon, was forced to retire. The vice-president of the company, Mike Peters, reports to Dr. Oputa. Mike Peters has been with the organization for more than five years and has only been appointed vice-president for about a year.

As a result of decrease in health services sales and other business, Dr. Oputa decided to eliminate layers of the corporate hierarchy. The new CEO found it challenging to implement changes in an organization where some managers were having difficulty accepting that there was immediate need for a change in culture and the way business used to be. There was little doubt that KOLLC needed to change radically in order to survive. Indeed, the changes in KOLLC have been dramatic, but this experience is far from unique in the world of business. Clearly, change has become the rule rather than the exception.

Dr. Oputa's new approach was built on the premise that KOLLC should consist of seven elements, divided into hard S's and the soft S's. The hard S's—Strategy, Structure, and System—are fairly easy to identify. They can be found in the KOLLC strategic statement, corporate plan, organizational chart, and other documentations. However, the four soft S's—Style, Staff, Skills, and Shared Values (or Super-ordinates Goals)—are more embedded in KOLLC and more challenging to locate. Thus, the implementation of organizational change became the major concern of Dr. Oputa.

Mike Peter's management style is quite different from that of Dr. Oputa. The differences in style created another set of tension between the two senior executives of the company. In addition to the problem that occurs between both of them, there were also problems with the two regional offices. The two regional directors also reported directly to the CEO. According to one regional director, the problem at the head office was as a result of Dr. Oputa's action. His autocratic leadership style had caused great strife among the regional directors who used to be consulted before decisions were made. The regional directors were split into two groups. Five members of the first group were hired by Dr. Oputa. Two members of the second group were in the organization before Dr. Oputa was named the CEO. The division was as a result of the way Dr. Oputa applied separate standards for each group of directors.

The conflict between Dr. Oputa and Peters was mainly over the best management approach on how to lead the company. It was not only employees that the company had to strive to keep happy; they had to keep their customers happy as well. For example, years ago, it was not usual for the two regional offices to be closed. Today, due to union activities and an innovative strategy of implementation, the company needed organizational change in the manner that is not necessarily acceptable to all employees. There was also the immediate need to enhance the effectiveness of the organization's solvency.

As soon as Dr. Oputa resumed duty in the company, he hired his own team of managers and promoted them as regional directors. He created five new regional branches and posted them to New York, Boston, Huston, San Francisco, and Miami, respectively. Peters found himself explaining elementary stuff to Dr. Oputa and his cohort whenever they visited the headquarters in Indianapolis.

When Dr. Oputa resumed duty he was told what the major problems of the company were, but instead of listening to Peters, the vice-president, he spent more time complaining about the past administration than cleaning up the problems in the company. From day one, he insisted upon a complete divorce from the past, and of course Peters was a part of the past.

In another development, most women in the organization complained about the glass ceiling in the company. However, since Dr. Oputa took over as the chief executive of the company two years ago, no woman had been promoted into a senior management position. In some cases, women in the company were not promoted or allowed to be head of any department. Sometimes women who took sick leave were automatically dismissed from the company for no other reason." Dr. Oputa was expected to address the issue of female staff being treated as second class employee in the organization. However, he felt that was a problem associated with the past and never introduced any new initiatives to correct the plight of women in he organization.

Six weeks after Dr. Oputa resumed duty as the chief executive of the company, he redesigned the institution without consulting with the five functional directors who reports to him. According to Dr. Oputa, the restructuring was based primarily on centralized management principles. Dr. Oputa reorganized the company into six divisions. Coordination mechanism were established so that accounting, purchasing, human resources, and other functions now operated on a more centralized basis. Many aspects of service delivery functions, such as career development, technology, pension, industrial development, and management information systems, were decentralized. As part of Dr. Oputa's reorganization of the company, he retired all the employees that were 55 years and older. He also removed women from all sectional head positions, because he felt they were always taking time off from work. The redesigning of the company was contrary to affirmative action and equal employment opportunity laws. It further led to high rate of turnover in the company. Another consequence of Dr. Oputa's reorganization was that some regional directors could not hire nor promote employees working under them. It was also ironic that the regional directors that Dr. Oputa hired when he resumed duty in the company were allowed to perform these centralized functions in their respective regions.

Mike Peters had assumed many characteristics of a typical pragmatic executive. He spent a great deal of time listening to the personal problems of his subordinates, and maintained close social ties with many of the men in the organization. Consequently, many employees sought Peters's advice and attention to register their complaints or concern with management. For example, many employees complained to Peters about the personnel policy that Dr. Oputa had installed. This involved a move away from female and other minority promotions that were formally based on seniority to one based on superior evaluation of subordinates. The employee asked Peters to intercede on their behalf. He did so, and insisted that their demands were fully justified in view of traditional management practices.

Although Dr. Oputa found it helpful to learn about the feelings of middle managers from Peters, he resented having to deal with Peters as an adversary rather than a colleague. Dr. Oputa became reluctant to ask Peters's opinion, because he invariably raised objections to changes that were contrary to past norms and customs. Other events had raised some doubts in Dr. Oputa's mind as to the soundness of Peters' judgment, which Dr. Oputa had never before questioned. For, instance, when Dr. Oputa wanted to dismiss a manager who, in his opinion, lacked initiative, leadership, and general competency, Peters defended the manager, noting that the company had never fired a manager. Peters also argued that the manager had been loyal and honest, and that the company was partially at fault for keeping him on for the last five years without sporting his incompetence and recommending further training. Dr. Oputa fired him anyway, only to discover two weeks later that Peters had interceded on behalf of the fired manager and had gotten a sister company to hire him. Dr. Oputa confronted Peters about the issue and he simply said that he had done what was expected of a superior in an organization where there was no consensus or participatory type of management.

Assignment

Each student is required to study the case study on Ojanigo Health Company and write a strategic plan. Papers should be approximately 10–15 pages in length. Students should rely upon information from the classroom texts, in addition to other peer reviewed scholarly journals, in compiling their papers.

10 Business and Government Relations in Uganda

Peter Ngwafu and Robert A. Dibie

Introduction

Uganda is a landlocked country located in Eastern Africa. It shares a boundary with Kenya, Tanzania, the Democratic Republic of the Congo, Rwanda, and South Sudan. Uganda has a population of 37.8 million people (World Bank, 2015). The gross domestic product (GDP) of the country in 2015 was US$1,766 (World Bank, 2015). The terrain of the country is mostly plateau, with a rim of mountains and a southeastern border on Lake Victoria. (GlobalEdge, 2016)

The country has transformed from a nation with a troubled past to one of relative stability and prosperity. It used to be a British colony, but achieved independence in 1962. Since its independence from Britain in 1962, Uganda has endured a military coup, followed by a brutal military dictatorship, which ended in 1979; disputed elections in 1980; and a five-year war that brought current President Yoweri Museveni to power in 1986 (British Broadcasting Corporation, 2016). President Museveni has been the commander-in-chief and head of government since 1986. Museveni was reported to have won the country's 2011 presidential elections after his administration orchestrated a 2005 constitutional amendment that lifted presidential term limits. President Museveni, the former rebel leader, won his fifth term in the February 20, 2016, Ugandan presidential elections, with over 60% of the ballot (British Broadcasting Corporation, 2016). Museveni has been credited for restoring relative stability and economic prosperity to Uganda following years of civil war and repression under former leaders Milton Obote and Idi Amin.

The country has experienced some economic growth, open markets, and abundant natural resources, which include at least 2.5 billion barrels of recoverable oil. These natural resources provide good opportunities for knowledgeable investors in Uganda (US Department of State, 2016). According to GlobalEdge (2016), Uganda maintains a liberal trade and foreign exchange regime, and largely adheres to IMF/World Bank programs to fight poverty, maintain macroeconomic stability and restructure the economy. The Government of Uganda is also reported to be revising a range of laws and regulations to improve government accountability, open markets, develop infrastructure, and build a more attractive environment for foreign investment (World Bank, 2016). Despite these positive government initiatives the country has a sluggish bureaucracy, poor infrastructure, insufficient power supply, high energy and production costs, non-tariff barriers, and severe corruption problems. The government has been reported to often interfere in the affairs of the private sector, and this practice constitutes a major challenge to investment in the country (US Department of State, 2012). In addition, as a result of the multiple levels of government in Uganda, numerous government agencies and an entrenched bureaucracy, disputes and tensions between these political institutions sometimes lead to conflicting and confusing policies and their implementation (U.S. & Foreign Commercial Service and U.S. Department of State, 2014).

Although the country has a mixed economic system in which there is a variety of private freedom, combined with centralized economic planning and government regulation, the supply of electricity remains one of the largest obstacles to investment in the country (British Broadcasting Corporation, 2016; GlobalEdge, 2016). According to the U.S. Department of State (2012), the demand for electricity in Uganda far exceeds supply. Only 5% of Uganda's rural population has access to electricity, and most people still rely on wood and charcoal for fuel. Consequently, the country's electricity network urgently needs renovation and expansion (U.S. & Foreign Commercial Service and U.S. Department of State, 2014).

Business and government relations in Uganda are somewhat mixed On the one hand, some businesses are impacted by government policies, while others strive not only to understand those government policies that affect their existence, but to devise strategies to successfully influence government decision making. Despite these shortcomings in 2012, the total trade was $9.3 billion, with $2.86 billion worth of exports, and $6.42 billion worth of imports. Trade contributed 42% of GDP. The trade balance improved from a deficit of $2.6 billion to $1.8 billion as a result of increased exports (U.S. & Foreign Commercial Service and U.S. Department of State, 2014).

This chapter investigates the nature of business and government relations in Uganda. It also explores the extent to which the public sector uses public policy and other means to influence the private sector's decision making and practices for the purpose of achieving economic development. The chapter provides a detailed description of the important role of both sides of this relationship with respect to corporate social responsibility and government regulation in Uganda. It argues that the Government of Uganda and its policies are crucial for the appropriate attainment of an effective business and government relationship in the country. It uses data derived from primary and secondary sources to analyze the current relationship between business and government in Uganda. The conceptual framework of this study is based on the new growth theory. The findings indicate that while there have been past weaknesses in the relationship between government and business in some industrial sectors due to inadequate enforcement of policies, the relationship in both sectors has improved over three decades. In addition, government policies have not been able to effectively galvanize the private sector and NGOs to create a national system of technological innovation and economic transformation. The national government and the leaders of Uganda are still very reluctant to leave economic outcomes in the country entirely up to market forces. The chapter recommends that appropriate collaboration between business and government be established so as to enhance efficient technological development and economic growth in Uganda in the future.

Business and Government Partnership Framework

An effective relationship between government and business hinges on the capacity of both entities to develop a framework that would spur economic growth within an economy. According to Te-Velde (2006: 3), in order for governments and businesses to benefit from such a mutual relationship, they must interact effectively so as to foster a more efficient allocation of scarce resources, conduct a more appropriate industrial policy, remove the biggest obstacles to growth, and create wealth more efficiently. Ferrell et al (2014) and Te-Velde (2006) contend that when both entities fail to work collaboratively or engage in destructive adversarial practices, economic activities that are designed to create wealth benefit the few at the expense of the many. Consequently, effective interactions between business and government are absolutely necessary for wealth creation and economic development.

The goal of economic freedom is not simply an absence of government coercion or constraint, but the creation and maintenance of a mutual sense of liberty for all, including the business sector (Porter 2002; Sen & TeVelde 2009)). In any nation, as individuals enjoy the blessings of economic freedom, they in turn have a responsibility to respect the economic rights and freedoms of others within the rule of law. This is why governments are instituted to ensure basic protections against the ravages of nature or the predations of one citizen against another (Cammett, 2007; Quareshi & TeVelde, 2007). As a result, positive economic rights such as property and contracts are given to society as well as individuals to defend against the destructive tendencies of others

Cortright (2001) contends that societies that generate and tolerate new ideas and continuously adapt to changing economic and technological approaches, establish a precondition for sustained economic growth. Cortright (2001) further maintains that a new growth theory and the increasing returns associated with knowledge have several implications for economic development policy. New growth theory underscores the importance of investing in new knowledge creation to sustain growth. He believes that policy makers will have to pay attention to all the factors that provide incentives for knowledge creation, such as research and development, the educational system, entrepreneurship, tolerance for diversity, and openness to trade (Cortright, 2001: 11). Herzberg & Wright 2005) contends that the emergence of new growth theory, new trade theory, and new institutional economics have inspired a significant shift toward comparing the market and governments, and that has spurred the consensus that government and markets play vital roles in transforming economies especially developing ones. Yifu (2010) also acknowledges that even developed economies need constant and strategic state action to support and regulate private businesses and help generate and disseminate on a large scale the technological progress that sustains economic growth (Willem 2009; Yifu 2010: 5).

A brief review of some of the contemporary perspectives that have been used to articulate government and business relations is helpful in providing some understanding of the nature of such relations. Over the past several decades, students and observers of government and business relations have used three perspectives to assess the nature of such relations. One perspective considers government and business as two actors, opposed to each other (Cammett, 2007). In the prevailing dominant mainstream view following the great recession, business and government are widely viewed as institutions that oppose each other. This "antiregulatory" or "limited 'government" view has been attributed to advocates of the notion that free markets with limited government intervention are ideal for the efficient functioning of nations' economies (Podolny, 2009; Schneider, 1998). The main thrust of this perspective is its emphasis on the belief that business relations with government should be predicated on the need to reduce government's role, as well as the costs and burdens on private business and the general economy with respect to government taxes, regulations, and policies.

Figure 10.1 shows that government is a social control mechanism that provides incentives either positively or negatively for business to respond to

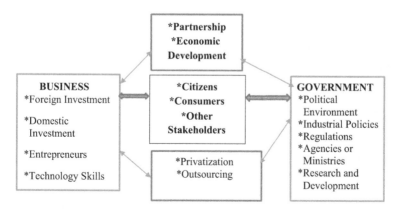

Figure 10.1 Business and government partnership framework
Source: Designed by authors

economic growth and social values that may not be adequately addressed through the market system. On the other hand, government's role involves establishing transparent rules of ownership and contract, creating an independent judiciary to settle disputes and provide due process, enacting favorable tax laws, ensuring public policies that are consistent over time, treating foreign corporations on the same basis as domestic companies (Dibie et al., 2015). Business freedom is about an individual's right to establish and run an enterprise without undue interference from the state. Burdensome and redundant regulations are the most common barriers to the free conduct of entrepreneurial activity. By increasing the costs of production, regulations can make it difficult for entrepreneurs to succeed in the marketplace. Although many regulations hinder business productivity and profitability, the most inhibiting to entrepreneurship are those that are associated with licensing new businesses. State intervention generates the same problems in the labor market that it produces in any other market. Government regulations take a variety of forms, including wage controls, restrictions on hiring and firing, and other constraints (Dibie et al., 2015).

By contrast, the other perspective on business and government relations is undergirded by the belief that government should support businesses and provide them with business performance and investment incentives, because businesses are the principal sources of jobs, innovation and sustenance of the economic well-being of society (Ferrell et al., 2014). As a result, advocates of this view argue that governments should therefore support businesses with grants, tax credits, and subsidies (Podolny, 2009; Meznar & Johnson, 2005).

The third perspective on business and government relations maintains that businesses should forge productive partnerships with governments in addressing key societal problems. This view clearly contrasts with the notion that government should be the regulator to ensure that governments act in a socially responsible manner (Meznar & Johnson, 2005). As a result of finding a new mechanism for constructive engagement between government, business, and other civic society organizations that is designed to help solve the serious economic and financial crisis that may arise in any country, businesses must take a pragmatic step and invest in research and development (R&D; Isaksson & Celik, 2013; Schepers, 2000). This is essential in providing a more constructive instrument for enhancing operations in the political environment where market regulations are enacted and implemented.

At first glance, these views may appear to be separate or independent from each other. However, a careful assessment indicates that they are, indeed, inextricably interrelated. For example, a given business can use some aspects of its relations with government to extract benefits for itself, such as the tax credits that it receives from government, while at the same time it can partner with government to accomplish a social purpose and in the end attempt to minimize its tax obligations (Meznar & Johnson, 2005; Sanyal & Guvenli, 2000). It is therefore important for businesses to understand how their efforts to operate profitably and to serve a social purpose are greatly impacted by government policies. In that regard, it is also important for businesses to endeavor to manage their relationships with all levels of governments effectively to ensure their own sustainability.

The new growth theory, according to Barros (1993), argues that the development of new knowledge is generally seen as an important deriver of economic growth. It stipulates that for economies to develop or grow, they must espouse nonphysical resources that are aimed at increasing the knowledge base (rather than land, labor, and capital, which were the central tenets of classical growth theory) and sustain the institutions that help develop and share knowledge. Furthermore, because this variant of new growth, theory holds that knowledge can generate increasing returns and drive economic growth; government should invest in human capital and the development of educational institutions and skills. The nature of government and business relations in Uganda is one that is projected to spur economic growth in the future. The country is reported to have a developing economy that stands to benefit from new knowledge and innovative economic development approaches (USAID 2007, UNIDO. (2007). Therefore, it could be argued that the new growth theory offers a theoretical foundation, which if properly explored and implemented, can shape the basis of government and business relations in Uganda. The new growth concept could also help a country to usher in the type of economic growth and development that the country needs at this point in its political and economic advancement. Seen in the context of government and business relations in Uganda, government should support private sector research and development and encourage inward or endogenous investment, which will bring new knowledge with it.

When businesses determine the extent to which government policy impacts their operations and profitability, they usually devise strategies for interacting with government. Typically, businesses respond reactively, interactively, and proactively to government policy. Reactive responses entail responding to government policy after it is implemented (Podolny, 2009). An interactive response, by contrast, involves engaging with government policy makers and actors (including the media) to try to influence public policy to serve the interests of the businesses. A proactive response approach entails acting to influence policies, and anticipating changes in public policy. Admittedly, for most businesses, a combination of the interactive and proactive approaches is the best strategy (Farrell et al., 2015; Dibie et al., 2015).

According to Allard and Martinez (2008) and Dawah (2006), cited in Goldsmith (2002: 40), "social capital reflects the capability of people to form organizations and take on group tasks, which they argue is important for social and economic progress." Lehne (2013) contends that unlike the other factors of production, social capital is intangible because it is based on a combination of personal connections, mutual obligations, and a shared sense of purpose. Public choice advocates, by contrast, present a less optimistic view of business and government relations. Inspired by economic or rational actor models as a means of explaining political decision making, public choice has been favored by economists and has shaped the development agendas or strategies of development agencies such as the World Bank. Goldsmith (2002) and Lehne (2013) argued that from the perspective of public choice, politics is essentially an issue of rent seeking behavior by influential but nonetheless obstructive interest groups. Economic rents are policy-induced gains that would be absent in a competitive market, and they include additional income derived from licenses, tariffs, tax incentives, public contracts, and direct subsidies.

Kalema argues that following independence in African countries, "the most successful local entrepreneurs were of non-indigenous communities that included the Indians in East Africa, and the Lebanese in West Africa, while European owned firms dominated banking, manufacturing, and large scale trade in both regions (Kalema, 2008: 4). Kalema also contends that political independence from colonial rule was viewed largely as a right toward economic independence that would end the economic dominance perpetuated by immigrant groups and usher in meaningful changes in the economic fabric of Africa's countries and their relations with developed economies. According to Kalema (2008) and Dicklitch and Howard-Hassmann (2007), systematic public-private sector dialogue is a relatively recent development in Africa, even as the experience of newly industrialized nations indicates that effective government and business relations are essential for private sector driven economic development. In essence, whereas government and business relations in Uganda and most of sub-Saharan Africa have improved over the past several decades, they remain essentially weak.

Analysis of Business and Government Relations

This chapter examines the nature of business and government relations in Uganda. It adopts a cross-sectional study design and employs both quantitative and qualitative methods of data collection in Uganda. Secondary data was obtained through an in-depth desk review and content analysis of relevant published and gray material (unpublished studies), policy and programs documents, and regulations and laws of Uganda. The main areas of business and government relations are considered as key in the economic growth of Uganda. While the poor are susceptible to diverse risks—political, environmental, social, and economic—the effects of these risks have significant differential impacts on citizens with higher risks and vulnerability to poverty among people in Uganda. Relations between business and government are crucial in explaining patterns of development in Uganda. Appropriate industrial policy is also seen as a key strategy for tackling the "poverty trap" delivery of citizens, which includes decision making through representation on the governance structures, policies, laws, and regulations. In addition, the key dimensions of accountability, including transparency and participation in decision making, planning, implementation, and evaluation of initiatives, are also very important to development in Uganda. Government-led development is not market-led but rather business-led development.

Although governments attempted to deliver on the promises of a success-ful post-independence African environment, the results were mixed. Nations such as Tanzania attempted to re-orient their economies toward socialism, while Kenya attempted to promote indigenous capitalists and attract foreign investment. The vast majority of post-independent African nations created state-owned enterprises (parastatals) or expanded those that were created during the colonial period as mechanisms for economic modernization and African economic empowerment (Dicklitch & Howard-Hassmann, 2007). The performance of these "parastatals" subsequently declined, as they were plagued by political interference and inexperienced management. In Uganda, the problem was exacerbated by the collapse of political institutions and the loss of professional civil servants (NSSF 2007; USAID 2007). The subse-quent privatization of state-owned enterprises in the 1990s and concerted efforts to foster domestic and foreign private investment resulted in the emergence of new business ventures, including commercial banks, telecom-munications firms, and manufacturing enterprises (World Bank, 2004).

The nation of Uganda had not always been a violent and anarchic place to do business or live (British Broadcasting Corporation, 2016). At inde-pendence in 1962, the economy was flourishing. This success, however, was short-lived. Unlike most African nations, Uganda was one of the few African countries that had a viable industrial sector before independence. The lit-erature maintains that there were small and medium industries, as well as large-scale industries. Following the creation of the Uganda Development Corporation (UDC) in 1952, priority was given to industrial advancement as an important component of the nation's development strategy. The UDC was responsible for promoting the establishment of industries, including joint ventures, negotiating finance and attracting direct foreign investment, and fostering the establishment of industrial research institutions and related support services (UNCTAD, 2007). Next, the Ugandan Manufacturing Association was created in the 1960s and revived in 1988; the association was supported by the United States Agency for International Development in the 1990s to create the Uganda National Forum as a voice for economic policy recommendations. Following the demise of the National Forum, the World Bank supported the creation of yet another group of business promo-tion organizations, known as the Private Sector Foundation (World Bank, 2014). Uganda's manufacturing sector was developed through import sub-stitution, with a focus on the production of consumer goods. Such industries relied heavily on imported factor inputs and were heavily protected and subsidized (UNCTAD 200, 4). In 1986, when Museveni and his guerilla army, the National Resistance Movement (NRM), took over Uganda, they inherited not only an overdeveloped state but a collapsed state and economy (World Bank, 2004; British Broadcasting Corporation, 2016).

According to Dicklitch and Howard-Hassmann (2007) the National Resistance Movement (NRM) regime has been credited with turning the Ugandan economy around and stabilizing the political arena. Uganda had the sixth fastest-growing economy in sub-Saharan Africa by 1996, and enjoyed an economic growth rate of 7.1% per annum from 1990 to 1998 (USAID, 2007: 20). According to the World Bank (2004), Uganda's economic success can be attributed to several factors. These include strong and single-minded political leadership; capable, committed, and trusted officials in key ministries; and pragmatic external donors prepared to engage with the government at the working level (World Bank, 2004). Good public policy is essential to successful economic growth and political stability.

In the process of rejuvenating Uganda's economic growth and sustainable development, the National Resistance Movement instituted its 10 Point Program for economic recovery in 1986 (Government of Uganda, 2003 and 2006). The economic growth program included state-led development; decentralization of power; corruption reform, and grassroots democracy via a newly implemented five-tier Resistance Council (RC) system, renamed the Local Council (LC) system in 1995 ((Dicklitch & Howard-Hassmann, 2007). It is interesting to note that the economic growth program fostered greater government intervention in the economy, government control over foreign exchange rates, and government control over the prices of essential imports (Morril et al 1997: 3–4). The political interference of the Government of Uganda included pushing the public owned joint venture partner to make new and expensive demands on foreign investors. The regulatory agencies of the government were also engaged in interpreting rules in a way that adversely affected business operations, suddenly enforcing certain laws and regulations vigorously or throwing roadblocks to inhibit the smooth operations of business ventures. These actions reveal that the Government of Uganda can play a major role in either creating or inhibiting appropriate conditions for conducting business (Government of Uganda, 2006). As a result of these interventionist policies of the Government of Uganda inflation escalated to over 300% by May 1987, and a further deterioration in most economic indicators followed (Dicklitch & Howard-Hassmann, 2007).

Allard and Martinez (2008) maintains that the nature of business associations in Uganda, and to some extent in most of Africa, can be explained using two perspectives: pluralism and public choice. Drawing from Pluralist interest groups theory, Goldsmith posits that interest groups such as the Uganda Manufacturing Association are "potential sources of socio-political diversity in developing countries" (Goldsmith, 2002: 40). In his view, pluralists view development as a decline of natural relationships followed by an emergence of voluntary and formal organizations, shaped by a new status (such as labor unions, professional bodies, or business associations). They observes further that these groups look for common ground as they negotiate and bargain over public policy matters, and in the process, win on some issues and lose on some. In addition Dawah (2006) believes that these processes contribute to social stability and enhance changes in the legal and regulatory environment that favor business expansion.

As impressive as the beginnings of Uganda's industrial development policy and strategy was, little attention was paid to human resources management development, especially the need to create a functional labor force that was consistent with its model of industrialization and economic development. Local entrepreneurial capabilities and expertise were not fostered and nurtured, and despite joint ventures which were tightly controlled by the government, private sector industries were mainly owned by the Asian community. Asian-owned businesses were subsequently transformed into government-owned enterprises after the expulsion of the Asian business community, beginning in 1972. According to the United Nations Industrial Development Organization (UNIDO), the industrialization process did not incorporate the use of technology and like most African countries Uganda did not embrace technology as an essential component of its industrial development policy (UNIDO, 2007: 4). As a result of these shortcomings, the prosperity and productivity that had been generated in the industrial sector was short lived. By 1975 manufacturing output in Uganda had plummeted precipitously; average growth was less than 5.0 % and by 1984 it was less than 3.0%. Clearly, private industry was in a difficult situation, and to address the problem several economic recovery programs, rehabilitation and development plans were introduced. The programs and development plans were specifically designed to reduce government control of industrial development and its control of the economy, and improve the efficiency and performance of industrial enterprises and businesses through the privatization of public enterprises and the strengthening of industrial support institutions (UNCTAD, 2007: 5).

From the mid-1970s through the early 1980s, Uganda witnessed a period of slow economic growth, and it was obvious that the country needed an economic development strategy that would spur growth in most sectors of the economy and energize a vibrant private sector. In order to foster the recovery that began in the mid-1980s and sustain greater growth, several policies and programs were implemented in the 1990s and beyond. These included the Industrialization Policy and Framework 1994–1999, the Structural Adjustment Programs (SAPs), Economic Recovery Program (ERP), and the Poverty Eradication Action Plan (PEAP). While the Industrialization Policy and Framework was established to promote investments that would increase exports, ensure the effective transfer of technology, and optimize the utilization of the countries natural resources, its primary objective was to usher in a swift transition from a public-sector-driven industrial development orientation to a private-sector-led industrial development approach. In this transitional process, the government facilitated the creation of appropriate environment for establishing industry and for supporting sustainable industrial development (UNIDO, 2007: 5).

Prior to the formulation and implementation of the industrial policy and framework, a number of industrial studies were conducted and funded by the World Bank to provide policy makers and the nation's development partners with reliable information for policy decisions, as well as possible opportunities for investment and development. The Ministry of Industry collaborated with external partners to organize round table discussions that brought together key stakeholders to review the process of industrial development; identify problems and constraints, opportunities, and challenges; and deliberate on possible policy options to facilitate and accelerate industrial development. Furthermore, strategic consultative groups were established to facilitate increased dialogue between the government and the private sector on critical economic and policy issues. The initial consultative efforts between the government and private sector were nurtured, and the government devoted its efforts toward creating an enabling environment. Physical infrastructure such as roads, electricity, and water supply were greatly enhanced and emphasis was given to investment that was aimed at attracting foreign investment (Vision 2030 -Uganda Integrated Industrial Policy, 2007).

Other reform initiatives that were aimed at improving government and private sector business practices in the 1990s included the establishment of simplified, appropriate, and contemporary legal and regulatory frameworks for small and medium size industries (that were better than the old structures), to ensure more effective management of these industries. Industrial institutions and industry support entities, such as the Uganda National Bureau of Standards, the Ugandan Industrial Research Institute, the Ugandan Council for Science and Technology, the Ugandan Investment Authority, the Ugandan Coffee Development Authority, and the Ugandan Revenue Authority, were also established and supported in the 1990s. Furthermore, the 1991 Investment Code provided tariff and non-tariff incentives for various private investments in the industrial sector. The UNIDO Report (2007: 6) indicated that the policy and institutional capacity building measures discussed previously resulted in impressive industrial growth of 11.8% in 1992, to 17% in 1998. Industrial contribution to the gross domestic product (GDP) increased from 10% in the 1980s to approximately 20% between 1997 and 1998. The share of manufacturing to GDP increased from 6.2% in 1992 to approximately 10% in 1995 (Government of Uganda, 2006). The Ugandan Ministry of Tourism, Trade, and Industry reported that the number of industrial establishments in the country increased from 1,320 in 1989 to approximately 11,968 by 2005 (Uganda National Commission, 2007).

Although Uganda offers a good example of the current regional shift toward establishing business associations in Africa as an attempt to demonstrate the relevance of effective government and business relations in economic development, it is important to begin by examining the extent to which the Government of Uganda and the nation's business policy development evolved before and after independence. One of the major predicaments facing the country all along is that the cost of transportation of goods and services has made the cost of doing business very expensive in Uganda. The Ugandan government has not invested much in the construction of good roads. Thus, high transportation costs are another constraint on Uganda's economy. The nation's dilapidated roads and bridges infrastructure needs considerable investment, its railway system is in disrepair, and air freight charges are among the highest in the region (World Bank Group, 2016). It is unfortunate to observe that a two-lane highway from Kenya remains the primary route for 80% of Uganda's trade, making transportation slow, costly, and susceptible to disruption (U.S. Department of State, 2012). Dependence on Kenya's road network has often caused obstruction to smooth business operation in Uganda. For instance, in 2007, election-related violence in Kenya virtually halted imports into Uganda for more than two months, causing a spike in commodity and fuel prices. Also a problem is landlocked Uganda's reliance on Kenya's Mombasa port, where chronic congestion increasingly results in costly delays. Uganda also relies on the refinery at Mombasa for all of Uganda's fuel, and the cost of transport to Uganda keeps fuel prices high (U.S. Department of State, 2012). In 2011, passenger traffic through Uganda's Entebbe International Airport was up 6.1% from 2010, with nearly 1.1 million people flowing through. In 2010, four new international carriers commenced flights to Entebbe, bringing the total number to 22 (World Bank Group, 2016).

The Ugandan economy has benefited from macroeconomic, export-led reform. It is reported that inflation rates dropped, growth rates increased, trade as a percentage of GDP increased from 27% in 1990 to 41% in 2004 (World Bank, 2005), and the overall economy stabilized. In spite of these positive results, economic growth is not necessarily sufficient to promote economic human rights. What was the impact of macroeconomic reform on Ugandan society? The percentage of people who were undernourished declined from 33 in 1980 to 19.1 in 2001 (UNCTAD, 2007). The infant mortality rate declined from 107 per thousand live births in 1980 to 81 in 2003 (Dicklitch & Howard-Hassmann, 2007), and the under-five mortality rate from 185 per thousand in 1980 to 140 in 2003 (Dicklitch & Howard-Hassmann, 2007). The literacy rate improved from 60.1% in 1980 to 70.1% in 1990 (Dicklitch & Howard-Hassmann, 2007). In 1997, Uganda introduced Universal Primary Education (UPE; World Bank Group, 2016). Primary school enrollment figures subsequently increased from 3.4 million in 1996 to 7.3 million in 2002 (UNCTAD, 2007, 20). Fifty-six percent of the population had sustainable access to an improved water source in 2002, as compared to 44% in 1990 (World Bank, 2015). The estimated gross domestic product per capita in constant 2000 international dollars, calculated as purchasing power per person, rose from $876 in 1982 to $1440 in 2004. Despite all these improvements, however, life expectancy decreased from 50.4 in 1980 to 42.7 in 2000 (Dicklitch & Howard-Hassmann, 2007; World Bank Group, 2016; World Bank, 2015).

Table 10.1 Current economic indicators of Uganda

Indicator	Percentage and US$	Year
Inflation, consumer prices (annual %)	4.288%	2014
External debt stocks, total (DOD, current US$)	$4,361,282,000	2013
Total tax rate (% of commercial profits)	36.5%	2014
Real interest rate (5 year average %)	18.649%	2014
Manufacturing, value added (% of GDP)	8.786%	2013
Current account balance (BoP), current US$)	$1,999,186,807	2013

Source: World Bank Group. (2016). *Ease of Doing Business in Uganda*. www.doingbusiness.org/data/exploreeconomies/uganda

In 2012, total trade was $9.3 billion, with $2.86 billion worth of exports, and $6.42 billion worth of imports. Trade contributed 42% of GDP. Trade balance improved from a deficit of $2.6 billion to $1.8 billion as a result of increased exports (U.S. Department of State, 2012). In addition, foreign direct investment (FDI) declined from $1.7 billion in 2012 to $1.2 billion in 2013, although the United Nations Conference on Trade and Development (UNCTAD) World Investment Report shows that Uganda remains the leading recipient of Foreign Direct Investment in the East African region (World Bank Group (2016).

The country benefited immensely from foreign donor aid, which was undoubtedly crucial to its reform efforts. Uganda became the first country to qualify for the World Bank and IMF-sponsored Heavily Indebted Poor Country (HIPC) debt relief initiative in 1998 (original) and 2000 (enhanced). In 2005, loans and grants from foreign donors accounted for 17% and 28% of the Ugandan budget respectively. Thus, 45% of the Ugandan budget was composed of Official Development Assistance (ODA) (Republic of Uganda 2004–5, 5). In June 2005, Uganda was granted 100% debt relief by the G8, relieving it of the burden of paying back loans from the IMF, World Bank, and African Development Bank (Republic of Uganda 2004–5, 5). Despite this support, it could be argued that foreign aid alone cannot account for Uganda's economic successes (World Bank Group, 2016; Dicklitch & Howard-Hassmann, 2007).

Given the uncertainty and the inadequacy that characterize the political and legal environment in Uganda, the issue of managing business and government relations has assumed considerable importance for the Government of Uganda. The country's traditional export crops have fluctuated substantially in quantity and dollar value over the past several years. Most industries in Uganda depend heavily on agriculture for raw material inputs (World Bank Group, 2016). President Museveni actively promotes value-added exports, such as roasted coffee, palm oil processing, and cotton yarn. Uganda hopes to expand its agricultural exports under the East

Table 10.2 Current business trade indicators of Uganda

Trade indicators	Percentage and US$	Year
Imports of goods and services (current US$)	$7,688,317,723	2014
Export of goods and services	$5,219,655,368	2014
Total merchandise trade (% of GDP)	30.932%	2014
FDI, net inflows (BoP, current US$)	$1,194,398,346	2013
Commercial service exports (current US$)	$2,169,622,885	2013
Total exports (2014)	$2,261,964,441	2014
Total imports (2014)	$6,073,527,801	2014
Trade balance (2014)	–$3,811,563,360	
Exports of goods and services (% of GDP)	19.84%	2014
Imports of goods and services (% of GDP)	29.22%	2014
Employment in agriculture (% of total employment)	65.6%	2009
Employment in industry (% of total employment)	6%	2009
Employment in services (% of total employment)	28.4%	2009

Source: GlobalEdge. (2016). *Uganda.* http://globaledge.msu.edu/countries/uganda/memo
World Bank (2015). *World Development Report.* New York: Oxford University Press, Washington D.C.

African Customs Union. Agricultural processing is starting to develop, and there are investment opportunities in processing and packaging coffee, edible oils, tropical fruits, fruit juices, and nontraditional crops such as vanilla (World Bank Group, 2016). The nation's top industries are in sugar, brewing, tobacco, and cotton textiles (GlobalEdge, 2016). Food processing equipment, including drying, storage, and treatment facilities; chemicals and additives used to preserve or process foods; canning, bottling, and other packaging equipment and related materials; repair and maintenance services; and consulting services on setup and operation of food processing equipment and system constitute the other industries (United States Foreign Commercial Service and U.S. Department of State, 2014).

The country's economy grew by 5.7% in fiscal year (FY) 2013/14, up from 5.1% the previous year. Economic growth is expected to accelerate 6% in FY 2014/15. The country, however, still is highly dependent on foreign aid (GlobalEdge, 2016). Uganda's gross domestic product (GDP) was $25.3 billion in FY 2013/14, and the World Bank reports that GDP per capita is $551. The service sector was the largest contributor to GDP in 2012 at 44.7%, and industry contributed about 26.6%. The agriculture and fishing sectors have stagnated at about 22% over the past years. Nonetheless, the sector provides approximately 66% of employment in Uganda. Of the

37 million people living in Uganda, 24.5% of the population lives on less than $1 per day (World Bank Group, 2016).

The nation's strong tradition of government led development has performed relatively well compared to the situation in which it was three decades ago. The protectionist trade policies and their effects on business have improved considerably. However, institutions needed to effectively coordinate collective private sector participation and inter collaboration have not quite emerged in Uganda. Despite this predicament, the Ugandan government continues to emphasize strengthening the country's road, rail, water, energy, and communications infrastructure. In FY 2013/14, the Ugandan Government invested nearly $1 billion in road construction and improvement, and this remained a priority in fiscal year 2014/15 (GlobalEdge, 2016).

The nation exported coffee, tea, tobacco, and cotton, Uganda's largest exports by value, and these have generally increased in quantity and dollar value, with some year-to-year fluctuations. Uganda is Africa's largest exporter of coffee, producing about 3.8 million bags of coffee in 2013, and the country benefited from a drought in Brazil that drove coffee prices higher (World Bank Group, 2016). Tea exports increased to $73.9 million in 2012 from 72.1 million in 2013. Cotton exports decreased from $105 million in 2010 to $76 million in 2012. Other important exports include fish, flowers, and cement. Tourism is a growing industry. In 2011, Uganda earned $805 million from 1.15 million visitors, up from $662 million earned in 2010 from 946,000 visitors. Tourism earned the country $834 million in 2012 (GlobalEdge, 2016; World Bank Group, 2016).

Table 10.3 Major traded goods in Uganda

Trade indicators	Percentage and US$	Year
09 (coffee and spices)	$498,665,616	2014
27 (oil and mineral fuels)	$184,032,783	2014
03 (seafood)	$134,790,626	2014
15 (fats and oils)	$102,471,339	2013
25 (natural minerals and stone)	$93,785,525	2013
72 (iron and steel)	$93,129,434	2014
41 (hides and leather)	$73,757,585	2014
24 (tobacco)	$66,017,739	2014
17 (sugar and confectionery)	$65,906,417	2014
10 (cereals)	$63,715,407	2014

Source: GlobalEdge. (2016). *Doing Business in Uganda*. http://globaledge.msu.edu/countries/uganda/memo

World Bank (2015). World Development Report. New York: Oxford University Press, Washington D.C.

The barriers to doing business in Uganda include high levels of corruption, poor infrastructure, a lack of access to affordable loan financing, low levels of human capacity, inefficient government services, complicated land laws, and frequent land disputes (United States Foreign Commercial Service, 2014). The World Bank (2014) Doing Business survey ranked Uganda 132nd out of 185 countries for ease of doing business. The country is also open to foreign investment and provides tax incentives for medium and long-term foreign investors (World Bank, 2014). The Heritage Foundation's 2011 Index of Economic Freedom ranked Uganda's economy 80th of 179 countries, based on ease of doing business, trade freedom, property rights, and fiscal and monetary policy (World Bank Group, 2016). Among the 46 sub-Saharan African countries on the index, Uganda's economy ranked as 7th freest overall, and as 3rd best on measures of responsible government spending and fiscal policies. However, due to perceptions that widespread corruption, even at the highest levels of government, makes it difficult for foreign businesses to compete effectively. Uganda ranked low at 31st of 46 sub-Saharan African countries on measures of corruption (Uganda Bureau of Statistics 2007; Uganda Ministry of Tourism 2008). Uganda also dropped from 2nd to 22nd of 46 on the Index's measure of monetary freedom, due to perceptions that government interference in the economy through state-owned enterprises leads to domestic price distortions (GlobalEdge, 2016).

According to the United States Department of State (2012) the country enjoys a unique location at the heart of Africa thus giving it an advantage for regional trade and investment. Uganda has seen its regional trade grow steadily with its neighbors South Sudan, the Democratic Republic of Congo, Kenya, Tanzania, and Rwanda. However, trade flows can be suddenly

Table 10.4 Major imported goods in Uganda

Trade Indicators	Amount in US$	Year
27 (oil and mineral fuels)	$1,444,391,091	2014
87 (motor vehicles and parts)	$543,671,648	2014
84 (industrial machinery)	$490,885,381	2014
85 (electrical machinery)	$373,963,024	2013
30 (pharmaceuticals)	$358,081,442	2013
15 (fats and oils)	$268,130,962	2014
39 (plastics)	$266,972,540	2014
72 (iron and steel)	$251,052,695	2014
10 (cereals)	$245,841,138	2014
25 (natural minerals and stone)	$137,803,925	2014

Source: World Bank Group. (2016). *Ease of Doing Business in Uganda*. www.doingbusiness. org/data/exploreeconomies/uganda

disrupted when conflict breaks out, as happened in South Sudan at the end of 2013 (World Bank, 2014). In addition, the United States exports to Uganda totaled $125 million in 2013. Major American exports to Uganda include machinery and machinery parts, electronics, transportation equipment, and optic and medical instruments. Prospects for US exports to Uganda include construction equipment, renewable energy technologies, oil production technologies, power generation, hydropower technologies, manufacturing and mining equipment, information and communication technology products, medical equipment and pharmaceuticals, supplies for food processing, agricultural inputs, cosmetics, and consumer goods (United States Department of State, 2016).

The World Bank (2014) Human Development Report revealed that the main areas of foreign investment in the country were manufacturing, financial services and real estate, and agriculture, forestry, and fish. Other areas of significant investment were in power, oil, construction, and mining. In 2011, Uganda Investment Authority began to more closely scrutinize foreign investment license applicants, rejecting a greater number of those lacking solid business plans and capital. In response to growing perceptions that foreign workers without work permits were taking local jobs, the government also began more strictly enforcing its foreign labor laws. Foreign investors in Uganda should be aware that projects that could impact the environment require an Environmental Impact Assessment (EIA) carried out by the National Environment Management Authority (NEMA). The requirement for EIAs applies to both local and foreign investors (World Bank Group, 2016).

The nation's inadequate electricity supply and poor road infrastructure are major impediments for investors and other businesses. Uganda's current energy supply of 340 megawatts falls far short of the 460 megawatts of current demand (United States Department of State, 2012). This power deficit, combined with the inability of the government to pay the bills for its overly subsidized power sector, resulted in chronic power blackouts in the second half of 2011. With demand for power increasing 10% per year, the government hopes to expand capacity to 1,045 megawatts within the next five years. The 250 megawatt hydropower dam at Bujagali Falls on the Nile River is expected to be fully operating to full capacity by 2015. The government is also fast-tracking the 600 megawatt Karuma Hydropower Project, but it will not go online until 2017, at the earliest (United States Department of State, 2012). In addition, full commissioning of the 250 megawatt Bujagali Hydropower Project in 2012 temporarily alleviated Uganda's power deficit, but demand is growing at 10% per year, and is gradually beginning to outstrip supply again. In 2013, the government held a groundbreaking ceremony for the construction of the Karuma hydropower project that will add another 600 megawatts of power to Uganda's grid, when it comes online, possibly in 2018. The country is also constructing a number of micro hydro projects along the Nile River, and is promoting development of renewable energy in Uganda (World Bank Group, 2016; GlobalEdge, 2016).

Table 10.5 Export and import partners

Export partners	Volume in US$	Import partners	Volume in US$
Kenya	$297,435,925	India	$1,490,195,385
South Sudan	$280,294,992	China	$739,643,124
European Union	$464 million	United States	$125,000,000
Nigeria	$1 million		
Rwanda	$245,334,653	Kenya	$593,887,653
Democratic Republic of the Congo	$181,680,327	United Arab Emirates	$401,281,096
Sudan	$105,091,081	Japan	$354,635,239
Italy	$98,546,964	South Africa	$259,880,085
Belgium	$89,828,683	Indonesia	$224,120,832
Netherlands	$89,422,112	Saudi Arabia	$177,006,442
Germany	$75,081,850	Germany	$117,666,552
China	$65,995,222	Bahrain	$101,480,737
United States	$34 million		

Source: GlobalEdge. (2016). *Doing Business in Uganda*. http://globaledge.msu.edu/ countries/ uganda/memo

World Bank (2015). *World Development Report*. New York: Oxford University Press, Washington D.C.

Globalization transformed international trade and developing nations opened up their economies to such trade, which had become important to every country's prosperity. While global economic activities have expanded, African countries, including Uganda, have failed to take advantage of the opportunities provided by globalization (World Bank Group, 2016). They have not bridged the digital gap, and their industries are faced with greater competition at home and in foreign markets. Capital mobility made possible by globalization means that government and businesses must compete for capital in the global market. Unfortunately, because of the complex and costly processes that such global transactions involve, it is unlikely that African countries are adequately equipped to compete for such resources. In essence, African nations do not only lack the capital resources but also the technological and advanced skills necessary to take advantage of globalization and become competitive across global markets (UNIDO, 2007: 47). The end of the 1990s called the government's attention to the fact that the private sector was going to play a vital role in the economic and industrial transformation of Uganda. To that end, several economic reforms were initiated to create an enabling environment for the private sector. These reforms included the effective implementation of the 1991 investment code, the privatization of public enterprises, the reduction of import tariffs, elimination of licensing requirements, lifting of import bans, elimination of export taxes, harmonization of tariffs within the East African Community, and trade liberalization in general (Government of Uganda, 2010). While impressive strides were achieved following the implementation of the reform measures, a 1998 World Bank firm level survey indicated that the competitiveness of the Ugandan private sector was constrained by serious structural problems (UNIDO, 2007:12; World Bank Group, 2016).

The National Planning Authority, in consultation with other government institutions and other stakeholders, developed a Uganda Vision 2040 to build on the progress that had been made in addressing the strategic issues that have constrained Uganda's socio-economic development since its independence in 1966, including ideological disorientation, weak private sector, underdeveloped human resources, inadequate infrastructure, small market, lack of industrialization, underdeveloped services sector, under-development of agriculture, and poor democracy, among others. It is conceptualized around strengthening the fundamentals of the economy to harness the abundant opportunities around the country. The opportunities include oil and gas, tour-ism, minerals, ICT business, abundant labor force, geographical location and trade, water resources, industrialization, and agriculture (Uganda Vision, 2040, 2013). The proposed enabling environment stipulated in Vision 2040 is one in which the private sector could increase its capacity to produce, create employment opportunities, and generate profit in a free and competitive business framework capable of attracting domestic and foreign investments. The government was expected to facilitate the process by adopting and implementing appropriate policies, as well as legal and regulatory frameworks aimed at promoting and developing micro and small enterprises (UNIDO, 2007: 13). The theme for the MTCS of 2000–2005 was "making institutions support private sector growth," with an emphasis on creating an enabling environment for private sector through various economic reforms, providing effective infrastructure and public entities, removing export impediments, and improving access to capital and credit for micro and small enterprises (World Bank Group, 2016).

In addition to what businesses required from the government, a number of nongovernmental and civil society organizations were established to foster the government-private sector dialogue and lay the foundation for an enabling environment within which businesses would thrive and grow. These included the Uganda and the Millennium Challenge Corporation, which was a partnership designed to fight public corruption by enhancing the ability of four key anti-corruption agencies to investigate, prosecute, and adjudicate corruption cases quickly and successfully (World Bank Group, 2016). This partnership also strengthened civil society organizations to use existing legal frameworks to better identify, monitor, expose, and secure public redress against public corruption. Also established was the businesses linkage program by Enterprise Uganda, which sought to develop a new generation of dynamic Uganda entrepreneurs by actively providing support to small and medium scale enterprises (SMEs) to improve their productivity, growth, and competitiveness. Enterprise Uganda accomplished this by structuring commercial business arrangements between successful global corporations and local SMEs through innovative and well-organized business linkages. Created in 1992 as an initiative of the Uganda Manufacturer's Association and the Presidential Economic Council, and sponsored by the World Bank and the United States Agency for International Development (USAID), the Uganda National Forum played a critical role in articulating and promoting business friendly policies that contributed to economic growth with equity.

The National Forum enjoyed impressive success in its first five years, and was instrumental in the establishment of the Private Sector Foundation of Uganda (PSFU). The Private Sector Foundation, formed in 1995, was aimed at addressing the challenges of a fragmented private voice in dialogue with the government. By 2001, the foundation had brought together 81 business associations and 24 corporations to lead the private sector in on policy and business environment issues with the government. The foundation also developed a reputable track record for managing private sector related projects, which were supported by development partners working closely with government through the Ministries of Finance and Trade, Energy, and Health (Government of Uganda, 2010). Business licensing reforms were also initiated by the Entebbe Municipality in partnership with the Uganda Private Sector Foundation, to streamline the process of obtaining business licenses and increase revenue to the local government from licensing through increased compliance levels and lower administrative costs. Streamlining the licensing process and reducing the number of required approvals and assessments reduced the cost of registering a business by up to 75% (Uganda Ministry of Finance, Planning and Economic Development 2015; GlobalEdge, 2016).

Promoting Effective Business and Government Relations

It is clear from the preceding discussion that in order to enhance more effective government and business relations in Uganda, the challenges that have been previously identified as inhibiting the creation of an enabling business environment will have to be addressed successfully. This can be accomplished by establishing a collaborative and integrative framework that incorporates the lessons learned from the literature that has examined various aspects of the nature of this relationship thus far (Ferrell et al., 2014). Such a framework must be driven by the existence of a mechanism for measuring, what Te-Velde (2006: 7) refers to as a measurement of the role of the private sector in business and government relations, based on the presence and length of existence of a central organization linking businesses and associations. In addition, a measurement of the role of the public sector in business and government relations should be based on the presence and length of existence of an investment promotion agency to promote business, as well as an assessment of the cooperation between the public and private sectors using several processes and procedures. The agency's operations must be independent from those of government, in order for it to credibly establish the effectiveness of such collaboration, and evaluation of the existence and effectiveness of laws. Such laws to protect business practices have to be transparent, and be devoid of collusive behavior. In addition to these measures, a credible framework for enhancing effective business and government relations must include demonstrated political support and commitment at the highest levels of government, especially in the early stages of policy dialogue. This is necessary to ensure follow up action on agreements reached by government and businesses in the country (Ferrell et al., 2014). Establishing the capacity and readiness for a robust public-private sector dialogue also requires both sides to be engaged in meaningful negotiation. This is vital because businesses perform well when government implements a clear development strategy shaped by a well-defined vision for the country's economic future. On the other hand, government should provide leadership for its attainment, and demonstrate its commitment through consistent investment in the necessary infrastructure, institutions, skills, and capabilities (Dibie et al., 2015; Kalema, 2007: 22–24).

In this regard, government must promote private sector governance by ensuring that the same attention and commitment that are given to the public sector are given to private sector institutions (Dibie et al., 2015).

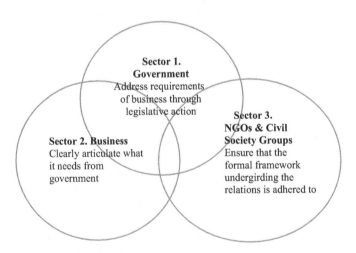

Figure 10.2 Framework for effective public and private sectors dialogue
Authors' own conceptualization

Government must also include corporate governance principles in legislation; create awareness of policies, laws, and regulations through information dissemination and consultation; encourage small and medium enterprises (SMEs) to operate professionally and transparently; and ensure that government and business work together to incorporate the principles of corporate governance in corporations' operations. It is also crucial for government to provide an appropriate environment for informal enterprises to operate (Graham 2002; Kalema, 2008: 25–27; Ferrell et al., 2014). Therefore, a framework for effective business and government relations must afford businesses the opportunity to effectively contribute to the sustainable development of the nation's economy.

Ultimately, the collaborative and integrative framework being proposed as a means of enhancing government and business relations in Uganda is one which must strive to bring all stakeholders together. Representatives of the public and private sectors and nongovernmental organizations must identify the challenges that have prohibited the creation of an enabling environment for dialogue. They should also establish mechanisms that would allow them to work collaboratively and transparently, and integrate key policy decisions aimed at promoting effective relations between government, business, and civil society organizations into a credible framework that would promote businesses and advance economic growth (Dibie et al., 2015).

Government should address the requests of business through legislative action or other institutionalized mechanisms that provide an enabling environment for supporting and enhancing business development. Business should clearly articulate what it needs from government. Nongovernmental organizations and civil society entities should also strive for the creation of a legal mechanism for ensuring that the formal framework undergirding the partnership between government and business is enforced, and where necessary, identify instances of violations for prosecution.

Economic freedom impacts the critical relationships between individuals, businesses, and the government (Miller & Kim, 2015; World Bank 2010). As a result, a free and open investment environment provides maximum entrepreneurial opportunities and incentives for expanded economic activity, greater productivity, and job creation. Furthermore, when business and economic processes are driven by supply and demand principles, markets provide real-time information on prices and the need immediate corrective action for those who have made bad decisions. It is very important to emphasize here that the Government of Uganda must allow the nation's economic processes to be driven by transparency in the market and the integrity of the information being made available to consumers. This new dimension also requires a prudent and effective regulatory system, through disclosure requirements and independent auditing. Furthermore, there is a crucial need to expand the financial opportunities in the country, as well as promote entrepreneurship. There is also the need to have an open banking environment that encourages competition in order to provide the most efficient financial intermediation between corporations, individuals, and government, as well as between investors and entrepreneurs (Dibie et al., 2015). Despite the fact that many regulatory activities in Uganda hinder business productivity and profitability, the most inhibiting to entrepreneurship are those that are associated with licensing new businesses. Consequently, in order for the government to solve this predicament, it must ensure transparency in dealing effectively with corruption. It has been argued that openness in regulatory procedures and processes can promote equitable treatment and greater efficiency (Ferrell et al., 2014). In that regard, expertise in the interaction between public governance and the efficient functioning of the commercial market in Uganda must be a key requirement to acquire before entering senior management positions in either business or government in Uganda.

Conclusion

This chapter has examined the nature of government and business relations in Uganda. It argues that a collaborative and integrative arrangement that brings together government, business, NGOs, or civil society organizations to formulate and implement industrial policy would foster the creation of an enabling environment for business promotion and economic growth in Uganda. In addition to creating better business and government relations, there is a need to increase the capacity of domestic corporations and the technological skills of workers in the country. Major Ugandan corporations should be the focus of innovation and technological development. Technological development depends critically on establishing solid business and government relations on one hand. On the other hand, attracting appropriate foreign investment and integrating principles of globalization into the economy of the country must also be addressed. Furthermore, the right political and economic environment must be provided in order to enhance the assimilation of foreign technology.

Attracting foreign investment to the country by the Government of Uganda could also galvanize the promotion and development of domestic entrepreneurs. The analysis of this paper reveals that a new industrial policy and dynamic regulation system can provide the underpinning rationale that will guide Uganda's economic growth, as long as an appropriate political environment is established to provide the framework in which both businesses and government agencies can operate as partners. However, the degree to which government hinders the free flow of foreign commerce has a direct bearing on the ability of corporations to pursue their economic goals and maximize their productivity and well-being.

The economic recovery program of the Government of Uganda has not been very effective in improving government and business relations. As a result, a more pragmatic government action is necessary for Ugandans to improve and defend themselves, promote a peaceful evolution of civil society, enjoy the fruits of their labor, and become entrepreneurs. This is why businesses and citizens are taxed to provide revenue for public safety, the protection of property, and the common defense. In addition, an appropriate business and government partnership could enhance the supply of public goods more efficiently. Some public goods, such as education, social services, protection of property rights, and sustainable development require the input of all stakeholders in Uganda. The simple truth is that the government cannot do it alone. The Government of Uganda definitely needs the private sector to effectively achieve its economic growth and sustainable development program. When government action rises beyond the minimal necessary level, however, it leads inevitably and quickly to the loss of freedom and the support of the business sector. The first freedom affected is often the economic freedom of both the public and private sectors. It is expected that a new industrial policy could foster the Government of Uganda's ability to attract multinational corporations to invest in the country, as well as increase its levels of foreign direct investment and industrial growth. A question for future research is whether close relations between business and government have any impact on capital flight in Uganda and how government has responded to it.

References

Allard, G. and Martinez, C. A. (2008). *The Influence of Government Policy and NGOs on Capturing Private Investment*. OECD Global Forum on International Investment. www.oecd.org/investment/globalforum/40400836.pdf. Accessed February 18, 2016.

Barros, R. A. (1993). Some Implications of New Growth Theory for Economic Development. *Journal of International Development*, 5(5), 531–558.

British Broadcasting Corporation. (2016). *Uganda Country Profile*. www.bbc.com/news/world-africa-14107906. Accessed February 18, 2016.

Cammett, M. (2007). Business-Government Relations and Industrial Change: The Politics of Upgrading in Morocco and Tunisia. *World Development*, 35(11), 1889–1903.

Cortright, J. (2001). *New Growth Theory, Technology and Learning: A Practical Guide*. Reviews of Economic Development Literature and Practice, No. 4.

Dewah, M. E. (2006). *The Practice of Public Policy Dialogue in Botswana, 1988–2007*. Center for International Private Enterprise, REFORM Case Study, No. 0708, November 2, 2007.

Dibie, R., Edoho, F. M. and Dibie, J. (2015). Analysis of Capacity Building and Economic Growth in Sub-Saharan Africa. *International Journal of Business and Social Science*, 6(12), 1–25.

Dicklitch, S. and Howard-Hassmann, R. H. (2007). Public Policy and Economic Rights in Ghana and Uganda. In Shareen Hertel and Lanse Minkler (Eds.), *Economic Rights: Conceptual, Measurement and Policy Issues*. Cambridge: Cambridge University Press, 325–344.

Ferrell, O. C., Hirt, G. A. and Ferrell, L. (2014). *Business: A Changing World*. New York: McGraw-Hill Press.

GlobalEdge. (2016). *Doing Business in Uganda*. Memo. http://globaledge.msu.edu/countries/uganda/. Accessed February 19, 2016.

Goldsmith, A. A. (2002). Business Associations and Better Governance in Africa. *Public Administration & Development*, 22, 39–49.

Government of Uganda. (2010). The Uganda Public Service Standing Orders 2010. http:// library.health.go.ug/publications/leadership-and-governance-governance/ laws-and-regulations/uganda-public-service. Accessed, September 2016.

Government of Uganda. (2006). Medium Term Competitiveness Strategy (MTCS)- Uganda's Public-Private Partnership for Competitiveness. Annual Report.

Government of Uganda. (2003). *Strategy to Develop Economic Growth*. Progress Report. www.finance.go.ug/dmdocuments/CG%202003%20Growth%20 Paper%20-%20Final.pdf. Accessed February 22, 2016.

Graham, C. (2002, April). *Strengthening Institutional Capacity in Poor Countries, No. 98*. Washington, DC: The Brookings Institution.

Harris, J. (2006). *Institutions and State Business Relations*. Briefing Note 2. London: IPPG.

Herzberg, B. and Wright, A. (2005). Competitiveness Partnerships: Building and Maintaining Public-Private Dialogue to Improve the Investment Climate. A Resource Drawn From the Review of 40 Countries' Experience.

Isaksson, M. and Celik, S. (2013). Equity Markets, Corporate Governance and Value Creation. *OECD Journal: Financial Market Trends*, 1, 1–45. http://dx.doi. org/10.1787/19952872. Accessed February 20, 2016.

Kalema, W. (2008). Enhancing Government/Business Relations and Mobilizing the Business Sector to Develop Productive Capacities in Least Developing Countries. New York: United Nations Conference on Trade & Development, UNCTAD.

Kalema, W. (2005). *Public-Private Sector Dialogue in Uganda's Reform Process, Development Outreach-Putting Knowledge to Work for Development*. www. publicprivatedialogue.org.

Lehne, R. (2013). *Government and Business: The Political Economy of the United States*. Washington, DC: Congressional Quarterly Press, 34–61.

Meznar, M. and Johnson, J. Jr. (2005). Business-Government Relations Within a Contingency Theory Framework: Strategy, Structure, Fit, and Performance. *Business & Society*, 44(2), 119–143.

Miller, T. and Kim, A. B. (2015). *Why Economic Freedom Matters*. www.heritage. org/index/book/chapter-2.

Morril, G., Kanyomozi, Y., Caroll, A. and Aggarwal, R. (1997, September). *Institutional Capacity for the Uganda National Forum*. The Uganda Mission of the United States Agency for International Development (USAID).

NSSF Strategic Planning Group. (2007). *NSSF 5 Year Corporate Strategic Plan*. Kampala Uganda.

Podolny, J. M. (2009). The Buck Stops (and Starts) at Business School. *Harvard Business Review*, 87(6), 62–72.

Porter, R. B. (2002). *Government-Business Relations in the United States*. Paper Presented at Conference Hosted by the John F. Kennedy School of Government at Harvard University, April 11–12.

Qureshi, M. and TeVelde, D. W. (2007). State-Business Relations, Investment Climate Reform and Firm Productivity in Sub-Saharan Africa. Discussion Paper 6. London: IPPG.

Republic of Uganda. *Uganda Development Corporation Act 1952*. www.ulii.org/ug/ legislation/consolidated-act/326. Accessed September 26, 2016.

Sanyal, R. N. and Guvenli, T. (2000). Relations Between Multinational Firms and Host Government: The Experience of American Owned Firms in China. *International Business Review*, 9, 119–134.

Schepers, S. (2010). Business-Government Relations: Beyond Lobbying. *Corporate Governance*, 10(4), 475–483.

Schneider, R. B. (1998). Business-Government Relations and Development. *Comparative Politics*, *31*, 101–122.

Sen, K. and Te Velde, D. W. (2009). State-Business Relations and Economic Growth in Sub-Saharan Africa. *Journal of Development Studies*, *45*(8), 1–17.

Te-Velde, D. W. (2006). *Measuring State Business Relations in Sub-Saharan Africa*. Discussion Paper 4. London: IPPG.

Uganda Bureau of Statistics. (2007). *Report on the Uganda Business Register 2006/2007, Kampala, Uganda*. www.ubos.org/onlinefiles/uploads/ubos/pnsd/NSS_MetaData Dic.pdf. Accessed February 22, 2016.

Uganda Ministry of Tourism, Trade and Industry. (2008). www.ugahicom.co.ke/index.php?option=com_content&view=article&id=115&Itemid=136.

Uganda National APRM Commission. (2007). *African Peer Review Mechanism (APRM) Uganda: A New Partnership for Africa's Development (NEPAD)*. Corporate Governance Thematic Area, Final Report.

Uganda Vision 2030. (2007). *Office of the President of Uganda, Kampala, Uganda*. https://images.search.yahoo.com/yhs/search;_ylt=A0LEVrcpjctW84s AOOUPxQt.;_ylu=X3oDMTByMjB0aG5zBGNvbG8DYmYxBHBvcwMxB HZ0aWQDBHNlYwNzYw—?p=Uganda+Vision+201%3A&fr=yhs-avg-fh_ lsonsw&hspart=avg&hsimp=yhs-fh_ lsonsw. Accessed February 22, 2016.

Uganda Vision 2040. (2013). A Transformed Ugandan Society From a Peasant to a Modern and Prosperous Country Within 30 Years. http://npa.ug/uganda-vision-2040/. Accessed February 22, 2016.

Ugandan Ministry of Finance, Planning and Economic Development. (2015). www.finance.go.ug/. Accessed February 22, 2016.

UNCTAD. (2007). The Least Developed Countries Report. United Nations Conference on Trade and Development. Geneva. http://unctad.org/en/Docs/ldc2007_ en.pdf. Accessed May 8, 2016.

UNIDO. (2007). Uganda: Integrated Industrial Policy for Sustainable Industrial Development and Competitiveness. Vienna, Austria.

US Department of States. (2016). Uganda Country Profile. www.regionalmms.org/images/CountryProfile/Uganda/Uganda%20Country%20Profile.pdf. Accessed September 27, 2016.

United States Department of State, (2012). Country Reports on Human Rights Practices – Uganda. www.refworld.org/docid/517e6dbef.html. Accessed December 15, 2016.

United States Agency for International Development (USAID). (2007). *Policy Reform: Lessons Learned*. Review of Economic Growth Related Policy Reform Activities in Developing Countries.

United States Foreign Commercial Service and U.S. Department of State. (2014). *Doing Business in Uganda: 2014 Country Commercial Guide for U.S. Companies*. http://photos.state.gov/libraries/adana/766947/public/doing-business-uganda 2014.pdf.

Willem, D. T. (2009) Effective State-Business Relations, Industrial Policy and Economic Growth. Westminster Bridge, London: ODI Publications.

World Bank. (2004). Uganda Investment Climate Assessment Report. Washington DC: World Bank Publication.

World Bank. (2005). *World Development Report: A Better Investment Climate for Everyone*. New York: Oxford University Press, Washington, DC.

World Bank. (2010). Innovation Policy: A Guide for Developing Countries. Washington, DC: Word Bank Publication.

World Bank. (2014). *Human Development Index*. New York: Oxford University Press, Washington, DC.

World Bank. (2015). *World Development Report*. New York: Oxford University Press, Washington, DC.

World Bank Group. (2016). *Ease of Doing Business in Uganda*. www.doingbusiness.org/data/exploreeconomies/uganda. Accessed February 19, 2016.

Yifu, J. L. (2010). Optimal Framework for State-Business Relations in Effective State-Business Relations, Industrial Policy and Economic Growth. Westminster Bridge, London: ODI Publications.

11 Business and Government Relations in Ethiopia

Josephine Dibie and Robert A. Dibie

Introduction

Ethiopia is Africa's second most populous country and has one of its fastest growing economies. The nation is known as the Federal Democratic Republic of Ethiopia, and it is located in the Northeastern Horn of Africa. It is bordered by Eritrea to the north and northeast, Djibouti and Somalia to the east, and Sudan and South Sudan in the southwest. The nation's population is approximately 91 million (United Nations Human Development Index, 2014). About 50% of the population are women (African Development Bank Report, 2013). Ethiopia has experienced some economic expansion of around 10% over the past five years. The country's economy has been enhanced by improved infrastructure and more effective mining and farming techniques, but growth remains highly vulnerable to external shocks (Index of Economic Freedom, 2016; Ezana, 2011). According to the United Nations Development Programme (UNDP) Human Development Report (2014), the economic growth of Ethiopia has reduced the percentage of the population living in poverty by 33% since 2000, but per capita income remains among the world's lowest, and many young people leave to seek opportunity elsewhere. The economy is based largely on agriculture and remains vulnerable to droughts and external shocks. The UNDP Human Development Report (2014) indicated that Ethiopia is one of the poorest countries in the world, with a per capita GNP of about US$1,589. The country has also had a growth rate of about 10.3%, and the inflation rate is reported to be about 7.4%.

The country is regarded as the only African nation that was never colonialized by Western industrialized imperialists. The capital of Ethiopia, Addis Ababa, is also the headquarters of the African Union. The nation has a federal government and 10 regional states. The states are Afa, Amhara, Tigray, Oromia, Gambella, Somalia Benishagul-Gumuz, Southern Nations Nationalist and Peoples region, and Harar, and the two administrative states are Addis Ababa City administration and Dire Dawa Council.

Ethiopia is a landlocked country. The nation has a traditional economic system in which the allocation of available resources is made on the basis of primitive methods, and many citizens engage in subsistence agriculture (GlobalEdge, 2016). Business and government relations in the country are still very weak, because the business environment is very difficult. Unlike most other countries, corporate financial information is rarely available and, when available, usually unreliable. The Government of Ethiopia's legal system makes debt collection very unpredictable (Gebeyaw & Chofana, 2012; Melese, 2012; U.S. Department of State). The institutional framework has very serious weaknesses. Intercompany transactions can thus be very difficult to manage in the highly risky environments of the country (GlobalEdge, 2016).

Tremendous progress has been made in Ethiopia compared to what the nation used to be 30 years ago. People live longer and have healthier lives, better water, and better air quality. However, there are still many social and economic problems to tackle. Several million people in Ethiopia are still not very lucky to have universal education, an assured food supply and clean, pipe water supply (UNDP, 2014). Something that becomes very clear from these challenges is the degree to which the Ethiopian Government has been able to collaborate with the business sector. The Government of Ethiopia has not effectively established or explores partnership with its private sectors to address its greatest challenges and opportunities, despite the fact that these issues are interrelated. Business on like government is better prepared in distilling their challenges into topics allowing them to identify the best, most achievable opportunities (Chambers 2005; Steven 2005). The failure of the Ethiopian Government to effective collaborate with the business sector to set national priorities indicates that sometimes it is not sure if the nation's monetary policy is the best way to achieve its priority programs. Forming partnership with the business sector and finding synergies between priorities are an additional bonus that may come from the government and citizens. But this has not been the case in Ethiopia (African Development Bank Report, 2013).

According to GlobalEdge (2016), when entrepreneurs draw up a business plan and try to get it underway, the Ethiopian Government bureaucratic and legal procedures to incorporate and register the new company are the first hurdles that must be overcome. On one hand, some have a straightforward and affordable process. On the other hand, others have procedures that are so burdensome that entrepreneurs have to bribe officials to speed up the process or they opt to run their business informally (GlobalEdge, 2016; World Bank, 2016). Further, it has been reported that recent economic crisis in Ethiopia have raised concerns about the design of bankruptcy systems and the ability of such system to help reorganized viable companies in the country. As a result of the bankruptcy process been so inefficient most creditors in Ethiopia hardly use it (World Bank, 2016). It could therefore be argued that business and government relations policy reform has not effectively improve contract enforcement outside of bankruptcy in the country.

The tax system in Ethiopia is progressive in nature. People working for the government and well established private organizations pay an individual income tax rate of 35% (Ethiopia Central Statistics, 2012). Most poor farmers in the rural areas do not pay tax because their income is difficult to access. The top corporate tax rate is about 30% after overhead cost. Other taxes include a value-added tax and a capital gains tax. The overall tax burden equals 12.4% of GDP (Ethiopia Central Statistical Authority, 2012). Government spending amounts to 17.8% of total domestic output, and the deficit has increased. Public debt amounts to about 22% of GDP (Index of Economic Freedom, 2016).

According to the World Bank (2016) ineffective and opaque regulatory requirements still increase the overall cost of conducting business in Ethiopia. The underdeveloped labor market continues to trap much of the labor force in the informal sector (Ethiopia Central Statistical Authority, 2012). The World Bank report (2016) reveals that the Ethiopian birr (currency) is overvalued, and the IMF warns of the risks of crowding out private-sector activity is eminent in the near future. Several subsidized parastatals have had to resort to non-concessional foreign loans to stay afloat. In addition, all lands are owned by the government. The state strongly influences lending and funds state-led development projects by forcing private banks to purchase treasury bills. Foreign ownership of banks remains prohibited (Index of Economic Freedom, 2016).

The development of entrepreneurship in Ethiopia has been faced with a lot of challenges such as technical skill, inadequate funds, incentives, well equipped vocational and technical training institutions, progressive educational system, and poor managerial skills. Many unemployed citizens in the country today are creative, but they are incapacitated because they do not have enough funds to start a business that could make them self-reliant (Dibie, 2014).

According to Gebeyaw and Chofana (2012) and Nzinga and Tsegay (2012), millions of Ethiopians, especially the youth and women, are unemployed, underemployed, or in the swelling ranks of the working poor. The 2010 urban employment survey by the Ethiopia Central Statistical Agency (2012) reported that 4,790,958 out of the 5,907,470 labor force were employed, with the remaining 1,116,512 people unemployed. This means that the urban population unemployment rate is about 18.9%. The corresponding female unemployment rate is reported to be 27.4% while the male unemployment rate is 11% (Ethiopia Central Statistical Authority, 2012).

This chapter examines the relationship between businesses and government in Ethiopia. It argues that while the Government of Ethiopia intervenes in the economy with laws and regulations designed to promote competition and to protect consumers, employees, and environment in the country, business entrepreneurs are also needed to risk their wealth, time, and efforts to develop for profit an innovative product or ways of doing something. The dynamics of development and participation at both national and grassroots levels in Ethiopia must involve business practices that foster new technology and innovative management techniques. At the same time, government has to take steps to maximize the disruptive effects of economic fluctuation and reduce unemployment. It uses data derived from primary and secondary sources to analyze the relationship between business and government in Ethiopia. The chapter recommends government, private sector, and NGOs should collaborate to establish a mechanism for a better and efficient approach to providing employment, goods, and services for all Ethiopian. It further suggests that appropriate monetary and fiscal policies are necessary for Ethiopia, to effectively address its sustainable development and capacity building problems.

Framework for Public and Private Sectors Partnership

It is no secret that domestic growth in Ethiopia is important because it provides a foundation for the future of business and government relations in the nation. Economic growth can contribute to advancements in all fields, creating beneficial outcomes and solutions to many economic problems. According to Froeb et al. (2016), economics can be used by business people to spot money-making opportunities. On the other hand, government plays a critical role in the wealth creating process by enforcing property rights and contracts mechanisms that facilitate voluntary transactions (Rondinelli 1993; Onah 2010). By making sure that buyers and sellers can keep the gains from trade, the Ethiopian legal system makes trade much more likely and is responsible for the nation's enormous wealth ability. Several scholars have contended that government collect taxes out of the total surplus created by business transaction. However, it should be noted that if tax is larger than the surplus, the transaction will not take place (Ferrell et al., 2016; Froeb et al., 2016; Miller et al., 2014; Schiller, 2011). The intended effect of a taxation is to raise revenue for the government; however, the unintended consequence of taxation is that it deters some wealth creating business transaction. Government policies designed to extend credits to businesses and to lower income citizens indirectly increase economic growth opportunities for both the public and private sectors. All these development tasks of business and government are most likely to occur at the national and regional levels, and are reminiscent of the strategic goals of accomplishing economic growth and sustainable development.

Business and government relations assume that several parties such as private corporations, government, and nongovernment organizations must combine forces in order to accomplish various developmental goals sustainably. Both the power and conflict inherent in business and government relationship arise from the notion of building new partnership between principal and agents, which have different constituencies and interests, along with divergent strategic and operational realistic. Despite the existence of business and government differences, the principal-agent model suggests that the relationship is primary one of delegation, in which the government provides organizational material or financial resources. On the other hand, the business organization carries out its mission with varying degrees of policy level direction by government to accomplish national economic development goals (Dibie, 2010; Dibie et al., 2015).

The missing component model is predicated on the idea that development can be effective by identifying the critically weak or missing element in developing a country's economic growth or assets, and by subsequently providing this component (OECD, 2007a; World Bank, 2003). In Ethiopia such missing components typically are identified as domestic saving, better governance for development, appropriate technology, intermediation between existing business and government relations stakeholders, and research and development. The efficacy of business and government relations in the drive for sustainable development is of paramount importance. Consequently, it will prove to be the means by which developing nations such like Ethiopia can lift themselves from underdevelopment and achieve the goals that are exemplified in the basic human needs in the country (Anderson, 2015; Schiller, 2011).

Encouraging new business development is an essential component of economic growth and poverty reduction in Africa (Dibie et al., 2015). According to the Organization for Economic Cooperation and Development (OECD) (2008), private business development is a very important source of innovation and employment generation. This is because a vibrant and competitive private sector can also empower poor people by providing them with better goods and services at more affordable prices. Peter (2013) contends that governments in African countries are beginning to realize the importance of fostering private business development as a key pillar to achieving their sustainable development goals. The international initiative for African development known as Enhanced Private Sector Assistance (EPSA) has taken a comprehensive approach to support private business development. According to OECD (2014), the EPSA has been channeling resources to five major areas of intervention: (1) creating an enabling environment for private business development; (2) promoting trade and foreign direct investment; (3) promoting the development of small and medium size enterprises (SMEs); (4) strengthening financial systems building comprehensive economic and social infrastructure; and (5) investing in areas that has not been fully exploited. In addition to the efforts of the EPSA, the African Development Bank has assisted its member states' governments in developing national strategies to enhance corporate governance, which is fundamental to attract and protect both domestic and foreign investors (African Development Bank, 2011; OECD, 2014; World Trade Organization, 2006). Despite the good intention of the Enhanced Private Sector Assistance in Africa, most countries in the continent continue to face the challenge of enhancing transparency and accountability in the design and implementation of policies aimed at fostering private business development. In the case of Ethiopia, limited private business development led growth has not benefited the society as a whole, due to inadequate implementation of appropriate policies by the government (Melese, 2012; Abebe & Aelmu, 2013).

Businesses in Ethiopia tend to face much larger regulatory burdens. Heavy regulation and weak property rights exclude the poor from doing business. Women, young people, and low-skilled workers are hurt the most. Economic growth is the only benefit of better business regulation and property protection. Thus, the Government of Ethiopia can use revenues to improve their health and education system, rather than support an overblown bureaucracy. The Government of Ethiopia has an obligation to seek new and even more effective ways of making tangible progress toward its sustainable development strategic policies. The attainment of the nation's sustainable development policies requires building organizational capacity (Anderson, 2015; Kraft & Furlong, 2016). All too often, the governments in the country, however, focus on creating new programs and keeping administrative costs low, instead of building the organizational capacity necessary to achieve their aspirations effectively and efficiently (Dibie, 2014). The nation must change both its public administrators and those that fund them. It must also recognize that excellence in programmatic innovation and implementation are insufficient for government institutions to achieve lasting economic growth results. As a result, great programs need great organizations and capacity building measures behind them (Miller et al., 2014). It should be noted that businesses react to incentives, costs, and constraints, which are often summarized as the business environment or more narrowly, as the investment climate. Influencing the environment for business and investment are the actions of government in shaping and implementing policies. Both good policies and good administration of policies are needed. One without the other would be ineffective.

Analysis of Business and Government Relations

The line of demarcation between the activities of the business and government in Ethiopia has never been firmly drawn for the past five decades. Ethiopia is Africa's second most populous country after Nigeria, with almost 91 million people has been growing with about 10% a year for the past decade before the severe impact of drought which slowed growth to about 8.1% in 2015 (World Bank, 2016). The Democratic Republic of Ethiopia economy is based on agriculture, which accounts for 46% of GDP in 2015 and 2016. On the other hand, the agriculture sector provides 85% of total employment in the country (GlobalEdge, 2016). As a result of the landlocked nature of the country, food processing, beverages, textiles, and leather are the major industrial sectors in the nation. However, the severe drought between 2014and 2016 has left almost one-fifth of Ethiopian citizens needing food aid and 400,000 people facing severe malnutrition (Woldenarriel 2011; World Bank, 2016).

The geography of Ethiopia consists of high plateau with the central mountain range divided by Great Rift Valley. The chief of state is the president, and the head of government is the prime minister. Ethiopia has a traditional economic system in which the allocation of available resources is made on the basis of primitive methods, and many citizens engage in subsistence agriculture. Ethiopia is a member of the Common Market for Eastern and Southern Africa (World Bank, 2016; GlobalEdge, 2016).

The national and regional governments in Ethiopia not only provide the framework of rules and the physical infrastructure so vital to the operations of market; they also play important participatory role in the market system of the nation. Through public corporations such as the Ethiopian Airlines that are independent, the Ethiopian Government today accounts for a significant share of the nation's commercial production. From this perspective, business and government sectors have worked in partnership to meet the challenges of building a nation and of developing an economic and technological system. This initiative would not only be responsive to the material aspiration of Ethiopia but also reflective of their social consciousness and industrial diversity.

The country is endowed with fertile land and large bodies of lakes and rivers. These natural resources offer opportunities for expansion of irrigated agriculture, fish production and hydroelectric power generation. Ethiopia is known as the water tower of Africa, and its hydropower potential is conservatively estimated at 45,000 MW, less than 5% of which is developed. With this potential, and provided that environmental and social sustainability issues are addressed effectively, the country could well meet its energy needs and leave a large surplus for export to the regional markets (African Development Bank Group, 2011; GlobalEdge, 2016).

Ethiopia is also very rich in renewable energy resources. While the total endowment of hydropower is estimated to be up to 45,000 MW per annum, only 3% of the country's hydropower potential is currently being exploited (GlobalEdge, 2016). The country is reported to be on the brink of an energy revolution, but requires significant assistance to realize its potential, particularly in the areas of geothermal, wind, solar, and biomass resources as long-term options for power generation for both local industrialization and as a potential source of sustainable development earnings (African Development Bank Group, 2011). It is also reported that the Ethiopian Electric Power Corporation has set concrete plans to achieve 75% energy access by 2015, and aspires to become a regional power exporter and green energy hub for East Africa (U.S. Department of State, 2013).

The environment in which change agents work in Ethiopia also plays a part in determining how effective business and government relations programs function or policies are implemented. The policy environment of the pre-1991 Ethiopia significantly restricted private sector investment if not considered totally banned under the Marxist-Leninist social policies of that regime. In that regime, the maximum capital investment allowable for private owners was limited to Br 250,000 (Ethiopian currency). With the complete demise of the socialist era in 1991, there has been significant economic reform measures undertaken to make the business environment congenial to entrepreneurship and private sector investment (Melese, 2012; Abebe & Aelmu, 2013). The government implemented extensive deregulation and liberalization policies due to proactive actions. The aim of this government initiative is to establish a cordial business environment for the promotion of private sector investment. The government has been providing diverse forms of support to entrepreneurs and industrialists that yielded significant and progressive record development in promotion of private investment in domestic and foreign investments. The supports mainly include provision of free land lease, subsidized credit services, reduction of tax rates, and tax relief for a specified period of time. The government is also providing training services and more importantly business development services to encourage the development of the flourishing Micro and Small Scale Enterprises (World Bank, 2016; African Development Bank Group, 2011). To curb the unemployment problem in urban areas, the government has been providing effective supports to the youth interested in the operation of micro and small enterprises on individual as well as group bases (Abebe & Aelmu, 2013; U.S. Department of State, 2013).

Cognizant of the social and political consequences of unemployment, the government has designed and implemented programs that targeted job creation over the last decade (ILO, 2012; Halie 2003). The most noticeable policy actions were the introduction of Micro and Small Businesses Development Strategy and Industrial Development Strategy, respectively, with the purpose of promoting private sector development so that the sector may plays significant role as a mechanism for economic growth and development (Melese, 2012; Abebe & Aelmu, 2013). Since the Micro and Small Enterprises Development Strategy was enacted in 2004, citizens of the country have been encouraged to enter into the micro and small enterprises in an organized way, with special support rendered by the government. The support includes provision of entrepreneurship and business management training; mutual guarantee credit services through micro finance institutions, market linkage services, relevant technology research, business development services, and basic infrastructure deemed necessary for their operation (Lishan 2012; Oliver de Sardan 2005). The government has shown its commitment to continue supporting the development of micro and small enterprises with a coordinated approach. To this end, the government established the Federal Micro and Small Enterprises Development Agency, and state governments stepped in by establishing similar agencies at regional levels. Ethiopia's policy of generating employment for citizens through enhanced skills development in the economically active population is similar to what is in practice in its counterparts of sub-Saharan African economies (African Development Bank Groups, 2011).

The African Development Bank (2013) reported that Ethiopia's economy grew by 10.3%, making the country one of Africa's top performing economies, and this strong growth is expected to continue in 2015 and 2016. The nation has also enacted prudent fiscal and monetary policy that has helped contain inflation to single digits since 2013. The right implementation of federalism and devolution of power to the regions are paving the way to overcome geographic and socio-economic barriers to inclusive growth and structural transformation (United Nations Economic Commission for Africa, 2011).

One of the greatest challenges facing Ethiopia today is restoring its economic strength and sustainability goals. The extent to which the government has been able to address the sustainability challenges of human resources capacity, as well as a holistic approach to capitalizing on the strengths of a diverse workforce, has not been encouraging. Despite the political and economic stability in the country for almost two decades, the nation has not been able to attract and retain a committed productive workforce in turbulent economic conditions that offer opportunity for financial success but severely ignored citizens capacity building (Ethiopian Economic Association [EEA], 2005–2006; World Bank, 2011).

According to the Ethiopia Central Statistical Agency report (2012), the agricultural sector is the dominant sector in the Ethiopian economy because it contributes over 41% of the nation's gross domestic product (GDP). The agricultural sector also contributes 60% of Ethiopia's exports, and is the major employer of approximately 83.5% of the country's population. In addition, the agricultural sector in Ethiopia is the major employer of the rural population. According to the African Development Bank Group Report (2011), agriculture practices such as smallholder farming and live-stock production composed the dominant sector in the economy. While the services sector has recently outstripped agriculture in terms of its share of GDP (currently estimated at 46%) agriculture remains critical for broad based growth. The agriculture sector accounts for 42% of GDP, 80% of employment, and 85% of Ethiopia's export earnings (African Development Bank Group, 2011).

The second largest contribution to the national GDP of Ethiopia comes from the service sector (Gebeyaw & Chofana, 2012; Melese, 2012). Recent reports revealed that the contribution of the service sector to Ethiopian gross domestic product is about 46% (Ethiopia Central Statistics Agency, 2012). Though the service sector of the economy has shown flamboyant performance with regard to its contribution to the GDP in recent years, it could not generate significant employment opportunity and does not pay as well as the industrial sector. As shown in Table 11.1, export revenues have more than doubled since 2004, reaching US$2 billion in 2010.

The industrial sectors contribution is very minimal, with about 13% comparative to the two dominant sectors in the Ethiopian economy. This indicates significant structural weakness of the economy. Employment opportunity in the urban areas is directly related to the development of the industrial sector of the economy. The low level of development in the industrial sector of the economy therefore is one of the major issues that explain unemployment problems.

Table 11.1 Ethiopia's economic indicators and trade statistics

No.	Indicators	Amount in US$	Year
1	GDP, PPP (current international)	$145,414,752,149	2014
2	GDP growth rate (annual %)	10.279%	2014
3	GDP per capita, PPP (current international)	$1,500	2014
4.	Inflation, consumer prices (annual %)	7.392%	2014
5	External debt stocks, total (DOD, current US$)	$12,556,584,000	2013
6	Imports of goods and services (current US$)	$16,182,860,468	2014
7	Exports of goods and services (current US$)	$6,474,165,408	2014
8	Total merchandise trade (% of GDP)	42.121% (2014)	2014
9	Commercial service exports (current US$)	$2,536,557,849	2012
10	Total exports	$5,666,889,414	2014
11	Total imports (2014)	$21,914,373,648	2014
12	Trade balance (2014)	$16,247,484,234	2014
13	Exports of goods and services (% of GDP)	11.64%	2014
14	Imports of goods and services (% of GDP)	29.1%	2014

Source: GlobalEdge. (2016). *Ethiopia Trade Statistics.* http://globaledge.msu.edu/countries/
ethiopia/trade stats. Accessed October 20, 2016.

World Bank Group. (2016). *Doing Business: Measuring Regulatory Quality and Efficiency.*
www.doingbusiness.org/~/media/GIAWB/Doing%20Business/Documents/Annual-Reports/
English/DB16-Full-Report.pdf. Accessed October 20, 2016.

The share of non-traditional exports, notably flowers, gold, meat, and leather products increased to 74.6% in 2010 from 60% (GlobalEdge, 2016). Ethiopia's 10 top export country partners are Kuwait, Somalia, Saudi Arabia, China, the Netherlands, the United States, Djibouti, Germany, Japan, and Switzerland. Over the same period, imports, especially for capital goods, grew rapidly (on average by about 27.4% per annum). Within a period of six years, FDI increased eightfold to reach US$950 million in 2010. Remittances grew, on average, by 34% per annum to reach US$2.2 billion. However, the current account deficits remained high, at an average of 6% of GDP, due to the fact that Ethiopia is an importer of oil and capital goods (GlobalEdge, 2016; African Development Bank Group, 2011).

The business climate and competitiveness in Ethiopia is improving considerably (World Bank, 2016). In 2010, the country was ranked 107 out of 183 countries in the world compared with 116 in 2009. The 2016 World Bank Doing Business report represents an improvement; however, impediments to private sector development remain in the country. For instance, access to credit and foreign exchange is limited. Although infrastructure services are improving, they are still inadequate, as reflected in frequent power outages and poor telecommunications services (National Bank of Ethiopia

Table 11.2 Ethiopia's top 10 export goods

No.	Export goods	Amount in US$	Year
1	Oil and mineral fuels	$1,078,389,430	2014
2	Coffee and spices	$1,061,588,945	2014
3	Vegetables	$936,985,108	2014
4	Oil seeds	$771,228,628	2014
5	Live plants	$679,689,982	2014
6	Live animals	$332,248,541	2014
7	Precious stones and metals	$176,757,059	2014
8	Hides and leather	$97,462,563	2014
9	Meat	$87,660,523	2014
10	Other Items	$44,336,681	2014

Source: GlobalEdge. (2016). *Ethiopia Trade Statistics*. http://globaledge.msu.edu/countries/ethiopia/tradestats. Accessed October 20, 2016.

2012). The business community also considers tax administration and enforcement procedures as burdensome. These are compounded by what the business community perceives as the lack of a level playing field vis-à-vis public enterprises and party affiliated businesses (African Development Bank Group, 2011). The Democratic Republic of Ethiopia has established partners with several western and Asian countries. The 10 most crucial partners where it imports goods from are China, the United States, Kuwait, Saudi Arabia, India, Japan, Indonesia, Turkey, and Germany (World Bank Group, 2016).

The Government of Ethiopia enacted a five-year Growth and Transformation Plan in 2010. The policy was intended to galvanize Ethiopia's openness to foreign investment. The Growth and Transformation Plan projects significant investment contributing to a per annum gross domestic product (GDP) growth rate of at least 11% (U.S. Department of State, 2013). Improving the quality of social services and infrastructure, ensuring macroeconomic stability, and enhancing productivity in agriculture and manufacturing are major objectives of the plan. The five year plan also puts a significant emphasis on developing local production to lessen Ethiopia's dependency on imported goods, and encourage investment in the export-oriented sectors of textiles/garments, leather/leather products, cut flowers, fruits and vegetables, and agro-processing (GlobalEdge, 2016).

According to World Bank's (2016) Doing Business report, the lack of competition, poor access to finance and land, low productivity, and resource allocation inefficiencies pose a major hindrance to Ethiopia's competitiveness. Even though the Government of Ethiopia recognizes the importance of private sector consultations in policy making, in reality the process is fraught with difficulties. The recently institutionalized Public Private Dialogue Forum is expected to improve business and government relations in the country.

According to the African Development Bank Group (2011) report in 2009, the Ethiopian government broadened its agricultural policy focus from increasing smallholder productivity, adding encouragement of private investment (both domestic and foreign) in larger-scale commercial farms to the existing priorities. In addition the Ministry of Agriculture of the country created a new Agricultural Investment Support Directorate that is tasked with negotiating long-term leases (all land is owned by the government) on more than seven million acres of land for these commercial farms (U. S. Department of State, 2013; GlobalEdge, 2016). The strategic plan of the ministry is to boost productivity, employment, technology transfer, and foreign exchange reserves by offering incentives to private investors. Since its establishment, the Ministry of Agriculture program has encountered some protests from individuals and groups claiming interests in land to be made available to new investors. In response to the predicaments created by the Ministry of Agriculture's program, the Government of Ethiopia established an Agricultural Transformation Agency (ATA) in 2010 with the intension of streamlining agricultural investments and improving the enabling environment for both smallholder and commercial agricultural development in the country (US State Department Report, 2013).

The Labor and Social Affairs Bureau of Addis Ababa (2013) reported that the current unemployment rate is about 20%, while youth unemployment ranges from 30% to 35% (Abebe & Aelmu, 2013). The Government of Ethiopia introduced measures in the past to address the unemployment predicament. These reform policies include labor market laws, and decentralization of public spending. They also created enabling entrepreneurship environments, to improve the quality of education, stimulated innovation and developed skills through Technical Vocational Education Training (TVET), private sectors involvement, as well as business development services (Ministry of Education, 2008). Despite, these policies by both the national and Addis Ababa city governments, the youth unemployment problems have not been effectively resolved. This policy dilemma has resulted in citizens further requesting different approaches to address the unemployment issue (SparkNotes, 2012; Nebil et al., 2010).

The Government of Ethiopia has introduced tools to facilitate trade—including single windows, risk-based inspections, and electronic data interchange systems. These changes help improve the trading environment and boost firms' international competitiveness. In addition, contract enforcement takes 530.00 days and costs 15.20% of the value of the claim in the country. Globally, Ethiopia stands at 84 in the ranking of 189 economies on the ease of enforcing contracts (World Bank, 2016). An important point to note is that the Government of Ethiopia has the ability to clarify the

Table 11.3 Ethiopia's top 10 import goods

No.	Import goods	Amount in US$	Year
1	Oil and mineral fuels	$3,869,389,450	2014
2	Industrial machinery	$2,936,129,287	2014
3	Electrical machinery	$1,977,441,553	2014
4	Motor vehicles and parts	$1,846,604,169	2014
5	Iron and steel articles	$1,068,831,784	2014
6	Plastics	$996,015,527	2014
7	Iron and steel	$869,629,628	2014
8	Cereals	$562,806,575	2014
9	Fats and oils	$511,133,667	2014
10	Fertilizers	$474,180,14	2014

Source: GlobalEdge. (2016). *Ethiopia Trade Statistics*. http://globaledge.msu.edu/countries/ethiopia/tradestats. Accessed October 20, 2016.

expectations of businesses, creditors, and debtors. However, the outcome of insolvency proceedings, well-functioning insolvency systems has not effectively facilitated access to finance such initiatives in the country. Thus, the country need a more viable businesses and sustainably strategy to grow the economy. Globally, Ethiopia stands at 114 in the ranking out of 189 countries' economies on the ease of resolving insolvency (World Bank, 2016). Table 11.3 shows the rankings for comparable economies in east Africa. The regional average ranking provides other useful benchmarks for assessing the efficiency of contract enforcement in Ethiopia. There are major challenges facing the country in respect of growth in the manufacturing sector and regulatory practices in all ramifications. The world bank data also shows the absolute distance to the best performance in each Doing Business indicator. An economy's distance to frontier score is indicated on a scale from 0 to 100, where 0 represents the worst performance and 100 the frontier (World Bank, 2016).

Protecting minority investors by the Government of Ethiopia matters for the ability of companies to raise the capital they need to grow, innovate, diversify, and compete effectively. Ferrel et al. (2016) contend that effective regulations define related-party transactions precisely, and promote clear and efficient disclosure requirements (World Bank, 2016). It also requires shareholder participation in major decisions of the company and sets detailed standards of accountability for company insiders. The Ethiopian economy has a score of 3.50 on the strength of minority investor protection index, with a higher score indicating stronger protections (World Bank, 2016). Globally, Ethiopia stands at 166 in the ranking of 189 nations' economies

Table 11.4 Ethiopia and other African countries' economies' rank on the ease of enforcing contracts and resolving insolvency

Name of country	Enforcing contract rank	Rank in resolving insolvency	Distance to frontier score
Uganda	78	104	58.67
Ethiopia	84	114	59.06
Kenya	102	144	56.25
South Africa	119	41	53.18
Eritrea	121	189	52.75
Rwanda	127	72	51.21
Egypt	155	119	44.6

Source: World Bank. (2016). *Doing Business: Measuring Regulatory Quality and Efficiency.* www.doingbusiness.org/~/media/GIAWB/Doing%20Business/Documents/Annual-Reports/ English/DB16-Full-Report.pdf. Accessed April 3, 2016

on the strength of minority investor protection index (World Bank, 2016). In many cases, it is not winning a case that is most important, but rather it is not losing either. A negotiated settlement may be more sensible than a long, drawn-out legal or labor fight in which even the winning side may be weaker and more frustrated.

Private sector development is very important in every civilized society with capitalist economic systems. The recent development in Ethiopia also follows this pattern. In transition economies like the Ethiopian economy, the development of the private sector requires support from the government (Dibie, 2014). Policies conducive to enhancement of the productivity of the private sector are important for this purpose. Equally important is the improvement of the linkage between the formal and informal sectors of the economy. The prevalence of informal economic activities is natural in Ethiopia, as it is in transition economies. That means improving the complementarities between the informal and formal sectors of the economy can enlarge the business activities, making more job opportunities.

Ethiopia is among the few countries in Africa where foreign and domestic private companies have the right to establish, acquire, own, and dispose of most forms of business enterprises. There is no right of private ownership of land. It is interesting to note that all land in the country is owned by the Government of Ethiopia and can be leased for up to 99 years. In November 2011, the government enacted a controversial urban land lease proclamation that allows the government to determine the value of land in transfers of leasehold rights, in an attempt to curb speculation by investors (U.S. Department of State, 2013; African Development Bank Group, 2011).

In addition, investors are allowed to import duty-free capital goods and construction materials necessary for the establishment of a new enterprise or for the expansion of an existing enterprise. The Government of Ethiopia also allows spare parts worth 15% of the value of the capital goods to be imported duty-free (African Development Bank Group, 2011). Like most public policies in the country, this privilege has its own setbacks. Importers may not be granted duty-free privilege if comparable capital goods or construction materials can be produced locally and have competitive prices, quality, and quantity. Further, imported duty-free capital goods can no longer be used as loan collateral. Travel agencies or tourism companies have increased duty-free privileges for the importation of goods such as vehicles, provided they are used solely in tourism activities (GlobalEdge, 2016; U.S. Department of State, 2013).

The fact that businesses in Ethiopia largely depend on government contracts and policies, and the notion that the country has never had a fully representative government political and military power disparity, tend to favor a single party. The Ethiopian People's Revolutionary Democratic Front (EPRDF) is the current ruling party. According to Schwikowski (2016), Ethiopia's military and security apparatus has remained the only source of EPRDR's strength and tight grip of power. The military top generals' power has also lead to the divergence in economic and domestic private investment opportunities, resulting in the Endowment Fund for Rehabilitation of Tigray (EFFORT). The military and politician capitalist own more than 50 companies in the country (Schwikowski, 2016). It is also reported that EFFORT has a business group affiliated to the government. The fact, however, is that administrators and politicians in the Government of Ethiopia are also owners of the companies under EFFORT. In addition, during the first decade of EPRDF's rule, Ethiopia suffered a serious setback in attracting foreign investment. This is because foreign investors were realizing the unhealthy governance system as a risk not worth taking (Schwikowski, 2016). It is also reported that in recent times the Government of Ethiopia often acts in the interest of domestic cronies, and foreign investors are needed to camouflage EFFORT's aggressive expansion. As a result, foreign investors have often been lured into joint ventures with party owned or affiliated domestic companies (Abebe & Aelmu, 2013; Schwikowski, 2016).

Ethiopia recently introduced a state-heavy model that seeks to industrialize the impoverished country within a decade by improving infrastructure and combining investment with cheap labor, land, and water to produce higher value goods. This Ethiopian Government project includes the African continents' largest hydropower dam, railroad, and the building of 700,000 low-cost apartments by 2020 (Un-Habitat 2011; World Bank, 2016). Investors such as Diageo Plc, the world's largest liquor manufacturer, and Unilever Plc are also exploring the expansion by building facilities in Ethiopia. It is estimated that during the first quarter of 2016, about 70% of construction materials were imported, including cables, steel, ceramic, locks, furniture, and electrical fittings. Cement plants built by companies including Dangote have made Ethiopia self-sufficient in the material. At the same time, manufacturing incentives provided by the government have attracted glass, paint, and steel factories to play a much needed role in the construction sector (Federal Government of Ethiopia, 2005; World Bank 2016). Despite these initiatives, the Government of Ethiopia has not been able to use construction as a means of improving domestic capacity building and good governance. Although the government wants to improve regulations and change attitudes so contractors could boost their skills and ethics, the construction industry still suffers from a lack of good governance (World Bank 2016; Abebe & Aelmu, 2013).

The Government of Ethiopia has constantly changed its investment code. There was an amendment to its investment code in 1996 and again in 2003. The current investment code, however, provides incentives for development-related investments, and has gradually removed most of the sectoral restrictions on investment. The current investment code prohibits foreign investment in banking, insurance, and financial services (World Bank, 2016). The other state-controlled sectors include telecommunications, power transmission and distribution, and postal services, with the exception of courier services. Another forum for business and government relations in Ethiopia is the manufacturing of weapons. The government mandates that the manufacturing of weapons and ammunition can only be undertaken as joint ventures with the state (U.S. Department of State, 2013).

Consequently, the Government of Ethiopia reserves other areas of investment for Ethiopian nationals only. The sector reserved for Ethiopian citizens include broadcasting; air transport services; travel agency services; forwarding and shipping agencies; retail trade and brokerage; wholesale trade (excluding supply of petroleum and its by-products as well as wholesale by foreign investors of their locally-produced products); most import trade; capital goods rentals; export trade of raw coffee, chat, oilseeds, pulses, hides, and skins bought from the market; live sheep, goats, and cattle not raised or fattened by the investor; construction companies, excluding those designated as grade one; tanning of hides and skins up to crust level; hotels (excluding star-designated hotels); restaurants and bars (excluding international and specialized restaurants); trade auxiliary and ticket selling services; transport services; bakery products and pastries for the domestic market; grinding mills; hair salons; clothing workshops (except garment factories); building and vehicle maintenance; saw milling and timber production; custom clearance services; museums, theaters, and cinema hall operations; and printing industries (World Bank, 2016; U.S. Department of State, 2013). It is interesting to note that the Government of Ethiopia has recently indicated an intension of bringing foreign private sector expertise to some of these sectors (U.S. Department of State, 2013). For example, Ethiopian-Americans can obtain a local resident card from the Ministry of Foreign Affairs that allows them to invest in many sectors closed to foreigners, and foreign companies can supply goods and services to Ethiopian corporations in the closed sectors provided weapons are not exchanged in the process (African Development Bank Groups, 2011).

One of the nice aspects of the 2003 investment code is that the policy allows new investors engaging in manufacturing, agro-processing activities, or the production of certain agricultural products, or who export at least 50% of their products or supply at least 75% of their product to an exporter as production inputs, are giving exempt from income tax for five years (African Development Bank Groups, 2011). In addition, an investor who exports less than 50% of his product or supplies his product only to the domestic market is income tax exempt for two years. Investors who expand or upgrade existing enterprises and export at least 50% of their output or increase production by 25% are eligible for income tax exemption for two years (U.S. Department of State, 2013). Further, an investor who invests in the "developing regions" of Gambella, Benishangul Gumuz, South Omo, Afar, or the Somali region are also eligible for an additional one-year income tax exemption. The policy also states that an investor who exports hides and skins after processing only up to crust level will not be entitled to the income tax incentive (Kibrom, 2010; Abebe & Aelmu, 2013; Melese, 2012). There is a special loan fund that was established through the Development Bank of Ethiopia to provide land at low lease rates for priority export areas such as floriculture, leather goods, textiles and garments, and agro-processing related products. An investor can borrow up to 70% of the cost of the project from this special fund without collateral upon presenting a viable business plan and 30% personal equity (GlobalEdge, 2016; Work Bank, 2016; U.S. Department of State, 2013).

In the mix of all the efforts put forward to improve business and government relations in Ethiopia, the nation's airline enterprise, the African's largest carrier by revenue, increased its profit by 12% to 3.53 billion Ethiopia birr ($165.4 million) in 2014–2015, despite declining air traffic in the continent (Mandel, 2012). The state-owned Ethiopia airline company recently ordered 20 Boeing 737 MAX 8s worth more than $2.1 billion, and has the option to purchase 15 more. The Government of Ethiopia has also exempted the airline from paying corporate income tax (African Development Bank 2011). Table 11.5 shows the number and investment capital of approved projects by ownership.

The implementation of Micro and Small Businesses Development Strategy and Industrial Development Strategy respectively has recorded enormous achievements in creation of employment opportunity in urban areas. It has benefited millions of citizens in Ethiopian urban areas since its inception. Statistical evidence from the Federal Micro and Small Enterprises Development Agency revealed that the sector created employment opportunity for more than 1.2 million unemployed citizens in 2011 in Ethiopian urban areas (Ethiopia Central Statistical Authority, 2012). The Micro and Small Enterprises Development Agency has managed to achieve encouraging results in supporting the development of enterprises that are employment

Table 11.5 Investment capital approved projects in the public and private sectors in Ethiopia, 1992–2011

Fiscal year	Domestic projects		Foreign projects		Public projects		Total projects	
	No. projects	Investment capital	No. projects	Investment capital	No. projects	Investment capital	No. projects	Investment capital*
1992/93	542	3,750	3	233	0	0.00	545	3,983.0
1993/94	521	2,926	4	438	1	57.00	526	3,421.0
1994/95	684	4,794	7	505	2	39.00	693	5,338.0
1995/96	897	6,050	10	434	1	6.00	908	6,490.0
1996/97	752	4,447	42	2,268	1	7.00	795	6,722.0
1997/98	816	5,819	81	4,106	1	14.00	898	9,939.0
1998/99	674	3,765	30	1,380	9	4,915.00	713	10,060.0
1999/00	561	6,740	54	1,627	9	5,760.00	624	14,127.0
2000/01	635	5,675.7	45	2,923	7	257.00	687	8,856.0
2001/02	756	6,117.3	35	1,474	10	1,598.80	801	9,190.2
2002/03	1,127	9,362.9	84	3,369	6	706.11	1,217	13,437.9
2003/04	1,862	12,177.7	347	7,205	16	1,837.04	2,225	21,220.0
2004/05	2,240	19,571.7	622	15,405	10	1,486.48	2,872	36,463.3
2005/06	5,100	41,841.1	753	19,980	6	18,215.08	5,859	80,036.3
2006/07	5,322	46,630.1	1,150	46,949	0	0.00	6,472	93,579.0
2007/08	7,307	77,868.2	1,651	92,249	3	261.56	8,961	170,378.5
2008/09	7,184	83,630.2	1,613	73,111	10	82,783.52	8,807	239,524.8
2009/10	5,080	40,852.2	1,413	55,169	3	393.89	6,496	96,415.4
2010/11	5,360	42,093	952	53,357	10	154,019	6,322	249,469
Total	47,420	424,111	8,896	382,182	105	272,356	56,421	1,078,650

Source: Ethiopian Investment Agency. (2011). *Number of Investment Capital of Approved Projects by Ownership*. Addis Ababa, EIV Publication.
* Investment capital is in millions of Birr (Ethiopian Currency)

intensive so far. There are large numbers of micro and small scale enterprises that have graduated from their original level and transformed to medium scale industries. This could galvanize the successful support rendered by the government to the development of the sector in the future (Gebeyaw & Chofana, 2012; Kibrom, 2010. According to the United Nations Economic Commission for Africa (2011), barriers to the creation and development of business opportunities, particularly in gaining access to financial, physical, and social capital, are basic problems for job creation for the citizens. This implies that periodic evaluation of the working policies and strategies with the aim of innovative amendment is vital to exploit the contribution of the private sector employment creation and poverty reduction.

Appropriate Governance of Business and Government Relations

For policy makers trying to improve their economy's regulatory environment for business, a good place to start is to find out how it compares with the regulatory environment in other economies. Nation capacity building is essentially a long-term process, and it needs long-term strategies and policies whose impact will prevent the emergence of conditions which give rise to stagnated economic growth (Mankiw, 2012; Miller, 2014).

Figure 11.1 shows an appropriate model that could be adopted to enhance business and government governance in Ethiopia and many countries in Africa and around the world. In order to make sure that buyers and sellers have the appropriate environment and keep the gain from trade an inclusive, the democratic and legal system makes trade more likely OECD 2014; Mankiw 2018).

The Republic of Ethiopia has abundant natural resources such as water, geothermal, solar, and wind resources. These natural resources offer opportunities for foreign and domestic business to develop clean energy enterprises in the nation. However, all future development should be required to meet the sustainability standards and expected rapid economic growth badly needed in the country (Mankiw, 2018). Although Ethiopia has enacted a vision to achieve middle income status by 2025, the country still needs to create an enabling political environment to attain the sustainable development and appropriate economic growth goals that may enhance the living standards of all citizens of the country. Given the heterogeneous nature of the Federal Democratic Republic of Ethiopia, a fundamental objective should be to revive the concept of nation-building, an inclusive political and governance system that could benefit all citizens, including rural and urban residences.

To ensure the right environment for industrial development as well as appropriate business and government relations, there is a need to develop a political system whose rules allow competition for power and which guarantee the possibility of alternate groups achieving power within a reasonable period of time (Smith-Sebasto, 2012). Term limit should be required by

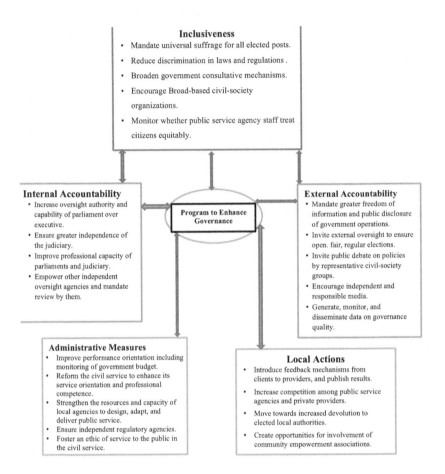

Inclusiveness
- Mandate universal suffrage for all elected posts.
- Reduce discrimination in laws and regulations .
- Broaden government consultative mechanisms.
- Encourage Broad-based civil-society organizations.
- Monitor whether public service agency staff treat citizens equitably.

Internal Accountability
- Increase oversight authority and capability of parliament over executive.
- Ensure greater independence of the judiciary.
- Improve professional capacity of parliaments and judiciary.
- Empower other independent oversight agencies and mandate review by them.

Program to Enhance Governance

External Accountability
- Mandate greater freedom of information and public disclosure of government operations.
- Invite external oversight to ensure open. fair, regular elections.
- Invite public debate on policies by representative civil-society groups.
- Encourage independent and responsible media.
- Generate, monitor, and disseminate data on governance quality.

Administrative Measures
- Improve performance orientation including monitoring of government budget.
- Reform the civil service to enhance its service orientation and professional competence.
- Strengthen the resources and capacity of local agencies to design, adapt, and deliver public service.
- Ensure independent regulatory agencies.
- Foster an ethic of service to the public in the civil service.

Local Actions
- Introduce feedback mechanisms from clients to providers, and publish results.
- Increase competition among public service agencies and private providers.
- Move towards increased devolution to elected local authorities.
- Create opportunities for involvement of community empowerment associations.

Figure 11.1 Enhance business and government governance model

Source: Organization for Economic Cooperation and Development (OECD). (2007a). *Business for Development: Fostering the Private Sector.* www.oecd.org/dev. Accessed April 4, 2016.

the provisions of the Constitution, and no president should be allowed to amend the constitution for his or her benefit.

The democratic political system should allow large numbers and groups to be involved in the selection or election of decision-makers at different levels of the power structure. Several important principles are absolutely critical to such a political system: (a) extensive devolution of power; (b) accumulation of wealth through the use of state institutions must be totally forbidden; (c) the principles of good and democratic governance must be fully implemented (i.e., transparency, accountability, independent judiciary, and completeness); (d) extensive involvement of indigenous independent civil society groups in national and local affairs, especially in the monitoring of policy implementation and service delivery (Dibie, 2014; OECD, 2007b; Froeb el al 2016).

In addition, the pathway program to enhance governance could be elaborated along five principles of good governance: (1) national actions to strengthen external accountability; (2) national checks and balances to strengthen internal accountability; (3) measures to enhance inclusiveness; (4) administrative reform to improve internal accountability; (5) local actions to strengthen external accountability; and (6) adoption of laws and regulations (OECD, 2007a; Jones, 2001; Katsioloudes, 2006).

The World Bank (2016) contends that inclusiveness is a value in its own right, and it is an indispensable ingredient in better accountability, especially external accountability (Mankiw, 2018). Therefore, the first step in enhancing inclusiveness is the adoption of laws and regulations that widen and secure access to widely acceptable basic rights and freedom. It is also very important that no one, including the president, should be above the laws of the country. Internal and external accountability mechanisms are not substitutes. As a matter of fact, they reinforce each another. Stronger mechanisms for external accountability will reveal weaknesses in internal accountability mechanisms, while stronger mechanisms and capacity for internal accountability are needed to generate the information about what the government wants to achieve (OECD, 2007a; Froeb et al 2016). Ethiopia also needs a better participatory process that gives voice to citizen concern and that builds a social consensus in which everyone feels he or she has a stake in the government and national economy (African Development Bank Report, 2013).

In order to establish vibrant or robust business and government relations that could enhance economic and sustainable development, a free market economy is important in a country. Unlike the case in Ethiopia, it is now clearly acknowledged that the economy should not be allowed to generate serious poverty, and those policies and affirmative action programs must be developed to minimize and reduce poverty (Kraft & Furlong, 2016; OECD, 2007a; Mankiw 2018). As it has been observed in many countries in Africa, poverty is an important cause of conflict (Schwikowski, 2016). Consequently, it is paramount that economic resources and development funds should be evenly distributed between the regions and groups in the Ethiopia. Clear and serious uneven distribution of economic resources between regions and ethnic groups is known to have led to conflict, and sometimes to serious secessionist rebellion in many African countries.

Finally, for Ethiopia to achieve positive result in its industrial and sustainable development, it is important to note, however, that there is no mystery to developing governance. Shared or inclusive governance requires open commitment followed by action (Dibie, 2014). Therefore, if the people and the government that are the primary actors in governance join together in the process, everyone in the country could have equal access to the fruits of faster growth, to better public services, and a future replete with the attributes of human and infrastructure development.

Conclusion

This chapter has examined the nature of business and government relations in Ethiopia. It argues that while the Government of Ethiopia intervenes in the economy with laws and regulations designed to promote competition and to protect consumers, employees, and environment in the country, business entrepreneurs are also needed to risk their wealth, time, and efforts to develop for profit an innovative product or ways of doing something. Choosing between alternative solutions to Ethiopia's challenges does not mean the nation should ignore the lower priority ones. It means if monetary and fiscal policies are effectively implemented, more people in the country will benefit more quickly if the higher priority items are tackled first. This may then free up resources to tackle the issues originally given lower priority. Trying to deal with every challenge at once simply reduces the level of effective help. Such additional help could come from the business and non-governmental organization sectors.

The respective roles of business and government are paramount in achieving sustainable development. The bone of contention, however, is that for national markets in Ethiopia to work efficiently and deliver desired outcomes, an effective government is also needed to create an enabling business environment. Therefore, it could be argued that good business and government relations in Ethiopia could lead to more robust provision of public goods, and facilitate adjustment and mitigation of negative externalities associated with private action, such as corruption, pollution, and other harmful environmental effects (Dibie et al., 2015).

How people perceive business and government relations in Ethiopia will largely determine whether capacity building and living standards improve or deteriorate. Growing human numbers, urban expansion, and resource exploitation do not resonate well for the future. Without seeking capacity building and practicing sustainable development behavior, the citizens of Ethiopia may face a deteriorating environment as well as even invite ecological disaster. The country will have to balance the need to match the promotion of job-created sectors such as agro-business, textile, and tradable services with the desire to capitalize on windfall gain generated by higher commodity prices (OECD, 2014; Froeb et al., 2016).

Appropriate government policies to enhance previously weak business and government relations might include grants and prizes for innovative projects and companies, joint research efforts involving domestic public research centers and corporations, long-term collaboration between universities, domestic training centers, and business associations (Dibie et al., 2015). In addition, in order to increase job absorption by the private sector, incentive packages, such as special tax breaks to promote persistent labor-intensive investments, should be considered by the government, rather than giving uniform tax advantages to all private corporations (Froeb et al., 2016; Ferrell et al 2016). Strategies for creating an enabling environment for the private sector and NGOs should be clearly defined in the national policy. In addition, the strategy that enhances the collaboration of government, the private sector, and NGOs to deal with unemployment should be designed and implemented accordingly. There should be periodic forums in which potential private sectors, NGOs, and government participate to discuss issues related to economic development strategies in Ethiopia. The established public labor-intensive infrastructure projects in urban areas, like cobblestone, housing, micro and small enterprises, and others, need to be strengthened and supported by government, private sectors, and NGOs, both technically and financially. Finally, the positive attributes of business and government relations and inclusive governance encompass material well-being, wider choices and opportunities for people to realize their potentials, and the guarantee of equity of treatment, freedom to choose, and full participation in the process by which citizens govern themselves in the country.

References

Abebe, T. and Aelmu, K. (2013). Analysis of Urban Youth Unemployment in Ethiopia: The Case of Addis Ababa. *Journal of International Politics and Development, 11*(1–2), 131–162.

African Development Bank Group. (2011). *Federal Democratic Republic of Ethiopia Country Strategy Paper 2011–2015*. www.afdb.org/fileadmin/uploads/afdb/Documents/Project-and-Operations/Ethiopia-2011–2015%20CSP%20ENG1.pdf. Accessed April 4, 2016.

African Development Bank Report. (2013). *Ethiopia Economic Outlook*. www.afdb.org/en/countries/east-africa/ethiopia/. Accessed April 4, 2016.

African Development Bank Report. (2004). *Ethiopia: Multi-Sector Country Gender Profile*. African Development Bank Publication, Addis Ababa.

Anderson, J. (2015). *Public Policy Making*. Stamford, CT: Cengage Learning.

Brooks, C. (2012). What Is Fiscal Policy? *Business News Daily*. www.businessnewsdaily.com/3484-fiscal-policy.html. Accessed April 12, 2014.

Chambers, R. (2005). *Ideas for Development*. London, UK: Earthscam Press.

Dibie, R. (2014). Comparative Perspective of Environmental Policies and Issues. New York, NY: Routledge Press.

Dibie, R. (2010). Social Impact of Environmental Policies in Ethiopia. *Journal of International Politics and Development, 8*(1), 1–32.

Dibie, R., Edoho, F. M. and Dibie, J. (2015). Analysis of Capacity Building and Economic Growth in Sub-Saharan Africa. *International Journal of Business and Social Science, 6*(12), 1–25.

Dye, T. (2011). *Understanding Public Policy*. 13th Edition. New York: Longman, 210–231.

Ethiopia Central Statistical Authority/CSA. (2011). *Urban Employment Unemployment Survey*. Addis Ababa, Ethiopia.

Ethiopia Central Statistical Authority. (2012). *Urban Employment Unemployment Survey*. Addis Ababa, Volume 1 and 2, Addis Ababa, Ethiopia.

Ethiopian Investment Agency. (2011). *Number of Investment Capital of Approved Projects by Ownership*. Addis Ababa, EIV Publication.

Ezana, H. W. (2011). Factors Influencing Affected Group Participation in Urban Redevelopment in Addis Ababa: The Case of Senga Tera-Fird Bet I Project. International Institute of Urban Management, Erasmus University of Rotterdam.

Federal Democratic Republic of Ethiopia. (2005). *Expropriation of Land for Public Purposes Proclamation No. 455/2005, Land Law Education.* Addis Ababa: Government of Ethiopia Press.

Federal Democratic Republic of Ethiopia. (1994). The Constitution of the Federal Democratic Republic of Ethiopia (Unofficial English Translation From the Amharic Original). Addis Ababa: Government Press.

Ferrell, O. C., Hiirt, G. and Ferrell, L. (2016). *Business: A Changing World.* New York, NY: McGraw-Hill Press.

Froeb, L. M., McCann, B., Shor, M. and Ward, M. (2016). *Managerial Economics: A Problem Solving Approach.* 4th Edition. Boston, MA: Cengage Learning.

Gebeyaw, T. and Chofana, T. (2012). *Socio-demographic Determinants of Urban Unemployment: The Case of Addis Ababa, Ethiopia.* www.slideshare.net/tesfayechofana/s-ocioeconomic-causes-of-unemployment-after-incorporation-of-commentsfinal-1. Accessed April 8, 2016.

GlobalEdge. (2016). *Ethiopia Trade Statistics.* http://globaledge.msu.edu/ countries/ethiopia/memo. Accessed October 20, 2016.

Haile, G. A. (2003). *The Incidence of Youth Unemployment in Urban Ethiopia.* NBE #2011. National Bank of Ethiopia: Annual Report.

Index of Economic Freedom. (2016). *Ethiopia.* www.heritage.org/index/country/ethiopia. Accessed March 21, 2016.

International Labor Organization (ILO). (2012). *Global Employment; A Global Goal a National Challenge.* The International Labor Organization, Geneva.

Jones, R. (2001). *Engineering Capacity Building in Developing Countries to Promote Economic Development.* www.worldexpertise.com/Engineering_Capacity_Building_in_Developing_Countries.htm. Accessed March 19, 2014.

Katsioloudes, M. (2006). Strategic Management: Global Culture Perspectives for Profit and Nonprofit Organizations. New York, NY: Elsevier Press.

Kibrom, T. (2010). *The Sources of Inflation in Ethiopia.* Saarbrücken, Germany: Lap Lambert Academic Publishing.

Kraft, M. and Furlong, S. (2016). *Public Policy: Politics, Analysis, and Alternatives.* Washington, DC: Congressional Press, 322–337.

Lehne, R. (2013). *Government and Business.* Washington, DC: Congressional Quarterly Press.

Lishan, S. (2010). Socio-Economic Impacts of Relocation in Addis Ababa: The Case of Relocatees From Sheraton Hotel and Economic Commission for Africa (ECA) Areas. Masters of Arts Education, Addis Ababa University, Addis Ababa.

Mandel, M. (2012). *Economics: The Basics.* New York, NY: McGraw-Hill Hill Press.

Mankiw, G. (2018). *Macroeconomics.* New York, NY: McGraw-Hill Press.

Melese, M. K. (2012). Employment Challenges in Eastern Africa in the Context of Ethiopia. Friedrich-Ebert-Stiftung, Nairobi, Kenya.

Miller, R., Benjamin, D. and North, D. (2014). *The Economics of Public Issues.* Boston, MA: Pearson.

Ministry of Education. (2008). National Technical & Vocational Education & Training (TVET)—Strategy Ministry of Education. Addis Ababa: Government Press.

National Bank of Ethiopia. (2012). *Sectorial Gross Domestic Product.* Addis Ababa: NBE Publication.

Nebil, K., Gezahegn, A. and Hayat, Y. (2010). *Enabling the Private Sector to Contribute to the Reduction of Urban Youth Unemployment in Ethiopia.* Addis Ababa Chamber of Commerce and Sectoral Associations, Addis Ababa.

Nwazor, J. C. (2012). Capacity Building, Entrepreneurship and Sustainable Development. *Journal of Emerging Trends in Educational Research and Policy Studies (JETERAPS)*, 3(1), 51–54.

Nzinga, H. B. and Tsegay, G. (2012). *Youth Unemployment: Ethiopia Country Study*. International Growth Centre Working Paper 12/0592, London School of Economics and Political Science.

Olivier de Sardan, J. P. (2005). Anthropology and Development: Understanding Contemporary Social Change. London, UK: Zed Books.

Onah, F. O. (2010). Urban Unemployment Situation in Nigeria. In E. O. Ezeani and O. A. Otaki (Eds.), Youth Unemployment in Nigeria: Some Implication for the Third Millennium. *Global Journal of Social Sciences*, 2(1), 21–26.

Organization for Economic Cooperation and Development (OECD). (2014). *Economic Development in Africa*. www.oecd.org/dev. Accessed March 22, 2016.

Organization for Economic Cooperation and Development (OECD). (2008). *Business for Development: Fostering the Private Sector*. www.oecd.org/dev. Accessed March 22, 2016.

Organization for Economic Cooperation and Development (OECD). (2007a). *Business for Development*. www.oecd.org/dev. Accessed April 4, 2016.

Organization for Economic Cooperation and Development (OECD). (2007b). *Public–Private Dialogue in Developing Countries*. www.oecd.org/dev. Accessed March 22, 2016.

Peter, L. (2013). *Economic and Political Reform in Africa*. Bloomington, IN: Indiana University Press.

Rondinelli, D. A. (1993). Development Projects as Policy Experiments: An Adaptive Approach to Development Administration. London, UK: Routledge Press.

Schiller, B. (2011). *Essentials of Economics*. New York, NY: McGraw-Hill Press.

Schwikowski, M. (2016). "Protests surge after mass panic in Ethiopia." www.dw.com/en/protests-surge-after-mass-panic-in-ethiopia/a-35961575. Accessed May 25, 2016.

Smith-Sebasto, N. (2012). *Sustainability*. New York, NY: McGraw-Hill Press.

SparkNotes. (2013). *Problems With Monetary Policy and Fiscal Policy*. www.sparknotes.com/economics/macro/policydebat. Accessed April 12, 2014.

Steven, K. (2005). *The Employment Intensity of Growth: Trends and Macroeconomic Determinants*. Employment Strategy Papers; International Labour Office.

U.S. Department of State Report. (2013). *Ethiopia 2013 Investment Climate Statement*. www.state.gov/e/eb/rls/othr/ics/2013/204639.htm. Accessed April 5, 2016.

UNDP. (2014). *Human Development Report*. New York: Oxford University Press.

UNECA. (2011). Africa Youth Report: Addressing the Youth Education and Employment Nexus in New Global Economy. www.uneca.org/sites/default/files/Publication Files/african_youth_report_2011_final.pdf. Accessed May 8, 2016.

Un-Habitat. (2011). *Condominium Housing in Ethiopia: The Integrated Housing Development Programme*. Housing Practices Series United Nations Human Settlements Programme: Nairobi, Kenya.

UNICEF. (2009). *Information by Country*. www.unicef.org/infobycountry/ethiopia_statistics.html#0 Accessed November 8, 2009.

United Nations. (2014). Combined 4th and 5th Periodic Report of the Federal Democratic Republic of Ethiopia to the United Nations Committee on the Rights of the Child 2006–2011. New York: United Nations Press.

United Nations Development Programme. (2013). *Human Development Report*. New York: Oxford University Press.

United Nations. (2012). *Human Development Index*. New York, NY: Oxford University Press.

United Nations. (2010). *Millennium Development Goals Report*. www.un.org/
millenniumgoals/pdf/MDG%20Report%202010%20En%20r15%20low%20
res%2020100615%20.pdf.

Woldengariel, T. (2011, February 8). Filtu Farmer Development Irrigation. *The Ethiopian Herald*, 2–4.

World Bank. (2011). Ethiopia Protection of Basic Services Phase 2 Project. Washington, DC: World Bank.

World Bank. (2003). Better Governance for Development in the Middle East and
North Africa: Enhancing Inclusiveness and Accountability. Washington, DC:
World Bank Publication.

World Bank Group. (2016). *Doing Business: Measuring Regulatory Quality and
Efficiency*. www.doingbusiness.org/~/media/GIAWB/Doing%20Business/Docu-
ments/Annual-Reports/English/DB16-Full-Report.pdf. Accessed October 20,
2016.

World Trade Organization. (2006). *World Trade Report*. Geneva: World Trade
Organization Publication.

Ya Ni, A. and Van Wart, M. (2016). *Building Business–Government Relations: A
Skills Approach*. New York: Routledge Press.

12 Corporate Takeover and Public Policy in South Africa

Kealeboga J. Maphunye and Robert A. Dibie

Introduction

The subjects of corporate takeover and public policy are of as much interest to political economists and political economy students and researchers as they are to policy makers and economic advisers. Furthermore, the concepts of corporate takeover, mergers, and acquisitions can be understood to be closely linked with corporate governance because of the implications of what relations develop once a takeover, merger or acquisition is effected (UNECA, 2007). Some argue that there is not a universally accepted definition of "corporate governance" but equally acknowledge that when defined broadly "corporate governance" refers to the private and public intuitions, including laws, regulations, and accepted business practices, which in the market economy govern the relationship between corporate managers and entrepreneurs ("corporate insiders") on one hand, and those who invest resources in corporations, on the other (Okeahalam & Akinboade, 2003). Similarly, corporate takeover is a practice that takes place according to the laws, regulations, and accepted norms and standards of business relations in a capitalist economy.

In South Africa takeover legislation is particularly suited to such the evaluation on how competence the national government has been in regulating corporate takeover. The government takeover legislation is one of the best mechanisms to examine business activities in the country because it has been one of the most active areas of corporate law making in the country. This is because takeovers are considered to play a critical role in protecting shareholders against management abuse and the distortion of corporate information (Gerald, 1989). Some scholars have argued that managers tend to incorporate in government with corporate law regimes that favor their own interest. In addition, as result of the fact that government has been very anxious to win chartering business, they have responded to this demand by allowing corporate executives to exploit company resources at the shareholders' expense. Consequently, the Government of South Africa, competing for chartering business, have been encouraged to replace the current system of regulation with a uniform national system (Triki & Chun 2011;

Vaughan & Rayan 2006). While protectionism may explain much of the current national government takeover legislation, some of the new policies have been enacted in response to the market for corporate charters. Despite, these measures, the lack of effective implementation strategies has caused the charting market to promote management interests rather than the shareholder interests in the country (UNECA, 2007; Behar & Hodge, 2008: 3–4). Thus, the lack of corrective government intervention has further galvanized management entrenchment legislation in South Africa.

However, in the areas of politics and public administration (in which policy is a familiar topic), corporate takeover is rarely linked to policy, although the relationship between these two concepts is critical. For instance, in many African countries (at least those that can be described as electoral democracies such as Botswana, Mauritius and South Africa), political parties and candidates are rarely quizzed about their specific policies toward corporate takeovers or how they will deal with this matter once elected to office.

Observers argue that in the developing world, South Africa was the first to develop a corporate governance code of best practice via the King Report of 1994 (Mangena & Chamisa, 2007: 5; Ellis et al 2015; Malin, 2004). Yet, even in South Africa, a country that has experienced the limits of inward-looking apartheid economy (Hart & Padayachee, 2000: 683) for many decades, the idea of a "corporate sector" was always contested. This is because the mere mention of a "South African business community" was almost always understood to refer to "the country's various business communities," given the racial discriminatory labor and other economic policies. Similarly, what in other countries could be easily classified as the "corporate" or "formal" sector, inevitably referred to "that sector made up of mainstream, formal sector firms, which continue[d] for the most part to be dominated by white, English-speaking South Africans, in terms of both ownership and management" (Handley, 2005: 212). Yet, the intricate nature of the apartheid system also entailed significant ownership and control of the media by English and Afrikaner groups "within the wider web of South African monopoly capital" (Tomaselli, 1997: 67), with further implications for domination and control of the country's related industries.

Admittedly, much has been written about the country's apparent political miracle, and the contribution of business to the political transition (Handley, 2005: 213, citing Ellis et al 2015; Mengena & Chamisa 2007). Some even argue that the "barriers of separating rich and poor, black, brown, and white, have come tumbling down; at least in theory" (Hart & Padayachee, 2000: 683). However, since the fall of apartheid it has increasingly become almost impossible to disentangle South Africa's political transformation (fundamental change) from economic transformation or the redress of centuries of economic exploitation of the country's indigenous population by former colonial masters and European settlers. Observers note that "Southern Africa has undergone rapid political and economic transformation in the past 15 years" (UNECA, 2007: 1). Thus,

South Africa's transformation process should be placed within this context, as it also determines the nature, scope, and essence of corporate takeovers or mergers in the country.

This chapter examines the challenges faced by South Africa's economic sector in addressing corporate takeovers and how the country's transformation policies intersect with this process. It seeks to answer questions such as: What is the nature of economic takeovers in the South African economic? How are they affected by policy formulation and implementation, including other policy requirements that are related to the country's transformation process? To what extent can the South African case help us understand corporate takeovers in the sub-region and elsewhere in the African continent? It relies on the extant literature, theoretical assumptions, media articles, and the country's laws and policies on transformation which promote or undermine corporate takeovers in the country. The chapter outlines the nature of accountability and the challenges faced by the country's economic cluster in enhancing South Africa's economic system. It argues that the South African government has scored several achievements in the economic front despite equally confronting some of the intractable problems ever faced by an African country. The question of corporate takeover is an important subject that underlines a significant part of economic development, trade, and the role of private companies in a country's economic growth. Yet, it is rarely linked with public policy in South Africa. Undoubtedly, this presents challenges for two sectors: government, which is usually keen to ensure that all the economic activities under its territory comply with policy obligations, and the private sector, which often complains about government overregulation and policy interference in the economic sphere. The chapter recommends a nationwide transformation, which inevitably affects business and economic relations. Policy makers in South African should no longer perceive the choice between regulatory and judicial means of enforcement as an either choice to make. Rather, they should see those measures as complementary means and mutually reinforcing mechanism for national economic growth and sustainable development. Through such transformation, the government could seek to ensure the equitable participation of all the country's racial groups in the running of the economy and wealth creation

Understanding Corporate Takeover

Corporate takeover depend on how business organizations incorporate politics and respond to what government does to deliberately and unintentionally promote or discourage business from becoming bigger (Schneider, 1998; Gerald, 1989). Most radical governments promote drastic transformation of dominant conglomerates. On the other hand, privatization programs are sometimes used to displace traditional big business and create huge new conglomerates. In most African countries, arbitrary, unstable, or highly interventionist government exacerbate political uncertainty, which in turn encourage conglomeration in order to diversify risk (Schneider, 1998; Greenfield, 1979). On the other hand, some countries that practice capitalism may also create huge conglomerates in order to maximize political influence.

There are several reasons why an acquiring company may wish to purchase another company. In most cases, some takeovers are thought to be strategic because there may be other reasons other than acquiring profit. On the other hand, some takeovers could be regarded as opportunistic (Gregg, 2002; Schneider, 1998). Corporate takeovers have been part the business cycle for many decades all over the world (Investopedia staff, 2015). As a result of the dynamic nature of the economic environment and business cycle, many corporations are often challenged to maximize their shareholder value. Through takeover, merger, and acquisition, a company could develop a competitive advantage and ultimately increase shareholder value (Schneider, 1998; Dibie et al., 2015).

Several scholars have investigated the dynamics of corporate entry and exist. Most of their finding reveals that company creation seems to be a process of search and experimentation (Ahn, 2001; Brandt, 2004b; Bartelsman et al., 2003). It has been argued that economic growth often leads to creative destruction as a mechanism that facilitates innovation and new technology adoption. Schumpeter (1954) argued that the innovation and technological change of a nation come from the entrepreneurs, or wild spirits. He contends that the doing of new things or the doing of things that are already being done in a new way stemmed directly from the efforts of entrepreneurs. This mind-set helps companies to shift resources from less productive unit to more productive ones (Cooper et al., 1997; Campbell, 1997). These scholars contend that the role of firm turnover is often dependent on the ability to adopt new technology. As a result, companies that enter with the state-of-the-art technology often would replace incumbents that rely on outdated production processes (Caballero & Hammour, 1994; Brandt, 2004a).

The product life cycle is another premise for corporate entry and existence. Industrial evolution often could arise due to companies' innovation and technological change (Klepper, 1996). It is often observed that companies' creation and product innovation, as well as high market shares, change rapidly as corporations enter the market. Further in the stages of a company product life cycle, market shares will stabilize and innovative efforts are increasingly devoted to improving the production process rather than to introducing new product variation (Brandt, 2004b). Thus, at the beginning of the product life cycle, most corporations are still small and there is uncertainty about user preferences and the technological means of satisfying them. In those stages, new corporations can compete with larger incumbents by entering with a new version of the product. On the other hand, as most successful corporations expand, the advantage of size in process research and development eventually puts entrants at such a cost disadvantage that entry decreases. As a result of this, dynamics of innovation and appropriate product life cycle incumbent corporations stabilize their market shares and compete more on the bases of their size and their process innovations. According to Brandt (2004b), it is possible that high rates at the beginning of the product life cycle could coincide with high output and employment growth, as both new and incumbent companies expand when there are still a lot of unexpected technological and business opportunities. In Schumpeter's (1983) view, technological innovation is at the cause of both cyclical instability and economic growth. As a result, fluctuations in innovation could cause fluctuation in investment and those cause cycles in economic growth. Schumpeter sees innovations as clustering around certain points in time periods that he refers to as "neighborhoods of equilibrium," when entrepreneurs perceive that risk and returns warrant innovative commitments. These clusters lead to long cycles by generating periods of acceleration in aggregate growth.

In South Africa it is often thought that new corporations tend to create and have positive impact on the production and output of growth. This is because new corporations' entrance normally has an advantage in innovating and adopting new technologies. According to the Schumpeterian model of creative destruction (Schumpeter, 1983, 1954; Aghion & Howitt, 1991), new companies are very important for the implementation of new ideas and new technologies; as a result they often galvanize high turnover, which might in turn lead to many companies both entering and existing the market. Schumpeter (1954) contends that the lifeblood of capitalism was "creative destruction." Companies rising and falling would unleash innovation and in the end make the economy stronger.

In addition Schumpeter (1954) argued that technological change needs to demonstrate that changes in the rate of innovation governs changes in the rate of new investments, and that the combined impact of innovation clusters takes the form of fluctuation in aggregate output or employment. The process of technological innovation involves extremely complex relations among a set of key variables: inventions, innovations, diffusion paths, and investment activities. The impact of technological innovation on aggregate output is mediated through a succession of relationships that have yet to be explored systematically in the context of long wave. New inventions are typically primitive, their performance is usually poorer than existing technologies, and the cost of their production is high (Schumpeter, 1983). A production technology may not yet exist, as is often the case in major chemical inventions and pharmaceutical inventions. The speed with which inventions are transformed into innovations and diffused depends on actual and expected trajectory of performance improvement and cost reduction (Mansfield, 1983). It is interesting to note that public policy makers often believe that institution that foster corporate entry may ultimately enhance the overall economic performance of their economic growth (Dibie et al., 2015; Evans, 1989).

As a result of lack of appropriate data, investigating the impact of policy and institution on company entry and survival in South Africa is very difficult. This is because parts of the regulatory framework are very old. The current method seeks to capture quantitative aspects of the number of years that creditors have claimed bankruptcy assets, the number of procedures necessary to start a new business, and whether or not there are convenient centralized departments or agencies for information on and insurance of licenses. In South Africa the source of collective action by business both as corporations and as associations are multiple and depend usually on prior government actions that promote or discourage various forms of corporate takeover in the country. This is true not only because of South Africa's corporate governance system that is composed of considerably more than its security laws and their enforcement, but also due to the danger that those with responsibility to regulate may be corrupted or duly influenced by those whose actions they are supposed to regulate or monitor.

The Political Economy of Corporate Takeover

Until a few years ago (at least two decades from 1994–2015), a mere mention of the term "corporate sector" let alone "corporate takeover" in South Africa implicitly or inevitably referred to the formal, white-male dominated part of the economy that essentially served the economic interests of the apartheid government. During the apartheid regime in South Africa, a small minority of white citizens controlled businesses and the economy in the country. A possible explanation for this view is the fact that the racial policies of the government of the day during the apartheid era were geared toward promoting socio-economic, political and other forms of empowerment for one race (whites) compared with the others who were legally classified as "non-whites."

Subsequent apartheid regimes have since 1948 vigorously promoted policies and laws that sought to exclude the equal participation of blacks in their country's economy, which denied them of their labor and other economic rights. Thus the "corporate sector" was almost always associated with the then apartheid system since this sector, like others in the economy, also perpetuated economic inequalities, albeit reluctantly sometimes, as the system did not always work in the interests of the white capitalist class in South Africa. For instance, in as much as some in the predominantly white business class would have wanted to establish close business ties and collaborate with the black entrepreneurs to capture the market in the black townships and other settlements, the system made this impossible, owing to a myriad of laws, policies, and rules that proscribed such collaboration across the color bar.

One observer argues that "by the late 1980s, the South African economy was both industrialized and relatively diversified but apartheid severely stunted the development of black entrepreneurs" (Handley, 2005: 212). To a large extent, this stunted development of black entrepreneurs inevitably resulted in the marginalization of any efforts within the black communities to participate equitably in any corporate takeovers, mergers, or acquisitions in the larger economy owing to racial and income inequalities.

Furthermore, such inequalities meant that the commanding heights of the economy remained in the predominantly white corporate sector, benefitting a small section of the population and therefore undermining even the effect of the "invisible hand" of the market forces. It is therefore not surprising that after the demise of apartheid, some advocated the view that "government policy formulation and implementation can only be understood in terms of the economic and political forces operating through the state and market" (Fine & Rustomjee, 1996, in Roberts, 1998: 319). In other words, in the South African context all economic activities, including takeovers, mergers, and acquisitions, should not just focus on the roles of the government and the private sector in economic activities individually but on how they both complement each other in such economic activities jointly (Fine & Rustomjee, 1996; Michie & Padayachee, 1997).

It is therefore argued that given the depth of the racial and income divides that prevailed, it would not have been unreasonable to predict a cycle of redistribution and macroeconomic populism after democratization, wreaking havoc with the economy and turning the country into a sham democracy (Rodrick, 2008: 770). Contrary to expectations just before 1994, however, no nationalizations or large-scale asset redistributions (Rodrick, 2008) occurred, although some disaffected sections of the population continue to call for such interventions by the state. Triki and Chun (2011) comments that while the political transition to democracy in South Africa has been internationally acclaimed, economic transformation has been much slower to occur and economic performance has been poor, especially regarding employment. This largely underscores the major political economy challenges facing South Africa; which also have a significant effect on the operations of the corporate sector.

Consequently, to South Africa's largely economically exploited and excluded black majority, corporate takeover or corporate governance in such a heavily constrained and racialized economic environment was a sham for two reasons: Firstly, it meant nothing because they regarded the capitalist owners of the means of production including the corporate sector as oppressors or promoters of the country's infamous apartheid system. To some extent, South Africa remains one of the most unionized societies, partly because the majority of trade unions that were formed before and during the apartheid era still view the predominantly white business sector as a major stumbling block for South Africa's democratic consolidation and economic transformation. According to observers:

South African mining unions grew stronger in the 1980s and 1990s. Increased power was demonstrated in a serious strike in 1987 and entrenched by the introduction of new labor legislation in 1995. Together with rigidities, this indicates the kind of employee power in which contract theories . . . may operate. In the gold industry, dramatic job losses led to the formation of a Gold Crisis Committee in the late 1990s, in which stakeholders agreed a formal procedure for negotiating terms of layoffs and improving coordination.

(Behar & Hodge, 2008: 3–4)

Barely two decades into the country's democracy, such employee power was demonstrated in the 2012 massive mineworkers' strike that brought the same industry virtually to a standstill and resulted in what is now known as the Marikana massacre whose tragic events in Marikana, near Rustenburg (North West Province), left 34 miners dead and 78 others wounded by police gunfire (Twala, 2012: 65).

Secondly, in almost all instances where such corporate takeovers were effected, the black population, the majority of whom were mere laborers in such body corporates, was almost always adversely affected. This situation was largely informed by the creation of artificial racial divides to prop up the apartheid economy through the generation of super profits using poor black labor that rarely, if at all, benefitted from the results of corporate takeovers. This is probably what prompted the United Nations and some lobby groups to advocate corporate social responsibility, the underlying principle that business leaders should care not only about making their companies profitable for the shareholders, but also about improving the lives of their workforce and the society as a whole (Ocampo, 2004: 249). Ironically, during its dying days some firms that supported apartheid tried fervently to project themselves as the champions of corporate social responsibility in Africa. But this was unmasked by the regime's unrelenting brutality toward its black citizens between 1970s and 1990s, which subsequently attracted economic sanctions from the international community.

To some extent, this situation remained largely unchanged for many years into South Africa's fledgling democracy, the main reason being that the country's key economic resources, especially main corporations, remained in the hands of a small minority of white business owners, the majority of whom were represented at the Johannesburg Stock Exchange (JSE). Thus, any takeover bids or actual takeovers of any corporate entity in the country inevitably became "politicized" and entangled in South Africa's calls for "economic transformation. Evidence suggests that "South Africa has undergone a remarkable transformation since its transition in 1994, but economic growth and employment generation have been disappointing. Most worryingly, unemployment is currently among the highest in the world" (Rodrick, 2008: 769). Evidence also suggests that takeovers, mergers, and acquisitions usually have adverse effects in the South African economy, especially in major industries such as mining (Behar & Hodge, 2008). Examining the employment effects of mergers using data from the South

African gold mining industry, it is argued that "public perception traditional associates mergers and acquisitions (M&A) with employment losses" (Behar & Hodge, 2008: 1, Vaughan & Ryan, 2006). Citing the "welfare loss to workers associated with retrenchments [which] can be pronounced in countries with high unemployment" such as South Africa, Behar and Hodge (2008: 1) cite the country's high unemployment rate of 25% (citing Statistics South Africa, 2007) and argue that "it is no surprise that employment consequences are a major concern." In a country with a militant and powerful trade union, and elaborate human rights that are enshrined in the constitution, loss of employment in South Africa is a serious policy matter that often sees a tug-of-war among corporate authorities, government, and employees.

Not surprising, therefore, 21 years (1994–2015) into democracy, there have been more vociferous calls for such transformation, which is usually associated with the need for nationalizing the mines, land, and certain public enterprises. Much of the argument has so far been articulated by those on the left of the South African political spectrum—especially sections of COSATU (Congress of South African Trade Unions), SACP (South African Communist Party), and ANC (African National Congress) "alliance" and opposition parties such as the Economic Freedom Fighters (EFF). During South Africa's national elections, the latter party was vociferous in advocating for nationalization of certain industries and effecting takeovers of some of them by the state to ensure wealth redistribution and economic freedom as the party's name suggests.

Attempts are usually made to compare South Africa to the rest of the African continent; indeed, the country shares similarities with many African countries despite its economic and other infrastructure that are relatively developed. However, observers caution that

> while South Africa resembles many African states in the disproportionate influence wielded by big business, and in the ethicized nature of the interactions between business and the state, it differs strikingly in . . . the size and strength of the country's indigenous business community vis-à-vis government."
>
> (Handley, 2005: 212–213)

In addition, the nature of the country's economy is also such that some corporate takeovers, mergers, and acquisitions arise from the links that local companies or firms have with their global parent holdings.

Some suggest that takeovers occur because of different opinions over asset values stemming from the acquirer's belief he can manage the assets better. This could lead to the immediate post-acquisition retrenchment. However, if successful, the acquirers would raise the value of the firm and, if anything, improve the standing of employees (Behar & Hodge, 2008: 2 Triki & Chun 2011).

The Nature of Economic Takeovers

The nature of economic takeover in South Africa takes different forms, which are in many ways related to the country's history of an economic sector divided or arranged according to race. South Africa's apartheid legislation categorized its nationals along four racial groups: White, "Colored," Indian, and Black (see Marks & Trapido, 1987; MacDonald, 2006). Ironically, such racial categories were retained by the new black-dominated government after the country's historic and founding elections that ushered in the current democratic dispensation. This supports proponents who argue that that race still matters in South Africa (MacDonald, 2006). Others argue that "South Africa has in the past been seen as a useful case study for investigations into racism and political change, yet with characteristics of both developed and developing countries it also provides opportunities for studies in corporate governance" (West, 2006). Other proponents of this view further argue that "the 'white race' spans Afrikaans and English-speakers; the 'African race' includes Sotho, Tswana, Xhosa, Zulus, and several other ethno-cultures besides" (MacDonald, 2006: 32). Thus, such racial categories continue to be used to implement policies such as Affirmative Action (AA) and BBBEE (Broad-Based Black Economic Empowerment) that are aimed at addressing the socio-economic, political, and other imbalances of the past by benefitting previously disadvantaged black communities.

Give the previous background of the country's demographics, economic takeovers and mergers including other economic activities in South Africa cannot be immune to the country's socio-economic and political dynamics. Hart and Padayachee (2000) note that in some South African communities, notably the Indian community, economic activities also included takeovers of family and other businesses. Soon after the demise of apartheid, some entrepreneurs from the Indian community took advantage of opportunities to take over and merge with other economic entities, especially in the clothing and textile industries. They include U.P. (Rajen) Pillay of the Coastal Group, who became "the first black stockbroker on the JSE [Johannesburg Stock Exchange]" (Hart & Padayachee, 2000: 695–696). Accordingly, for more than a century they endured a racial politics of segregation that forced them into a closed corporate community, a small minority squeezed between South Africa's whites and blacks (p. 687). Essentially, this community was forced to conduct business with relatives, which was the same with colored (mixed race) and black communities and in the process reduced the income and economic opportunities that access to a wider, non-racial, market would provide.

More than two decades after democracy, corporate takeovers in such communities have not changed much and are adversely affected by conglomerates that "still obstruct the progress of newer South African capitalists and many of the leading banks are tied to traditional [read white] producers such as the major mining companies)," to whom they offer preferential interest rates, passing off the costs to other customers (Hart & Padayachee, 2000: 697). A few years before the demise of the apartheid regime, many black entrepreneurs were optimistic about the removal of the vestiges of petty apartheid, which essentially entailed piece-meal reforms of the racial system, as they thought that such reforms would open up many opportunities hitherto closed to them by institutionalized racism in the economy. However, they were soon disappointed to discover that the major banks and other financial lending institutions were not prepared to extend loans, capital and other forms of assistance to them. The major reason for this scenario is that the majority of the shareholders and stakeholders behind those banks (e.g., ABSA Bank, First National Bank, Standard Bank South Africa, West Bank) were largely white and therefore served the interests of this community. Thus most black entrepreneurs looked to the informal sector, which became what some called the employer of last resort (Rodrik, 2008: 782).

Corporate takeovers in South Africa have also affected the public sector and involved the privatization of its State Owned Enterprises. As UNECA reports, "between 2001 and 2004, significant stakes in State entities such as Telkom, Transnet, Eskom and Denel, were to be put for sale to private investors. These four companies accounted for about 75% of the total assets of the 15 biggest State enterprises in South Africa" (UNECA, 2007: 20). Over the years, such takeovers, mergers, or privatization of state assets have had mixed results and in some cases may have disadvantaged workers in the related industries owing to reductions in labor because of mechanization of operations.

Corporate takeovers that occur in South Africa's different economic sectors often have far-reaching effects that may result in high unemployment in the country (Rodrik, 2008). Further, such takeovers often transcend the country's borders and affect the economies of many of its Southern African Development Community (SADC) neighbors such as Botswana, Lesotho, Swaziland, Namibia, Zimbabwe, Mozambique, Malawi, and Zambia. Undoubtedly, South Africa remains a regional economic power bloc with significant influence and impact in the region's geo-political dynamics. Thus, economic relations in the southern African region are systematically linked and promoted through initiatives such as the New Partnership for Africa's Development (NEPAD), African Peer Review Mechanism (APRM), and global organizations such as the OECD (Organization for Economic Cooperation and Development) (UNECA, 2007: 15–16).

Largely, these countries are involved in cross-border trade (some through the Southern African Customs Union, SACU) but usually South African firms such as retail giants Shoprite; fuel companies Engen, Shell, and BP; hotel chains and fast food giants such as Nandos, Chicken Licken; transport sector, rail, and other economic conglomerates dominate the markets in these countries. Needless to add, some fast food chains (e.g., franchises such as Kentucky Fried Chicken, McDonald's); the automobile industry (e.g., Volkswagen, Toyota, Nissan, FIAT, BMW, Ford, General Motors, Mercedes

Table 12.1 Stock exchange and market capitalization in Southern Africa in 2002

Country	Name of stock exchange	Stock market capitalization ($US million)
South Africa	JSE Securities Exchange	182,616
Zimbabwe	Zimbabwe Stock Exchange	11,689
Botswana	Botswana Stock Exchange	1,717
Zambia	Lusaka Stock Exchange	231
Namibia	Namibia Stock Exchange	201
Swaziland	Swaziland Stock Exchange	146
Malawi	Malawi Stock Exchange	107

Source: Adapted from UNECA (2007: 19)

Benz; Barnes & Morris, 2004: 790); and other famous supermarket chains are local properties of international companies in the United States, Europe, Asia, and elsewhere in the globe. Table 12.1 indicates the volume of trade in the regional stock exchanges.

Multinational corporations in South Africa generally define the nature of the country's corporate takeovers, mergers, and acquisitions. In the automobile industry, for instance, it is argued that:

> In 1990, only two of the assemblers (BMW and Volkswagen) were Multinational Corporation (MNC) owned and embedded in their global corporate structure. By 2001 this had changed dramatically. All domestic assemblers were at least partly controlled by MNCs, with five completely owned and controlled by their global parent companies. Automakers (Nissan) and Samcor (Ford) have only recently been incorporated into MNC parent companies. Toyota Japan became the majority shareholder of Toyota SA in mid-202. Delta Motor Corporation, with 49% general Motors Shareholding, can still be considered a South African-owned company. Despite ongoing speculation that General Motors is to purchase the company, its ownership remains unresolved.
>
> (Barnes & Morris, 2004: 794–795)

As scholars suggest, the question of corporate takeovers, mergers, and acquisitions have to be understood within the context of the theory of corporate governance. This theory "is frequently described in terms of two apparently opposing models: the shareholder and stakeholder models" (West, 2006: 433, Handley 2005; Turnbull, 1997). Basically, the shareholder model posits that "the corporation is an extension of its owners (the shareholders)" (West, 2006: 433), which suggests that such owners essentially determine any attempts or opportunities by the corporation to take over others, merge with, or acquire over any other corporations. On the other hand, the stakeholder model is based on the view of the corporation as a social entity that has responsibility (accountability) to a variety of stakeholders, usually encompassing owners, suppliers, customers, employees, management, government, and local communities (West, 2006: 434, Maphunye 2011). In the South African situation that is usually affected by racial categories, both these models would inevitably be influenced by (racial) opinions about the merits or demerits of takeovers, mergers, and acquisitions.

The shareholder model is bound to play a significant role in influencing business and labor policy owing to the ANC's recent tendency of co-opting the private sector in its election campaigns and other political activities (Southall, 2004). Thus, it is argued that "Black economic empowerment' (BEE) is one of the most contested terms in South Africa today. Some fear that 'affirmative action' points to the ANC wanting to 'take over everything whites have built up'" (Southall, 2004: 313). Yet, the stakeholder model can equally suggest an even more comprehensive role of the ANC's stakeholders in the policy process. This is also owing to the strong influence of the ANC's "alliance" partners and other stakeholders in the governance process, which can determine the shape, size, and extent of takeovers in the South Africa.

Thus, the question of economic takeovers, mergers, and acquisitions in South Africa remains a contested terrain with mixed implications for the private corporate sector, as it is for the majority black entrepreneurs, the majority of whom tend to view the formal business sector with suspicion owing to historical tendencies of business to exclude black business through covert or blatant economic discrimination.

Economic Transformation and Its Effect on Corporate Takeovers

The installation of South Africa's post-apartheid government of national unity (GNU) was underpinned by many compromises that made it difficult for the governing ANC to implement radical policies by resolving decades of apartheid misrule. However, more than 20 years since 1994, fundamental economic change or "transformation" remains outstanding. This means that for any socio-economic, political, and other activities in South Africa's calendar, such transformation must be visibly enforced, as it has significant implications for the country's politics. Thus, as part of effecting corporate takeovers, mergers, or acquisitions, companies are frequently forced to factor transformation into their operations. Specifically, they have to demonstrate the extent to which economic activities such as corporate takeovers not only benefit the poorest sectors of the economy but also how many women and blacks (colored, Indians, and black Africans) accrue opportunities from such activities.

Of course, to those who may be unaware of the entrenchment of apartheid racism in the economy, such measures may seem odd and probably disadvantageous to the unfettered growth of the economy based on the "invisible hand" of market forces. The ANC government itself has frequently been accused by the country's big business of meddling in the economy with its "interventionist" policies that seek to empower the previously marginalized sectors of the economy.

However, on the positive side, focus on transformation has ensured that the different firms and industries are diversified and led by people from across the different racial, gender, and cultural divides of the country's multi-racial society. In policy terms, this move has legitimized the practices of many industries, including their corporate takeover strategies. The biggest challenge facing the government's current BEEE policies is to demonstrate clearly using measurable outputs and outcomes that show exactly how many previously disadvantaged groups and individuals benefit from such policies (anecdotal evidence suggests that the "previously advantaged" groups continue to enjoy more benefits). Furthermore, this has resulted in the development of various government, business, and labor forums that were unthinkable barely a few decades ago. Such forums include BUSA (Business Unity South Africa), BMF (Black Management Forum), and NEDLAC (National Economic Development and Labor Council). Individuals from these entities nowadays play a role in international trade relations such as the IBSA (India-Brazil-South Africa) trilateral forum and lately BRICSA (Brazil-Russia-India-China-South Africa).

The Challenges of Corporate Takeover

The African continent generally experiences many other challenges pertaining to corporate governance. For instance, research evidence from elsewhere in Africa suggests that "there is a preponderance of closely-held family owned and managed businesses. In Nigeria, the informal nature of most businesses and the high level of government ownership of enterprises pose challenges to the practice of corporate governance" (Okeahalam & Akinboade, 2003: 20). This might be different to the South African economy in the sense that the country's businesses (especially the formal white-dominated sector) has over the years grown into formal entities that are listed in the Johannesburg Stock Exchange (JSE). Yet, South Africa may be described as "a country of two nations" which former president Thabo Mbeki's (1998) said was characterized by one very rich, highly advanced, and predominantly white nation, which was juxtaposed to another, very poor, downtrodden, and highly economically disadvantaged and dependent on the former. At the time Mbeki propounded this view, some among the country's white population were beginning to express concern that he was deviating from Nelson Mandela's policies of reconciliation and racial harmony aimed at nation-building. However, to many in the previously disadvantaged communities, Mbeki's speech was welcomed as a true reflection of the country's majority black population. "The second and larger nation of

South Africa," Mbeki (1998) argued in his parliamentary speech, "is black and poor, with the worst affected being women in the rural areas, the black rural population in general and the disabled. This nation lives under conditions of a grossly underdeveloped economic, physical, educational, communication and other infrastructure."

Lessons from Corporate Takeover

A careful but brief analysis of the South African case suggests a few lessons about corporate takeovers in Africa and the rest of the developed world. First, the South African situation clearly suggests that a country that does not develop corporate governance guidelines and principles for its businesses and companies may experience difficulties, especially if the country has had a difficult and racially divided past.

Second, and probably against the traditional advice that the state must keep away from the economy, some kind of intervention by the state could assist the economy to ameliorate the adverse results of corporate takeovers, mergers, and acquisitions on vulnerable sectors and communities. Recently, South Africa tried to emulate the examples of the "Asian Tigers" by attempting to follow the economic growth path of developmental states (Maphunye, 2011). Undoubtedly, countries such as Taiwan, Singapore, Japan, Malaysia, Indonesia, South Korea, and Thailand enjoyed relatively higher growth rates a few decades ago. South Africa's situation differs fundamentally from that of the "tiger economies," because some countries in this group did not always achieve such remarkable growth rates based on democratic socio-economic, political, and other practices.

Third, and most important, there will be need for compromises from the different economic, social, political, and other actors in a country to ensure its economic growth and recovery. It is acknowledged that the South African model of compromise and reconciliation continuously baffles those who had thought that the country would experience a devastating civil war. Admittedly, it may never apply anywhere else in the world given the uniqueness of the country's historical experiences. Even in the short-term economic growth and recovery may be difficult to discern; but in the long term (all other things remaining equal), the economies of scale and other benefits of corporate takeovers, mergers, and acquisitions may prove beneficial for developing countries such as South Africa.

Conclusion

This chapter has examined the issue of corporate takeovers and its impact in South Africa. Admittedly, such takeovers have negative and positive implications for a country's economy and have affected employers, workers, public officials, and communities in the country. Accordingly, recent corporate takeovers have compounded the social and economic problems of communities affected by the earlier rounds of industrial restructuring and plant closings (Jonas, 1992: 348). In terms of public policy, such problems may have devastating damages on the image and support of the government and relevant politicians.

In South Africa more work remains to be done, some of which will only be possible when comparable company entry and survival data is available. It would be desirable to find more data to help estimate the impact of different regulatory indicators and to be able to determine the variable that capture the dynamics of the companies' financial system, such as high risks capital. Much of this depends on the availability of comparable business dynamics data from decade to decade in the country. On one hand, the Schumpeter creative destruction model ascribes to an important role for technological change and productivity growth. On the other hand, the product life cycle explains why entry rates decline as industries become more mature and the most successful incumbent grow. In order to exploit the importance of these two theories in the country, the Government of South African should be very conscious not to use their regulatory mechanism to hinder firm entry or corporate takeover. Since entry companies know little about their chances to survive, government policy that could make corporations exist or discourage companies from entry should be avoided as much as possible.

As countries around the world continue to grapple with the challenges of an increasingly globalized economic order, perhaps the so-called "emerging markets" such as South Africa have lessons that they can share with their more developed counterparts. These lessons could be in the area of corporate social responsibility to ensure that economic activities such as corporate takeovers, mergers, and acquisitions do not adversely affect all those whose lives depend on corporations that may decide to take over others or merge them in line with their economic strategies. However, in such initiatives, collaboration with different stakeholders is key. It is very important to note that variation in collective action by corporations in turn may have their own impact on preference formation on the part of the Government of South Africa.

References

Aghion, P. and Howitt, P. (1991). A Model of Growth Through Creative Destruction. *Econometrica*, 60(2), 323–351.

Ahn, S. (2001). Firm Dynamics and Productivity Growth: A Review of Micro Evidence From OEED Countries. OCED Economic Department Working Paper No. 297, OCED, Paris.

Barnes, J. and Morris, M. (2004). The German Connection: Shifting Hegemony in the Political Economy of the South African Automotive Industry. *Industrial and Corporate Change*, 13(5), 789–814.

Bartelsman, E. J., Scapetta, S. and Schivardi, F. (2003). *Comparative Analysis of Firm Demographics and Survival: Micro-Level Evidence for the OECD Countries*. OECD Economics Department Working Paper No. 348, OCED, Paris.

Behar, A. and Hodge, J. (2008). The Employment Effects of Mergers in a Declining Industry: The Case of South African Gold Mining. *The B.E. Journal of Economic Analysis & Policy*, 8(1), Article 29, 1–18.

Brandt, N. (2004a). *Business Dynamics in Europe*. STI Working Paper 2004, OCED, Paris.

Brandt, N. (2004b). *Business Dynamics, Regulation and Performance*. OCED Science, Technology and Industry Working Paper No. 3, OCED, Paris.

Caballero, R. J. and Hammour, M. L. (1994). The Cleansing Effect of Creative Destruction. *American Economic Review*, 84(5), 1350–1368.

Campbell, J. (1997). *Entry, Exist, Technology and Business Cycles*. National Bureau of Economic Research Working Paper No. 5955.

Cooper, R., Haltiwanger, J. and Power, L. (1997). *Machine Replacement and the Business Cycle*. National Bureau Economic Research Working Paper No. 5260.

Dibie, R., Edoho, F. M. and Dibie, J. (2015). Analysis of Capacity Building and Economic Growth in Sub-Saharan Africa. *International Journal of Business and Social Science*, 6(12), 120–157.

Evans, P. (1989). The State as Problem and Solution. In Stephen Haggard and Robert Haufman (Eds.), *The Politics of Economic Adjustment*. Princeton, NJ: Princeton University Press, 73–95.

Fine, B. and Rustomjee, Z. (1996). South Africa's Political Economy: From Minerals-Energy Complex to Industrialisation? London: Hurst.

Ellis, K., Lamont, B., Reus, T. H., and Falfman. L. (2015). Mergers and Acquisitions in Africa: A Review and an Emerging Research Agenda. Journal Africa Journal of Management, 1(2), 137–171.

Gerald, A. E. (1989). State Competence to Regulate Corporate Takeover Lesson From State Takeover Status. *Hofstra Law Review*, 17(2), 535–542.

Greenfield, S. (1979). *Entrepreneurs in Cultural Context*. Albuquerque: University of New Mexico Press.

Gregg, J. (2008). Takeover and Leverage Buyouts. In David R. Henderson Edited by David R. Henderson. *The Concise Encyclopedia of Economics*. 2008. Library of Economics and Liberty. www.econlib.org/library/Enc/Intro.html. Accessed May 9, 2016.

Handley, A. (2005). Business, Government and Economic Policymaking in the New South Africa, 1990–2000. *Journal of Modern African Studies*, 43(2), 211–239.

Hart, K. and Padayachee, V. (2000). Indian Business in South Africa After Apartheid: New and Old Trajectories. *Comparative Studies in Society and History*, 42(4), 683–712.

Investopedia Staff. (2015). *Merger and Acquisition: Understanding Takeovers*. www.investopedia.com/articles/01/050901.asp. Accessed January 29, 2016.

Jonas, A. E. G. (1992). Takeover and the Politics of Community: The Case of Norton Company in Worcester. *Economic Geography*, 68(4), 348–372.

Klepper, S. (1996). Entry, Exit, Growth, and Innovation Over the Product Life Cycle. *American Economic Review*, 86(3), 562–583.

MacDonald, M. (2006). *Why Race Matters in South Africa*. Cambridge: Harvard University Press.

Mangena, M. and Chamisa, E. (2007, November). Corporate Governance and Incidences if Listing Suspension by the JSE Securities Exchange of South Africa: An Empirical Analysis. Working Paper No. 07/31.

Mansfield, E. (1983). Long Waves and Technological Innovation. *The American Economic Review*, 73(2), 141–145.

Maphunye, K. J. (2011). The Relevance of the Developmental State Model to South Africa's and Botswana's Public Services. *Journal of Public Administration*, 46(1), 608–621.

Marks, S. and Trapido, S. (Eds.) (1987). The Politics of Race, Class and Nationalism in Twentieth-Century South Africa. London and New York: Routledge.

Mbeki, T. (1998, 29 May). Statement of Deputy President Thabo Mbeki at the Opening of the Debate in the National Assembly, on 'Reconciliation and Nation Building'. National Assembly Cape Town. www.dfa.gov.za/docs/speeches/1998/mbek0529.htm. Accessed January 28, 2016.

Michie, J. and Padayachee, V. (Eds.) (1997). *The Political Economy of South Africa's Transition.* London: Dryden.

Ocampo, J. A. (2004). Corporate Social Responsibility. *Natural Resources Forum,* 28, 249–250.

Okeahalam, C. C. and Akinboade, A. (2003). *A Review of Corporate Governance in Africa: Literature, Issues and Challenges.* www.researchgate.net/publication/237256378. Accessed January 28, 2016.

Roberts, J. (1998). Economy Policy and Industrial Restructuring in South Africa—Political Economy Approaches. *International Review of Applied Economics,* 12(2), 317–324.

Rodrik, D. (2008). Understanding South Africa's Economic Puzzles. *Economics of Transition,* 16(4), 769–797.

Schneider, B. R. (1998). Business-Government and Development. *Comparative Politics,* 31, 101–122.

Schumpeter, J. (1983). The Theory of Economic Development: An Inquiry Into Profits, Capital, Credit, Interest, and the Business Cycle. New Brunswick, NJ: Transaction Books.

Schumpeter, J. (1954). *Economic Doctrine and Method: An Historical Sketch.* New York: Oxford University Press.

Southall, R. (2004). The ANC & Black Capitalism in South Africa. *Review of African Political Economy,* 100, 313–328.

Tomaselli, K. G. (1997). Ownership and Control in the South African Print Media: Black Empowerment After Apartheid, 1990–1997. *Ecquid Novi: African Journalism Studies,* 18(1), 67–68.Triki, T. and Chun, O. M. (2011). Does Good Governance Create Value for International Acquirers in Africa: evidence from US acquisitions. African Development Bank. https://core.ac.uk/download/pdf/6633184.pdf. Accessed May 9, 2016.

Twala, T. (2012). The Marikana Massacre: A Historical Overview of the Labour Unrest in the Mining Sector in South Africa, Policy Brief. *Southern African Peace and Security Studies,* 1(2), 61–67.

UNECA. (2007). An Overview of Corporate Governance and Accountability in Southern Africa. Addis Ababa: UN Economic Commission for Africa.

Vaughn, M. and Ryan, L. V. (2006). Corporate Governance in South Africa: Bellwether for the Continent? *Corporate Governance,* 14(5), 504–512.

West, A. (2006). Theorising South Africa's Corporate Governance. *Journal of Business Ethics,* 68, 433–448.

13 Business and Government Relations in Cameroon

Wilfred Gabsa

Introduction

The Republic of Cameroon is one of the countries in West Africa. It is located to the east of Nigeria. It also has boundaries with Central African Republic to the northeast, the Republic of Chad to the north, the Republic of Congo to the east, and the Democratic Republic of Equatorial Guinea and Gabon Republic to the southeast, respectively. The Atlantic Ocean and the Bight of Biafra is located to the south of Cameroon (Government of Cameroon, 2015). The country has a mixed economic system that includes a variety of private freedoms, combined with centralized economic planning and government regulation. It is reported that the nation has a population of approximately 22.77 million people in 2015 (Global Edge, 2016; BBC News, 2016). The Republic of Cameroon in 2014 had a GDP per capita $2,972 (World Bank Group, 2016).

Cameroon has a very interesting history as a former colony of several European countries such as Portugal, Holland, France, Germany, and Britain. The Portuguese set up sugar plantations and began slave trade in Cameroon, in about 1520 (Yanou & Foyam, 2008). The colony was later taken over by the Dutch in the 1600s. In 1884 the West African colony of called Cameroon came under the control of German (Yanou & Foyam, 2008). The colony expanded and in 1911, under the Treaty of Fez, it was handed over to Germans (Hope, 1997). In 1916 the British and French troops forced the German settlers to leave Cameroon. According to its history, 3 years later, Cameroon was divided under the London Declaration—80% to the French and 20% to the British (BBC News, 2016; Yanou & Foyam, 2008).

In 1958 French Cameroon was granted self-government with Ahmadou Ahidjo as prime minister. The country becomes independent two years later in 1960, and Ahidjo became its first president (Hope, 1997; Yanou & Foyam, 2008). As a result of a United Nations sponsored referendum, the (British) Southern Cameroons joined the Republic of Cameroon to become the Federal Republic of Cameroon, while Northern Cameroon join Nigeria (Hope, 1997; GlobalEdge, 2016; BBC News, 2016). Further, in 1982 the then Prime Minister Paul Biya succeeds Ahidjo, who resigns, only to flee the country the following year after Biya accuses him of masterminding a coup (Yanou & Foyam, 2008; Hope. 1997). Biya was elected president in 1984, and continues to rule the country with a new name the Republic of Cameroon (BBC New, 2016). Under the presidency of Paul Biya, for more than three decades the Cameroon's government system is considered to take the form of a multiparty presidential democracy. The chief of state is the president, and the head of government is the prime minister (United States Embassy, Yaoundé, 2015).

The Republic of Cameroon is considered to have one of the largest economies in sub-Saharan Africa and a landscape rich in natural resources and biodiversity; Cameroon has the potential to become an economic stalwart and serious regional player (Cameroon Economic Review, 2015). In the last two decades, Cameroon's economic growth has fluctuated tremendously to the extent that it affected both public and private businesses in various ways. In spite of the fluctuation, it has never crossed the range of 8%; it has remained stagnant at a rate of 7%, according to some commentators. The economic crisis of the mid-1980s did not show any sign of moderation in Cameroon but made life difficult for many; it made life for consumers, purchasers, and the government very difficult. Like in many other African countries, the crisis produced disastrous results—among other things, poverty and socioeconomic inequalities increased, the external debt burden became heavier, the brain drain intensified, capital flight deepened, the balance of payments weakened, the physical infrastructure deteriorated, unemployment and crime escalated, famine and malnutrition became pronounced, budget deficits soared, agricultural productivity declined, urbanization burgeoned, environmental degradation expanded, political and civil strife worsened, and corruption became more rampant (Hope, 1997). The crisis was seen as an inevitable outcome of the failure of the post-independent State to formulate and implement adequate development policy and its inability to contend with an adverse international economic environment at that time. It was then thought that the State was not the best-fit economist or entrepreneur, and calls began inevitably to multiply, calling on States to lessen their grip on the economy by reviewing the nature of business-government relations. This notwithstanding, the State has remained ever present in economic life—playing a major role as regulator, referee, or market controller. Even economic rescue plans proposed and imposed by international financiers had to be implemented by the State—thereby giving the impression that no matter what economic problem there is, the State is an inevitable actor. The economic failures and dysfunctionalities of the time forced many States to bow to the internationally imposed Structural Adjustment Program (SAP). Initially suggested and imposed by international financial institutions, the Structural Adjustment Program (SAP) was an economic rescue plan introduced after the collapse or at least near collapse of the economy in 1986. It involved internal and external adjustment to the new economic order.

Internally, the government was compelled to introduce adjustment measures ranging from reduction in its expenditures to revamping the hitherto dormant and/or nonproductive public and private sectors.

The objective of Chapter 13 is to investigate the nature of business and government relations in Cameroon. It examines the strengths, weaknesses, opportunities, and threats to business with a focus on the nature, role, and impact of public policy on the private sector in general. It argues that although the State remains the major regulator of the economy in Cameroon, its economic reform policies since the 1990s have been to strategically associate the private sector in the process of economic decision making. The sustainable development strategic plan of the country includes increasing production, enhancing trade and distribution of agricultural crops, and attracting appropriate technology and economic growth. The chapter uses secondary data to make an argument that the business sector has not been left out in economic policies of the nation, given the right to private ownership through privatization. It also evaluates the economic road maps of the country, such as vision 2035, Growth and Employment Strategy Paper (GESP), Poverty Reduction and Employment Strategy Paper (DSCE), and recently, the Three Year Emergency Plan. The main thrust is a focus on government's role in the economy based on past and current experiences. It seeks to contribute to the course of economic policies with regard to the processes by which those policies are developed in Cameroon. The chapter concludes that the nature of business-government relations has improved significantly over the last two decades, to the extent that the roles played by the State as well as the private sector are complementary.

Business-Government Relations Background in Cameroon

The development of Cameroon's economy has always been a business of government. When Cameroon became independent, the government initiated a number of economic policies that defined business-government relations. Ahmadou Ahidjo, president of the first Republic, introduced the notion of *balanced development* and *planned liberalism* as the frameworks of Cameroon's economy. While balanced development meant that the fruits of development will be distributed throughout the national territory so that enclaved regions will not be discriminated against in terms of spreading development projects, planned liberalism on the other hand meant that while the State would play a key role in economic development, the creative force of the private sector would not be neglected or minimized (Awung & Atanga, 2011). Government through this policy encouraged private foreign investors to invest in the industrial sector. To that effect, the National Investment Corporation (NIC) was established in 1964 to undertake joint ventures with foreign investors for industrial development (Awung & Atanga, 2011). This in essence meant that although government was willing to do business with the private sector, it wanted it to operate under its control. This is the kind of mixed type economic system that manifested in Cameroon. This system was envisaged by French authorities and it was therefore a continuation of an economic policy thought of, and planned by, foreign administrations. The Five-Year-Development Plan, which laid the conditions for public investment and facilitated the flow of development assistance from foreign partners, was formulated by French technocrats and was to run from 1960 to 1965 (Awung & Atanga, 2011). It relied heavily on French public and private capital, and to encourage the private sector, the investment code provided for many tax exemptions to foreign investors and guaranteed the repatriation of profits (Hope, 1997; Awung & Atanga, 2011).

The main objective of the first Five Year Plan (1961–1966) was to integrate the country politically and economically and to improve the standard of living of the population. This was mainly to be achieved by doubling the per capita income from 21,500 CFA francs in 1961 to 43,000 CFA francs in 1980.

The second development plan (1966–1971) further focused again on doubling the per capita income by 1980 and aiming to reduce socioeconomic inequalities between the regions of the country. The third plan overtly highlighted government's interest toward the private sector. It stressed increased production and productivity of all sectors of the economy with significant investment expenditures directed toward the private sector (Ajab, 2002). This plan, which ran from 1971 to 1976, saw the allocation of 63% of total investment budget to productive projects compared with 46% of the second plan (Ajab, 2002).

The fourth development plan (1976–1981) coincided with the oil boom period. By 1985 oil's share in GDP had increased to 18% and to 45% of government revenue and 35% of exports. It was also the period when there were increases in world commodity prices. The plan stressed large public projects and import substitution industry, and salaries of civil servants were regularly increased with the main public salary scales established in 1970.

The fifth plan (1981–1986) took into consideration the oil boom and constraints on investment absorptive capacity. However, it was through the fourth and fifth plans that the public sector grew rapidly at the expense of the private sector and the agricultural sector. The reason is that significant allocation went more, to administrative equipment and ministerial buildings and little to the agricultural sector that until further notice remains the backbone of every developing economy.

From 1986, an attempt was made to implement the sixth plan, but it did not work because the economy had collapsed and the structural adjustment program was already being applied. An austerity program to rescue the economy was launched in 1987, but whether it succeeded or not remains a topic for another debate. The program affected both the public and private sectors. For example, while private sector incomes and subsidies declined, civil servants' salaries were maintained up to 1993 instead of increasing as it was the case in the previous years. The austerity program was partly to reconstitute public savings and restore budgetary balance. Submerged by internal and external economic constraints, the government was compelled to reduce its grip on the economy by introducing more realistic economic liberalization measures. The introduction of economic liberalism as a general economic framework was a direct result of the collapse of the economy and the failure of the sixth plan after 1986. Economic liberalism was not implemented out of sheer governmental will. It was out of sociopolitical and economic necessity that government took the initiative to liberalize the economy (World Bank Group, 2016; GlobalEdge, 2016). Economic liberalism was first expressed in total price liberalization as a measure to encourage the private sector. However, it was shortly after 1990 that significant liberalization measures were carried out. With regard to trade liberalization, tariffs were reduced well below the levels agreed by the Central African Custom Union, and all quantitative restriction was eliminated, with reduction in exemptions. The private sector increasingly became associated in the process of economic production and growth.

Business and Government Relations Determents

The Democratic Republic of Cameroon has modest oil resources and favorable agricultural conditions. The country has one of the best-endowed primary commodity economies in sub-Saharan Africa (Cameroon Economic Review, 2015). The major business opportunities in the country are petroleum production and refining, aluminum production, food processing, electricity, and consumer goods. Cameroon exports oil and petroleum, aluminum, cocoa, and wood (GlobalEdge, 2016). For the past two decades the private sector has played a major role in job creation and rejuvenating the economic growth in the country. The Government of Cameroon has been stable for the past three decades. In addition, the political and business environment have encouraged and rewarded innovation and entrepreneurship, as well as galvanized international trade and foreign investment in the country.

What factors determine public and private sector relations in Cameroon? Under what conditions or circumstances is the public and private sector likely to cooperate or not? Both internal and external factors have determined the nature of public and private sector relations.

Internally, an unfavorable investment climate, particularly inappropriate infrastructure, is discouraging the emancipation of the private sector (Cameroon Economic Update, 2012). Poor infrastructure and an unfavorable investment climate continue to hamper economic activity. Although Cameroon is endowed with significant natural resources, including oil, high value timber species, and agricultural products (coffee, cotton, cocoa), untapped resources such as natural gas, bauxite, diamonds, gold, iron, and

Table 13.1 Cameroon's economic and trade indicators

No.	Economic and trade indicator	Amount in US$	Year
1	GDP, PPP (current international)	$67,686,481,734	2014
2	GDP per capita, PPP (current international)	$2,972	2014
	GDP growth rate (annual %)	5.927%	2014
3	Imports of goods and services (current US$)	$9,984,169,170	2014
4	Exports of goods and services (current US$)	$6,966,360,244	2014
5	Trade balance	–$2,401,618,990	2014
6	Total merchandise trade (% of GDP)	36.926%	2014
7	Commercial service exports (current US$)	$1,887,949,820	2013
8	Inflation, consumer prices (annual %)	1.948% (2014)	2014
9	External debt stocks, total (DOD, current US$)	$4,922,311,000 (2013)	2014
10	Labor force, total	9,176,788 (2014)	2014
11	Employment in agriculture (% of total employment)	53.3% (2010)	2014
12	Employment in industry (% of total employment)	12.6% (2010)	2014
13	Employment in services (% of total employment)	34.1% (2010)	2014
14	Unemployment rate	4.3% (2014)	2014

Source: Global Edge. (2016). *Cameroon Economic and Trade Statistics.* http://globaledge.msuedu/countries/cameroon/tradestats.

cobalt, economic growth has been lagging behind the average growth rate because of the poor state of infrastructure.

In 2010 the Logistics Performance Index—reflecting the operators' perceptions of the logistic "friendliness" of countries—ranked Cameroon 105 out of 155 countries. The quality of trade and transport infrastructure (e.g., ports, railroads, roads, information technology) and the efficiency of the clearance process (i.e., speed, simplicity, and predictability of formalities) by border control agencies are the dimensions that received the lowest scores. The number of documents required to import or export goods, for instance, is far higher in Cameroon than on average in sub-Saharan Africa, and illustrates these administrative hurdles.

The geo-strategic location of Cameroon is another determinant of the public and private sector relations. Due to its strategic location neighboring Nigeria and Gabon, and potential crossing point to the landlocked countries of Central Africa (Chad and the CAR), Cameroon is a natural hub for the region with the port of Douala as the main entrance. However, in addition to poor infrastructure quality, significant deficiencies in logistics, such as cartels, prevent Cameroon from playing the role of effectively inviting foreign private investors—for example, costs inflation and lengthy delays for cargo bound inland to CAR and Chad.

Turning to agriculture, recent data are lacking for a proper discussion on policies to improve competitiveness and labor productivity in this sector. Growth in agriculture is nevertheless thought to be hampered by among other factors: (1) limited access to improved inputs (such as high yielding improved varieties, certified seeds, and fertilizers); (2) poor rural infrastructure (marketing and transport); (3) weak linkages to markets and market information; (4) limited access to credit; and (5) weak producer organizations and low productivity techniques. Studies on Western and Central Africa tend to show, for instance, that up to 50% of crops could be lost because of poor roads, hampering their timely transport to consumers. Preliminary estimations on the Batibo-Ekok corridor would confirm that up to 40% of production could be lost because of lack of appropriate roads and transport services. However, governmental focus on agricultural activities may reduce the potential for it to adopt inclusive measures.

Government subsidies have determined to some extent the public-private relations. Fuel subsidies are a source of concern. The costs in terms of GDP related to the decision to freeze retail fuel prices are the highest in the region, benefitting mostly the richest segment of the population. SONARA, the national oil refinery, has been benefitting from assistance to compensate it for its revenue shortfalls stemming from government's policy to freeze retail prices of petroleum products (diesel, gasoline, kerosene, and LPG). Subsidies for energy products are provided both directly to SONARA through direct budgetary transfers from the treasury and indirectly through tax reductions on the prices of energy products. In 2011, the subsidies reached 2.6% of GDP (14% of the budget), the highest level in the CEMAC zone.

Externally, global financial crisis can affect the nature of the public-private relationship, particularly with regard to foreign private investors and the ability of government to regulate the private sector. For example, the 2008–2009 global financial crisis propagated to financial institutions globally and resulted in a sharp tightening of credit conditions globally. As a result, international trade declined and real global activity contracted. Indeed, Cameroon's financial sector was not directly exposed to the global financial crisis, but indirectly it was affected through the following ways: deteriorating terms of trade (15%); slower world demand for oil, timber, rubber, cotton, and aluminum, resulting in the reduction of export volumes of 4.8%; tighter international liquidity conditions that led to reduction in capital inflows and the postponement of some investments; and a slight decline in remittances (0.5%; Cameroon Economic Update, 2012). Sovereign debt crisis in advanced economies, particularly in the Euro zone, clouded the economic outlook and made foreign private investment particularly challenging. It was believed that an inclusive business public policy would lessen the weight of the debt crisis on foreign investors and strengthen the relationship between the public and foreign private sector.

Private Sector Potentials in Cameroon

In Cameroon there are basically two types of private sectors: the national and foreign private sectors. The national private sector is the major actor when it comes to the development of the production sector. A large share of the labor force in Cameroon is occupied in the private sector (Cameroon Economic Update, 2012). As in other parts of Africa, the formal manufacturing and service sectors have the potential to be an important source of employment, but because they hire such a small share of the labor force, even with very high growth rates, they will not be able to absorb more than a fraction of the new entrants. Most Cameroonians are thus likely to continue working in low-productivity agriculture and non-agriculture informal sector activities over the next two decades.

This observation calls for greater emphasis on measures to increase the productivity, and hence the earnings, of those employed in the informal private sector, while at the same time working to create more jobs in the formal public sector. Like most Africans, Cameroonians already have jobs; they cannot afford otherwise. The problem is that these jobs have extremely low productivity and generate low earnings. Labor productivity enhancement can come from two sets of interventions: (1) those that improve the supply of labor; and (2) those that stimulate the demand for goods and services produced, and hence for labor.

The informal sector—agriculture and non-agriculture—remains the main provider of employment in Cameroon, with more than 90% of the overall labor force. Informality is predominant in urban as well as rural areas and represents the main employer for men as well as for women. Overall the formal private sector represents less than 4% of the labor force, employing essentially men in urban areas. Because it may be easier to enter, most young people find jobs in the informal sector. In 2010, about 92% of young people employed were in the informal sector.

In spite of the fact the private sector is the major actor when it comes to the development of the production sector, it faces the following difficulties: malfunctions that penalize free enterprise and creativity, administrative bottlenecks and high transaction cost, poor governance and incivility, anti-competitive practices such as contraband, customs fraud, falsification, dumping, and absence of support infrastructure and so on. It is against this backdrop that economists find that the strategy of the complementary role of the public and private sectors in promoting the growth of the economy remains valid (Raipuria & Mehta, 1991). Nevertheless, the validity will also have to depend on the nature of government's economic regulatory powers. These predicaments lead to, on one hand, limited participation of the poor in the development process of the country. On the other hand, minimal infrastructure development has prevented large members of the lower economic class group of citizens to effectively connect to the market that is controlled by the business sector. Thus institutional capacities are essential to ensure pragmatic reforms.

Nature of Business Response to Regulation

Political scientists consider the State as society's shaping organism. This is because the State holds the monopoly of the use or threat of use of physical and symbolic violence. As modern political systems, States have always engaged in the regulation of society's major sectors, including the political, economic, and socio-cultural sectors. However, the problem has always been on the degree to which States intervene to regulate these sectors. The economic sector is one of those crucial sectors to which modern States have not been indifferent. In some cases, States have appropriated the economy as their private business, defining its pattern and deciding who does and gets what, when, and how. But the challenges of modern economic systems, globalization, technological advancement, and economic crisis have compelled modern States to review their economic interventionism policies.

In Cameroon, the State means all public institutions provided for in the constitution. When we get into the constitution, we observe that generally the State is represented in three main structures or institutions: the executive, the judiciary, and the legislative. Amongst them all, however, the executive is the most powerful because it is headed by a chief executive (President of the Republic) who takes major decisions that affect the entire nation with or without the consent of other institutions. It was the President of the Republic who promulgated law No. 2002/04 of April 19, 2002, relating to the Republic of Cameroon's Investment Charter. This law defines the role of the State in the economy as being to issue laws and regulations; supervise, facilitate, and regulate economic and social activities and the development of basic and information infrastructure; provide training; ensure security; and compensate for market failures. To that end, the State organizes, controls, and secures all markets through appropriate regulation and effective supervision. What we consider as an inclusive economic role of the State is that of recognizing the key role of entrepreneurs, investors, and private enterprise as crucial factors in wealth and job creation, and thereof, to develop a genuine partnership with the private sector and civil society in order to improve the distribution of resources, particularly in areas where the market has limitations.

As economic overseer, the Government of Cameroon makes sure that the private sector complies with competition rules by avoiding fraudulent practices and by discouraging conduct conducive to corruption within the private sector; takes steps to preserve the interests of consumers and users; organizes its various sectors and branches in such a way as to promote among its members respect for morality in business and the judicious application of the ethical rules connected with each professional activity; and cooperates reliably with the State and its organs with a view to ensuring the success of national economic policy.

Also, as an economic regulator, the government is a party to both bilateral and multilateral agreements relating to investment guarantees. It is a party to: the Convention on the Recognition and Enforcement of Foreign Arbitral Awards (New York Convention), concluded under United Nations auspices; the Convention on the Settlement of Investment Disputes, which established the International Centre for Settlement of Investment Disputes (ICSID) (Washington Convention); the Convention Establishing the Multilateral Investment Guarantee Agency (MIGA) of October 11, 1985 (Seoul Convention), intended to ensure against non-commercial risks; the OHADA treaty, in implementation of which simple and modern legal rules based on international practice have been developed in the area of business law. Through its membership of OHADA, the State has available to it both ad hoc and institutional arbitration mechanisms based on the most effective international instruments, such as the 1985 Model Law on International Commercial Arbitration of the United Nations Commission on International Trade Law (UNCITRAL) and the 1998 Rules of Arbitration of the International Chamber of Commerce.

In addition, the State is a party to the Partnership Agreement of June 23, 2000, between the members of the African, Caribbean and Pacific Group of States, on the one hand, and the European Community and its member states, on the other (ACP-EC Partnership Agreement), which establishes an arbitration mechanism for the settlement of disputes between African, Caribbean, and Pacific States and entrepreneurs, suppliers, or providers of services financed by the European Development Fund (EDF). However, the State is yet to establish a national court of arbitration for the settlement of industrial and commercial disputes as spelled out in article 12 of the Cameroon Investment Charter of 2002. Furthermore, the State has created institutions for the promotion and facilitation of investments and exports, which are the Council for Regulation and Competitiveness; the Investment Promotion Agency; the Export Promotion Agency; and most importantly, institutions for the promotion of private initiatives such as the Industrial Partnership Council; an Entrepreneurship Institute; a Monitoring Center for Industry and Trade; a Standards and Quality Agency; and an Intellectual Property Center.

One of the traditional economic regulatory mechanisms of the State is the tax system that has improved over the years in Cameroon. According to Cameroon's Investment Charter, tax and customs have been transformed from an economic disincentive into a private sector incentive mechanism. The tax and customs is not only based on the principle of equity among the various taxpayers and reductions, but the process has been simplified and harmonized in order to ensure the same level of transparency, fluidity, and legibility for all investors. Although the taxes and customs duties are collected in amounts that are similar or equivalent to international norms, the State reserves the right to adjust the amount to the specific nature of and developments of different industries. But perhaps what private investors have been long awaiting is the possibility of the State to reduce stamp duties and registration taxes. This disposition is not only an imposition of the Investment Charter but the value-added-tax (VAT) has also been imposed as a neutral levy for investment and wealth generation. Apart from the regulatory frameworks noted, the State accumulated and preserved fiscal savings as a countercyclical fiscal measure. This method was particularly instrumental in limiting the effects of the 2008–2009 global financial crisis on the country.

The informal sector was also affected by State policies. As opposed to the formal sector, which was constantly submitted to State rules and regulations, the informal sector which operated clandestinely and at the fringes of law was systematically neglected (Yuh, 2009). It was not until the late 1980s, with the economic crisis that the economic potential of the informal sector was acknowledged and appropriate measures taken to regulate it (World Bank Group, 2016). A study by Alia and his colleagues suggests that the increase in informal household investment has a positive effect on the performance of the informal sector and led to a decrease in household poverty in this sector (Alia et al., 2015). The regulation of the informal sector in Cameroon began with a process of formalization that is the presence of the State in informal sector activities through institutions such as the Support Program for Rural and Urban Youths (PAJER-U), Women Empowerment Center (WECs), and the National Employment Fund (NEF), which culminated into the Integrated Support Project for Informal Sector Actors (PIAASI)—the only State institution responsible solely for informal sector issues. According to Joseph Yuh (2009), the formalization process also involved the removal of the informal sector from the confines of clandestine activities by granting it formal sector characteristics such the promotion and protection of the rights of workers and the rationalization of the sector (Yuh, 2009). To that effect, private sector reacted by creating bodies such as the National Street Vendor's Association (ANESCAM) and the National Association of Operators of the Informal Sector and of the Fight against Poverty in Cameroon (ANOSILP), which now operate within the confines of well-defined legal and institutional framework (World Bank Group, 2016).

The response of the private sector to the role of government in business in Cameroon was also championed by corporate activists and trade union reactions. Indeed, students of economics are of the opinion that as a method of reallocating assets and functions from the public sector to the private sector, privatization appears to be a factor that could play a serious role in the quest for growth (Filipovic, 2005). How has business responded to the privatization? The association of Cameroon businessmen and entrepreneurs known in French as "Groupement" Inter-Patronal du Cameroon

(GICAM) has come out strongly to formulate demands to government for the amelioration of the business climate in Cameroon. One of the requests of GICAM is the establishment of an Investment Code (Code d'incitation à l'Investissement). In 2004, GICAM went into negotiations with government on how the business climate could be improved in Cameroon. The outcome of the negotiation was a proposal for government to adopt and enact into law a National Investment Code that will accelerate economic development and growth. (GICAM Bulletin, 2013). Apart from this request, other requests included the creation of economic, industrial, and agricultural zones; the respect of the deadline for the realization of infrastructural works such as the Lom Pangar and Memve'ele dams, the Kribi deep sea port, the second bridge on the Wouri, the east and west routes of Douala, and the Douala-Yaounde double highway; the participation of at least 30% of national enterprises in the realization the huge construction works noted; the implementation of the recommendations of the Cameroon Business Forum; the acceleration of road networks; and the free movement of people and goods in the Central African subregion.

Following from these regulatory policies, we notice that indeed the government is making an effort to deregulate the economy. Economic policies are increasingly becoming flexible, even if this is not at the pace that would have been expected. According to the Doing Business report year from 2010 to 2015, in 2010, Cameroon made starting a business easier by exempting newly formed companies from paying the business license tax for their first 2 years of existence; in 2011, it made starting a business easier by establishing a new one-stop shop and abolishing the requirement for verifying business premises and its corresponding fees, and in 2012, another effort was made by replacing the requirement for a copy of the founders' criminal records with one for a sworn declaration at the time of the company's registration, and by reducing publication fees (World Bank, 2014). These are indeed positive signs of economic inclusiveness, but perhaps the most important is to discover how Cameroon has so far fared with privatization.

The Political Economy of Privatization

Privatization is part of the process by which the economy is liberalized. Privatization has been considered as any material transaction by which the State's ultimate ownership of corporate entities is reduced (OECD, 2010). This definition focuses on transfer of corporate assets to the private sector rather than a transfer merely of activities.

It follows that privatization in principle means the process of transfer of ownership, sometimes also of permanent or long-term user ship, of a formerly common or public good to individuals and/or groups operating for private profit (i.e., its passage from public to segregated owner and/or user ship). According to Dibie (2000), privatization is construed as the divestiture of State assets to private receivers, the transfer from State management to private auspices, and/or the consignment of State-run services to private suppliers (Dibie, 2000). It is the divestiture, or transfer of ownership and/or operational control, of productive economic entities to private owners, operators, and investors (Nellis, 2006).

The practice of modern privatization in Africa in general and Cameroon in particular was introduced by the colonial State. There is evidence that privatization played an important role in the establishment of colonialism. In fact, privatization and colonialism were intertwined. Almost all political colonization processes in Africa between the seventeenth and the twentieth century were preceded by economic privatization processes made possible by the ascent of entrepreneurial capital and financial liberalism supported by the political and military powers of the European nation-states. In essence, colonialism was an economic expansionism through the medium of privatization followed by political annexation. It was typically carried out in four steps: (1) a contract that opened a country up for trade and allowed foreign enterprises to exploit resources; (2) the resulting dependency of rulers and governments on Western credits to buy their goods and services; (3) the sale of land in exchange for credits and capital, resulting in the private ownership of large portions by foreign investors; and (4) the "protection" of these private assets through the creation of protectorates, and as a consequence often the annexation of a country by—or its inclusion into—the colonizing motherland. It was essentially for economic reasons that in 1884, the German government annexed the German Kamerun coast and later decided to penetrate the interior in order to discover and colonize new resources (Yanou & Foyam, 2008). Indigenous resources such as land and labor were privatized, and indigenes did not accept this and had to go to war with the Germans in order to resist this German-led privatization scheme. The Cameroon Development Corporation (CDC) was created in 1946 as an agro-industrial corporation on land confiscated by the Germans from indigenous Bakweri people of today's South West Region (World Ban Group, 2016; Yanou & Foyam, 2008). The Woermann, Jantzen, and Thoermalen firms were German firms that were firmly established at the coast of present-day Cameroon. When Britain and France took over Cameroon in 1916, they continued with the same capitalist economic system introduced by the Germans.

Generally, the failure of public enterprises to live up to the expectations of creditors and financiers has been put forward as the main reason behind privatization in developing countries (World Bank Group, 2016; Nellis, 2006). Rather than contribute to State budgets, public enterprises drained them. A high percentage failed to produce a sufficient quantity or a high quality of service or product. Particularly troublesome was a widespread failure to charge cost-covering tariffs in infrastructure/utility public enterprises; subsidies from government and soft budgets kept them afloat. These flaws eventually posed large financial burdens on government budgets—and attracted the attention of the international financial institutions and donors (Nellis, 2006). John Nellis (2006) explains the origin of the shortcomings in the mixing of social and political with economic objectives which weakened managerial autonomy, commercial performance, and efficiency. According to him,

> Government owners decreed that public enterprises operate in a commercial, efficient and profitable manner. At the same time they insisted that they finance their actions with debt rather than equity, provide goods and services at prices less than cost, generate employment, receive their inputs from state-sanctioned suppliers, choose plant location on political rather than commercial criteria, hire their staff on the basis of who rather than what they knew, etc.
>
> (Nellis, 2006)

According to Awung and Atanga (2011) the increasing revenue accruing from the Cameroon State—largely from the retention of farmer's surplus, and later from oil—led to the proliferation of parastatals as major players in the economy (Awung & Atanga, 2011). By 1988, for example, there were some 200 State-owned corporations covering virtually every sector of the national economy such as the Cameroon Shipping Lines (CAMSHIP) in the transport sector, the Cameroon Development Corporation (CDC) in the agricultural sector, the National Petroleum Corporation (SNH) in the oil sector, the Cameroon Telecommunications (INTELCAM/CAMTEL) in the telecommunications sector, the National Water Corporation (SNEC) in the water sector, the National Electricity Corporation (SONEL) in the energy sector, the Inter-Communal Fund for Equipment and Mutual Assistance (FEICOM) in the local government sector, the National Social Insurance Fund (CNPS) in the social sector, the National Oil Refinery (SONARA) in the oil refinery sector, and the National Cotton Development Corporation (SODECOTON) in the cotton sector, just to name these few.

However, these parastatals began operating at a loss by 1988 and the State was compelled to subsidies them to the tune of 150 billion Francs CFA annually. Worst of all, government involvement was seen to have ruined the management of the economy in some way. For example, governmental control of the National Produce Marketing Board (NPMB) limited the rural farmers' access to the international market and enabled the State to retain the surplus revenue derived from business with rural farmers (World Bank Group, 2016). In addition, as intermediary between the national private sector and the international private sector, the State was in a position to set a ceiling on national private sector's ability to have access to international business opportunities. Privatization was therefore seen as the "only" practical solution to economic difficulties and the problems of economic development but, again, the reasons behind privatization have varied from one State to another. Apart from being seen as solution to economic difficulties, privatization is inherently good following the findings of economist Adnan Filipovic (2005), who contends that privatization does not only create strong incentives that induce productivity but may also improve efficiency, provide fiscal relief, encourage wider ownership, and increase the availability of credit for the private sector (Filipovic, 2005).

In Cameroon, it was in 1989 that the President of the Republic was given the powers to decide on privatization (Loi, 1989). But it was in June 1990 that the President of the Republic for the first time signed an ordinance on the objectives and principles that govern privatization in Cameroon (BBC, 2o16). The basic official objectives of privatization are to reorganize public finance, to stimulate the private sector and promote investments, to increase market competition, and to redirect national savings toward productive investments. In article 3 of the 1990 ordinance, the privatization operations are carried out in the following ways: through total or partial transfer to the private sector of State shares in public enterprises, total or partial transfer of State assets to the private sector of the enterprise to be privatized, acceptance of investment capital or an increase of capital thereof from private physical and moral investors, through leasing to private physical and moral persons, through management contract of the public enterprise by private physical and moral persons. Although the ordinance does not say anything about the practical modalities of the privatization process, an effort was made to ensure transparency in the operation given that the privatization process had to be preceded by two major principles—namely, a preliminary evaluation of the public enterprise and an eventual competitive bidding system. According to the Ministry of the Economy and Finance (now Ministry of Finance), the principles that govern privatization are guarantees that rules of competition and transparency are respected, preliminary evaluation of the enterprises to be privatized, systematic reservation of a substantial capital of the enterprise to private nationals and staff, and the participation of all parties in the decision-making process.

In practice, although the privatization process began in the early 1990s, it was in 1999 that the President of the Republic signed a decree short listing the following public and para-public enterprises for privatization: Cimenteries Industrielles du Cameroun (CIMENCAM), Société Camerounaise des Dépôts Pétroliers (SCDP), Société Nationale de Eaux du Cameroun (SNEC), Société Nationale d'Electricité du Cameroun (SONEL), Cameroon Telecommunications (CAMTEL), and Cameroon Telecommunications-Mobiles (CAMTEL-MOBILE) (Government of Cameroon Decret No. 99/210). Out of a total of 171 public enterprises, 30 were shortlisted for privatization, but as of August 2013, 23 of the 30 were effectively privatized, as Table 13.2 indicates.

The observation that we can make from the table is that virtually every sector of the economy was affected by privatization: the primary, secondary, and tertiary. This is a display of government's commitment to reduce the grip of the State on economic activities. The second observation is that the majority of shareholders are foreigners. Together, foreigners account for 78.2% of capital shareholding in privatization in Cameroon. Cameroonians have been major shareholders in only three enterprises (namely, CAMSHIP,

Table 13.2 Enterprises privatized up to 2013

Enterprise	Date of transfer	Transferee	Share capital sold to foreigners	Major shareholder
1. BICEC	31 December 1999	Banques populaires	71% (France)	Foreigners
2. CAMSHIP	13 February 1997	Private foreign group	48.41% (France & Germany)	Cameroon
3. CAMSUCO	22 December 1998	SOMDIAA (JLV)	75% (France)	France
4. CAMTEL MOBILE	15 February 2000	MTN	100% (South Africa)	Foreigner
5. CEPER	14 September 1998	MUPEC	0%	Cameroon
6. CHOCOCAM	11 December 1995	Tiger Brands	74.41% (France)	Foreigner
7. CIMENCAM	ND	Lafarge Group	55% (France)	Foreigner
8. COCAM	19 December 1992	Khoury Group	87.6% (India & Pakistan)	Foreigner
9. HEVECAM	9 December 1996	GMG Investment	90% (USA)	Foreigner
10. Tea estate of CDC	18 October 2002	BROBON FINEX LIMITED	60% (South Africa)	Foreigner
11. OCB	15 February 1992	Compagnie frutière de Marseille	60% (France)	Foreigner
12. ONDAPB	13 February 1995	Fadil Private Foreign Group Daniel Yok (Muyuka)	34% (France)	Cameroon
13. REGIFERCAM	1 March 1999	BOLLORE-COMAZAR	77% (France & South Africa)	Foreigner
14. SCDM	30 June 1994	Hobum Afrika	86.61% (Germany)	Foreigner
15. SCM	1989	Private Cameroonian	0%	Cameroonian
16. SEPBC	11 April 1992	Foreign Private	70% (France)	Foreigner
17. SNEC	2 May 2008	ONEP Group	Morocco	ND

Enterprise	Date of transfer	Transferee	Share capital sold to foreigners	Major shareholder
18. SOCAMAC	3 October 1993	GEODIS	15% (France)	Foreigner
19. SOCAPALM	19 February 1999	PALCAM SOGEPART	90% (France)	Foreigner
20. SOCAR	July 1999	Chanas Assurances S.A	70%	Foreigner
21. SOFIBEL	13 December 1995	Fadil Group	50%	ND
22. SONEL	18 July 2001	AES Corp	51% (USA)	Foreigner
23. SPFS-SRL	13 February 1995	Fadil Group & others	63.49% (Switzerland)	Foreigner

Source: Republic of Cameroon Government of Decret No. 99/210 of 1990.

CEPER, and ONDAPB) while the other enterprises were bought over by foreigners (namely, the United States, Germany, France, South Africa, Switzerland, India, and Morocco). The question now is to know why fewer Cameroonians have been less responsive to privatization. Could it be that they could not afford to compete with foreign entrepreneurs? Could the problem be with the procedures of privatization itself? Could it also have been the willingness of government to have fewer Cameroonians own or partly own or run former public enterprises? Whatever interpretation one may give to the passive participation of Cameroonians in the privatization enterprise, the overall rate of privatization today stands at between 60% and 62%. In the eye of some commentators, this rate comes at a time when other important State-owned enterprises such as SCDP, CAMTEL, and CAMAIR-CO are still in the privatization pipeline (BBC News, 2016).

Public–Private Partnership and New Business Opportunities

The private sector is a partner to the recent economic development plans established by government as part of its economic development strategy. In its Vision 2035, Cameroon wants to be for the next 25 to 30 years an "Emerging, Democratic and United Country in Diversity" (GlobalEdge, 2016). Economically, Vision 2035 intends to transform Cameroon's economy into an emerging one that is based on sub-regional, regional, and global integration. At the macro-economic level, the vision highlights the need to accelerate growth by stepping up forest, agro-pastoral, and fishing activities and ensuring an industrial technological advancement with emphasis on the processing of local commodities. The vision also envisages changing the

Table 13.3 Cameroon's top 10 companies

No.	Names of companies	Types of business
1	SONARA	Oil and gas
2	SABC	Beverages
3	TOTAL	Cameroon oil and gas
4	Eneo Cameroon	Electricity
5	Group CFAO	Services
6	MTN Cameroon Telecom	Telecom
7	SODECOTON	Agroindustry
8	CAMTEL	Telecoms
9	Afriland First Bank	Financial services
10	Orange Cameroon	Telecom
11	ALUCAM	Manufacturing
12	Oil Libya	Oil and gas
13	Group PHP	Agroindustry
14	CDC	Agroindustry
15	CIMENCAM	Manufacturing
16	Dangote Cement	Manufacturing

Source: Cameroon Economic Review (2015). *United States and Cameroon Relations.* 1st Quarter, *1*(1), (February). 7–10

structure of the economy; from a primary sector economy (agriculture and extraction) and informal tertiary activities to a more powerful secondary sector, and an intensive primary sector, a professional, specialized tertiary sector that creates decent jobs. For this goal to be achieved, the vision advocates the stepping up of investments as growth engine through the formation of partnerships with the private sector.

Cameroon's top economic sectors that have potential business opportunities are (1) Agro-industry, (2) Energy; (3) Oil and Gas; (4) Mining; (5) Public Sector Infrastructure, Utilities; (5) Transport; (6) Services; (7) Manufacturing; (8) Telecommunication; (9) Financial Services; and (10) Tourism.

That is why in the Poverty Reduction Strategy Paper (PRSP), the economic role of the State is defined as one of partnership with the private local sector, civil society, and technical and financial international partners. The objectives of this paper is to increase growth rate to an average of 5.5% annually between 2010 and 2020, reduce under-employment from 75.8% to at least 50% by 2020, reduce poverty by 28% in 2020, and meet the Millennium Development Goals (MDG) by 2020. However, the 5.5% annual increase in growth rate has not been met, although partnership with the private sector has been strengthened. Elaborated in 2003 with the participation of public authorities, economic operators, civil society, and development partners, PRSP is now considered as the framework of reference that defines the terms of partnership between the public and private sector. For example, one of the strategic management functions of the State to enhance public-private partnership (PPP), as spelt out in the PRSP, is to fight against contraband, fraud, and other illicit traffics as a means to protect the private sector.

In order to further strengthen the relations between the public and private sector, the government has made an effort to promote Development Partnerships with the Private Sector (DPP) in key areas, sometimes with the assistance of foreign development bodies. It established a general legal framework for PPP in the years 2006 to 2009, and some partnerships for larger infrastructure projects (highways, port, and shopping malls) have been concluded. Such PPPs are considered an important option for major public works in Cameroon's Growth and Employment Strategy Paper (GESP; World Bank Group, 2016). A DPP-Day was organized in June 2013 to inform and familiarize stakeholders from the public and private sector with the concept of Social Contract Partnerships (SCP) within the framework of the Partnership Landscape Analysis (PLA). Various projects were presented as examples. The DPP-day is followed up with public and private stakeholders interested in DPP and in new forms of cooperation.

The Support Council for the Realization of Partnership Contracts (CARPA) is a public body in charge of the development and implementation of partnerships and multi-actor development planning with the private sector and other relevant actors in Cameroon. The main objective of this body is to have the private sector involved in and contribute to the realization of development goals. Table 13.4 summarizes recent and ongoing DPP.

The table reveals that DPP is concerned with almost all sectors, even though third party contribution is insignificant. It also indicates that the years between 2011 and 2013 marked a turning point in DPP, given that seven DPPs were initiated and concretized. This DPP trend is expected to continue, particularly with the introduction of the Three-Year Economic Emergency Plan.

The Three-Year Economic Emergency Plan launched by the president of the republic in response to the failure of the PRSP to increase annual growth rate by 5.5% is another economic plan that has enhanced PPP. This three-year development plan earmarked for execution by the government concerns all 10 regions and will cost FCFA 925 billion. Seen as an innovative program, the plan, which has seven sectors, also contains the names of banks that will finance the projects, as well as the conditions for success and follow-up so as to guarantee the required results. The plan is due to receive support from private financial institutions, as indicated in Table 13.5.

It is observed from the table that five private financial institutions are effectively involved in the economic development of Cameroon. And this is the testimony of the government's inclusive economic policy.

Table 13.4 Cameroon's ongoing development partnerships with the private sector (DPP)

Title	Partner	Start	End	Public contribution	Private contribution	Contribution by third partners	Total	Sector
Charcoal production from sawmill waste	SFID	03/11	12/13	112,700 Euros	118,583 Euros		231,283 Euros	Environment
The Business Coalition Against Corruption in Cameroon	BCA	12/11	11/13	192,950 Euros	200,000 Euros		392,950 Euros	Good governance
Access to solar energy under a bottom pyramid approach	TOTAL	12/11	11/13	154,950 Euros	154,950 Euros		309,900 Euros	Energy
Partnership in Sustainable Development in Massok, Songloulou, and Pouma	AES-SONEL	12/11	12/13	186,411 Euros	200,873 Euros		387,284 Euros	Sust. economic development
Mutual health insurance for cocoa farmers	Société Jaco SA	01/13	12/13	10,210 Euros	14,230 Euros		24,440 Euros	Health
Viable agricultural lending based on good agricultural practices and farmer business skills	CAMCUL	02/12	12/13	90,000 Euros	90,000 Euros		180,000 Euros	Agriculture
Support for production and marketing of charcoal	GRUMCAM	03/12	12/13	20,000 Euros	22,000 Euros		42,000 Euros	Environment
Workplace program: HIV/AIDS, tuberculosis, and malaria prevention	GFBC	01/07	12/13	727,521 Euros	1,010,899 Euros	353,578 Euros	2,091,998 Euros	Health

Source: GIZ, Cooperation with the Private Sector in Cameroon, *Country Report*, 2013.

Table 13.5 Private banking support for the three-year economic emergency plan

No.	Banking institution	Amount in US dollars
1	Deutsche Bank	17 million
2	BGFI Cameroon	200 million
3	Ecobank	70 million
4	Standard Chartered Bank Cameroon	600 million
5	Bank Atlantic Cameroon	380 million

Source: Cameroon Economic Review (2015: 9).

Conclusion

This chapter has examined business and government relations in Cameroon. It argues that although the State remains the major regulator of the economy in Cameroon, its economic reform policies since the 1990s has been to strategically associate the private sector in the process of economic decision making. The sustainable development strategic plan of the country includes increasing production, enhancing trade and distribution of agricultural crops, and attracting appropriate technology and economic growth.

After exploring the connection between business and government in Cameroon and some policy options of the government in dealing with the challenges that beset this sector, it is important to state clearly that there is every evidence that the government or the State has done a lot to correct the ills of the past in the country. In addition, the Government of Cameroon has done much to protect its population as well as local business from the power of ruthless multinational corporations. On the other hand, the fact remains true that a lot still has to be done for the local consumers as well as for the local, small, and medium size companies that struggle beyond reasonable measure for their ends to meet.

The domestic inheritance of mistrust and cynicism between government and business is profound. The testimonies of some members of the Cameroon corporate world complain incessantly about all kinds of harassments, and sometimes they worry that there is a huge divide between what the law prescribes and what actually occurs. Elsewhere such complaints have been attributed to a system of government that existed prior to the opening up of the economy (Honore @ Nkama 2009). However, the central contention is that a mutually beneficial *modus vivendi* between business and government in the SADC, and Africa more broadly, can only be achieved once the domestic relationship is grounded on trust, free and open communication, and mutuality of interest.

In this chapter, economic diplomacy is seen as the crafting of enabling policy and departmental strategies to facilitate and enhance the country's strategic objectives in Africa and globally. Within this spectrum are aspects such as, but not limited to, the promotion of regional integration strategies; deep engagement with new partnership projects; trade negotiations, a proper management and reform of the customs sector, and the drive toward a greater free trade zone. At this level, the Government of Cameroon is doing more than enough under the distinguished guidance of the President of the Republic and Head of State. On the other, the Government of Cameroon continues to confront the challenges of its economic growth in all ramifications. Although, there are incremental progress in finance, markets, planning and regional development, higher education, professional training, scientific research and geological research, trade and industry, commerce, and so on. Some scholar have argued that negotiating and signing cooperation ties that boost the local economy, the population, and eventually the multinational or international interest is essential (Ferragina et al 2012; Oyejide 2009). This must to a very great extent, given greater prominence to economic diplomacy in its foreign interactions, recognizing the centrality of this to Cameroon's economic interests. In still the same vein, financial and commercial diplomacy, which are major aspects of economic diplomacy, should also be taken good care of in the system. Procedures and rules should be redefined and refined so that there is little interaction between potential buyers, consumers, and traders.

The interest of this chapter was to describe the nature of business and government relations in the economy of Cameroon. The findings reveal that although the State is ever present in the economy, public-private sector relationship has improved tremendously. Public-private partnership is a reality, and this is as a result of the efforts of the government in regulating and implementing an inclusive economic policy through progressive economic deregulation. However, much still remains to be done for consumers and local producers to be well protected against merciless multinationals, most of whom depend on our weak economies for their survival and growth.

References

Ajab, A. A. (2002). *An Examination of the Sources of Economic Growth in Cameroon*. AER Research Paper No. 116, African Economic Research Consortium, Nairobi, The Regal Press.

Alia, D. Y. et al. (2015). Economic Policies and Informal Sector Performance in Cameroon: A CGE Analysis. In *Ministry of Economy, Planning and Regional Development*. Cameroon.

Awung, J. W. and Atanga, M. (2011). Economic Crisis and Multi-Party Politics in Cameroon. *Journal on Democracy and Human Rights*, 5(1), 94–127.

BBC News. (2016). *Cameroon Country Profile*. www.bbc.com/news/world-africa-13146029. Accessed October 21, 2016.

Cameroon Economic Review. (2015, February). *United States and Cameroon Relations*. 1st Quarter, 1(1), 7–10.

Cameroon Economic Update. (2012, January). Unlocking the Labor Force: An Economic Update on Cameroon With a Focus on Employment. Issue No. 3.

GICAM Bulletin (2015): Note sur la Crise Economique; 107e Assamblee Generale; Yaounde, Cameroon (May), Government Press, 9–21

Dibie, R. (2000). Understanding Public Policy in Nigeria: A Twenty-First Century Approach, Lagos, Nigeria: Mbeyi & Associates.

Ferragina, E. Seeleibe-Kaiser and Tominson, M. (2012). "Unemployment Protection and Family Policy at the Turn of the 21st Century: A Dynamic Approach to Welfare Regime Theory. http://onlinelibrary.wiley.com/doi/10.1111/j.1467-9515.2012. 00855.x/full. Accessed May 2016.

Filipovic, A. (2005, August). Impact of Privatization on Economic Growth. *Issues in Political Economy*, 4–36

GIZ. (2013). *Cooperation With the Private Sector in Cameroon, Country Report.* Yaounde: Government of Cameroon Publication.

Global Edge. (2016). *Cameroon Economic and Trade Statistics.* http://globaledge. msuedu/countries/cameroon/tradestats. Accessed October 20, 2016.

Government of Cameroon. (1999). *Decret No. 99/210 du 22 of September (1999).* Portant admission de certaines entreprises du secteur public et para-public à la procédure de privatisation.

Honore, A. and Nkama, G. (2009). "Analyzing the Impact of the Global Economic and Financial Crisis in Cameroon." UNDP Yaounde, Cameroon. http://dspace. africaportal.org/jspui/bitstream/123456789/32291/1/Nkama-Financial.pdf?1. Accessed September 15, 2016.

Hope, K. R. (1997). African Political Economy: Contemporary Issues in Development. New York: M.E Sharpe.

Law No. 2002/04 of 19th April. (2002). *Relating to the Republic of Cameroon's Investment Charter.* Yaoundé: Government of Cameroon Publication.

Loi No. 89/030 du 29 Décembre. (1989). Habilitant le Président de la République à légéferer par Ordinance en matière de privatisation des entreprises publiques et para-publiques.

Nellis, J. (2006). *Privatization in Developing Countries: A Summary Assessment.* Center for Global Development, Working Paper No. 87.

Organization for Economic Co-operation and Development (OECD). (2010). *Privatization in the 21st Century: Summary of Rect Experiences.* https://link.springer. com/article/10.1057/eps.2010.27. Accessed September 15, 2016.

Oyejide, A. (2009): Impact of the Glbal Crisis on Africa's Trade and Investment; Addis Ababa, Ethiopia: UNDP Publication.

Raipuria, K. and Mehta, R. (1991). Role of Public and Private Sectors in India's Development: Selected Simulations From a Macroeconomic Model. *Economic and Political Weekly*, 26(31–32), 1873–1875.

United States Embassy Yaounde- Cameroon. (2016). *Doing Business in Cameroon.* https://yaounde.usembassy.gov/doing-business-local.html. Accessed October 20, 2016.

World Bank. (2014). *Doing Business 2015: Going Beyond Efficiency.* Washington, DC: World Bank Group.

World Bank Group. (2016). World Bank Publication (2016). *Doing Business: Assessing Business Environment in Cameroon.* www.doingbusiness.org/ExploreEconomies/Default.aspx?economyid=101. Accessed October 21, 2016.

Yanou, M. and Foyam, J. (2008). Trade Unions, Labor Contracts and Industrial Peace: The Case of Tole Tea Estate. *Revue Africaine des Sciences Juridiques FSJP UYII*, 5(1), 25–32.

Yuh, J. (2009). A Descriptive Analysis of the Rights of Workers in the Informal Sector in Cameroon. *CJDHR*, 3(2), 17–25.

14 Business and Government Relations in Tanzania

Chinyeaka Justine Igbokwe-Ibeto

Introduction

A number of theoretical models provide many compelling reasons why effective business and government relations (GBRs) would stimulate economic growth and national development. Indeed, the relationship between the state and business in forging economic growth and development has been an enduring area of research for both economists and political scientists since the Industrial Revolution of the seventeenth century. Since independence in 1961, the relationship between the state and business community in the United Republic of Tanzania has varied. Tanzania, like any other developing economy, is faced with its challenges in government business relations. However, significant measures have been taken to liberalize the Tanzanian economy along market lines and encourage both foreign and domestic private investment. Beginning in 1986, following the voluntary retirement of President Julius Nyerere, the Government of Tanzania embarked on an adjustment program to dismantle state economic controls and encourage more active participation of the private sector in the economy. Apart from pursuing a vigorous free-market economic, industrial, and trade policy, it also adopted a liberalized investment policy, with the goal of attracting foreign investment as well as promoting joint ventures between foreign and local investors. Certain social, political, and economic patterns of change have emerged, such as a comprehensive package of policies that reduced the budget deficit and improved monetary control, substantially depreciated the overvalued exchange rate, liberalized the trade regime, removed most price controls, eased restrictions on the marketing of food crops, freed interest rates, and initiated a restructuring of the financial sector and an expanding private sector and the establishment of legal and regulatory structures (UNCTAD, 2010).

The economy of Tanzania is overwhelmingly agricultural; plantations grow cash crops, including coffee, sisal, tea, cotton, pyrethrum, cashews, tobacco, sugarcane, and cloves (cultivated in Zanzibar and Pemba). Most of the population, however, is engaged in subsistence farming, growing corn, wheat, cassava, bananas, fruits, and vegetables. In addition, large numbers of cattle, sheep, and goats are raised. Timber is important and includes mahogany, teak, ebony, camphor wood, and mangrove. Manufactures include processed agricultural goods, beverages, wood products, and basic consumer items. Refined petroleum, fertilizer, aluminum goods, and construction materials are also produced. Diamonds, tanzanite, and other gemstones are mined; other minerals extracted in significant quantities include gold, salt, gypsum, phosphates, and kaolin. There are also tin mines in northwest Tanzania and coal and iron ore deposits near Lake Nyasa. Natural gas from deposits around Songo Island, off the south central coast, are used to produce electricity (Makoye, 2013).

Accounting for less than 10% of GDP, Tanzania's industrial sector is one of the smallest in Africa. It was hard hit during the 2002–2003 drought years and again in 2005–2006 by persistent power shortages caused by low rainfall in the hydroelectric dam catchment area, a condition compounded by years of neglect and bad management at the state-controlled electric company. The main industrial activities (90%) are dominated by small and medium sized enterprises (SMEs) specializing in food processing including dairy products, meat packing, preserving fruits and vegetables, production of textile and apparel, leather tanning and plastics. A few larger factories (10%) manufacture cement, rolled steel, corrugated iron, aluminum sheets, cigarettes, beer and bottling beverages, fruit juices, and mineral water. Other factories produce raw materials, import substitutes, and processed agricultural products. Poor infrastructure in water and electricity supply systems continues to hinder factory production. In general, Tanzania's manufacturing sector targets primarily the domestic market with limited exports.

Despite Tanzania's past record of political stability, an unattractive investment climate has discouraged foreign investment. Government steps to improve government business relations include redrawing tax codes, floating the exchange rate, licensing foreign banks, and creating an investment promotion center to cut red tape. In terms of mineral resources and the largely untapped tourism sector, Tanzania could become a viable and attractive market for US goods and services.

Zanzibar's economy is based primarily on the production of cloves (90% grown on the island of Pemba), the principal foreign exchange earner (World Bank, 2012). Exports have suffered with the downturn in the clove market. In 1992, the government designated two export-producing zones and encouraged the development of offshore financial services. Zanzibar still imports much of its staple requirements, petroleum products, and manufactured articles. Tourism is a promising sector, and a number of new hotels and resorts have been built in recent years.

The Government of Zanzibar legalized foreign exchange bureaus on the islands before the mainland Tanzania moved to do so. The effect was to increase the availability of consumer commodities. Furthermore, with external funding, the Government of Zanzibar plans to make the port of Zanzibar a free port. In 2007, the rehabilitation of Zanzibar's sport facilities commenced with assistance from European donors. The island's manufacturing sector is limited mainly to import substitution industries, such as cigarettes, shoes, and process agricultural products.

Cognizant of the enormous danger posed by the dwindling economy, an Investment Policy Review (IPR) was conducted and published in 2002 by the Tanzanian government. The report recommended a strategic thrust for investment promotion, along with strategies for creating a more attractive and enabling environment for investors in the country, such as strengthening the investment framework as well as reducing the cost of doing business. It also addressed the issue of continued privatization, stimulating human resource development (HRD), infrastructure development, as well as building a dynamic and robust business enterprise sector (UNCTAD, 2010).

Since the IPR was published, foreign direct investment (FDI) inflows into the country have witnessed a steady increase, at an annual average of 28% since 2003 (UNCTD, 2011). However, it appears the overall progress made in implementation of IPR has generated a mixed bag. Therefore, this chapter seeks to x-ray the efficacy or otherwise of institutional arrangements put in place by various governments to promote government business relations in Tanzania aimed at promoting economic growth and national development.

The chapter adopts a qualitative approach of the disciplines of business management, political science, economics, and organizational management to explore business and government relations in Tanzania. Secondary data include review of statutory literature such as the Constitution of the United Republic of Tanzania, Acts of Parliament, Statutes, Ujamaa policy, codes, contracts, rules, and procedures and conventions establishing institutions. The chapter examines how business and government relations has improved lives, strengthened communities, and fostered civic engagement through consumer protection and employment. Both the private and public sectors in Tanzania have expanded the ability of informal organizations to fight poverty. Rather than providing services to low income individuals and communities, the government in Tanzania has collaborated with businesses in the country to strengthen and support entrepreneurs. This in return has helped NGOs, businesses, and government by building infrastructure, enhancing technology, expanding community partnership, securing long-term resources, coordinating training for citizens, and alleviating poverty in the country. The purpose here is to examine the characteristics of formal and informal rules and regulations governing the establishment and operation of businesses, how these have evolved over time, and how they may have impacted on economic growth in Tanzania.

Conceptualizing Business and Government Relations

Most of the development theories that emerged in the early nineteenth century examined economic and political relations among both developed and developing countries. While many theorists commented on the relations between the state and society which also comprised economic groups, development remained the overarching focus of such studies; much of what was discussed had direct bearings on the relationship between emergent states in the developing world and how economic agents interacted (Ackah et al., 2010). The relationship between states and markets were then conceived in ideological terms. Capitalists who wrote after Adam Smith emphasized the importance of markets in generating wealth. Most observers and commentators claim that markets can self-regulate. Marxists writers, on the other hand, introduce class relations to showcase how state and markets operate with claims that dominant classes who control wealth creation in most polities capture the state to pass laws and institutions that favor their interest. In between these two extreme positions on state and markets, many variant views were suggested to explain specific circumstances.

Economic theorists such as Martinussen (1997) see the state as "an important initiator and catalyst of growth and development." However, what still remains contentious is how states are conceptualized. Martinussen (1997) went further to list two major approaches and four dimensions of the state. A "society-centered" approach attaches much importance to societal structures and social forces that exert greater impact on what becomes the state such that state power, apparatus, and functions derive from economic agents and social forces of societies (Poulantzas, 1978). "State-centered" approaches give greater autonomy to state apparatuses and state personnel who act independently of economic agents, social classes, or interest groups (OECD, 2010). A cardinal point about discretionary powers of political leaders is shared by dialectic modernization theorists like (Balile, 2013), who argue that African rulers' personality takes precedence over rules. State-business relations take place in such political environments where patron-client relationships exist throughout Africa (Chapain et al 2013).

According to Ackah et al. (2010), in the absence of a legal framework that ensures security of property; impartial public services that directly facilitate production; and the regulation of foreign economic relations that maximizes national interest, informal ties like blood relations, ethnic origins, and personal access to political leadership dictate the pace of GBR in many parts of Africa. At this juncture, it is imperative we have a brief review of Ujamaa policy under Nyerere.

An Overview of Julius Nyerere's Ujamaa Philosophy

Mwalimu Kambarage Julius Nyerere, the central character in this review, will be recognized by the readers as an enormously creative conceptualizer, a far-sighted pioneer, a selfless role model, an almost dangerously courageous champion of righteous campaigns in Africa and the Third World as a whole, a fearless confronter of nations and institutions that tried to interfere with Tanzania's self-determination, a unifier of a vast and diverse economy and people, and a man of the people. Julius Nyerere was the President of the

United Republic of Tanzania between April 1964 and October 1985, when he retired out of his own free will but continued to influence the Tanzania political scene until his death on October 14, 1999, in a London hospital from leukemia. He was the architect of an exemplary mode of uniting two sovereign states in Africa (UNDP, 2012) in which, despite the existence of all the ingredients of disunity, has endured for over four decades now.

A plethora of published works exist on Nyerere and the Ujamaa experiment in Tanzania, particularly in the 1970s when the reforms in Tanzania caught world attention, leading to the long-drawn debate about the merits and demerits of the experiment. Indeed, the discourse over Ujamaa became a thriving industry for academics and popular writers.

According to Mesaki and Malipula (2011), Julius Nyerere's central domestic preoccupations during the period of his presidency were fourfold: (i) promoting the development of Tanzanian economy, which he saw as a sine qua non for the accomplishment of most if not all other objectives; (ii) securing and retaining national control of the direction of Tanzania's economic development; (iii) creating political institutions that would be widely participatory and that would sustain the extraordinary sense of common purpose which in its early years united Tanzanians under his leadership and that of the Tanzanian African National Union (TANU); (iv) building a just society in Tanzania, free of severe income inequalities, in which all would share the benefits of development as it was accomplished (Pratt, 1999). In a policy booklet published in March 1967 on "Education for Self-Reliance," Nyerere spelled out the values and objectives of the society he envisioned as follows: "we want to create a socialist society which is based on three principles: equality and respect for human dignity; sharing of the resources which are produced by our efforts; work by everyone and exploitation by none" (Mesaki & Malipula, 2011).

At the heart of Nyerere's core values was an affirmation of the fundamental equality (Balile, 2013) of all humankind and a commitment to the building of social, economic, and political institutions, which would reflect and ensure this equality. He frequently presented his views on socialism as an expression of values, which he felt to be an essential ethical component of a departing African way of life. Nyerere recognized that the social values of traditional Tanzania were rapidly being undermined. Even before 1967, Nyerere argued that Tanzanians must find a way to progress economically and would not undermine the communal equality of their society. Nyerere realized, from the earliest days of his leadership, that his society needed modern educated men and women to lead it forward but that the members of these elites were bound to be tempted to set their aspirations by reference to the levels of material welfare enjoyed by the elites of other much richer societies. He knew very well that the material ambitions of the emerging African bourgeoisie were powerful and hard to contain. His socialist doctrine was eloquently expounded in the famous Arusha Declaration, a doctrine he had formulated and had the blessings of the ruling party, TANU.

The Arusha Declaration of 1967 was one of his most influential pieces of writing. The declaration defined the meaning of socialism in the context of Tanzania.

Inherent in the declaration was the rejection of material wealth for its own sake. It was a commitment to the belief that there are more important things in life than the amassing of riches and that if the pursuit of wealth clashes with things like human dignity and social equality, then the latter will be given priority. His faith in socialism was an expression of values which he felt to be the distinctive ethical core of departing African traditional way of life. His blueprint was his vision of traditional African culture. In pre-colonial Africa, he argued that the three aforementioned sectors were self-reliant, democratic, and egalitarian, respectively. Nyerere's vision of traditional Africa was largely characterized by equality.

Nyerere also wrote about a person's right "to live in dignity and equality with others." According to Pratt (1999), Nyerere strive to achieve material "equity"—not necessarily equality, but less stratification in wealth. According to Mesaki and Malipula (2011), ingrained in the Arusha Declaration was a clear-cut code of ethics for party leaders to abide with which excluded economic exploitation of the masses by those in positions of control in the top echelons of the government.

From a religious point of view, it amounted to a covenant between the party/government and the people as a woman missionary put it, "Nyerere's ujamaa philosophy acknowledged the deeply human and indeed religious aspirations it signified. Ujamaa looked at the traditional extended family as a symbol. To Balile (2013), Ujamaa signified the hope of turning the whole nation into relatives who would care for each other . . . it was utopian in the sense of providing a vision of alternative social relations, especially in contrast to the increasingly capitalist relations, that had come into the country through colonialism." Mesaki and Malipula (2011) refers to Ujamaa as a paradoxical occasion in which Nyerere is said to have likened Tanzanian socialism to "the religion of socialism and self-reliance" without elaborating.

Prior to his death in 1999, Nyerere was asked about the continued validity of the Arusha Declaration, to which he retorted, "I still travel with it. I read it over and over to see what I would change. May be I would improve on the Kiswahili that was used but the declaration is still valid, I would not change a thing" (See *New Internationalist Magazine* Issue 309, 1999). According to Mesaki and Malipula (2011), shortly after he voluntarily stepped down as President of Tanzania in 1985, Nyerere had declared that "although socialism has failed in Tanzania, I will remain a socialist because I believe socialism is the best policy for poor countries like Tanzania."

Beyond Failure of Ujamaa as a Development Paradigm

The issue that two decades of nationalization and the village oriented (Ujamaa) policy of Julius Nyerere neither helped launch Tanzania into economic prosperity nor ensured its economic self-reliance is now hardly a matter for contention (Chapain et al, 2013). What remains an issue of debate, however, is what broad interpretations can be made on the influence and legacy of Ujamaa as a development strategy. The quest for answers to this question has attracted the attention of several scholars who basically fall into two opposing schools of thought (Green, 1995; Yeager, 1989; OCED 2003; Ergas, 1980; Hyden, 1980; Freyhold, 1979; Raikes, 1975).

According to Nursey-Bray (1980), the first school of thought argues that the Ujamaa policies were unmitigated failures and that Under Nyerere, Tanzania's economic progress was distorted and resources wasted in the "slavish adherence to ideology," giving rise to a marginalized rural sector and a corrupt and inefficient bureaucracy.

It is thus concluded that Nyerere's idealism was detrimental to the country's development. Through his failed economic schemes, he left this country poorer than it would have been under less utopian-minded leadership. Proponents of the second school, while conceding that the economic achievements of Ujamaa were quite modest, point to significant successes in social welfare terms, such as the provision of health and educational facilities; a movement toward greater social equality in income distribution; the maintenance of political stability; and the achievement of a substantial degree of harmony between the country's ethnic groups. It is thus contended that quite apart from the criterion of economic performance, it is necessary to examine the extent of social progress, which attended Nyerere's development strategy (Ishemo, 2000; Pratt, 1999; Legum & Mmari, 1995). These are issues worth addressing in any appraisal of Ujamaa as a development experiment.

Although Ujamaa can be described as a kind of state corporatism, the party-state system sought to mediate interests in such a way as to achieve the creation of a self-reliant socialization without the reliance on an elite vanguard group. While in certain instances state officials used coercive means to ensure the implementation of Ujamaa policies, especially the village oriented program, only the most sanguine Nyerere bashers would argue that he was a dictator. To World Bank (2009), Mutahaba and Okema (1990), Nyerere sought to institutionalize a relatively participatory political and social process from the early days of independence and throughout the transition to a multi-party system. In this regard, the village orientation scheme, in spite of some of the abuses associated with it implementation process, was a harbinger of social welfare development. The Ujamaa villages were seen as the most important units for the provision of social resources to the majority of the people. Under the policy of education for self-reliance, these villages became very important centers for the promotion of literacy among both adults and children. According to Samoff (1990), by the early 1980s, even in the face of economic difficulties, Tanzania had one of the highest literacy rates in Africa, with every village boasting of at least a primary school. Ninety percent of these villages had at least one village cooperative store, while over 60% had relatively easy access to safe and clean water supply, a health center, or dispensary (Africa Now, 1981). As a result, a village oriented program provided a bridge in the gulf between urban and rural dwellers by ensuring the latter's access to basic social amenities.

Despite wide criticism and agreement on the failure of Nyerere's economic policies, several writers have identified Tanzania's most notable national achievement as its ability to create a strong sense of national identity among Tanzanians and in the advances made in terms of social welfare. Few sub-Saharan African countries have achieved the level of national unification that Tanzania did under the leadership of Nyerere. Under Nyerere and his successor, Ali Hassan Mwiyi (1985–1995), the Tanzanian mainland was largely spared the ethnic and regionalist politics that have proved so dysfunctional in Kenya, so catastrophic in Rwanda and Burundi, and so prevalent throughout the rest of the continent (Chapain et al, 2013; UNCTAD, 2011). Whether these social and political gains of the Ujamaa policy really adequately compensate for its economic shortcomings is open to debate. What is important, however, is to recognize the need to transcend the emphasis on purely economic and GDP criteria in evaluating the legacy of Ujamaa. The relative political stability that Tanzania (unlike most of her neighbors) enjoyed during the Nyerere years is one that cannot be appreciated in economic terms. Indeed, the legacy of stability that Nyerere's policies promoted in Tanzania has allowed the country to remain one of the most stable countries in Africa (Ibhawoh & Dibua, 2013).

Strengthen Business and Government Relations

Following failure of Ujamaa as a development policy, the Government of Tanzania began to search for a paradigm shift in its development approach. It will be recalled that an Investment Policy Review (IPR) was conducted in 2002 and one of the recommendation of IPR is the strengthening of investment framework in Tanzania. In the past two decades, the Government of Tanzania has made significant progress in the paradigm shift from a centrally planned economy to a market based regime (World Bank, 2012). The reform process has been maintained at a rate that has outpaced reforms to the statutes (UNCTD, 2011). As a result, the IPR identified several key legislative areas affecting FDI, which should be brought in line with the reformed government business relations. These include the following.

Employment and Labor Laws

The IPR was primarily concerned with the difficulty that investors in the United Republic of Tanzania were facing in terminating or laying off employees. Investors were wary of creating jobs and hiring permanent workers until the worker's competence had been proved. The IPR also noted that the labor laws from before the 1990s were onerous and complex. During the drafting of the IPR, the Ministry of Labor was working to reform labor laws. Initially, this entailed simplifying existing legislation and processes. A new law—the Employment and Labor Relations Act—was introduced in 2004, becoming effective in 2007 (see section 4.4).

Commercial Disputes, Contract Law, the Arbitration Act and the Companies Act

Commercial dispute settlement and contract enforcement were identified as problematic for investors. The laws were considered outdated and inconsistent, and were found to have gaps with regard to modern business organizations, modern commercial practices, and modern business systems and technologies.

Commercial dispute settlement and arbitration is dealt within the 1997 Investment Act, which has yet to be updated. Contract enforcement is codified in the Law of Contract Act, 1961, which also has not been updated. The new 2002 Companies Act, which came into effect in 2006, repealed the Companies Ordinance (Cap. 212), 1932. Some salient aspects of the new Act are reducing the minimum number of people required to establish a company to two, and reducing the amount of information required in the memorandum to the registrar (a document necessary for business registration). In the past, new companies were required to list explicitly all activities of the company. This has been simplified so that companies can now describe their intended activities in more general terms. Changing the activities or reducing capital investment no longer requires court approval, unless there is a challenge by shareholders or creditors (UNCTAD 2011; UNDP 2012). It should be noted that the mainland Tanzanian and Zanzibar Governments do not have the same laws and regulations, and that they enforce them separately. For the purposes of this chapter, only the mainland is being assessed.

Tourism and Fishing

As strategic priorities, both tourism and fishing have been governed by outdated laws which were drawn up in a less internationally competitive market. To begin to attract FDI to these sectors, once FDI in lead sectors such as mining was established, the IPR recognized the importance of modernizing the regulations governing these sectors. In line with the IPR recommendation, the Government replaced the Hotel Act, 1963, and the Tourist Agency Licensing Act, 1969, with the Tourism Act, 2008. It also replaced Fisheries Act No. 6 of 1970 with Fisheries Act No. 22 of 2003.

The Fair Trade Practices Act of 1994 and the Fair Trade Practices Commission

The Fair Trade Practices Act of 1994 was passed to address competition issues that the newly established market economy was facing. In 2001 it was amended and became the Fair Competition Act (UNDESA, 2010). At that time, the Act addressed economic regulation and competition together. The Appellant Mechanism Tribunal was not established in accordance with the Act and the Commissioner acted in the capacity of advisor, while one person made rulings. The IPR recommended that the Fair Competition Act be reviewed and the Fair Trade Practices Commission be strengthened.

A new Competition Act was introduced in 2003, which separated economic and competition regulation, and established the Fair Competition Commission (FCC) along with other regulatory bodies for areas such as marine and surface transport, energy and water, communications, and aviation (World Bank 2009, OECD 2010). Companies or individuals can now approach the FCC or the other regulatory bodies listed previously with complaints, and if unsatisfied with the decision, can appeal through the Appellant Tribunal established by the new Act. The Tribunal is chaired by a High Court judge, with final decisions being made jointly by five commissioners.

The FCC has been strengthened, although there has been some decline in resources since the World Bank shifted responsibility for funding to the Government in 2009. Training uses up a large portion of the budget, as many of the staff recruited are not well versed in competition-related issues and regulations. The FCC does recoup approximately 5% to 10% of its budget through fines for anticompetitive offenses. In addition to the ability to impose fines, the FCC can impose compliance orders and order companies to pay compensation for damage.

Investment Climate

The government has undertaken a number of measures to improve the government relations. The most notable of these are the passage of Tanzania Investment Act of 1997 (repealing the 1990 NIPPA) and of the 1998 Mining Act. The latter has had a far-reaching impact on establishing clear incentives for the mining industry in Tanzania. In addition the Tanzania Investment Center was established in the place of the Investment Promotion Center and mandated as a "one-stop" center to facilitate the process of setting up business operations in Tanzania (see Doingbuiness.org).

However, the IPR found that the 1997 Act was rapidly becoming obsolete. It no longer had relevance to issues such as the functions of the Tanzania Investment Centre (TIC), and it contained references to Acts no longer in existence (e.g., the Sales Tax Act which was replaced by the VAT Act) and to the Certificate of Incentives. As a result, the IPR recommended that the Act be replaced by a new and up-to-date Act. Other areas that the IPR felt required review were the minimum investment thresholds, which may exclude some investments. The IPR recommended that these be lowered to levels that would be competitive with other African countries. It also prescribed a review of the vague and unspecified investment incentives included in the Act, which could lead to Report on the Implementation of the Investment Policy Review United Republic of Tanzania arbitrariness or discrimination among investors. So far, the Act has not been revised; however, TIC has created a Certificate of Incentives that provides clear, specific incentives for investors (World Bank, 2012).

The legal framework for FDI thus has become increasingly transparent. For example, foreign investment law protects against expropriation and guarantees investors' rights to repatriate profits, dividends, loan repayments, and fees (KPMG, 2012). In 1999 a commercial court was established to expedite resolution of commercial disputes and to facilitate enforcement of legal contracts, with the aim of keeping the average period for case resolution to six months or less.

Initiatives such as the Investors' Round Table (IRT) and the program for business environment strengthening in Tanzania (BEST) were instituted to seek investors' views and provide strategic focus for the government's efforts to create an environment supportive of private investment. In this context, the then president Benjamin Mkapa met biannually with chief executive officers (CEOs) of global companies interested in investing in Tanzania. Finally, the National Business Council and the Private Sector Foundation were established by local businesses, in conjunction with the government, to enhance public–private sector partnerships. Despite some improvement in the legal and regulatory framework, many challenges remain.

Table 14.1 Contract enforcement in selected African countries, 2012

Country	Number of procedures[a]	Duration[b]	Formalism index[c]
Kenya	25	255	3.09
Mozambique	18	240	4.48
South Africa	11	84	1.68
Tanzania	14	127	3.82
Uganda	16	99	2.60

Source: World Bank (2012)
a. Covers all independent procedural actions mandated by law or court regulation that demand interaction between the parties or between them and the judge or court officer.
b. Measures the total of average duration of the procedure in calendar days, including duration until completion of service of process, duration of trial, and duration of enforcement.
c. The formalism index, which ranges from 0.0 to 7.0, is an index of the degree of formalism in the procedures to resolve disputes. The index measures substantive and procedural statutory intervention in judicial cases at lower-level civil trial courts.

Table 14.2 Trade restrictiveness ratings

	1997	1998	1999	2000	2001	2002	2003
Tanzania	7	7	6	6	5	5	5
Uganda	5	2	2	2	2	2	2
Kenya	6	6	6	6	6	6	6
India	10	10	10	10	8	8	8
Pakistan	8	8	7	7	7	6	6

Source: IMF Staff Calculation, 2003.
Note: 1 = Most Open; 10 = Most Restrictive.

Tanzania has continuously liberalized its trade regime, as demonstrated by the improvement in the IMF's trade restrictiveness ratings for Tanzania. Apart from Uganda, the simple average tariff in Tanzania is lower in comparison with other comparator countries—for example, 30% in India, 17% in Pakistan, and 19% in Kenya.

Bilateral Investment Treaties and Double Taxation Treaties

To increase the attractiveness of the United Republic of Tanzania as a destination for foreign investment, a number of bilateral investment treaties (BITs) and double taxation treaties (DTTs) can be increased, with special emphasis on current and potential sources of FDI, such as France, Japan, and the United States. In addition, it now considers dynamic, developing countries from Asia, such as Malaysia, Singapore, and Thailand, as well as South Africa. There has been some progress made in this area, particularly as it relates to regional agreements. As a member of the East African Community, the United Republic of Tanzania has participated in the common market since July 2010. Included in the protocol establishing the common market is the gradual harmonization of taxation between all member States. Although the Blue Book advised ratification of the EAC DTT, it is still under negotiation, following a review after the entry of Burundi and Rwanda into the EAC. In addition to the good progress made regionally in this area, there has been some momentum in signing new BITs and DTTs, notably with South Africa. According to UNCTAD (2011), the new BITs and DTTs in force include the following.

Reducing the Cost of Doing Business

The cost of doing business is fairly high in the United Republic of Tanzania. Recognizing its negative implication and the importance of pursuing policies and procedures that would reduce these costs, the Tanzanian Government in 2002 launched the Business Environment Strengthening for Tanzania (BEST) program. BEST is a five-year multi-sector program intended to reduce the administrative and regulatory burden of doing business, to improve the commercial and judicial system, and to strengthen the advocacy role of the private sector. As part of the program, the Better Regulation Unit (BRU) was established to oversee implementation (see Doingbuiness.org). The BEST program was identified as a clear path to reducing the cost of doing business and to creating an enabling investment climate. In particular, the IPR strongly supported the idea that a BRU be established to implement the BEST program (see Doingbuiness.org).

The progress made in the reforms was highlighted when, in 2005–2006, the United Republic of Tanzania was ranked tenth out of 175 economies for improvements made in easing the conditions for doing business (World Bank, 2012). Priority is given to the following areas of the BEST program: regulatory improvements in business licensing and registration, taxation, land, labor, import and export procedures, commercial dispute resolution, and using private sector organizations to help identify and remove barriers. However, lately progress has slowed, although work is ongoing.

Business Licensing and Registration

Since 1999, the Business Registrations and Licensing Agency (BRELA) of Tanzania has retained responsibility for business start-up processes. In the past, these processes were viewed as revenue streams. In the process of streamlining and reforming these processes and the accompanying regulations, there has been a shift toward more facilitation and less revenue collection. The new Business Activities Registration Act of 2007 has been introduced, and is being implemented jointly by BRELA and BRU. The Business Activities Registration Act of 2007 was designed to eliminate the general licenses for businesses, leaving only sector-specific licenses such as mining licenses. In the past, BRELA's only activity was licensing businesses, but under the Business Activities Registration Act of 2007, BRELA will register businesses as well. However, presently the only registration system in place is a business name registration, which provides, for a fee, the legal right for a business to be the sole user of the name in question. Although deemed to be voluntary, no transaction can be carried out using an unregistered business name (e.g., opening a company bank account). Therefore registration is, in effect, required. The BRELA registration and licensing system has been computerized, most especially in several of BRELA's regional offices. Table 14.3 outlines the procedures involved in setting up a business in Tanzania. It also details the time involved and the associated costs.

Table 14.3 Procedures for setting up a new business in Tanzania

	Procedure	Time to complete	Cost of completion
1	Apply for clearance of the proposed company name at the Business Registration and Licensing Authority (BRELA)	1 day	No Charge
2	Apply for a certificate of incorporation and of commencement to Registrar of Companies	7 days	TzS 206,200
3	Apply for taxpayer identification number (TIN) with the Tanzania Revenue Authority	2 days	No charge
4	Income tax officials inspect the office site of the new company	1 day simultaneous with procedure 3	No charge
5	Apply for PAyE with the Tanzania Revenue Authority	1 day, simultaneous with procedure 4	No charge
6	Apply for business license from the regional trade officer (depending on the nature of business)	6 days	TzS 1,000
7	Receive a land and town inspection of the premises	1 day	Transport cost, trivial
8	Have the health officer inspect the premises and obtain his signature	1 day, simultaneous with procedure 6	Transport cost, trivial
9	Apply for VAT certificate with the Tanzania Revenue Authority	4 days	No charge
10	Receive VAT/stamp duty inspection	1 day, simultaneous with procedure 9	No charge
11	Register for the workmen's compensation insurance at the National Insurance Corporation or other alternative insurance policy	1 day	No charge
12	Obtain registration number at the National Social Security Fund (NSSF)	7 days	No charge

Source: KPMG Services Proprietary Limited (2012)

Taxation

In this area, BRU is not applying the BEST program. Instead, the World Bank has provided $7 million in funding to review the taxation system (World Bank, 2012). There have been some regulatory changes in the interim. In 2006, the Revenue Authority Act, Cap. 399, was introduced, which according to TIC has reduced the number of tax requirements. The Act introduced a system that allowed investors to defer a portion of their tax payments due in advance.

Tax incentives for investors seem to be operating smoothly; however, TIC is concerned that TRA's allegations that abuses are occurring will lead to the removal of goods deemed to be capital goods. TRA has implemented an Audit on Exemptions Unit to address possible abuses, while TIC is working with TRA to ensure that investors are not unfairly harassed. In general, progress has been made in modernizing and simplifying tax regulations, and more progress can be made.

The Government of Tanzania through TRA has done much to enhance transparency in tax administration. In this regard, a quarterly stakeholders' forum has been put in place, with the participation of representatives from the private sector, tax consultants, and various representatives of government departments. TRA also introduced a taxpayers' charter informing the public of TRA initiatives and new developments with regard to tax, and a taxpayers' service center to handle enquiries and suggestions and to provide a hotline for complaints. A whistle-blowing mechanism has also been included in TRA's strategic planning.

Land

Access to land is a delicate issue in the United Republic of Tanzania, and for investors it is also one of the most problematic. There are two land laws that were enacted in 1999: (a) the Land Act No. 4 and (b) the Village Land Act No. 5. By 2003, neither Act had been implemented. Recognizing the need for prioritization to implement the many elements of the Acts, consultants were hired to develop a detailed strategic plan. The Strategic Plan for Implementation of New Land Laws (SPILL) was completed in April 2005. Several projects were identified as necessary for implementation of SPILL. These included land registration and land information, a geodetic network and mapping, implementation of the Village Land Act, house registration in unplanned urban settlements, a dispute-resolution mechanism, and capacity-building. A $30 million project to implement SPILL was funded through the World Bank's Tanzania Private Sector Competitiveness Project, with implementation planned for the period from 2006 to 2012 (World Bank, 2012).

To facilitate land access for investors, TIC has created a "land bank." Through the land bank, TIC maintained reserved tracts of land for investors.

These tracts would have the appropriate infrastructure and leasing permits already in place. However, the project has been delayed as the Government of and TIC stalled negotiations on whether TIC should pay rent for the unused reserved land. There is also some question as to how the program would work in relation to export processing zones, and who would fund the infrastructure development in the reserved tracts of the land bank.

Labor

The Employment and Labor Relations Act of 2004 was introduced but became effective in 2007. It addresses issues such as leave, wages, severance pay, maternity, contracts, and collective bargaining. Some of the provisions related to hiring and termination include a probation period where unfair termination does not apply to workers employed for six months or less, and "fair" termination being deemed to be related to the employee's conduct, capacity, or compatibility, or being based on the operational requirements of the employer. Furthermore, an employment contract can be for an unspecified period of time, for a specified period of time, or can be a contract for a specific task (UNCTD, 2011).

Labor regulations pertaining specifically to foreign investors are contained in the Investment Act of 1997. Because no new investment Act has been introduced, these regulations have remained unchanged. There are two kinds of work permit for foreigners in Tanzania. The class a permit is given to investors and their family members. The class B permit is issued for qualified labor. The maximum number of foreign employees with a class B permit per investment allowed under the 1997 Act is five (UNCTD, 2011). There is, however, a provision in the Act allowing investors to request and be allowed more. For example, permit records from 2008 indicate that, on average, 6.7 class B permits were granted per investment. Given the skill shortage, five foreign workers is rather low for a management team of any sizeable enterprise of the type that the United Republic of Tanzania would like to attract.

To increase local labor skills, an additional requirement has been placed on the use of expatriate labor: the direct assistants of foreign employees must be Tanzanian. Unfortunately, the workers' level of skills is usually low, requiring companies to invest significantly in training the indigenous labor.

Import and Export Procedures

A serious concern impacting the costs of doing business relates to customs processes. One issue is the lack of clarity about which agencies are responsible for the various customs functions. To address this issue, the Government is considering establishing a body to oversee all port organizations. The customs system, which is not operating smoothly, is also contributing to the high costs of doing business in the United Republic of Tanzania. An initiative is under way to streamline the clearance and customs processes of the five agencies involved. Unfortunately, the lack of computerization across all agencies is slowing progress in this area. For example, Port Authority operations are not computerized, and all data is recorded manually on paper. Although UNCTAD's Automated System for Customs Data (ASYCUDA++) is in use, it does not seem to be connected to all the customs-related areas that would normally provide input to the system.

Commercial Dispute Resolution

Accessibility to the Commercial Court, court procedures, and corruption were all problems confronting investors when seeking dispute resolution in Tanzania. However, these areas receive special attention in Tanzanian reform efforts. Thus, capacity in the area of administrative support to commercial courts has been improved. Better Regulation Unit (BRU) implemented BEST in the commercial court system. Thus far, BRU has been able to integrate the commercial courts into the Court of Appeals and has enabled cases to be heard by the High Court. In the past, if there was a dispute, the Ministry was the highest authority; under the new process, the case will move through the judicial system. A Civil Justice Technical Working Group, funded through BEST, is working to close loopholes in the operations of the commercial courts. The challenge that continues to face the court system is capacity. Resolving a case is a lengthy and time-consuming process for investors. The judicial committees handle corruption issues through a bottom-up approach, which helps ensure that concerns at each level are brought to the attention of senior government officials.

National Business Council and the National Investment Steering Committee

The Tanzanian National Business Council (TNBC) and the National Investment Steering Committee (NISC) is vital to the improvement of government business relations. While the TNBC have continued to make efforts to remove barriers to efficient business operation, and vigorous follow-up to problems identified subsequently, the NISC strongly pursue links with the business community and actively monitor the government business relations.

The TNBC has been found to be a useful forum. The primary benefit of the TNBC is the meetings that it holds between the private and public sector prior to the Government's decision on the annual budget. This allows the private sector to make input. Although the TNBC forum is commendable, there is a lack of follow-up or tracking of the agreements and decisions reached in the meetings, which causes the TNBC to fall short of achieving the outcome hoped for (UNCTD, 2011). This shortcoming is primarily due to the fact that the TNBC lacks a fully functional secretariat (UNCTD, 2011).

Ensuring Continued Success of Privatization

Another recommendation of IPR is for the government to ensure continued success in privatization. In order to achieve this endeavor, the Tanzanian government came up with the following.

Privatization of Utilities and Infrastructure:

In 2002, the IPR found that the privatization program was successful and urged the Government to move more quickly in privatizing utilities. Since then, the results of privatization have been more mixed. Whereas privatization of manufacturing, the financial sector, hotels, and other sectors has been largely successful, with only a few negative experiences (e.g., turning a manufacturing plant into a warehouse), privatizations of infrastructure and utilities have not been as successful. In 2003, a 10-year lease with a firm from the United Kingdom for supplying water in Dar-es-Salaam was terminated after only two years, as improvements in service delivery and infrastructure had failed to (UNCTD, 2011). The privatization of railways has been problematic too. In 2006, Tanzania Railways was leased to Rail India Technical and Economic Services (RITES), giving RITES a 51% stake in the operation of Tanzania Railways' passenger and freight services for 25 years. In 2010, both the Government and RITES, dissatisfied with the partnership, were seeking early termination of the agreement. The sale in 2002 to South African Airways of a 49% stake of Air Tanzania Company Limited was initially considered to be a success. However, differences in business approaches led to the dissolution of the partnership in 2006 and to the Government buying out South African Airways. In addition to these examples and in common with many developing countries (see UNCTAD, 2018), the United Republic of Tanzania has faced difficulties in privatizing the landline telecommunications and electricity sectors.

In search for appropriate partners for assistance in developing utilities and infrastructure, the IPR identified the Asia-Africa Investment Technology Promotion Centre (AAITPC) as a potential partner and framework to link investors in Asia with government projects in the United Republic of Tanzania. The best known example to have come through the AAITPC is the RITES investment in Tanzania Railways. China and India has most of the bilateral institutions and agreements with the Tanzanian Government (UNCTD, 2011).

The National Development Corporation (NDC) is an important factor in building infrastructure through private investment in Tanzania. It is mandated to initiate, develop, and guide the implementation of projects in partnership with the private sector, and to initiate development of export processing zones. In order to help NDC acquire the necessary capacity, the government approved the involvement of private sector executives to NDC.

Implementation of Effective Infrastructure Development

Infrastructure was identified by the Government of Tanzania as an opportunity to attract foreign investment and other forms of involvement. The focus was on Airports, Dar-es-Salaam Port, and EPZs as opportunities suited to FDI. We shall at this juncture examine efforts and successes recorded so far in this sector. The Government uses its experience with the privatization of Kilimanjaro International Airport to develop a partnership model that is attractive to foreign investors and beneficial for the country. Kilimanjaro International Airport was privatized in 1998, through a 25-year lease contract with the Kilimanjaro Airports Development Company owned by United Kingdom firm Mott MacDonald and Tanzanian firm Inter-Consult. However, dissatisfied with the progress recoded, the Government took over the airport in 2009. This experience, however, did not stopped government from privatizing Nyerere International Airport in Dar-es-Salaam.

The potential of Dar-es-Salaam Port was recognized by the government. Thus, the Government transformed it into a major shipping and cargo center because it felt that it could become a top provider of port services, through either a joint venture or hiring the appropriate experts. The challenges facing the Tanzania Port Authority, which owns and operates the port, include storage capacity, non-computerized processing (including customs handling), and a history of corruption. Despite being poorly outfitted and losing market share to other regional ports, Dar-es-Salaam Port's cargo volume continues to grow. This indicates that port services continue to be in high demand, and that growth could be much higher if the proper infrastructure and management are in place. Cargo has been increasing at a rate of 15% annually since 2004 (Balile, 2013). Unfortunately, the development of container storage has not kept pace, creating significant delays since 2009. Dar-es-Salaam Port had lost 30% of its traffic to the ports of Mombasa (Kenya) and Beira (Mozambique) (Reuters Africa, 2009).

Recent steps to alleviate the capacity problems include the establishment of inland container depots. A dry port at Isaka is being built from an existing railway terminal; and construction of another dry port is planned in Mbeya, to service Malawi. The effect of implementing dry docks and of streamlining procedures has improved port operation. For example, waiting times at sea have been reduced from 14 to 4 days for all but oil tankers (UNCTAD 2011).

Multi-facility Economic Zones:

Frequently, EPZs are used to attract FDI in countries where infrastructure is a challenge; industrial parks are then developed separately to encourage domestic production. Rather than pursuing two separate initiatives, the United Republic of Tanzania developed multi-facility economic zones (MFEZs) which would combine domestic production and export-oriented industries in one facility. Through cost-sharing with the private sector, and implementation of the regulatory environment envisaged by the BEST program combined with efficient administration, MFEZs could provide the best possible business environment within a limited geographical area.

The creation of "township" economic zones mirroring China's approach to industrial organization improved government business relations in

Tanzania. The incentives offered in EPZs are not dependent upon "zone" incentives but rather on the amount of exports. Currently, there are 18 companies operating under EPZ status in industrial parks, and 15 single factory units with EPZ status. EPZ enterprises are nearly evenly divided between local and foreign companies (UNDP, 2012). The foreign companies are primarily from China, Denmark, India, and Japan. The majority of companies are in engineering, followed by textiles, agro-processing, and mineral processing. In addition, there are 14 sites designated for EDZ development. Priority is being given to the zones at the ports of Mtwara and Tanga, at the coastal town of Bagamoyo (50 km north of Dar-es-Salaam), and at the northern, inland town of Arusha.

Stimulating Human Resource Development and Linkages

As in other developing countries, skills shortages pose problems for investors in the United Republic of Tanzania. The government has made efforts to address this shortage of skills of the private sector through curriculum changes, training programs in partnership with the private sector, and the development of domestic–foreign partnership programs. Although there is a shortage of skilled workers in the United Republic of Tanzania, there is also the problem of workers having skill sets that do not meet the needs of a modern, market economy (UNDP 2012). The government has expanded the provision of higher education and revising curriculums to better meet the private sector's needs. There has not been an expansion in higher education or technical training, but there has been some attempt to reform technology-related education. COSTECH, in partnership with United Nations Educational and Scientific and Cultural Organization (UNESCO), is working on this aspect of university education reform, including adding an element of entrepreneurship training to science departments in universities.

There are also several private associations that provide training. The Tanzania Chamber of Commerce, Industry and Agriculture (TCCIA), with support from international development agencies, provides training for SMEs, focusing on transforming subsistence farmers into commercial farmers as well as on business management. To improve the skills and experience of Tanzanian workers, the government developed linkage programs based on sectors. Although energy, mining, and agribusiness are all of fundamental importance to attracting FDI, the government focused on the easier tourism sector. No "sector" linkage program has materialized. There are three linkage programs. The TCCIA hosts regional trade fairs to help promote business linkages, and engages in "matchmaking" when foreign delegations visit. SIDO, under the Ministry of Trade, Industry, and Marketing, provides workshops for small and medium-sized enterprises (SMEs) on business linkages, and encourages SMEs to become suppliers to large companies. Finally, UNCTAD launched a business linkages program in June 2009 in collaboration with TIC. These three programs benefited from coordination and sector emphasis.

The Role of Business and Government Sectors in the Economy

The Government of Tanzania (GOT) generally has a favorable attitude toward foreign direct investment (FDI) and has had considerable success in attracting FDI. However, the legacy of state oriented approach has not yet been overcome, and some officials remain suspicious of foreign investors and free competition. After several years of growing FDI, new FDI in 2009 declined modestly due to the global economic crisis to US$650 million from 2008's record US$744 million.

Tanzania's Capital Account regime restricts the free flow of investment in and out of the country. Non-citizens cannot buy bonds and other debt securities in the domestic market. In addition, Tanzanians cannot sell or issue securities abroad, unless approved by the Capital Markets and Securities Authority (CMSA). The Dar-es-Salaam Stock Exchange (DSE) forbids companies with more than 60% foreign ownership from listing. Under the terms of the planned East African Community (EAC) monetary union, all EAC residents are expected to receive national treatment thereafter.

There are no laws or regulations that limit or prohibit foreign investment, participation, or control, and firms generally do not restrict foreign participation in practice. In 2010, new legislation required foreign-owned telecommunications firms to list on the DSE within three years and gave the Minister of Energy and Minerals discretion to require foreign mining companies to give the government a free carried share of ownership in order to receive a Mining Development Agreement. Foreign investors generally receive national treatment; however, the Tourism Act of 2008 bars foreign companies from engaging in mountain guiding activities. According to the legislation, only Tanzanian citizens can operate travel agencies and car rental services and engage in tour guiding.

The Tanzanian Investment Center (TIC), established by the Tanzanian Investment Act of 1997, is the focal point for all investors' inquiries, screens foreign investments, and facilitates project start-ups. TIC has been given authority to manage public private partnerships (PPPs) for foreign companies under the 2010 PPP legislation that set a framework for Build-Operate-Transfer arrangements with private companies. Filing with TIC is not mandatory, but offers incentives for joint ventures with Tanzanians and wholly owned foreign projects above US$300,000. The review process takes up to 10 days and involves multiple GOT agencies, which are required by law to cooperate fully with TIC in facilitating foreign investment, but in practice can create bureaucratic delays.

Land ownership remains restrictive in Tanzania; under the Land Act of 1999, all land in Tanzania belongs to the state. Procedures for obtaining a lease or certificate of occupancy can be complex and lengthy, both for citizens and foreign investors. Less than 10% of land has been surveyed, and registration of title deeds is currently manual and mainly handled at the local level. Noncitizen investors may occupy land for investment purposes through a government-granted right of occupancy or through sub-leases through a granted right of occupancy. Foreign investors can also partner with Tanzanian leaseholders. Rights of occupancy and derivative rights may be granted for periods up to 99 years and are renewable.

The Economic Processing Zones Act 2006 authorized the establishment of Special Economic Zones (SEZs) to encourage Greenfield investments in the light industry, agro-processing industry, and agriculture sectors. The GOT's Export Processing Zones Authority (EPZA) continues to promote Export Processing Zones (EPZ) to attract investments in agricultural value added processing, textiles, and electronics. EPZA has earmarked 4000 hectares for export clusters, though on-site infrastructure and facilities are lacking. Six zones have already been developed; one is owned by the GOT and the rest by the private sector. (40 companies in total, mostly foreign textile exporters) In early 2011 EPZA announced the Tanzania Revenue Authority had opened an office in its Mabibo EPZ, streamlining seamless tax and revenue procedures for participants.

Nyerere's Legacy and the Economic Development Impact

To characterize Nyerere's legacy is neither easy nor straightforward. We have dwelt on the earlier mentioned core values of Julius Nyerere's Ujamaa and the underpinnings of this rare breed of African politicians. In assessing Nyerere's political legacy, Mazrui (2005) argues that

> Nyerere's policies of Ujamaa amounted to a case of heroic failure. They were heroic because Tanzania was one of the few African countries which attempted to find its own route to development instead of borrowing the ideologies of the West. But it was a failure because the economic experiment did not deliver the goods of development.

On the other hand, Nyerere's policies of nation-building amount to a case of unsung heroism. With wise and strong leadership, coupled with brilliant policies of cultural integration, he took one of the poorest countries in the world and made it a proud leader in African affairs and an active member of the global community (Mazrui. 2005). Balile (2013) and Mesaki, and Malipula (2011) hailed Nyerere as

> "a creative conceptualizer, a far-sighted pioneer, a selfless role model, an almost dangerously courageous champion of righteous campaigns in Africa and the Third World as a whole, a fearless confronter of nations and institutions that tried to interfere with Tanzania's self-determination, a unifier of a vast and diverse economy and people, and a man of the people" (Mesaki & Malipula, 2011).

Stoger-Eising (2000), Onimode (1988), and Biersteker (1992) contend that the quest for an African way, which neither denies the appeal of universals nor rejects local exigencies, but builds on local inventiveness, is the challenge that currently confronts the development project in Tanzania. The deconstructing of Ujamaa was a challenge to which Nyerere was so acutely conscious and responsive (Balile, 2013). It is from this perspective that we can understand Ujamaa's emphasis on self-reliance and non-exploitative development (Richards, 1985).

The Way Forward

The imperatives of formalized GBRs in Tanzania cannot be overemphasized: For example, in Mauritius, the Joint Economic Council (JEC) is an influential private sector actor in GBRs, and measured GBRs led to higher growth in a regression over the period 1970–2005. Budget proposals, which include suggestions for better industrial policies, are frequently taken up by government budgets. This constitutes an important economic function of effective GBRs. The World Bank (2009) report indicated that a favorable collaboration between the state and business may have positive consequences for the growth of the economy as a whole, as long as certain mechanisms are in place which facilitate the following: transparency (the flow of accurate and reliable information, both ways, between the business and government); reciprocity between the business and the government; credibility (such that the market is able to believe what the state actors say); and high levels of trust through transparency, reciprocity, and credibility. Hence, appropriate government policies, necessary for promoting economic growth in general and private sector development in particular, are made possible by efficient and fruitful state-business relations and dialogues.

No doubt, an effective GBR could help Tanzania reduce policy uncertainties in the economy. Expectations play a major role in the activities of firms and investors, particularly when it comes to savings decisions, the type of investment to undertake or the type of goods to produce, the period of production, the quantities to be produced, the technology to be used, how and where to market what has been produced, and even how pricing of the commodities should be done (Chapain et al 2013). All these decisions are taken based on anticipated market conditions and expected profitability. The OECD (2010) report argues that uncertainty tends to have significant negative effects on investment, especially when investment involves large sunk and irreversible costs.

There is urgent need for an effective liaison between the state and the market results in tailor-made, accurate, and efficient government policies and institutions in Tanzania. In other words, an effective GBR will ensure that government policies toward businesses are appropriate and of good quality. This is because, in the presence of such an effective relationship between the state and the market, the design of government policies will be done, among other things, using the input of and in consultation with the private sector. Regular interactions and sharing of information will ensure that the private sector objectives coincide with public action and that local level issues are input into the centralized policy processes.

Beyond formal GBRs, there are also informal GBRs. For example, the Ghana experience shows that more developed social networks (politicians, civil servants) of firms (in a sample of 256) lead to better firm performance. Such informal GBRs may provide a stepping stone toward formalization (te Velde, 2010). Business association membership is frequently associated with better firm performance. In several African case studies, membership leads to better firm performance by reducing policy uncertainty and lobbying, although individual lobbying remains important.

Conclusion

This chapter has examined the relationship between business and government in forging economic growth and development in Tanzania. The relationship between the business and government in Tanzania under Julius Nyerere was a (Ujamaa) socialist state. However, leaders after him adopted the neo-liberal market approach. This study employed a multi-disciplinary approach and qualitative aspects of the disciplines of political science, economics, and organizational management. It seeks to provide an understanding of what constitutes effective business and government relations in Tanzania.

The analysis provided in this chapter reveals how progress in business and government relations in the country has been mixed. Noticeable gains have been made in improving the investment framework and in reducing the cost of doing business. The progress in these areas, although good, has been limited by slow implementation. A similar situation exists regarding progress in infrastructure development, where the absence of an implemented PPP policy remains a bottleneck for many projects. Human resource development and investment promotion are the areas in which the least progress was made. The education and training system has largely remained unchanged despite recommendations for change. All of the recommendations, if implemented, could enhance business and government relations and attract more foreign direct investment into the country.

References

Ackah, C., Aryeetey, E., Ayee, J. and Clottey, E. (2010). *State-Business Relations and Economic Performance in Ghana*. Institutions and Pro-Poor Growth (IPPG), London: DFID.

Balile, D. (2013). *Political Battle Heats Up in Tanzania Over Constitutional Review Bill*. Sabahi http://sabahionline.com/en_GB/articles/hoa/articles/features/2013/09/30/feature-01. Accessed January 15, 2016.

Chapain, C, Clifton, N. and Comunian, R. (2013). "Understanding Creative Regions: Bridging the Gap between Global Discourses and Regional and National Contexts." *Regional Studies 47* (2), 12–33

Dibua, J. I. (1998). Journey to Nowhere: Neo-Liberalism and Africa's Development Crisis. *Comparative Studies in South Asia, Africa and the Middle East, XVIII*(2), 119–130.

Ergas, Z. (1980). Why Did the Ujamaa Village Policy Fail?—Towards a Global Analysis. *Journal of Modern African Studies, 18* (3), 34–59.

Green, H. R. (1995). *Ujamaa: Success or Failure?* African Development, January. www.afroarticles.com/article-dashboard. Accessed October 21, 2016.

Hyden, G. (1980). Beyond Ujamaa in Tanzania: Underdevelopment and an Uncaptured Peasantry. Berkeley: University of California Press.

Ishemo, S. L. (2000). Tributes to Mwalimu J.K Nyerere. *Review of African Political Economy,* 27, 1–23.

Legum, C. and Mmari, G. (eds). (1995). *Mwalimu: The Influence of Nyerere.* Lawrenceville: Africa World Press.

Makoye, K. (2013). *Tanzania: Government Hopes New Tanzanian Constitution Bans Child Marriage.* All Africa. http://allafrica.com/stories/201310140133. html. Accessed November 29, 2015.

Martinussen, J. (1997). Society, State and Market: A Guide to Competing Theories of Development. London: Zed Books Ltd.

Mazrui, A. (2005). *The Africans Triple Heritage.* Boston, MA: Little Brown and Company.

Mesaki, S. and Malipula, M. (2011). "Julius Nyerere's influence and legacy: From a proponent of familyhood to a candidate for sainthood." International Journal of Sociology and Anthropology *3* (3),. 93–100.

Nursey-Bray, P. F. (1980). Tanzania: The Development Debate. *African Affairs, 79,* 23–47.

Nyerere, J. (1961). Scramble for Africa: Address to the World Assembly of Youth. Dar-es-Salaam: Government Printer.

Onimode, B. (1988). *Apolitical Economy of the African Crisis.* London and Atlantic Highlands, NJ: Zed Books & the Institute for African Alternatives.

Organization for Economic Co-operation and Development (OECD) Report. (2010). *Tanzanian Profile.* http://dx.doi.org/10.1787/9789264077478-124-en. Accessed November 7, 2015.

Organization for Economic Co-Operation and Development (OECD). (2003). www. oecd.org/dev. Accessed November 7, 2015.

Poulantzas, N. (1978). *State, Power and Socialism.* London: New Left Books.

Pratt, C. (1976). *The Critical Phase in Tanzania, 1945–67: Nyerere and the Emergence of a Socialist Strategy.* Cambridge and New York: Cambridge University Press.

Raikes, P. L. (1975). Ujamaa and Rural Socialism. *Review of African Political Economy, 3,* 31–57.

Richards, P. (1985). Indigenous Agricultural Revolution: Ecology and Food Production in West Africa. London and Boulder, CO: Hutchinson & Westview.

Samoff, J. (1990). Modernizing a Socialist Vision: Education in Tanzania. In M. Carnoy and J. Samoff (Eds.), *Education and Social Transition in the Third World.* Princeton, NJ: Princeton University Press, 121–139.

Stoger-Eising,V. (2000). Ujamaa Revisited: Indigenous and European Influences in Nyerere's Social and Political Thought. *Africa, 17* (1), 37–58.

te Velde, D. W. (Ed.). (2010). State-Business Relations and Economic Performance in Sub-Saharan Africa, in Effective State-Business Relations, Industrial Policy and Economic Growth. London: ODI Publications.

United Nations Conference on Trade and Development (UNCTD). (2011). *Report on the Implementation of the Investment Policy Review, United Republic of Tanzania*. New York and Geneva: United Nations:

UNCTAD), 2010 United Nations Development Programme (UNDP)/United Nations Conference on Trade and Development (UNCTAD). 2010. Creative Economy. Report 2010, Geneva and New York, NY: UNDP and UNCTAD Publication.

United Nations Development Program (UNDP). (2012). *Human Development Report*. UNDP, New York: Oxford University Press.

United Nations Development Program (UNDP). (2014). *Human Development Report*. UNDP, New York: Oxford University Press.

United Nations, Department of Economic and Social Affairs. (2010). Country Profile: United Republic of Tanzania, http://esa.un.org/unpd/wpp/country-profiles/pdf/834.pdf. Accessed September 15, 2016.

World Bank. (2009). Sub-Saharan Africa-From Crisis to Sustainable Growth: A Long-Term Perspective Study. Washington, DC: The World Bank.

World Bank. (2010). *World Bank Development Indicators*. Washington, DC: World Bank.

World Bank. (2012). *World Bank Development Report*. New York: Oxford University Press.

Yeager, R. (1989). *Tanzania: An African Experiment*. CO: Westview Press.

15 Business and Government Relations in Kenya

Robert A. Dibie, Josephine Dibie, and Omolara Quadri

Introduction

The Republic of Kenya is a country in east Africa. It has a boundary with the Indian Ocean to the east, the Republic of Ethiopia to the north, Somalia to the northeast, and Tanzania to the south. Other countries having boundaries with Kenya are South Sudan to the northwest and Uganda to the west. Lake Victoria is located southwest of the country. According to World Bank Group (2016) Kenya has a population of about 44.86 million people. The gross domestic product (GDP) of Kenya was US$132.5 billion in 2014, while its GDP per capital was US$2,942 in the same year. (GlobalEdge, 2016). Kenya gained its independence from Britain on December 12, 1963. The nation became a republic in 1964 and Jomo Kenyatta was elected the first president of the new country in the same year. The current president is Uhuru Kenyatta, and he is the son of Kenya's founding president Jomo Kenyatta. Uhuru Kenyatta was elected president in April 2013 (BBC, 2016; Lubale, 2012; Government of Kenya, 2015). The nation is famous for its glacier, abundant wildlife, lakes, and safari parks. The administrative capital of the country is Nairobi. Nairobi is also the largest city in the country. Kenya is endowed with gold, limestone, soda ash, salt, rubies, fluorspar, garnets, wildlife, hydropower, water, and arable land (Kenya Business and Development Profile, 2011).

The country's economy is classified as a mixed system with various private freedoms. The economic system in the country supports the means of production under private ownership. At the same time, profit-seeking enterprises and the accumulation of capital remains the fundamental driving force in all the economic activities in the country. However, the government tends to centralize its economic planning and regulation activities. The current relationship between business and government is neither totally free nor capitalist or socialist. Over the past two decades the increased business and government relations activity in Kenya as well as the integration of active civil society role has reinvigorated the economy in such a way that the system has been regarded as a new form of shared governance (Central Intelligent Agency, 2016).

According to the World Bank Group (2016) Kenya has made significant structural and economic reforms that have contributed to sustained economic growth in the past decade. Despite these positive economic growth trends, the country is still faced with some development challenges. The economic growth and development challenges include poverty, inequality among gender, lack of infrastructure, corruption, and vulnerable of the economy to internal and external shocks (Doing Business in Kenya, 2016). Although the country's growth is projected to rise to 5.9% in 2016 and 6.1 % in 2017, the positive outlook is predicated on infrastructure investments. Fiscal consolidation is expected to ease pressure on domestic interest rates and increase credit applications by the private sector (Lubale, 2012; Kenyan Business Development Profile, 2011). There is also the dilemma of sustainable development in the area of poverty, inequality, effective governance, inadequate environmental protection, low investment, and low firm productivity in the country (Lubale, 2012; Abdullah, 2015; Ashe-Edmunds, 2015). The government has not been able to come up with appropriate fiscal and monetary policies that could adequately galvanize the economy to achieve rapid, sustained growth rates that may transform the lives of ordinary citizens in Kenya (Blanchard, 2013).

The Government of Kenya is on a recovery path after many decades of economic decline and misrule. The traits associated with invulnerability play a big role in the ability of the country to achieve its sustainable development goals. Kenya continues to gain substantial growth in almost all its sectors (US Department of State, 2016). Consequently, the nation's economy has been maintaining the momentum that it had started in 2003 with most sectors recording accelerated growth despite the post-election setback of 2008 (BBC, 2016). In the past three decades the government administration tends to benefit some people at the expense of a larger segment of the citizens. The new democratic principles embraced in Kenya in 2013 have promised a renewed commitment to develop policies that are responsive to economic growth in the country. In addition, the promotion of political stability has made the country a crucial and enabling environment for investment. The nation is currently engaged in the renovation and development of infrastructure in a bid to make the cost of doing business in the country affordable (GlobalEdge, 2016). According to a World Bank Group (2016) report, Kenya's key economic challenge is to increase its real GDP growth rate. Kenya continues to face challenges associated with corruption, high unemployment, tribal tensions, land titles, insecurity due to sporadic aggression by Al Shabab terrorist group from Somalia, and poverty (US Department of State, 2016; BBC, 2016).

According to the US Department of State (2016) report, the agricultural sector is the largest employer in Kenya, contributing 23.4% of GDP. The nation's agricultural major exports are tea, coffee, cut flowers, and vegetables. Kenya is reported to be the world's leading exporter of black tea. Tea is one of Kenya's top foreign exchange earners (Freeman & Kaguongo,

2003; World Bank Group, 2016). The climate and vegetation in the country provides a favorable weather conditions and a stable foreign exchange rate boosted tea export earnings. In recent years, tea production increased by 40% to a record level of 441 million kilograms, valued at US$1.2 billion (World Bank Group, 2016). Occasionally, however, the weather in some parts of the country could be very hot and unconducive for agricultural crops. As a result of a major drought in 2011, tea exports fell by 5% to 421 million kilograms (US Department of State, 2016).

One other area that needs substantial improvement in Kenya is its roads. Although the country has a few good roads, the decapitated conditions of some of its rural roads are terrible, especially during the rainy season. The nation's capital city Nairobi is the commercial center and transportation hub of Eastern and Central Africa and the largest metropolitan town between Cairo and Johannesburg. At the nation's eastern coast is Port of Mombasa. The city of Mombasa is considered to be the most important sea port in the region, supplying the shipping needs of more than a dozen countries despite equipment deficiencies, inefficiency, and corruption (GlobalEdge, 2016). It has been reported that the Government of Kenya has been unable to provide a secure environment for businesses and families, particularly in urban settings (Blanchard, 2013). Frequent property crime and violence are major concerns and have become an unavoidable cost of doing business for companies in Kenya (Blanchard, 2013; BBC, 2016; Dagne, 2011).

This chapter examines business and government relations in Kenya. It argues that the Government of Kenya is not doing enough to encourage businesses to conform to the nation's business ethics standards, values, and attitudes. The chapter also explores how the Government of Kenya has responded to basic ethical and corporate social responsibility concerns in the country in the form of codified laws and regulations. Data were derived through interviews, observation, and a review of print and electronic documentation on business and government relations in Kenya. The chapter explores the efficacy of laws and regulations as an effective tool for dealing with consumer protection, employees, safe products, investors, the communities, and societies in Kenya. The chapter contributes to the body of literature on the techniques used by the government of any developing nation to promote competition, protect consumers, employees, and the environment. Result of the analysis of data shows that successful business and government relations can contribute significantly to the quality of the nation's economic growth. It recommends strategies for the institutionalization of successful business and government relations to improve the economy of Kenya.

Business Practice and the Economy Framework

According to Ferrell et al. (2016) an economy system is a mechanism that most societies use to distribute their resources, and to produce goods and services. In addition, the major issue of economics is how to fulfill the unlimited demand for goods and services in a world of limitation or where scarcity of resources exists. In most countries the factors of production are controlled by government planning, while in other countries government regulates business to preserve competition and protect consumers and employees (Lehne, 2013; Kuye & Ogundele, 2013)

In the twenty-first century entrepreneurs are constantly changing the business practices in many African countries with new technology and innovative management techniques (Dibie et al., 2015). Businesses create jobs and pay taxes, making it natural for the government to want to help them start and thrive. Municipalities, counties, states, and the federal government all offer direct and indirect assistance to individual businesses and industries through a variety of monetary grants, paid research, legislation, and workers training (Dibie et al., 2015; Ashe-Edmunds, 2015). Although businesses play an essential role in any country, society is increasingly demanding that business people behave ethically and socially responsible toward not only their customers but also their investors, employees, government regulators, the natural environment, and communities (Ferrell et al., 2017).

The stakeholder theory presents an argument that investors, entrepreneurs, government, business owners, and civil society organizations should be involved to implement socially responsible activities in order to enhance their performance, values, economic growth, and reputation. (Donaldson & Preston, 1995). The theory also suggests that because these groups have a stake in the success and outcome of a business, they are called stakeholders. Businesses are required to abide by laws and government regulations as well as act in an ethical and socially responsible manner. In the process of abiding by the laws, businesses are also required to adapt economic, technology, and social changes without harming members of the society. This is the reason why some companies' corporate social responsibility strategy has reflected eco-friendly or green product oriented (Dibie & Dimitriou, 2016).

Employees and customers of businesses who are also classified as stakeholders frequently influence the corporate management strategies and performance in different ways. The stakeholder theory also postulates that sustainability should be evaluated on the basis of those stakeholders who benefit the most from pro-social and environmental initiatives. This is because they are the target audience of each business practice. The stakeholder theory perceives sustainability as activities that demonstrate the inclusion of all stakeholders such as civil society organizations, employees, customers, communities, suppliers, local governments, and other businesses in an ethical and responsible manner (Ferrrell et al 2017). "Ethical and responsible manner," as used in this chapter, means treating stakeholders in a manner deem acceptable in civilized societies (Hopkins, 2003; Dahlsrud, 2008; Perez & del Bosque, 2014). This pragmatic influence of stakeholders could also stimulate businesses to strive to satisfy all citizens or customers of their products or services in the long run. By engaging in such practices, businesses tend to maximize their reputation and values. Creating a reputation as an eco-friendly business could also improve the company's employees' organizational commitment as well as enhance performance and retention (Singh et al., 2014; Kang et al., 2012; Lee & Park, 2009). Therefore, it could be argued that corporate social responsibility is a close concept of how firms have mobilized their activities toward addressing environmental issues in the areas where they are located. Figure 15.1 shows the relationship between business stakeholders and government.

Figure 15.1 shows that various stakeholders are involved in the business and government relations of any country. At the center of the relation is government, business owners, employees, and customers. The other set of stakeholders are those that are actively involved in activities relating to management, marketing, and financing the business. Employees are responsible for the work that goes on within a business (Griffin et al 2017). Further entrepreneurs are constantly changing the business practices of any country with new technology, and innovative management techniques (Nelson & Quick 2013; Hanson 2009). On the hand from regulation activities, government also enacts monetary and fiscal policies to minimize the disruptive effects of economic fluctuations and reduce unemployment (Froeb et al., 2016; McGuigan et al., 2014).

Beyond the business and nongovernmental sectors, the current structure of governance arrangement in Kenya tends to create the wrong kind of incentives for most participants that are engaged in infrastructure development (Abdullah, 2015). This is because once the traditional incentives permeate all aspects of infrastructure development, changing these positive

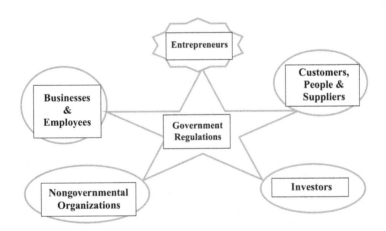

Figure 15.1 The relationship between business stakeholders and government

Source: Dibie, R., and Dimitriou, C. (2016). Evaluation of Sustainable Environmental Initiatives in Hotels in Southern Nigeria. *Journal of Applied and Theoretical Environmental Sciences,* 2(2), 25–56

or corrupt factors becomes very difficult. The bone of contention is that many well-placed individuals in the current administration and government of the country benefit from the current system (Wang & Ahmend 2007; Henderson 2007; Mankiw 2018). Consequently, appropriate government regulations of businesses in the country and corporate social responsibility (CSR) could be seen as a vital part of the armory for achieving a stronger business and government relations, as well as sustainable development in Kenya in the future. It is anticipated that companies with good corporate social responsibility can enhance employee effective organizational commitment by improving their working environment, promoting employee participation in socially responsible actions, and fostering a good corporate image that makes employees feel proud of their companies' ethical, legal, and discretionary actions (Maignan & Ferrell, 2001; Wang, 2014). Therefore the positive image that can accrue when corporations in Kenya are seen to behave well and act as good citizens in the society could be regarded as a critical ingredient for achieving good business and government relations as well as economic growth in the country.

Nature of Business and Government Relations

Kenya's economy is the largest and most diverse in East Africa, although it has faced increased challenges in recent years (World Bank Group, 2016). The economy was hit hard by the 2007–2008 post-election crisis. The global economic downturn, and a 2011–2012 regional drought, also negatively affected Kenya's economy (GlobalEdge, 2016; Blanchard, 2013). About a decade ago, the economy of the country was stagnant. According to the World Bank Group (2016), Kenya's economy has shown some growth since the 1990s. For instance, the GDP grew an estimated 5.6% in 2010 but declined a little bit to 4.5% in 2011 and then increased positively to 5.9 % in 2012 (World Bank Group, 2016; BBC, 2016). Despite the fact that the economic growth rate has increased systematically in the past few years with an average of 5.2% to 6%, the Government of Kenya has not been able to effectively resolve its development predicaments (Blanchard, 2013; Abdullah, 2015).

Some of the crucial economic generating sources such as high fuel and electricity costs, inflation, poor transportation infrastructure, and inadequate power supply continue to hamper multiple economic growth in the both the business and government sectors (BBC, 2016). As a remedy to the slow economic growth, the Government of Kenya enacted a policy to implement privatization, deregulation, and trade liberalization initiatives (Government of Kenya, 2015). However, high tariff rates continue to hinder investment (Blanchard, 2013). Agricultural products dominate exports to Europe, while manufactured goods, primarily apparel made from imported fabrics, dominate exports to the United States (US Department of State, 2016). Table 15.1 shows some Kenyan economic indicators.

Table 15.1 Kenya's economic indicators

Economic factor	Amount in US$	Year
GDP, PPP (current international)	$132,530,497,155	2014
GDP per capita, PPP (current international)	$2,954	2014
GDP growth rate (annual %)	5.328%	2014
Imports of goods and services (current US$)	$20,643,637,216	2014
Exports of goods and services (current US$)	$9,993,414,632	2014
Trade balance	-$10,857,516,704	2014
External debt stocks, total (DOD, current US$)	$13,471,481,000	2013
Commercial service exports (current US$)	$4,027,047,728	2014
Employment in agriculture (% of total employment)	61.1%	2005
Employment in industry (% of total employment)	6.7%	2005
Employment in services (% of total employment)	32.2%	2005

Source: GlobalEdge. (2016). *Kenya Economy.* http://globaledge.msu.edu/countries/kenya/economy. Accessed August 31, 2016.

Doing Business in Kenya (2016). *Embassy of the United States.* Nairobi, Kenya. https://nairobi.usembassy.gov/doing-business-local.html. Accessed September 3, 2016.

The strategic framework for a more robust business and government relations in Kenya was laid out in a major policy pronouncements since 2003. The major objective of this policy is to focus on a private business sector driven development process. This is the main goal of Kenya's Economic Recovery Strategy for Wealth and Employment Creation, the Private Sector Development Strategy (PSDS), and the recent Vision 2030. The new 2030 is the country's new development blueprint covering the period 2008 to 2030 (Kenya Vision 2030). This initiative constitutes a strategy to turn Kenya into a newly industrializing, middle-income country with an annual average growth rate of 10%. The major goals of the Vision 2030 are: (1) economic; (2) social; and (3) political governance reform anticipated to provide a high quality life to all its citizens by the year 2030 (Kenya Vision 2030).

Table 15.2 shows the export and import goods of Kenya. About 75% of Kenyans are engaged largely in subsistence farming. Coffee, tea, corn, wheat, sisal, and pyrethrum are grown in the highlands, mainly on small African-owned farms formed by dividing some of the large, formerly European-owned estates. Coconuts, pineapples, cashew nuts, cotton, and sugarcane are grown in the lower-lying areas. Much of the country is savanna, where large numbers of cattle are pastured. Kenya also produces dairy goods, pork, poultry, and eggs. The country's industries include food processing, flour milling, and horticulture (Government of Kenya, 2015; World Bank Group, 2016).

The Government of Kenya has largely steered the economy through stable growth, registering 5.6% in 2010, even after a period of prolonged

Table 15.2 Kenya's major export and import goods

Export	Amount in US$	Year
Coffee and spices	$1,421,943,629	2014
Live plants	$537,984,621	2014
Vegetables	$262,860,967	2014
Oil and mineral fuels	$218,377,556	2014
Plastics	$169,346,435	2014
Natural minerals and stone	$165,514,302	2013
Tobacco	$161,169,785	2014
Iron and steel	$151,540,111	2005
Preserved fruits and vegetables	$151,495,158	2005
Apparel: knit	$141,376,437	2005
Oil and mineral fuels	$3,882,648,081	2014
Industrial machinery	$1,821,438,047	2014
Motor vehicles and parts	$1,320,587,763	2014
Electrical machinery	$1,244,662,658	2014
Iron and steel	$775,497,275	2014
Plastics	$707,089,290	2014
Cereals	$577,125,085	2014
Fats and oils	$562,664,803	2014
Pharmaceuticals	$446,549,558	2014
Iron and steel articles	$410,079,336	2014
Trade Balance	−$10,857,516,704	2014

Source: GlobalEdge. (2016). *Kenya Economy.* http://globaledge.msu.edu/countries/kenya/economy. Accessed August 31, 2016.

Doing Business in Kenya. (2016). *Embassy of the United States.* Nairobi, Kenya. https://nairobi.usembassy.gov/doing-business-local.html. Accessed September 3, 2016.

drought and famine in parts of the country. This incremental economic growth was partially due international developments such as increased oil prices. The economic growth is also associated with macroeconomic stability, increased credit to the private sector, and improved weather conditions (Michuki, 2012). Meanwhile most business sectors of the economy are recording positive growths of varying magnitude, but best performers are the construction, mining, and quarrying industry (10%), electricity and water supply (9.9%), financial intermediation (8.8%), and agriculture and forestry (6.3%) (World Bank Group, 2016). Despite these positive outcomes, Kenya's population growth continually exceeds the rate of economic growth, resulting in large national budget deficits and high unemployment.

The country's well-developed transportation system has suffered from neglect in recent years (World Bank Group, 2016).

According to Kenya's Business Development Profile (2011) the Government of Kenya has instituted various reforms in the energy sectors to enhance power production and reduce overdependence on hydro-electric power. These measures include the separation of power generation (KENGEN) from its distribution (KP&LC), establishment of Rural Electrification Authorities and Geothermal Power Generation Authority, and the licensing of Independent Power Producers (IPPs). Major efforts are being made to diversify into wind, bio-diesel, and solar power generation. New sources of energy will be found through exploitation of geothermal power, coal, renewable energy sources, and connecting Kenya to energy-surplus countries in the region (Government of Kenya, 2007).

In the past decade, the Government of Kenya has reinvigorated its Meat Commission, Cooperative Creameries, Rift Valley Textile Mills, and other factories. Further, it rehabilitated its cotton, coconut, and cashew nut production, to mention a few initiatives. In order to enhance competiveness of local goods, the government has enforced international quality and environmental standards that are being policed by regulatory authorities, such as the National Environmental Managements Authority (NEMA) and the Kenyan Bureau of Standards (KEBS). Meanwhile the Kenyan Anti-counterfeit Authority has been established to cushion local manufacturers against competition from sub-standard goods (Kenya Business and Development Profile, 2011).

Corruption used to be a major problem in doing business with both the government and the private sectors in the past three decades in Kenya. However, since President of Uhuru Kenyatta resumed office as head of state, the incidence of corruption has declined in Kenya, even though it remains a major problem. A recent evaluation by Transparency International (TI) has ranked Kenya below all its neighboring countries, except Rwanda, on corruption prevalence. One of the advantages of a coalition government is that each side keeps a watchful eye on the other and will "blow the whistle" at the earliest opportunity in order to gain political mileage.

It takes a lot of effort for a nation to change from developing status to an industrialized country classification (Kenyan Association of Manufacturers, 2015). However, Kenya's manufacturing sector is relatively well advanced as compared to that of its neighboring countries. Indeed, the country is a net exporter of manufactured goods to the East and Central African region. According to Vision 2030, contribution of the manufacturing sector to GDP ought to grow from 10% to 20% by the year 2030 for Kenya to be considered as a newly industrializing country (Kenyan Business Development Profile, 2011; Michuki, 2011). The Ministry of Industrialization continues to collaborate with the business sector to work toward the realization of this objective.

Further, Kenya businesses also manufacture consumer goods such as plastic, furniture, batteries, clothing, and cigarettes. Petroleum is refined and aluminum, steel, and building materials are produced (BBC, 2016). Another challenge, however, is that the industrial development of Kenya has been hampered by shortages in hydroelectric power and by inefficiency and corruption in the public sector, but steps have been taken to privatize some state-owned companies. The chief minerals produced are limestone, soda ash, gemstones, salt, and fluorspar. Kenya attracts many tourists, largely lured by its coastal beaches and varied wildlife, which is protected in the expansive Tsavo National Park (8,034 sq. mi/20,808 sq. km) in the south-east (Blanchard, 2013; GlobalEdge, 2016; BBC, 2016).

Major Economic Challenges

Kenya's development priorities set out in Vision 2030, which aspire to promote political and macroeconomic stability, sustained economic growth, and social development, underpinned by rapidly expanding infrastructure, are a major economic challenge (BBC, 2016). The Vision aims for growth rates of 10% to reach upper middle income status (currently defined as a gross national income [GNI] per capita of $3,945) (World Bank Group, 2016). Kenya's GNI per capita was $760 in 2009. Economic growth in Kenya has been volatile, most notably slumping from 7% in 2007 to under 2% in 2008 following domestic and international shocks. Growth was provisionally 5% in 2011. Progress toward these goals requires increased investment and significantly improved productivity. An increase in aid to 2015 could make this achievable more quickly, improving Kenya's off-track performance on the Millennium Development Goals (notably child and maternal mortality) and reducing inequality. Aid could gradually be replaced by investment later in the decade, including from public finance such as the CDC Group (Kenya Operational Plan, 2012).

Unemployment and underemployment is currently at 40% of the labor force, and it is estimated to be about 20 million people (World FactBook, 2008). Unemployment for age 15–34 years, standing at 25% in 2005–2006, has increased over the years. The largest rise in the working-age population was recorded among the age cohort of 15–34 years, where the working-age population increased from 9.7 million persons in 1998/99 to 13.1 million persons in 2005/2006. The overall labor force participation rate was slightly over 72% in 2005/2006, with the male labor force participation being higher than the female participation rate (Blanchard, 2013; World Bank Group, 2016).

Social disparities are vast and reflect differences in economic development opportunities that are compounded by inequalities based on gender, age, social class, geographical distribution, and access to social services. Particularly women and youth in Kenya face special problems arising from poverty, forced early marriage, domestic violence, HIV and AIDS, lack of access to health services, and an unfavorable business environment. Even though Kenya ratified the UN Convention on the Elimination of All Forms of Discrimination against Women and has enacted legislation to implement its provisions in 1984, gender disparities remain widespread. Much of the problem lies with traditional practices that favor men in access to education, land, and inheritance, financial services, employment, and access to positions of political power. Poverty, especially income poverty, remains one of the most daunting challenges for Kenyans today (Blanchard, 2013; GlobalEdge, 2016). The national population in 2009 stood at 38.6 million people and is growing by an average of one million per year. The high rate of population growth is bound to have adverse effects on the economy due to increased public spending, and high dependency ratios. More than half (58%) of Kenyans live below poverty line, on less than $2 a day (Abdullah, 2015; GlobalEdge, 2016; World Fact Book, 2008). This means that most citizens of Kenya have inadequate access to basic needs such as food, water, shelter, clothing, and educational and health facilities.

There is a growing recognition of the potential impact of social protection in reducing poverty, child labor, and inequality, especially given the global economic downturn. Another major challenge in Kenya is gender equality and high unemployment among educated women (Kenya Economy, 2005; Dagne, 2011).World Bank Group, 2016). There is the crucial need for the promotion of women equal right in the country (GlobalEdge, 2016). More robust social protection delivery mechanisms using gender audits to inform analysis and to mainstream may be helpful in this regard. The examination of the differing needs constraints and opportunities and the impact of these differences in women's and men's access to social protection will be critical for developing a better government relationships dynamics in Kenya. Definitely without the equal contribution of women in the nation's sustainable development processes, Kenya can never be an industrialize country as proposed by its Vision 2030. The Government of Kenya recognizes the need to ensure that women are not penalized career-wise for their reproductive role. To this effect, the Government of Kenya has proposed the National Social Security Fund regarding the introduction of a maternity grant, which would be a major step toward addressing the pervasive gender inequities in the Kenyan workplace. A government mandated maternity grant would help ensure that women have financial security during maternity leave and also help reduce discriminatory hiring practices against women (Summary of Key Investment Opportunities in Kenya, 2014; Dagne, 2011).

Private and Public Sectors Partnership

The private sector in Kenya has emerged as an increasing important area to reinvigorate the process of seeking economic growth for the country. As a result of paradigm adjustment, economic growth is now realized to be best achieved through the promotion of the private sector in the country. The

Government of Kenya enacted the Private Public Partnership Act of 2013. The objective of this policy is to establish a legal framework for business and government relations in the development of infrastructure in the country (Government of Kenya, 2015). The National Treasury Ministry Private Public Partnership (2013) policy also specified 47 areas of priority that the government was interested in developing in the same year.

In the past few years the Government of Kenya has introduced initiatives to sell several of its public corporations. The government acknowledges that privatization of public corporation could strengthen the private sector more through the sales of shares, public-private partnership, negotiated sale of assets, and contracting out of services to the private sector. The public corporations selected for privatization were in the heavy equipment industry, food processing, and packaging, the Kenyan Electricity Generating Company, the Kenyan Ports Authority, various hotels, sugar, cement, dairy, wine, and meat processing companies, industrial equipment, education, energy, mining, finance, and agribusiness (Kenya National Treasury Ministry Private Public Partnership, 2013).

The Government of Kenya has implemented extensive deregulation and liberalization policies due to its proactive actions of Vision 2030. The aim of this government initiative is to establish an enabling business environment for the promotion of private sector investment in the country (Kenya Business Development Strategy, 2011). In addition, the Government of Kenya has been providing supports of diverse form to entrepreneurs and industrialists that yield significant and progressive records in the promotion of private investment. These initiatives include the provision of free land lease, subsidized credit services, reduction of tax rates, tax relief for a specific period of time, training services, and more importantly business development services to encourage the development of the flourishing micro and small-scale enterprises (Dibie et al., 2015).

The Government of Kenya requires businesses operating in the country to obtain one or more licenses and permits, depending on the activities of their enterprise. There are normally two types of business licenses: (1) sectoral specific licenses, and (2) non-sector-specific or cross-cutting licenses (Kenya Business Development Strategy, 2011; Government of Kenya, 2013). The sector-specific licenses are issued to business organizations in specific lines of industry (i.e., telecom, banking, and mining) by the agency responsible for regulating the sector. On the other hand, the non-sector specific or cross-cutting licenses are issued to business organizations that undertake activities that are subject to regulation but may fall across many types of production of goods and services. Business that fall into this category include environmental companies, immigration workers, consulting firms, and construction corporations (Government of Kenya, 2013). It is also important to note that all private businesses and NGOs in Kenya must also obtain a single business permit, which is issued by the local government authority where the business is physically located.

The most noticeable policy actions were the introduction of micro and small business development and industrial strategies with the purpose of promoting private sector development so as to significantly enhance its role as a mechanism for economic growth and development. The Government of Kenya support for micro and small enterprise development strategy includes provision of entrepreneurship and business training, mutual guarantee credit services through micro finance institutions, market linkage services, relevant technology research, business development services, and basic infrastructure that are deemed necessary for their operations (Blanchard, 2013; (Michuki, 2012).

Foreign Investment

The Government of Kenya is committed to attracting foreign investors to the country. As a result of this commitment, it has enacted the 2013 Private Public Partnership Act and the Foreign Investment Act and the Investment Promotion Act of 2004, respectively. Some provisions of the Kenyan 2010 Constitutions and the Companies Ordinance provide some level of protection for foreign direct investment in the country. The government of the country has also established the Kenyan Investment Authority to spearhead the promotion of investment in the nation (Government of Kenya, 2015). Despite these policies, industrial foreign ownership percentage is somewhat restricted. For instance, foreign ownership in the shipping industry is restricted to 49%, mining 65%, and telecommunication 80%. Other industrial sectors restriction includes stock market 75% and the construction industry 30% (Government of Kenya, 2015).

China is increasingly investing in the country. It is now estimated that there are 44 firms from mainland China operating in Kenya (GlobalEdge, 2016). Over the past four decades Chinese companies have helped Kenya build several projects—namely, Moi International Sports Center in Nairobi's central business district, a new teaching hospital at the brand new Moi University in Eldoret, and the Gambogi-Serem highway—and provided teaching equipment at Egerton University (Chege, 2014). It is also reported that China provides about 10 scholarships annually to Kenya and two top-level military exchanges per year as well (Summary of Key Investment Opportunities in Kenya, 2014; Dagne, 2011). There continue to be many Chinese construction companies in Kenya. The most successful so far is the China Road and Bridge Company, and it has attracted admiration and condemnation in equal measure. Since entering the Kenyan market in 1985, it has built more than 750 miles of trunk roads. By 2005, it had completed 11 projects worth nearly US$250 million. Among these are the Gambogi-Serem and Nairobi Road (Chege, 2014). Chinese construction companies also helped the Government of Kenya build a US$52 million sports stadium with a seating capacity of 60,000 people, an Olympic-size swimming pool, and a modern gymnasium to host the fourth All-Africa games in 1987 (Dagne, 2011).

Kenyan companies have led the way in developing mobile phone-based banking systems that have revolutionized financial transactions for increasing numbers in the developing world (US Department of State, 2016). US foreign direct investment in Kenya has grown in recent years, and the US government has proposed a new trade and investment partnership with the East African Community (EAC), of which Kenya is a member. The United States plans to engage with the EAC in a Commercial Dialogue, only one of four such dialogues worldwide.

For more than a decade, Demark has been committed to supporting development of the business sector in Kenya. This relationship has also been on the basis of partnerships between Kenyan and Danish companies to facilitate knowledge transference from Denmark to Kenya; thus Danish companies gain access to new markets and cheap production methods and facilities. In 2005 assistance entered a new dimension with the launching of the Business Sector Program Support (BSPS). This program supports the business sector both on a macro, meso, and micro level by assisting not only government but also private sector partners in creating an enabling environment for business (Kenyan Business Development Profile, 2011).

In addition, through its Danida Business Partnerships Program, the Danish Embassy in Kenya has committed itself to increase the quality and quantity of long-term partnerships between Danish business investors and Kenyan business partners. The program is designed to achieve this objective by promoting investment and trade opportunities for Danish investors in doing commercial business with Kenyan partners. At the present time the Danida Business Program (DBP) has supported more than 50 partnerships at different stages in all sectors of the Kenyan economy (Kenyan Business Development Profile, 2011). In the past few years Kenya's chief agricultural exports (i.e., tea and coffee) have been fluctuating in their world prices, and periodic droughts have had tremendous economic impact. Petroleum products, flowers, and fish are also exported. The leading imports are machinery, transportation equipment, petroleum products, motor vehicles, iron and steel, and plastics. Major trading partners in Kenya are the United States, Great Britain, Uganda, and the United Arab Emirates. In addition, the nation has bilateral investment agreement with Argentina, Bulgaria, Burundi, Poland, India, Pakistan, Thailand, Russia, Finland, France, Germany, Iran, Italy, Libya, United Kingdom, the Netherlands, Switzerland, Slovakia, and many countries in Africa (Summary of Key Investment Opportunities in Kenya, 2014). It is interesting to note that that at the present time, there is no prohibition on acquisition of Kenyan companies by foreign-owned firms, nor are there regulations restricting joint venture arrangements between Kenyans and foreigners.

Investment Opportunities for New Business

Despite infrastructure deficits, corruption, political uncertainty, an untapped informal sector, weak transportation infrastructure and interrupted supply of electricity power challenges that prevent the acceleration of economic growth and a robust private sector in Kenya, some new initiatives have been introduced (BBC, 2016; GlobalEdge, 2016). There are many investment opportunities in Kenya. It is interesting to note however that the nations has just started exploring these opportunities in the recent past two decades. According to the Government of Kenya (2015) report and the US Department of State (2016) report, Kenya seems to have turned its attention to exploring gas, oil, and minerals. This means there has been a shift from market foreign direct investment to resource seeking foreign direct investment activities in the country. This shift to resource exploration also requires all investors in the country to comply with environmental standards that are set by the National Environment Management Authority (Kenya Business and Development Profile, 2011; Government of Kenya, 2015).

One of the recent positive accomplishments of the Government of Kenya is that it has eliminated many business licenses from 697 in 2007 to just 16 (World Bank Group, 2016). The government has also established the e-registry to systematically speed up the registration of new companies, foster more transparency, as well as reduce cost of regulating the business sector (Summary of Key Investment Opportunities in Kenya, 2014; Dafflon & Madies, 2013).

While agriculture is the major economic driver of the economy, it suffered a US$300 million loss in assets due to post-election violence in 2008 as a result of destruction of farms and dairies (Dagne, 2011). Despite these shortcomings, the agricultural and tourism sectors have since rejuvenated their productivity and growth. Currently agriculture is reported to be providing livelihood to approximately 75% of the population (GlobalEdge, 2016; BBC, 2016). There is considerable opportunity for more diversification and expansion of the agricultural sector through accelerated food crop production, processing and marketing storage, and transportation; intensified irrigation; and additional value added (Best Business Ideas in Kenya, 2016). There are also many opportunities for improvement in technology update, infrastructure, packaging, and food processing. These are areas for future investments (Dafflon & Madies, 2013). According to the Government of Kenya Vision 2030 report, the communications, energy, building and construction, and pharmaceuticals sectors are major industrial sectors that need to expand. Specific areas of interest to business are eco-tourism, power generation equipment, telecommunications equipment, agricultural inputs, and food processing; these are major business and investment opportunities in Kenya. Tourism, agriculture, transport and infrastructure, manufacturing processing and packaging equipment, road construction, cement production, motor vehicles parts, among others are also potential areas of investment (Kenyan Business Development Profile, 2011).

In accordance with the provisions of Vision 2030, the Government of Kenya has introduced many initiatives to foster its economic development agenda. The government has invited the private sector to invest in power generation for sale to the national grid (Blanchard, 2013). The projected growth in electricity demand, therefore, could present several opportunities for investment in the energy sector. In addition to power supply opportunities for private sector investments, the Government of Kenya has created some programs for helping business entrepreneurs start to continue to grow and relocate to specific rural and urban areas in the country. Dafflon and Madies (2013) contend that the government often gives loans as start-up incentives and taking steps to create a "business-friendly" environment. These incentives include tax credits, worker training, free land, zoning changes, low-interest loans, infrastructure improvements, and help with fast-tracking licensing and permitting. In addition, Government agencies such as the US Small Business Administration provide loan guarantees to small business, encouraging local banks to work with start-ups or area business that wish to expand (World Bank Group, 2016; US Department of State, 2016). Further, the National Government of Kenya also provides grants to academic institutions working to develop new technologies that will benefit industry, with the caveat that the institutions share the technologies with industry. In some instances, the government will provide grants to private companies making a new product or service that will improve a vital area of Kenya's economy. On one hand, the National Governments help improve the infrastructure needed for businesses to thrive whenever it might be too costly for any one business to fund. Such support includes building and maintaining roads, bridges, rail lines, airports, seaports, and energy transmission lines and telecommunications systems. On the other hand, the Kenyan government often works with trade schools, community colleges, and universities to provide free workers' training. This gesture of the government has enhanced businesses in the country to have access to trained workers.

According to Abdullah (2015) and Ashe-Edmunds (2015), Kenya has a well-developed construction industry. With increase in population, opportunities exist in the construction of residential, commercial, and industrial buildings, including prefabricated low-cost housing. Extensive opportunities for investment exist particularly in the area of upgrading slums and informal settlements, urban renewal, construction of middle and low income housing, and manufacture and supply of building materials and components. In addition, a mirage of opportunities for direct and joint-venture investments exist in the manufacturing sector, including agro-processing, manufacture of garments, assembly of automotive components and electronics, plastics, paper, chemicals, pharmaceuticals, and metal and engineering products for both domestic and export markets (Doing Business in Kenya, 2016; World Bank Group, 2016; Central Intelligent Agency, 2016).

While government fiscal and monetary policies will remain a key factor of economic growth in Kenya, the private sector tourism industry is growing as a result of the liberalization measures. The diversification of tourist generating markets and continued government commitment to providing an enabling environment, coupled with successful tourism promotion and political stability, has resulted in positive growth. Enormous opportunities exist for investment in film production; recreation, and entertainment facilities in the following areas. The World Bank Group (2016) report reveals that the tourism industry in Kenya is the third largest foreign exchange earner. Through direct investments or joint ventures with Kenyan entrepreneurs, there are several opportunities in the tourism industry for construction of tourist hotels and game lodges all over the country.

It is interesting to note, however, that foreign ownership of equity in insurance and telecommunication companies is restricted to 66.7% and 80%, respectively. In addition, telecommunication companies are given a three year's grace period to find local investors to achieve the local ownership requirement (Government of Kenya, 2015). This incentive reveals that the Government of Kenya has made computer and Internet services one of its major economic recovery priorities. As a result, there are great opportunities for investment in this industrial sector. On the other hand, technology licenses are subject to scrutiny by the Kenyan Industrial Property Office to ensure that they are in line with the Industrial Property Act of the country. The bone of contention is that as the private sector is the main generator of economic growth and job creation, the Government of Kenya has a strong interest in ensuring that their business environment encourages and rewards entrepreneurship and innovation. This is very important, because such initiatives could galvanize private businesses in the county to expand and forge international trade and investment linkages, as well as benefit from the globalization processes.

Policy Recommendations

The analysis of business and government relations in Kenya reveals that both sectors cannot exist without each other. As a result the regulations of producers, buyers and exporters of agricultural goods can affect business growth, and in turn, the growth of the agricultural sector as a whole. Such regulations can take the form of licensing and registration requirements for the sale or purchase of certain agricultural products, or may involve special registration requirements for agricultural production contracts. It is recommended that the Government of Kenya impose special licensing regimes on the domestic market of certain agricultural plant (i.e., coffee, tea, cut flowers) products. These requirements can determine whether farmers are permitted to sell regulated crops, or if those crops can be bought only by licensed buyers. On the other hand, business firms in the country must legally do all it can to ensure a pragmatic commitment to corporate social responsibility. This could enable them to step up their ethical behavior, protect the environment more than the current situation, and adopt pragmatic corporate social responsibility practices.

The Government of Kenya is encouraged to do more in forming a conducive partnership with nongovernment organization (NGOs), community-based organizations, and other civil society groups, because these groups could enhance appropriate modifications to sustainable development policies in the country. In addition, with the growing demand for food and increasing export opportunities in regional trade, farmers will need to transport their produce to these markets to benefit from their potential. It is recommended that the Government of Kenya construct better roads as well as establish modern environmental friendly transport systems in the country. There is the immediate need to reduce transport costs, because such expenses continue to increase the price farmers pay for inputs as well as decrease their profit or income. High transportation cost also decreases the incentive to invest in their farms. Positive and transparent regulations practices could positively affect the availability, efficiency, effectiveness, reliability, and safety of transport services, as well as enhance sustainable development.

Since the government sector cannot provide all the jobs to solve the unemployment problems in Kenya, it is very crucial for the government to provide more incentives that could attract many international investors and corporations to the country (Mankiw 2018). There is also the need for the Government of Kenya, private sector, NGOs, and other civil society organizations to form partnerships in an integrated manner to create employment opportunities. To this effect, the introduction of micro and small business development and industrial development strategies with the purpose of promotion of private sector development as a mechanism for economic growth and development is strongly recommended (Dibie, 2014).

Although the Government of Kenya has taken a number of measures to deal with the problem of corruption, tackling corruption is another serious challenge facing the country's public and private sectors. Completely rooting out official corruption may require removing many senior members of the government from power and prosecution of former senior government officials. According to Dibie (2014), in order to escape the vicious cycle that corruption has created for disadvantaged groups, people need to be able to speak up for their rights and demand accountability from their leaders, ensuring access to basic social services and resources. If the social contract between the government and the people fails, the poor citizens may be forced to compromise on the quality of their livelihoods and their social and human rights. There is a common joke that when corrupt Kenyan political leaders die, they are often buried with their stolen wealth, houses, and dozens of expensive cars and jets. If this is not the case, they need to learn how to be accountable, transparent, and work diligently to provide for the basic needs of citizens. Further, programs that could enable disadvantaged people to take part in the development processes by opening dialogue between them and their governments should be established. If people have a say in how they are governed (participatory governance) and officials are accountable to the people they serve (social accountability), poor people become aware of their power as well as recognize their constitutional rights to demand accountability from their political leaders and public administrators. Participatory social accountability tools increase contact between citizens and governments, and therefore increase transparency, accountability, and good governance. These factors could also reduce the opportunities for people in authority to abuse their power. Increased citizen participation means better informed communities, more public oversight, and less corruption in planning and monitoring local development. This creates a win-win situation: the poor benefit from local development, and people in power benefit from being considered champions of integrity, and the community prospers (Stiwati et al., 2015; Dibie et al., 2015; Ya Ni & Van Wart, 2016).

The Government of Kenya should create an enabling environment that could enhance the private sector to provide a framework and incentives for innovation and delivery of goods and services. Therefore, there is a crucial need in Kenya to look for greater synergies between the means of more investment in private sector activities that benefit poor people. According to Dibie et al. (2015), the Kenyans themselves will need to proactively rebuild their country. Enhancing capacity building that leads to domestic economic growth in the country countries is important because it will provide a foundation for the future of the societies in the nation.

Economic growth can contribute to advancements in manufacturing, production, employment, and social well-being of citizens, as well as creating beneficial outcomes and solutions to many economic problems in the country (Mankiw, 2012). Economic growth is important because it keeps all sectors in the country moving in a positive, productive direction (Mankiw 2018; Mandel, 2012). Increased economic growth in Kenya may enhance or increase employment opportunities. The neoclassical approach to economic growth prescribes two basic premises: a free market economy and appropriate fiscal and monetary policies in the economic development of a country.

Clear and serious uneven distribution of economic resources between regions and ethnic groups is known to have led to conflict and sometimes to serious secessionist rebellion. An enabling environment free of conflict is where economic growth can take place. Helping citizens meet their needs such as job creation and full employment will also reduce conflict. In addition, good governance and minimal government intervention in the private production of goods and services, minimal management of industry strategies, and a more regulatory approach to social and individual responsibilities could rejuvenate sustainable development in the country (Ya Ni & Van Wart, 2016). However, more important than learning about market, technology, competitors, customers, or suppliers, Kenya's leaders must prepare for and look forward to learning about the concept of servant leadership and the type of economic development legacy that they want to leave behind.

The notion of power in Kenya has both positive and negative connotations and often produces feelings of ambivalence in the country. The Government of Kenya must view power as located in each person, not centralized in an elite group, and it must treat the legitimate exercise of power as a right that belongs to all citizens. The cooperative arrangements of networks where everybody is working together toward achieving a common goal could serve to enhance civility that is necessary for effective governance. The governance network will provide the opportunities for citizen participation. The cooperative network will enhance more effective regulatory control, and the expression of public sector values within the marketplace in Kenya. This will happen as a result of the sense of shared responsibility and the dependent relationship. Judicial reform and a free media is also an important instrument to encourage participation of civil society groups and citizens in conflict resolution in the country. Participatory social accountability tools will increase contact between citizens and governments, and therefore increase transparency, accountability, and good governance. Therefore, the positive attributes of inclusive governance encompass material well-being, wider choices, and opportunities for people to realize their potentials, and the guarantee of equity of treatment, freedom to choose, and full participation in the process by which citizens govern themselves in Kenya.

Conclusion

This chapter has examined the nature of business and government relations in Kenya. It argues that the relationship between business and government in Kenya is tantamount to satisfying the needs of all stakeholders and ensuring sustainable development in the country. On one hand, the government regulates business and control of the economy through fiscal and monetary policies. On the other hand, businesses influence government in its regulation through pressure groups and public opinion, as well as by producing goods and services.

The evaluation of business-government relations in Kenya reveals that the government of the country does not effectively provide the enabling environment due to corruption and political sentiments. This predicament has affected the way businesses are required to comply with the laws and regulations that are implemented by the government. The Government of Kenya introduced a robust Vision 2030 development plan in 2006. This very ambitious agenda postulates a strategy to turn Kenya into a newly industrializing, middle-income country that will provide a high quality life to all its citizens by the year 2030. However, achieving such high growth will depend on improved economic governance and greater economic reform in order to improve the country's investment climate. According to Dibie et al. (2015), recognizing the complex nature of business and government relations in Africa, and the ability of the Kenyan Government to detect incredibly weak warning signs, and taking appropriate decisive action when ideal are the hallmarks of achieving the goal of Vision 2030 and sustainable development in the country.

Kenya has developed several partnerships with foreign businesses from China, Japan, the United States, the Netherlands, and several other African countries. It is necessary for the Government of Kenya to be careful in entering such extensive partnership. This is because most African governments, business entrepreneurs, intellectuals, and policy makers have been previously manipulated in the hands of foreign corporations. The Kenyan case with foreign business partnership demonstrates that there are severe challenges as well as opportunities for the country in its emerging economic relationships with foreign corporations and NGOs. While previous partnership had advanced mutual gain in some cases, it has also fostered exploitation in other areas. Therefore, there is a crucial need for an objective analysis of the current nature of partnership with foreign business in order to work out new modalities of reform.

The chapter also explored strategic imperative approaches such as inclusiveness, responsiveness, and efficiency in business and government relations in Kenya, trust creation, and confidence building. Others scholars also contend that good governance in Africa should include (1) national actions to strengthen external accountability; (2) national checks and balances to strengthen internal accountability; (3) measures to enhance inclusiveness; (4) administrative reform to improve internal accountability; (5) local actions to strengthen external accountability; and (6) adoption of laws and regulations (Sitawati et al., 2015; Dibie et al 2015, Teece, 2007; Uwazie, 2014).

Despite its good industrial development initiatives, the government has been unable to provide a secure environment for businesses and families, particularly in urban settings. Property crime and violence are major concerns and have become an unavoidable cost of doing business for companies in Kenya. One fact is that Kenyan citizens alone can develop their nation. The people of Kenya must be the change they wish to see in their country, and they must develop a common sense of economic and sustainable development goals.

References

Abdullah, S. (2015, June 9). *Economic Relations on Kenya*. The National Staff. www.thenational.ae/uae/government/sheikh-abdullah-discusses-economic-relations-on-kenya-visit. Accessed August 31, 2016.

Ashe-Edmunds, S. (2015). *Role of Government in Promoting Small Business*. http://smallbusiness.chron.com/role-government-promoting-small-business-60657.html. Accessed August 31, 2016.

Best Business Ideas in Kenya. (2016). www.africa-do-business.com/kenya.html. Accessed August 30, 2016.

Blanchard, L. P. (2013). *U.S.-Kenya Relations: Current Political and Security Issues*. Congressional Research Service, 7–5700: United States, Government Press.

British Broadcasting Corporation. (2016). *Kenya Country Profile*. www.bbc.com/news/world-africa-13681341. Accessed August 31, 2016.

Central Intelligent Agency. (2016). *The World Factbook*. www.cia.gov/library/publications/the-world-factbook/. Accessed August 30, 2016.

Chege, M. (2014). *Economic Relations Between Kenya and China, 1963–2007*. https://csis-prod.s3.amazonaws.com/s3fs-public/legacy_files/files/media/csis/pubs/080603.chege_kenyachina.pdf. Accessed September 23, 2016.

Dafflon, B. and Madies, T. (2013). The Political Economy of Decentralization in Sub-Saharan Africa: A New Implementation Model in Burkina Faso, Ghana, Kenya and Senegal. African Development Series, Washington, DC. World Bank Publication.

Dagne, T. (2011). *Kenya: Current Conditions and the Challenges Ahead*. Congressional Research Service, 7–5700: United States, Government Press.

Dahlsrud, A. (2008). How Corporate Social Responsibility Is Defined: An Analysis of 37 Definitions. *Corporate Social Responsibility Environment Management*, 15, 1–13.

Dibie, R. (2014). Civil Society and Conflict Resolution in the Niger Delta of Nigeria. In E. Uwazie (Ed.), *Alternative Dispute Resolution and Peace-building in Africa*. Newcastle upon Tyne, UK: Cambridge Scholars Publishing.

Dibie, R. and Dimitriou, C. (2016). Evaluation of Sustainable Environmental Initiatives in Hotels in Southern Nigeria. *Journal of Applied and Theoretical Environmental Sciences*, 2(2), 25–56.

Dibie, R., Edoho, F. M. and Dibie, J. (2015). Analysis of Capacity-Building in Africa. *International Journal of Business and Social Sciences*, 4(12), 233–243.

Doing Business in Kenya. (2016). *Embassy of the United States*. Nairobi, Kenya. https://nairobi.usembassy.gov/doing-business-local.html. Accessed September 3, 2016.

Donaldson, T. and Preston, L. E. (1995). The Stakeholder Theory of the Corporation: Concept, Evidence, and Implications. *Academy of Management Review*, 20(1), 65–91.

Ferrell, C., Fraedrich, J. and Farrell, L. (2017). *Business Ethics: Ethical Decision Making and Cases*. 10th Edition. Stanford, CT: Cengage Learning Press.

Ferrell, O. C., Hirt, G. and Ferrell, L. (2016). *Business: A Changing World*. New York: McGraw-Hill Press.

Freeman, H. A. and Kaguongo, W. 2003. Fertilizer Market Liberalization and Private Retail Trade in Kenya. *Food Policy*, 28(5–6), 505–518.

Froeb, L. M., McCann, B. T., Shor, M. and Ward, M. R. (2016). *Managerial Economics: A Problem Solving Approach*. Stamford, CT: Cengage Learning.

GlobalEdge. (2016). *Kenya Economy*. http://globaledge.msu.edu/countries/kenya/economy. Accessed August 31, 2016.

Government of Kenya. (2015). www.commonwealthofnations.org/sectors-kenya/government/. Accessed September 3, 2016.

Government of Kenya. (2013). *How to Use the E-Registry*. www.businesslicense.or.ke/index.Php/index/index/id/3. Accessed August 28, 2016.

Government of Kenya. (2007). *Vision 2030*. www.usaid.gov/sites/default/files/documents/1860/3%29%20Vision%202030%20Abridged%20version.pdf. Accessed August 28, 2016.

Griffin, R., Phillips, M. and Gully, S. M. (2017). *Organizational Behavior: Managing People and Organizations*. Boston, MA: Cengage Learning, 69–71.

Hanson, S. (2009). *Corruption in Africa*. www.cfr.org/africa-sub-saharan/corruption-sub-saharan-africa/p19984. Accessed April 14, 2016.

Henderson, J. (2007). Corporate Social Responsibility and Tourism: Hotel Companies in Phuket, Thailand, After the Indian Ocean Tsunami. *Hospitality Management*, 26, 228–239.

Hopkins, M. (2003). *The Planetary Bargain-CSR Matters*. London, UK: Earthscan.

Kang, K. H., Sein, L., Heo, C. Y. H. and Lee, S. (2012). Views on Environmentalism and Consumers' Willingness to Pay for Environmental Sustainability in the Hotel Industry. *International Journal of Hotel Management*, 28(1), 105–112.

Kenya Association of Manufacturers. (2015). www.kam.co.ke. Accessed August 30, 2016.

Kenya Business Development Strategy. (2011). The Feed the Future (FTF) Multi-Year Strategies. https://feedthefuture.gov/sites/default/files/resource/files/KenyaFeedthe FutureMultiYearStrategy.pdf. Accessed August 31, 2016.

Kenya Economy. (2005). www.infoplease.com/encyclopedia/world/kenya-government. html. Accessed August 29, 2016.

Kenya National Treasury Ministry Private Public Partnership. (2013). http://ppunit. go.ke. Accessed September 2, 2016.

Kenya Operational Plan 2011–2015 Department for International Development. (2012). www.gov.uk/government/uploads/system/uploads/attachmentdata/file/ 67399/kenya-2011.pdf. Accessed August 31, 2016.

Kuye, O. L. and Ogundele, O. J. K. (2013). Strategic Roles of Business, Government and Society: The Nigerian Situation. *International Journal of Business and Social Sciences*, 4(12), 233–243.

Lee, S. and Park, S. Y. (2009). Do Social Responsibility Activities Help Hotels and Casinos Achieve Their Financial Goals? *International Journal of Hospitality Management*, 43, 13–32.

Lehne, R. (2013). *Government and Business*. Washington, DC: Congressional Quarterly Press.

Lubale, G. (2012). *An Introduction to the County Governments of Kenya*. http:// gabriellubale.com/an-introduction-to-the-county-governments-of-kenya/. Accessed September 3, 2016.

McGuigan, J. R., Moyer, R. C. and Harris, F. H. (2014). *Managerial Economics: Application, Strategy and Tactics*. Stamford, CT: Cengage Learning.

Maignan, I. and Ferrell, O. C. (2001). Antecedents and Benefits of Corporate Citizenship: An Investigation of French Businesses. *Journal of Business Research*, 51(1), 37–51.

Mandel, M. (2012). *Economics: The Basics*. New York, NY: McGraw-Hill Press.

Mankiw, C. N. (2018). *Principles of Macroeconomics*. Mason, OH: South Western/ Cengage Learning.

Michuki, W. (2012). *The Role of Government in the Promoting Private Sector Development in Kenya*. www.slideshare.net/subsahara/wanja-michuki. Accessed August 28, 2016.

Nelson, D. and Quick, J. C. (2013). *Organizational Behavior: Science, the Real World and You*. Mason, OH: South-Western Press/Cengage Learning.

Perez, A. and del Bosque, I. R. (2014). Sustainable Development and Stakeholder Relations Management: Exploring Sustainability Reporting in the Hospitality Industry From a SD-SRM Approach. *International Journal of Hospitality*, 42, 174–187.

Singh, N., Cranage, D. and Lee, S. (2014). Green Strategies for Hotels: Estimation of Recycling Benefits. *International Journal of Hospitality Management*, 43, 13–32.

Sitawati, R., Winata, L. and Mia, L. (2015). Competitive Strategy and Sustainable Performance: The Application of Sustainable Scorecard. *Issues in Social Environmental Accounting*, 9(1), 51–75.

Summary of Key Investment Opportunities in Kenya. (2014). *Ministry of State for Planning, National Development and Vision 2030*. Nairobi, Kenya: Government Press.

Teece, D. (2007). Explicating Dynamic Capabilities: The Nature and Micro-Foundations of Sustainable Enterprise Performance. *Strategic Management Journal*, 28(13), 1319–1350.

US Department of State. (2016). *Doing Business in Kenya*. http://nairobi.usembassy. gov/doing-business-local.html. Accessed September 23, 2016.

Uwazie, E. (2014). *Alternative Dispute Resolution and Peace-building in Africa.* Newcastle upon Tyne, UK: Cambridge Scholars Publishing.

Wang, C. (2014). Do Ethical and Sustainable Practices Matter? Effects of Corporate Citizenship on Business Performance in Hospitality Industry. *International Journal of Contemporary Hospitality Management*, 26(6), 930–947.

Wang, C. L. and Ahmed, P. K. (2007). Dynamic Capabilities: A Review and Research Agenda. *International Journal of Management Review*, 9(1), 31–51.

World Bank. (2012). *Africa Can Help Feed Africa: Removing Barriers to Regional Trade in Food Staples.* Washington, DC: World Bank.

World Bank Group. (2016). www.worldbank.org/en/country/kenya/overview. Accessed September 23, 2016.

World Bank (2016). *Doing Business: Assessing Business Environment in Kenya.* www.doingbusiness.org/ExploreEconomies/Default.aspx?economyid=101. Accessed August 30, 2016.

World Factbook (2008). Kenya's Uncertain Democracy: The Electoral Crisis of 2008. https://books.google.com/books?id=1cXdAAAAQBAJ&pg=PA18&dq=World+Factbook+2008+Kenya. Accessed May 10, 2016. &hl=en&sa=X&ved=0ahUKEwiis6ney e TTAhVpiVQKHazzAfUQ6AEIKzAC#v=onepage&q=World%20Factbook%202008%20Kenya&f=false - Page 18

Ya Ni, A. and Van Wart, M. (2016). *Building Business–Government Relations: A Skills Approach.* New York: Routledge Press.

Case Study

Panoramic Corporate Social Responsibility Debacle

The Department of Environment (DE) recently hired a new secretary named Dr. Ajiri Maro. Dr. Maro is an accomplished civil servant, having previously served as director in several federal agencies and boards. The Department of Environment has four major divisions that help implement and regulate environmental policy issues all over the country. The Department of Environment is assigned by the national government to manage all environmental concerns in the country Environmental concerns in the country has been creating ethical issues for individuals, organizations, and public policy makers. The desire for sustainable business means that social responsibility, ethics, and special initiatives must be used to implement effective changes. The Department of Environment defines sustainability from a business perspective as the potential for long-term protection of the natural environment, including the ecosystem, biological entities, as well as for mutually beneficial interactions among nature and individual, organizations, and business strategies.

All the employees in the four divisions were constantly expected to meet high expectations of safety. As a reward for their performance, employees were able to advance upward, receive better pay, or obtain career advancement. The career prospect of employees in the Department of Environment was seen as a forum for positive reinforcement. This is because work processes were historically treated as having more value than their outcome.

Just after two months in his new position, Dr. Maro had a meeting with all the directors in the Department of Environment. In that meeting, Dr. Maro contends that the state of the environment in the business sector was really bad, and as a result things have to change. He indicated that the lack of compliance in the business sector was due to internal leadership issues and unethical behavior in the Department of Environment. He argued that a performance evaluation system may have to be introduced to constantly evaluate staff performance and the nature of rewards. He was also not sure whether the work made a difference to other employees or to the organization as a whole. In addition, Dr. Maro suggested that he had decided to move away from the old hierarchical control system in the department to a vertical hierarchy, with the compartmentation of all activities. As a result, the new structure of the department must reflect this tendency. After his speech, Dr. Maro called for a motion to adopt what he had just proposed. No motion was forthcoming. His deputy, Dr. Ogaga, requested to be recognized to give a short speech. Dr. Ogaga was allowed to give a short speech.

In his speech, Dr. Ogaga thanked the new secretary to the Department of Environment, and he moved forward to state that while Dr. Maro's views of the department might be correct, they did not correlate with the past independent assessment of the staff's performance. Dr. Ogaga ended his speech by calling for motion that the senior staff of the department should be given some time to review the proposal of Dr. Maro. Dr. Ogaga's motion was seconded and passed unanimously. The issues that came up from this meeting are that Dr. Maro was not fully aware of the professional intractable attachment to the process and the functional activities that made it up. The staff of the department had generally come to prize their work activities once they become experts at and are rewarded for doing them.

At the next meeting, Dr. Ogaga; Dr. Akoko, the Director of the Environmental Protection Agency; as well as Mrs. Ojemeh, Director of Occupational Safety and Health, jointly proposed a motion that the staff should disregard what was proposed by Dr. Maro in the last meeting. This is because their various staffs find it challenging to adjust or even eliminate what they do in the face of a lack of evidence that it produces anything meaningful or sustainable.

Dr. Maro was highly offended by the motion that defeated his new proposal. He immediately jumped to his feet and left the board room. On reaching his office, he asked his administrative assistant to write a letter to Dr. Ogaga, Mrs. Ojemeh, and Dr. Akoko, asking them to resign immediately or they will be fired. In his letter Dr. Maro reiterated that the chief lesson that he has learned in his various leadership roles is that the only way to make an employee trustworthy is by trusting him or her. In addition, the surest way to make staff untrustworthy is to distrust them. It is therefore paramount to always help employees increase their self-esteem by letting them know that you appreciate their efforts. This is necessary; hence you make it a point to praise your staff in the presence of those closest to them.

Dr. Maro noted that 70% to the staff that had resigned in Dr. Ogaga's division did so because they did not feel valued or trusted. These data are an indictment of how poorly Dr. Ogaga has treated his staff over the five past years. The bone of contention is that it has cost the Department of Environment more than $500,000 to conduct new job searches to hire the replacement of the 120 employees that resigned in Dr. Ogaga's division. Dr. Maro stated that Dr. Ogaga had allowed Dr. Akoko and Mrs. Ojemeh to manipulate him. Dr. Ogaga had also allowed his two friends, Ojemeh and Akoko, to influence his decisions through him (Dr. Maro). The golden rule of leadership is "do to others whatever you would like them to do to you." Thus, a good business relationship and friendship should be based on the golden rule, because this ethical practice would have resulted in a win-win situation for Dr. Ogaga. However, since this is not the case, Dr. Ogaga, Dr. Akoko, and Mrs. Ojemeh need to go, because their obstructive leadership style has cost the Department of Environment approximately $3 million in the past five years. Other senior colleagues intervened and pleaded for leniency. As a result of their intervention, Dr. Maro had to change his decision from firing Ogaga, Akoko, and Ojemeh to recommending their immediate retirement.

After almost two months of the leadership debacle, Dr. Maro's attention was drawn to other serious management issues in the Environmental Protection Agency (EPA) that he was asked to also lead by the executive branch of the government. At the EPA, the relationship among senior administrators was cordial yet somewhat strained. This is because the leaders dealing with complex issues on how to regulate the corporations in the energy and manufacturing industries in the country often disagree on the appropriate methods to adopt. In the past, although the acting director of the EPA, Mr. Odudu, often publicly stated that he wanted to hear all sides of the issues facing the agency, he also constantly interrupted the discussion or attempted to change the topic when other senior administrators openly disagreed in their view of the problem. This interruption was typically followed by an awkward silence in the group. In many instances, when a solution to a pressing problem did not appear forthcoming, senior administrators either moved on to another issue, or they informally voted on proposed options, letting majority rule decide the outcome. In addition, some senior administrators rarely discussed the need to move on or vote; rather, these behaviors emerged informally over time and became the acceptable way of dealing with difficult issues.

Many companies that were regulated by the EPA had realized the importance of sustainability to their customers. As a result, they implemented extensive waste management and recycling programs. Other companies introduced large scale environmental initiatives, particularly those regarding energy saving and recycling. One of the companies regulated by the EPA prohibited trucks from idling their engines outside any of their buildings. The same company had collected more than 80 million pounds of electronic waste for recycling. To ensure that corporations are acting in a socially responsible manner, the EPA inspectors monitor many corporations' recycling practices to enhance compliance. A national reputable company headed by Dr. Ikede was found to have been dumping his recycled computers, asbestos, lead, and engine oil into a distance city landfill. While the environmental benefits of recycling have been made quite clear by the EPA to include reduction in waste, decreased gas emission, energy savings, and more, the strict recycling policy of the EPA continues to encourage manufacturing corporations to take greater responsibility in product design. As a result of violating these laws, Dr. Ikede was arrested. In the process of writing his statement at the EPA office, Dr. Ikede confessed that the director of the EPA knew all along that his corporation was dumping waste in the landfill. The name of the EPA director was Mr. Makunju. Dr. Ikede stated that he normally paid Mr. Makunju $20,000 every six months to cover up the waste disposal crime.

There were several other problems reported about the EPA. Several minority staff complained that their voices and perspectives were not respected by their white bosses. In addition, Black and Hispanic CEOs of corporations that the EPA had regulated complained that senior administrators do not reply their phone calls. These practices have negatively affected the reputation of the EPA among Blacks and Hispanic citizens that are CEOs of corporations that the agency previously regulated. These minority groups often argue that the EPA board needs to ensure that decisions affecting them are environmentally sensitive to the needs of their communities. Apparently there are no Black or Hispanic senior staff working in the EPA.

Many EPA inspectors that were assigned to ensure that major corporations in the country did not pollute the environment by emitting fossil fuels did not perform their duties diligently. Some of the inspectors were given expensive gifts by corporations' chief executive officers. In some cases, their boss Mr. Odudu was invited to play golf with the CEOs of the corporations that he inspected. During such events, he was also given millions of dollars and expensive cars as gifts. Some other corporations often send his wife and children on expensive holiday trips to the Bahamas. Two of the major corporations that Mr. Odudu's staff recently inspected and certified for excellent emission standards had plants that caught fire. The emergency experts from the Occupations Health and Safety (OHS) Agency discovered that there were high rates of fossil fuel emission from the burned plants. The CEO of the corporation called Mr.

Odudu to issue altered certificate of compliance. Mr. Odudu ultimately decided not to disclose the poor compliance information and indulge in unethical behavior by signing the compliance certificate. Eventually the OSH Agency concluded that it was impossible to identify who was at fault for the usual high emissions.

About a month before Dr. Maro was assigned to address the debacle in the EPA, a white woman named Ms. Abiola, working in one the divisions of the EPA, described her male boss who refused to pay her any respect. Ms. Abiola complained that her supervisor constantly micromanaged her duties. As a result of the interference of her boss Ms. Abiola believes that her colleagues, supervisor, and EPA did not benefit from her unproductive circumstance working environment. Instead of other senior administrators to advise her boss not to micromanage her, they kept quiet. The situation warranted a manager from one of the corporations who came out of town to do business with the EPA to advise Ms. Abiola to accept responsibility for her own personal fulfillment as well as find ways to expand her potential. The visiting manager also reiterated that she needed to find a new way to use her capacities to serve the needs of others and the EPA. Ms. Abiola's case reveals that effective followers are far from powerless, and they know it. Therefore, they do not despair in their position, nor do they resent or manipulate others.

Ms. Jumoke, who had just completed her master's in public management, was hired by the EPA. She was very thrilled to put into practice all that she had learned about environmental policy in graduate school. When she started her new job, nobody told her where her duties began and ended. Those things were never actually spelled out in an agreement, and the boundaries remained vague and confusing. Ms. Jumoke suddenly realized that there was little or no discussion of her vision or any mention about how she could fit into the future being laid out for her. Ms. Jumoke wanted to feel like an EPA staff member and not a sidekick to the senior administrators. At the same time, she did not want to push so hard that the senior administrators become concerned that they made a mistake in selecting her. Ms. Jumoke was not the only staff facing a lack of defined job description. Many line managers were also not living up to the expectations of empowering their junior staff. The situation in the Environmental Protection Agency shows that attempts to achieve collaboration, empowerment, and diversity in the institution have failed because the senior staff believe in an old paradigm that values control, stability, and homogeneity. It was difficult for senior administrators to let go of methods and practices that have made them and the EPA successful in the past.

In the first meeting that Dr. Maro had with the senior administrators of the EPA, he suggested that the leadership problem facing the agency entails high interdependence among the functional administrators. Consequently, high coordination among senior administrators is needed to resolve the predicament. He contended that the EPA senior administrators' meetings also seem to include many issues that are complex and not easily solved, so there is probably a relatively high amount of uncertainty in the technology or work process. The causes of the problem or acceptable solutions are not readily available. As a result, senior administrators must process considerable information during problem-solving, especially when there are different perceptions and opinions about the issues. It is paramount that senior administrators in the EPA must realize that their staffs are constantly exposed to a variety of information. They know when their leaders are being phony.

Dr. Maro decided to decentralize the structure of the Environmental Protection Agency. The new divisions created were (1) Human Resources; (2) Industrial Inspections; (3) Occupational Safety; (4) Technology Transfer; and (5) Pollution Control. He gave five new division heads CEO-like authority. He also created a compelling vision for EPA for the agency to implement a strategy to support the vision, and launched a marketing campaign to build the EPA service standard and reputation. The new vision of the EPA called for a shift from a stand-alone service agency to an e-services public agency. The two remaining senior administrators Mr. Odudu and Mrs. Kolo were assigned to marketing responsibilities that focus on building positive relations with key industrial clients. In addition, the structural changes were supported with new compensation systems in the EPA. Dr. Maro also stated that everybody deserves a returned phone call. All employees of the EPA must return phone calls of CEOs of corporation, as well as those of citizens that are calling to inquire information about environmental protection and pollution control issues. According to him, that is the standard operating procedure. The most important part of a relationship with people or corporations is communication. We have to nurture relationships with citizens and corporations or anybody that wants to talk to us about our organization.

The EPA senior and managerial rewards, traditionally in the form of raises and bonuses, were revamped to include retirement investment and overall agency performance. Dr. Maro contends that it is not only salary that motivates staff. How much they are respected, cordial relationships with colleagues, and whether they feel they have a career with the EPA are also very important. By paying close attention to the implementation of structural and personnel changes, Dr. Maro helped the EPA make great strides in institutionalizing cooperation and individual coordination. Thus, he rejuvenated the perception of reality and dispelled the negative doubt that often influences behavior in the workplace. Leaders who persistently promote performance and humanity devote considerable energy to reading and responding to followers' feelings, needs, and actions. He challenged the new directors and their environmental inspectors to continue to main high ethical standards regarding corporations, employees, vendors, and the environment.

Assignment

Conduct a critical analysis of the problems facing the Department of Environment and the Environment Protection Agency (EPA). In what ways have the employees of both the Department of Environment and EPA enhanced or reduced leadership creativity in their respective organizations? Make appropriate recommendations on how to resolve the problems in both organizations.

16 Business and Government and Capacity Building in Africa

Robert A. Dibie and Felix M. Edoho

Introduction

African countries collectively have more than one billion people who are consumers (World Bank, 2016). Satisfying the needs of these huge consumers constitutes and poses great challenges to businesses and governments in the African continent. In spite of these challenges, the people in sub-Saharan African countries need to eat, drink clean water, live in houses, and wear clothes. They also need electricity, cell phones, good education, medical care, computers, roads, automobiles, air conditioners, and so on (Dibie et al 2015). Various forms of multinational and domestic businesses have been exploring the great consumer market in sub-Saharan Africa. Although the business system has served the African society somewhat well, criticism of business and its practices has become commonplace in recent decades. According to Mahajan (2009) and Sandbrook (1993), the business system and government suffered a major blow when the International Monetary Fund (IMF) and the World Bank prescribed a series of structural adjustment programs that African countries adopted. The structural adjustment programs heightened the public's awareness of the impact that businesses can have on unemployment and inflation (World Bank, 2014; Ayeni & Adelabu, 2012; United Nations Human Development Report, 2014).

One of the greatest challenges facing Africa today is restoring its economic growth and sustainability goals. During the 1980s and early 1990s, some African countries were plagued with severe political instability and poverty (Ezana, 2011; UNDP, 2014). Fortunately, these challenges have been followed by a favorable democratic and environmental renaissance (Gwin, 2014). Indeed, the current positive conditions have become a catalyst for economic growth, bringing affordable energy, jobs, revenues, and an accompanying resurgence of manufacturing and agricultural products (United Nations Human Development Index, 2014). Many scholars have described the social, economic, and institutional problems in sub-Saharan Africa to be associated with its inadequate capacity building efforts (Gwin, 2014; James, 1998; Eade, 2005; Edoho, 1998; Hayami & Gogo, 2005).

The principal institutional mechanism for developing human capital is the formal education system of primary, secondary, and tertiary training (Nsubuga, 2003; Afolabi, 2002; Ayeni & Adelabu, 2012; Gwin, 2014; James, 1998). However, the education institutions all over the continent are poorly equipped, managed, and have provided educational access to the poor and rural people. In some cases, there has been a negative connection between the education system and the skills needed for economic growth (World Bank, 2014; UNDP, 2014).

According to Helpman (2004), one of the reasons for the gap between African countries and those of developed countries is the fact that nations in the African continent have failed to focus on increasing their research and development (R&D) initiatives. African countries, rather than developing their own R&D, tend to benefit from the ones that take place in the industrialized countries. Another major problem is that these R&D benefits are larger when measured in consumption rather than GDP units (Gilpin, 2001). This means that the output gains of the developed countries far exceed the output gains of African countries. Sengupta (2011) contends that most African countries are characterized by high income inequality, whereby several million citizens are placed in extreme poverty. This kind of problem limits the benefits of equally shared growth in the continent. As a result, inequality further augments the adverse effect of market and policy failure on economic growth.

A World Bank (2014) report indicated that although basic socioeconomic conditions in Africa are gradually improving, market and policy failure problems continue to constitute a weak foundation for expanding public sector and business capacities. The political situation in many African countries has further prevented the national governments from integrating formal rules with informal norms in ways that ensure good governance (Nwazor, 2012). According to Hayami and Gogo (2005), Dibie (2014), and the World Bank (2014), consensus building on how to move forward is often a difficult thing to do in a political atmosphere that constantly generates a complex configuration of losers and winners. Concern for capacity building in the sub-Saharan African region led to the creation of the African Capacity Building Initiative (ACBI) in 1991. The ACBI framework called for increased participation and leadership of African citizens in the development assistance projects. It also proposed a radical change of the traditional attitudes on the part of donors toward technical assistance.

The relatively underdevelopment and poor capacity building in Africa are also caused by brain drain. Brain drain designates the international transfer of human capital from the African continent to various Western developed countries (Alamiirew, 2008). Mohamedbhai (2007), UNDP (2014), and Gwin (2014) contend that the African continent losses about 73,000 professional personnel annually, and currently more than 41,000 of its PhD holders are living in Europe, Canada, or the United States. Another major problem of capacity building is that 55% of the medical doctors trained in

Africa leave the continent to practice in Western Europe or North America (Gwin, 2014). Therefore, it could be argued that capacity building should be a very difficult thing to achieve in Africa because (1) the continent presently lacks professional or expert human capital; (2) the continent presently lacks international communication technology; (3) the governments do not regard development as a process that could be cumulative as well; (4) the governments fail to see sustainable development as a process that requires all stakeholders or citizens collaboration; and (5) the governments fail to take stakeholders as altruist when it comes to contributing to development, and never care to seek diaspora expertise to augment home-country development efforts (Nwazor, 2012; Onah, 2010)

The ability to deal with economic, capacity building, and social challenges, as well as engage in responsible and ethical business practices, provide high quality products and services, as well as develop methods and measures to determine if the government is meeting the needs of its citizens (Sengupa, 2011; Dibie, 2010). The extent to which African governments have been able to address the sustainability challenges of human resource capacity building, as well as a holistic approach to capitalizing on the strengths of a diverse workforce, has not been encouraging (Smith-Sebasto, 2012). Despite the political and economic stability in some African countries for almost two decades, the affected governments have not been able to attract and retain a committed productive workforce in turbulent economic conditions that offer opportunity for financial success. Further, most African countries have severely ignored youth capacity building (World Bank, 2013).

According to the United Nations Human Development Index (2012), youth between 16 and 25 represent more than 60% of Africa's total population and account for 45% of the total labor force (World Bank, 2014). In Ghana, Nigeria, Zimbabwe, Kenya, and Ethiopia, it is estimated that the youth represent 25% of the nations' working-age population, and this figure may increase in the next two decades (Nwazor, 2012; Gwin, 2014). In addition to youth population growth, increased poverty, environmental degradation, and unemployment are problems facing most countries in sub-Saharan Africa. It is expected that this increase in the number of youth will not decline in the next four decades or more (UNDP, 2013). To compound the capacity building problems in the continent, the high cost of seeking educational and vocational skills is increasingly causing millions of unemployed and underemployed youth in several African countries to turn to crime (Dibie et al 2015).

The underlying problems have resulted in a large number of youth under 25 years old to seek employment every year. Several youth of this age group have also left the continent in search of domestic employment in Arab and Western industrialized countries (Nebil et al., 2010; Abebe & Aelmu, 2013). Further, the lack of employment opportunities has given rise to other economic and social problems in the society, such as increased crimes rates, suicides, poverty, alcoholism, and prostitution (Rafik et al., 2010; Dibie et al 2015). In addition, the lack of employment opportunities in several countries in Africa has spilled over to health issues, low household income, stagnated government revenue, and hence, deplorable GDP and the inability to effectively implement sustainable development strategic plans (Peters, 2013; Dibie et al., 2015).

According to Kraft and Furlong (2013), Rafik et al. (2010), the five major economic goals that governments in Africa have not been able to effectively use to promote economic growth include low levels of unemployment, low levels of inflation, a positive balance of trade, and the management of deficits and debt. There is very scanty evidence to show that the governments of Ethiopia, Kenya, Uganda, Senegal, Sierra Leone, Liberia, Tanzania, and Zimbabwe have effectively utilized these economic growth policy instruments (Eade, 2005; Gilpin, 2001; Gwin, 2014). Although enhanced capacity is central to some African countries' development, several sub-Saharan nations continue to trade off infrastructure development for social services programs, corruption, unfruitful agriculture projects, strengthening public institution, improving public performance, increasing employment, and fostering appropriate skills for manufacturing and production.

Capacity building in the African continent therefore lacks a fully articulated framework for assessing economic growth and sequencing appropriate interventions as well as determining results for both the public and private sectors (Sengupa, 2011; Gwin, 2005). As a result, new ways of building sub-Saharan African citizens' capacity to realize a more effective environment would have to come from entrepreneurship, experimentation, and learning of skills that are appropriate for its sustainable development process. The simulation of capacity building in the public and private sector of several African countries must address the human, organizational, and institutional capacity dimensions (Dibie, 2014; James, 1998). According to Gwin (2005), capacity building efforts will succeed only where they take adequate account of the prevailing local politics and institutions, and are African-owned rather than donor-driven.

This chapter examines how government and businesses in sub-Saharan Africa seek to enhance their human, institutional, and infrastructure capacity in order to secure a stable and sustainable economy. It argues that technical capacity building will serve as a lever for economic growth and social development. Capacity building is a continuous process of development that could be accomplished through the participation of the citizens in their own development. The dynamics of development and participation at both national and grassroots levels must involve the exposure of government change agents to participatory learning and action models. The chapter uses data derived from primary and secondary sources to analyze the capacity building problems. The conceptual framework is based on the social constructionist, building block model of development, monetarists, and the Keynesian theories.

Framework for Capacity Building and Economic Growth

Business is a more inviting target than government, however, because it is seen as being motivated only by profit; government is not seeking profit but is charged with acting in the public interest (Carroll & Buchholtz, 2015). Understanding that business and government relations are embedded in a macro-environment provides Africans with a constructive way of understanding the kinds of issues that constitute the broad arena in which business functions in the continent. According to Lahne (2013), an assessment of the activities of government in the past four decades in sub-Saharan Africa will also help us judge contemporary proposals for government action. What is interesting, however, is that African governments have not been able to effectively control all aspects of their economic activity in order to increase the wealth, unity, and power of their respective nations (Dibie, 2014). As a result, most government efforts in the poststructural adjustment era to respond to business activities have been were more significant as symbols than as accomplishments (Sengupta, 2011; Moorhead & Griffin, 2014). Therefore, business and government role in capacity building that leads to domestic economic growth in many African countries is important because it will provide a foundation for the future of the societies in the continent. Economic growth can contribute to advancements in manufacturing, production, employment, and social well-being of citizens, creating beneficial outcomes and solutions to many economic problems (Mankiw, 2018). Economic growth as a result of business and government partnership is important because it keeps all nations moving in a positive, productive direction (Mandel, 2012). Increased economic growth in Africa may enhance or increase employment opportunities.

The neoclassical approach to economic growth prescribes two basic premises. On the one hand, it postulates the competitive model of equilibrium, where markets play a critical role in allocating resources efficiently (Sengupta & Phillip, 2009). The neoclassical approach suggests that markets for labor, capital, and finance following competitive rules help secure optimal allocation of inputs and outputs (Samuelson & Marks, 2015). On the other hand, the neoclassical approach assumes that technology is given. Solow (1956) used the interpretation that the technology in the production is exogenous. From this perspective, it could be argued that investing in R&D and human capital by the governments of African countries could result in enough capacity to address their sustainable development challenges. Despite its crucial contribution, the neoclassical approach fails to explain the most basic fact of actual growth behavior. Unfortunately, this means that the long-term rate of national growth is determined outside the model and is independent of preferences (Sengupta, 2011).

In the era of globalization and modern information technology, high-tech industries of the twenty-first century tend to invest in knowledge capital and have played very important role as engines of economic, capacity building, social and sustainable growth (Ebert & Griffin, 2015). In addition, several of the subsectors of the information technologies and communication sectors specializing in software services and managerial skills in the arena of international outsourcing are highly labor-intensive (Sengupta, 2011; Helpman, 2004). While industrialized countries are able to export the spillover of global R&D and innovation technology to other countries of the world, the authors of this chapter wonder why African countries cannot emulate such entrepreneurial strategies. The endogenous growth theory has attempted to incorporate these spillover effects and impact of market expansion in sustaining economic rate in the long run (Sengupta, 2011). Schumpeter's (1947) concept of the dynamic competition is essentially based on the notion of dynamic efficiency through flexibility in a hypercompetitive framework. The concept explains a process of innovation involving technical change that is embodied in physical capital (Nelson & Winter, 1982; Heerje, 1988). The recent upsurge in knowledge capital and information technology has surpassed the Schumpeterian innovation concept in two ways. The first is the rapid development of high-tech industries with significant increasing returns to scale, and it has helped to expand the global market. Second, the market structure has become more and more hypercompetitive (Hayami & Gogo, 2005; Sengupta, 2011). Figure 16.1 represents the concept of tapping talent for capacity building model.

Figure 16.1 also shows a comprehensive model of success factors in tapping diaspora expertise.

It also shows that the idea platform for development is a partnership-in-planning model. This should be a partnership through which the change agent as an outsider closely collaborates with the beneficiaries of a particular program or project in all the stages of planning and implementation.

The model attempts to explain that the process of achieving capacity building success in Africa may require a complicated interplay of factors such as shared governance leadership skills, host and origin country political will, state of the art universities, appropriate transfer of technology, appropriate incentives to attract the right experts, and institutional and expert collaboration (Boxer, 2011; Ebert & Griffin, 2015; Samuelson & Marks, 2015).

Tapping talent for a capacity building model presents an argument that change initiatives do not come about as a due process following the crafting of strategy and policy (Lehne, 2013; Boxer, 2011). The theory stipulates that without leadership collaboration, even the most capacity building creative policy will fail (Ikharehon, 2007; Porter, 2006; Kraft & Furlong, 2013). It also suggests that attending to host country factors, continental factors, original country factors, expert factors, and organizational factors could determine the likelihood that African countries or governments could achieve full capacity building and sustainable development in the future.

According to Dye (2013) the lack of leadership could pose a major challenge and barrier to the implementation of any capacity building project and

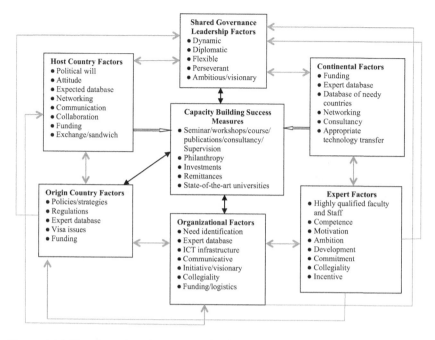

Figure 16.1 Tapping talent for capacity building model

Source: Adopted from Boxer, Lionel. (2011, January). Preparing Leaders for Sustainable Future. *International Journal of Business Insights and Transformation*, 3, 34–43; Bekele, T. A., and Alamirew, B. (2009). Optimal Tapping of Diaspora Expertise for African development: A Model of Success. *Ethiopian Students' Union in Oslo Bulletin*, 1(1), 1–12.

sustainable policy. Potterfield (1999) contends capacity building involves mobilizing people to gain the skills and knowledge that will allow them to overcome obstacles in life or work environment, and ultimately help them develop within themselves or in the society. It also involves increasing the educational, economic, social, political, gender, or spiritual strength of an individual, group, or society (Ebert & Griffin, 2015). In some societies or nations, those who had previously suffered from discrimination based on disability, gender, race, ethnicity, religion, or economic status could be trained to attain equal status, just like others that have been enjoying freedom (Blanchard et al., 1993).

UNDP (2003) defined capacity building to cover human resources development and the strengthening of managerial systems, institutional development that involves community participation, and creation of an enabling environment. Capacity building in the context of development implies a dynamic process that enables individuals and agencies to develop the critical social and technical capacities to identify and analyze problems as well as proffer solutions to them. Azikiwe (2008), Dibie et al (2015), and Theron

(2008) contend that capacity development takes place at three different levels: (a) the individual level; (b) the organizational level; and (c) the societal level. These three levels are interlinked and interdependent. An investment in capacity development must design and account for impact at these multiple levels. Figure 16.2 shows the capacity building model.

Figure 16.2 describes capacity building as a process of change and the systematic management of transformation. It involves the transformation of peoples, institutional and society's capacity (World Bank, 2013). Capacity building, according to Chambers (2005), requires commitment, vision of leadership, viable institution and respective organizations, material, financial, and skilled human resources.

Capacity building is the sustainable creation of solutions and stabilization of capacity in order to reduce poverty, enhance self-reliance, and improve peoples' lives (UNDP, 2009). These definitions suggest that capacity building should be treated as a goal in its own right, not merely as a means for achieving other development. Further, the definitions pointed out that support for capacity building needs to address four very important dimensions of public sector capacity, such as (1) human capacity (individuals with skills to analyze development needs, design and implement strategies, policies, and programs, deliver services, and monitor results; Ebert & Griffin, 2015); (2) organizational capacity (groups of individual bounds by a common purpose, with clear objectives and the internal structures, processes, systems, staffing, and other resources to achieve them; Samuelson & Marks, 2015); (3) institutional capacity (the formal rule of the game and informal

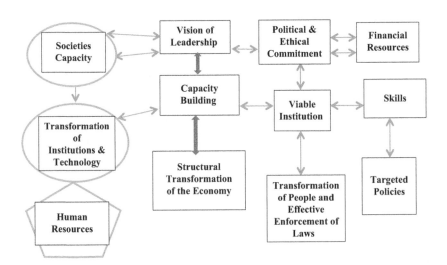

Figure 16.2 Reflection of capacity building impact
Source: Designed by authors

norms such as collecting taxes, reporting on the use of public funds and regulating private business; Gwin, 2014; UNDP, 2009); and (4) community capacity building (CCB), which refers to capacity as a conceptual approach to development that focuses on understanding the obstacles that inhibit people, governments, international organizations, and nongovernmental organizations from realizing their development goals, while enhancing the abilities that will allow them to achieve measurable and sustainable results (Linnell, 2003; Dibie et al 2015). In addition, Kaplan (2000) contends that NGO capacity building is a way to strengthen an organization so that it can perform the specific mission it has set out to do and thus survive as an organization. Another type of capacity building is the organizational form that is focused on developing capacity within organizations like NGOs. It refers to the process of enhancing an organization's abilities to perform specific activities (Ebert & Griffin, 2015). An organizational capacity building approach is used by NGOs to develop internally so they can better fulfill their defined mission (Eade, 2005).

Developing national capacity is tantamount to laying a solid endogenous foundation for sustained economic growth and the virtuous circle of self-regenerating development. In the public sector, the national efforts toward capacity building should cut across all sectors of the economy and all levels of government. In the private sector, capacity building should cut across all functional areas of the organization. In this context, Edoho (1998: 235) conceptualized capacity building as the continuous improvements in the ability of the individuals and society to control the forces of nature and to harness them for their benefit. It has to do with developing the skill and knowledge base of the society to enable it to improve the material conditions of its citizens. Thus, capacity is the amalgam of a society's stock of managerial, scientific, technological, entrepreneurial, and institutional capabilities.

A nation's focus on what development policies and investments work best to strengthen the abilities, networks, skills, and knowledge base cannot be that of intervention (Mankiw, 2018). The bone of contention is that capacity building is about capable and transformational states, which enable progressive and resilient societies to achieve their own development objectives over time. Ideally, the transfer of knowledge should be in both directions, whereby a mutually beneficial and empowering social learning process and a partnership in planning through which the change agent acts as a mediator between types of knowledge system. The challenge of capacity building is to see what responsible well-being might mean for all people, in their relation with themselves, with others, and with the environment. According to Dibie (2014) and Helpman (2004), the major principles by which capacity building may create positive impact on people are in the areas of sustainability and equity. Capacity development is about who and how and where the decisions are made, management takes place, services are delivered, and results are monitored and evaluated.

This is because the overarching ends are human well-being supported by capability and livelihood. Sustainability and equity in the implementation of appropriate economic policies are necessary instruments for achieving good quality of livelihood and security (Carroll & Buchholtz, 2015). Capacity building for a society or nation can enhance the ability of citizens to become more economically and socially secured, and be able to contribute effectively to the sustainable development process of African countries. The question in the case of sub-Saharan Africa is, do the beneficiaries experience a life-changing reality that builds their capacity, empowers them, and establishes honor, dignity, and self-esteem? The action research conducted in several African countries does not show total appreciation of this kind of reality.

Many scholars have described the five major economic goals that government should attempt to promote in their strategic development plans. These sustainable development goals include economic growth, low levels of unemployment, low levels of inflation, a positive balance of trade, and management of deficits and debt (Kraft & Furlong, 2013; Mankiw, 2018; Mandel, 2012; Ferrell et al., 2015). Economic growth means an increase in the production of goods and services each year, and it is expressed as gross domestic product (GDP). Stable prices or low levels of inflation or an increase in the cost to goods and services measured by the Customer Price Index reflects every change in the pricing goods and services (Mankiw, 2018). A positive balance of trade is an economic goal that positively reflects the role of African countries in an international economy. In addition, full employment benefits might further galvanize the African economy. If unemployment goes up, the governments lose revenues because of the loss of wage taxes. The government will have increased expenses due to welfare and unemployment expense paid to the workers (Mankiw, 2018; Peters, 2013).

Governments have numerous strategic options at their disposal to try to influence the performance of the economy. Analysts believe that the two most popular options include fiscal policy and monetary policy. Other options include regulation and tax policy. The first policy that the government of African countries uses is fiscal policy. In Chad Brooks's article, "What Is Fiscal Policy?" (2012), he states, "One of the factors that helps determine a country's economic direction is fiscal policy." The government uses fiscal policy to influence the economy by adjusting revenue and spending levels. Fiscal policy can also be used in combination with monetary policy. There are two main tools of fiscal policy. These tools include taxes and spending. Brooks (2012) and Brooks (2012) contend that taxes influence the economy by determining how much money the government has to spend in certain areas and how much money individuals have to spend. It is crucial for governments to find the right balance and to make sure that the economy doesn't lean too far either way.

There are two types of fiscal policy: expansionary and contractionary. The first type, expansionary fiscal policy, is designed to stimulate the economy. Expansionary fiscal policy is used during a recession and times of high unemployment or other low periods of the business cycle. It involves the government spending more money, lowering taxes, or both (Mankiw 2018). The goal is to place more money in the hands of the consumers so they can spend more and stimulate the economy. The second type, contractionary fiscal policy, is used to decrease economic growth, such as when inflation is growing too rapidly. Contractionary fiscal policy also raises taxes and cuts spending. Fiscal policies are tied into the federal budget each year. The federal budget gives an overview of the government's spending plans for the fiscal year and how it plans to pay for that spending through either new or existing taxes (Mandel 2012; Mankiw 2018).

The monetary policy determines the amount of money flowing through the economy and can affect the direction of a nation's economy. Monetary policy is set by the various Central Banks of African countries and influences the economic activity by controlling the country's money supply and credit. The central banks can control monetary policy by fluctuating rates of interest and changing the amount of money banks must have in their reserves (Mandel, 2012; Mankiw, 2018). The monetary policies goals are to encourage maximum employment, stabilize prices, and moderate long-term interest rates. According to Mankiw (2018) and Mandel (2012), when implemented correctly, monetary policy stabilizes prices and wages, which in turn leads to an increase in jobs and long-term economic growth (Brooks, 2012). The key to monetary policy is finding the perfect balance; if you let the money supply grow too rapidly, it increases inflation, while letting it grow too slowly stunts economic growth.

Economic theory on employment and unemployment has contributed to the problem of low rates employment in many African countries. The problems with supply and the demand sides of the labor market in the country, as well the lack of a transparent labor market information system, has galvanized severe economic growth problems in the continent. According to Schiller (2011), supply side factors such as demographic structure, education, and training policies could affect the labor market outcomes in any nations' economy. Demand side issues including aggregate demand of the economy, and the absorptive capacity of the economy for labor through development of enterprises and job creation institutions are potential factors that affect the unemployment rate in any country (Schiller, 2011; Lehne, 2013). In addition to the ineffective labor market information system, the institutional and fiscal and monetary policies have a major role in the interaction of the supply and the demand sides of the labor market in many African countries (UNDP, 2007; World Bank, 2013). The Phillips curve represents the relationship between the rate of inflation and the unemployment rate. W. H. Phillips (Mankiw, 2018) believes that there is a consistent inverse relationship: when unemployment was high, wages increased slowly; when unemployment was low, wages rose rapidly (Mankiw, 2018; Hoover, 2008).

According to Anderson (2015) and Dibie (2014), in order to tackle the unemployment and capacity building gap between basic education, vocational training, and the job market lifelong learning problems, the following factors are required: (1) skills provider and employers; and (2) skills development and industrial investment, trade, technology, and environmental policies. Further, this also occurs through institutions such as (1) inter-ministerial mechanisms (linked to national development framework); (2) social dialogue; (3) skills forecasting and labor market information system; (4) value chain; (5) industrial clusters; (6) social inclusiveness; (7) maintaining employability of workers and sustainability of enterprises; (8) matching demand and supply of skills; and (9) sustaining a dynamic development process (R. Jones, 2001; Lehne, 2013). It could be argued therefore that African nations must change both the orientation of their public administrators and those that fund them. As a result, great programs need great organizations and capacity building measures behind them (Miller et al., 2014).

According to Dibie (2014), in order to avoid authoritarianism in African countries, a focus must be directed at developing the abilities and skills of national and local governments so that shared governance and sustainable development can be diffused across all states and regions. Capacity building in governments often involves providing the tools to help citizens best fulfill their responsibilities. These include building up a government's capacity to budget, collect revenue, create and implement laws, promote civic engagement (Chambers, 2002), be transparent and accountable, and fight corruption (Dibie et al 2015).

Analysis of Business and Government Role in Capacity Building

The post-independence African states have not been in the right environment in which change agents and elites work together to play major part in determining how effective business-government and capacity building programs function or are implemented. Bereketeab (2014) and Homer-Dixon (2001) describe the African environment as a continent with three scarcity sources. The sources are (1) supply induced scarcity; (2) demand induced scarcity; and (3) structural scarcity. On one hand, the supply induced scarcity refers to scarcity arising from the decrease of renewable resources. On the other hand, the demand induced scarcity relates to demographical change where population increase is greater than available resources. The structural scarcity relates to a shortage of resources arising from unequal access to resources. Unequal access to resources also relates to vulnerability and issues of distribution. The issue of distribution is also associated with the nature of the political system and the types of public policies that are implemented by the African governments (Bereketeab, 2014; Hauge & Ellingsen, 1998).

According to James (1998), the accomplishment of independence left most African countries with a small ruling elite who, although they had political power, were not necessarily rich. Rather than embarking on laying the foundation for capacity-building, these elites were more determined to amass wealth at the expense of national development. It has been nearly over 50 to 60 years since most African countries achieved their independence; yet this pattern of elite corrupt and unethical practices still continues. The ruling Africa elites are more determined than ever to focus their attention on their particular ethnic groups by mobilizing the rural population behind their self-aggrandizement. As a result, ethnic issues continue to hinge upon who runs the government, since the government is the largest employer (Nnoli, 1995; James, 1998; Dibie, 2014). The lack of unity to establish a national political will to focus on state building and sustainable development is central to the flaws of capacity building in the African continent. The political conflict over the years in the Democratic Republic of Congo, Liberia, Libya, Northern Sudan, Nigeria (with Boko Haram issues), Sierra Leone, South Sudan, Mali, Burkina Faso, Rwanda, Uganda, Zimbabwe, and the Central African Republic are a few examples of the factors militating against capacity building in the African continent.

Some African countries are enjoying higher levels of economic growth and well-being, but insecurity, as well as natural or human-induced disasters, persists in some parts of the region (Fisher & Anderson, 2015). According to the United Nations 2104 Human Development Report (HDR; 2014), several nations in sub-Saharan Africa have not been able to successfully intensify their battle against deprivation and prevent crises from setting back recent development advances. The HDR (2014) also reveals that 77% of the African population is in vulnerable employment. Many of the unemployed and those that are in vulnerable employment are youths. These unemployed youth have become recruiting avenues for Boko Haram, Al-Shabaab, and other militant groups. Thus, measures to create equal access to jobs, health care, and education opportunities have an important role to play in promoting sustainable development and capacity building. McBride and Sherraden (2004) contend that the outcome of sustainable development programs can range from peace and international understanding, to improved job skills and education, to sustained civic engagement. Dibie (2014) pointed out that achieving sustainability requires addressing agriculture, justice and equity, wood, products, water supplies, biodiversity, climate change, manufacturing and industry, fisheries, and forests. Sustainability transcends and supersedes environmentalism. Sustainability involves a transformation from a wasteful, consumptive behavior to a more pragmatic modest life style. Sustainability is based on what can be referred to as the triple bottom line: *People, Planet,* and *prosperity for all.*

The 2014 United Nations Human Development report indicated that gender inequality remains a major barrier to capacity building and other forms of human development. Girls and women have made major strides since 1990, but they have not yet gained gender equity. The disadvantages facing women and girls are a major source of inequality. Table 16.1 shows how women and girls are discriminated against in health, education, political representation, the labor market, and so on.

Table 16.1 shows that in 2013, sub-Saharan Africa countries had the second highest rate of progress in the Human Development Index (HDI), which combines achievements in income, health, and education. Rwanda and Ethiopia achieved the fastest growth, followed by Angola, Burundi, Mali, Mozambique, the United Republic of Tanzania, and Zambia. Despite this milestone accomplishment, a recent troubling finding shows that 585 million people in sub-Saharan Africa, the equivalent of 72% of the region's population, are living in multidimensional poverty (HDR, 2014). This group of poor people also suffers deprivation in education, health, and living standards, and they are at risk of falling back into poverty (HDR, 2014). Table 16.2 shows the average expenditure of health as percentage of GDP of selected African countries in comparison to three Western industrialized countries. Table 16.2 shows the world expenditure on health in comparison to what African countries are spending.

These groups often do not experience improvements in their standard of living because they have limited political participation, livelihood options, and access to basic social services, and even when they do escape poverty, they can relapse rapidly into precariousness when crises hit (Gwin, 2014; Fisher & Anderson, 2015). Deprivation in health, education, and living standards in Africa often could spill over to affect individuals or even entire communities over a life-span, based on gender, ethnicity, geographic location, and other factors. For example, the report shows that the region has the world's highest disparities in health, and shows considerable gender inequalities in income, educational attainment, and access to reproductive health services.

According to Gilpin (2001), economic globalization has led to key development in trade, finance, and foreign direct investment by multinational corporations. In addition to impact of globalization, the last four decades have experienced deregulation and privatization. These two economic factors have opened national economics to imports. Technological advance in communications and transportation tend to have reduced costs and thus significantly encourage trade expansion (Falk, 1999; Gilpin, 2001). While several countries and businesses are taking advantage of these economic and technological changes, more and more businesses have participated in the international market, and several African countries have not been fully engaged in the dynamics of technological advances, deregulation, and privatization. They are somewhat excluded because of their low capacity. The only area African countries have favorable improvement in is in the exportation of food and raw materials. The World Bank (2012) reported that Africa accounted for only 2% of total world trade.

Table 16.1 Expenditure on education, public (% of GDP)

HDI rank	Country	Share of seats in parliament, 2013	Life expectancy at birth, female, 2013	Life expectancy at birth, male, 2013	Mean years of schooling, female, 2002–2012	Mean years of schooling, male, 2002–2012	Estimated GNI per capita (2011 PPP$), female, 2013	Estimated GNI per capita (2011 PPP$), male, 2013
109	Botswana	7.9	66.8	62.1	11.7	11.6	11,491	18,054
110	Egypt	2.8	2.8	73.6	68.8	12.7	13.3	4,225
118	S. Africa	41.1	58.8	54.7	—	—	8,539	15,233
138	Ghana	10.1	62.1	60.2	10.9	12.1	2,937	4,138
140	Congo	9.6	60.2	57.4	10.9	11.3	4,222	5,597
147	Kenya	19.9	63.6	59.8	10.7	11.3	1,763	2,554
151	Rwanda	51.9	65.7	62.4	10.3	10.2	1,263	1,550
152	Nigeria	6.6	52.8	52.2	8.2	9.8	4,068	6,594
156	Zimbabwe	35.1	60.8	58.8	9.1	9.5	1,124	1,496
173	Ethiopia	25.5	65.3	62.0	8.0	9.0	1,090	1,515
	Tanzania	36.0	62.9	60.2	9.0	9.3	1,501	1,903
	Senegal	42.7	64.9	61.9	7.8	8.1	1,642	2,717

Source: World Bank (2013). *World Development Indicators 2013*. Washington, DC: World Bank.

Table 16.2 Expenditure on health, public (% of GDP)

HDI Rank	Country	2007	2008	2009	2010	2011
1	Norway	8.7	8.6	9.7	9.3	9.1
5	United States	16.2	16.6	17.7	17.6	17.9
8	Canada	10.0	10.3	11.4	11.4	11.2
109	Botswana	7.2	4.4	4.9	5.1	5.1
110	Egypt	4.9	4.8	5.0	4.7	4.9
118	S. Africa	7.8	8.0	8.7	8.7	8.5
138	Ghana	6.0	5.6	5.0	5.2	4.8
140	Congo D. R.	2.5	2.1	2.3	2.3	2.5
147	Kenya	4.4	4.2	4.6	4.4	4.5
151	Rwanda	9.4	9.2	10.0	10.4	10.8
152	Nigeria	7.0	6.3	6.8	5.4	5.3
156	Ethiopia	3.9	4.0	4.4	4.4	4.7
163	Tanzania	5.7	5.4	5.6	7.2	7.3
180	Senegal	5.9	7.3	0.1	7.5	8.5

Source: World Bank. (2013). *World Development Indicators 2013*. Washington, DC: World Bank. http://data.worldbank.org. Accessed March 4, 2015.

Dimension of African Labor Market

Two essential dimensions of the labor market are the demand and supply sides of the economy (Samuelson & Marks, 2015). The number of officials trained in the African continent by IMF increased steadily during the mid-1990s. The driving forces for this increase in officials trained by the IMF certainly lie in the interplay between demand and supply. On one hand, the demand side of the African labor market is associated with the ability of the economy to generate employment opportunity for various skill categories. The demand factors also include the political and economic development, African countries openness, and financial crisis, which further lets governments in the continent feel the need to request training and loans from the World Bank and IMF (Samuelson & Marks, 2015; Mankiw, 2018). On the other hand, the supply side of the labor market deals with whether the current labor force in the continent countries match with the type of skills that the economy demands. In addition to the labor market, public and private institutions such as the governance of labor market-industrial relations and labor market services play a significant role in employment promotion. This implies that an ineffective management of labor market institutions has also led to high unemployment in sub-Saharan African countries.

The Demand Side of Labor Market Issues

According to the World Bank report (2013)), the agricultural sector is the dominant sector in the African economy because it contributes over 41% of the continent's gross domestic product (GDP). The agricultural sector also contributes to 60% of African nations' exports, and is the major employer of approximately 83.5% of the continent's population. In addition, the agricultural sector in several African countries is the major employer of the rural population. As a result, job opportunities for urban youths in the agricultural sector are limited. The second largest contribution to the national GDP of African countries comes from the service sector (Arezki et al., 2012; UNEC, 2011).

The industrial sectors contribution is very minimal, with about 13% comparative to the two dominant sectors in the African economy (UNEC, 2011). This indicates significant structural weakness of the economy. Employment opportunity for urban youth is directly related to the development of the industrial sector of the economy. The low level of development in the industrial sector of the economy therefore is one of the major issues that explain the high unemployment problem (Bereketeab, 2014; Hayami & Gogo, 2005). Table 16.3 shows the environmental problems in some African countries due to inadequate government policy, business compliance, capacity building, and economic growth.

Table 16.3 shows that some nations in Africa have great problems in dealing with more recent environmental problems created by industrialization, heavy automobile traffic, large quantities of solid waste, and informal society activities. Dye (2013) and Smith-Sebasto (2012) contend that the environmental problems of African nations are as serious and urgent as the problems of underdevelopment. As alluded to earlier in this chapter, the problem of governance in some of these African nations is even more serious and urgent (Collier & Hoeffler, 2014).

Growth oriented development strategies in several African countries have failed to fully comprehend the range of economic activities that should take places in communities, cities, and rural and urban towns, especially the non-monetary and sustainable activities within the plan or policy. Several scholars have attributed the demand side problems of the labor market in African economies to be the result of weakness of the economies, saturated public services, and small private sector bases that are unable to employ large numbers of people (Schiller, 2011; Mankiw, 2012; Adebayo, 1999; Rondinelli, 1993; UNEC, 2011). A study by Gwin (2014) reveals that the education systems in African countries have failed to promote vocational and technical trainings.

The Supply Side of Labor Market Issues

To supplement the demand side of the labor market, the government of some African countries has introduced specific and employment or job

Table 16.3 Environmental problems due to inadequate capacity building initiatives

Type of Environmental Problems	Ghana	South Africa	Nigeria	Kenya	Botswana	Egypt	Demo. Republic of Congo
Garbage collection problem	X	X	X	X	X	X	X
Inadequate landfill	X	X	X	X	X	X	X
Foul odors due to waste dumped in gullies	X	PX	X	X	X	X	X
Waste dumped on the streets	X	X	X	X	X	X	X
Sewage treatment	X	X	X	X	X	X	X
Effect of informal sector	X	X	X	X	X	X	X
Improper disposal of waste engine oil and car batteries	X	PX	X	X	X	X	X
Drainage problems when it rains	X	PX	X	X	X	X	X
Burning refuse	X	X	X	X	X	X	X
Use of firewood	X	X	X	X	X	X	X

Source: Focus group meeting in Africa 2013–2015.
Key X = excessive problem; PX = partial problem.

creation targeted programs. One of such programs is the cobblestone project in urban Ethiopia, which was initiated by the Engineering Capacity Building Program supported by the German Development Cooperative (GTZ). Since 2007, the Engineering Capacity Building Program has been training the youth in traditional crafting of cobblestone paving, with the dual objective of creating jobs for youth and creating clean, attractive pavement roads in Ethiopian towns. It is based on the principle of local resource utilization in a labor intensive manner to pave roads and public spaces using an environmentally amicable approach adopted from the German experiences. The project created jobs for the youth organized to operate micro and small enterprises. This means construction of pavements in towns and cities enabled creation of new micro and small enterprises, thereby boosting housing investment. Available evidence shows that the project has resulted in the creation of more than 2,000 micro and small enterprises and employed more than 90,000 youth in urban areas of Ethiopia by the end of 2011 (Ezana, 2011).

According to the United Nations Millennium Development Goals (2010) Report, the net primary education enrollment rate in the Central, Western,

Eastern, and Southern African regions combined increased from 58% in 1999 to 76% in 2008, while in North Africa, it increased from 86% in 1999 to 94% in 2008. However, the increase in primary education enrollment rates has not necessarily been followed by an equivalent increase in secondary and tertiary education rates, especially for young women and girls. According to UNEC (2011), when it comes to tertiary education among youth populations in Africa, the gross enrollment rate for tertiary education level is very low. The pattern for Ethiopia, Somalia, Sudan, Eritrea, Chad, Niger, Mali, and Libya is similar, as the increase in primary education enrollment has not been accompanied by an equivalent rise in secondary and tertiary education enrollment. The participation of women and young girls is significantly lower at the tertiary level compared with the participation in primary education due to early marriage traditions (UNEC, 2011).

In the past three decades the new education system that was introduced by many African countries has been partially successful. According to Afolabi (2002) and Olagboye (2004), the new education system stipulates that only those who score qualifying results on national examinations offered at the end of the twelfth grade can be admitted to polytechnics or universities. Despite the good intentions of several African countries' governments to introduce new educational systems, they have failed to sustain the quality and standards that were originally intended. Most public schools are dilapidated and inadequate to provide quality education. Polytechnics and vocational training institutions lack appropriate equipment (Dibie, 2014; UN Human Development Report, 2014). Dibie et al (2015) and Duze and Ogbah (2013) contend that classrooms in most of the public schools were inadequate in terms of decency, space, furniture, ventilation, and insulation from heat and cold. The toilets in universities and polytechnics do not have running water. Institutions that have generating electricity plants cannot effectively maintain them. The governments of many African countries cannot also effectively manage a national electricity system. As a result, schools and industries are often in darkness (Baker & Berstein, 2012; Duze & Ogbah, 2013).

There is also clear evidence that certain aspects of school buildings have negatively impacted students' health and learning in several ways. When deprived of natural light, studies have shown that children's melatonin cycles are disrupted, thus likely having an impact on their alertness during school (Figueiro & Rea, 2010). Teachers report higher levels of comfort in their classrooms when they have access to thermal controls like thermostats or operable windows (Heschong, 2003; Lackney, 2001). It has been reported that when ventilation rates are at or below minimum standards (roughly 15 cfm per student), an associated decrease of 5%–10% occurs in certain aspects of student performance tests (Baker & Berstein, 2012; Armstrong & Fukam, 2009).

The questions that the authors of this chapter beg to ask at this point are as follows: Are some African countries actually serious about capacity building for their citizens? If the answer is positive, why are the respective governments in the continent unable to provide state of the arts building, furniture, and equipment that could contribute to positive learning environment, quality education, and capacity building process for all citizens to work toward the attainment of sustainable development? The quality of the school buildings, equipment, and furniture, as well as provision of instructional resources facilities for teachers, will determine the government commitment to capacity building for higher performance in the public and private sectors.

Appropriate Solutions and Policy Strategies

In establishing supply side policies for capacity building, government will have to work with the business sector to place equal emphasis on the demand side of the labor market as well. In other words, it is necessary to try to reduce unemployment by addressing the lack of skills or poor attitudes of young people while concentrating on promoting economic growth and job creation. In this regard, in the recent double digit economic growth that some African countries have witnessed in the past two years, self-assessment should also lead both the public and private sectors to improve in areas where weaknesses are identified. According to Berman et al. (2016), deficiencies in capacity building can be reduced through self-study and reading training inside or outside the organization, and formal education. In a competitive market, lack of appropriate knowledge, skills, self-discipline, and abilities may be a weakness because basic qualifications may affect the level of performance (Carroll & Buchholtz, 2015). Figure 16.3 shows policies for reducing vulnerability in Africa.

Figure 16.3 shows that structural transformation of the economies of African countries are necessary in order to provide more jobs by using targeted policies that support the development of strategic sectors and actives. This means that government investment into infrastructure development has to maintain its momentum, and private sector development in the industrial sector has to be encouraged. Many African countries are faced with the challenges of underemployment. As a result of these delicate challenges, the labor market policies are not enough, considering that most jobs are in the informal economy (Ebert & Griffin, 2015). Therefore, pursuing full employment and reducing employment related vulnerability in the future requires policies that promote job-creating growth, and that extend a social protection framework for all in both the formal and informal sectors all over the Africa continent.

Entrepreneurship has to be promoted making it easier to start and run enterprises in order to provide more and better jobs for young people, and employment creation has to be enhanced, placing job creation at the center of macroeconomic policy. Central to the promotion of economic growth and development is the promotion of investment in the real sector of the

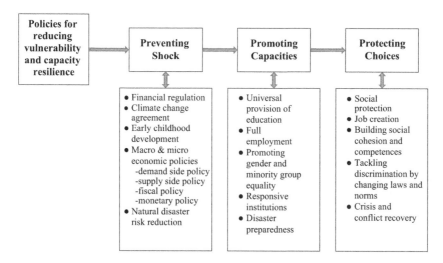

Figure 16.3 Policies for reducing capacity building vulnerability
Source: United Nations Human Development Report 2014

economy (Echebiri 2005; Ezana 2011; World Bank 2016). The development of micro and small enterprises has to be strengthened, encouraged, and facilitated by the government offices in charge of this responsibility, because the sector practically proved to be one of the fundamental solutions to urban capacity building in sub-Saharan Africa.

Enhancing the labor market information system through investments to improve information resources for employment creation is essential to avoid the mismatch between skills that educators entrust to their graduates and the technical skills that the economy requires (Dibie & Dibie, 2014). High quality labor market information and career guidance can help citizens make better informed decisions about their future, including the selection of academic and vocational programs. The development of labor market information is also useful for the effective design and implementation of appropriate policies. Further, measures that can enable the African people to have improved access to valuable information and opportunities so that they might make informed decisions about their lives are important. To this end, it is important to enhance the capacity of the labor market institutions.

A labor market study by World Bank (2007) proved that both the private sector brokers and the public sector labor market information providers are weak to serve the market function properly. The situation in Ethiopia, Zimbabwe, South Africa, Benin, Senegal, Kenya, and Nigeria with this regard is similar to that of many sub-Saharan African economies (Dibie, 2014). The relevant labor market institutions that are causes of youth unemployment in Africa include labor demand barriers, such as observed discrimination by employers toward gender on the grounds of lack of experience, and information gaps between job seekers and potential employers (United Nations Economic Commission for Africa, 2011). Hence strengthening the labor-market information system is therefore very important, so that it can play its intermediation role between the supply side and the demand side.

Demand-Side Policy

Supply-side interventions by government can only be successful with complementary efforts that help expand job opportunities for all citizens in both the business and public sector. In an environment with low labor demand, young people will have a hard time finding a job, no matter what their skills level and educational attainment are (Mankiw 2018; Mandel 2012). Thus programs that generate jobs and foster local businesses are vital to reduce the prevalence of unemployment in urban areas (Ikatu, 2010). The following strategies are critical for the government to explore in the near future.

1. Reduce entry barriers by reducing experience requirements.
2. Avoid discrimination on the basis of gender during the recruitment process.
3. Avoid discrimination during the recruitment process on the basis of relationships, economic status, ethnicity, disability, and so on.
4. Financially and/or technically support entrepreneurship.
5. Organize and provide financial and technical support for youth to start their business.
6. Increase interests for government organization to hire qualified staff.
7. Provide incentives for private sectors and NGOs to encourage them in hiring new graduates from universities and polytechnics.
8. Promote investment in public works and labor-intensive infrastructure projects that can absorb new graduates in the respective nations (Ravans 2011; Ezana 2011; Anderson 2015).

Supply-Side Policy

The government supply side policies enable the citizens to get prepared for the labor demand market (Mankiw, 2018). Thus, attention to the strategies listed is very essential. It is very important for the government to help citizens gain skills and training or education that has high labor market demand for the sustainable future. Furthermore, the Government of African countries should establish training institutions at national and regional levels that exclusively focus on providing the needed skills for people in their country Oluwagbuyi & Adaramola 2013). This kind of vocational training institutions could galvanize people to start their own businesses. The following supply side policy strategies are options for the African countries governments to explore in the near future.

1. Establish national vocational and technical training institutions that could provide appropriate training in the utilization of advanced technologies.
2. Create an opportunity for youth to easily join technical vocational educational training in order to gain education that leads to high skills in technological areas and experience in self-job creation.
3. Create awareness for unemployed citizens to explore employment opportunities.
4. Encourage citizens to develop skill in technical and vocational training institutes.
5. Establish policies for citizens to participate in apprenticeship or internship when they are still in school to gain practical skills.
6. Help graduates get adequate training/education that has high demand in the market.
7. Give training that helps citizens to start their own business rather than searching from other sectors.
8. Produce enough food.
9. Preserve the integrity of ecosystems.
10. Use resources efficiently (land, water, energy).
11. Use renewable energy, and recycle nutrients.

(Dibie & Dibie, 2014; Dye 2013).

Capacity building is a continuous process of development that could be accomplished through the participation of the citizens in their own development. The dynamics of development and participation at both national and grassroots levels in African countries must involve the exposure of government change agents to participatory learning and action (Boxer, 2011; Smith-Sabasto, 2012). Sustainable development goals in sub-Saharan Africa should be based on the following orientations and alternative approaches. According to Tucker (2014) and Theron (2008), the following are areas where a nation could focus its capacity-building efforts:

1. **Organizational training.** This informal practical training in group dynamics, simple bookkeeping, and accounting, adult literacy, banking, and proposal writing.
2. **Technical training.** Technical capability is needed for developing countries to engage effectively in the global economy; direct foreign investment, international trade, mobility of engineers, and the flow of work to countries with cost-effective talent will result. This is based on needs and priorities defined by the people themselves. Training opportunities in various skills need to be arranged either externally or internally (Dibie et al 2015; World Bank 2013).

3. **Indigenous science and technology capacity.** Indigenous science and technology capacity is needed to ensure that international aid funds are utilized effectively and efficiently—for initial project implementation, for long-term operation and maintenance, and for the development of capacity to do future projects. And a sufficient pool of engineers can enable a developing country to address the UN's Millennium Development Goals effectively, including poverty reduction, safe water and sanitation, and so on (Dibie et al 2015)

4. **Technical workforce pool.** In order to stimulate job formation in developing countries, a technical workforce pool is needed, made up of people who are specifically educated and prepared to engage in entrepreneurial start-up efforts that meet local needs.

5. **Leadership development.** This is informal training in leadership development and the planning, implementation, and evaluation of projects.

6. **External linkages and capacity building.** People need to be assisted in establishing linkages and building networks with external agencies. Part of this process is helping people acquire the skills, confidence, and capacity required in establishing and maintaining such linkages (Dibie et al 2015).

7. **Exchange of experiences.** People should be assisted in arranging visits and exchange with similar groups, projects, training and research centers, and attending internships, on-the-job training sections, job-related conferences, workshops, and fieldtrips (Chambers, 2002; 2005).

8. **Support and encouragement.** The presence of the change agent living and working in the country and sharing the experiences and problems of the people is often a decisive factor in encouraging people to persevere in their early efforts to improve their own lives. Once a sustainable participatory development projects has been initiated, it should be backed by a continuous process with a goal to achieve a visible end (Samuelson & Marks, 2015).

9. **International experience.** The formulation of policies for a developmental state not only requires ongoing work within the state, but also the capacity to rapidly learn from international experience. It should be the objective of government in the medium term to strengthen its engagement with society and with social partners (Dibie & Dibie, 2014). Without this capacity, it is more likely that the environment for engagement will be reactive, and that productive partnerships will not emerge (Ya Ni & Van Wart 2016).

10. **Economic sustainability strategy.** Economic sustainability is an actionable strategy companies engage in to ensure they remain a growing concern. Different strategies include lean accounting or management, competitive market analysis, product differentiation, concentrated growth, or similar strategies (Gwin, 2014). A nation's operating environment will rarely remain static; external forces will pressure the country to make changes to public and business practices that could enhance

sustainability (Carroll & Buchholtz, 2015). Using one or more of these strategies can ensure the country remains competitive and stable in all economies.

Finally, it is very important to note that capacity building projects that have foundation behavior and attitudes, methods, and sharing planted in the humanist advancement offer not only the basis for self-reliance and participatory development but a means to citizens' empowerment.

Conclusion

This chapter has examined the problem of the business and government role in capacity building and economic growth in sub-Saharan African countries. It argues that capacity building efforts in sub-Saharan Africa are incomplete because the respective governments fail to incorporate vulnerability and resilience in their analysis. Although the governments of most African countries now regulate every facet of business operations, this approach has not been very successful in enhancing capacity-building. The creation of new businesses and productive corporations are often regarded as key to economic growth in sub-Saharan Africa economies. Sustained progress in capacity building and economic growth in Africa is a matter of expanding people's choice and keeping these choices secured (United Nations Human Development Report, 2014). Capacity building in Africa will also require visionary and ethical leaders that are committed to structural transformation of institutions, people, skills, and appropriate policies to address vulnerability. Such leaders will enact appropriate fiscal and monetary policies to provide universal education, full employment, promotion of gender, and minority group equity programs, as well as ethical responsive institutions. Building social cohesion and competences, as well as tacking discrimination by effectively adopting new laws and norms, will enhance capacity building.

Technical capacity building in Africa will serve as a lever for economic and social growth in the continent (R. Jones, 2001; Carroll & Buchholtz, 2015). This fact is currently being recognized as an important priority in the global sustainable community. Despite the increasing significance of the market and economic globalization, economic outcomes in Africa are determined not only by economic forces but also by governments and their policies (Sengupa, 2011; Gilpin, 2001). Yet African countries and their national societies differ fundamentally in the degree to which their governments play a meaningful role in the economy and in the ways in which they attempt to manage their economies (Samuelson & Marks, 2015; Gilpin, 2001).

In order to increase job absorption by the private sector, incentive packages, such as special tax breaks to promote persistent labor-intensive investments, should be considered by the government rather than giving uniform tax advantages to all private firms (M. Jones, 2001; Ebert & Griffin, 2015). Strategies for creating an enabling environment for the private sector and

NGOs should be clearly defined in the national policy. In addition, the strategy that enhances the collaboration of government, the private sector, and NGOs to deal with urban and rural unemployment should be designed and implemented accordingly. There should be periodical forums in which potential private sectors, NGOs, and government participate to discuss national economic transformation issues (Dibie & Dibie, 2014; Sengupa, 2011).

Finally, how people preserve or abuse the African environment will largely determine whether capacity building and citizens' living standards improve or deteriorate. Growing human numbers, urban expansion, and resource exploitation do not resonate well for the future. Without seeking capacity building and practicing sustainable development behavior, the citizens of African countries may face a deteriorating environment as well as even invite ecological disaster that they probably do not have the skills to address (Dibie, 2014; Carroll & Buchholtz, 2015). The strategy of economic adjustment can mean letting the market work and implementing judicious interventionist policies to shift the African economy away from those industries and economic activities in which it is losing comparative advantage and toward those in which it is gaining advantage (Mankiw 2018; (Sengupa, 2011; Gwin, 2014). African governments may have to expand regional economic and political integration in order to better address some of their economic growth problems.

References

Abebe, T. and Aelmu, K. (2013). Analysis of Urban Youth Unemployment in Ethiopia: The Case of Addis Ababa. *Journal of International Politics and Development*, 11(1–2), 131–162.

Adebayo, A. (1999). Youth Unemployment and National Directorate of Employment and Self-Employment Programs. *Nigerian Journal of Economics and Social Studies*, 41(1), 81–102.

Afolabi, F. O. (2002). The School Building and Its Environment: Implication on the Achievement of Functional Universal Basic Education Program in Ondo State. In T. Ajayi, J. O. Fadipe, P. K. Ojedele, and E. E. Oluchukwu (Eds.), *Planning and Administration of Universal Basic Education in Nigeria*. Abuja, Nigeria: National Institute for Educational Administration and Planning (NIEPA) Publication, 101–110.

Alamiirew, B. (2008). *Migration Brain Drain and Remittances*. Paper Presented at the 4th General Assembly of Ethio_Europe Research and Innovation Link, University of Giessen, Germany.

Anderson, J. (2015). *Public Policy Making*. Stamford, CT: Cengage Learning.

Arezki, R., Dupuy, A. and Gelb, A. (2012). Resource Windfalls, Optimal Public Investment and Redistribution: The Role of Total Factor Productivity and Administrative Capacity. IMF Working Paper. www.imf.org/external/pubs/ft/wp/2012/wp12200.pdf. Accessed April 10, 2015.

Armstrong, S. and Fukami, C. (2009). *The Sage Handbook of Management, Learning, and Development*. Los Angeles: Sage Press.

Ayeni, A. J. and Adelabu, M. (2012). Improving Learning Infrastructure and Environment for Sustainable Quality Assurance Practice in Secondary Schools in

Ondo State, Nigeria. *International Journal of Research Studies in Education,* 1(1), 61–68.

Azikiwe, U. (2008). *Standard in Tertiary Education: Capacity Building and Sustainable Development in Nigeria.* A Lead Paper Presented at the Annual Conference of the Faculty of Education, Nnamdi Azikiwe University, Awka, and Anambra State, Nigeria.

Baker, L. and Berstein, H. (2012). *The Impact of School Buildings on Student Health and Performance.* http://media.mhfi.com/documents/GreenSchoolsWP-2012. pdf. Accessed March 2015.

Bekele, T. A. and Alamirew, B. (2009). Optimal Tapping of Diaspora Expertise for African Development: A Model of Success. *Ethiopian Students' Union in Oslo Bulletin,* 1(1), 1–12.

Bereketeab, R. (2014). Environmental Change, Conflicts and Problems of Sustainable Development in the Horn of Africa. *African and Asian Studies,* 13, 291–314.

Berman, E., Bowman, J., West, J. and Van Wart, M. (2016). *Human Resource Management in Public Service.* Los Angeles, CA: Sage Press.

Blanchard, K. H., Zigarmi, D. and Nelson, R. B. (1993). Situational Leadership After 25 Years: A Retrospective. *The Journal of Leadership Studies,* 1(1), 21–36.

Boex, J. and Yilmaz, S. (2010). *An Analytical Framework for Assessing Decentralized Local Governance and the Local Public Sector.* Urban Institute Center on International Development and Governance.

Boxer, L. (2011, January). Preparing Leaders for Sustainable Future. *International Journal of Business Insights and Transformation,* 3, 34–43.

Brooks, C. (2012). What Is Fiscal Policy? *Business News Daily.* www.businessnewsdaily.com/3484-fiscal-policy.html. Accessed April 12, 2014.

Carroll, A. and Buchholtz, A. (2015). *Business and Society: Ethics, Sustainability and Stakeholder Management.* Stamford, CT: Cengage Learning.

Chambers, R. (2005). *Ideas for Development.* London, UK: Earthscam Press.

Chambers, R. (2002). Participatory Workshop: A Sourcebook of 21 Sets of Ideas and Activities. London, UK: Earthscan Press.

Collier, P. and Hoeffler, A. (2004). Greed and Grievance in Civil War. *Oxford Economic Papers,* 56, 563–595.

Dibie, R. (2010). Social Impact of Environmental Policies in Ethiopia. *Journal of International Politics and Development,* 8(1), 1–32.

Dibie, R. (2014). Comparative Perspective of Environmental Policies and Issues. New York, NY: Routledge Press.

Dibie, R. and Dibie, J. (2014). The Dichotomy of Capacity Building and Unemployment in Ethiopia. *Africa's Public Service Delivery and Performance Review,* 2(3), 25–76.

Dibie, R., Edoho, F.M., and Dibie, J. (2015). "Analysis of Capacity Building and Economic Growth in Su-Saharan Africa." *Journal of Business and Economic Policy.* 2(4), 1–20.

Duze, C. and Ogbah, R. (2013). Retaining and Developing Quality Teachers: Critical Issues for Administrators in Nigeria Secondary Schools. *Journal of Sociological Research,* 4(1), 145–161.

Dye, T. (2013). *Understanding Public Policy.* 13th Edition. New York: Longman, 210–231.

Eade, D. (2005). Capacity-Building: An Approach to People Centered Development. London, UK: Oxfam Press, 30–39.

Ebert, R. and Griffin, R. (2015). *Business Essentials.* Boston, MA: Pearson.

Echebiri, R. N. (2005). Characteristics and Determinants of Urban Youth Unemployment in Umuahia, Nigeria: Implications for Rural Development and Alternative Labor Market Variables. A Paper Presented at the ISSER/Cornell/World Bank Conference on "Shared Growth in Africa" held in Accra, Ghana, July 21–24.

Edoho, F. M. (1998). Management Capacity Building: A Strategic Imperative for African Development in the 21st Century. In V. U. James (Ed.), *Capacity Building in Developing Countries: Human and Environmental Dimensions*. Westport, CT: Praeger, 228–251.

Ezana, H. W. (2011). Factors Influencing Affected Group Participation in Urban Redevelopment in Addis Ababa: The Case of Senga Tera-Fird Bet I Project. International Institute of Urban Management, Erasmus University of Rotterdam.

Falk, R. (1999). *Predatory Globalization*. London, UK: Oxford Polity Press.

Ferrel, O. C., Hiirt, G. and Ferrell, L. (2015). *Business: A Changing World*. New York, NY: McGraw-Hill Press.

Figueiro, M. and Rea, M. S. (2010). Lack of Short-Wavelength Light During the School Day Delays Dim Light Melatonin Onset (DLMO) in Middle School Students. *Neuroendocrinology Letters*, 31(1), 21–48.

Fisher, J. and Anderson, J. (2015). Authoritarianism and the Securitization of Development in Africa. *International Affairs*, 91, 131–151.

Gilpin, R. (2001). Global Political Economy: Understanding the International Economic Order. Princeton, NJ: Princeton University Press.

Gwin, C. (2014). Capacity Building in Africa. An OECD Evaluation of World Bank Support. Herbdon, VA: World Bank Publication.

Gwin, C. (2005). Capacity Building in Africa: An OECD Evaluation of World Bank Support. Herndon, VA: World Bank Publication.

Hauge, W. and Ellingsen, T. (1998). Beyond Environmental Scarcity: Causal Pathways to Conflict. *Journal of Peace Research*, 35(3), 299–317.

Hayami, Y. and Gogo, Y. (2005). *Development Economics*. New York: Oxford University Press.

Heerje, A. (1988). Schumpeter and Technology Change. In H. Hanusch (Ed.), *Evolutionary Economics: Applications of Schumpeter's Ideas*. New York: Cambridge University Press, 45–67.

Helpman, E. (2004). *The Mystery of Economic Growth*. Cambridge, MA: Harvard University Press.

Heschong, L. (2003). Windows and Classrooms: A Study of Student Performance and the Indoor Environment. (P500-03-082-A-7). California Energy Commission.

Homer-Dixon, T. F. (2001). *Environment, Scarcity, and Violence*. Princeton, NJ: Princeton University.

Hoover, K. D. (2008). *Phillips Curve. Library of Economics and Liberty*. www.econlib.org/library/Enc/PhillipsCurve.html. Accessed April 11, 2014.

Ikatu International. (2010). Global Youth Employment: An Overview of Need and Interventions. Revised Report.

Ikharehon, J. I. (2007). Capacity Building for National Sustainable Development. The Nigerian Experience. *Journal of Social Sciences*, 154, 25–29.

James, V. (1998). Capacity Building in Developing Countries: Human and Environmental Dimensions. Westport, CT: Greenwood Press.

Jones, M. (2001, February 1). Sustainable Organizational Capacity Building: Is Organizational Learning a Key? *International Journal of Human Resource Management*, 12, 91–98.

Jones, R. (2001). *Engineering Capacity Building in Developing Countries to Promote Economic Development*. www.worldexpertise.com/Engineering_Capacity_Building_in_Developing_Countries. htm. Accessed March 19, 2014.

Kaplan, A. (2000). Capacity Building: Shifting the Paradigms of Practice. *Development in Practice*, 10(3/4), 517–526.

Kraft, M. and Furlong, S. (2013). *Public Policy: Politics, Analysis, and Alternatives*. Washington, DC: Congressional Press, 322–337.

Lackney, J. A. (2001). *The State of Post-Occupancy Evaluation in the Practice of Educational Design.* Paper presented at the Environmental Design Research Association, EDRA 32, Edinburgh, Scotland.

Lahne, R. (2013). *Government and Business.* Washington, DC: Congressional Quarterly Press.

Linnell, D. (2003). *Evaluation of Capacity Building: Lessons From the Field.* Washington, DC: Alliance for Nonprofit Management.

McBride, A. M. and Sherraden, M. (Eds.). (2004). Civic Service: Toward a Global Research Agenda [Special Issue]. *Nonprofit and Voluntary Sector Quarterly, 33*(4).

Mahajan, V. (2009). *Africa Rising.* Upper Saddle River, NJ: Pearson Education Inc.

Mandel, M. (2012). *Economics: The Basics.* New York, NY: McGraw-Hill Hill Press.

Mankiw, G. (2018). *Macroeconomics.* New York, NY: McGraw-Hill Press.

Miller, R., Benjamin, D. and North, D. (2014). *The Economics of Public Issues.* Boston, MA: Pearson.

Mohamedbhai, G. (2007). *Higher Education Reform in Africa.* Paper presented at the 19th Annual European Association for International Education Conference, Trondhein, Norway, September 12–15.

Moorhead, G. and Griffin, R. (2014). *Organizational Behavior: Managing People and Organization.* Stamford, CT: Cengage Learning.

Nebil, K., Gezahegn, A. and Hayat, Y. (2010). *Enabling the Private Sector to Contribute to the Reduction of Urban Youth Unemployment in Ethiopia.* Addis Ababa Chamber of Commerce and Sectoral Associations, Addis Ababa.

Nelson, R. and Winter, S. (1982). *An Evolutionary Theory of Economic Change.* Cambridge, MA: Belknap Press.

Nnoli, O. (1995). *Ethnicity and Development in Nigeria.* Aldershot, Hants, UK: Avebury Press.

Nsubuga, Y. (2003). Analysis of Leadership Styles and School Performance of Secondary Schools in Uganda. http://docs.mak.ac.ug/sites/default/files/JournalArticle%5B1%5D.pdf. Accessed March 18, 2015.

Nwazor, J. C. (2012). Capacity Building, Entrepreneurship and Sustainable Development. *Journal of Emerging Trends in Educational Research and Policy Studies (JETERAPS), 3*(1), 51–54.

Olagboye, A. A. (2004). *Introduction to Educational Management in Nigeria.* Ibadan: Daily Graphics (Nigeria) Limited.

Oluwagbuyi, O. L. and Adaramola, A. O. (2013). Triple Bottom Line Reporting: An Assessment of Sustainability in Banking Industry in Nigeria. *Asian Journal of Finance and Accounting, 5*(2), 57–72.

Onah, F. O. (2010). Urban Unemployment Situation in Nigeria. *Journal of Social Sciences, 2*(1), 21–26.

Peters, G. (2013). *American Public Policy.* Washington, DC: Congressional Quarterly Press.

Porter, T. B. (2006). Co-Evolution as a Research Framework for Organization and the Natural Environment. *Organization and Environment, 19*(4), 479–503.

Potterfield, T. A. (1999). The Business of Employee Empowerment: Democracy and Ideology in the Workplace. Westport, CT: Greenwood Publishing Group.

Rafik, M., Ahmad, I., Ullah, A. And Khan, Z. (2010). Determinants of Unemployment: A Case Study of Pakistan Economy (1998–2008). *Abasyn Journal of Social Sciences, 3* (1), 23–47.

Revans, R. W. (2011). *ABC's of Action Learning.* Burlington, VT: Gower Press.

Rondinelli, D. A. (1993). Development Projects as Policy Experiments: An Adaptive Approach to Development Administration. London, UK: Routledge Press.

Samuelson, W. and Marks, S. (2015). *Managerial Economics*. 8th Edition. Hoboken, NJ: John Wiley and Sons.

Sandbrook, R. (1993). *The Politics of African's Economic Recovery*. New York: Cambridge University Press.

Schiller, B. (2011). *Essentials of Economics*. New York, NY: McGraw-Hill Press.

Schumpeter, J. (1947). *Capitalism, Socialism, and Democracy*. 2nd Edition. New York Harper Brothers Press.

Sengupta, J. (2011). Understanding Economic Growth: Modern Theory and Experience. New York: Springer Press.

Sengupta, J. and Phillip, F. (2009). *Efficiency Market Dynamics and Industry Growth*. New York: Palgrave Macmillan.

Smith-Sebasto, N. (2012). *Sustainability*. New York, NY: McGraw-Hill Hill Press.

Solow, R. M. (1956). A Contribution to the Theory of Economic Growth. *Quarterly Journal of Economics*, 70, 65–94.

Theron, F. (2008). *The Development Change Agent*. Pretoria, South Africa: Van Schail Press.

Tucker, I. (2014). *Survey of Economics*. Mason, OH: Thompson Higher Education.

UNECA. (2011). Africa Youth Report: Addressing the Youth Education and Employment Nexus in New Global Economy. www.uneca.org/sites/default/files/ PublicationFiles/african_youth_report_2011_final.pdf. Accessed September 15, 2016.

United Nations. (2010). *Millennium Development Goals Report*. www.un.org/ millenniumgoals/pdf/MDG%20Report%202010%20En%20r15%20low%20 res%2020100615%20.pdf.

United Nations. (2012). *Human Development Index*. New York, NY: Oxford University Press.

United Nations Development Program (UNDP). (2014). *Human Development Report*. UNDP, New York: Oxford University Press.

United Nations Development Program (UNDP). (2013). *Human Development Report*. UNDP, New York: Oxford University Press.

United Nations Development Program (UNDP). (2009). World Survey on the Role of Women in Development. Women's Control Over Economic Resources and Access to Financial Resources, Including Microfinance. New York: United Nations Press.

United Nations Development Program (UNDP). (2007). *Human Development Report*. UNDP, New York: Oxford University Press.

United Nations Development Program (UNDP). (2004, 2005 and 2006). *Human Development Report*. UNDP, New York: Oxford University Press.

United Nations Development Program (UNDP). (2003). *Human Development Report*. UNDP, New York: Oxford University Press.

World Bank. (2016). *World Bank Development Report*. New York: Oxford University Press.

World Bank. (2014). *World Bank Development Report*. New York: Oxford University Press.

World Bank. (2013). *World Bank Development Report*. New York: Oxford University Press.

Ya Ni, A. and Van Wart, M. (2016). *Building Business–Government Relations: A Skills Approach*. New York: Routledge Press.

Index

For Product Safety Concerns and Information please contact our EU
representative GPSR@taylorandfrancis.com Taylor & Francis Verlag GmbH,
Kaufingerstraße 24, 80331 München, Germany

Printed and bound by CPI Group (UK) Ltd, Croydon, CR0 4YY
01/05/2025
01858436-0001